THE COMPLETE RESULTS & LINE-UPS OF THE UEFA EUROPA LEAGUE 2018-2021

Dirk Karsdorp

British Library Cataloguing in Publication Data
A catalogue record for this book is available from the British Library

ISBN: 978-1-86223-472-7

Copyright © 2021, SOCCER BOOKS LIMITED (01472 696226)
72 St. Peter's Avenue, Cleethorpes, N.E. Lincolnshire, DN35 8HU, England
Web site   www.soccer-books.co.uk
e-mail   info@soccer-books.co.uk

All rights are reserved. No part of this publication may be reproduced, stored in a retrieval system or transmitted, in any form or by any means, electronic, mechanical, photocopying, recording, or otherwise, without the prior written permission of Soccer Books Limited.

Printed in the UK by 4edge Ltd.

FOREWORD

Between the years of 1971 and 2009, the UEFA Cup was the second most important European Club competition, having itself superseded both the Fairs Cup and the European Cup-Winners' Cup competitions. From 1995 onwards, the Intertoto Cup also became an official UEFA competition and was, effectively, their third-ranked club competition until it ended in 2008.

From 2009, in an attempt to streamline their club tournaments, UEFA decided to end both the UEFA Cup and the Intertoto Cup competitions, replacing them with a single highly-ranked competition which was named the UEFA Europa League.

This publication provides a comprehensive statistical record of this competition from the first game in the qualifying stages of the 2018/2019 competition through to the 2021 Final itself. Similar publications covering the Europa League from 2009-2012, 2012-2015 and 2015-2018 are also available from Soccer Books Limited as are books covering the UEFA Cup and a selection of other European competitions including the Champions League and the earlier European Cup. Please check the back page of this book for a listing of these and many other publications.

Although the contents of this book are, we believe, as accurate as possible, it is not always easy to obtain reliable statistics for such a pan-European competition. On occasions, different sources can provide different information for the same match, particularly in relation to attendances. In such cases as this the most trustworthy information which could be discovered was used in this book.

Michael Robinson
Editor

UEFA EUROPA LEAGUE 2018-2019

PRELIMINARY ROUND

26.06.18 Estadi Comunal, Andorra la Vella:
UE Sant Julià – Gzira United 0-2 (0-1)
UE Sant Julià: Nico Ratti, Enric Pi, Nicolae Vasile, Pedro Muñoz, Jonny, Walter Balufo, Francisco Girau (69' Luis Blanco), José Aguilar Gómez (87' Daniel "Dani" Gonzalez), Alberto Molina, Vincent Ramaël, Joel Méndez (82' Diego Nájera). Coach: Jesús Barón Tellez.
Gzira United: Justin Haber, Clifford Baldacchino, Rodolfo Soares, Thomas Veronese, Prince Mambouana, Nicky Muscat (62' Zachary Scerri), Andrew Cohen, Roderick Briffa, Édinson Bilbao Zarate, Amadou Samb (90+3' Luca Brincat), Emmanuel Okoye (70' Jorginho). Coach: Darren Abdilla.
Goals: 20' Amadou Samb 0-1 (p), 87' Jorginho 0-2.
Referee: Denys Shurman (UKR)   Attendance: 380.

Joel Méndez missed a penalty kick (44').

28.06.18 Victoria Stadium, Gibraltar: Europa FC – Prishtina KF 1-1 (1-0)
Europa FC: Javi Muñoz, Ibrahim Ayew, Iván Moya, Jesús Toscano, Guille Roldán, Toni García, Martín Belfortti, Liam Walker, Mustapha Yahaya, Enrique Carreño, Rubo Blanco (69' Joselinho). Coach: Juan Gallardo Fernández.
Prishtina KF: Visar Bekaj, Armend Dallku, Arago Jamal, Ahmet Haliti, Përparim Osmani, Argjend Mustafa, Meriton Korenica, Gauthier Mankenda, Ergyn Ahmeti (82' Lorik Boshnjaku), Ahmed Januzi (87' Arbër Hoxha), Khalid Abdul Basit (65' Alen Jasharovski). Coach: Mirel Josa.
Goals: 45' Enrique Carreño 1-0 (p), 50' Meriton Korenica 1-1.
Referee: João Capela (POR)   Attendance: 350.

28.06.18 MFA Centenary Stadium, Ta'Qali:
Birkirkara FC – KÍ Klaksvík 1-1 (0-0)
Birkirkara FC: Kristijan Naumovski, Edward Herrera, Cain Attard, Arian Mrsulja, Eduardo Mancha, Mislav Andjelkovic, Uchenna Umeh, Jake Grech, Fabiano, Michael Mifsud, Marcelinho (81' Stanimir Miloskovic). Coach: Paul Zammit.
KÍ Klaksvík: Kristian Joensen, Marko Dusak (71' Steinbjørn Olsen), Deni Pavlovic, Ólafur Niclasen (87' Mikkjal á Bergi), Semir Hadzibulic, Boris Dosljak, Hørdur Askham, Jákub Andreasen, Jóannes Bjartalíd (82' Ronni Møller-Iversen), Jóannes Danielsen, Páll Klettskard. Coach: Mikkjal Kjartansson Thomassen.
Goals: 72' Michael Mifsud 1-0, 88' Deni Pavlovic 1-1.
Referee: Besfort Kasumi (KOS)   Attendance: 954.

28.06.18   Park Hall Stadium, Oswestry: Cefn Druids AFC – FK Trakai 1-1 (0-0)
Cefn Druids AFC: Michael Jones, Neil Ashton, Nathan Peate, Aaron Simpson, Naim Arsan, Matty Owen, Alec Mudimu (76' Fisnik Hajdari), Ryan Kershaw (82' Iwan Cartwright), Arkadiusz Piskorski, James Davies, Jordan Evans. Coach: Huw Griffiths.
FK Trakai: Tomas Svedkauskas, Valdemars Borovskis, Evgeniy Osipov, Justinas Janusevskis, Kevin Ntika Bondombe (71' Edvinas Baniulis), Vaidas Silénas, Valentin Jeriomenko, Donatas Kazlauskas, Modestas Vorobjovas (56' Rokas Masenzovas), Svajūnas Cyzas (63' Etienne Mukanya), Dmitriy Otstavnov. Coach: Jose Antonio Vicuña Ochandorena.
Goals: 48' James Davies 1-0, 86' Donatas Kazlauskas 1-1.
Referee: Christopher Jäger (AUT)   Attendance: 742.

(Cefn Druids AFC played their home match at Park Hall Stadium instead of their regular stadium, The Rock which does not meet UEFA requirements)

28.06.18   Estadi Comunal, Andorra la Vella:
            UE Engordany – SS Folgore/Falciano 2-1 (1-0)
UE Engordany: Jesús Coca, Christian Cellay, Walter Wagner (67' Fábio Serra Alves), Miguel Ruiz, Rafael Brito, Mateo Rodríguez Firpo, Mario Spano, Christopher Pousa, Larsen Touré, Luigi San Nicolas (83' Brian Figliamonte), Sebastián Gómez (87' Jorge Sebastian Varela). Coach: José Luis Mengual Pradcs.
SS Folgore/Falciano: Filippo Giannelli, Manuel Muccini, Francesco Sartori, Nicola Marini, Fabio Sottile, Luca Bezzi, Stefano Sacco, Andrea Nucci, Lorenzo Dormi (66' Umberto Semeraro), Imre Badalassi (85' Alessandro Bianchi), Martin Lago Ramiro (75' Marco Bernardi). Coach: Oscar Lasagni.
Goals: 39' Christian Cellay 1-0, 72' Umberto Semeraro 1-1, 86' Miguel Ruiz 2-1.
Referee: Kári Jóannesarson á Høvdanum (FAR)   Attendance: 432.

28.06.18   Stadio Tullo Morgagni, Forlì: SP Tre Fiori – Bala Town FC 3-0 (3-0)
SP Tre Fiori: Giorgio Pizzolato, Matteo Andreini, Guido Ghetti, Davide Bologna, Davide Succi, Luca Filippi, Giacomo Pracucci, Andrea Tamagnini, Danny Gasperoni (76' Davide Pasolini), Alessandro Teodorani (84' Nicola Della Valle), Mirco Vassallo (87' Sossio Aruta). Coach: Matteo Cecchetti.
Bala Town FC: Ashley Morris, Stuart Jones Jr., Andrew Burns, Anthony Miley (79' Mike Hayes), Sean Smith, Chris Venables, Robert Pearson, Nathan Burke, Andrew Mangan, Steven Tames (54' Ian Sheridan), Kieran Smith (69' Evan Horwood). Coach: Colin Caton.
Goals: 7' Anthony Miley 1-0 (og), 32' Giacomo Pracucci 2-0, 36' Mirco Vassallo 3-0.
Referee: Stanislav Todorov (BUL)   Attendance: 542.
Sent off: 80' Giacomo Pracucci.

(SP Tre Fiori played their home match at Stadio Tullo Morgagni instead of their regular stadium, San Marino Stadium, due to renovation)

28.06.18   Gundadalur, Tórshavn: B36 Tórshavn – St. Joseph's FC 1-1 (1-1)
B36 Tórshavn: Rói Hentze, Odmar Færø, Alex Mellemgaard, Erlendur Magnusson, Eli Nielsen, Meinhard Olsen (70' Hannes Agnarsson), Benjamin Heinesen, Andrias Eriksen (23' Magnus Holm Jacobsen), Robert Hedin Brockie, Kaimar Saag, Lukasz Cieslewicz. Coach: Jákup á Borg.
St. Joseph's FC: Jamie Robba, Mauri Torres, Iván Lobato, Samuel Fernández, José Otero, Daniel Guerrero, Domingo Ferrer (81' Carlos Pomares), Pedrito, Pedro Muñoz, Ernesto Cornejo (73' Joselu), Boro (80' Dexter Panzavechia). Coach: Raúl Procopio.
Goals: 33' Lukasz Cieslewicz 1-0 (p), 41' Boro 1-1 (p).
Referee: Jari Järvinen (FIN)   Attendance: 200.

05-07-18 Victoria Stadium, Gibraltar: St. Joseph's FC – B36 Tórshavn 1-1 (0-1, 1-1)
St. Joseph's FC: Félix Romero, Pecci, Mauri Torres, Iván Lobato (74' José Otero), Samuel "Samu" Fernández, Daniel Guerrero, Domingo Ferrer (94' Dexter Panzavechia), Pedrito, Pedro Muñoz, Ernesto Cornejo (54' John-Paul Duarte), Boro (67' Joselu). Coach: Raúl Procopio.
B36 Tórshavn: Rói Hentze, Odmar Færø, Alex Mellemgaard, Erlendur Magnusson, Eli Nielsen, Meinhard Olsen, Benjamin Heinesen (76' Magnus Holm Jacobsen), Andrias Eriksen (49' Bjarni Petersen), Robert Hedin Brockie, Kaimar Saag (61' Hannes Agnarsson, 98' Hugin Samuelsen), Lukasz Cieslewicz. Coach: Jákup á Borg.
Goals: 14' Lukasz Cieslewicz 0-1 (p), 88' José Otero 1-1.
Referee: Christophe Pires Martins (LUX)   Attendance: 536.

B36 Tórshavn won on penalties after extra time (2-4).
Penalties: Duarte 1-0, Jacobsen 1-1, Muñoz 2-1, Mellemgaard 2-2, Pedrito missed, Olsen 2-3, "Samu" missed, Færø 2-4.

05-07-18 Alytus Stadium, Alytus: FK Trakai – Cefn Druids AFC 1-0 (1-0)
FK Trakai: Tomas Svedkauskas, Valdemars Borovskis, Evgeniy Osipov, Rokas Masenzovas, Kevin Ntika Bondombe, Diniyar Bilyaletdinov (73' Etienne Mukanya), Vaidas Silénas, Valentin Jeriomenko, Donatas Kazlauskas, Justinas Marazas (83' Rokas Gedminas), Edvinas Baniulis (25' Svajūnas Cyzas). Coach: Jose Antonio Vicuña Ochandorena.
Cefn Druids AFC: Michael Jones, Neil Ashton, Nathan Peate, Aaron Simpson (86' Alun Morris), Naim Arsan, Matty Owen (69' Jonathan Taylor), Alec Mudimu, Ryan Kershaw, Arkadiusz Piskorski, James Davies, Jordan Evans. Coach: Huw Griffiths.
Goal: 29' Diniyar Bilyaletdinov 1-0 (p).
Referee: Dejan Jakimovski (MKD)   Attendance: 850.

(FK Trakai played their home match at Alytus Stadium instead of their regular stadium, Vilniaus LFF stadionas, due to a music event held there)

05-07-18 Stadiumi Olimpik Adem Jashari, Mitrovica: Prishtina KF – Europa FC 5-0 (3-0)
Prishtina KF: Visar Bekaj, Armend Dallku, Arago Jamal, Ahmet Haliti, Përparim Osmani, Argjend Mustafa, Meriton Korenica (75' Mërgim Pefqeli), Gauthier Mankenda, Ergyn Ahmeti, Ahmed Januzi (66' Alen Jasharovski), Khalid Abdul Basit (69' Lorik Boshnjaku). Coach: Mirel Josa.
Europa FC: Javi Muñoz, Alberto Merino (46' Rubo Blanco), Ibrahim Ayew, Iván Moya, Jesús Toscano, Guille Roldán (58' Joselinho), Toni García, Martín Belfortti, Liam Walker, Mustapha Yahaya, Enrique Carreño (71' Michael Yome). Coach: Juan Gallardo Fernández.
Goals: 9' Armend Dallku 1-0 (p), 13' Gauthier Mankenda 2-0, 35' Armend Dallku 3-0 (p), 59' Ahmed Januzi 4-0, 86' Mërgim Pefqeli 5-0.
Referee: Ioannis Papadopoulos (GRE)   Attendance: 1,140.

(Prishtina KF played their home match at Stadium Olimpik Adem Jashari instead of their regular stadium, Stadiumi Fadil Vokrii, due to renovation)

05-07-18 MFA Centenary Stadium, Ta'Qali: Gzira United – UE Sant Julià 2-1 (0-0)
Gzira United: Justin Haber, Clifford Baldacchino, Rodolfo Soares, Thomas Veronese, Prince Mambouana, Andrew Cohen, Roderick Briffa, Édinson Bilbao Zarate, Zachary Scerri (89' Juan Corbalan), Amadou Samb (73' Jorginho), Emmanuel Okoye (70' Nicky Muscat).
Coach: Darren Abdilla.
UE Sant Julià: Nico Ratti, Enric Pi (57' Diego Nájera), Nicolae Vasile, Pedro Muñoz (76' Daniel "Dani" Gonzalez), Jonny, Walter Balufo, Jamal Zarioh Taouil, Luis Blanco, José Aguilar Gómez (48' Francisco Girau), Vincent Ramaël, Joel Méndez.
Coach: Jesús Barón Tellez.
Goals: 62' Joel Méndez 0-1, 65' Amadou Samb 1-1 (p), 90+2' Édinson Bilbao Zarate 2-1.
Referee: Juxhin Xhaja (ALB)   Attendance: 649.
Sent off: 90' Luis Blanco.

05-07-18 Corbett Sports Stadium, Rhyl: Bala Town FC – SP Tre Fiori 1-0 (0-0)
Bala Town FC: Ashley Morris, Stuart Jones Jr., Andrew Burns (88' Joshua Jones), Anthony Miley, Sean Smith (67' Evan Horwood), Chris Venables, Robert Pearson, Nathan Burke, Andrew Mangan (54' Steven Tames), Ian Sheridan, Kieran Smith. Coach: Colin Caton.
SP Tre Fiori: Giorgio Pizzolato, Matteo Andreini, Guido Ghetti, Davide Bologna, Davide Succi (71' Enrico Magnani), Luca Filippi (82' Alessandro Caforio), Davide Pasolini, Andrea Tamagnini, Alessandro Teodorani (90+6' Simone Matteoni), Acquarelli Miacol, Mirco Vassallo. Coach: Matteo Cecchetti.
Goal: 77' Nathan Burke 1-0.
Referee: Kristoffer Hagenes (NOR)   Attendance: 610.

(Bala Town FC played their home match at Corbett Sports Stadium instead of their regular stadium, Maes Tegid which does not meet UEFA requirements)

05-07-18 Gundadalur, Tórshavn: KÍ Klaksvík – Birkirkara FC 2-1 (1-0)
KÍ Klaksvík: Kristian Joensen, Ísak Simonsen, Deni Pavlovic, Ólafur Niclasen, Semir Hadzibulic (86' Steinbjørn Olsen, 90+3' Hjalgrím Elttør), Boris Dosljak, Hørdur Askham, Jákub Andreasen, Jóannes Danielsen, Ronni Møller-Iversen, Páll Klettskard.
Coach: Mikkjal Kjartansson Thomassen.
Birkirkara FC: Kristijan Naumovski, Cain Attard, Arian Mrsulja, Eduardo Mancha, Mislav Andjelkovic, Uchenna Umeh (79' Gianluca Zammit), Jake Grech (73' Stanimir Miloskovic), Neil Micallef (61' Edward Herrera), Fabiano, Michael Mifsud, Marcelinho.
Coach: Paul Zammit.
Goals: 45+2' Deni Pavlovic 1-0, 59' Páll Klettskard 2-0, 90' Marcelinho 2-1.
Referee: Kristoffer Karlsson (SWE)   Attendance: 1,100.

(KÍ Klaksvík played their home match at Gundadalur instead of their regular stadium, Vid Djúpumyrar)

05-07-18   Stadio Tullo Morgagni, Forlì: SS Folgore/Falciano – UE Engordany 1-1 (0-0)
SS Folgore/Falciano: Filippo Giannelli, Manuel Muccini, Francesco Sartori, Nicola Marini, Fabio Sottile, Luca Bezzi (39' Umberto Semeraro), Stefano Sacco, Andrea Nucci (65' Marco Domeniconi), Lorenzo Dormi, Imre Badalassi, Martin Lago Ramiro (57' Marco Bernardi). Coach: Oscar Lasagni.
UE Engordany: Jesús Coca, Christian Cellay, Miguel Ruiz, Rafael Brito, Mateo Rodríguez Firpo, Edu Peppe (42' Christopher Pousa), Mario Spano, Hamza Bouharma (79' Jorge Sebastian Varela), Larsen Touré (70' Luigi San Nicolas), Sebastián Gómez, Fábio Serra Alves. Coach: José Luis Mengual Prades.
Goals: 86' Stefano Sacco 1-0, 90+6' Francesco Sartori 1-1 (og).
Referee: Zbynek Proske (CZE)   Attendance: 349.

(SS Folgore/Falciano played their home match at Stadio Tullo Morgagni instead of their regular stadium, San Marino Stadium, due to renovation)

FIRST QUALIFYING ROUND

10.07.18   Mikheil Meskhi sakhelobis Stadioni, Tbilisi:
          FC Samtredia – Tobol Kustanai 0-1 (0-0)
FC Samtredia: Sergey Pogorily, Ivan Fatic, Giorgi Guruli, Jemal Gogiashvili, Oleg Mamasakhlisi, Visako Bachiashvili, Roman Chachua (86' Shota Kerdzevadze), Avto Endeladze (76' Giorgi Akhaladze), Giorgi Pantsulaia (72' Lasha Kutchukhidze), Iinters Gui, Tamaz Makatsaria. Coach: Giorgi Tsetsadze.
Tobol Kustanai: Dmytro Nepogodov, Viktor Dmitrenko, Fernander Kassaï, Dmitry Miroshnichenko, Jaba Kankava, Azat Nurgaliev, Artūras Zulpa, Nika Kvekveskiri, Tanat Nuserbayev (87' Samat Zharynbetov), Bayurzhan Turysbek (79' Zhasulan Moldakaraev), Maxim Fedin. Coach: Vladimir Nikitenko.
Goal: 90+5' Maxim Fedin 0-1.
Referee: Timothy Marshall (NIR)   Attendance: 778.

(FC Samtredia played their home match at Mikheil Meskhi sakhelobi Stadioni instead of their regular stadium, Erosi Manjgaladze Stadium)

11.07.18   Banants Stadium, Yerevan: FC Banants Yerevan – FK Sarajevo 1-2 (1-2)
FC Banants Erevan: Aram Ayrapetyan, Vahagn Ayvazyan, Borislav Jovanovic, Edward Kpodo, Narek Petrosyan, Ognjen Krasic (67' Karen Melkonyan), Aram Bareghamyan, Igor Stanojevic (85' Wal), Solomon Udo, Kwasi Sibo, Lester Peltier (89' Fagner). Coach: Aram Voskanyan.
FK Sarajevo: Bojan Pavlovic, Dusan Hodzic (73' Halid Sabanovic), Nihad Mujakic, Emir Halilovic, Amar Rahmanovic, Anel Hebibovic, Milos Stanojevic (78' Alen Mustafic), Joachim Adukor, Mersudin Ahmetovic, Krste Velkoski, Aladin Sisic (82' Haris Handzic). Coach: Husref Musemic.
Goals: 16' Mersudin Ahmetovic 0-1, 21' Emir Halilovic 0-2, 34' Vahagn Ayvazyan 1-2.
Referee: Rohit Saggi (NOR)   Attendance: 3,000.

11.07.18   FFM Training Centre Petar Milosevski, Skopje:
FK Rabotnicki Skopje – Budapest Honvéd FC 2-1 (1-1)
FK Rabotnicki Skopje: Daniel Bozinovski, Dejan Mitrev, Leon Najdovski, Dusan Stevic, Sebastián Herrera, Ljubomir Stevanovic (88' Nehar Sadiki), Ostoja Stjepanovic, Oliver Peev, Petar Petkovski (79' Geoffrey Charles Chinedu), Joel Bopesu, Nikolce Sarkoski (70' Filip Petkovski). Coach: Djordje Jovanovski.
Budapest Honvéd FC: Dávid Gróf, Dino Skvorc, Bence Batik, Krisztián Vadócz, Eke Uzoma (72' Tonci Kukoc), Djordje Kamber, Gergö Nagy, Filip Holender (86' Fousseni Bamba), Dániel Gazdag, Danilo, Dániel Lukàcs (66' Milán Májer). Coach: Attila Supka.
Goals: 34' Petar Petkovski 1-0, 45+1' Gergö Nagy 1-1, 60' Nikolce Sarkoski 2-1.
Referee: Kristo Tohver (EST)   Attendance: 730.

(FK Rabotnicki Skopje played their home match at FFM Training Centre Petar Milosevski instead of their regular stadium, Telekom Arena, which was used for KF Shkëndia 79 match the day before)

11.07.18   Rheinpark Stadion, Vaduz: FC Vaduz – Levski Sofia 1-0 (1-0)
FC Vaduz: Andreas Hirzel, Maximilian Göppel, Nils von Niederhäusern, Philipp Muntwiler, Milan Gajic, Marco Mathys, Christopher Drazan (69' Gabriel Lüchinger), Sandro Wieser, Jodel Dossou (63' Maurice Brunner), Mohamed Coulibaly (86' Boris Babic), Igor Tadic. Coach: Roland Vrabec.
Levski Sofia: Bozhidar Mitrev, Aymen Belaïd, David Jablonsky, Milos Cvetkovic, Ivan Goranov, Jordi Gómez, Gabriel Obertan, Davide Mariani (79' Stanislav Kostov), Anthony Belmonte, Jerson Cabral (59' Stanislav Ivanov), Sergiu Bus (74' Iliya Dimitrov). Coach: Delio Rossi.
Goal: 14' Mohamed Coulibaly 1-0.
Referee: Fran Jovic (CRO)   Attendance: 1,243.

11.07.18   Gundadalur, Tórshavn: KÍ Klaksvík – FK Zalgiris 1-2 (0-1)
KÍ Klaksvík: Kristian Joensen, Ísak Simonsen, Deni Pavlovic (53' Jóannes Bjartalíd, 87' Kristoffur Jakobsen), Ólavur Niclasen, Semir Hadzibulic, Boris Dosljak, Hørdur Askham, Jákup Andreasen, Jóannes Danielsen, Ronny Møller-Iversen (80' Steinbjørn Olsen), Páll Klettskard. Coach: Mikkjal Kjartansson Thomassen.
FK Zalgiris: Dziugas Bartkus, Venelin Filipov (82' Marquinhos Carioca), Rolandas Baravykas, Mamadou Mbodj, Saulius Mikoliūnas, Donovan Slijngard, Liviu Antal, Slavko Blagojevic, Jérémy Manzorro (64' Serge Nyuiadzi), Marko Tomic, Louis Ogana (74' Tomás Malec). Coach: Valdas Urbonas.
Goals: 40' Liviu Antal 0-1, 60' Jóannes Bjartalíd 1-1 (p), 90+2' Mamadou Mbodj 1-2.
Referee: Alain Durieux (LUX)   Attendance: 487.

(KÍ Klaksvík played their home match at Gundadalur instead of their regular stadium, Vid Djúpumyrar)

11.07.18   Stade Émile Mayrisch, Esch-sur-Alzette: CS Fola Esch – Prishtina KF 0-0
CS Fola Esch: Thomas Hym, Rodrigue Dikaba, Billy Bernard, Tom Laterza, Peter Chrappan, Mehdi Kirch (46' Enis Saiti), Veldin Muharemovic, Ryan Klapp, Corentin Koçur (69' Ken Corral), Samir Hadji, Moussa Seydi (46' Cédric Sacras). Coach: Thomas Klasen.
Prishtina KF: Visar Bekaj, Armend Dallku, Arago Jamal, Ahmet Haliti, Armend Thaçi, Argjend Mustafa, Meriton Korenica (90+2' Abdul Bashiru), Gauthier Mankenda (80' Mërgim Pefqeli), Ergyn Ahmeti, Ahmed Januzi (84' Lorik Boshnjaku), Khalid Abdul Basit. Coach: Mirel Josa.
Referee: Ívar Orri Kristjánsson (ISL)   Attendance: 1,007.

11.07.18   Mourneview Park, Lurgan: Glenavon FC – Molde FK 2-1 (1-1)
Glenavon FC: Jonny Tuffey, Rhys Marshall, Andrew Doyle, Caolan Marron, Gary Muir, Andrew Hall, Stephen Murray (90+2' Dylan King), Mark Sykes, Joshua Daniels (90+5' Jordan Jenkins), Niall Grace, Stephen Donnelly (72' Robbie Norton). Coach: Gary Hamilton.
Molde FK: Andreas Linde, Vegard Forren, Ruben Gabrielsen, Kristoffer Haugen, Christoffer Remmer, Petter Strand (70' Fredrik Brustad), Etzaz Hussain (60' Daniel Chima Chukwu), Babacar Sarr, Eirik Hestad, Fredrik Aursnes, Erling Håland (82' Tobias Svendsen). Coach: Ole Gunnar Solskjær.
Goals: 36' Eirik Hestad 0-1, 37' Rhys Marshall 1-1, 59' Joshua Daniels 2-1.
Referee: Mads-Kristoffer Kristoffersen (DEN)   Attendance: 631.

12.07.18   Vazgen Sargsyan anvan Hanrapetakan Marzadasht, Yerevan:
         Pyunik Yerevan FC – Vardar Skopje 1-0 (1-0)
Pyunik Yerevan FC: Evgeni Kobozev, Vyacheslav Dmitriev, Maksim Zhestokov, Serob Grigoryan, Maksim Trusevich, Denis Voynov (58' Robert Hakobyan), Didier Kadio, Alik Arakelyan (65' Robert Minasyan), Vahagn Hayrapetyan, Petros Avetisyan, Mohamed Konaté (75' Ruslan Koryan). Coach: Andrey Talalaev.
Vardar Skopje: Filip Gacevski, Goran Popov, Evgen Novak, Tigran Barseghyan (75' Maksim Maksimov), Kosta Manev, Kristijan Tosevski, Darko Micevski, Clarence Bitang, Besar Iseni (67' Ali Adem), Matej Cvetanoski, Willian Lira (46' Jakub Berisha). Coach: Boban Babunski.
Goal: 28' Mohamed Konaté 1-0.
Referee: Michal Ocenás (SVK)   Attendance: 2,000.

(Pyunik Yerevan FC played their home match at Vazgen Sargsyan anvan Hanrapetakan Marzadasht instead of their regular stadium, Pyunik Stadium)

12.07.18   Olimpiskā centra Ventspils Stadionā, Ventspils:
         FK Ventspils – Luftëtari Gjirokastër 5-0 (5-0)
FK Ventspils: Maksims Uvarenko, Abdoul Mamah, Vitālijs Jagodinskis, Medzit Neziri, Hélio Batista, Ritvars Rugins (89' Raens Tālbergs), Abdullahi Alfa, Giuly Mandzhgaladze, Tosin Aiyegun, Vasili Pavlov (63' Nikita Kolesovs), Adeleke Akinyemi. Coach: Dejan Vukicevic.
Luftëtari Gjirokastër: Hrvoje Bukovski, Nemanja Janicic, Ledio Liçaj, Jackson, Oltion Rapa, Vladan Milosavljev (63' Maldin Ymeraj), Erjon Vuçaj, Behar Ramadani (82' Donald Rapo), Albano Aleksi, Dejvi Bregu, Vasil Shkurtaj. Coach: Milos Kostic.
Goals: 8', 12', 24' Adeleke Akinyemi 1-0 (p), 2-0, 3-0, 37' Tosin Aiyegun 4-0 (p), 43' Adeleke Akinyemi 5-0.
Referee: Vasilis Dimitriou (CYP)   Attendance: 2,300.

12.07.18   Mikheil Meskhis Sakhelobis Stadioni, Tbilisi:
         FC Chikhura Sachkhere – Beitar Jerusalem 0-0
FC Chikhura Sachkhere: Dino Hamzic, Davit Maisashvili, Lasha Chikvaidze, Bakari Mirtshkulava, Davit Megrelishvili, Revaz Chiteishvili, Denis Dobrovolski (62' Demur Chikhladze), Irakli Lekvtadze (79' Giorgi Bukhaidze), Teimurazi Markozashvili (57' Mikheil Sardalishvili), Irakli Bugridze, Giorgi Gabedava. Coach: Samson Pruidze.
Beitar Jerusalem: Itamar Nitzan, Carlos Cuéllar (90' Michael Siroshtein), Tal Kachila, Matan Peleg, Or Zehavi, Erik Sabo, Ofir Kriaf, Ya'akov Berihon (58' Lior Inbrum), David Keltjens, Jakub Sylvestr (65' Gaëtan Varenne), Idan Vered. Coach: Guy Luzon.
Referee: Kai Erik Steen (NOR)   Attendance: 1,220.

(FC Chikhura Sachkhere played their home match at Mikheil Meskhis Sakhelobis Stadioni instead of their regular stadium, Central Stadium Sachkhere)

12.07.18 Stadiumi Selman Stërmasi, Tirana: FK Partizani Tirana – NK Maribor 0-1 (0-0)
FK Partizani Tirana: Alban Hoxha (I), Renaldo Kalari (57' Jurgen Bardhi), Egzon Belica, Renato Gojkovic, Libanot Ibrahimi, Gerhard Progni (64' Stefan Nikolic), Bruno Telushi, Ardit Hila, Lorenc Trashi, Jasir Asani, Esat Mala (74' Besart Abdurahimi). Coach: Skënder Gega.
NK Maribor: Jasmin Handanovic, Marko Suler, Mitja Viler, Martin Milec, Sasa Ivkovic, Blaz Vrhovec, Amir Dervisevic, Martin Kramaric (64' Dino Hotic), Marcos Tavares (80' Jan Mlakar), Gregor Bajde (87' Dare Vrsic), Luka Zahovic. Coach: Darko Milanic.
Goal: 50' Gregor Bajde 0-1.
Referee: Jérôme Brisard (FRA)   Attendance: 1,050.

12.07.18 Stadion Ob Jezeru, Velenje: Rudar Velenje – SP Tre Fiori 7-0 (1-0)
Rudar Velenje: Marko Pridigar, Josip Tomasevic, Klemen Bolha, Robert Pusaver, Ivan Vasiljevic, Damjan Trifkovic (64' Ante Solomun), Domagoj Muic (57' Vlatko Simunac), Anze Pisek, Dominik Radic, Djair Parfitt-Williams, Milan Tucic (72' Tim Vodeb).
Coach: Marijan Pusnik.
SP Tre Fiori: Giorgio Pizzolato, Matteo Andreini, Guido Ghetti, Dario Merendino (52' Filippo Matteoni), Davide Bologna (72' Nicola Della Valle), Luca Filippi, Mattia Costantini, Davide Pasolini, Alessandro Teodorani, Marco De Angelis (81' Alessandro Caforio), Mirco Vassallo. Coach: Matteo Cecchetti.
Goals: 33' Milan Tucic 1-0, 48' Dominik Radic 2-0, 49' Djair Parfitt-Williams 3-0, 59' Milan Tucic 4-0, 75' Nicola Della Valle 5-0 (og), 78' Dominik Radic 6-0, 84' Ante Solomun 7-0.
Referee: Luis Godinho (POR)   Attendance: 923.

12.07.18 Telia 5G-areena, Tampere: Ilves Tampere – Slavia Sofia 0-1 (0-0)
Ilves Tampere: Mika Hilander, Jani Tanska, Tuomas Rannankari, Felipe Aspegren, Tatu Miettunen, Eero Tamminen, Lauri Ala-Myllymäki (83' Niklas Jokelainen), Mame Thiaw, Tuure Siira (83' Alim Moundi), Iiro Järvinen (87' Matias Ojala), Marius Noubissi.
Coach: Jarkko Wiss.
Slavia Sofia: Georgi Petkov, Aleksandar Aleksandrov, Emil Martinov, Andrea Hristov, Momchil Tsvetanov (90+2' Ivailo Dimitrov), Galin Ivanov, Slavcho Shokolarov (69' Georgi Yomov), Milen Gamakov, Yanis Karabelyov, Dimitar Velkovski, Milcho Angelov (87' Tsvetelin Chunchukov). Coach: Zlatomir Zagorcic.
Goal: 80' Momchil Tsvetanov 0-1.
Referee: Krzysztof Jakubik (POL)   Attendance: 1,511.

12.07.18 Qäbälä Sähär stadionu, Qabala: Gabala FK – Progrès Niederkorn 0-2 (0-0)
Gabala FK: Dmitro Bezotosniy, Ilgar Gurbanov, Vojislav Stankovic (72' Lalawelé Atakora), Urfan Abbasov, Bahlul Mustafazade, Asif Mammadov, Sabien Lilaj, Elvin Jamalov (56' Tamkim Khalilzade), Steeven Joseph-Monrose, Rauf Aliyev, Segun Adeniyi (76' Roman Huseynov). Coach: Senan Gurbanov.
Progrès Niederkorn: Sebastian Flauss, Mario Mutsch, Adrien Ferino, Marvin da Graça, Jordan Gobron, Tim Hall, Emmanuel Françoise, Sébastien Thill, Yannick Bastos (84' Yann Matias Marques), Olivier Thill (80' Ben Vogel), Mayron De Almeida (89' Dino Ramdedovic).
Coach: Paolo Amodio.
Goals: 51' Mayron De Almeida 0-1, 61' Olivier Thill 0-2 (p).
Referee: Veaceslav Banari (MOL)   Attendance: 1,600.

12.07.18 Lahden Stadion, Lahti: FC Lahti – FH Hafnarfjördur 0-3 (0-2)
FC Lahti: Damjan Siskovski, Mikko Hauhia, Kalle Taimi, Artem Vyatkin, Santeri Hostikka, Artjom Dmitrijev, Xhevdet Gela (73' Pavel Osipov), Loorents Hertsi, Aleksi Paananen, Teemu Jäntti (46' Stenio, 56' Ville Salmikivi), Henri Anier. Coach: Toni Korkeakunnas.
FH Hafnarfjördur: Gunnar Nielsen, Pétur Vidarsson, Hjörtur Valgardsson, Vidar Ari Jónsson, Rennico Clarke (56' Edi Gomes), Davíd Vidarsson, Gudmundur Kristjánsson (77' Robbie Crawford), Halldór Björnsson (69' Jónatan Jónsson), Brandur Hendriksson Olsen, Atli Gudnason, Steven Lennon. Coach: Ólafur Kristjánsson.
Goals: 4' Halldór Björnsson 0-1, 18' Steven Lennon 0-2, 90+1' Robbie Crawford 0-3.
Referee: Yaroslav Kozyk (UKR)   Attendance: 3,178.

12.07.18 A. Le Coq Arena, Tallinn: JK Narva Trans – FK Zeljeznicar Sarajevo 0-2 (0-1)
JK Narva Trans: Artur Kotenko, Igor Ovsjannikov (78' Arbër Basha), Viktor Plotnikov (31' Eduard Golovljov), Tanel Tamberg, Dante Leverock, Irie Elysée (84' Matheus), Dmitri Proshin, Denis Polyakov, Artjom Skinjov, Aleksandr Zakarlyuka, Dmitriy Barkov. Coach: Adyam Kuzyaev.
FK Zeljeznicar Sarajevo: Vedran Kjosevski, Jadranko Bogicevic, Sinisa Stevanovic, Milos Bakrac, Ivan Curjuric (84' Semir Dacic), Antonio Pavic, Filip Arezina (75' Haris Hajdarevic), Jovan Blagojevic, Anel Sabanadzovic, Sulejman Krpic, Dzenan Zajmovic (71' Mladen Veselinovic). Coach: Slobodan Krcmarevic.
Goals: 15' Artur Kotenko 0-1 (og), 74' Anel Sabanadzovic 0-2.
Referee: Daniyar Sakhi (KAZ)   Attendance: 263.

(JK Narva Trans played their home match at A. Le Coq Arena instead of their regular stadium, Narva Kreenholmi staadion)

12.07.18 Vilniaus LFF stadionas, Vilnius: FK Trakai – Irtysh Pavlodar 0-0
FK Trakai: Tomas Svedkauskas, Valdemars Borovskis, Evgeniy Osipov, Rokas Masenzovas (60' Justinas Janusevskis), Kevin Ntika Bondombe, Diniyar Bilyaletdinov, Vaidas Silénas, Valentin Jeriomenko (40' Modestas Vorobjovas), Donatas Kazlauskas, Svajūnas Cyzas, Justinas Marazas (75' Etienne Mukanya). Coach: Kibu Vicuña.
Irtysh Pavlodar: Nikita Kalmykov, Aleksandr Kislitsyn, Milos Stamenkovic, Adrian Avramia, Dimitriy Schmidt, Sergey Kislyak, Ilya Kalinin (90+3' Vladimir Vomenko), Adrián Gómez, Doru Popadiuc (79' Kirill Shestakov), Carlos Fonseca, Ruslan Esimov. Coach: Oyrat Saduov.
Referee: Fábio Veríssimo (POR)   Attendance: 400.

12.07.18 Kadrioru staadion, Tallinn: FCI Levadia Tallinn – Dundalk FC 0-1 (0-0)
FCI Levadia Tallinn: Sergei Lepmets, Markus Jürgenson, Dmitri Kruglov, Maksim Podholjuzin, Igor Dudarev, Evgeny Kharin (75' Mark Oliver Roosnupp), Yuriy Tkachuk, Rasmus Peetson (67' Muamer Svraka), Marcelin Gando (56' Pavel Marin), Nikita Andreev, Roman Debelko. Coach: Aleksandar Rogic.
Dundalk FC: Gary Rogers, Brain Gartland, Dane Massey, Sean Gannon, Sean Hoare, Chris Shields, Robbie Benson, Dylan Connolly (88' John Mountney), Jamie McGrath (81' Krisztián Adorján), Patrick Hoban, Michael Duffy (90+4' Ronan Murray). Coach: Stephen Kenny.
Goal: 53' Dylan Connolly 0-1.
Referee: Bojan Nikolic (SER)   Attendance: 1,343.

12.07.18 Savon Sanomat Areena, Kuopio: Kuopion PS – FC København 0-1 (0-0)
Kuopion PS: Otso Virtanen, Henri Toivomäki, Lum Rexhepi, Luis Murillo, Juho Pirttijoki, Petteri Pennanen, Joni Mäkelä (61' Saku Savolainen), Ville Saxman, Ilmari Niskanen, Rasmus Karjalainen (89' Eetu Pellikka), Ats Purje (78' Rangel). Coach: Jani Honkavaara.
FC København: Stephan Andersen, Pierre Bengtsson (66' Nicolai Boilesen), Sotirios Papagiannopoulos, Peter Ankersen, Denis Vavro, Ján Gregus (63' Carlo Holse), Rasmus Falk, Zeca, Robert Skov, Dame N'Doye, Kenan Kodro (84' Mads Roerslev Rasmussen).
Coach: Ståle Solbakken.
Goal: 75' Robert Skov 0-1.
Referee: Kirill Levnikov (RUS)   Attendance: 2,890.

12.07.18 Stadions Daugava, Liepāja: FK Liepāja – BK Häcken 0-3 (0-0)
FK Liepāja: Arsen Beglaryan, Sady Guèye, Seydina Keita, Vladimir Kamess (64' Verners Apins), Igors Kozlovs, Dmitrijs Hmizs (76' Cristián Torres), Jānis Ikaunieks, Raivis Jurkovskis, Leonel Strumia, Kristers Tobers, Mārtins Kigurs (55' Girts Karlsons).
Coach: Tamaz Pertia.
BK Häcken: Peter Abrahamsson, Kari Arkivuo, Emil Wahlström, Johan Hammar, Gustav Berggren, Erik Friberg (72' Alexander Faltsetas), Adam Andersson, Viktor Lundberg (56' Daleho Irandust), Mervan Çelik, Paulinho Guerreiro (84' Alhassan Kamara), Nasiru Mohammed. Coach: Andreas Alm.
Goals: 74' Daleho Irandust 0-1, 77' Paulinho Guerreiro 0-2, 82' Mervan Çelik 0-3.
Referee: Marco Guida (ITA)   Attendance: 2,234.

12.07.18 Alytaus m. centrinis stadionas, Alytus:
          FC Stumbras – Apollon FC Limassol 1-0 (0-0)
FC Stumbras: Rodrigo Josviaki, Lukas Cerkauskas, Matheus Bissi, Rimvydas Sadauskas, Jardel Nazaré, André Almeida, Dominykas Galkevicius (82' Levan Matcharashvili), Agostinho Cá, Marcos Junior (86' Amran Al-Jassasi), Lucas Villela, Nasro Bouchareb (67' Liu Yuhao).
Coach: Mariano Barreto.
Apollon FC Limassol: Bruno Vale, Charis Kyriakou, Kévin Bru (76' Antreas Karo), André Schembri (68' Ioannis Pittas), Héctor Yuste, Giorgos Vasiliou, Sasa Markovic, Esteban Sachetti, João Pedro, Fotis Papoulis (88' Luca Polizzi), Adrián Sardinero.
Coach: Sofronis Avgousti.
Goal: 90+1' Levan Matcharashvili 1-0.
Referee: Georgi Vadachkoria (GEO)   Attence: 800.

(FC Stumbras played their home match at Alytaus m. centrinis stadionas instead of their regular stadium, Stepono Dariaus ir Stasio Giréno stadionas, due to reconstruction)

12.07.18   Dalga Arena, Baku: Neftçi PFC Baku – Újpesti FC 3-1 (1-1)
Neftçi PFC Baku: Sälahät Agayev, Ruslan Abisov, Anton Krivotsyuk, Sony Mustivar, Goran Paracki, Rahman Hajiyev (77' Slavko Bralic), Kyrylo Petrov, Magomed Mirzabekov, Namig Alasgarov (42' Emin Makhmudov), Bagaliy Dabo (90' Kwame Karikari), Dário Júnior da Silva. Coach: Roberto Bordin.
Újpesti FC: Filip Pajovic, Mijusko Bojovic, Branko Pauljevic, Róbert Litauszki, Dzenan Burekovic, Dániel Nagy (90' Viktor Angelov), Benjámin Balász, Bojan Sankovic, Donát Zsótér (74' Kristóf Szűcs), Benjámin Cseke, Soma Novothny (82' Patrik Tischler). Coach: Nebojsa Vignjevic.
Goals: 9' Dániel Nagy 0-1, 23', 72' Bagaliy Dabo 1-1, 2-1, 90+2' Emin Makhmudov 3-1.
Referee: Dennis Higler (HOL)   Attendance: 4,000.

(Neftçi PFC Baku played their home match at Dalga Arena instead of their regular stadium, Bakcell Arena)

12.07.18   Brandywell Stadium, Derry: Derry City FC – FK Dinamo Minsk 0-2 (0-1)
Derry City FC: Gerard Doherty, Daniel Seaborne, Darren Cole, Conor McDermott, Dean Shiels, Aaron McEneff, Jamie McDonagh, Ben Fisk (78' Gavin Peers), Rory Hale (6' Ronan Hale), Aaron Splaine, Alistair Roy (60' Rory Patterson). Coach: Kenny Shiels.
FK Dinamo Minsk: Andrey Gorbunov, Yuriy Ostroukh (77' Roman Begunov), Nino Galovic, Maksim Shvetsov, Maksim Zhavnerchik, Seidu Yahaya, Uros Nikolic, Nikita Kaplenko (29' Filipp Ivanov), Artem Gurenko, Vladimir Khvashchinskiy (67' Artem Solovey), Anton Saroka. Coach: Sergei Gurenko.
Goals: 2' Nino Galovic 0-1, 64' Vladimir Khvashchinskiy 0-2.
Referee: Nikola Popov (BUL)   Attendance: 1,467.
Sent off: 81' Conor McDermott.

12.07.18   Corbett Sports Stadium, Rhyl:
            Connah's Quay Nomads FC – Shakhtyor Soligorsk 1-3 (0-2)
Connah's Quay Nomads FC: John Danby, George Horan, Laurence Wilson, Danny Holmes, John Disney, Michael Parker (66' Declan Poole), James Owen (81' Noah Edwards), Michael Bakare, Callum Morris, Ryan Wignall (86' Nathan Woolfe), Andrew Owens.
Coach: Andrew Morrison.
Shakhtyor Soligorsk: Andrey Klimovich, Pavel Rybak, Igor Kuzmenok, Igor Burko, Mikhail Shibun, Roger Cañas (83' Luka Simunovic), Aleksandr Selyava, Yuri Kovalev (80' Pyry Soiri), Július Szöke, Max Ebong Ngome, Elis Bakaj (73' Denis Laptev).
Coach: Sergey Tashuev.
Goals: 20' Max Ebong Ngome 0-1, 34' Elis Bakaj 0-2, 75' Mikhail Shibun 0-3, 89' Callum Morris 1-3 (p).
Referee: Juri Frischer (EST)   Attendance: 577.

(Connah's Quay Nomads FC played their home match at Corbett Sports Stadium instead of their regular stadium, Deeside Stadium)

12.07.18   Stadionul Zimbru, Chisinau: CS Petrocub Hîncesti – NK Osijek 1-1 (0-0)
CS Petrocub Hîncesti: Dumitru Celeadnic, Maxim Potîrniche, Victor Mudrac, Vlad Slivca, Artur Patras (56' Maxim Cojocaru), Alexandru Vremea (71' Ion Sandu), Dan Taras, Vladimir Ambros, Jessie Guera Djou, Donalio Melachio Douanla, Vladislav Ivanov (59' Sergiu Matei). Coach: Lilian Popescu.
NK Osijek: Marko Malenica, Borna Barisic, Stjepan Radeljic, Tomislav Sorsa, Mile Skoric, Gabrijel Boban (84' Marin Pilj), Haris Hajradinovic (55' Domagoj Pusic), Benedik Mioc, Petar Bockaj (71' Dmitriy Lepa), Danijel Loncar, Mirko Maric. Coach: Zoran Zekic.
Goals: 52' Mirko Maric 0-1, 65' Vladimir Ambros 1-1.
Referee: Karim Abed (FRA)   Attendance: 2,700.

(CS Petrocub Hîncesti played their home match at Stadionul Zimbru instead of their regular stadium, Stadionul Municipal Hîncesti)

12.07.18   Stadio Antonis Papadopoulos, Larnaca:
         Anorthosis Famagusta FC – KF Laçi 2-1 (0-1)
Anorthosis Famagusta FC: Mário Felgueiras, Gordon Schildenfeld, Konstantinos Sotiriou, Erwin Koffi, Danijel Pranjic, João Victor, Rayo, Nosa Igiebor (34' Giorgos Economides), Sekou Cissé, Michal Duris, Beka Mikeltadze (81' Nikos Englezou). Coach: Roni Levy.
KF Laçi: Gentian Selmani, Taulant Sefgjinaj, Erion Hoxhallari, Eglentin Gjoni, Andi Hadroj (90' Redon Xhixha), Ndricim Shtubina, Nikola Eller, Fjoart Jonuzi, Regi Lushkja, Vice Kendes, Myrto Uzuni. Coach: Besnik Prenga.
Goals: 21' Erion Hoxhallari 0-1, 52' Danijel Pranjic 1-1 (p), 59' Sekou Cissé 2-1.
Referee: José María Sánchez Martínez (ESP)   Attendance: 2.

12.07.18   Groupama Aréna, Budapest: Ferencvárosi TC – Maccabi Tel Aviv 1-1 (0-0)
Ferencvárosi TC: Dénes Dibusz, Endre Botka, Miha Blazic, Abraham Frimpong, Stefan Spirovski, Lukács Böle, Fernando Gorriarán, Davide Lanzafame (75' Leandro de Almeida), Kjartan Finnbogason (80' Dániel Böde), Roland Varga (76' Ivan Petryak), Gergö Lovrencsics. Coach: Thomas Doll.
Maccabi Tel Aviv: Predrag Rajkovic, Eitan Tibi, Avi Rikan (85' Sheran Yeini), Saborit, Elazar Dasa, Jair Amador, Eyal Golasa (64' Eliran Atar), Dor Mikha, Dor Peretz, Vidar Kjartansson (79' Omer Atzili), Aaron Schoenfeld. Coach: Vladimir Ivic.
Goals: 61' Stefan Spirovski 1-0, 90+1' Eliran Atar 1-1.
Referee: Ricardo De Burgos Bengoetxea (ESP)   Attendance: 14,127.

12.07.18   MFA Centenary Stadium, Ta'Qali: Balzan FC – Keshla FK 4-1 (3-1)
Balzan FC: Steve Sultana, Elkin Serrano, Steven Bezzina, Ivan Bozovic, Michael Johnson, Cadú, Nenad Sljivic (85' Ricardo Correa), Milos Lepovic, Alfred Effiong (63' Uros Ljubomirac), Lecão, Bojan Kaljevic (78' Andrija Majdevac). Coach: Marko Micovic.
Keshla FK: Kamran Agayev, Dênis, Tarlan Guliyev, Azer Salahli, Slavik Alkhasov, Sertan Taskin (84' Hervé Tchami-Ngangoue), Ebrima Sohna, Fuad Bayramov (60' Milos Bosancic), Vagif Javadov (63' Mammad Guliev), Andre Clennon, César Meza Colli.
Coach: Yuriy Maksimov.
Goals: 12' Alfred Effiong 1-0, 21' Lecão 2-0, 29' César Meza Colli 2-1 (p),
34' Bojan Kaljevic 3-1, 55' Cadú 4-1.
Referee: Volen Chinkov (BUL)   Attendance: 504.

12.07.18   CSR Orhei. Orhei: FC Milsami Orhei – Slovan Bratislava 2-4 (0-3)
FC Milsami Orhei: Radu Mîtu, Vadim Bolohan, Constantin Bogdan, Artur Craciun, Alexandru Antoniuc, Andrei Cojocari, Gheorghe Andronic (58' Romeo Surdu), Mihai Platica, Maxim Antoniuc (46' Vasile Jardan), Igor Bugaev, Sergiu Platica. Coach: Veaceslav Rusnac.
Slovan Bratislava: Michal Sulla, Mitch Apau, Vasil Bozhikov, Artem Sukhotsky, Dávid Holman (68' Vukan Savicevic), Joeri de Kamps, Nono Delgado, Kenan Bajric, "Moha" Mohammed Rharsalla, Aleksandar Cavric (81' Dejan Drazic), Andraz Sporar (87' Filip Holosko). Coach: Martin Sevela.
Goals: 10' Mohammed Rharsalla 0-1, 22' Andraz Sporar 0-2,
41' "Moha" Mohammed Rharsalla 0-3, 59' Igor Bugaev 1-3, 75' Romeo Surdu 2-3,
79' Artur Craciun 2-4 (og).
Referee: Vitali Romanov (UKR)   Attendance: 3,000.

12.07.18   Stadion Bâlgarska Armija, Sofia: CSKA Sofia – Riga FC 1-0 (0-0)
CSKA Sofia: Vytautas Cerniauskas, Nikolaj Bodurov, Kristiyan Malinov, Boris Sekulic, Bozhidar Chorbadzhiyski, Geferson, Valentin Antov, Rúben Pinto, Tiago Rodrigues, Jorginho (89' Tonislav Yordanov), Henrique (46' Edwin Gyasi). Coach: Nestor El Maestro.
Riga FC: Roberts Ozols, Vladislavs Gabovs, Antons Kurakins, Stefan Panic, Volodymyr Baenko, Antonijs Cernomordijs, Tomislav Saric, Ivan Enin, George Davies, Darko Lemajic, Milan Vusurovic (90+1' Kriss Kārklins). Coach: Viktor Skripnik.
Goal: 49' Tiago Rodrigues 1-0.
Referee: Mario Zebec (CRO)   Attendance: 7,500.

12.07.18   Stadion Pecara, Siroki Brijeg: Siroki Brijeg – NK Domzale 2-2 (0-2)
Siroki Brijeg: Luka Bilobrk, Josip Kvesic (46' Dejan Cabraja), Josip Barisic, Stipo Markovic, Bernardo Matic, Dominik Kovacic, Luka Begonja, Josip Corluka, Mateo Maric (61' Boze Vukoja), Drazen Bagaric, Tomislav Turcin (85' Eliomar). Coach: Boris Pavic.
NK Domzale: Dejan Milic, Matija Sirok, Gaber Dobrovoljc, Tilen Klemencic, Dario Melnjak, Senijad Ibricic, Zeni Husmani, Lovro Bizjak (90+1' Nermin Haljeta), Adam Gnezda Cerin, Agim Ibraimi (85' Zan Zuzek), Shamar Nicholson (76' Tonci Mujan). Coach: Simon Rozman.
Goals: 12' Lovro Bizjak 0-1, 26' Dario Melnjak 0-2, 47' Tomislav Turcin 1-2,
83' Stipo Markovic 2-2.
Referee: Petr Ardeleánu (CZE)   Attendance: 2,500.

12.07.18   Stade Josy Barthel, Luxembourg:
              Racing FC Union Luxembourg – FC Viitorul Constanta 0-2 (0-1)
Racing FC Union Luxembourg: Romain Ruffier, Thomas Birk, Pit Simon, Pape Ibra M'Boup, Kevin Nakache, Tarek Nouidra (87' Julien Humbert), Benoît Nyssen, Daniël Alves da Mota (90' Benssad Sulejmani), Sebastian Szimayer (80' Florik Shala), Edis Osmanovic, Jonathan Hennetier. Coach: Patrick Grettnich.
FC Viitorul Constanta: Valentin Cojocaru, Sebastian Mladen, Tudor Baluta, Bradley de Nooijer (78' Radu Boboc), Mailson Lima, Vlad Achim, Bogdan Tîru, Ianis Hagi (86' Alexi Pitu), Ionut Vîna, Alexandru Matan (58' Lyes Houri), Denis Dragus. Coach: Gheorghe Hagi.
Goals: 23' Denis Dragus 0-1, 82' Ianis Hagi 0-2 (p).
Referee: Alex Troleis (FAR)   Attendance: 1,383.

(Racing FC Union Luxembourg played their home match at Stade Josy Barthel instead of their regular stadium, Stade Achille Hammerel)

12.07.18 Gundadalur, Tórshavn: B36 Tórshavn – OFK Titograd Podgorica 0-0
B36 Tórshavn: Rói Hentze, Odmar Færø, Alex Mellemgaard, Bjarni Petersen, Erlendur Magnusson (69' Benjamin Heinesen), Ragnar Samuelsen (83' Gilli Samuelsen), Eli Nielsen, Meinhard Olsen, Magnus Holm Jacobsen (76' Hugin Samuelsen), Kaimar Saag, Lukasz Cieslewicz. Coach: Jákup á Borg.
OFK Titograd Podgorica: Damir Ljuljanovic, Milos B.Radulovic, Ivan Novovic, Branko Ojdanic, Marko Roganovic, Jovan Nikolic, Vasko Kalezic, Marko Milickovic, Ivica Jovanovic (71' Mirko Raicevic), Pjeter Ljuljdjuraj, Zoran Petrovic (61' Vojin Pavlovic).
Coach: Aleksandar Miljenovic.
Referee: Aleksandrs Anufrijevs (LAT)   Attendance: 611.

12.07.18 Ernest Pohl Stadiu, Zabrze: Górnik Zabrze – FC Zaria Balti 1-0 (0-0)
Górnik Zabrze: Tomasz Loska, Dani Suárez, Adrian Gryszkiewicz, Przemyslaw Wisniewski, Szymon Matuszek, Angulo, Adam Wolniewicz, Adam Ryczkowski (46' Marcin Urynowicz), Maciej Ambrosiewicz (81' Daniel Liszka), Szymon Zurkowski, Jesús Jiménez (75' Rafal Wolsztynski). Coach: Marcin Brosz.
FC Zaria Balti: Vladimir Livsit, Oleg Ermak, Ion Burlacu, Felipe Alves (70' Rodrigo Bostan), Lucas Silva, Daniel Dumbravanu, Rúben Gómez, Serghei Alexeev, Conrado (81' Guilherme), Vadim Gulceac, Jean Patric (61' Georgi Ovsyannikov). Coach: Vlad Goian.
Goal: 87' Angulo 1-0.
Referee: Filip Glova (SVK)   Attendance: 19,528.
Sent off: 90+2' Szymon Zurkowski.

12.07.18 Estadi Comunal, Andorra la Vella: UE Engordany – FK Kairat 0-3 (0-2)
UE Engordany: Jesús Coca, Christian Cellay, Walter Wagner (74' Luigi San Nicolas), Miguel Ruiz, Rafael Brito, Mateo Firpo, Mario Spano, Christopher Pousa, Larsen Touré (90' Rodrigo Guida), Sebastián Gómez, Fabio Serra (62' Brian Figliamonte). Coach: José Prades.
FK Kairat: Vladimir Plotnikov, Sheldon Bateau, Gafurzhan Suyumbaev, Aleksandr Sokolenko, Ákos Elek, Isael (64' Vyacheslav Shvyrev), Bauyrzhan Islamkhan (73' Georgiy Zhukov), Nuraly Alip, Andrey Arshavin, Juan Felipe Alves, Aderinsola Eseola (58' Márton Eppel).
Coach: Carlos Alós Ferrer.
Goals: 5' Walter Wagner 0-1 (og), 25' Bauyrzhan Islamkhan 0-2 (p), 90' Márton Eppel 0-3.
Referee: Iwan Arwel Griffith (WAL)   Attendance: 657.

12.07.18 Hásteinsvöllur, Vestmannaeyjar: ÍB Vestmannaeyja – Sarpsborg 08 0-4 (0-0)
ÍB Vestmannaeyja: Halldór Geirsson, Yvan Erichot (15' Sigurdur Arnar Magnússon), David Atkinson, Sindri Snær Magnússon, Kaj Leo í Bartalsstovu, Atli Arnarson (63' Jonathan Franks), Priestley Griffiths, Dagur Hilmarsson, Felix Örn Fridriksson, Gunnar Thorvaldsson (76' Ágúst Björnsson), Shahab Zahedi Tabar. Coach: Kristján Gudmundsson.
Sarpsborg 08: Aslak Falch, Amin Askar, Joackim Jørgensen, Joachim Thomassen, Joonas Tamm, Matti Lund Nielsen (85' Muhammed Usman), Ole Halvorsen, Kristoffer Zachariassen, Tobias Heintz (76' Kristoffer Larsen), Patrick Mortensen, Rashad Muhammed (71' Harmeet Singh). Coach: Geir Bakke.
Goals: 59' Rashad Muhammed 0-1, 66' Patrick Mortensen 0-2, 90+1' Ole Halvorsen 0-3, 90+4' Amin Askar 0-4.
Referee: Nick Walsh (SCO)   Attendance: 673.

12.07.18   Tallaght Stadium, Dublin: Shamrock Rovers FC – AIK Solna 0-1 (0-0)
Shamrock Rovers FC: Gavin Bazunu, Joey O'Brien (83' Roberto Lopes), Sean Kavanagh, Lee Grace, Sam Bone, Ronan Finn, Greg Bolger (78' Aaron Bolger), Ethan Boyle, Dylan Watts, Daniel Carr (75' Aaron Green), Joel Coustrain. Coach: Stephen Bradley.
AIK Solna: Oscar Linnér, Per Karlsson, Haukur Hauksson, Daniel Sundgren, Alexander Milosevic, Robin Jansson, Tarik Elyounoussi (90+2' Stefan Silva), Ahmed Yasin (79' Denni Avdic), Enoch Adu, Kristoffer Olsson, Henok Goitom. Coach: Rikard Norling.
Goal: 74' Daniel Sundgren 0-1.
Referee: Alexander Harkam (AUT)   Attendance: 2,817.

12.07.18   Stadion Kraj Bistrice, Niksic: FK Rudar Pljevlja – Partizan Beograd 0-3 (0-1)
FK Rudar Pljevlja: Vuk Radovic, Radule Zivkovic, Filip Mitrovic, Alphonse Soppo, Armin Bosnjak, Nemanja Sekulic, Milija Golubovic (74' Aleksandar Macanovic), Perisa Pesukic, Milos Zecevic, Radomir Djalovic (74' Velizar Janketic), Edvin Kuc (60' Marko Vukovic). Coach: Vuko Bogavac.
Partizan Beograd: Vladimir Stojkovic, Marc Valiente (77' Nemanja Miletic (I)), Sasa Zdjelar, Zlatan Sehovic, Svetozar Markovic, Gabriel Enache, Marko Jevtovic (71' Marko Jankovic), Seydouba Soumah, Danilo Pantic, Nemanja Nikolic (64' Nebojsa Kosovic), Ricardo Gomes. Coach: Miroslav Djukic.
Goals: 44' Marko Jevtovic 0-1 (p), 50' Seydouba Soumah 0-2, 57' Ricardo Gomes 0-3.
Referee: Stuart Steven Attwell (ENG)   Attendance: 3,150.

(FK Rudar Pljevlja played their home match at Stadion Kraj Bistrice instead of their regular stadium, Stadion pod Golubinjom)

12.07.18   Stadion Pod Goricom, Podgorica: FK Buducnost Podgorica – AS Trencín 0-2 (0-2)
FK Buducnost Podgorica: Milan Mijatovic, Vladan Adzic, Luka Mirkovic, Ilija Tucevic, Stefan Milic, Miljan Vlaisavljevic, Milos Mijic (87' Dusan Bakic), Petar Vukcevic (48' Bojan Roganovic), Milan Djurisic, Igor Ivanovic, Balsa Sekulic (79' Mihailo Perovic). Coach: Zoran Govedarica.
AS Trencín: Igor Semrinec, Jamie Lawrence, Martin Sulek, Keston Julien, Reuben Yem, Ashraf El Mahdioui, Abdul Zubairu, Joey Sleegers, Antonio Mance (59' Emeka Umeh), Hamza Catakovic, Philip Azango (84' Philippe van Arnhem). Coach: Ricardo Moniz.
Goals: 27' Hamza Catakovic 0-1, 30' Antonio Mance 0-2.
Referee: Mete Kalkavan (TUR)   Attendance: 2,000.

12.07.18   Ibrox Stadium, Glasgow: Glasgow Rangers FC – KF Shkupi 2-0 (1-0)
Glasgow Rangers FC: Allan McGregor, James Tavernier, Connor Goldson, Jon Flanagan, Ross McCrorie, Nikola Katic, Jamie Murphy, Scott Arfield (67' Oviemuno Ejaria), Josh Windass (79' Glenn Middleton), Candeias (56' Ryan Jack), Alfredo Morelos. Coach: Steven Gerrard.
KF Shkupi: Suat Zendeli, Muharem Bajrami (46' Amir Bilali), Blagojce Ljamcevski (61' Bunjamin Shabani), Toni Tipuric, Muarem Muarem, Ermadin Adem, Stephan Vujcic, Ron Broja, Basilio Nchama (90+2' Besart Krivanjeva), Blaze Ilijoski, Kristijan Stojkovski. Coach: Zekirija Ramadani.
Goals: 23' Jamie Murphy 1-0, 90+2' James Tavernier 2-0 (p).
Referee: Christian Dingert (GER)   Attendance: 49,309.

12.07.18   Stadion Karadjordje, Novi Sad: Spartak Subotica – Coleraine FC 1-1 (0-1)
Spartak Subotica: Nikola Peric, Stefan Milosevic (75' Vladimir Torbica), Andrija Vukcevic, Noboru Shimura, Dejan Kerkez, Nemanja Calasan, Mile Savkovic, Bojan Cecaric (46' Ognjen Djuricin), Nemanja Glavcic, Milan Marcic, Dejan Djenic (35' Samuel Afum).
Coach: Vladimir Gacinovic.
Coleraine FC: Christopher Johns, Aaron Traynor, Gareth McConaghie, Adam Mullan, Stephen O'Donnell, Stephen Lowry, Darren McCauley (81' Ciaron Harkin), Aaron Burns, Ian Parkhill, Bradley Lyons (90+2' Matthew Kirk), Eoin Bradley (65' Jamie McGonigle).
Coach: Oran Kearney.
Goals: 23' Darren McCauley 0-1, 90+4' Mile Savkovic 1-1 (p).
Referee: Aleksei Matyunin (RUS)   Attendance: 976.

(Spartak Subotica played their home match at Stadion Karadjordje instead of their regular stadium, Subotica City Stadium)

12.07.18   Solitude, Belfast: Cliftonville FC – FC Nordsjælland 0-1 (0-1)
Cliftonville FC: Brian Neeson, Jamie McGovern (62' Ryan Catney), Garry Breen, Liam Bagnall, Jamie Harney, Levi Ives, Christopher Curran, Conor McMenamin (74' Stephen Garrett), Rory Donnelly, Ryan Curran, Joe Gormley. Coach: Barry Gray.
FC Nordsjælland: Nicolai Larsen, Karlo Bartolec, Mads Pedersen, Andreas Skovgaard, Mathias Jensen, Victor Nelsson, Andreas Skov Olsen (57' Matias Rasmussen), Mikkel Damsgaard, Mikkel Rygaard Jensen (87' Nicklas Strunck Jakobsen), Godsway Donyoh (71' Martin Frese), Benjamin Hansen. Coach: Kasper Hjulmand.
Goal: 19' Andreas Skov Olsen 0-1.
Referee: Sándor Andó-Szabó (HUN)   Attendance: 1,170.

12.07.18   INEA stadion, Poznan: KKS Lech Poznan – Gandzasar FC Kapan 2-0 (2-0)
KKS Lech Poznan: Jasmin Buric, Thomas Rogne, Rafal Janicki, Volodymyr Kostevych, Vernon, Tomasz Cywka, Mihai Radut (58' Pedro Tiba), Maciej Makuszewski, Maciej Gajos, Darko Jevtic (69' Niklas Bärkroth), Christian Gytkjær (86' Pawel Tomczyk).
Coach: Ivan Djurdjevic.
Gandzasar FC Kapan: Gevorg Kasparov, Ara Khachatryan (82' Vardan Pogosyan), Vukasin Tomic, Hayk Ishkhanyan, Aleksandr Sverchinski, Gegham Harutyunyan, Christian Alex Júnior, Artur Yuspashyan (59' Gevorg Ohanyan), Wbeymar Angulo, Lubambo Musonda, Gevorg Nranyan (90+4' Davit Minasyan). Coach: Ashot Barseghyan.
Goals: 10', 15' Christian Gytkjær 1-0, 2-0 (p).
Referee: Yigal Frid (ISR)

Match was played behind closed doors.

12.07.18   Easter Road Stadium, Edinburgh: Hibernian FC Edinburgh – NSÍ Runavík 6-1 (4-0)
Hibernian FC Edinburgh: Ádám Bogdán, Steven Whittaker, Lewis Stevenson, Paul Hanlon, Darren McGregor (60' Danny Swanson), Efe Ambrose, Vykintas Slivka, Stephen Mallan, Martin Boyle, Florian Kamberi (51' Simon Murray), Oliver Shaw (82' Marvin Bartley). Coach: Neil Lennon.
NSÍ Runavík: Tordhur Thomsen, Einar Tróndargjógv Hansen, Pól Justinussen, Jóhan Davidsen (46' Per Langgaard), Jens Joensen, Fródi Benjaminsen, Bárdur Jögvansson-Hansen, Árni Frederiksberg (46' Jann Benjaminsen), Betuel Hansen (40' Magnus Olsen), Petur Knudsen, Klæmint Andrasson Olsen. Coach: Sámal Hentze.
Goals: 3', 21' Florian Kamberi 1-0 (p), 2-0, 29' Oliver Shaw 3-0, 43' Stephen Mallan 4-0, 48' Florian Kamberi 5-0, 53' Petur Knudsen 5-1, 84' Stephen Mallan 6-1.
Referee: Manfredas Lukjancukas (LIT)   Attendance: 12,501.
Sent off: 33' Einar Tróndargjógv Hansen.

12.07.18   MOL Aréna, Dunajská Streda: DAC Dunajská Streda – Dinamo Tbilisi 1-1 (1-1)
DAC Dunajská Streda: Patrik Macej, Lubomír Satka, Milan Simcák (46' Zsolt Kalmár), Timotej Záhumensky, Marin Ljubicic, Erik Pacinda (79' Marko Divkovic), Tomás Huk, Kristián Kostrna, Krisztopher Vida (67' Maksym Tretyakov), Christián Herc, Vakoun Issouf Bayo. Coach: Marco Rossi.
Dinamo Tbilisi: Demetre Buliskeria, Gudzha Rukhaia, Luka Lochoshvili, Davit Kobouri, Nika Ninua, Levan Kharabadze, Dmitriy Ivanisenya, Akaki Shulaia (80' Bakar Kardava), Otari Kiteishvili, George Ivanishvili (46' Mikheil Ergemlidze), Budu Zivzivadze (73' Mate Vatsadze). Coach: Kakhaber Katcharava.
Goals: 15' Budu Zivzivadze 0-1, 30' Vakoun Issouf Bayo 1-1.
Referee: Irfan Peljto (BIH)   Attendance: 8,759.

12.07.18   Gradski Stadion Cair, Nis: Radnicki Nis – Gzira United 4-0 (1-0)
Radnicki Nis: Mladen Zivkovic, Aleksandar Todorovski, Radovan Pankov, Djordje Crnomarkovic, Aleksandar Stanisavljevic (69' Sasa Stojanovic), Petar Grbic (83' Aleksandar Jovanovic (I)), Dusan Micic, Nikola Stankovic, Ryota Noma, Sladan Nikodijevic (46' Marko Mrkic), Nermin Haskic. Coach: Nenad Lalatovic.
Gzira United: Justin Haber, Clifford Baldacchino, Rodolfo Soares, Thomas Veronese, Destin Prince Mambouana (81' Sacha Borg), Roderick Briffa (79' Luca Brincat), Édison Bilbao Zárate, Juan Corbalan, Zachary Scerri (63' Nikolai Muscat), Amadou Samb, Jorginho. Coach: Darren Abdilla.
Goals: 14' Radovan Pankov 1-0, 53' Nermin Haskic 2-0, 55' Marko Mrkic 3-0, 85' Nermin Haskic 4-0.
Referee: Jason Lee Barcelo (GIB)   Attendance: 8,500.

12.07.18   Samsung völlurinn, Gardabær: UMF Stjarnan – JK Nõmme Kalju 3-0 (1-0)
UMF Stjarnan: Haraldur Björnsson, Baldur Sigurdsson, Brynjar Gudjónsson, Daníel Laxdal, Thorsteinn Már Ragnarsson (58' Jóhann Laxdal), Heidar Ægisson, Alex Thór Hauksson (74' Sölvi Fodilsson), Gudmundur Hafsteinsson (56' Eyjólfur Hédinsson), Gunjón Baldvinssòn, Thórarinn Valdimarsson, Hilmar Árni Halldórsson. Coach: Rúnar Sigmundsson.
JK Nõmme Kalju: Vitali Teles, Maximiliano Uggè, Trevor Elhi, William Gustavo, Andriy Markovych, Igor Subbotin, Réginald Mbu-Alidor, Aleksandr Volkov (70' Kasper Paur), Marko Brtan, Liliu, Rimo Hunt (46' Deniss Tjapkin). Coach: Sergey Frantsev.
Goals: 19' Hilmar Árni Halldórsson 1-0 (p), 49' Baldur Sigurdsson 2-0, 70' Gunjón Baldvinsson 3-0.
Referee: Radek Príhoda (CZE)   Attendance: 980.

17.07.18   Telekom Arena, Skopje: KF Shkupi – Glasgow Rangers FC 0-0
KF Shkupi: Suat Zendeli, Toni Tipuric, Amir Bilali, Besart Krivanjeva, Muarem Muarem (90+2' Fatih Ismaili), Ermadin Adem, Stephan Vujcic (76' Suhejlj Muharem), Ron Broja, Basilio Nchama (37' Bunjamin Shabani), Blaze Ilijoski, Kristijan Stojkovski.
Coach: Zekirija Ramadani.
Glasgow Rangers FC: Allan McGregor, James Tavernier, Connor Goldson, Jon Flanagan, Ross McCrorie, Nikola Katic, Jamie Murphy (90+1' Andrew Halliday), Ryan Jack, Josh Windass (64' Glenn Middleton), Candeias (72' Oviemuno Ejaria), Alfredo Morelos.
Coach: Steven Gerrard.
Referee: Halil Umut Meler (TUR)   Attendance: 4,750.

(KF Shkupi played their home match at Telekom Arena instead of their regular stadium, Cair Stadium)

17.07.18   Bozsik-József-Stadion, Budapest:
            Budapest Honvéd FC – FK Rabotnicki Skopje 4-0 (2-0)
Budapest Honvéd FC: Dávid Gróf, Eke Uzoma (68' Tonci Kukoc), Tibor Heffler, Dino Skvorc, Bence Batik, Krisztián Vadócz, Djordje Kamber, Gergö Nagy (86' Nikolasz Kovács), Dániel Gazdag, Filip Holender (83' Dániel Lukàcs), Danilo. Coach: Attila Supka.
FK Rabotnicki Skopje: Daniel Bozinovski, Dejan Mitrev, Leon Najdovski, Dusan Stevic, Sebastián Herrera, Ljubomir Stevanovic, Ostoja Stjepanovic, Oliver Peev, Petar Petkovski (70' Filip Petkovski), Joel Bopesu, Nikolce Sarkoski (70' Geoffrey Charles Chinedu).
Coach: Djordje Jovanovski.
Goals: 6', 16' Filip Holender 1-0, 2-0, 63', 84' Danilo 3-0 (p), 4-0.
Referee: Marius Avram (ROM)   Attendance: 64.
Sent off: 62' Sebastián Herrera.

Referee Marius Avram was injured in the 29th minute injured and replaced by Iulian Calin.

17.07.18   Vivacom Arena – Georgi Asparuhov Stadium, Sofia:
            Levski Sofia – FC Vaduz 3-2 (1-1)
Levski Sofia: Bozhidar Mitrev (46' Martin Polacek), Aymen Belaïd, David Jablonsky, Milos Cvetkovic, Ivan Goranov, Jordi Gómez, Gabriel Obertan, Davide Mariani, Anthony Belmonte (65' Stanislav Kostov), Jerson Cabral, Sergiu Bus (83' Iliya Dimitrov). Coach: Delio Rossi.
FC Vaduz: Andreas Hirzel, Maximilian Göppel, Nils von Niederhäusern, Philipp Muntwiler, Milan Gajic, Marco Mathys, Christopher Drazan (46' Gabriel Lüchinger), Sandro Wieser, Jodel Dossou (76' Maurice Brunner), Mohamed Coulibaly (87' Mario Bühler), Igor Tadic.
Coach: Roland Vrabec.
Goals: 25' Mohamed Coulibaly 0-1, 35' Sergiu Bus 1-1, 53' Aymen Belaïd 2-1, 55' Igor Tadic 2-2, 85' Jerson Cabral 3-2.
Referee: Rob Harvey (IRL)   Attendance: 6,100
Sent off: 90+4' Stanislav Kostov.

Sergiu Bus missed a penalty kick (76').

FC Vaduz won on away goals.

18.07.18   Stadion Grbavica, Sarajevo: FK Zeljeznicar Sarajevo – JK Narva Trans 3-1 (2-1)
FK Zeljeznicar Sarajevo: Vedran Kjosevski, Jadranko Bogicevic, Sinisa Stevanovic, Milos Bakrac, Ivan Curjuric (78' Haris Hajdarevic), Antonio Pavic, Filip Arezina, Jovan Blagojevic (84' Semir Dacic), Anel Sabanadzovic, Sulejman Krpic, Dzenan Zajmovic (74' Mladen Veselinovic). Coach: Slobodan Krcmarevic.
JK Narva Trans: Artur Kotenko, Igor Ovsjannikov (75' Vadim Mihhailov), Viktor Plotnikov, Tanel Tamberg, Dante Leverock, Irie Elysée (36' Matheus), Dmitri Proshin, Denis Polyakov, Artjom Skinjov (62' Arbër Basha), Aleksandr Zakarlyuka, Dmitriy Barkov.
Coach: Adyam Kuzyaev.
Goals: 5' Viktor Plotnikov 0-1, 25' Dzenan Zajmovic 1-1, 29', 82' Sulejman Krpic 2-1, 3-1.
Referee: Catalin Gaman (ROM)   Attendance: 7,603.

19.07.18   Ortaliq Stadion, Kostanay: Tobol Kustanai – FC Samtredia 2-0 (1-0)
Tobol Kustanai: Dmytro Nepogodov, Viktor Dmitrenko, Fernander Kassaï, Dmitry Miroshnichenko (75' Aslan Darabaev), Marat Bystrov (69' Samat Zharynbetov), Jaba Kankava, Azat Nurgaliev, Artūras Zulpa, Nika Kvekveskiri, Bayurzhan Turysbek (63' Tanat Nuserbaev), Maxim Fedin. Coach: Vladimir Nikitenko.
FC Samtredia: Sergey Pogorily, Ivan Fatic, Giorgi Guruli, Jemal Gogiashvili, Oleg Mamasakhlisi (67' Michael Olaitan), Visako Bachiashvili, Giorgi Akhaladze (77' Anatoli Mesiachenko), Jaba Lipartia, Avto Endeladze, Iinters Gui, Tamaz Makatsaria (71' Zaur Khabeishvili). Coach: Giorgi Tsetsadze.
Goals: 12' Bayurzhan Turysbek 1-0, 83' Aslan Darabaev 2-0.
Referee: Tihomir Pejin (CRO)   Attendance: 8,012.

19.07.18   Ortaliq Stadion, Almaty: FK Kairat – UE Engordany 7-1 (4-0)
FK Kairat: Vladimir Plotnikov, Gafurzhan Suyumbaev, Aibol Abiken, Ákos Elek (46' Sheldon Bateau), Magomed Paragulgov, Islambek Kuat, Bauyrzhan Islamkhan (57' Georgiy Zhukov), Yan Vorogovskiy, Márton Eppel, Juan Felipe Alves, Aderinsola Eseola (46' Vyacheslav Shvyrev). Coach: Carlos Alós Ferrer.
UE Engordany: Jesús Coca, Christian Cellay, Walter Wagner, Miguel Ruiz, Rafael Brito (57' Mateo Firpo), Mario Spano, Christopher Pousa (71' Morgan Lafont), Hamza Bouharma, Luigi San Nicolas (62' Fábio Serra), Sebastián Gómez, Brian Figliamonte. Coach: José Prades.
Goals: 4', 11' Márton Eppel 1-0, 2-0, 42' Aderinsola Eseola 3-0, 44' Márton Eppel 4-0, 53' Bauyrzhan Islamkhan 5-0, 72' Morgan Lafont 5-1, 75' Márton Eppel 6-1,
87' Yan Vorogovskiy 7-1.
Referee: Jovan Kaludjerovic (MNE)   Attendance: 10,500.

19.07.18   Vazgen Sargsyan anvar Hanrapetakan Marzadasht, Yerevan:
            Gandzasar FC Kapan – KKS Lech Poznan 2-1 (0-0)
Gandzasar FC Kapan: Grigor Meliksetyan, Ara Khachatryan, Vukasin Tomic, Hayk Ishkhanyan, Aleksandr Sverchinski, Gegham Harutyunyan, Christian Alex Júnior, Artur Yuspashyan (64' Gevorg Ohanyan), Wbeymar Angulo, Lubambo Musonda, Gevorg Nranyan (83' Vardan Pogosyan). Coach: Ashot Barseghyan.
KKS Lech Poznan: Matús Putnocky, Nikola Vujadinovic, Piotr Tomasik, Rafal Janicki, Vernon, Tomasz Cywka, Lukasz Tralka, Maciej Makuszewski, Maciej Gajos (60' Mihai Radut), Pedro Tiba (60' Darko Jevtic), Christian Gytkjær. Coach: Ivan Djurdjevic.
Goals: 50' Lubambo Musonda 1-0, 67' Gegham Harutyunyan 2-0, 90+5' Lukasz Tralka 2-1.
Referee: Mohammed Al-Hakim (SWE)   Attendance: 1,645.

19.07.18   Ortaliq Stadion, Pavlodar: Irtysh Pavlodar – FK Trakai 0-1 (0-1)
Irtysh Pavlodar: Nikita Kalmykov, Aleksandr Kislitsyn, Milos Stamenkovic, Dimitriy Schmidt (75' Vladimir Vomenko), Ilya Kalinin, Kirill Shestakov, Adrián Gómez, Doru Popadiuc, Gbolahan Salami, Carlos Fonseca (65' Arman Smailov), Ruslan Esimov.
Coach: Oyrat Saduov.
FK Trakai: Tomas Svedkauskas, Valdemars Borovskis, Evgeniy Osipov, Justinas Janusevskis, Kevin Ntika Bondombe (70' Valentin Jeriomenko), Diniyar Bilyaletdinov, Vaidas Silénas, Donatas Kazlauskas (85' Rokas Gedminas), Modestas Vorobjovas, Svajūnas Cyzas (73' Aleksandras Levsinas), Justinas Marazas. Coach: Kibu Vicuña.
Goal: 19' Svajūnas Cyzas 0-1.
Referee: Luca Barbeno (SMR)   Attendance: 6,250.

19.07.18   Stadionul Central, Ovidiu:
   FC Viitorul Constanta – Racing FC Union Luxembourg 0-0
FC Viitorul Constanta: Valentin Cojocaru, Sebastian Mladen, Tudor Baluta, Bradley de Nooijer, Vlad Achim, Bogdan Tîru, Lyes Houri (83' Alexi Pitu), Ianis Hagi (56' Mihai Vodut, Ionut Vîna, Denis Dragus (55' Alexandru Matan), Mailson Lima. Coach: Gheorghe Hagi.
Racing FC Union Luxembourg: Romain Ruffier, Thomas Birk, Henrique, Pape Ibra M'Boup (80' Benssad Sulejmani), Julien Humbert, Kevin Nakache, Tarek Nouidra, Florik Shala (75' Sebastian Szimayer), Daniël Alves da Mota, Edis Osmanovic, Jonathan Hennetier.
Coach: Patrick Grettnich.
Referee: Alexandr Aliyev (KAZ)   Attendance: 2,130.

19.07.18   Stadyen Dynama, Minsk: FK Dinamo Minsk – Derry City FC 1-2 (1-1)
FK Dinamo Minsk: Sergey Ignatovich, Roman Begunov, Maksim Shvetsov, Maksim Zhavnerchik, Seidu Yahaya, Artem Solovey (6' Vladimir Khvashchinskiy), Aleksandr Sachivko, Artem Bykov, Uros Nikolic, Artem Gurenko (85' Yuriy Ostroukh), Anton Saroka (63' Filipp Ivanov). Coach: Sergei Gurenko.
Derry City FC: Gerard Doherty, Gavin Peers, Daniel Seaborne, Darren Cole, Dean Shiels (72' Ronan Hale), Aaron McEneff, Jamie McDonagh, Ben Fisk (89' Ben Doherty), Rory Hale, Aaron Splaine, Alistair Roy. Coach: Kenny Shiels.
Goals: 7' Alistair Roy 0-1, 28' Aleksandr Sachivko 1-1, 75' Ronan Hale 1-2.
Referee: Jens Maae (DEN)   Attendance: 13,750.

19.07.18   Stadiumi Laçi, Laçi: KF Laçi – Anorthosis Famagusta FC 1-0 (0-0)
KF Laçi: Gentian Selmani, Taulant Sefgjinaj, Erion Hoxhallari, Eglentin Gjoni, Andi Hadroj (64' Abdurraman Fangaj), Ndricim Shtubina (80' Ded Bushi), Nikola Eller, Fjoart Jonuzi (80' Redon Xhixha), Regi Lushkja, Vice Kendes, Myrto Uzuni. Coach: Besnik Prenga.
Anorthosis Famagusta FC: Mário Felgueiras, Gordon Schildenfeld, Konstantinos Sotiriou (90' Nikos Englezou), Erwin Koffi, Danijel Pranjic, João Victor, Rayo, Nosa Igiebor, Sekou Cissé, Michal Duris, Beka Mikeltadze (51' Nika Kacharava). Coach: Roni Levy.
Goal: 88' Myrto Uzuni 1-0.
Referee: Donatas Rumsas (LIT)   Attendance: 1,950.

KF Laçi won on away goals.

19.07.18 Kadrioru staadion, Tallinn: JK Nõmme Kalju – UMF Stjarnan 1-0 (0-0)
JK Nõmme Kalju: Pavel Londak, Maximiliano Uggè, Trevor Elhi, Deniss Tjapkin (80' Alex Tamm), William Gustavo, Andriy Markovych, Igor Subbotin, Réginald Mbu-Alidor, Aleksandr Volkov (24' Kasper Paur), Liliu (71' Marko Brtan), Rimo Hunt.
Coach: Sergey Frantsev.
UMF Stjarnan: Haraldur Björnsson, Baldur Sigurdsson, Brynjar Gudjónsson, Daníel Laxdal, Eyjólfur Hédinsson (58' Gudmundur Hafsteinsson), Thorsteinn Már Ragnarsson (60' Jóhann Laxdal), Heidar Ægisson, Alex Thór Hauksson, Gunjón Baldvinsson, Thórarinn Valdimarsson, Hilmar Árni Halldórsson (81' Jósef Kristinn Jósefsson). Coach: Rúnar Sigmundsson.
Goal: 88' Alex Tamm 1-0.
Referee: Giorgi Kruashvili (GEO)   Attendance: 1,455.

(JK Nõmme Kalju played their home match at Kadrioru staadion instead of their regular stadium, Hiiu staadion)

19.07.18 Stadion Vasil Levski, Sofia: Slavia Sofia – Ilves Tampere 2-1 (1-0)
Slavia Sofia: Antonis Stergiakis, Aleksandar Aleksandrov, Emil Martinov, Andrea Hristov, Momchil Tsvetanov (84' Vladislav Uzunov), Galin Ivanov (90+3' Filip Krastev), Milen Gamakov, Yanis Karabelyov, Dimitar Velkovski, Georgi Yomov (67' Slavcho Shokolarov), Milcho Angelov. Coach: Zlatomir Zagorcic.
Ilves Tampere: Mika Hilander, Jani Tanska (76' Tariq Kazi), Felipe Aspegren, Tatu Miettunen (62' Iiro Järvinen), Diogo Tomas, Matias Ojala, Eero Tamminen (69' Santeri Haarala), Lauri Ala-Myllymäki, Mame Thiaw, Tuure Siira, Marius Noubissi. Coach: Jarkko Wiss.
Goals: 36' Galin Ivanov 1-0, 55' Marius Noubissi 1-1, 56' Galin Ivanov 2-1.
Referee: Nenad Djokic (SER)   Attendance: 3,400.

(Slavia Sofia played their home match at Stadion Vasil Levski instead of their regular stadium, Slavia Stadium)

19.07.18 Aker Stadion, Molde: Molde FK – Glenavon FC 5-1 (2-0)
Molde FK: Andreas Linde, Vegard Forren, Ruben Gabrielsen (46' Stian Gregersen), Kristoffer Haugen, Christoffer Remmer, Etzaz Hussain, Babacar Sarr, Eirik Hestad, Mattias Mostrøm (74' Fredrik Aursnes), Fredrik Brustad (61' Ibrahima Wadji), Daniel Chima Chukwu.
Coach: Ole Gunnar Solskjær.
Glenavon FC: James Taylor, Andrew Doyle, Dylan King, Caolan Marron, Gary Muir, Andrew Hall (84' Jordan Jenkins), Stephen Murray, Mark Sykes, Joshua Daniels (90+2' Jack O'Mahony), Niall Grace, Stephen Donnelly (46' Robbie Norton). Coach: Gary Hamilton.
Goals: 28' Etzaz Hussain 1-0 (p), 34', 59' Eirik Hestad 2-0, 3-0, 62' Vegard Forren 3-1 (og), 90' Eirik Hestad 4-1, 90+4' Babacar Sarr 5-1.
Referee: Alexandru Tean (MOL)   Attendance: 5,150.

19.07.18 MFA Centenary Stadium, Ta'Qali: Gzira United – Radnicki Nis 0-1 (0-1)
Gzira United: Anthony Curmi, Clifford Baldacchino, Rodolfo Soares, Sacha Borg, Thomas Veronese, Andrew Cohen (65' Emmanuel Okoye), Roderick Briffa, Édison Bilbao Zárate, Juan Corbalan (82' Christian Sammut), Zachary Scerri, Jorginho (75' Luca Brincat).
Coach: Darren Abdilla.
Radnicki Nis: Mladen Zivkovic, Aleksandar Todorovski, Radovan Pankov, Djordje Crnomarkovic (35' Taras Bondarenko), Aleksandar Stanisavljevic, Petar Grbic (46' Aleksa Jovanovic (II)), Dusan Micic, Nikola Stankovic, Ryota Noma, Nermin Haskic (63' Sladan Nikodijevic), Marko Mrkic. Coach: Nenad Lalatovic.
Goal: 7' Radovan Pankov 0-1.
Referee: Suren Baliyan (ARM)   Attendance: 509.

19.07.18   Stadions Skonto, Riga: Riga FC – CSKA Sofia 1-0 (1-0, 1-0)
Riga FC: Roberts Ozols, Vladislavs Gabovs (66' Kriss Kārklins), Antons Kurakins (119' Thiago Primão), Stefan Panic, Volodymyr Baenko, Antonijs Cernomordijs, Tomislav Saric, Bogdan Vastsuk, Ivan Enin (101' Armands Pētersons), George Davies (80' Milan Vusurovic), Darko Lemajic. Coach: Viktor Skripnik.
CSKA Sofia: Vytautas Cerniauskas, Nikolaj Bodurov, Kristiyan Malinov, Boris Sekulic (91' Steven Pereira), Bozhidar Chorbadzhiyski, Geferson, Valentin Antov (60' Henrique, 105+1' Janio Bikel), Rúben Pinto, Tiago Rodrigues, Kiril Despodov, Jorginho (61' Edwin Gyasi).
Coach: Nestor El Maestro.
Goal: 44' Antonijs Cernomordijs 1-0.
Referee: Furkat Atazhanov (KAZ)   Attendance: 3,100.
Sent off: 74' Tiago Rodrigues, 109' Stefan Panic, 130' Volodymyr Baenko,
130' Bogdan Vastsuk, 130' Nikolaj Bodurov, 130' Kristiyan Malinov.

Kiril Despodov missed a penalty kick (89').

CSKA Sofia won on penalties after extra time (5-3).
Penalties: Malinov 1-0, Lemajic missed, Bodurov 2-0, Thiago Primão 2-1, Geferson 3-1, Kārklins 3-2, Gyasi 4-2, Baenko 4-3, Despodov 5-3.

19.07.18   Stadión Pasienky, Bratislava: Slovan Bratislava – FC Milsami Orhei 5-0 (3-0)
Slovan Bratislava: Michal Sulla, Mitch Apau, Vasil Bozhikov, Artem Sukhotsky, Ibrahim Rabiu, Dávid Holman, Nono Delgado (58' Vukan Savicevic), Kenan Bajric, "Moha" Mohammed Rharsalla, Aleksandar Cavric (48' Boris Cmiljanic), Andraz Sporar (74' Dejan Drazic). Coach: Martin Sevela.
FC Milsami Orhei: Radu Mîtu, Vadim Bolohan, Constantin Bogdan (54' Sergiu Platica), Dinu Graur, Artur Craciun, Alexandru Antoniuc (81' Ion Ibrean), Andrei Cojocari, Mihai Platica, Vadim Rata, Andrei Rusmac, Romeo Surdu (34' Igor Bugaev). Coach: Veaceslav Rusnac.
Goals: 15', 25' Andraz Sporar 1-0, 2-0, 33' "Moha" Mohammed Rharsalla 3-0, 52' Boris Cmiljanic 4-0, 77' "Moha" Mohammed Rharsalla 5-0.
Referee: Nejc Kajtazovic (SVN)   Attendance: 3,175.

19.07.18   Vilniaus LFF stadionas, Vilnius: FK Zalgiris – KÍ Klaksvík 1-1 (1-0)
FK Zalgiris: Dziugas Bartkus, Rolandas Baravykas, Mamadou Mbodj, Saulius Mikoliūnas, Donovan Slijngard, Tomas Simkovic, Liviu Antal (36' Serge Nyuiadzi), Slavko Blagojevic, Marquinhos Carioca (46' Venelin Filipov), Jérémy Manzorro (66' Louis Ogana), Marko Tomic. Coach: Valdas Urbonas.
KÍ Klaksvík: Kristian Joensen, Ísak Simonsen (90+2' Óli Poulsen), Deni Pavlovic, Ólavur Niclasen, Semir Hadzibulic, Boris Dosljak (75' Jóannes Bjartalíd), Hørdur Askham, Jákup Andreasen, Jóannes Danielsen, Ronny Møller-Iversen (87' Kristoffur Jakobsen), Páll Klettskard. Coach: Mikkjal Kjartansson Thomassen.
Goals: 6' Liviu Antal 1-0, 66' Ronny Møller-Iversen 1-1.
Referee: Milovan Milacic (MNE)   Attendance: 2,500.

19.07.18   Stadiumi Olimpik Adem Jashari, Mitrovica: Prishtina KF – CS Fola Esch 0-0
Prishtina KF: Visar Bekaj, Armend Dallku, Arago Jamal, Ahmet Haliti, Armend Thaçi, Argjend Mustafa, Meriton Korenica, Gauthier Mankenda (76' Mërgim Pefqeli), Ergyn Ahmeti (98' Lorik Boshnjaku), Alen Jasharovski (93' Arbër Hoxha), Khalid Abdul Basit.
Coach: Mirel Josa.
CS Fola Esch: Thomas Hym, Rodrigue Dikaba, Billy Bernard (46' Julien Klein), Tom Laterza (66' Gérard Mersch), Peter Chrappan, Mehdi Kirch (105' Cédric Sacras), Veldin Muharemovic, Enis Saiti (72' Stefano Bensi), Ryan Klapp, Samir Hadji, Ken Corral.
Coach: Thomas Klasen.
Referee: Urs Schnyder (SUI)   Attendance: 2,300.

(Prishtina KF played their home match at Stadiumi Olimpik Adem Jashari instead of their regular stadium, Stadiumi Fadil Vokrii, due to renovation)

CS Fola Esch won on penalties after extra time (5-4).
Penalties: Bensi 1-0, Dallku 1-1, Sacras missed, Korenica 1-2, Hadji 2-2, Thaçi 2-3, Chrappan 3-3, Pefqeli missed, Muharemovic missed, Hoxha missed, Dikaba missed, Boshnjaku missed, Klapp 4-3, Haliti 4-4, Mersch 5-4, Jamal missed.

19.07.18   Boris Paichadze Dinamo Arena, Tbilisi:
  Dinamo Tbilisi – DAC Dunajská Streda 1-2 (1-0)
Dinamo Tbilisi: Demetre Buliskeria, Gudzha Rukhaia, Luka Lochoshvili, Davit Kobouri, Nika Ninua, Levan Kharabadze, Dmitriy Ivanisenya, Akaki Shulaia, Otari Kiteishvili, Budu Zivzivadze (74' Mate Vatsadze), Mikheil Ergemlidze (88' George Ivanishvili).
Coach: Kakhaber Katcharava.
DAC Dunajská Streda: Patrik Macej, Éric Davis (57' Zsolt Kalmár), Lubomír Satka, Timotej Záhumensky, Marin Ljubicic (72' Máté Vida), Erik Pacinda, Tomás Huk, Kristián Kostrna, Krisztopher Vida (80' Maksym Tretyakov), Christián Herc, Vakoun Issouf Bayo.
Coaches: Marco Rossi & Peter Hyballa.
Goals: 41' Budu Zivzivadze 1-0, 86', 90+4' Vakoun Issouf Bayo 1-1, 1-2.
Referee: Dimitar Meckarovski (MKD)   Attendance: 6,111.

19.07.18   Neo GSP Stadium, Nicosia: Apollon FC Limassol – FC Stumbras 2-0 (1-0)
Apollon FC Limassol: Bruno Vale, Valentin Roberge, Charis Kyriakou, André Schembri (83' Emilio Zelaya), Héctor Yuste, Giorgos Vasiliou, Esteban Sachetti, João Pedro, Fotis Papoulis (90' Ioannis Pittas), Anton Maglica, Adrián Sardinero (68' Sasa Markovic).
Coach: Sofronis Avgousti.
FC Stumbras: Rodrigo Josviaki, Lukas Cerkauskas, Matheus Bissi, Rimvydas Sadauskas, Jardel Nazaré, André Almeida, Agostinho Cá, Marcos Junior (56' Dominykas Galkevicius), Levan Matcharashvili (74' Alsény Bah), Lucas Villela, Nasro Bouchareb (46' Liu Yuhao).
Coach: Mariano Barreto.
Goals: 7', 62' Héctor Yuste 1-0, 2-0.
Referee: Eldorjan Hamiti (ALB)   Attendance: 2,556.

(Apollon FC Limassol played their home match at Neo GSP Stadium, Nicosia, instead of their regular stadium, Tsirio Stadium, Limassol)

19.07.18   Stadionul Zimbru, Chisinau: FC Zaria Balti – Górnik Zabrze 1-1 (1-0)
FC Zaria Balti: Vladimir Livsit, Oleg Ermak, Ion Burlacu, Lucas Silva, Daniel Dumbravanu, Rúben Gómez, Rodrigo Bostan (73' Cristian Dros), Georgi Ovsyannikov, Guilherme, Conrado, Vadim Gulceac (87' Serghei Alexeev). Coach: Vlad Goian.
Górnik Zabrze: Tomasz Loska, Dani Suárez, Wiktor Biedrzycki (73' Michal Koj), Adrian Gryszkiewicz, Przemyslaw Wisniewski, Szymon Matuszek, Angulo, Adam Wolniewicz, Adam Ryczkowski (54' Daniel Smuga), Maciej Ambrosiewicz (59' Daniel Liszka), Jesús Jiménez. Coach: Marcin Brosz.
Goals: 7' Guilherme 1-0, 85' Daniel Smuga 1-1.
Referee: Rahim Hasanov (AZE)   Attendance: 1,300.

(FC Zaria Balti played their home match at Stadionul Zimbru instead of their regular stadium, Stadionul Orasenesc)

19.07.18   Telekom Arena, Skopje: Vardar Skopje – Pyunik Yerevan FC 0-2 (0-0)
Vardar Skopje: Filip Gacevski, Evgen Novak, Vladica Brdarovski (86' Filip Najdovski), Tigran Barseghyan, Kosta Manev, Kristijan Tosevski, Jovan Popzlatanov (71' Besar Iseni), Darko Micevski, Clarence Bitang, Jakub Berisha (46' Willian Lira), Maksim Maksimov. Coach: Boban Babunski.
Pyunik Yerevan FC: Evgeni Kobozev (46' Andrija Dragojevic), Vyacheslav Dmitriev, Maksim Zhestokov, Serob Grigoryan, Maksim Trusevich (61' Vitali Stezhko), Denis Voynov, Didier Kadio, Alik Arakelyan, Vahagn Hayrapetyan, Ruslan Koryan (70' Bacar Baldé), Mohamed Konaté. Coach: Andrey Talalaev.
Goals: 85', 89' Bacar Baldé 0-1, 0-2.
Referee: Ian McNabb (NIR)   Attendance: 5,823.

19.07.18   Friends Arena, Solna: AIK Solna – Shamrock Rovers FC 1-1 (0-1, 0-1)
AIK Solna: Oscar Linnér, Per Karlsson, Daniel Sundgren, Alexander Milosevic, Rasmus Lindkvist (83' Nicolás Stefanelli), Robin Jansson, Tarik Elyounoussi (109' Haukur Hauksson), Ahmed Yasin, Enoch Adu, Denni Avdic (63' Kristoffer Olsson), Stefan Silva (63' Henok Goitom). Coach: Rikard Norling.
Shamrock Rovers FC: Gavin Bazunu, Joey O'Brien, Sean Kavanagh, Roberto Lopes, Lee Grace, Sam Bone (84' Greg Bolger), Ronan Finn, Ethan Boyle, Dylan Watts (93' David McAllister), Daniel Carr (67' Aaron Bolger), Joel Coustrain (68' Aaron Green). Coach: Stephen Bradley.
Goals: 19' Daniel Carr 0-1, 94' Nicolás Stefanelli 1-1.
Referee: Nicolas Laforge (BEL)   Attendance: 8,115.

AIK Solna won after extra time.

19.07.18   Stadyen Budaunik Stroitel, Soligorsk:
Shakhtyor Soligorsk – Connah's Quay Nomads FC 2-0 (1-0)
Shakhtyor Soligorsk: Andrey Klimovich, Pavel Rybak, Igor Kuzmenok (45+1' Maksim Bordachev), Siarhei Matveichyk, Mikhail Shibun, Roger Cañas, Aleksandr Selyava, Yuri Kovalev, Július Szöke, Max Ebong Ngome (83' Pyry Soiri), Elis Bakaj (65' Denis Laptev). Coach: Sergey Tashuev.
Connah's Quay Nomads FC: John Danby, George Horan (46' Jonathan Spittle), Laurence Wilson, Danny Holmes, John Disney, Michael Parker (66' Declan Poole), James Owen (53' Noah Edwards), Michael Bakare, Callum Morris, Ryan Wignall, Andrew Owens.
Coach: Andrew Morrison.
Goals: 24' Elis Bakaj 1-0 (p), 82' Maksim Bordachev 2-0.
Referee: Admir Sehovic (BIH)   Attendance: 2,700.
Sent off: 62' Andrew Owens.

19.07.18   Winner Stadium, Netanya: Maccabi Tel Aviv – Ferencvárosi TC 1-0 (1-0)
Maccabi Tel Aviv: Predrag Rajkovic, Eitan Tibi, Avi Rikan (89' Sheran Yeini), Saborit, Elazar Dasa, Jair Amador, Dor Mikha, Roslan Barski, Dor Peretz, Vidar Kjartansson (66' Aaron Schoenfeld), Eliran Atar (73' Omer Atzili). Coach: Vladimir Ivic.
Ferencvárosi TC: Dénes Dibusz, Marcel Heister, Miha Blazic, Abraham Frimpong, Stefan Spirovski, Lukács Böle, Ivan Petryak (74' Dániel Böde), Fernando Gorriarán, Davide Lanzafame (63' Roland Varga), Kjartan Finnbogason, Gergö Lovrencsics.
Coach: Thomas Doll.
Goal: 45+1' Eliran Atar 1-0.
Referee: Hugo Miguel (POR)   Attendance: 8,256.

(Maccabi Tel Aviv played their home match at Winner Stadium instead of their regular stadium, Bloomfield Stadium, due to renovation)

19.07.18   Dalga Arena, Baku: Keshla FK – Balzan FC 2-1 (1-0)
Keshla FK: Kamran Agayev, Adrian Scarlatache, Dênis, Tarlan Guliyev, Slavik Alkhasov, Sertan Taskin (85' Mammad Guliev), Ebrima Sohna, Milos Bosancic (74' Hervé Tchami-Ngangoue), Andre Clennon, Bakhodir Nasimov (64' Amit Yunanov), César Meza Colli.
Coach: Yuriy Maksimov.
Balzan FC: Steve Sultana, Elkin Serrano, Steven Bezzina, Ivan Bozovic, Uros Ljubomirac (59' Lecão), Michael Johnson, Cadú, Nenad Sljivic, Milos Lepovic, Alfred Effiong (69' Justin Grioli), Bojan Kaljevic (85' Andrija Majdevac). Coach: Marko Micovic.
Goals: 11' César Meza Colli 1-0 (p), 90+1' Slavik Alkhasov 2-0, 90+6' Andrija Majdevac 2-1.
Referee: Mikhail Vilkov (RUS)   Attendance: 2,215.
Sent off: 90+7' Andrija Majdevac.

(Keshla FK played their home match at Dalga Arena instead of their regular stadium, Inter Arena)

19.07.18 Sarpsborg Stadion, Sarpsborg: Sarpsborg 08 – ÍB Vestmannaeyja 2-0 (1-0)
Sarpsborg 08: Aslak Falch, Joackim Jørgensen, Joachim Thomassen, Bjørn Utvik, Jon-Helge Tveita, Kristoffer Zachariassen (70' Ole Halvorsen), Tobias Heintz, Muhammed Usman, Patrick Mortensen (62' Rashad Muhammed), Mikkel Agger, Kristoffer Larsen (67' Harmeet Singh). Coach: Geir Bakke.
ÍB Vestmannaeyja: Halldór Geirsson, David Atkinson, Sindri Snær Magnússon, Kaj Leo í Bartalsstovu (70' Ágúst Björnsson), Alfred Már Hjaltalín, Atli Arnarson (60' Jonathan Franks), Priestley Griffiths (80' Róbert Eysteinsson), Dagur Hilmarsson, Felix Örn Fridriksson, Sigurdur Arnar Magnússon, Shahab Zahedi Tabar. Coach: Kristján Gudmundsson.
Goals: 13', 82' Mikkel Agger 1-0, 2-0.
Referee: Genc Nuza (KOS)   Attendance: 3,552.

19.07.18 Bravida Arena, Göteborg: BK Häcken – FK Liepāja 1-2 (1-1)
BK Häcken: Peter Abrahamsson, Emil Wahlström, Alexander Angelin, Johan Hammar (90' Kari Arkivuo), Gustav Berggren, Rasmus Lindgren, Erik Friberg (69' Alexander Faltsetas), Adam Andersson (76' Karl Bohm), Viktor Lundberg, Alhassan Kamara, Nasiru Mohammed. Coach: Andreas Alm.
FK Liepāja: Arsen Beglaryan, Deniss Ivanovs, Sady Guèye, Seydina Keita, Vladimir Kamess, Dmitrijs Ilmizs (52' Cristián Torres), Raivis Jurkovskis, Leonel Strumia, Kristers Tobers (79' Kristaps Grebis), Mārtins Kigurs (63' Benjamin Teidi), Girts Karlsons. Coach: Tamaz Pertia.
Goals: 11' Sady Guèye 0-1, 42' Nasiru Mohammed 1-1, 86' Girts Karlsons 1-2.
Referee: Sergey Ivanov (RUS)   Attendance: 1,713.

19.07.18 Stade Parc des Sports, Differdange: Progrès Niederkorn – Gabala FK 0-1 (0-1)
Progrès Niederkorn: Sebastian Flauss, Mario Mutsch, Adrien Ferino, Marvin da Graça, Jordan Gobron, Tim Hall, Emmanuel Françoise (85' Yann Matias Marques), Sébastien Thill, Yannick Bastos (29' Alexander Karapetyan), Olivier Thill (90' Ben Vogel), Mayron De Almeida. Coach: Paolo Amodio.
Gabala FK: Dmitro Bezotosniy, Ilgar Gurbanov, Rasim Ramaldanov, Urfan Abbasov, Javid Hüseynov, Asif Mammadov (55' Lalawelé Atakora), Sabien Lilaj, Tamkim Khalilzade, Steeven Joseph-Monrose, Rauf Aliyev, Segun Adeniyi. Coach: Senan Gurbanov.
Goal: 28' Steeven Joseph-Monrose 0-1.
Referee: Keith Kennedy (NIR)   Attendance: 1,842.
Sent off: 79' Tamkim Khalilzade.

(Progrès Niederkorn played their home match at Stade Parc des Sports, Differdange, instead of their regular stadium, Stade Jos Haupert, Niederkorn)

19.07.18 Right to Dream Park, Farum: FC Nordsjælland – Cliftonville FC 2-1 (0-1)
FC Nordsjælland: Nicolai Larsen, Mads Aaquist (66' Andreas Skov Olsen), Viktor Tranberg (46' Mikkel Rygaard Jensen), Clinton Antwi, Ulrik Jenssen, Nicklas Strunck Jakobsen, Victor Nelsson, Ibrahim Sadiq (46' Godsway Donyoh), Jacob Christensen, Mikkel Damsgaard, Nikolai Baden Frederiksen. Coach: Kasper Hjulmand.
Cliftonville FC: Brian Neeson, Jamie McGovern, Garry Breen, Liam Bagnall, Jamie Harney, Levi Ives, Christopher Curran (84' Stephen Garrett), Rory Donnelly, Ryan Curran (64' Conor McDonald), Joe Gormley, Jay Donnelly (73' Conor McMenamin). Coach: Barry Gray.
Goals: 6' Joe Gormley 0-1 (p), 58' Godsway Donyoh 1-1, 83' Jamie Harney 2-1 (og).
Referee: Eitan Shemeulevitch (ISR)   Attendance: 1,592.

19.07.18   Teddi Malcha Stadium, Jerusalem:
      Beitar Jerusalem – FC Chikhura Sachkhere 1-2 (0-0)
Beitar Jerusalem: Itamar Nitzan, Carlos Cuéllar, Michael Siroshtein (78' Ya'akov Berihon), Tal Kachila, Matan Peleg (58' Gaëtan Varenne), Or Zehavi, Erik Sabo, Ofir Kriaf, Lior Inbrum, Jakub Sylvestr, Idan Vered. Coach: Guy Luzon.
FC Chikhura Sachkhere: Dino Hamzic, Davit Maisashvili, Lasha Chikvaidze, Bakari Mirtshkulava, Davit Megrelishvili, Revaz Chiteishvili, Denis Dobrovolski (71' Levan Kakubava), Irakli Lekvtadze (59' Mikheil Sardalishvili), Teimurazi Markozashvili, Irakli Bugridze (72' Kakha Kakhabrishvili), Giorgi Gabedava. Coach: Samson Pruidze.
Goals: 62' Idan Vered 1-0, 73' Levan Kakubava 1-1, 83' Giorgi Gabedava 1-2 (p).
Referee: Marco Di Bello (ITA)   Attendance: 1,300.

19.07.18   Svangaskard, Toftir: NSÍ Runavík – Hibernian FC Edinburgh 4-6 (3-3)
NSÍ Runavík: Eli Joensen, Pól Justinussen, Jens Joensen, Per Langgaard, Pætur Hentze, Fródi Benjaminsen, Bárdur Jögvansson-Hansen, Petur Knudsen, Jann Benjaminsen (88' Mórits Heini Mortensen), Magnus Olsen (71' Betuel Hansen), Klæmint Andrasson Olsen (74' Jann Mortensen). Coach: Sámal Hentze.
Hibernian FC Edinburgh: Ádám Bogdán, Steven Whittaker (77' Vykintas Slivka), Lewis Stevenson, Efe Ambrose, David Gray, Ryan Porteous, Marvin Bartley (88' James Gullan), John McGinn, Stephen Mallan, Florian Kamberi, Oliver Shaw (78' Danny Swanson). Coach: Neil Lennon.
Goals: 1' Efe Ambrose 1-0 (og), 6' Klæmint Andrasson Olsen 2-0, 10' John McGinn 2-1, 16' Lewis Stevenson 2-2, 35' Klæmint Andrasson Olsen 3-2, 45+1' David Gray 3-3, 50' Efe Ambrose 3-4, 57' Klæmint Andrasson Olsen 4-4, 70', 77' Stephen Mallan 4-5, 4-6.
Referee: Luis Teixeira (POR)   Attendance: 587.

19.07.18   Elbasan Arena, Elbasan: Luftëtari Gjirokastër – FK Ventspils 3-3 (1-2)
Luftëtari Gjirokastër: Shkelzen Ruçi (45+2' Hrvoje Bukovski), Nemanja Janicic, Lejdi Liçaj (46' Aurel Demo), Oltion Rapa, Donald Rapo (71' Donaldo Açka), Vladan Milosavljev, Erjon Vuçaj, Behar Ramadani, Maldin Ymeraj, Albano Aleksi, Vasil Shkurtaj. Coach: Milos Kostic.
FK Ventspils: Maksims Uvarenko, Abdoul Mamah, Vitālijs Jagodinskis (64' Nikita Kolesovs), Medzit Neziri, Hélio Batista, Ritvars Rugins (46' Raens Tālbergs), Abdullahi Alfa, Giuly Mandzhgaladze, Tosin Aiyegun, Vasili Pavlov (46' Kaspars Kokins), Adeleke Akinyemi. Coach: Dejan Vukicevic.
Goals: 44' Vasil Shkurtaj 1-0 (p), 45+4', 45+8' Adeleke Akinyemi 1-1, 1-2, 55' Maldin Ymeraj 2-2, 61' Vladan Milosavljev 3-2, 90+3' Abdullahi Alfa 3-3.
Referee: Anders Poulsen (DEN)   Attendance: 270.

(Luftëtari Gjirokastër played their home match at Elbasan Arena instead of their regular stadium, Stadiumi Gjirokastra)

19.07.18   Telia Parken, København: FC København – Kuopion PS 1-1 (0-0)
FC København: Jesse Joronen, Sotirios Papagiannopoulos, Nicolai Boilesen, Denis Vavro, Mads Roerslev Rasmussen (71' Peter Ankersen), Ján Gregus, Rasmus Falk (90+4' Andreas Bjelland), Zeca, Viktor Fischer, Dame N'Doye, Kenan Kodro (70' Robert Skov). Coach: Ståle Solbakken.
Kuopion PS: Otso Virtanen, Henri Toivomäki, Lum Rexhepi, Luis Murillo, Juho Pirttijoki, Petteri Pennanen, Joni Mäkelä (71' Ats Purje), Ville Saxman, Ilmari Niskanen, Saku Savolainen, Rangel (61' Rasmus Karjalainen). Coach: Jani Honkavaara.
Goals: 75' Rasmus Karjalainen 0-1, 81' Denis Vavro 1-1 (p).
Referee: Vilhjálmur Thórarinsson (ISL)   Attendance: 7,145.

19.07.18   Olimpijski Stadion Asim Ferhatovic Hase, Sarajevo:
             FK Sarajevo – FC Banants Erevan 3-0 (2-0)
FK Sarajevo: Bojan Pavlovic, Nihad Mujakic, Selmir Pidro (81' Milos Stanojevic), Emir Halilovic, Amar Rahmanovic, Anel Hebibovic, Joachim Adukor, Alen Mustafic, Mersudin Ahmetovic (74' Haris Handzic), Krste Velkoski, Aladin Sisic (68' Sevkija Resic).
Coach: Husref Musemic.
FC Banants Erevan: Anatoliy Ayvazov, Vahagn Ayvazyan, Borislav Jovanovic, Edward Kpodo, Narek Petrosyan, Aram Bareghamyan, Igor Stanojevic (66' Karen Melkonyan), Solomon Udo (75' Aram Loretsyan), Kwasi Sibo, Lester Peltier, Wal (46' Ognjen Krasic).
Coach: Aram Voskanyan.
Goals: 31' Nihad Mujakic 1-0, 38' Mersudin Ahmetovic 2-0, 72' Sevkija Resic 3-0.
Referee: Lionel Tschudi (SUI)   Attendance: 8,125.

19.07.18   Ljudski vrt, Maribor: NK Maribor – FK Partizani Tirana 2-0 (1-0)
NK Maribor: Jasmin Handanovic, Marko Suler, Mitja Viler, Martin Milec, Sasa Ivkovic, Blaz Vrhovec, Amir Dervisevic, Dino Hotic (83' Aleks Pihler), Martin Kramaric (78' Dare Vrsic), Luka Zahovic, Jan Mlakar (78' Marcos Tavares). Coach: Darko Milanic.
FK Partizani Tirana: Alban Hoxha (I), Sodiq Atanda, Renato Gojkovic, Libanot Ibrahimi, Gerhard Progni (66' Renaldo Kalari), Bruno Telushi, Ardit Hila, Lorenc Trashi, Jasir Asani (76' Stefan Nikolic), Jurgen Bardhi (56' Besart Abdurahimi), Esat Mala.
Coach: Skënder Gega.
Goals: 31' Amir Dervisevic 1-0, 90+3' Marcos Tavares 2-0.
Referee: Paul Tierney (ENG)   Attendance: 6,876.

19.07.18   Furbalovy stadión Spartak Myjava, Myjava:
             AS Trencín – FK Buducnost Podgorica 1-1 (0-0)
AS Trencín: Igor Semrinec, Jamie Lawrence, Martin Sulek, Keston Julien, Reuben Yem, Ashraf El Mahdioui, Abdul Zubairu, Joey Sleegers, Antonio Mance (90+3' Emeka Umeh), Hamza Catakovic, Philip Azango. Coach: Ricardo Moniz.
FK Buducnost Podgorica: Milan Mijatovic, Vladan Adzic, Luka Mirkovic, Ilija Tucevic (77' Dusan Bakic), Dominique Correa, Bojan Roganovic, Stefan Milic, Miljan Vlaisavljevic, Milos Mijic, Balsa Boricic (73' Balsa Sekulic), Igor Ivanovic (89' Mihailo Perovic).
Coach: Zoran Govedarica.
Goals: 70' Antonio Mance 1-0, 90' Mihailo Perovic 1-1.
Referee: Sergey Lapochkin (RUS)   Attendance: 1,520.

(AS Trencín played their home match at Furbalovy stadión Spartak Myjava instead of their regular stadium, Stadión na Sihoti, due to renovation)

19.07.18   Stadion Pod Goricom, Podgorica:
OFK Titograd Podgorica – B36 Tórshavn 1-2 (1-0)
OFK Titograd Podgorica: Damir Ljuljanovic, Milos B.Radulovic, Ivan Novovic, Branko Ojdanic (81' Mirko Raicevic), Marko Roganovic, Jovan Nikolic, Vasko Kalezic, Marko Milickovic (73' Ognjen Gasevic), Ivica Jovanovic, Pjeter Ljuljdjuraj, Zoran Petrovic (32' Vojin Pavlovic). Coach: Aleksandar Miljenovic.
B36 Tórshavn: Rói Hentze, Odmar Færø, Alex Mellemgaard, Bjarni Petersen, Erlendur Magnusson, Eli Nielsen, Meinhard Olsen, Benjamin Heinesen (71' Hugin Samuelsen), Magnus Holm Jacobsen (80' Robert Hedin Brockie), Kaimar Saag (87' Gilli Samuelsen), Lukasz Cieslewicz. Coach: Jákup á Borg.
Goals: 4' Zoran Petrovic 1-0, 51' Benjamin Heinesen 1-1, 83' Milos B.Radulovic 1-2 (og).
Referee: Omar Pashayev (AZE)   Attendance: 2,050.

(OFK Titograd Podgorica played their home match at Stadion Pod Goricom instead of their regular stadium, Mladost Stadium)

19.07.18   Stadion Partizana, Beograd: Partizan Beograd – FK Rudar Pljevlja 3-0 (2-0)
Partizan Beograd: Filip Kljajic, Marc Valiente (57' Svetozar Markovic), Nemanja Miletic (I), Sasa Zdjelar, Gabriel Enache, Seydouba Soumah (57' Zoran Tosic), Danilo Pantic, Nemanja Miletic (II), Ognjen Ozegovic (63' Ricardo Gomes), Djordje Ivanovic, Armin Djerlek. Coach: Miroslav Djukic.
FK Rudar Pljevlja: Vuk Radovic, Zeljko Tomasevic (61' Radule Zivkovic), Filip Mitrovic, Alphonse Soppo, Armin Bosnjak, Aleksandar Macanovic (46' Velizar Janketic), Dejan Kotorac (68' Edvin Kuc), Nemanja Sekulic, Milija Golubovic, Radomir Djalovic, Marko Vukovic. Coach: Vuko Bogavac.
Goals: 11' Danilo Pantic 1-0, 44' Ognjen Ozegovic 2-0, 83' Ricardo Gomes 3-0.
Referee: Daniele Doveri (ITA)   Attendance: 5,869.

19.07.18   The Showgrounds, Coleraine: Coleraine FC – Spartak Subotica 0-2 (0-1)
Coleraine FC: Christopher Johns, Aaron Traynor, Gareth McConaghie, Adam Mullan (85' James McLaughlin), Stephen O'Donnell, Stephen Lowry, Darren McCauley, Aaron Burns (60' Jamie McGonigle), Ian Parkhill (60' Ciaron Harkin), Bradley Lyons, Eoin Bradley. Coach: Oran Kearney.
Spartak Subotica: Nikola Peric, Andrija Vukcevic, Branimir Jocic, Noboru Shimura (66' Vladimir Torbica), Dejan Kerkez, Nemanja Calasan, Mile Savkovic, Nemanja Glavcic (75' Milan Marcic), David Dundjerski, Samuel Afum (83' Bojan Cecaric), Ognjen Djuricin. Coach: Vladimir Gacinovic.
Goals: 33' Mile Savkovic 0-1, 90+2' Bojan Cecaric 0-2.
Referee: Trustin Farrugia Cann (MLT)   Attendance: 1,602.

19.07.18   Stadion Gradski vrt, Osijek: NK Osijek – CS Petrocub Hîncesti 2-1 (1-1)
NK Osijek: Marko Malenica, Borna Barisic, Stjepan Radeljic, Tomislav Sorsa, Gabrijel Boban (22' Dmitriy Lepa, 66' Domagoj Pusic), Benedik Mioc, Petar Bockaj (78' Haris Hajradinovic), Robert Mudrazija, Daniel Loncar, Mirko Maric, Ezekiel Henty. Coach: Zoran Zekic.
CS Petrocub Hîncesti: Dumitru Celeadnic, Maxim Potîrniche, Ion Sandu, Victor Mudrac, Maxim Cojocaru, Vlad Slivca (70' Sergiu Matei), Dan Taras (60' Artur Patras), Vladimir Ambros, Jessie Guera Djou, Donalio Melachio Douanla, Vladislav Ivanov (54' Alexandru Vremea). Coach: Lilian Popescu.
Goals: 15' Robert Mudrazija 1-0, 22' Vladimir Ambros 1-1 (p), 61' Borna Barisic 2-1.
Referee: Dimitrios Massias (CYP)   Attendance: 2,233.

19.07.18   Stadio Tullo Morgagni, Forlì: SP Tre Fiori – Rudar Velenje 0-3 (0-1)
SP Tre Fiori: Giorgio Pizzolato, Matteo Andreini, Guido Ghetti, Davide Succi, Luca Filippi, Mattia Costantini (63' Davide Pasolini), Nicola Della Valle (72' Espedito Marinaro), Andrea Tamagnini (82' Simone Matteoni), Alessandro Teodorani, Acquarelli Miacol, Mirco Vassallo. Coach: Matteo Cecchetti.
Rudar Velenje: Marko Pridigar, Josip Tomasevic, Klemen Bolha (67' Domagoj Muic), Robert Pusaver, Ivan Vasiljevic, Damjan Trifkovic (46' Djair Parfitt-Williams), Anze Pisek, Ante Solomun, Dominik Radic (46' Vlatko Simunac), Milan Tucic, Abu Kamara.
Coach: Marijan Pusnik.
Goals: 43' Klemen Bolha 0-1, 47' Vlatko Simunac 0-2, 71' Abu Kamara 0-3.
Referee: Fyodor Zammit (MLT)   Attendance: 245.

(SP Tre Fiori played their home match at Stadio Tullo Morgagni instead of their regular stadium, San Marino Stadium, due to renovation)

19.07.18   Oriel Park, Dundalk: Dundalk FC – FCI Levadia Tallinn 2-1 (2-1)
Dundalk FC: Gary Rogers, Brain Gartland, Dane Massey, Sean Gannon, Sean Hoare, Chris Shields, Robbie Benson, Dylan Connolly (62' Krisztián Adorján), Jamie McGrath, Patrick Hoban (90+2' Georgie Kelly), Michael Duffy (83' Karolis Chvedukas).
Coach: Stephen Kenny.
FCI Levadia Tallinn: Sergei Lepmets, Markus Jürgenson (88' Rasmus Peetson), Dmitri Kruglov, Maksim Podholjuzin, Igor Dudarev, Muamer Svraka, Evgeny Kharin (80' Kirill Nesterov), Yuriy Tkachuk, Marcelin Gando (64' Mark Oliver Roosnupp), Nikita Andreev, Roman Debelko. Coach: Aleksandar Rogic.
Goals: 31' Patrick Hoban 1-0, 33' Michael Duffy 2-0, 42' Roman Debelko 2-1.
Referee: Adrien Jaccottet (SUI)   Attendance: 3,000.

19.07.18   Sportni Park, Domzale: NK Domzale – Siroki Brijeg 1-1 (1-0)
NK Domzale: Dejan Milic, Matija Sirok, Gaber Dobrovoljc, Tilen Klemencic, Dario Melnjak, Senijad Ibricic, Zeni Husmani, Lovro Bizjak (90+2' Andraz Kirm), Adam Gnezda Cerin, Agim Ibraimi (80' Zan Zuzek), Shamar Nicholson (67' Tonci Mujan). Coach: Simon Rozman.
Siroki Brijeg: Luka Bilobrk, Josip Barisic, Stipo Markovic (83' Josip Kvesic), Bernardo Matic, Dominik Kovacic, Danijel Kozul (46' Mateo Maric), Luka Begonja, Eliomar (60' Dejan Cabraja), Josip Corluka, Drazen Bagaric, Tomislav Turcin. Coach: Boris Pavic.
Goals: 11' Dario Melnjak 1-0, 73' Bernardo Matic 1-1.
Referee: Antti Munukka (FIN)   Attendance: 2,000.

NK Domzale won on away goals.

19.07.18   Szusza Ferenc Stadion, Budapest: Újpesti FC – Neftçi PFC Baku 4-0 (2-0)
Újpesti FC: Filip Pajovic, Mijusko Bojovic, Branko Pauljevic, Róbert Litauszki, Dzenan Burekovic, Dániel Nagy (88' Benjámin Cseke), Bojan Sankovic, Donát Zsótér (81' Benjámin Balász), Alassane Diallo, Obinna Nwobodo, Soma Novothny (90+1' Patrik Tischler).
Coach: Nebojsa Vignjevic.
Neftçi PFC Baku: Sälahät Agayev, Ruslan Abisov (41' Tural Akhundov), Slavko Bralic, Anton Krivotsyuk (54' Kwame Karikari), Sony Mustivar, Goran Paracki, Rahman Hajiyev (78' Mirabdulla Abbasov), Kyrylo Petrov, Magomed Mirzabekov, Bagaliy Dabo, Dário Júnior da Silva. Coach: Roberto Bordin.
Goals: 19' Róbert Litauszki 1-0, 21' Bojan Sankovic 2-0, 49' Donát Zsótér 3-0, 65' Obinna Nwobodo 4-0.
Referee: Ioannis Papadopoulos (GRE)   Attendance: 3,738.

19.07.18 Kaplakrikavöllur, Hafnarfjördur: FH Hafnarfjördur – FC Lahti 0-0
FH Hafnarfjördur: Gunnar Nielsen, Hjörtur Valgardsson, Vidar Ari Jónsson, Edi Gomes, Rennico Clarke, Davíd Vidarsson, Gudmundur Kristjánsson, Kristinn Steindórsson, Brandur Hendriksson Olsen (86' Robbie Crawford), Atli Gudnason (65' Zeiko Lewis), Steven Lennon (76' Geoffrey Castillion). Coach: Ólafur Kristjánsson.
FC Lahti: Oskari Forsman, Mikko Hauhia, Kalle Taimi, Pavel Osipov, Artem Vyatkin, Santeri Hostikka, Paavo Voutilainen (59' Fareed Sadat), Artjom Dmitrijev (87' Eemelie Virta), Loorents Hertsi, Aleksi Paananen (74' Xhevdet Gela), Henri Anier.
Coach: Toni Korkeakunnas.
Referee: Espen Eskås (NOR)   Attendance: 742.

SECOND QUALIFYING ROUND

Bye: Cork City FC.

26.07.18 Stadion Neftyanik, Ufa: FC Ufa – NK Domzale 0-0
FC Ufa: Aleksandr Belenov, Bojan Jokic, Denis Tumasyan, Ionut Nedelcearu, Jemal Tabidze, Veroljub Salatic, Ivan Paurevic, Dmitri Zhivoglyadov, Ivan Oblyakov (76' Catalin Carp), Sylvester Igboun, Vyacheslav Krotov (46' Kehinde Fatai). Coach: Sergei Tomarov.
NK Domzale: Dejan Milic, Matija Sirok, Gaber Dobrovoljc, Tilen Klemencic, Dario Melnjak, Senijad Ibricic, Zeni Husmani, Lovro Bizjak (90+1' Zan Zuzek), Adam Gnezda Cerin, Agim Ibraimi (83' Shamar Nicholson), Andraz Kirm. Coach: Simon Rozman.
Referee: Donatas Rumsas (LTU)   Attendance: 11,210.

26.07.18 Olimpiskā centra Ventspils Stadionā, Ventspils:
    FK Ventspils – Girondins de Bordeaux 0-1 (0-1)
FK Ventspils: Maksims Uvarenko, Abdoul Mamah, Vitālijs Jagodinskis (55' Nauris Bulvītis), Medzit Neziri, Hélio Batista, Ritvars Rugins (46' Pedro Mendes), Abdullahi Alfa, Giuly Mandzhgaladze, Tosin Aiyegun, Vasili Pavlov (89' Raens Tālbergs), Adeleke Akinyemi.
Coach: Dejan Vukicevic.
Girondins de Bordeaux: Benoît Costil, Igor Lewczuk, Pablo Castro, Maxime Poundjé, Jules Koundé, Jaroslav Plasil, Younousse Sankharé, Lukas Lerager, Aurélien Tchouaméni (89' Otávio), Zaydou Youssouf (64' Nicolas de Préville), François Kamano (77' Gaëtan Laborde).
Coach: Gustavo Poyet.
Goal: 3' Zaydou Youssouf 0-1.
Referee: Sergey Lapochkin (RUS)   Attendance: 3,055.

26.07.18 Slokas Stadionā, Jūrmala: FK Spartaks Jūrmala – SP La Fiorita 6-0 (3-0)
FK Spartaks Jūrmala: Jevgenijs Nerugals, Gints Freimanis, Aleksandar Kosoric, Mārcis Oss, Ingus Slampe, Artemiy Maleev (71' Ingars Stuglis), Oleg Dmitriev, Evgeni Kobzar, Denis Davydov (17' Ariagner Smith), Diego Aguirre (53' Ricards Korzāns), Vitor Faísca.
Coach: Aleksandr Grishin.
SP La Fiorita: Gianluca Vivan, Samuele Olivi, Roberto Di Maio, Marco Gasperoni, Riccardo Mezzadri (68' Alessandro D'Addario), Damiano Tommasi (70' Simone Loiodice), Luca Righini, Adolfo José Hirsch, Armando Amati, Andy Selva (78' Fabrizio Castellazzi), Danilo Rinaldi. Coach: Gianluca Procopio.
Goals: 6' Evgeni Kobzar 1-0, 20' Artemiy Maleev 2-0, 26' Evgeni Kobzar 3-0, 64' Ingus Slampe 4-0, 66' Ariagner Smith 5-0, 73' Ingars Stuglis 6-0.
Referee: Vitaliy Meshkov (RUS)   Attendance: 648.

26.07.18   Ortaliq Stadion, Almaty: FK Kairat – AZ Alkmaar 2-0 (1-0)
FK Kairat: Vladimir Plotnikov, Sergey Politevich, Sheldon Bateau, Gafurzhan Suyumbaev, Isael, Islambek Kuat (85' Magomed Paragulgov), Bauyrzhan Islamkhan, Yan Vorogovskiy, Andrei Arshavin (90+1' Georgiy Zhukov), Juan Felipe Alves, Aderinsola Eseola (78' Márton Eppel). Coach: Carlos Alós Ferrer.
AZ Alkmaar: Marco Bizot, Ron Vlaar, Jonas Svensson, Pantelis Hatzidiakos, Thomas Ouwejan, Fredrik Midtsjø, Mats Seuntjens, Guus Til, Oussama Idrissi, Fred Friday, Myron Boadu (72' Iliass Bel Hassani). Coach: John van den Brom.
Goals: 12', 50' Aderinsola Eseola 1-0, 2-0.
Referee: Aliyar Aghayev (AZE)   Attendance: 20,000.

26.07.18   Ortaliq Stadion, Kostanay: Tobol Kustanai – Pyunik Yerevan FC 2-1 (0-0)
Tobol Kustanai: Dmytro Nepogodov, Viktor Dmitrenko, Fernander Kassaï, Dmitry Miroshnichenko, Marat Bystrov (68' Tanat Nuserbaev), Jaba Kankava, Azat Nurgaliev (90+1' Samat Zharynbetov), Artūras Zulpa, Nika Kvekveskiri, Maxim Fedin, Juan Lescano (72' Bayurzhan Turysbek). Coach: Vladimir Nikitenko.
Pyunik Yerevan FC: Evgeni Kobozev, Vyacheslav Dmitriev, Maksim Zhestokov, Serob Grigoryan, Maksim Trusevich, Denis Voynov (81' Albert Bogatyrev), Didier Kadio, Alik Arakelyan (62' Rumyan Hovsepyan), Vahagn Hayrapetyan, Petros Avetisyan, Mohamed Konaté (69' Ruslan Koryan). Coach: Andrey Talalaev.
Goals: 49' Maxim Fedin 1-0, 80' Azat Nurgaliev 2-0, 90' Ruslan Koryan 2-1.
Referee: Juri Frischer (EST)   Attendance: 7,700.

26.07.18   Stadionul Central, Ovidiu: FC Viitorul Constanta – Vitesse Arnhem 2-2 (1-0)
FC Viitorul Constanta: Valentin Cojocaru, Sebastian Mladen, Tudor Baluta, Bradley de Nooijer, Vlad Achim, Bogdan Tîru, Ianis Hagi, Ionut Vîna, Alexandru Matan (30' Lyes Houri), Denis Dragus (73' Andrei Artean), Mailson Lima (73' Srdjan Luchin).
Coach: Gheorghe Hagi.
Vitesse Arnhem: Eduardo, Alexander Büttner, Rasmus Thelander, Vyacheslav Karavaev, Jake Clarke-Salter, Roy Beerens, Thulani Serero, Navarone Foor (84' Matús Bero), Thomas Bruns (69' Hilary Gong), Tim Matavz, Bryan Linssen. Coach: Leonid Slutsky.
Goals: 44', 49' Denis Dragus 1-0, 2-0, 54' Tim Matavz 2-1, 72' Bryan Linssen 2-2.
Referee: Davide Massa (ITA)   Attendance: 2,543.
Sent off: 79' Andrei Artean.

26.07.18   Stadion Ob Jezeru, Velenje: Rudar Velenje – Fotbal Club FCSB 0-2 (0-1)
Rudar Velenje: Marko Pridigar, Josip Tomasevic, Klemen Bolha, Robert Pusaver, Ivan Vasiljevic, Damjan Trifkovic (73' Tim Vodeb), Domagoj Muic, Anze Pisek, Dominik Radic, Djair Parfitt-Williams (56' Abu Kamara), Milan Tucic (69' Vlatko Simunac).
Coach: Marijan Pusnik.
Fotbal Club FCSB: Cristian Balgradean, Marko Momcilovic, Junior Maranhão, Daniel Benzar, Bogdan Planic, Filipe Teixeira (82' Lucian Filip), Mihai Pintilii, Kamer Qaka, Olimpiu Morutan (68' Antonio Jakolis), Harlem Gnohéré (46' Florin Tanase), Dennis Man.
Coach: Nicolae Dica.
Goals: 5' Dennis Man 0-1, 74' Filipe Teixeira 0-2.
Referee: Hüseyin Göçek (TUR)   Attendance: 450.

26.07.18   Ramaz Shengelias Sakhelobis Stadioni, Kutaisi:
Torpedo Kutaisi – Víkingur Gøta 3-0 (1-0)
Torpedo Kutaisi: Rion Kvaskhvadze, Mamuka Kobakhidze, Giorgi Kimadze, Levan Gegetchkori, Oleksandr Azatsky, Lazar Marin (46' Milos Lacny), Levan Kutalia, Marek Hlinka (70' Giorgi Kukhianidze), Arfang Daffé (59' Grigol Dolidze), Mate Tsintsadze, Tornike Kapanadze. Coach: Kakhaber Chkhetiani.
Víkingur Gøta: Elias Rasmussen, Atli Gregersen, Hanus Jacobsen, Dennis Nieblas, Gunnar Vatnhamar, Elias Jóhannesson Lervig (90' Tonni Thomsen), Sølvi Vatnhamar, Karl Løkin, Hedin Hansen (59' Hans Jákup Lervig), Filip Djordjevic, Adeshina Lawal (80' Andreas Olsen). Coach: Sigfríður Clementsen.
Goals: 27' Tornike Kapanadze 1-0, 73' Giorgi Kimadze 2-0, 84' Levan Kutalia 3-0).
Referee: Artyom Kuchin (KAZ)   Attendance: 4,585

26.07.18   MFA Centrenary Stadium, Ta'Qali: Balzan FC – Slovan Bratislava 2-1 (1-0)
Balzan FC: Steve Sultana, Elkin Serrano, Steven Bezzina, Ivan Bozovic, Uros Ljubomirac, Michael Johnson, Cadú (82' Dale Camilleri), Nenad Sljivic, Milos Lepovic, Lecão (76' Ricardo Correa), Bojan Kaljevic (63' Alfred Effiong). Coach: Marko Micovic.
Slovan Bratislava: Michal Sulla, Mitch Apau, Vasil Bozhikov, Artem Sukhotsky, Ibrahim Rabiu (72' Dejan Drazic), Dávid Holman (46' Vukan Savicevic), Nono Delgado, Kenan Bajric, "Moha" Mohammed Rharsalla, Aleksandar Cavric (72' Boris Cmiljanic), Andraz Sporar. Coach: Martin Sevela.
Goals: 17' Bojan Kaljevic 1-0, 67' Uros Ljubomirac 2-0, 74' Vukan Savicevic 2-1.
Referee: Jens Maae (DEN)   Attendance: 558.

26.07.18   Sammy Ofer Stadium, Haifa: Hapoel Haifa – FH Hafnarfjördur 1-1 (0-0)
Hapoel Haifa: Ernestas Setkus, Nisso Kapiloto, Dor Malul, Risto Mitrevski, Hen Dilmoni, Rasmus Sjöstedt (58' Ness Zamir), Gil Vermouth, Radu Gînsari (84' Guy Hadida), Gal Arel, Eli Elbaz (64' Thanasis Papazoglou), Maxim Plakushchenko. Coach: Nir Klinger.
FH Hafnarfjördur: Gunnar Nielsen, Hjörtur Valgardsson, Vidar Ari Jónsson, Edi Gomes, Rennico Clarke, Davíd Vidarsson, Gudmundur Kristjánsson, Brandur Hendriksson Olsen (60' Robbie Crawford), Atli Gudnason (75' Pétur Vidarsson), Steven Lennon, Jákup Thomsen (82' Kristinn Steindórsson). Coach: Ólafur Kristjánsson.
Goals: 53' Edi Gomes 0-1, 65' Thanasis Papazoglou 1-1.
Referee: Srdjan Jovanovic (SER)   Attendance: 3,950.

26.07.18   Mikheil Meskhis Sakhelobis Stadioni, Tbilisi:
FC Chikhura Sachkhere – NK Maribor 0-0
FC Chikhura Sachkhere: Dino Hamzic, Davit Maisashvili (88' Davit Megrelishvili), Lasha Chikvaidze, Bakari Mirtshkulava, Revaz Chiteishvili, Levan Kakubava, Irakli Lekvtadze (49' Kakha Kakhabrishvili), Teimurazi Markozashvili, Irakli Bugridze, Giorgi Gabedava, Mikheil Sardalishvili (78' Denis Dobrovolski). Coach: Samson Pruidze.
NK Maribor: Jasmin Handanovic, Marko Suler, Mitja Viler, Sasa Ivkovic, Blaz Vrhovec, Amir Dervisevic (60' Alexandru Cretu), Aleks Pihler, Dino Hotic, Marcos Tavares, Gregor Bajde (81' Jasmin Mesanovic), Luka Zahovic (63' Dare Vrsic). Coach: Darko Milanic.
Referee: Kevin Blom (HOL)   Attendance: 3,500.

(FC Chikhura Sachkhere played their home match at Mikheil Meskhis Sakhelobis Stadioni instead of their regular stadium, Central Stadium Sachkhere)

26.07.18   Stade Jos Nusbaum, Dudelange: F91 Dudelange – Drita Gjilan 2-1 (0-1)
F91 Dudelange: Jonathan Joubert, Tom Schnell, Jerry Prempeh, Aniss El Hriti, Marc-André Kruska, Jordann Yéyé (54' Dominik Stolz), Edisson Jordanov, Clément Couturier (59' Mario Pokar), Danel Sinani, Nicolas Perez (74' Patrick Stumpf), David Turpel.
Coach: Dino Toppmöller.
Drita Gjilan: Edvan Bakaj, Liridon Leci, Viktor Kuka, Ardian Limani, Arbër Shala, Haxhi Neziraj (80' Eri Lamçja), Drilon Musaj (74' Përparim Livoreka), Bujar Shabani, Xhevdet Shabani, Betim Haxhimusa (89' Zgjim Mustafa), Endrit Krasniqi. Coach: Bekim Isufi.
Goals: 45+2' Xhevdet Shabani 0-1, 66' Nicolas Perez 1-1, 81' David Turpel 2-1 (p).
Referee: Leontios Trattou (CYP)   Attendance: 737
Sent off: 81' Endrit Krasniqi.

26.07.18   Red Bull Arena, Leipzig: RB Leipzig – BK Häcken 4-0 (2-0)
RB Leipzig: Péter Gulácsi, Willi Orban, Lukas Klostermann, Ibrahima Konaté, Stefan Ilsanker, Kevin Kampl, Diego Demme, Bruma (85' Niclas Stierlin), Marcelo Saracchi (68' Nordi Mukiele), Jean-Kévin Augustin, Matheus Cunha (89' Fabrice Hartmann).
Coach: Ralf Rangnick.
BK Häcken: Peter Abrahamsson, Kari Arkivuo, Johan Hammar, Rasmus Lindgren, Erik Friberg, Alexander Faltsetas (83' Gustav Berggren), Adam Andersson, Daleho Irandust (46' Nasiru Mohammed), Mervan Çelik (71' Viktor Lundberg), Paulinho Guerreiro, Alhassan Kamara. Coach: Andreas Alm.
Goals: 35' Bruma 1-0, 39' Matheus Cunha 2-0, 50' Kevin Kampl 3-0,
84' Jean-Kévin Augustin 4-0.
Referee: Aleksandar Stavrev (MKD)   Attendance: 18,126.
Sent off: 81' Stefan Ilsanker.

26.07.18   Stadion pod Bijelim Brijegom, Mostar: Zrinjski Mostar – FC Valletta 1-1 (0-0)
Zrinjski Mostar: Ivan Brkic (45' Antonio Soldo), Pero Stojkic, Slobodan Jakovljevic, Ognjen Todorovic, Milos Filipovic (64' Marko Bencun), Hrvoje Barisic, Frane Cirjak, Marin Galic, Nemanja Bilbija, Amer Bekic (70' Milos Acimovic), Semir Pezer. Coach: Ante Mise.
FC Valletta: Henry Bonello, Joseph Zerafa, Ryan Camilleri, Steve Borg (49' Juan Gill), Rowen Muscat, Raed Ibrahim Saleh Al Mukhaini, Kyrian Nwoko (65' Bogdan Gavrila), Santiago Malano, Miguel Alba (86' Jean Borg), Matteo Piciollo, Mario Fontanella.
Coach: Danilo Doncic.
Goals: 51' Nemanja Bilbija 1-0, 90' Mario Fontanella 1-1.
Referee: Neil Doyle (IRL)   Attendance: 3,100.

26.07.18   Neo GSP Stadium, Nicosia: APOEL Nicosia – FC Flora Tallinn 5-0 (2-0)
APOEL Nicosia: Boy Waterman, Zhivko Milanov, Carlão, Yohan Tavares, Nicolas Ioannou (81' Nektarios Alexandrou), Nuno Morais, Giorgos Efrem (76' Moussa Al Taamari), Lucas Souza, Ghayas Zahid, Roland Sallai, Mickaël Poté (66' Dellatorre). Coach: Bruno Baltazar.
FC Flora Tallinn: Mait Toom, Gert Kams, Kevin Aloe, Jürgen Lorenz, Madis Vihmann, Aleksandr Dmitrijev, Maksim Gussev (76' Frank Liivak), German Slein, Mihkel Ainsalu (70' Markus Poom), Rauno Alliku, Rauno Sappinen. Coaches: Jürgen Henn & Arno Pijpers.
Goals: 25' Yohan Tavares 1-0, 44' Lucas Souza 2-0, 47' Nuno Morais 3-0 (p),
73' Roland Sallai 4-0, 78' Dellatorre 5-0.
Referee: Marco Fritz (GER)   Attendance: 9,836.

26.07.18   Aker Stadion, Molde: Molde FK – KF Laçi 3-0 (2-0)
Molde FK: Andreas Linde, Vegard Forren, Ruben Gabrielsen, Kristoffer Haugen, Christoffer Remmer, Etzaz Hussain (68' Leke James), Babacar Sarr, Eirik Hestad, Fredrik Aursnes, Pawel Cibicki (65' Magnus Eikrem), Erling Håland (74' Petter Strand). Coach: Ole Gunnar Solskjær.
KF Laçi: Gentian Selmani, Marko Radas, Taulant Sefgjinaj, Erion Hoxhallari, Eglentin Gjoni, Ndricim Shtubina (48' Abdurraman Fangaj), Nikola Eller, Fjoart Jonuzi, Regi Lushkja (90+1' Serxho Ujka), Vice Kendes, Myrto Uzuni. Coach: Besnik Prenga.
Goals: 6' Erling Håland 1-0 (p), 24' Eirik Hestad 2-0, 79' Leke James 3-0.
Referee: Adrien Jaccottet (SUI)   Attendance: 4,179.

26.07.18   Vilniaus LFF stadionas, Vilnius: FK Zalgiris – FC Vaduz 1-0 (0-0)
FK Zalgiris: Dziugas Bartkus, Rolandas Baravykas, Mamadou Mbodj, Saulius Mikoliūnas, Donovan Slijngard, Tomas Simkovic (63' Serge Nyuiadzi), Liviu Antal, Slavko Blagojevic, Jérémy Manzorro (77' Domantas Simkus), Marko Tomic, Louis Ogana (84' Tomás Malec). Coach: Valdas Urbonas.
FC Vaduz: Andreas Hirzel, Maximilian Göppel, Sadik Vitija, Philipp Muntwiler, Milan Gajic, Marco Mathys (46' Gabriel Lüchinger), Christopher Drazan, Sandro Wieser, Maurice Brunner (74' Jodel Dossou), Mohamed Coulibaly, Igor Tadic (90+1' Boris Babic).
Coach: Roland Vrabec.
Goal: 86' Liviu Antal 1-0.
Referee: István Vad (II) (HUN)   Attendance: 3,000.

26.07.18   Winner Stadium, Netanya: Maccabi Tel Aviv – Radnicki Nis 2-0 (0-0)
Maccabi Tel Aviv: Predrag Rajkovic, Eitan Tibi, Avi Rikan (46' Eyal Golasa), Saborit, Elazar Dasa, Jair Amador, Dor Mikha (85' Roslan Barski), Dor Peretz, Vidar Kjartansson, Eliran Atar (66' Matan Hozez), Omer Atzili. Coach: Vladimir Ivic.
Radnicki Nis: Mladen Zivkovic, Aleksandar Todorovski, Andrija Mijailovic (74' Sladan Nikodijevic), Radovan Pankov, Taras Bondarenko, Aleksandar Stanisavljevic (62' Aleksandar Jovanovic (I)), Petar Grbic, Dusan Micic, Nikola Stankovic, Ryota Noma, Marko Mrkic (46' Aleksa Jovanovic (II)). Coach: Nenad Lalatovic.
Goals: 51', 69' Vidar Kjartansson 1-0, 2-0 (p).
Referee: Paolo Mazzoleni (ITA)   Attendance: 8,161.
Sent off: 79' Omer Atzili.

(Maccabi Tel Aviv played their home match at Winner Stadium instead of their regular stadium, Bloomfield Stadium, due to renovation)

26.07.18   Stadion Bâlgarska Armija, Sofia:
           CSKA Sofia – FC Admira Wacker Mödling 3-0 (3-0)
CSKA Sofia: Vytautas Cerniauskas, Boris Sekulic, Bozhidar Chorbadzhiyski, Steven Pereira, Geferson, Rúben Pinto, Edwin Gyasi (81' Tonislav Yordanov), Janio Bikel, Kiril Despodov, Maurides (72' Valentin Antov), Jorginho (90' Angel Lyaskov). Coach: Nestor El Maestro.
FC Admira Wacker Mödling: Andreas Leitner, Stephan Zwierschitz, Bjarne Thoelke, Sebastian Bauer, Milos Spasic, Wilhelm Vorsager, Morten Hjulmand (46' Daniel Toth), Marco Kadlec (83' Marcus Maier), Dominik Starkl, Sinan Bakis, Marin Jakolis (70' Patrick Schmidt). Coach: Ernst Baumeister.
Goals: 29', 34' Kiril Despodov 1-0, 2-0, 38' Maurides 3-0 (p).
Referee: John Beaton (SCO)   Attendance: 6,200.

26.07.18   Bozsik-József-Stadion, Budapest:
Budapest Honvéd FC – Progrès Niederkorn 1-0 (0-0)
Budapest Honvéd FC: Dávid Gróf, Eke Uzoma, Tibor Heffler, Dino Skvorc, Bence Batik, Krisztián Vadócz, Djordje Kamber, Gergö Nagy (88' Zsolt Pölöskei), Dániel Gazdag, Filip Holender (74' Botond Baráth), Dániel Lukàcs (51' Dominik Cipf). Coach: Attila Supka.
Progrès Niederkorn: Sebastian Flauss, Mario Mutsch (79' Ben Vogel), Adrien Ferino, Marvin da Graça, Jordan Gobron, Tim Hall, Yann Matias Marques, Emmanuel Françoise (69' Alexander Karapetyan), Sébastien Thill, Olivier Thill, Mayron De Almeida (90+4' Romeu Torres). Coach: Paolo Amodio.
Goal: 82' Botond Baráth 1-0.
Referee: Mohammed Al Hakim (SWE)   Attendance: 2,447.

26.07.18   Tele2 Arena, Stockholm: Djurgårdens IF – FC Mariupol 1-1 (0-1)
Djurgårdens IF: Andreas Isaksson, Erik Johansson, Marcus Danielsson, Niklas Gunnarsson (65' Jacob Une-Larsson), Jonathan Augustinsson, Haris Radetinac (77' Jonas Olsson), Jonathan Ring, Fredrik Ulvestad, Kerim Mrabti, Jesper Karlström (73' Kevin Walker), Aliou Badji. Coach: Özcan Melkemichel.
FC Mariupol: Rustam Khudzhamov, Sergey Yavorskiy, Maksym Bilyi, Igor Kyryukhantsev (87' Pavel Polegenko), Besir Demiri, Oleksiy Bykov, Igor Tyshchenko, Vyacheslav Churko (76' Sergiy Gorbunov), Dmytro Myshnov (82' Sergiy Chobotenko), Oleksandr Pikhalyonok, Ruslan Fomin. Coach: Oleksandr Babych.
Goals: 37' Sergey Yavorskiy 0-1, 90+4' Aliou Badji 1-1.
Referee: Miroslav Zelinka (CZE)   Attendance: 11,200.

26.07.18   Stadion Miejski, Bialystok: Jagiellonia Bialystok – Rio Ave FC 1-0 (1-0)
Jagiellonia Bialystok: Marián Kelemen, Lukasz Burliga, Nemanja Mitrovic, Guilherme, Ivan Runje, Mateusz Machaj (71' Martin Pospísil), Arvydas Novikovas (83' Patryk Klimala), Przemyslaw Frankowski, Bartosz Kwiecien (75' Rafal Grzyb), Taras Romanczuk, Cillian Sheridan. Coach: Ireneusz Mamrot.
Rio Ave FC: Giorgi Makaridze, Jonathan Buatu, Nélson Monte, Matheus Reis, Toni Borevkovic, Tarantini (76' João Schmidt), Leandrinho, Diego Lopes (18' Bruno Moreira), Gabrielzinho, Galeno (81' Damien Furtado), Gelson Dala. Coach: José Gomes.
Goal: 9' Mateusz Machaj 1-0.
Referee: Ricardo de Burgos Bengoetxea (ESP)   Attendance: 13,725.

26.07.18   Stadyen Budaunik Stroitel, Soligorsk:
Shakhtyor Soligorsk – KKS Lech Poznan 1-1 (0-0)
Shakhtyor Soligorsk: Andrey Klimovich, Maksim Bordachev, Pavel Rybak, Siarhei Matveichyk, Igor Burko, Roger Cañas, Aleksandr Selyava, Yuri Kovalev, Július Szöke, Max Ebong Ngome (46' Sergey Balanovich), Elis Bakaj (73' Denis Laptev).
Coach: Sergey Tashuev.
KKS Lech Poznan: Jasmin Buric, Thomas Rogne, Rafal Janicki, Volodymyr Kostevych, Vernon, Tomasz Cywka (90+3' Lukasz Tralka), Mihai Radut (77' Maciej Gajos), Maciej Makuszewski, Pedro Tiba, Darko Jevtic (70' João Amaral), Christian Gytkjær.
Coach: Ivan Djurdjevic.
Goals: 53' Elis Bakaj 1-0, 89' João Amaral 1-1.
Referee: Svein Oddvar Moen (NOR)   Attendance: 3,700.

26.07.18   Right to Dream Park, Farum: FC Nordsjælland – AIK Solna 1-0 (1-0)
FC Nordsjælland: Nicolai Larsen, Karlo Bartolec, Mads Pedersen, Andreas Skovgaard, Ulrik Jenssen, Victor Nelsson, Magnus Andersen (72' Nicklas Strunck Jakobsen), Andreas Skov Olsen (85' Mathias Rasmussen), Jacob Christensen, Mikkel Damsgaard (90+1' Benjamin Hansen), Mikkel Rygaard Jensen. Coach: Kasper Hjulmand.
AIK Solna: Oscar Linnér, Per Karlsson, Daniel Sundgren, Alexander Milosevic, Rasmus Lindkvist (46' Heradi Rashidi), Robin Jansson, Tarik Elyounoussi (80' Henok Goitom), Sebastian Larsson, Enoch Adu, Kristoffer Olsson, Nicolás Stefanelli. Coach: Rikard Norling.
Goal: 11' Magnus Andersen 1-0.
Referee: Sébastien Delferière (BEL)   Attendance: 3,474.

Tarik Elyounoussi missed a penalty kick (50').

26.07.18   Linzer Stadion, Linz: LASK Linz – Lillestrøm SK 4-0 (2-0)
LASK Linz: Alexander Schlager, Emanuel Pogatetz, Christian Ramsebner, Gernot Trauner, Reinhold Ranftl (84' Dominik Frieser), Maximilian Ullmann, James Holland, Thomas Goiginger, Peter Michorl, Yusuf Otubanjo (68' Samuel Tetteh), João Victor Santos Sá (77' Florian Jamnig). Coach: Oliver Glasner.
Lillestrøm SK: Marko Maric, Frode Kippe, Marius Amundsen, Mats Haakenstad, Simen Rafn, Aleksander Melgalvis (87' Stefan Antonijevic), Fredrik Krogstad, Ifeanyi Matthew, Erling Knudtzon, Thomas Olsen (82' Moses Ebiye), Gary Martin (76' Simen Mikalsen).
Coach: Jörgen Lennartsson.
Goals: 6' Thomas Goiginger 1-0, 45+1' James Holland 2-0, 70' Thomas Goiginger 3-0, 90+1' Dominik Frieser 4-0.
Referee: Aleksei Eskov (RUS)   Attendance: 8,304.

26.07.18   Stadyen DASK Brestski, Brest: FK Dynamo Brest – Atromitos FC 4-3 (2-0)
FK Dynamo Brest: Pavel Pavlyuchenko, Oleg Veretilo, Giannis Kargas, Zeljko Filipovic (45' Pavel Nekhaychik), Oleksandr Noyok, Pavel Savitskiy, Chidi Osuchukwu (63' Andrey Zaleski), Roman Yuzepchuk (76' Maksim Vitus), Gaby Kiki, Oleksiy Khoblenko, Joel Fameyeh. Coach: Aleksey Shpilevski.
Atromitos FC: Nikola Mirkovic, Madson, Dimitrios Chatziisaias, Dimitris Giannoulis, Spyros Risvanis, Theodoros Vasilakakis (46' Iraklis Garoufalias), Azer Busuladzic, Spyridon Natsos, Georgios Manousos (76' Armin Mujakic), Efthymios Koulouris, Bruno Souza (46' Clarck N'Sikulu). Coach: Damir Canadi.
Goals: 5' Zeljko Filipovic 1-0, 13', 61', 70' Pavel Savitskiy 2-0 (p), 3-0, 4-0,
74' Georgios Manousos 4-1, 80' Oleg Veretilo 4-2 (og), 88' Efthymios Koulouris 4-3.
Referee: José María Sánchez Martínez (ESP)   Attendance: 9,530.

26.07.18   Park Hall Stadium, Oswestry: The New Saints – Lincoln Red Imps 2-1 (1-1)
The New Saints: Paul Harrison, Christopher Marriott, Blaine Hudson, Kane Lewis, Benjamin Cabango, Aeron Edwards, Jon Routledge, Daniel Redmond (88' Adrian Cieslewicz), Tom Holland, Jamie Mullan, Dean Ebbe (40' Greg Draper). Coach: Scott Ruscoe.
Lincoln Red Imps: Lolo Soler, Joseph Chipolina (84' André dos Santos), Oli (65' Louie Annesley), Ryan Casciaro, Jean Garcia, Diego Gámiz, Álex Moreno, Juan Montesinos, Falu Aranda (64' Juanma Ortiz), Anthony Hernandez, Sykes Garro, Coach: Yiyi.
Goals: 6' Dean Ebbe 1-0, 31' Joseph Chipolina 1-1, 83' Blaine Hudson 2-1.
Referee: Thorvaldur Árnason (ISL)   Attendance: 632.

26.07.18   Estadi Comunal, Andorra la Vella: FC Santa Coloma – Valur Reykjavík 1-0 (0-0)
FC Santa Coloma: Eloy Casals, Ildefons Lima, Marc Rebés, Albert Mercadé (61' André Azevedo), Andreu Ramos, Jaime Noguerol, Moisés San Nicolás, Yago Pérez (87' Víctor Rodríguez), Loren Burón (72' Ibán Parra), Aleix Cistero, Juanma Torres.
Coach: Marc Rodríguez Rebull.
Valur Reykjavík: Anton Ari Einarsson, Birkir Sævarsson, Bjarni Eiríksson, Eidur Sigurbjörnsson, Sebastian Hedlund, Haukur Sigurdsson (86' Kristinn Halldórsson), Kristinn Sigurdsson, Sigurdur Lárusson (74' Andri Adolphsson), Einar Karl Ingvarsson (74' Gudjón Lydsson), Tobias Thomsen, Dion Jeremy Acoff. Coach: Ólafur Jóhannesson.
Goal: 72' Bjarni Eiríksson 1-0 (og).
Referee: Sebastian Coltescu (ROM)   Attendance: 385.

26.07.18   Stadion Kraj Bistrice, Niksic: FK Sutjeska Niksic – FC Alashkert 0-1 (0-1)
FK Sutjeska Niksic: Vladan Giljen, Darko Bulatovic, Stefan Cicmil, Dragan Grivic, Marko Cetkovic (83' Milutin Osmajic), Stefan Stefanovic (77' Vladan Bubanja), Stefan Loncar (46' Saleta Kordic), Nemanja Nedic, Luka Merdovic, Stefan Denkovic, Veljko Vukovic.
Coach: Nikola Rakojevic.
FC Alashkert: Ognjen Cancarevic, Gagik Daghbashyan, Oliver Práznovsky, Taron Voskanyan, Goran Antonic, Mladen Zeljkovic, Artur Yedigaryan, Jefferson (67' Danilo Sekulic), Mihran Manasyan (56' Artak Yedigaryan), Artak Grigoryan, Uros Nenadovic (84' Gustavo Marmentini dos Santos). Coach: Varuzhan Sukiasyan.
Goal: 11' Mladen Zeljkovic 0-1.
Referee: Alain Bieri (SUI)   Attendance: 2,000.

26.07.18   Stadion Stozice, Ljubljana: Olimpija Ljubljana – Crusaders FC 5-1 (1-0)
Olimpija Ljubljana: Aljaz Ivacic, Branko Ilic, Aris Zarifovic, Dino Stiglec, Macky Frank Bagnack, Matic Crnic, Daniel Avramovski (79' Stefan Savic), Tomislav Tomic (64' Asmir Suljic), Danijel Miskic, Nik Kapun, Kingsley Boateng (86' Haris Kadric). Coach: Ilija Stolica.
Crusaders FC: Sean O'Neill, Sean Ward, Billy Joe Burns, Howard Beverland, Colin Coates, David Cushley (59' Paul Heatley), Declan Caddell (82' Rodney Brown), Philip Lowry (73' Ross Clarke), Jordan Forsythe, Matthew Snoddy, Michael Carvill. Coach: Stephen Baxter.
Goals: 30' Kingsley Boateng 1-0, 56' Matic Crnic 2-0, 68' Kingsley Boateng 3-0, 73' Branko Ilic 3-1 (og), 75' Matic Crnic 4-1, 90+2' Haris Kadric 5-1.
Referee: Enea Jorgji (ALB)   Attendance: 2,980.

26.07.18   Arena Zabrze, Zabrze: Górnik Zabrze – AS Trencín 0-1 (0-1)
Górnik Zabrze: Tomasz Loska, Dani Suárez, Adrian Gryszkiewicz, Daniel Liszka (79' Wiktor Biedrzycki), Przemyslaw Wisniewski, Szymon Matuszek, Angulo, Adam Wolniewicz, Daniel Smuga (61' Marcin Urynowicz), Szymon Zurkowski, Jesús Jiménez. Coach: Marcin Brosz.
AS Trencín: Igor Semrinec, Jamie Lawrence, Martin Sulek, Keston Julien (89' Lukás Skovajsa), Reuben Yem, Ashraf El Mahdioui, Abdul Zubairu, Joey Sleegers (73' Osman Bukari), Antonio Mance, Hamza Catakovic (83' Desley Ubbink), Philip Azango.
Coach: Ricardo Moniz.
Goal: 39' Philip Azango 0-1.
Referee: Mattias Gestranius (FIN)   Attendance: 12,859.

26.07.18   Gundadalur, Tórshavn: B36 Tórshavn – Besiktas JK 0-2 (0-2)
B36 Tórshavn: Rói Hentze, Odmar Færø, Alex Mellemgaard (41' Benjamin Heinesen), Bjarni Petersen, Erlendur Magnusson, Meinhard Olsen, Andrias Eriksen, Robert Hedin Brockie, Magnus Holm Jacobsen (79' Hugin Samuelsen), Kaimar Saag (60' Michal Przybylski), Lukasz Cieslewicz. Coach: Jákup á Borg.
Besiktas JK: Tolga Zengin, Adriano, Caner Erkin, Gökhan Gönül, Gary Medel, Fatih Aksoy, Ryan Babel, Jeremain Lens (85' Vágner Love), Necip Uysal, Tolgay Arslan (78' Dorukhan Toköz), Cyle Larin (74' Mustafa Pektemek). Coach: Senol Günes.
Goals: 8' Jeremain Lens 0-1, 26' Gökhan Gönül 0-2.
Referee: Evgen Aranovskiy (UKR)   Attendance: 1,634.

26.07.18   Luminus Arena, Genk: KRC Genk – CS Fola Esch 5-0 (4-0)
KRC Genk: Nordin Jackers, Sebastien Dewaest, Bojan Nastic, Jhon Lucumí, Pozuelo (63' Zinho Gano), Ruslan Malinovskiy (46' Ibrahima Seck), Sander Berge, Joakim Mæhle, Leandro Trossard, Mbwana Samatta (75' Jakub Piotrowski), Edon Zhegrova. Coach: Philippe Clement.
CS Fola Esch: Thomas Hym, Rodrigue Dikaba, Peter Chrappan, Julien Klein, Mehdi Kirch, Cédric Sacras, Veldin Muharemovic, Ryan Klapp (80' Moussa Seydi), Gérard Mersch, Samir Hadji (84' Dejvid Sinani), Ken Corral (66' Stefano Bensi). Coach: Thomas Klasen.
Goals: 4' Ruslan Malinovskiy 1-0, 19' Pozuelo 2-0, 25' Leandro Trossard 3-0, 28' Sebastien Dewaest 4-0, 73' Leandro Trossard 5-0 (p).
Referee: Martin Strömbergsson (SWE)   Attendance: 10,300.

26.07.18   Stadion Poljud, Split: Hajduk Split – Slavia Sofia 1-0 (0-0)
Hajduk Split: Josip Posavec, André Fomitschow, Zoran Nizic, Borja López, Ádám Gyurcsó, Mijo Caktas, Hamza Barry, Josip Juranovic, Fran Tudor (46' Ahmed Said), Ante Palaversa (53' Toma Basic), Mirko Ivanovski (76' Ivan Delic). Coach: Zeljko Kopic.
Slavia Sofia: Georgi Petkov, Aleksandar Aleksandrov, Emil Martinov, Aleksandar Stanisavljevic, Andrea Hristov, Momchil Tsvetanov (71' Slavcho Shokolarov), Galin Ivanov (90+4' Georgi Yomov), Yanis Karabelyov, Dimitar Velkovski, Vladislav Uzunov, Milcho Angelov (86' Tsvetelin Chunchukov). Coach: Zlatomir Zagorcic.
Goal: 79' Ahmed Said 1-0.
Referee: István Kovács (ROM)   Attendance: 26,103.
Sent off: 84' Aleksandar Aleksandrov.

26.07.18   Kybunpark, St. Gallen: FC St. Gallen – Sarpsborg 08 2-1 (1-1)
FC St. Gallen: Dejan Stojanovic, Milan Vilotic, Andreas Wittwer, Nicolas Lüchinger (84' Leonel Mosevich), Silvan Hefti, Marco Aratore (75' Nassim Ben Khalifa), Jordi Quintillà, Dereck Kutesa (46' Yannis Tafer), Vincent Sierro, Majeed Ashimeru, Roman Buess. Coach: Peter Zeidler.
Sarpsborg 08: Aslak Falch, Amin Askar, Joackim Jørgensen, Joonas Tamm, Matti Lund Nielsen, Ole Halvorsen, Jon-Helge Tveita, Kristoffer Zachariassen, Tobias Heintz (23' Kristoffer Larsen, 72' Harmeet Singh), Patrick Mortensen, Rashad Muhammed (66' Mikkel Agger). Coach: Geir Bakke.
Goals: 6' Tobias Heintz 0-1, 41' Silvan Hefti 1-1, 66' Roman Buess 2-1.
Referee: Fábio Veríssimo (POR)   Attendance: 6,335.
Sent off: 4' Milan Vilotic.

26.07.18   MAPEI Stadium – Città del Tricolore, Reggio Emilia:
            Atalanta Bergamo – FK Sarajevo 2-2 (2-0)
Atalanta Bergamo: Etrit Berisha, Andrea Masiello, Rafael Tolói, Hans Hateboer, Robin Gosens (83' Marco Tumminello), Gianluca Mancini (75' José Palomino), "Papu" Alejandro Gómez, Marco D'Alessandro (54' Duván Zapata), Marten de Roon, Matteo Pessina, Musa Barrow.
Coach: Gian Piero Gasperini.
FK Sarajevo: Bojan Pavlovic, Amer Dupovac, Nihad Mujakic, Selmir Pidro, Emir Halilovic (84' Milos Stanojevic), Amar Rahmanovic, Anel Hebibovic, Joachim Adukor, Mersudin Ahmetovic (60' Haris Handzic), Krste Velkoski, Aladin Sisic (85' Benjamin Tatar).
Coach: Husref Musemic.
Goals: 11' Rafael Tolói 1-0, 45+3' Gianluca Mancini 2-0, 67' Haris Handzic 2-1, 72' Aladin Sisic 2-2.
Referee: Tamás Bognár (HUN)   Attendance: 7,518.

(Atalanta Bergamo played their home match at MAPEI Stadium – Città del Tricolore instead of their regular stadium, Stadio Atleti Azzurri d'Italia, as it wasn't given a UEFA licence to hold games)

26.07.18   Stadion Partizana, Beograd: Partizan Beograd – FK Trakai 1-0 (0-0)
Partizan Beograd: Vladimir Stojkovic, Marc Valiente, Sasa Zdjelar, Zlatan Sehovic, Svetozar Markovic, Gabriel Enache, Nebojsa Kosovic, Seydouba Soumah, Danilo Pantic (68' Marko Jankovic), Ricardo Gomes, Djordje Ivanovic (81' Sasa Ilic). Coach: Miroslav Djukic.
FK Trakai: Tomas Svedkauskas, Valdemars Borovskis, Evgeniy Osipov, Justinas Janusevskis, Diniyar Bilyaletdinov, Vaidas Silénas, Valentin Jeriomenko, Donatas Kazlauskas (58' Kevin Ntika Bondombe), Modestas Vorobjovas, Svajūnas Cyzas (76' Aleksandras Levsinas), Justinas Marazas (88' Rokas Masenzovas). Coach: Kibu Vicuña.
Goal: 57' Justinas Janusevskis 1-0 (og).
Referee: Georgi Kabakov (BUL)   Attendance: 6,210.
Sent off: 53' Modestas Vorobjovas.

26.07.18   Stadion Grbavica, Sarajevo:
            FK Zeljeznicar Sarajevo – Apollon FC Limassol 1-2 (0-1)
FK Zeljeznicar Sarajevo: Vedran Kjosevski, Jadranko Bogicevic, Milos Bakrac, Matej Rodin, Ivan Curjuric, Stojan Vranjes (70' Jovan Blagojevic), Antonio Pavic, Filip Arezina (84' Mladen Veselinovic), Anel Sabanadzovic, Sulejman Krpic, Dzenan Zajmovic (46' Asim Zec).
Coach: Slobodan Krcmarevic.
Apollon FC Limassol: Bruno Vale, Valentin Roberge, Charis Kyriakou, Richard Soumah (46' Giorgos Vasiliou), Héctor Yuste, Sasa Markovic (67' Facundo Pereyra), Esteban Sachetti, João Pedro, Fotis Papoulis (84' André Schembri), Anton Maglica, Adrián Sardinero.
Coach: Sofronis Avgousti.
Goals: 23' Jadranko Bogicevic 0-1 (og), 79' Esteban Sachetti 0-2, 90' Sulejman Krpic 1-2.
Referee: Alexander Harkam (AUT)   Attendance: 11,821.

26.07.18   Pittodrie Stadium, Aberdeen: Aberdeen FC – Burnley FC 1-1 (1-0)
Aberdeen FC: Joe Lewis, Shay Logan, Graeme Shinnie, Thomas Hoban, Michael Devlin, Dominic Ball, Scott McKenna, Niall McGinn (79' Scott Wright), Gary Mackay-Steven, Lewis Ferguson (57' Stephen Gleeson), Sam Cosgrove (77' Stevie May). Coach: Derek McInnes.
Burnley FC: Nick Pope (14' Anders Lindegaard), Stephen Ward, Matthew Lowton, Ben Mee, James Tarkowski, Aaron Lennon, Jack Cork, Jóhann Gudmundsson, Ashley Westwood, Jeffrey Hendrick (67' Samuel Vokes), Chris Wood. Coach: Sean Dyche.
Goals: 19' Gary Mackay-Steven 1-0 (p), 80' Samuel Vokes 1-1.
Referee: Daniel Siebert (GER)   Attendance: 20,313.

26.07.18   Oriel Park, Dundalk: Dundalk FC – AEK Larnaca 0-0
Dundalk FC: Gary Rogers, Brain Gartland, Dane Massey (81' Dean Jarvis), Sean Hoare, Daniel Cleary, Chris Shields, Robbie Benson, Dylan Connolly (84' Ronan Murray), Jamie McGrath (67' Patrick McEleney), Patrick Hoban, Michael Duffy. Coach: Stephen Kenny.
AEK Larnaca: Toño, Mikel González, Truyols, Thomas Ioannou, Igor Carioca, Ivan Trickovski, Jorge Larena (83' Nacho Cases), Acorán, Joan Tomás (62' Tete), Hector Hevel, Apostolos Giannou (90' Onisiforos Roushias). Coach: Andoni Iraola.
Referee: Harald Lechner (AUT)   Attendance: 3,000.

26.07.18   Stadion Karadjordje, Novi Sad: Spartak Subotica – AC Sparta Praha 2-0 (1-0)
Spartak Subotica: Nikola Peric, Andrija Vukcevic (74' Samuel Afum), Branimir Jocic, Noboru Shimura, Dejan Kerkez, Nemanja Calasan, Nemanja Tekijaski, Mile Savkovic, Bojan Cecaric (86' Milan Marcic), Nemanja Glavcic, Ognjen Djuricin (75' Stefan Milosevic).
Coach: Vladimir Gacinovic.
AC Sparta Praha: Florin Nita, Semih Kaya, Uros Radakovic, Alexandru Chipciu, Tal Ben Chaim (61' Vukadin Vukadinovic), Nicolae Stanciu, Martin Frydek, Guélor Kanga, Srdjan Plavsic (46' Josef Sural), Jirí Kulhánek, Benjamin Tetteh (84' Mihailo Ristic).
Coach: Pavel Hapal.
Goals: 8' Nemanja Calasan 1-0, 57' Ognjen Djuricin 2-0.
Referee: Pawel Raczkowski (POL)   Attendance: 4,000.

(Spartak Subotica played their home match at Stadion Karadjordje instead of their regular stadium, Subotica City Stadium)

26.07.18   Stadion Gradski vrt, Osijek: NK Osijek – Glasgow Rangers FC 0-1 (0-1)
NK Osijek: Marko Malenica, Borna Barisic, Tomislav Sorsa (46' Petar Bockaj), Domagoj Pusic (80' Haris Hajradinovic), Mile Skoric, Benedik Mioc (62' Dmitriy Lepa), Alen Grgic, Robert Mudrazija, Danijel Loncar, Mirko Maric, Ezekiel Henty. Coach: Zoran Zekic.
Glasgow Rangers FC: Allan McGregor, James Tavernier, Connor Goldson, Jon Flanagan, Nikola Katic, Jamie Murphy (68' Josh Windass), Ryan Jack, Ryan Kent, Oviemuno Ejaria (78' Ross McCrorie), Lassana Coulibaly, Alfredo Morelos (90+4' Glenn Middleton).
Coach: Steven Gerrard.
Goal: 18' Alfredo Morelos 0-1.
Referee: Pawel Gil (POL)   Attendance: 7,112.

26.07.18   Easter Road Stadium, Edinburgh:
   Hibernian FC Edinburgh – Asteras Tripolis FC 3-2 (0-2)
Hibernian FC Edinburgh: Ádám Bogdán, Steven Whittaker (46' David Gray), Lewis Stevenson, Paul Hanlon (90+4' Ryan Porteous), Darren McGregor, Efe Ambrose, Vykintas Slivka, John McGinn, Stephen Mallan, Martin Boyle, Florian Kamberi. Coach: Neil Lennon.
Asteras Tripolis FC: Georgios Athanasiadis, Konstantinos Triantafyllopoulos, Giorgos Kyriakopoulos, Triantafyllos Pasalidis, Matías Iglesias, Juan Munafo, Franco Bellocq (55' Martín Rolle), Nikolaos Kaltsas (77' Ángel Martínez), Michalis Manias, Kosmas Tsilianidis (86' Ioannis Christopoulos), Giannis Kotsiras. Coach: Savvas Pantelidis.
Goals: 12', 35' Giorgos Kyriakopoulos 0-1, 0-2, 64' Efe Ambrose 1-2, 77' David Gray 2-2, 90+3' Florian Kamberi 3-2.
Referee: Andreas Ekberg (SWE)   Attendance: 14,148.
Sent off: 84' Triantafyllos Pasalidis.

26.07.18   Samsung völlurinn, Gardabær: UMF Stjarnan – FC København 0-2 (0-0)
UMF Stjarnan: Haraldur Björnsson, Baldur Sigurdsson, Jósef Kristinn Jósefsson, Óttar Bjarni Gudmundsson, Daníel Laxdal, Jóhann Laxdal, Eyjólfur Hédinsson (67' Alex Thór Hauksson), Thorsteinn Már Ragnarsson (85' Sölvi Fodilsson), Gunjón Baldvinsson, Thórarinn Valdimarsson (62' Gudmundur Hafsteinsson), Hilmar Árni Halldórsson.
Coach: Rúnar Sigmundsson.
FC København: Stephan Andersen, Pierre Bengtsson, Sotirios Papagiannopoulos, Denis Vavro, Mads Roerslev Rasmussen, Ján Gregus, Rasmus Falk (46' Viktor Fischer), Zeca (46' Robert Skov), Nicolaj Thomsen, Dame N'Doye (64' Carlo Holse), Kenan Kodro.
Coach: Ståle Solbakken.
Goals: 52' Kenan Kodro 0-1, 58' Viktor Fischer 0-2.
Referee: Robert Schörgenhofer (AUT)   Attendance: 1,050.

26.07.18   MOL Aréna, Dunajská Streda:
            DAC Dunajská Streda – FK Dinamo Minsk 1-3 (1-1)
DAC Dunajská Streda: Patrik Macej, Lubomír Satka, Milan Simcák, Marin Ljubicic, Erik Pacinda, Tomás Huk, Zsolt Kalmár (74' Máté Vida), Kristián Kostrna, Krisztopher Vida (87' Maksym Tretyakov), Christián Herc (42' Éric Davis), Vakoun Issouf Bayo.
Coach: Peter Hyballa.
FK Dinamo Minsk: Andrey Gorbunov, Igor Shitov, Luis Rocha, Roman Begunov, Nino Galovic, Maksim Zhavnerchik, Seidu Yahaya, Filipp Ivanov (72' Aleksandr Makas), Nikita Korzun (81' Dinko Trebotic), Uros Nikolic, Vladimir Khvashchinskiy (61' Artem Gurenko).
Coach: Sergei Gurenko.
Goals: 24' Roman Begunov 0-1, 45' Erik Pacinda 1-1 (p), 77' Aleksandr Makas 1-2, 90+4' Uros Nikolic 1-3.
Referee: Sergiy Boyko (UKR)   Attendance: 9,227.
Sent off: 39' Milan Simcák.

26.07.18   Estadio Ramón Sánchez Pizjuán, Sevilla: Sevilla FC – Újpesti FC 4-0 (3-0)
Sevilla FC: Tomás Vaclík, Nicolás Pareja, Daniel Carriço, Sergio Escudero, Guilherme Arana (77' Borja Lasso), Jesús Navas (58' Sébastien Corchia), Franco Vázquez, Pablo Sarabia (70' Pejiño), Roque Mesa, Nolito, Wissam Ben Yedder. Coach: Pablo Machín.
Újpesti FC: Filip Pajovic, Mijusko Bojovic, Branko Pauljevic, Róbert Litauszki, Dzenan Burekovic, Dániel Nagy (33' Benjámin Balász), Bojan Sankovic, Donát Zsótér (64' Razvan Horj), Alassane Diallo, Obinna Nwobodo, Soma Novothny. Coach: Nebojsa Vignjevic.
Goals: 7' Jesús Navas 1-0, 32' Wissam Ben Yedder 2-0 (p), 43' Pablo Sarabia 3-0, 90+2' Franco Vázquez 4-0.
Referee: Andris Treimanis (LAT)   Attendance: 29,671.
Sent off: 31' Branko Pauljevic.

31.07.18   Vazgen Sargsyan anvan Hanrapetakan Marzadasht, Yerevan:
Pyunik Yerevan FC – Tobol Kustanai 1-0 (0-0)
Pyunik Yerevan FC: Andrija Dragojevic, Vyacheslav Dmitriev, Maksim Zhestokov, Serob Grigoryan, Maksim Trusevich, Denis Voynov (46' Mohamed Konaté), Didier Kadio, Rumyan Hovsepyan (46' Alik Arakelyan), Vahagn Hayrapetyan, Petros Avetisyan, Ruslan Koryan (76' Albert Bogatyrev). Coach: Andrey Talalaev.
Tobol Kustanai: Dmytro Nepogodov, Viktor Dmitrenko (89' Aslan Darabaev), Fernander Kassaï, Dmitry Miroshnichenko, Marat Bystrov (79' Juan Lescano), Jaba Kankava, Azat Nurgaliev, Artūras Zulpa, Nika Kvekveskiri, Tanat Nuserbaev, Maxim Fedin (90+2' Bayurzhan Turysbek). Coach: Vladimir Nikitenko.
Goal: 82' Mohamed Konaté 1-0.
Referee: Petr Ardeleánu (CZE)   Attendance: 8,000.
Sent off: 89' Petros Avetisyan.

Pyunik Yerevan FC won on away goals.

01.08.18   Stade Émile Mayrisch, Esch-sur-Alzette: CS Fola Esch – KRC Genk 1-4 (0-2)
CS Fola Esch: Emanuel Cabral, Rodrigue Dikaba, Peter Chrappan, Julien Klein (77' Guillaume Mura), Mehdi Kirch (66' Corentin Koçur), Dejvid Sinani, Bruno Freire, Stefano Bensi (83' Lucas Raposo), Samir Hadji, Ken Corral, Roman Pierrard. Coach: Thomas Klasen.
KRC Genk: Nordin Jackers, Bojan Nastic, Dries Wouters, Jhon Lucumí, Rubin Seigers, Ibrahima Seck, Manuel Benson, Bryan Heynen (66' Nikolaos Karelis), Jakub Piotrowski, Zinho Gano, Edon Zhegrova. Coach: Philippe Clement.
Goals: 13' Edon Zhegrova 0-1, 16' Bryan Heynen 0-2, 59' Zinho Gano 0-3,
61' Stefano Bensi 1-3, 63' Edon Zhegrova 1-4.
Referee: Filip Glova (SVK)   Attendance: 1,550.

02.08.18   Stadiumi Laçi, Laçi: KF Laçi – Molde FK 0-2 (0-2)
KF Laçi: Gentian Selmani, Marko Radas (73' Ndricim Shtubina), Taulant Sefgjinaj, Erion Hoxhallari, Eglentin Gjoni, Abdurraman Fangaj (76' Ded Bushi), Nikola Eller, Fjoart Jonuzi, Regi Lushkja, Vice Kendes (82' Serxho Ujka), Myrto Uzuni. Coach: Besnik Prenga.
Molde FK: Andreas Linde, Vegard Forren, Ruben Gabrielsen, Kristoffer Haugen, Petter Strand, Magnus Eikrem (60' Pawel Cibicki), Babacar Sarr (46' Isak Ssewankambo), Fredrik Aursnes, Stian Gregersen, Mattias Moström, Daniel Chima Chukwu (60' Leke James). Coach: Ole Gunnar Solskjær.
Goals: 41' Fredrik Aursnes 0-1 (p), 45+1' Petter Strand 0-2.
Referee: Kristo Tohver (EST)   Attendance: 420.

02.08.18   AEK Arena – George Karapatakis, Larnaca: AEK Larnaca – Dundalk FC 4-0 (3-0)
AEK Larnaca: Toño, Mikel González, Truyols, Thomas Ioannou, Igor Carioca, Ivan Trickovski, Jorge Larena (70' Nacho Cases), Acorán (86' Joan Tomás), Hector Hevel, Apostolos Giannou, Tete (81' Konstantinos Konstantinou). Coach: Andoni Iraola.
Dundalk FC: Gary Rogers, Brain Gartland, Dean Jarvis, Sean Hoare (65' Dane Massey), Daniel Cleary (46' Sean Gannon), Chris Shields, Robbie Benson, Dylan Connolly (46' Patrick McEleney), Jamie McGrath, Patrick Hoban, Michael Duffy. Coach: Stephen Kenny.
Goals: 13' Ivan Trickovski 1-0, 21' Tete 2-0, 38' Ivan Trickovski 3-0, 87' Joan Tomás 4-0.
Referee: Fran Jovic (CRO)   Attendance: 3,991.

02.08.18 Vilniaus LFF stadionas, Vilnius: FK Trakai – Partizan Beograd 1-1 (1-1)
FK Trakai: Tomas Svedkauskas, Valdemars Borovskis, Evgeniy Osipov, Justinas Janusevskis, Diniyar Bilyaletdinov, Vaidas Silėnas, Valentin Jeriomenko, Donatas Kazlauskas, Lajo Traore (58' Etienne Mukanya), Svajūnas Cyzas, Justinas Marazas (86' Elvinas Alisauskas).
Coach: Kibu Vicuña.
Partizan Beograd: Vladimir Stojkovic, Marc Valiente, Nemanja Miletic (I), Sasa Zdjelar, Gabriel Enache, Nebojsa Kosovic, Seydouba Soumah, Marko Jankovic (88' Djordje Ivanovic), Danilo Pantic (75' Armin Djerlek), Nemanja Miletic (II), Ricardo Gomes (82' Ognjen Ozegovic). Coach: Miroslav Djukic.
Goals: 9' Evgeniy Osipov 1-0, 45+3' Nemanja Miletic (I) 1-1.
Referee: Stephan Klossner (SUI)   Attendance: 1,980.
Sent off: 53' Seydouba Soumah.

02.08.18 Stadyen Dynama, Minsk: FK Dinamo Minsk – DAC Dunajská Streda 4-1 (1-0)
FK Dinamo Minsk: Andrey Gorbunov, Igor Shitov, Luis Rocha, Roman Begunov, Nino Galovic, Maksim Shvetsov, Seidu Yahaya, Filipp Ivanov (61' Aleksandr Makas), Nikita Korzun, Uros Nikolic (70' Dinko Trebotic), Vladimir Khvashchinskiy (57' Artem Gurenko).
Coach: Sergei Gurenko.
DAC Dunajská Streda: Patrik Macej, Éric Davis, Souleymane Koné (18' Lubomír Satka), Marin Ljubicic, Tomás Huk, Zsolt Kalmár, Kristián Kostrna (79' Dominik Spiriak), Krisztopher Vida, Máté Vida, Christián Herc, Vakoun Issouf Bayo (41' Marko Divkovic).
Coach: Peter Hyballa.
Goals: 19' Uros Nikolic 1-0, 47' Vladimir Khvashchinskiy 2-0, 51' Filipp Ivanov 3-0 (p), 58' Uros Nikolic 4-0, 73' Krisztopher Vida 4-1.
Referee: Antti Munukka (FIN)   Attendance: 9,450.

02.08.18 Stadion Vasil Levski, Sofia: Slavia Sofia – Hajduk Split 2-3 (1-1)
Slavia Sofia: Antonis Stergiakis, Emil Martinov, Aleksandar Stanisavljevic, Momchil Tsvetanov (58' Slavcho Shokolarov), Galin Ivanov (90+1' Filip Krastev), Milen Gamakov, Yanis Karabelyov, Dimitar Velkovski, Georgi Yomov, Vladislav Uzunov, Tsvetelin Chunchukov (71' Milcho Angelov). Coach: Zlatomir Zagorcic.
Hajduk Split: Marin Ljubic, André Fomitschow, Borja López, Bozo Mikulic, Ádám Gyurcsó (66' Michele Sego), Mijo Caktas, Hamza Barry (77' Stipe Vucur), Dino Besirovic (7' Stanko Juric), Toma Basic, Josip Juranovic, Ahmed Said. Coach: Zeljko Kopic.
Goals: 25' Stanko Juric 0-1, 45' Galin Ivanov 1-1 (p), 55' Mijo Caktas 1-2 (p), 70' Georgi Yomov 2-2, 87' Mijo Caktas 2-3.
Referee: Daniele Doveri (ITA)   Attendance: 2,100.

(Slavia Sofia played their home match at Stadion Vasil Levski instead of their regular stadium, Slavia Stadium)

02.08.18 Bravida Arena, Göteborg: BK Häcken – RB Leipzig 1-1 (0-0)
BK Häcken: Jonathan Rasheed, Kari Arkivuo (81' Elohor Ekpolo), Johan Hammar, Gustav Berggren, Rasmus Lindgren, Erik Friberg (64' Kevin Ackermann), Adam Andersson, Viktor Lundberg, Mervan Çelik, Alhassan Kamara, Nasiru Mohammed (64' Daleho Irandust).
Coach: Andreas Alm.
RB Leipzig: Marius Müller, Willi Orban, Lukas Klostermann, Ibrahima Konaté (64' Oliver Bias), Emil Forsberg (63' Erik Majetschak), Diego Demme, Massimo Bruno, Marcelo Saracchi, Niclas Stierlin, Jean-Kévin Augustin, Matheus Cunha (70' Lukas Krüger).
Coach: Ralf Rangnick.
Goals: 47' Massimo Bruno 0-1, 85' Daleho Irandust 1-1.
Referee: Mete Kalkavan (TUR)   Attendance: 2,968.

02.08.18   Åråsen Stadion, Lillestrøm: Lillestrøm SK – LASK Linz 1-2 (0-1)
Lillestrøm SK: Matvei Igonen, Frode Kippe (62' Stefan Antonijevic), Marius Amundsen, Simen Mikalsen, Mats Haakenstad, Simen Rafn, Erik Brenden, Fredrik Krogstad, Ifeanyi Matthew, Erling Knudtzon (62' Thomas Olsen), Gary Martin (73' Kristoffer Ødemarksbakken). Coach: Jörgen Lennartsson.
LASK Linz: Alexander Schlager, Christian Ramsebner, Gernot Trauner, Reinhold Ranftl, Markus Wostry, Maximilian Ullmann, Florian Jamnig, James Holland (57' Fabian Benko), Thomas Goiginger (46' Dominik Frieser), Peter Michorl, Samuel Tetteh (73' Yusuf Otubanjo). Coach: Oliver Glasner.
Goals: 35' Thomas Goiginger 0-1, 65' Samuel Tetteh 0-2, 79' Thomas Olsen 1-2.
Referee: Vilhjálmur Thórarinsson (ISL)   Attendance: 1,975.

02.08.18   Rheinpark Stadion, Vaduz: FC Vaduz – FK Zalgiris 1-1 (1-0)
FC Vaduz: Andreas Hirzel, Mario Bühler, Maximilian Göppel, Sadik Vitija, Philipp Muntwiler, Marco Mathys (85' Noah Blasucci), Christopher Drazan (74' Boris Babic), Sandro Wieser, Jodel Dossou (72' Maurice Brunner), Mohamed Coulibaly, Igor Tadic.
Coach: Roland Vrabec.
FK Zalgiris: Dziugas Bartkus, Rolandas Baravykas, Mamadou Mbodj, Saulius Mikoliūnas, Donovan Slijngard, Tomas Simkovic, Liviu Antal (90+3' Serge Nyuiadzi), Slavko Blagojevic, Jérémy Manzorro (65' Domantas Simkus), Marko Tomic, Louis Ogana (90+2' Tomás Malec). Coach: Valdas Urbonas.
Goals: 34' Jodel Dossou 1-0, 66' Tomas Simkovic 1-1.
Referee: Anastasios Papapetrou (GRE)   Attendance: 853.

02.08.18   Tele2 Arena, Stockholm: AIK Solna – FC Nordsjælland 0-1 (0-1)
AIK Solna: Oscar Linnér, Per Karlsson, Daniel Sundgren, Alexander Milosevic, Tarik Elyounoussi (82' Denni Avdic), Sebastian Larsson, Panajotis Dimitriadis (46' Enoch Adu), Kristoffer Olsson, Heradi Rashidi, Henok Goitom (71' Stefan Silva), Nicolás Stefanelli. Coach: Rikard Norling.
FC Nordsjælland: Nicolai Larsen, Ulrik Jenssen, Karlo Bartolec (89' Mads Aaquist), Mads Pedersen, Andreas Skovgaard, Victor Nelsson, Magnus Andersen, Jacob Christensen, Mikkel Damsgaard, Mikkel Rygaard Jensen (67' Mathias Rasmussen), Andreas Skov Olsen (83' Nicklas Strunck Jakobsen). Coach: Kasper Hjulmand.
Goal: 29' Andreas Skov Olsen 0-1.
Referee: Jérôme Brisard (FRA)   Attendance: 10,946.

02.08.18   BSFZ-Arena, Maria Enzersdorf:
          FC Admira Wacker Mödling – CSKA Sofia 1-3 (0-1)
FC Admira Wacker Mödling: Manuel Kuttin, Stephan Zwierschitz (84' Wilhelm Vorsager), Sebastian Bauer, Milos Spasic, Emanuel Aiwu (46' Bjarne Thoelke), Marcus Maier, Morten Hjulmand, Dominik Starkl (71' Marco Kadlec), Sinan Bakis, Marin Jakolis, Patrick Schmidt. Coach: Ernst Baumeister.
CSKA Sofia: Vytautas Cerniauskas, Boris Sekulic (75' Aleksandar Dyulgerov), Bozhidar Chorbadzhiyski, Steven Pereira, Geferson, Rúben Pinto, Tiago Rodrigues, Janio Bikel, Kiril Despodov (46' Valentin Antov), Maurides (74' Edwin Gyasi), Jorginho.
Coach: Nestor El Maestro.
Goals: 14', 53' Maurides 0-1, 0-2, 55' Sinan Bakis 1-2, 80' Jorginho 1-3.
Referee: Pol van Boekel (HOL)   Attendance: 2,400.

02.08.18   Generali Arena, Praha: AC Sparta Praha – Spartak Subotica 2-1 (1-0)
AC Sparta Praha: Florin Nita, Semih Kaya, Costa Nhamoinesu (85' Bogdan Vatajelu), Uros Radakovic, Alexandru Chipciu (90+6' Lukas Stetina), Josef Sural, Nicolae Stanciu, Martin Frydek, Guélor Kanga, Srdjan Plavsic, Benjamin Tetteh. Coach: Zdenek Scasny.
Spartak Subotica: Nikola Peric, Andrija Vukcevic, Branimir Jocic, Noboru Shimura, Dejan Kerkez, Nemanja Calasan (36' Milan Marcic), Nemanja Tekijaski, Mile Savkovic, Bojan Cecaric (90+4' Vladimir Torbica), Nemanja Glavcic, Ognjen Djuricin (56' Dejan Djenic). Coach: Vladimir Gacinovic.
Goals: 28' Josef Sural 1-0, 66' Srdjan Plavsic 2-0, 75' Bojan Cecaric 2-1 (p).
Referee: Sebastian Coltescu (ROM)   Attendance: 12,068.
Sent off: 82' Milan Marcic, 90+8' Josef Sural.

02.08.18   Neo GSP Stadium, Nicosia:
            Apollon FC Limassol – FK Zeljeznicar Sarajevo 3-1 (1-1)
Apollon FC Limassol: Bruno Vale, Valentin Roberge, Charis Kyriakou, André Schembri (46' Facundo Pereyra), Héctor Yuste, Giorgos Vasiliou, Esteban Sachetti, João Pedro, Fotis Papoulis, Anton Maglica (46' Emilio Zelaya), Adrián Sardinero (73' Kevin Bru).
Coach: Sofronis Avgousti.
FK Zeljeznicar Sarajevo: Vedran Kjosevski, Jadranko Bogicevic, Milos Bakrac, Aldin Sehic (57' Sinia Stevanovic), Ivan Curjuric, Stojan Vranjes, Antonio Pavic, Mladen Veselinovic (46' Dzenan Zajmovic), Anel Sabanadzovic (64' Jovan Blagojevic), Sulejman Krpic, Asim Zec. Coach: Milomir Odovic.
Goals: 2' Fotis Papoulis 1-0 43' Asim Zec 1-1, 57', 90' Fotis Papoulis 2-1 (p), 3-1.
Referee: Nikola Popov (BUL)   Attendance: 3,400.

(Apollon FC Limassol played their home match at Neo GSP Stadium, Nicosia, instead of their regular stadium, Tsirio Stadium, Limassol)

02.08.18   Stadion Chornomorets, Odessa: FC Mariupol – Djurgårdens IF 2-1 (0-0, 1-1)
FC Mariupol: Rustam Khudzhamov, Sergey Yavorskiy, Maksym Bilyi (105' Sergiy Chobotenko), Pavel Polegenko, Besir Demiri (116' Joyskim Dawa), Oleksiy Bykov, Igor Tyshchenko (110' Igor Kyryukhantsev), Vyacheslav Churko (73' Vladislav Vakula), Dmytro Myshnov, Oleksandr Pikhalyonok, Ruslan Fomin. Coach: Oleksandr Babych.
Djurgårdens IF: Andreas Isaksson, Jonas Olsson, Erik Johansson, Jacob Une-Larsson (105' Johan Andersson), Jonathan Augustinsson, Haris Radetinac (89' Dzenis Kozica), Jonathan Ring (101' Marcus Danielsson), Fredrik Ulvestad, Kerim Mrabti, Jesper Karlström (99' Kevin Walker), Aliou Badji. Coach: Özcan Melkemichel.
Goals: 63' Oleksandr Pikhalyonok 1-0, 77' Aliou Badji 1-1, 97' Ruslan Fomin 2-1 (p).
Referee: Rob Harvey (IRL)   Attendance: 5,077.

(FC Mariupol played their home match at Stadion Chornomorets in Odessa instead of their regular stadium, Volodymyr Boiko Stadium in Mariupol, due to the war conditions in Eastern Ukraine)

FC Mariupol won after extra time.

02.08.18   Stadio Peristeriou, Athens: Atromitos FC – FK Dynamo Brest 1-1 (0-0)
Atromitos FC: Nikola Mirkovic, Madson, Emanuel Sakic (75' Georgios Manousos), Dimitrios Chatziisaias, Dimitris Giannoulis, Spyros Risvanis, Javier Umbides, Kyriakos Kivrakidis, Armin Mujakic (60' Theodoros Vasilakakis), Kostas Kotsopoulos (60' Clarck N'Sikulu), Efthymios Koulouris. Coach: Damir Canadi.
FK Dynamo Brest: Aleksandr Gutor, Maksim Vitus, Oleg Veretilo, Giannis Kargas, Zeljko Filipovic (82' Saliw Babawo), Oleksandr Noyok, Pavel Savitskiy, Chidi Osuchukwu, Roman Yuzepchuk, Oleksiy Khoblenko (69' Pavel Nekhaychik), Joel Fameyeh (46' Nivaldo). Coach: Aleksey Shpilevski.
Goals: 80' Georgios Manousos 1-0, 90+5' Pavel Nekhaychik 1-1.
Referee: Eitan Shemeulevitch (ISR)   Attendance: 2,420.
Sent off: 63' Armin Mujakic.

02.08.18   Stade Parc des Sports, Differdange:
        Progrès Niederkorn – Budapest Honvéd FC 2-0 (1-0)
Progrès Niederkorn: Sebastian Flauss, Mario Mutsch, Marvin da Graça, Jordan Gobron, Tim Hall, Yann Matias Marques, Emmanuel Françoise (73' Yannick Bastos), Sébastien Thill (65' Metin Karayer), Olivier Thill, Alexander Karapetyan, Mayron De Almeida (88' Adrien Ferino). Coach: Paolo Amodio.
Budapest Honvéd FC: Dávid Gróf, Eke Uzoma (87' Tonci Kukoc), Tibor Heffler, Dino Skvorc, Bence Batik, Krisztián Vadócz, Djordje Kamber, Gergö Nagy, Filip Holender (72' Dániel Lukàcs), Bence Banó-Szabó (33' Botond Baráth), Danilo. Coach: Attila Supka.
Goals: 21' Mayron De Almeida 1-0, 84' Yann Matias Marques 2-0.
Referee: Karim Abed (FRA)   Attendance: 1,852.

(Progrès Niederkorn played their home match at Stade Parc des Sports, Differdange, instead of their regular stadium, Stade Jos Haupert, Niederkorn)

02.08.18   Gradski Stadion Cair, Nis: Radnicki Nis – Maccabi Tel Aviv 2-2 (1-2)
Radnicki Nis: Mladen Zivkovic, Nikola Aksentijevic, Radovan Pankov, Djordje Crnomarkovic, Aleksandar Stanisavljevic, Petar Grbic, Dusan Micic, Nikola Stankovic, Ryota Noma (55' Sasa Stojanovic), Nermin Haskic (82' Sladjan Nikodijevic), Lazar Randjelovic (73' Marko Mrkic). Coach: Nenad Lalatovic.
Maccabi Tel Aviv: Predrag Rajkovic, Eitan Tibi, Saborit (55' Sheran Yeini), Elazar Dasa, Jair Amador, Eyal Golasa, Dor Mikha, Dor Peretz, Vidar Kjartansson (83' Chikeluba Ofoedu), Eliran Atar (63' Roslan Barski), Aaron Schoenfeld. Coach: Vladimir Ivic.
Goals: 33' Radovan Pankov 0-1 (og), 38' Eliran Atar 0-2, 44',
58' Aleksandar Stanisavljevic 1-2, 2-2.
Referee: Radu Petrescu (ROM)   Attendance: 7,588.

02-08-18   Telia Parken, København: FC København – UMF Stjarnan 5-0 (3-0)
FC København: Stephan Andersen, Pierre Bengtsson (46' Denis Vavro), Sotirios Papagiannopoulos, Michael Lüftner, Mads Roerslev Rasmussen, William Kvist, Ján Gregus, Rasmus Falk (46' Nicolaj Thomsen), Viktor Fischer (53' Bashkim Kadrii), Kenan Kodro, Carlo Holse. Coach: Ståle Solbakken.
UMF Stjarnan: Haraldur Björnsson, Baldur Sigurdsson (62' Thorri Geir Rúnarsson), Jósef Kristinn Jósefsson (52' Thórarinn Valdimarsson), Brynjar Gudjónsson, Daníel Laxdal, Jóhann Laxdal, Eyjólfur Hédinsson, Thorsteinn Már Ragnarsson (70' Sölvi Fodilsson), Alex Thór Hauksson, Gunjón Baldvinsson, Hilmar Árni Halldórsson. Coach: Rúnar Sigmundsson.
Goals: 4' Viktor Fischer 1-0, 24' Carlo Holse 2-0, 39', 47', 74' Kenan Kodro 3-0, 4-0, 5-0.
Referee: Paul Tierney (ENG)   Attendance: 8,726.

02.08.18   Vodafone Stadyumu, Istanbul: Besiktas JK – B36 Tórshavn 6-0 (2-0)
Besiktas JK: Tolga Zengin, Adriano, Caner Erkin, Gökhan Gönül, Gary Medel, Fatih Aksoy (46' Oguzhan Özyakup), Ryan Babel (77' Vágner Love), Jeremain Lens (62' Gökhan Töre), Necip Uysal, Tolgay Arslan, Cyle Larin. Coach: Senol Günes.
B36 Tórshavn: Trygvi Ashkam, Odmar Færø, Bjarni Petersen, Erlendur Magnusson, Eli Nielsen, Meinhard Olsen, Benjamin Heinesen, Andrias Eriksen, Robert Hedin Brockie, Michal Przybylski (62' Hugin Samuelsen), Lukasz Cieslewicz (20' Kaimar Saag, 71' Magnus Holm Jacobsen). Coach: Jákup á Borg.
Goals: 31' Cyle Larin 1-0, 43' Caner Erkin 2-0, 61' Cyle Larin 3-0, 74' Oguzhan Özyakup 4-0, 79' Cyle Larin 5-0, 90+3' Vágner Love 6-0 (p).
Referee: Carlos Xistra (POR)   Attendance: 23,929.

02.08.18   GelreDome, Arnhem: Vitesse Arnhem – FC Viitorul Constanta 3-1 (1-0)
Vitesse Arnhem: Eduardo, Alexander Büttner, Rasmus Thelander, Vyacheslav Karavaev, Jake Clarke-Salter (57' Maikel van der Werff), Thulani Serero, Navarone Foor, Matús Bero (57' Thomas Bruns), Roy Beerens, Tim Matavz, Bryan Linssen (90+2' Hilary Gong).
Coach: Leonid Slutsky.
FC Viitorul Constanta: Valentin Cojocaru, Sebastian Mladen, Tudor Baluta (71' Robert Hodorogea), Bradley de Nooijer, Vlad Achim, Bogdan Tîru, Lyes Houri (46' Andrei Ciobanu), Ianis Hagi, Ionut Vîna, Denis Dragus (77' Alexandru Matan), Mailson Lima.
Coach: Gheorghe Hagi.
Goals: 23' Tim Matavz 1-0, 2-0 Bryan Linssen 2-0, 50' Denis Dragus 2-1, 77' Roy Beerens 3-1.
Referee: Kevin Clancy (SCO)   Attendance: 9,876.

02.08.18   Stadio Theororos Kolokotronis, Tripoli:
             Asteras Tripolis FC – Hibernian FC Edinburgh 1-1 (0-1)
Asteras Tripolis FC: Georgios Athanasiadis, Konstantinos Triantafyllopoulos, Giorgos Kyriakopoulos, Matías Iglesias, Juan Munafo, Franco Bellocq (57' Anastasios Douvikas), José Luis Valiente (90+1' Lucas Salas), Nikolaos Kaltsas (78' Martín Rolle), Michalis Manias, Kosmas Tsilianidis, Giannis Kotsiras. Coach: Savvas Pantelidis.
Hibernian FC Edinburgh: Ádám Bogdán, Lewis Stevenson, Paul Hanlon, Darren McGregor (78' Steven Whittaker), Efe Ambrose, David Gray, Vykintas Slivka (89' Marvin Bartley), John McGinn, Stephen Mallan (90+2' Ryan Porteous), Martin Boyle, Florian Kamberi.
Coach: Neil Lennon.
Goals: 44' John McGinn 0-1, 56' Kosmas Tsilianidis 1-1.
Referee: Benoît Millot (FRA)   Attendance: 3,870.
Sent off: 48' Michalis Manias.

02.08.18 Olimpijski Stadion Asim Ferhatovic Hase, Sarajevo:
FK Sarajevo – Atalanta Bergamo 0-8 (0-5)
FK Sarajevo: Bojan Pavlovic, Amer Dupovac, Nihad Mujakic, Selmir Pidro, Emir Halilovic, Amar Rahmanovic (75' Milos Stanojevic), Anel Hebibovic, Joachim Adukor, Mersudin Ahmetovic (69' Haris Handzic), Krste Velkoski, Aladin Sisic (83' Benjamin Tatar).
Coach: Husref Musemic.
Atalanta Bergamo: Etrit Berisha, Andrea Masiello, Rafael Tolói (75' Timothy Castagne), José Palomino, Hans Hateboer, Robin Gosens, "Papu" Alejandro Gómez, Marten de Roon (55' Duván Zapata), Remo Freuler (81' Luca Valzania), Matteo Pessina, Musa Barrow.
Coach: Gian Piero Gasperini.
Goals: 4' José Palomino 0-1, 15' "Papu" Alejandro Gómez 0-2, 18' Andrea Masiello 0-3, 28' "Papu" Alejandro Gómez 0-4, 39' Mersudin Ahmetovic 0-5 (og),
51', 70', 87' Musa Barrow 0-6, 0-7, 0-8.
Referee: Stuart Attwell (ENG)   Attendance: 23,820.

02.08.18 Ljudski vrt, Maribor: NK Maribor – FC Chikhura Sachkhere 2-0 (0-0)
NK Maribor: Jasmin Handanovic, Marko Suler, Mitja Viler, Sasa Ivkovic, Blaz Vrhovec, Amir Dervisevic, Aleks Pihler, Dino Hotic (89' Dare Vrsic), Marcos Tavares, Gregor Bajde (75' Jasmin Mesanovic), Luka Zahovic (86' Alexandru Cretu). Coach: Darko Milanic.
FC Chikhura Sachkhere: Dino Hamzic, Davit Maisashvili, Lasha Chikvaidze (81' Demur Chikhladze), Bakari Mirtshkulava, Revaz Chiteishvili, Levan Kakubava (86' Giorgi Bukhaidze), Teimurazi Markozashvili, Irakli Bugridze, Giorgi Gabedava, Mikheil Sardalishvili, Kakha Kakhabrishvili (67' Davit Megrelishvili). Coach: Samson Pruidze.
Goals: 70' Luka Zahovic 1-0, 90+6' Marcos Tavares 2-0.
Referee: Halil Umut Meler (TUR)   Attendance: 7,166.

02.08.18 Stadion Pasienky, Bratislava: Slovan Bratislava – Balzan FC 3-1 (1-0)
Slovan Bratislava: Michal Sulla, Kornel Saláta, Mitch Apau, Vasil Bozhikov, Nono Delgado, Kenan Bajric, Vukan Savicevic (82' Joeri de Kamps), "Moha" Mohammed Rharsalla, Aleksandar Cavric (75' Boris Cmiljanic), Andraz Sporar, Dejan Drazic (87' Filip Holosko). Coach: Martin Sevela.
Balzan FC: Steve Sultana, Elkin Serrano, Steven Bezzina (83' Andrija Majdevac), Ivan Bozovic, Uros Ljubomirac, Michael Johnson, Cadú, Nenad Sljivic, Milos Lepovic (76' Ricardo Correa), Lecão (62' Alfred Effiong), Bojan Kaljevic. Coach: Marko Micovic.
Goals: 7' Aleksandar Cavric 1-0, 70', 71' Andraz Sporar 2-0, 3-0, 77' Cadú 3-1.
Referee: Alexandre Boucaut (BEL)   Attendance: 4,176.

02.08.18 Arena Nationala, Bucuresti: Fotbal Club FCSB – Rudar Velenje 4-0 (1-0)
Fotbal Club FCSB: Cristian Balgradean, Junior Maranhão, Bogdan Planic, Mihai Balasa, Mihai Pintilii (59' Kamer Qaka), Antonio Jakolis, Ovidiu Popescu, Dragos Nedelcu, Olimpiu Morutan, Florin Tanase (46' Harlem Gnohéré), Florinel Coman (74' Daniel Benzar).
Coach: Nicolae Dica.
Rudar Velenje: Anze Malnar, David Kasnik, Josip Tomasevic, Klemen Bolha, Robert Pusaver, Ivan Vasiljevic, Domagoj Muic, Anze Pisek, Matej Santek (51' Djair Parfitt-Williams), Ante Solomun (62' Damjan Trifkovic), Vlatko Simunac (56' Abu Kamara). Coach: Marijan Pusnik.
Goals: 22' Florin Tanase 1-0 (p), 49' Olimpiu Morutan 2-0, 68' Florinel Coman 3-0, 90+3' Daniel Benzar 4-0.
Referee: Sergey Ivanov (RUS)   Attendance: 7,030.

02.08.18 Furbalovy stadión Spartak Myjava, Myjava: AS Trencín – Górnik Zabrze 4-1 (2-0)
AS Trencín: Igor Semrinec, Jamie Lawrence, Lukás Skovajsa, Martin Sulek, Reuben Yem, Ashraf El Mahdioui (90+1' Philippe van Arnhem), Abdul Zubairu, Joey Sleegers, Antonio Mance (90+1' Emeka Umeh), Hamza Catakovic, Philip Azango (86' Osman Bukari).
Coach: Ricardo Moniz.
Górnik Zabrze: Tomasz Loska, Dani Suárez, Adrian Gryszkiewicz, Daniel Liszka (46' Daniel Smuga), Przemyslaw Wisniewski, Szymon Matuszek, Angulo, Adam Wolniewicz, Marcin Urynowicz (46' Konrad Nowak), Szymon Zurkowski, Jesús Jiménez (73' Adam Ryczkowski).
Coach: Marcin Brosz.
Goals: 10' Angulo 1-0 (og), 20' Hamza Catakovic 2-0, 59' Philip Azango 3-0, 60' Daniel Smuga 3-1, 90' Hamza Catakovic 4-0.
Referee: Ole Hobber Nilsen (NOR)   Attendance: 1,897.

(AS Trencín played their home match at Furbalovy stadión Spartak Myjava instead of their regular stadium, Stadión na Sihoti, due to renovation)

02.08.18   Vazgen Sargsyan anvan Hanrapetakan Marzadasht, Yerevan:
           FC Alashkert – FK Sutjeska Niksic 0-0
FC Alashkert: Ognjen Cancarevic, Artak Yedigaryan, Oliver Práznovsky, Taron Voskanyan, Goran Antonic, Mladen Zeljkovic (87' Artem Simonyan), Artur Yedigaryan (66' Danijel Stojkovic), Danilo Sekulic, Jefferson, Artak Grigoryan, Uros Nenadovic (79' Edgar Manucharyan). Coach: Varuzhan Sukiasyan.
FK Sutjeska Niksic: Vladan Giljen, Darko Bulatovic, Stefan Cicmil, Dragan Grivic, Marko Cetkovic (55' Vladan Bubanja), Stefan Stefanovic, Nemanja Nedic (85' Saleta Kordic), Bojan Bozovic, Luka Merdovic, Stefan Denkovic, Veljko Vukovic (65' Zarko Grbovic).
Coach: Nikola Rakojevic.
Referee: Ivaylo Stoyanov (BUL)   Attendance: 6,735.

02.08.18   MFA Centenary Stadium, Ta'Qali: FC Valletta – Zrinjski Mostar 1-2 (0-1)
FC Valletta: Henry Bonello, Joseph Zerafa, Ryan Camilleri, Steve Borg (81' Juan Gill), Rowen Muscat, Bogdan Gavrila (71' Kyrian Nwoko), Raed Ibrahim Saleh Al Mukhaini, Santiago Malano (88' Jean Borg), Miguel Alba, Matteo Piciollo, Mario Fontanella.
Coach: Danilo Doncic.
Zrinjski Mostar: Antonio Soldo, Pero Stojkic (46' Advan Kadusic), Slobodan Jakovljevic, Ognjen Todorovic, Milos Filipovic (90' Toni Jovic), Hrvoje Barisic, Edin Rustemovic, Marin Galic, Nemanja Bilbija, Marko Perisic (53' Neven Lastro), Semir Pezer. Coach: Ante Mise.
Goals: 31' Hrvoje Barisic 0-1, 56' Steve Borg 1-1, 66' Milos Filipovic 1-2.
Referee: Rade Obrenovic (SVN)   Attendance: 1,310.
Sent off: 50' Marin Galic.

02.08.18   A. Le Coq Arena, Tallinn: FC Flora Tallinn – APOEL Nicosia 2-0 (2-0)
FC Flora Tallinn: Mait Toom, Gert Kams, Kevin Aloe (81' Erik Sorga), Henrik Pürg, Madis Vihmann, Aleksandr Dmitrijev, Zakaria Beglarishvili, Maksim Gussev (67' Joseph Saliste), Markus Poom, Rauno Alliku, Frank Liivak (70' Mark Anders Lepik).
Coaches: Jürgen Henn & Arno Pijpers.
APOEL Nicosia: Boy Waterman, Zhivko Milanov, Carlão (46' Praxitelis Vouros), Yohan Tavares, Nicolas Ioannou, Nuno Morais, Giorgos Efrem (46' Reza Ghoochannejhad), Lucas Souza, Ghayas Zahid (59' Savvas Gentsoglou), Moussa Al Taamari, Dellatorre.
Coach: Bruno Baltazar.
Goals: 32' Gert Kams 1-0, 37' Markus Poom 2-0.
Referee: Amaury Delerue (FRA)   Attendance: 801.

02.08.18   Victoria Stadium, Gibraltar: Lincoln Red Imps – The New Saints 1-1 (1-0)
Lincoln Red Imps: Lolo Soler, Joseph Chipolina, Bernardo Lopes, Ryan Casciaro, Diego Gámiz, André dos Santos, Montesinos Romero (81' Jack Sergeant), Juanma Ortiz (75' Calderón), Anthony Hernandez, Lee Casciaro, Sykes Garro (46' Pedro Corral). Coach: Yiyi.
The New Saints: Paul Harrison, Christopher Marriott, Blaine Hudson, Kane Lewis, Benjamin Cabango, Aeron Edwards, Jon Routledge, Daniel Redmond (68' Adrian Cieslewicz), Tom Holland (79' Greg Draper), Jamie Mullan, Kurtis Byrne (46' Dean Ebbe).
Coach: Scott Ruscoe.
Goals: 41' Montesinos Romero 1-0, 82' Dean Ebbe 1-1.
Referee: Petri Viljanen (FIN)   Attendance: 546.

02.08.18   Svangaskard, Toftir: Víkingur Gøta – Torpedo Kutaisi 0-4 (0-2)
Víkingur Gøta: Elias Rasmussen, Atli Gregersen, Hanus Jacobsen, Gunnar Vatnhamar (70' Hedin Hansen), Elias Jóhannesson Lervig, Sølvi Vatnhamar (69' Adrian Cascaval), Karl Løkin, Filip Djordjevic, Hjalti Strømsten, Andreas Olsen (70' Dennis Nieblas), Adeshina Lawal. Coach: Sigfríður Clementsen.
Torpedo Kutaisi: Rion Kvaskhvadze, Davit Khurtsilava, Mamuka Kobakhidze, Giorgi Kimadze, Levan Gegetchkori, Oleksandr Azatsky, Grigol Dolidze (75' Anri Chichinadze), Marek Hlinka, Merab Gigauri (46' Giorgi Kukhianidze), Mate Tsintsadze, Milos Lacny (60' Tornike Kapanadze). Coach: Kakhaber Chkhetiani.
Goals: 11' Milos Lacny 0-1, 24' Mamuka Kobakhidze 0-2, 59' Oleksandr Azatsky 0-3, 81' Tornike Kapanadze 0-4.
Referee: Simon Lee Evans (WAL)   Attendance: 300.

(Víkingur Gøta played their home match at Svangaskard, Toftir, instead of their regular stdium Sarpugedi, Nordragøta)

02.08.18   Sportni Park, Domzale: NK Domzale – FC Ufa 1-1 (0-0)
NK Domzale: Dejan Milic, Matija Sirok, Gaber Dobrovoljc, Tilen Klemencic, Dario Melnjak, Senijad Ibricic, Zeni Husmani, Lovro Bizjak, Adam Gnezda Cerin (90' Zan Zuzek), Agim Ibraimi, Tonci Mujan (76' Shamar Nicholson). Coach: Simon Rozman.
FC Ufa: Aleksandr Belenov, Bojan Jokic, Denis Tumasyan, Ionut Nedelceanu, Jemal Tabidze, Veroljub Salatic, Ivan Paurevic, Dmitri Zhivoglyadov (56' Aleksandr Sukhov), Ivan Oblyakov (73' Catalin Carp), Kehinde Fatai (69' Azamat Zaseev), Sylvester Igboun.
Coach: Sergei Tomarov.
Goals: 50' Lovro Bizjak 1-0, 87' Bojan Jokic 1-1.
Referee: Arnold Hunter (NIR)   Attendance: 2,500.

FC Ufa won on away goals.

02.08.18   AFAS Stadion, Alkmaar: AZ Alkmaar – FK Kairat 2-1 (1-1)
AZ Alkmaar: Marco Bizot, Ron Vlaar (57' Myron Boadu), Jonas Svensson, Pantelis Hatzidiakos, Thomas Ouwejan, Fredrik Midtsjø, Teun Koopmeiners, Guus Til, Oussama Idrissi, Dorin Rorariu (53' Iliass Bel Hassani), Fred Friday. Coach: John van den Brom.
FK Kairat: Vladimir Plotnikov, Sergey Politevich, Sheldon Bateau, Gafurzhan Suyumbaev, Isael, Islambek Kuat, Bauyrzhan Islamkhan (61' Ákos Elek), Yan Vorogovskiy, Andrei Arshavin (70' Stanislav Lunin), Juan Felipe Alves, Aderinsola Eseola (75' Márton Eppel).
Coach: Carlos Alós Ferrer.
Goals: 28' Bauyrzhan Islamkhan 0-1 (p), 41' Guus Til 1-1, 90+4' Teun Koopmeiners 2-1 (p).
Referee: Dimitar Meckarovski (MKD)   Attendance: 9,437.

02.08.18   Turf Moor, Burnley: Burnley FC – Aberdeen FC 3-1 (1-1, 1-1)
Burnley FC: Anders Lindegaard, Stephen Ward (91' Charlie Taylor), Matthew Lowton, Ben Mee, James Tarkowski, Aaron Lennon (87' Dwight McNeil), Jack Cork, Jóhann Gudmundsson, Ashley Westwood (105' Jeffrey Hendrick), Samuel Vokes, Chris Wood (46' Ashley Barnes). Coach: Sean Dyche.
Aberdeen FC: Joe Lewis, Andrew Considine, Shay Logan, Graeme Shinnie, Thomas Hoban (88' Dominic Ball), Michael Devlin, Scott McKenna, Niall McGinn (81' Scott Wright), Gary Mackay-Steven, Lewis Ferguson (105' Chris Forrester), Sam Cosgrove (100' Stevie May). Coach: Derek McInnes.
Goals: 6' Chris Wood 1-0, 27' Lewis Ferguson 1-1, 102' Jack Cork 2-1, 114' Ashley Barnes 3-1 (p).
Referee: Massimiliano Irrati (ITA)   Attendance: 17,404.

Burnley FC won after extra time.

02.08.18   Ibrox Stadium, Glasgow: Glasgow Rangers FC – NK Osijek 1-1 (0-0)
Glasgow Rangers FC: Allan McGregor, James Tavernier, Connor Goldson, Jon Flanagan, Nikola Katic, Ryan Jack, Ryan Kent, Oviemuno Ejaria (90+3' Andrew Halliday), Lassana Coulibaly (75' Scott Arfield), Candeias (85' Josh Windass), Alfredo Morelos. Coach: Steven Gerrard.
NK Osijek: Marko Malenica, Guti, Borna Barisic, Mile Skoric, Haris Hajradinovic, Benedik Mioc (80' Marin Pilj), Alen Grgic, Petar Bockaj (66' Tomislav Sorsa), Robert Mudrazija, Mirko Maric (66' Tomislav Strkalj), Ezekiel Henty. Coach: Zoran Zekic.
Goals: 53' Nikola Katic 1-0, 89' Connor Goldson 1-1 (og).
Referee: Dennis Higler (HOL)   Attendance: 48,202.

02.08.18   Stade Matmut-Atlantique, Bordeaux:
           Girondins de Bordeaux – FK Ventspils 2-1 (1-0)
Girondins de Bordeaux: Benoît Costil, Igor Lewczuk, Pablo Castro, Maxime Poundjé, Jules Koundé, Jaroslav Plasil, Younousse Sankharé, Aurélien Tchouaméni (68' Valentín Vada), Zaydou Youssouf (83' Otávio), Nicolas de Préville, François Kamano (68' Gaëtan Laborde). Coach: Gustavo Poyet.
FK Ventspils: Maksims Uvarenko, Abdoul Mamah, Vitālijs Jagodinskis (68' Nauris Bulvītis), Medzit Neziri, Hélio Batista, Pedro Mendes, Abdullahi Alfa (74' Raens Tālbergs), Giuly Mandzhgaladze, Tosin Aiyegun, Vasili Pavlov (46' Ritvars Rugins), Adeleke Akinyemi. Coach: Dejan Vukicevic.
Goals: 9' François Kamano 1-0, 48' Jules Koundé 2-0, 66' Adeleke Akinyemi 2-1.
Referee: Hugo Miguel (POR)   Attendance: 15,863.

02.08.18   Sarpsborg Stadion, Sarpsborg: Sarpsborg 08 – FC St. Gallen 1-0 (1-0)
Sarpsborg 08: Alexander Vasyutin, Amin Askar, Joackim Jørgensen, Joachim Thomassen, Joonas Tamm, Matti Lund Nielsen, Ole Halvorsen, Jon-Helge Tveita, Kristoffer Zachariassen, Patrick Mortensen, Rashad Muhammed (90+1' Harmeet Singh). Coach: Geir Bakke.
FC St. Gallen: Dejan Stojanovic, Andreas Wittwer, Nicolas Lüchinger, Silvan Hefti, Leonel Mosevich (82' Dereck Kutesa), Yannis Tafer, Marco Aratore (46' Nassim Ben Khalifa), Jordi Quintillà, Vincent Sierro, Majeed Ashimeru, Roman Buess (73' Cedric Itten). Coach: Peter Zeidler.
Goal: 31' Patrick Mortensen 1-0.
Referee: Frank Schneider (FRA)   Attendance: 5,460.

Sarpsborg 08 won on away goals.

02.08.18 INEA stadion, Poznan: KKS Lech Poznan – Shakthtyor Soligorsk 3-1 (1-0, 1-1)
KKS Lech Poznan: Jasmin Buric, Thomas Rogne, Rafal Janicki (46' Maciej Orlowski), Volodymyr Kostevych, Vernon, Tomasz Cywka, Maciej Makuszewski, Maciej Gajos (89' Mihai Radut), Pedro Tiba (97' Lukasz Tralka), Darko Jevtic (66' João Amaral), Christian Gytkjær. Coach: Ivan Djurdjevic.
Shakhtyor Soligorsk: Andrey Klimovich, Maksim Bordachev, Pavel Rybak, Siarhei Matveichyk, Igor Burko, Roger Cañas (73' Vitaly Lisakovich), Aleksandr Selyava, Yuri Kovalev, Július Szöke (91' Mikhail Shibun), Max Ebong Ngome (46' Sergey Balanovich), Elis Bakaj (64' Denis Laptev). Coach: Sergey Tashuev.
Goals: 15' Christian Gytkjær 1-0, 79' Denis Laptev 1-1, 94', 118' Christian Gytkjær 2-1, 3-1.
Referee: Christian Dingert (GER)   Attendance: 16,507.
Sent off: 117' Sergey Balanovich, 120' Denis Laptev, 120+1' Pavel Rybak.

KKS Lech Poznan won after extra time.

02.08.18   Estádio do Rio Ave Futebol Clube, Vila do Conde:
Rio Ave FC – Jagiellonia Bialystok 4-4 (2-1)
Rio Ave FC: Giorgi Makaridze, Jonathan Buatu, Nadjack, Nélson Monte, Matheus Reis, Tarantini (70' Nikola Jambor), Leandrinho (89' Ricardo Schutte), Bruno Moreira, Gabrielzinho (80' Damien Furtado), Galeno, Gelson Dala. Coach: José Gomes.
Jagiellonia Bialystok: Marián Kelemen, Lukasz Burliga, Nemanja Mitrovic, Guilherme, Ivan Runje, Mateusz Machaj (61' Martin Pospísil), Arvydas Novikovas (87' Rafal Grzyb), Przemyslaw Frankowski, Bartosz Kwiecien (75' Karol Swiderski), Taras Romanczuk, Cillian Sheridan. Coach: Ireneusz Mamrot.
Goals: 6' Cillian Sheridan 0-1, 27', 45+2' Galeno 1-1, 2-1, 56' Taras Romanczuk 2-2, 63' Gelson Dala 3-2, 72' Martin Pospísil 3-3, 79' Taras Romanczuk 3-4, 84' Damien Furtado 4-4.
Referee: Marco Di Bello (ITA)   Attendance: 5,930.

02.08.18   Szusza Ferenc Stadion, Budapest: Újpesti FC – Sevilla FC 1-3 (0-1)
Újpesti FC: Filip Pajovic, Mijusko Bojovic, Róbert Litauszki (89' Razvan Horj), Dzenan Burekovic, Dániel Nagy (67' Kristóf Szücs), Benjámin Balász, Bojan Sankovic, Donát Zsótér, Alassane Diallo, Obinna Nwobodo, Soma Novothny (66' Patrik Tischler).
Coach: Nebojsa Vignjevic.
Sevilla FC: Sergio Rico, Gabriel Mercado, Daniel Carriço, Sergio Escudero, Sébastien Corchia, Sergi Gómez, Éver Banega (72' Roque Mesa), Franco Vázquez, Pablo Sarabia (65' Nolito), Pejiño, Wissam Ben Yedder (66' Luis Muriel). Coach: Pablo Machín.
Goals: 36', 50' Pablo Sarabia 0-1, 0-2, 77' Donát Zsótér 1-2, 83' Luis Muriel 1-3.
Referee: Kirill Levnikov (RUS)   Attendance: 9,785.

02.08.18   Kaplakrikavöllur, Hafnarfjördur: FH Hafnarfjördur – Hapoel Haifa 0-1 (0-0)
FH Hafnarfjördur: Gunnar Nielsen, Pétur Vidarsson (79' Atli Gudnason), Hjörtur Valgardsson, Vidar Ari Jónsson, Edi Gomes, Rennico Clarke, Davíd Vidarsson, Gudmundur Kristjánsson, Brandur Hendriksson Olsen, Robbie Crawford (80' Jákup Thomsen), Steven Lennon.
Coach: Ólafur Kristjánsson.
Hapoel Haifa: Ernestas Setkus, Gabriel Tamas, Nisso Kapiloto, Dor Malul, Hen Dilmoni, Rasmus Sjöstedt, Gil Vermouth, Radu Gînsari, Gal Arel (58' Guy Hadida), Thanasis Papazoglou (90+1' Risto Mitrevski), Maxim Plakushchenko (64' Eli Elbaz).
Coach: Nir Klinger.
Goal: 68' Eli Elbaz 0-1.
Referee: Sergey Tsinkevich (BLS)   Attendance: 1,136.

02.08.18   Stadiumi Olimpik Adem Jashari, Mitrovica: Drita Gjilan – F91 Dudelange 1-1 (1-0)
Drita Gjilan: Edvan Bakaj, Liridon Leci, Fidan Gërbeshi, Ardian Limani, Arbër Shala (63'
Albin Krasniqi), Haxhi Neziraj (76' Eri Lamçja), Drilon Musaj, Bujar Shabani, Xhevdet
Shabani, Betim Haxhimusa, Përparim Livoreka (79' Zgjim Mustafa). Coach: Bekim Isufi.
F91 Dudelange: Jonathan Joubert, Tom Schnell, Jerry Prempeh, Aniss El Hriti (81' Kevin
Malget), Marc-André Kruska, Dominik Stolz, Edisson Jordanov, Clément Couturier, Danel
Sinani, David Turpel (90' Stélvio), Edis Agovic (34' Patrick Stumpf).
Coach: Dino Toppmöller.
Goals: 26' Ardian Limani 1-0, 46' Patrick Stumpf 1-1.
Referee: Michael Tykgaard (DEN)   Attendance: 2,200.
Sent off: 87' Zgjim Mustafa.

(Drita played their home match at Stadiumi Olimpik Adem Jashari, Mitrovica, instead of their regular stadium Gjilan City Stadium, Gjilan)

02.08.18   Stadio Tullo Morgagni, Forli (ITA): SP La Fiorita – FK Spartaks Jūrmala 0-3 (0-2)
SP La Fiorita: Gianluca Vivan, Samuele Olivi, Roberto Di Maio, Marco Gasperoni, Riccardo
Mezzadri, Damiano Tommasi (87' Alessandro Guidi), Luca Righini, Adolfo José Hirsch (54'
Samuel Pancotti), Simone Loiodice (72' Tiziano Mottola), Armando Amati, Danilo Rinaldi.
Coach: Gianluca Procopio.
FK Spartaks Jūrmala: Mārcis Melecis, Gints Freimanis (51' Ioan Calin Revenco), Pāvels
Mihadjuks, Mārcis Oss, Aleksejs Visnakovs (46' Kaspars Svārups), Ingars Stuglis, Oleg
Dmitriev, Diego Aguirre, Ricards Korzāns, Vitor Faísca (61' Edgars Vardanjans), Ariagner
Smith. Coach: Aleksandr Grishin.
Goals: 26' Ariagner Smith 0-1, 45+2' Diego Aguirre 0-2, 65' Ariagner Smith 0-3.
Referee: Alan Mario Sant (MLT)   Attendance: 224.
Sent off: 32' Luca Righini.

(SP La Fiorita played their home match at Stadio Tullo Morgagni, Forli, Italy, instead of their regular stadium San Marino Stadium, Serravalle, due to renovation).

02.08.18   Seaview, Belfast: Crusaders FC – Olimpija Ljubljana 1-1 (1-1)
Crusaders FC: Sean O'Neill, Sean Ward, Billy Joe Burns, Colin Coates, Kyle Owens (61'
David Cushley), Rodney Brown, Declan Caddell, Jordan Forsythe, Paul Heatley (73' Ross
Clarke), Matthew Snoddy, Michael Carvill (90+5' Philip Lowry). Coach: Stephen Baxter.
Olimpija Ljubljana: Nejc Vidmar, Branko Ilic, Aris Zarifovic, Dino Stiglec, Vitalijs
Maksimenko, Rok Kronaveter, Matic Crnic (90'+3 Matevz Turkus), Stefan Savic (76' Asmir
Suljic), Tomislav Tomic, Nik Kapun, Haris Kadric (46' Kingsley Boateng).
Coach: Aleksandar Linta.
Goals: 15' Nik Kapun 0-1, 41' Paul Heatley 1-1.
Referee: Oliver Drachta (AUT)   Attendance: 1,080.

02.08.18   Vodafone-Völlurin, Reykjavík: Valur Reykjavík – FC Santa Coloma 3-0 (0-0)
Valur Reykjavík: Anton Ari Einarsson, Birkir Sævarsson, Bjarni Eiríksson, Eidur
Sigurbjörnsson, Sebastian Hedlund, Gudjón Lydsson (67' Einar Karl Ingvarsson), Haukur
Sigurdsson, Kristinn Sigurdsson, Sigurdur Lárusson (79' Andri Adolphsson), Patrick Pedersen
(90' Tobias Thomsen), Dion Jeremy Acoff. Coach: Ólafur Jóhannesson.
FC Santa Coloma: Eloy Casals, Ildefons Lima, Marc Rebés, Albert Mercadé (54' André
Azevedo), Andreu Ramos, Jaime Noguerol (66' Chus Sosa), Moisés San Nicolás, Yago Pérez,
Loren Burón, Aleix Cistero (80' Ibán Parra), Juanma Torres. Coach: Marc Rodríguez Rebull.
Goals: 53' Sigurdur Lárusson 1-0, 63' Bjarni Eiríksson 2-0, 90+4' Andri Adolphsson 3-0.
Referee: Irfan Peljto (BIH)   Attendance: 825.

THIRD QUALIFYING ROUND

07.08.18   Vazgen Sargsyan anvar Hanrapetakan Marzadasht, Yerevan:
Pyunik Yerevan FC – Maccabi Tel Aviv 0-0
Pyunik Yerevan FC: Andrija Dragojevic, Vyacheslav Dmitriev, Maksim Zhestokov, Serob Grigoryan (68' Sergey Kolychev), Maksim Trusevich, Denis Voynov, Didier Kadio, Rumyan Hovsepyan, Alik Arakelyan, Vahagn Hayrapetyan (43' Albert Bogatyrev), Mohamed Konaté (66' Ruslan Koryan). Coach: Andrey Talalaev.
Maccabi Tel Aviv: Predrag Rajkovic, Eitan Tibi, Saborit, Elazar Dasa, Jair Amador, Eyal Golasa (60' Roslan Barski), Dor Mikha, Dan Glazer, Eliran Atar (67' Chikeluba Ofoedu), Aaron Schoenfeld (88' Vidar Kjartansson), Omer Atzili. Coach: Vladimir Ivic.
Referee: Pol van Boekel (HOL)   Attendance: 12,500.

09.08.18   Stadion Neftyanik, Ufa: FC Ufa – Progrès Niederkorn 2-1 (1-0)
FC Ufa: Aleksandr Belenov, Bojan Jokic, Denis Tumasyan, Catalin Carp, Ionut Nedelcearu, Jemal Tabidze, Veroljub Salatic, Ondrej Vanek (56' Azamat Zaseev), Dmitri Zhivoglyadov, Ivan Oblyakov (83' Kehinde Fatai), Sylvester Igboun. Coach: Sergei Tomarov.
Progrès Niederkorn: Sebastian Flauss, Mario Mutsch, Marvin da Graça, Jordan Gobron, Metin Karayer (79' Romeu Torres), Tim Hall, Yann Matias Marques (66' Adrien Ferino), Emmanuel Françoise (71' Yannick Bastos), Olivier Thill, Alexander Karapetyan, Mayron De Almeida. Coach: Paolo Amodio.
Goals: 38' Sylvester Igboun 1-0, 63' Ivan Oblyakov 2-0, 80' Olivier Thill 2-1.
Referee: Stephan Klossner (SUI)   Attendance: 6,794.

09.08.18   Vazgen Sargsyan anvan Hanrapetakan Marzadasht, Yerevan:
FC Alashkert – CFR Cluj 0-2 (0-1)
FC Alashkert: Ognjen Cancarevic, Gagik Dagbashyan, Artak Yedigaryan, Oliver Práznovsky, Taron Voskanyan, Danijel Stojkovic, Artur Yedigaryan (52' Danilo Sekulic), Gustavo Marmentini dos Santos (53' Edgar Manucharyan), Jefferson (65' César Romero), Artak Grigoryan, Uros Nenadovic. Coach: Varuzhan Sukiasyan.
CFR Cluj: Giedrius Arlauskis, Andrei Muresan, Paulo Vinícius, Camora, Cristian Manea, Ovidiu Hoban, Damjan Djokovic, Mihai Bordeianu (82' Alexandru Ionita (II)), Alexandru Paun, Sebastian Mailat (63' Valentin Costache), George Tucudean (68' Robert Tambe). Coach: Toni Conceição.
Goals: 5', 49' George Tucudean 0-1, 0-2 (p).
Referee: Sergey Boyko (UKR)   Attendance: 9,000.

09.08.18   Stadions Skonto, Riga: FK Spartaks Jūrmala – FK Sūduva Marijampolé 0-1 (0-0)
FK Spartaks Jūrmala: Jevgenijs Nerugals, Gints Freimanis, Aleksandar Kosoric, Mārcis Oss, Ingus Slampe, Aleksejs Visnakovs, Artemiy Maleev, Evgeni Kobzar (82' Ricards Korzāns), Kaspars Svārups (76' Diego Aguirre), Vitor Faísca, Ariagner Smith.
Coach: Aleksandr Grishin.
FK Sūduva Marijampolé: Ivan Kardum, Vaidas Slavickas, Algis Jankauskas, Vitaly Gayduchik, Andro Svrljuga, Aleksandar Zivanovic, Guilherme Finkler (90+1' Povilas Leimonas), Robertas Vézevicius (73' Julius Kasparavicius), Jovan Cadenovic, Ovidijus Verbickas (88' Daniel Offenbacher), Rigino Cicilia. Coach: Vladimir Cheburin.
Goal: 52' Guilherme Finkler 0-1.
Referee: Thorvaldur Árnason (ISL)   Attendance: 1,435.

(FK Spartaks Jūrmala played their home match at Stadions Skonto, Riga, instead of their regular stadium Slokas Stadionā, Jūrmala)

09.08.18   Sammy Ofer Stadium, Haifa: Hapoel Haifa – Atalanta Bergamo 1-4 (1-2)
Hapoel Haifa: Ernestas Setkus, Gabriel Tamas, Nisso Kapiloto, Dor Malul, Hen Dilmoni, Rasmus Sjöstedt, Gil Vermouth (59' Guy Hadida), Radu Gînsari (59' Eli Elbaz), Almog Buzaglo, Thanasis Papazoglou (69' Gal Arel), Maxim Plakushchenko. Coach: Nir Klinger.
Atalanta Bergamo: Pierluigi Gollini, Andrea Masiello, Rafael Tolói, José Palomino, Hans Hateboer, Robin Gosens, "Papu" Alejandro Gómez (83' Andreas Cornelius), Marten de Roon, Remo Freuler, Matteo Pessina (60' Mario Pasalic), Duván Zapata (63' Musa Barrow). Coach: Gian Piero Gasperini.
Goals: 7' Almog Buzaglo 1-0, 18 Hans Hateboer 1-1, 20' Duván Zapata 1-2, 65' Mario Pasalic 1-3, 86' Musa Barrow 1-4.
Referee: Harald Lechner (AUT)   Attendance: 6.412.

09.08.18   Red Bull Arena, Leipzig: RB Leipzig – CS Universitatea Craiova 3-1 (1-0)
RB Leipzig: Yvon Mvogo, Willi Orban (61' Emil Forsberg), Lukas Klostermann, Ibrahima Konaté, Stefan Ilsanker, Kevin Kampl, Diego Demme, Bruma (62' Marcel Sabitzer), Marcelo Saracchi, Jean-Kévin Augustin (75' Yussuf Poulsen), Matheus Cunha. Coach: Ralf Rangnick.
CS Universitatea Craiova: Mirko Pigliacelli, Renato Kelic, Ivan Martic, Marius Briceag, Tiago Ferreira (79' Matteo Fedele), Nicusor Bancu, Isaac Donkor, Alexandru Mateiu, Alexandru Mitrita (85' Jovan Markovic), Alexandru Cicaldau, Valentin Mihaila (27' Raoul Baicu). Coach: Devis Mangia.
Goals: 25' Ibrahima Konaté 1-0, 77' Matheus Cunha 2-0, 87' Yussuf Poulsen 3-0, 90+3' Ivan Martic 3-1.
Referee: Pawel Gil (POL)   Attendance: 16,648.

09.08.18   Ludogorets Arena, Razgrad: PFC Ludogorets Razgrad – Zrinjski Mostar 1-0 (1-0)
PFC Ludogorets Razgrad: Renan, Cosmin Moti, Cicinho, Rafael Forster, Svetoslav Dyakov (68' Jacek Góralski), Lucas Sasha (78' Gustavo Campanharo), Wanderson (82' João Paulo), Natanael Pimienta, Claudiu Keserü, Marcelinho, Jody Lukoki. Coach: Paulo Autuori.
Zrinjski Mostar: Antonio Soldo, Slobodan Jakovljevic, Neven Lastro, Advan Kadusic, Ante Vrljicak (78' Marko Perisic), Ognjen Todorovic (75' Nemanja Bilbija), Samir Bekric, Milos Filipovic, Toni Jovic (85' Kristijan Stanic), Frane Cirjak, Semir Pezer. Coach: Ante Mise.
Goal: 16' Cosmin Moti 1-0.
Referee: Vitaliy Meshkov (RUS)   Attendance: 3,574.

09.08.18   Bolshaya Sportivnaya Arena, Tiraspol:
            FC Sheriff Tiraspol – Valur Reykjavík 1-0 (0-0)
FC Sheriff Tiraspol: Serghei Pascenco, Petru Racu, Ante Kulusic, Mateo Susic, Veaceslav Posmac, Cristiano, Antun Palic (46' "Jô" Joálisson), Yuri Kendysh, Ziguy Badibanga, Al-Haji Kamara (81' Wilfried Balima), Gerson Rodrigues (59' Rifet Kapic). Coach: Goran Sablic.
Valur Reykjavík: Anton Ari Einarsson, Bjarni Eiríksson, Eidur Sigurbjörnsson, Arnar Geirsson, Sebastian Hedlund, Kristinn Sigurdsson, Sindri Björnsson (68' Einar Karl Ingvarsson), Ólafur Finsen, Ívar Jónsson (78' Sigurdur Lárusson), Patrick Pedersen, Dion Jeremy Acoff (90+2' Kristinn Halldórsson). Coach: Ólafur Jóhannesson.
Goal: 85' Ziguy Badibanga 1-0.
Referee: Arnold Hunter (NIR)   Attendance: 4,803.

09.08.18   Yaakov Turner Toto Stadium, Beer Sheva:
             Hapoel Be'er Sheva – APOEL Nicosia 2-2 (1-2)
Hapoel Be'er Sheva: David Goresh, Ben Bitton, Loai Taha, Shir Tzedek, Oren Biton, John Ogu, Maor Melikson (65' Hen Ezra), Hanan Maman (83' Ben Sahar), Daniel Einbinder, Eden Ben Basat (59' Tomás Pekhart), Anthony Nwakaeme. Coach: Barak Bakhar.
APOEL Nicosia: Boy Waterman, Carlão, Emilio N'Sue (90+2' Zhivko Milanov), Praxitelis Vouros, Caju, Nuno Morais, Tomás De Vincenti (60' Savvas Gentsoglou), Lucas Souza, Roland Sallai, Moussa Al Taamari (72' Nicolas Ioannou), Dellatorre. Coach: Bruno Baltazar.
Goals: 13' Nuno Morais 0-1 (p), 28' Dellatorre 0-2, 42' John Ogu 1-2,
70' Anthony Nwakaeme 2-2.
Referee: Aleksey Eskov (RUS)   Attendance: 9,311.
Sent off: 79' Dellatorre.

09.08.18   Mikheil Meskhis Sakhelobis Stadioni, Tbilisi:
             Torpedo Kutaisi – FK Kukësi 5-2 (4-1)
Torpedo Kutaisi: Rion Kvaskhvadze, Mamuka Kobakhidze (79' Davit Khurtsilava), Giorgi Kimadze, Levan Gegetchkori, Oleksandr Azatsky, Lazar Marin, Grigol Dolidze (72' Arfang Daffé), Giorgi Kukhianidze, Marek Hlinka, Mate Tsintsadze, Milos Lacny (67' Tornike Kapanadze). Coach: Kakhaber Chkhetiani.
FK Kukësi: Stivi Frashëri, Ylli Shameti, Rustem Hoxha, William Cordeiro (74' Vangjel Zguro), Simon Rrumbullaku, Harallamb Qaqi, Irakli Dzaria (63' Donjet Shkodra), Arbër Çyrbja (63' Sebino Plaku), Besar Musolli, Haris Harba, Reginaldo. Coach: Armando Cungu.
Goals: 3', 15' Giorgi Kukhianidze 1-0, 2-0, 22' Haris Harba 2-1, 28' Lazar Marin 3-1,
31' Giorgi Kimadze 4-1, 86' Tornike Kapanadze 5-1, 88' Sebino Plaku 5-2 (p).
Referee: Alan Mario Sant (MLT)   Attendance: 4,521.

(Torpedo Kutaisi played their home match at Mikheil Meskhis Sakhelobis Stadioni, Tbilisi, instead of their regular stadium Ramaz Shengelias Sakhelobis Stadioni, Kutaisi)

09.08.18   Stadyen Dynama, Minsk: FK Dinamo Minsk – Zenit St. Petersburg 4-0 (3-0)
FK Dinamo Minsk: Andrey Gorbunov, Igor Shitov, Luís Rocha, Roman Begunov, Nino Galovic, Maksim Shvetsov, Seidu Yahaya, Filipp Ivanov (82' Artem Gurenko), Nikita Korzun, Uros Nikolic (79' Aleksandr Makas), Vladimir Khvashchinskiy (61' Nikita Kaplenko).
Coach: Sergei Gurenko.
Zenit St. Petersburg: Yuriy Lodygin, Branislav Ivanovic, Aleksandr Anyukov, Miha Mevlja, Oleg Shatov, Hernani, Elmir Nabiullin, Matías Kranevitter (83' Magomed Ozdoev), Daler Kuzyaev, Emiliano Rigoni (46' Aleksandr Erokhin), Sebastián Driussi (46' Anton Zabolotny).
Coach: Sergey Semak.
Goals: 12' Uros Nikolic 1-0, 32' Vladimir Khvashchinskiy 2-0, 41' Nino Galovic 3-0,
67' Uros Nikolic 4-0.
Referee: Anastasios Papapetrou (GRE)   Attendance: 21,750.

09.08.18   Merkur Arena, Graz: SK Sturm Graz – AEK Larnaca 0-2 (0-0)
SK Sturm Graz: Jörg Siebenhandl, Fabian Koch, Anastasios Avlonitis, Lukas Spendlhofer, Dario Maresic, Stefan Hierländer, Peter Zulj, Sandi Lovric (64' Markus Lackner), Philipp Hosiner (57' Emeka Eza), Markus Pink, Lukas Grozurek (46' Philipp Huspek).
Coach: Heiko Vogel.
AEK Larnaca: Toño, Mikel González, Truyols (80' Tete), Thomas Ioannou (59' Daniel Mojsov), Igor Carioca, Ivan Trickovski (77' Joan Tomás), Jorge Larena, Acorán, Nacho Cases, Hector Hevel, Apostolos Giannou. Coach: Andoni Iraola.
Goals: 46' Truyols 0-1, 74' Ivan Trickovski 0-2.
Referee: Mohammed Al-Hakim (SWE)   Attendance: 7.612.
Sent off: 90+4' Stefan Hierländer.

09.08.18   Andruv stadion, Olomouc: SK Sigma Olomouc – FK Kairat 2-0 (1-0)
SK Sigma Olomouc: Milos Buchta, Michal Veprek, Jan Sterba, Václav Jemelka, Václav Pilar (64' Martin Hála), Martin Sladky, Jakub Plsek (85' Jakub Yunis), David Houska, Simon Falta, Lukás Kalvach, Martin Nespor (75' Tomás Zahradnícek). Coach: Václav Jílek.
FK Kairat: Vladimir Plotnikov, Sergey Politevich, Sheldon Bateau, Gafurzhan Suyumbaev, Ákos Elek, Isael, Bauyrzhan Islamkhan (79' Ivo Ilicevic), Stanislav Lunin, Andrei Arshavin (53' Islambek Kuat), Juan Felipe Alves, Aderinsola Eseola (57' Márton Eppel).
Coach: Carlos Alós Ferrer.
Goals: 21' Martin Sladky 1-0, 50' Václav Pilar 2-0.
Referee: Massimiliano Irrati (ITA)   Attendance: 6,118.
Sent off: 38' Gafurzhan Suyumbaev, 68' Michal Veprek.

09.08.18   Stadion Chornomorets, Odessa: FC Mariupol – Girondins de Bordeaux 1-3 (1-2)
FC Mariupol: Rustam Khudzhamov, Sergey Yavorskiy, Pavel Polegenko, Besir Demiri, Oleksiy Bykov, Joyskim Dawa (66' Vladislav Vakula), Igor Tyshchenko (82' Sergiy Gorbunov), Vyacheslav Churko (46' Andriy Boryachuk), Dmytro Myshnov, Oleksandr Pikhalyonok, Ruslan Fomin. Coach: Oleksandr Babych.
Girondins de Bordeaux: Benoît Costil, Pablo Castro, Maxime Poundjé, Milan Gajic (78' Igor Lewczuk), Jules Koundé, Jaroslav Plasil, Younousse Sankharé (87' Valentín Vada), Aurélien Tchouaméni, Zaydou Youssouf (78' Lukas Lerager), Gaëtan Laborde, François Kamano.
Coach: Gustavo Poyet.
Goals: 7' Dmytro Myshnov 1-0, 33', 37' Gaëtan Laborde 1-1, 1-2,
49' Aurélien Tchouaméni 1-3.
Referee: Ivan Bebek (CRO)   Attendance: 6,587.

(FC Mariupol played their home match at Stadion Chornomorets in Odessa instead of their regular stadium, Volodymyr Boiko Stadium in Mariupol, due to the war conditions in Eastern Ukraine)

09.08.18   Stadión pod Dubnom, Zilina: AS Trencín – Feyenoord Rotterdam 4-0 (3-0)
AS Trencín: Igor Semrinec, Jamie Lawrence, Lukás Skovajsa, Martin Sulek, Reuben Yem, Ashraf El Mahdioui, Abdul Zubairu (83' Desley Ubbink), Joey Sleegers (85' Osman Bukari), Antonio Mance, Hamza Catakovic, Philip Azango. Coach: Ricardo Moniz.
Feyenoord Rotterdam: Justin Bijlow, Jan-Arie van der Heijden, Bart Nieuwkoop (90' Lutsharel Geertruida), Sven van Beek, Calvin Verdonk, Jens Toornstra, Jordy Clasie, Sofyan Amrabat, Steven Berghuis, Sam Larsson (61' Jean-Paul Boëtius), Dylan Vente.
Coach: Giovanni van Bronckhorst.
Goals: 6', 37' Antonio Mance 1-0, 2-0, 44' Philip Azango 3-0, 63' Antonio Mance 4-0.
Referee: Robert Schörgenhofer (AUT)   Attendance: 6,817.

(AS Trencín played this home match at Stadión pod Dubnom, Zilina, instead of their regular stadium, Stadión na Sihoti, Trencín, due to renovation)

09.08.18   Neo GSP Stadium, Nicosia: Apollon FC Limassol – FK Dynamo Brest 4-0 (0-0)
Apollon FC Limassol: Bruno Vale, Valentin Roberge, Charis Kyriakou, Facundo Pereyra, Héctor Yuste, Giorgos Vasiliou, Esteban Sachetti (77' Kévin Bru), Emilio Zelaya (73' Anton Maglica), João Pedro, Fotis Papoulis, Adrián Sardinero (83' Sasa Markovic).
Coach: Sofronis Avgousti.
FK Dynamo Brest: Aleksandr Gutor, Oleg Veretilo, Andrei Zaleski, Pavel Nekhaychik, Zeljko Filipovic (59' Pavel Savitskiy), Oleksandr Noyok, Chidi Osuchukwu (46' Oleksiy Khoblenko), Roman Yuzepchuk, Gaby Kiki, Nivaldo, Joel Fameyeh (83' Sergey Krivets).
Coach: Aleksey Shpilevski.
Goals: 46', 58' Emilio Zelaya 1-0, 2-0, 87' Sasa Markovic 3-0, 90+2' Oleg Veretilo 4-0 (og).
Referee: Carlos Xistra (POR)   Attendance: 3.590.
Sent off: 66' Andrei Zaleski.

(Apollon FC Limassol played their home match at Neo GSP Stadium, Nicosia, instead of their regular stadium, Tsirio Stadium, Limassol)

09.08.18   Stadion Miejski, Bialystok: Jagiellonia Bialystok – KAA Gent 0-1 (0-0)
Jagiellonia Bialystok: Marián Kelemen, Jakub Wójcicki, Nemanja Mitrovic, Guilherme, Ivan Runje, Arvydas Novikovas (80' Karol Swiderski), Martin Pospísil (84' Mateusz Machaj), Przemyslaw Frankowski, Bartosz Kwiecien, Taras Romanczuk, Cillian Sheridan (72' Roman Bezjak). Coach: Ireneusz Mamrot.
KAA Gent: Colin Coosemans, Nana Asare, Igor Plastun, Sigurd Rosted, Thomas Foket, Vadis Odjidja-Ofoe (89' Brecht Dejaegere), Franko Andrijasevic, Birger Verstraete, Jean-Luc Dompé, Giorgi Chakvetadze (67' Roman Yaremchuk), Taiwo Awoniyi (69' Jonathan David).
Coach: Yves Vanderhaeghe.
Goal: 85' Jonathan David 0-1.
Referee: Ali Palabiyik (TUR)   Attendance: 15,591.

09.08.18   Right to Dream Park, Farum: FC Nordsjælland – Partizan Beograd 1-2 (0-1)
FC Nordsjælland: Nicolai Larsen, Benjamin Hansen (65' Mathias Rasmussen), Karlo Bartolec, Mads Pedersen, Andreas Skovgaard, Victor Nelsson, Magnus Andersen, Jacob Christensen (78' Nicklas Strunck Jakobsen), Mikkel Damsgaard, Mikkel Rygaard Jensen (65' Mohammed Kudus), Andreas Skov Olsen. Coach: Kasper Hjulmand.
Partizan Beograd: Vladimir Stojkovic, Marc Valiente, Nemanja Miletic (I), Sasa Zdjelar, Svetozar Markovic, Goran Zakaric (70' Milan Smiljanic), Nebojsa Kosovic (78' Nemanja Nikolic), Marko Jankovic (90+1' Gabriel Enache), Danilo Pantic, Nemanja Miletic (II), Ricardo Gomes. Coach: Zoran Mirkovic.
Goals: 10' Ricardo Gomes 0-1, 64' Goran Zakaric 0-2, 71' Mathias Rasmussen 1-2.
Referee: Alejandro Hernández Hernández (ESP)   Attendance: 6,079.

09.08.18   Vasil Levski National Stadium, Sofia: CSKA Sofia – FC København 1-2 (1-0)
CSKA Sofia: Vytautas Cerniauskas, Boris Sekulic, Bozhidar Chorbadzhiyski, Steven Pereira, Rúben Pinto, Edwin Gyasi (37' Jorginho), Tiago Rodrigues (44' Aleksandar Dyulgerov), Janio Bikel, Angel Lyaskov, Kiril Despodov (78' Valentin Antov), Maurides.
Coach: Nestor El Maestro.
FC København: Jesse Joronen, Andreas Bjelland (45+2' Denis Vavro), Sotirios Papagiannopoulos, Peter Ankersen, Nicolai Boilesen, Rasmus Falk (76' Ján Gregus), Zeca, Viktor Fischer, Nicolaj Thomsen (62' Robert Skov), Dame N'Doye, Kenan Kodro.
Coach: Ståle Solbakken.
Goals: 15' Maurides 1-0, 64' Denis Vavro 1-1, 74' Kenan Kodro 1-2 (p).
Referee: Bart Vertenten (BEL)   Attendance: 18,100.
Sent off: 41' Bozhidar Chorbadzhiyski.

(CSKA Sofia played their third qualifying round home match at Vasil Levski National Stadium, instead of their regular stadium Stadion Bâlgarska Armija)

09.08.18   Stadion Stozice, Ljubljana: Olimpija Ljubljana – HJK Helsinki 3-0 (1-0)
Olimpija Ljubljana: Aljaz Ivacic, Branko Ilic, Aris Zarifovic, Dino Stiglec, Rok Kronaveter (78' Marko Gajic), Marko Putincanin, Matic Crnic, Daniel Avramovski (84' Stefan Savic), Tomislav Tomic, Nik Kapun, Issah Abass (70' Asmir Suljic). Coach: Aleksandar Linta.
HJK Helsinki: Maksim Rudakov, Rafinha (89' Macauley Chrisantus), Hannu Patronen, Mikko Sumusalo, Faith Obilor, Anthony Annan, Moshtagh Yaghoubi, Sebastian Dahlström (63' Jordan Domínguez), Riku Riski, Evans Mensah (80' Nikolai Alho), Klauss.
Coach: Mika Lehkosuo.
Goals: 38' Issah Abass 1-0, 50' Rok Kronaveter 2-0 (p), 59' Issah Abass 3-0.
Referee: Benoît Millot (FRA)   Attendance: 4,900.
Sent off: 83' Matic Crnic.

09.08.18   Basaksehir Fatih Terim Stadyumu, Istanbul:
            Istanbul Basaksehir FK – Burnley FC 0-0
Istanbul Basaksehir FK: Mert Günok, Manuel da Costa, Gaël Clichy, Alexandru Epureanu, Júnior Caiçara, Eljero Elia (84' Kerim Frei), Emre Belözoglu, Mahmut Tekdemir, Edin Visca, Irfan Kahveci (58' Milos Jojic), Rijad Bajic (89' Stefano Napoleoni). Coach: Abdullah Avci.
Burnley FC: Joe Hart, Phil Bardsley, Ben Mee, James Tarkowski, Charlie Taylor, Jack Cork, Jóhann Gudmundsson (62' Samuel Vokes), Ashley Westwood, Jeffrey Hendrick, Jon Walters, Ashley Barnes (78' Aaron Lennon). Coach: Sean Dyche.
Referee: Srdan Jovanovic (SER)   Attendance: 4,503.

09.08.18 Luminus Arena, Genk: KRC Genk – KKS Lech Poznan 2-0 (1-0)
KRC Genk: Danny Vukovic, Sebastien Dewaest, Jere Uronen, Jhon Lucumí, Joakim Mæhle, Pozuelo, Ruslan Malinovskiy, Sander Berge, Leandro Trossard (82' Edon Zhegrova), Mbwana Samatta (65' Zinho Gano), Dieumerci N'Dongala. Coach: Philippe Clement.
KKS Lech Poznan: Jasmin Buric, Thomas Rogne (68' Nikola Vujadinovic), Volodymyr Kostevych, Vernon, Maciej Orlowski, Tomasz Cywka, Lukasz Tralka, Maciej Makuszewski (54' Kamil Józwiak), Maciej Gajos, Darko Jevtic (74' Pawel Tomczyk), Christian Gytkjær. Coach: Ivan Djurdjevic.
Goals: 44' Ruslan Malinovskiy 1-0, 56' Mbwana Samatta 2-0.
Referee: Marius Avram (ROM)   Attendance: 13,540.

09.08.18 GelreDome, Arnhem: Vitesse Arnhem – FC Basel 0-1 (0-0)
Vitesse Arnhem: Eduardo, Alexander Büttner (87' Max Clark), Maikel van der Werff, Vyacheslav Karavaev, Jake Clarke-Salter, Thulani Serero, Navarone Foor, Thomas Bruns (70' Hilary Gong), Roy Beerens, Tim Matavz, Bryan Linssen. Coach: Leonid Slutsky.
FC Basel: Jonas Omlin, Marek Suchy, Silvan Widmer, Éder Álvarez Balanta, Eray Cümart, Valentin Stocker (79' Kevin Bua), Luca Zuffi, Fabian Frei, Raoul Petretta, Ricky van Wolfswinkel, Albian Ajeti (90+2' Dimitri Oberlin). Coach: Marcel Koller.
Goal: 90+3' Ricky van Wolfswinkel 0-1.
Referee: Georgi Kabakov (BUL)   Attendance: 11,532.

09.08.18 Stadio Georgios Karaiskáki, Piraeus: Olympiakos Piraeus – FC Luzern 4-0 (3-0)
Olympiakos Piraeus: Andreas Gianniotis, Jagos Vukovic, Omar Elabdellaoui, Roderick Miranda, Kostas Tsimikas, Lazaros Christodoulopoulos (78' Marius Vrousai), Kostas Fortounis (86' Ioannis Fetfatzidis), Andreas Bouchalakis, Daniel Podence, Mohamed Camara (90' Vasilios Torosidis), Guerrero. Coach: Pedro Martins.
FC Luzern: Mirko Salvi, Christian Schwegler (58' Ruben Vargas), Simon Grether, Lucão, Yannick Schmid, Silvan Sidler, Idriz Voca, Christian Schneuwly (58' Marvin Schulz), Pascal Schürpf, Valeriane Gvilia, Blessing Eleke (74' Shkelqim Demhasaj). Coach: René Weiler.
Goals: 10', 33' Lazaros Christodoulopoulos 1-0, 2-0, 36', 84' Guerrero 3-0, 4-0.
Referee: François Letexier (FRA)   Attendance: 19,208.

09.08.18 Vodafone Stadyumu, Istanbul: Besiktas JK – LASK Linz 1-0 (1-0)
Besiktas JK: Tolga Zengin, Pepe, Caner Erkin, Gökhan Gönül, Gary Medel, Ryan Babel, Jeremain Lens (71' Ricardo Quaresma), Necip Uysal, Tolgay Arslan, Oguzhan Özyakup (80' Vágner Love), Cyle Larin (88' Álvaro Negredo). Coach: Senol Günes.
LASK Linz: Alexander Schlager, Emanuel Pogatetz, Christian Ramsebner, Gernot Trauner, Reinhold Ranftl, Maximilian Ullmann, James Holland, Thomas Goiginger, Peter Michorl (90+2' Dogan Erdogan), Dominik Frieser (67' Florian Jamnig), Samuel Tetteh (78' Yusuf Otubanjo). Coach: Oliver Glasner.
Goal: 6' Ryan Babel 1-0.
Referee: Bartosz Frankowski (POL)   Attendance: 24,476.

09.08.18   Slavutych-Arena, Zaporizhya: Zorya Luhansk – Sporting Braga 1-1 (0-0)
Zorya Luhansk: Luis Felipe, Vitaliy Vernidub, Oleksandr Svatok, Oleksandr Tymchyk, Bogdan Mykhaylychenko, Dmytro Khomchenovsky, Igor Kharatin, Oleksandr Karavayev, Silas (66' Artem Gordienko), Bohdan Lednev (71' Vladyslav Kochergin), Rafael Ratão (74' Vladyslav Kabayev). Coach: Yuriy Vernydub.
Sporting Braga: Matheus Magalhães, Raúl Silva, Ricardo Esgaio, Marcelo Goiano, Nuno Sequeira, Bruno Viana, Claudemir, Fransérgio, João Novais (89' Ricardo Ryller), Ricardo Horta (89' Fábio Martins), Wilson Eduardo (78' Dyego Sousa). Coach: Abel Ferreira.
Goals: 69' Ricardo Horta 0-1, 72' Oleksandr Karavayev 1-1.
Referee: Tobias Welz (GER)   Attendance: 5,365.

(Zorya Luhansk played their home match at Slavutych-Arena, Zaporizhya, instead of their regular stadium Avanhard Stadium, Luhansk, due to the war conditions in Eastern Ukraine)

09.08.18   Turner's Cross, Cork: Cork City FC – Rosenborg BK 0-2 (0-2)
Cork City FC: Mark McNulty, Damien Delaney, Steven Beattie, Shane Griffin, Sean McLoughlin, Jimmy Keohane, Conor McCormack (61' Gearóid Morrissey), Barry McNamee (46' Kieran Sadlier), Garry Buckley, Graham Cummins, Karl Sheppard (72' Ronan Coughlin). Coach: John Caulfield.
Rosenborg BK: André Hansen, Tore Reginiussen, Even Hovland, Vegar Hedenstad, Birger Meling, Mike Jensen, Anders Trondsen (87' Olaus Skarsem), Marius Lundemo, Nicklas Bendtner, Alexander Søderlund (78' Erik Botheim), Jonathan Levi. Coach: Rini Coolen.
Goals: 22', 44' Jonathan Levi 0-1, 0-2.
Referee: Petr Ardeleánu (CZE)   Attendance: 5,488.

09.08.18   Cardiff City Stadium, Cardiff: The New Saints – FC Midtjylland 0-2 (0-2)
The New Saints: Paul Harrison, Simon Spender, Christopher Marriott, Blaine Hudson, Benjamin Cabango, Aeron Edwards, Jon Routledge, Daniel Redmond (84' Joash Nembhard), Tom Holland (79' Kurtis Byrne), Jamie Mullan, Dean Ebbe (69' Adrian Cieslewicz). Coach: Scott Ruscoe.
FC Midtjylland: Jesper Hansen, Kian Hansen, Marc Hende (61' Joel Andersson), Bubacarr Sanneh, Alexander Munksgaard, Rasmus Nicolaisen, Jakob Poulsen, Gustav Wikheim, Mikkel Duelund, Paul Ebere Onuachu (79' Mayron George), Awer Mabil (62' Ayo Simon Okosun). Coach: Jess Thorup.
Goals: 9', 27' Paul Ebere Onuachu 0-1, 0-2.
Referee: Peter Královic (SVK)   Attendance: 863.

(The New Saints played their home match at the Cardiff City Stadium, Cardiff, instead of their regular stadium Park Hall Stadium, Oswestry)

09.08.18   Sarpsborg Stadion, Sarpsborg: Sarpsborg 08 – NK Rijeka 1-1 (0-0)
Sarpsborg 08: Alexander Vasyutin, Amin Askar (84' Tobias Heintz), Joackim Jørgensen, Joachim Thomassen, Joonas Tamm, Matti Lund Nielsen (83' Harmeet Singh), Ole Halvorsen, Jon-Helge Tveita, Kristoffer Zachariassen, Patrick Mortensen, Rashad Muhammed (86' Jørgen Larsen). Coach: Geir Bakke.
NK Rijeka: Simon Sluga, Roberto Puncec, Dario Zuparic, Mario Pavelic, Leonard Zuta, Srdan Grahovac, Domagoj Pavicic (82' Antonio Colak), Dario Canadija, Alexander Gorgon, Héber (66' Zoran Kvrzic), Boadu Maxwell Acosty (90+1' Luka Capan). Coach: Matjaz Kek.
Goals: 72' Kristoffer Zachariassen 1-0, 83' Alexander Gorgon 1-1.
Referee: Kevin Clancy (SCO)   Attendance: 5.944.

09.08.18 Easter Road Stadium, Edinburgh: Hibernian FC Edinburgh – Molde FK 0-0
Hibernian FC Edinburgh: Ross Laidlaw, Lewis Stevenson, Paul Hanlon, Efe Ambrose, David Gray, Ryan Porteous, Marvin Bartley (81' Emerson Hyndman), Vykintas Slivka, Stephen Mallan, Martin Boyle (90+4' Jamie MacLaren), Florian Kamberi (81' Oliver Shaw).
Coach: Neil Lennon.
Molde FK: Andreas Linde, Vegard Forren, Ruben Gabrielsen, Kristoffer Haugen, Petter Strand, Magnus Eikrem (62' Leke James), Etzaz Hussain, Babacar Sarr, Eirik Hestad (90+1' Pawel Cibicki), Stian Gregersen, Daniel Chima Chukwu (72' Mattias Mostrøm).
Coach: Ole Gunnar Solskjær.
Referee: Ádám Farkas (HUN)   Attendance: 16,339.

09.08.18 Stadion Poljud, Split: Hajduk Split – Fotbal Club FCSB 0-0
Hajduk Split: Josip Posavec, André Fomitschow, Stipe Vucur, Borja López, Bozo Mikulic, Ádám Gyurcsó (56' Michele Sego), Mijo Caktas, Hamza Barry (76' Márkó Futács), Josip Juranovic, Stanko Juric, Mirko Ivanovski (64' Ahmed Said). Coach: Zeljko Kopic.
Fotbal Club FCSB: Cristian Balgradean, Marko Momcilovic (45' Junior Maranhão), Romario Sandu Benzar, Bogdan Planic, Mihai Balasa, Filipe Teixeira, Mihai Pintilii, Lucian Filip, Harlem Gnohéré, Florin Tanase (87' Olimpiu Morutan), Dennis Man (47' Antonio Jakolis).
Coach: Nicolae Dica.
Referee: Tiago Martins (POR)   Attendance: 25,764.

09.08.18 Ibrox Stadium, Glasgow: Glasgow Rangers FC – NK Maribor 3-1 (1-1)
Glasgow Rangers FC: Allan McGregor, James Tavernier, Connor Goldson, Jon Flanagan, Nikola Katic, Scott Arfield, Ryan Kent (87' Ross McCrorie), Oviemuno Ejaria (78' Jamie Murphy), Lassana Coulibaly, Candeias, Alfredo Morelos (88' Umar Sadiq).
Coach: Steven Gerrard.
NK Maribor: Jasmin Handanovic, Marko Suler, Mitja Viler, Sasa Ivkovic, Denis Klinar, Blaz Vrhovec, Amir Dervisevic, Aleks Pihler, Marcos Tavares (79' Dare Vrsic), Gregor Bajde (61' Jasmin Mesanovic), Luka Zahovic. Coach: Darko Milanic.
Goals: 6' Alfredo Morelos 1-0, 40' Mitja Viler 1-1, 50' James Tavernier 2-1 (p), 86' Lassana Coulibaly 3-1.
Referee: Roi Reinshreiber (ISR)   Attendance: 48,001.

09.08.18 Stadion Rajko Mitic, Beograd: Spartak Subotica – Brøndby IF 0-2 (0-1)
Spartak Subotica: Nikola Peric, Stefan Milosevic, Andrija Vukcevic (69' Vladimir Torbica), Noboru Shimura, Nemanja Calasan, Nemanja Tekijaski, Bojan Cecaric, Nemanja Glavcic, David Dundjerski (89' Tim Chow), Dejan Djenic, Ognjen Djuricin (69' Samuel Afum).
Coach: Vladimir Gacinovic.
Brøndby IF: Marvin Schwäbe, Benedikt Röcker, Johan Larsson, Anthony Jung, Hjörtur Hermannsson, Kasper Fisker (67' Lasse Vigen Christensen), Dominik Kaiser, Josip Radosevic, Simon Tibbling (46' Hany Mukhtar), Kamil Wilczek (84' Mikkel Uhre), Ante Erceg.
Coach: Alexander Zorniger.
Goals: 29' Dominik Kaiser 0-1, 47' Hany Mukhtar 0-2.
Referee: Kevin Blom (HOL)   Attendance: 4,000.

(Spartak Subotica played their home match at Stadion Rajko Mitic, Beograd, instead of their regular stadium, Subotica City Stadium, Subotica)

09.08.18   Stadion Miejski Legii Warszawa im. Marszalka Józefa Pilsudskiego, Warszawa:
Legia Warszawa – F91 Dudelange 1-2 (1-1)
Legia Warszawa: Arkadiusz Malarz, Michal Pazdan, Iñaki Astiz, Dominik Nagy, Mateusz
Wieteska, Krzysztof Maczynski, Michal Kucharczyk, Chris Philipps, Cafú (46' José Kanté),
Sebastian Szymanski (65' Mateusz Zyro), Carlitos López (82' Mateusz Holownia).
Coach: Aleksandar Vukovic.
F91 Dudelange: Jonathan Joubert, Tom Schnell, Jerry Prempeh, Aniss El Hriti, Marc-André
Kruska, Stélvio (73' Mario Pokar), Dominik Stolz, Edisson Jordanov, Clément Couturier (80'
Nicolas Perez), Danel Sinani, Patrick Stumpf (58' David Turpel). Coach: Dino Toppmöller.
Goals: 24' Clément Couturier 0-1, 27' Carlitos López 1-1, 62' David Turpel 1-2 (p).
Referee: Halis Özkahya (TUR)   Attendance: 9,923.
Sent off: 44' Iñaki Astiz.

09.08.18   Stadión Pasienky, Bratislava: Slovan Bratislava – SK Rapid Wien 2-1 (1-1)
Slovan Bratislava: Dominik Greif, Kornel Saláta, Mitch Apau, Vasil Bozhikov, Dávid Holman
(46' Vukan Savicevic), Nono Delgado (87' Ibrahim Rabiu), Kenan Bajric, "Moha" Mohammed
Rharsalla, Aleksandar Cavric, Andraz Sporar, Dejan Drazic (90+1' Adam Laczkó).
Coach: Martin Sevela.
SK Rapid Wien: Richard Strebinger, Mario Sonnleitner, Marvin Potzmann, Boli Bolingoli-
Mbombo, Mateo Barac, Christoph Knasmüllner (68' Andrei Ivan), Stefan Schwab, Thomas
Murg (78' Jérémy Guillemenot), Dejan Ljubicic, Deni Alar, Veton Berisha.
Coach: Goran Djuricin.
Goals: 12' Stefan Schwab 0-1, 29' Vasil Bozhikov 1-1, 49' Mateo Barac 2-1 (og).
Referee: Pawel Raczkowski (POL)   Attendance: 9,563.

Deni Alar missed a penalty kick (83').

09.08.18   Estadio Ramón Sánchez Pizjuán, Sevilla: Sevilla FC – FK Zalgiris 1-0 (1-0)
Sevilla FC: Tomás Vaclík, Daniel Carriço, Aleix Vidal, Guilherme Arana, Joris Gnagnon, Juan
Berrocal, Éver Banega (74' Ganso), Ibrahim Amadou, Pejiño (59' Luis Muriel), Nolito (74'
Pablo Sarabia), Wissam Ben Yedder. Coach: Pablo Machín.
FK Zalgiris: Dziugas Bartkus, Rolandas Baravykas, Mamadou Mbodj, Saulius Mikoliūnas (74'
Serge Nyuiadzi), Donovan Slijngard, Tomas Simkovic, Liviu Antal (90' Venelin Filipov),
Slavko Blagojevic, Jérémy Manzorro (77' Domantas Simkus), Marko Tomic, Louis Ogana.
Coach: Valdas Urbonas.
Goal: 34' Éver Banega 1-0.
Referee: Bojan Pandzic (SWE)   Attendance: 26,189.

16.08.18   Ortaliq Stadion, Almaty: FK Kairat – SK Sigma Olomouc 1-2 (0-1)
FK Kairat: Stas Pokatilov, Sergey Politevich, Ákos Elek, Isael, Islambek Kuat, Bauyrzhan
Islamkhan, Stanislav Lunin (57' Aleksandr Sokolenko), Nuraly Alip (34' Márton Eppel),
Andrei Arshavin (74' Georgiy Zhukov), Juan Felipe Alves, Aderinsola Eseola.
Coach: Carlos Alós Ferrer.
SK Sigma Olomouc: Milos Buchta, Jan Sterba, Martin Hála, Václav Jemelka, Martin Sladky,
Jakub Plsek (80' Jakub Yunis), David Houska, Tomás Zahradnícek (67' Budge Manzia),
Simon Falta, Lukás Kalvach, Martin Nespor (63' Jirí Texl). Coach: Václav Jílek.
Goals: 19' Martin Nespor 0-1, 51' David Houska 0-2, 61' Márton Eppel 1-2.
Referee: Sandro Schärer (SUI)   Attendance: 20,000.
Sent off: 75' Juan Felipe Alves, 90+4' Isael.

16.08.18   Stade Parc des Sports, Differdange: Progrès Niederkorn – FC Ufa 2-2 (1-0)
Progrès Niederkorn: Sebastian Flauss, Adrien Ferino, Marvin da Graça (70' Romeu Torres), Jordan Gobron, Metin Karayer, Tim Hall, Sébastien Thill, Yannick Bastos, Olivier Thill (86' Ben Vogel), Alexander Karapetyan, Mayron De Almeida. Coach: Paolo Amodio.
FC Ufa: Aleksandr Belenov, Bojan Jokic, Pavel Alikin, Catalin Carp (46' Ondrej Vanek), Ionut Nedelcearu (82' Denis Tumasyan), Jemal Tabidze, Veroljub Salatic, Ivan Paurevic, Dmitri Zhivoglyadov, Ivan Oblyakov, Sylvester Igboun (80' Vyacheslav Krotov). Coach: Sergei Tomarov.
Goals: 2' Pavel Alikin 1-0 (og), 51' Ivan Paurevic 1-1, 72' Mayron De Almeida 2-1, 90+3' Ivan Paurevic 2-2.
Referee: Manuel Schüttengruber (AUT)   Attendance: 1,736.

(Progrès Niederkorn played their home match at Stade Parc des Sports, Differdange, instead of their regular stadium, Stade Jos Haupert, Niederkorn)

16.08.18   AEK Arena – Georgios Karapatakis, Larnaca:
           AEK Larnaca – SK Sturm Graz 5-0 (1-0)
AEK Larnaca: Toño, Mikel González, Daniel Mojsov, Truyols, Igor Carioca, Ivan Trickovski, Jorge Larena (78' Jean Luc Assoubre), Acorán, Hector Hevel, Apostolos Giannou (81' Florian Taulemesse), Tete (69' Nacho Cases). Coach: Andoni Iraola.
SK Sturm Graz: Tobias Schützenauer, Thomas Schrammel, Fabian Koch, Lukas Spendlhofer, Dario Maresic (46' Philipp Huspek), Markus Lackner, Peter Zulj, Sandi Lovric, Raphael Obermair, Philipp Hosiner (73' Emeka Eza), Markus Pink (63' Anastasios Avlonitis). Coach: Heiko Vogel.
Goals: 8' Ivan Trickovski 1-0, 65' Jorge Larena 2-0 (p), 67', 80' Ivan Trickovski 3-0, 4-0, 86' Florian Taulemesse 5-0.
Referee: Paolo Valeri (ITA)   Attendance: 4,145.
Sent off: 59' Sandi Lovric.

Coach Andoni Iraola was sent to the stands (42').

16.08.18   Telia 5G-areena, Helsinki: HJK Helsinki – Olimpija Ljubljana 1-4 (0-1)
HJK Helsinki: Maksim Rudakov, Rafinha, Mikko Sumusalo, Faith Obilor, Roni Peiponen, Anthony Annan, Jordan Domínguez (64' Macauley Chrisantus), Riku Riski, Nikolai Alho (46' Sebastian Dahlström), Evans Mensah, Klauss (73' Eetu Vertainen). Coach: Mika Lehkosuo.
Olimpija Ljubljana: Aljaz Ivacic, Branko Ilic, Aris Zarifovic, Dino Stiglec, Rok Kronaveter (65' Asmir Suljic), Marko Putincanin, Stefan Savic, Daniel Avramovski, Tomislav Tomic (62' Macky Frank Bagnack), Nik Kapun, Issah Abass (76' Goran Brkic). Coach: Aleksandar Linta.
Goals: 20' Issah Abass 0-1, 72' Daniel Avramovski 0-2, 75' Rafinha 0-3 (og), 85' Macauley Chrisantus 1-3, 90+2' Goran Brkic 1-4 (p).
Referee: Evgen Aranovskiy (UKR)   Attendance: 4,127.

16.08.18   Telia Parken, København: FC København – CSKA Sofia 2-1 (1-0)
FC København: Jesse Joronen, Andreas Bjelland, Peter Ankersen, Nicolai Boilesen, Denis Vavro, Ján Gregus (60' William Kvist), Zeca, Viktor Fischer, Nicolaj Thomsen, Robert Skov (86' Kenan Kodro), Dame N'Doye (90+1' Pieros Sotiriou). Coach: Ståle Solbakken.
CSKA Sofia: Vytautas Cerniauskas, Nikolaj Bodurov, Kristiyan Malinov (72' Janio Bikel), Boris Sekulic, Steven Pereira, Rúben Pinto, Edwin Gyasi (46' Evandro), Tiago Rodrigues, Angel Lyaskov, Kiril Despodov (79' Stanislav Manolev), Maurides. Coach: Nestor El Maestro.
Goals: 23' Dame N'Doye 1-0, 58' Evandro 1-1, 64' Dame N'Doye 2-1.
Referee: Halil Umut Meler (TUR)   Attendance: 10,078.

16.08.18   Stadionul Ion Oblemenco, Craiova:
   CS Universitatea Craiova – RB Leipzig 1-1 (0-1)
CS Universitatea Craiova: Mirko Pigliacelli, Renato Kelic, Ivan Martic (73' Tiago Ferreira), Marius Briceag, Nicusor Bancu, Isaac Donkor, Alexandru Mateiu, Alexandru Mitrita (51' Andrei Burlacu), Matteo Fedele (80' Jovan Markovic), Alexandru Cicaldau, Raoul Baicu. Coach: Devis Mangia.
RB Leipzig: Yvon Mvogo, Willi Orban, Nordi Mukiele, Ibrahima Konaté, Emil Forsberg, Kevin Kampl, Diego Demme (72' Stefan Ilsanker), Marcel Sabitzer (64' Bruma), Marcelo Saracchi, Yussuf Poulsen, Matheus Cunha (46' Jean-Kévin Augustin). Coach: Ralf Rangnick.
Goals: 39' Marcel Sabitzer 0-1, 85' Raoul Baicu 1-1.
Referee: Miroslav Zelinka (CZE)   Attendance: 12,050.

16.08.18   Stadion Petrovskiy, St. Petersburg:
   Zenit St. Petersburg – FK Dinamo Minsk 8-1 (1-0, 4-0)
Zenit St. Petersburg: Andrei Lunev, Branislav Ivanovic, Aleksandr Anyukov, Miha Mevlja, Christian Noboa (103' Igor Smolnikov), Aleksandr Erokhin (102' Róbert Mak), Leandro Paredes, Hernani (61' Sebastián Driussi), Elmir Nabiullin (59' Anton Zabolotny), Daler Kuzyaev, Artem Dzyuba. Coach: Sergey Semak.
FK Dinamo Minsk: Andrey Gorbunov, Igor Shitov, Luís Rocha (92' Aleksey Gavrilovich), Roman Begunov, Nino Galovic, Maksim Shvetsov, Seidu Yahaya, Dinko Trebotic (72' Giorgi Navalovski), Filipp Ivanov (65' Aleksandr Makas), Nikita Korzun, Vladimir Khvashchinskiy (55' Nikita Kaplenko). Coach: Sergei Gurenko.
Goals: 22' Leandro Paredes 1-0, 66' Christian Noboa 2-0, 75', 78' Artem Dzyuba 3-0, 4-0, 99' Seidu Yahaya 4-1, 109' Sebastián Driussi 5-1, 115' Artem Dzyuba 6-1 (p), 120+2', 120+3' Róbert Mak 7-1 (p), 8-1.
Referee: Sébastien Delferière (BEL)
Sent off: 72' Leandro Paredes, 120+1' Maksim Shvetsov.

Zenit St. Petersburg won after extra time.

(Zenit St. Petersburg played their third qualifying round home match at smaller stadium, Petrovsky Stadium, instead of their regular stadium Krestovsky Stadium, due they had to play behind closed doors)

16.08.18   Aker Stadion, Molde: Molde FK – Hibernian FC Edinburgh 3-0 (1-0)
Molde FK: Andreas Linde, Vegard Forren, Ruben Gabrielsen, Kristoffer Haugen, Christoffer Remmer, Etzaz Hussain, Eirik Hestad, Fredrik Aursnes, Stian Gregersen (71' Petter Strand), Pawel Cibicki (58' Magnus Eikrem), Erling Håland (83' Leke James).
Coach: Ole Gunnar Solskjær.
Hibernian FC Edinburgh: Ádám Bogdán, Lewis Stevenson (88' David Gray), Paul Hanlon, Efe Ambrose, Ryan Porteous, Marvin Bartley (40' Emerson Hyndman), Vykintas Slivka, Stephen Mallan, Martin Boyle, Jamie MacLaren (76' Oliver Shaw), Florian Kamberi.
Coach: Neil Lennon.
Goals: 35' Erling Håland 1-0, 66' Fredrik Aursnes 2-0, 82' Erling Håland 3-0.
Referee: Dennis Higler (HOL)   Attendance: 4,368.

16.08.18   Vilniaus LFF stadionas, Vilnius: FK Zalgiris – Sevilla FC 0-5 (0-3)
FK Zalgiris: Dziugas Bartkus, Rolandas Baravykas, Mamadou Mbodj, Saulius Mikoliūnas (46'
Serge Nyuiadzi), Donovan Slijngard, Tomas Simkovic, Liviu Antal, Slavko Blagojevic,
Jérémy Manzorro (54' Domantas Simkus), Marko Tomic, Louis Ogana (65' Tomás Malec).
Coach: Valdas Urbonas.
Sevilla FC: Tomás Vaclík, Daniel Carriço, Sergio Escudero (46' Guilherme Arana), Aleix
Vidal, Sergi Gómez, Joris Gnagnon, Éver Banega (55' Juan Berrocal), Pablo Sarabia (46' Luis
Muriel), Ibrahim Amadou, Nolito, Wissam Ben Yedder. Coach: Pablo Machín.
Goals: 6' Nolito 0-1, 7', 44' Pablo Sarabia 0-2, 3-0, 80' Guilherme Arana 0-4, 83' Nolito 0-5.
Referee: Enea Jorgji (ALB)   Attendance: 5,000.

16.08.18   Stadionul Dr. Constantin Radulescu, Cluj-Napoca:
           CFR Cluj – FC Alashkert 5-0 (2-0)
CFR Cluj: Cosmin Vatca, Andrei Muresan, Paulo Vinícius, Camora, Andrei Peteleu,
Emmanuel Culio (64' Alexandru Ionita (II)), Ovidiu Hoban, Damjan Djokovic (56' Mihai
Bordeianu), Alexandru Paun, George Tucudean, Billel Omrani (69' Sebastian Mailat).
Coach: Toni Conceição.
FC Alashkert: Ognjen Cancarevic, Gagik Dagbashyan, Artak Yedigaryan, Oliver Práznovsky,
Mladen Zeljkovic, Danijel Stojkovic, Artur Yedigaryan, Danilo Sekulic (58' César Romero),
Edgar Manucharyan (63' Artem Simonyan), Artak Grigoryan, Uros Nenadovic (58' Artak
Dashyan). Coach: Varuzhan Sukiasyan.
Goals: 19' Emmanuel Culio 1-0 (p), 45+1' Billel Omrani 2-0, 58' Ovidiu Hoban 3-0,
62' Billel Omrani 4-0, 90+2' Sebastian Mailat 5-0.
Referee: Vilhjálmur Alvar Thórarinsson (ISL)   Attendance: 5,500.

16.08.18   Marijampoles sporto centro stadione, Marijampolé:
           FK Sūduva Marijampolé – FK Spartaks Jūrmala 0-0
FK Sūduva Marijampolé: Ivan Kardum, Vaidas Slavickas, Algis Jankauskas, Vitaly
Gayduchik, Andro Svrljuga, Guilherme Finkler (87' Julius Kasparavicius), Povilas Leimonas,
Robertas Vézevicius (90+5' Marius Cinikas), Jovan Cadenovic, Ovidijus Verbickas (71'
Daniel Offenbacher), Rigino Cicilia. Coach: Vladimir Cheburin.
FK Spartaks Jūrmala: Jevgenijs Nerugals, Gints Freimanis, Aleksandar Kosoric, Mārcis Oss,
Ingus Slampe, Aleksejs Visnakovs, Artemiy Maleev, Evgeni Kobzar (83' Ricards Korzāns),
Kaspars Svārups (46' Diego Aguirre), Vitor Faísca, Ariagner Smith.
Coach: Tomas Razanauskas.
Referee: Ola Hobber Nilsen (NOR)   Attendance: 2,417.

16.08.18   MCH Arena, Herning: FC Midtjylland – The New Saints 3-1 (1-1)
FC Midtjylland: Jesper Hansen, Zsolt Korcsmár, Kian Hansen, Joel Andersson, Rasmus
Nicolaisen, Jakob Poulsen, Mads Thychosen, Frank Onyeka (61' Ayo Simon Okosun), Mayron
George, Paul Ebere Onuachu (84' Michael Baidoo), Awer Mabil (73' Bozhidar Kraev).
Coach: Jess Thorup.
The New Saints: Paul Harrison, Simon Spender, Christopher Marriott, Blaine Hudson,
Benjamin Cabango, Aeron Edwards, Jon Routledge, Daniel Redmond (70' Adrian Cieslewicz),
Tom Holland (79' Kurtis Byrne), Jamie Mullan, Dean Ebbe (74' Greg Draper).
Coach: Scott Ruscoe.
Goals: 16' Mayron George 1-0, 22' Dean Ebbe 1-1, 62', 80' Ayo Simon Okosun 2-1, 3-1.
Referee: Irfan Peljto (BIH)   Attendance: 4.368.

16.08.18 Neo GSP Stadium, Nicosia: APOEL Nicosia – Hapoel Be'er Sheva 3-1 (0-1)
APOEL Nicosia: Boy Waterman, Carlão, Emilio N'Sue, Praxitelis Vouros, Caju, Nuno Morais, Tomás De Vincenti, Lucas Souza, Ghayas Zahid (75' Savvas Gentsoglou), Roland Sallai (89' Nicolas Ioannou), Moussa Al Taamari (83' Zhivko Milanov). Coach: Bruno Baltazar.
Hapoel Be'er Sheva: David Goresh, Samuel Scheimann, Matan Ohayon, Ben Bitton, Loai Taha, John Ogu, Hen Ezra (76' Ben Sahar), Daniel Einbinder (67' Hanan Maman), Marwan Kabha (82' Maor Melikson), Eden Ben Basat, Anthony Nwakaeme. Coach: Barak Bakhar.
Goals: 19' Eden Ben Basat 0-1, 64' Anthony Nwakaeme 1-1 (og), 79', 90+3' Lucas Souza 2-1, 3-1.
Referee: Mattias Gestranius (FIN)   Attendance: 10,891.

16.08.18 Elbasan Arena, Elbasan: FK Kukësi – Torpedo Kutaisi 2-0 (1-0)
FK Kukësi: Faton Maloku, Ylli Shameti, William Cordeiro, Simon Rrumbullaku, Edis Malikji, Albi Alla, Irakli Dzaria (68' Donjet Shkodra), Besar Musolli (83' Sebino Plaku), Valon Ethemi (52' Arbër Çyrbja), Haris Harba, Reginaldo. Coach: Armando Cungu.
Torpedo Kutaisi: Rion Kvaskhvadze, Davit Khurtsilava, Mamuka Kobakhidze, Giorgi Kimadze (83' Levan Gegetchkori), Oleksandr Azatsky, Lazar Marin, Grigol Dolidze (62' Levan Kutalia), Giorgi Kukhianidze, Marek Hlinka (69' Merab Gigauri), Mate Tsintsadze, Milos Lacny. Coach: Kakhaber Chkhetiani.
Goals: 29', 76' Reginaldo 1-0 (p), 2-0 (p).
Referee: Alain Bieri (SUI)   Attendance: 200.

(FK Kukësi played their home match at Elbasan Arena, Elbasan, instead of their regular stadium Stadiumi Zeqir Ymeri, Kukës)

16.08.18 Winner Stadium, Netanya: Maccabi Tel Aviv – Pyunik Yerevan FC 2-1 (0-1)
Maccabi Tel Aviv: Predrag Rajkovic, Eitan Tibi, Saborit, Elazar Dasa, Jair Amador, Dor Mikha, Roslan Barski, Dor Peretz (79' Dan Glazer), Vidar Kjartansson (46' Itay Shechter), Eliran Atar, Omer Atzili (87' Matan Hozez). Coach: Vladimir Ivic.
Pyunik Yerevan FC: Andrija Dragojevic, Vyacheslav Dmitriev, Maksim Zhestokov, Serob Grigoryan (45' Sergey Kolychev), Vitali Stezhko, Maksim Trusevich, Denis Voynov (68' Karlen Mkrtchyan), Rumyan Hovsepyan, Alik Arakelyan, Vahagn Hayrapetyan, Mohamed Konaté (59' Ruslan Koryan). Coach: Andrey Talalaev.
Goals: 11' Denis Voynov 0-1, 55' Dor Mikha 1-1, 68' Eliran Atar 2-1.
Referee: Ville Nevalainen (FIN)   Attendance: 8,932.

(Maccabi Tel Aviv played their home match at Winner Stadium instead of their regular stadium, Bloomfield Stadium, due to renovation)

16.08.18 Swissporarena, Luzern: FC Luzern – Olympiakos Piraeus 1-3 (0-1)
FC Luzern: Mirko Salvi, Simon Grether, Lucão, Marvin Schulz, Silvan Sidler, Idriz Voca, Christian Schneuwly (66' Ruben Vargas), Pascal Schürpf, Valeriane Gvilia (81' Shkelqim Demhasaj), Filip Ugrinic (67' Stefan Wolf), Blessing Eleke. Coach: René Weiler.
Olympiakos Piraeus: Andreas Gianniotis, Jagos Vukovic, Omar Elabdellaoui, Roderick Miranda, Kostas Tsimikas, Lazaros Christodoulopoulos, Kostas Fortounis (63' Ioannis Fetfatzidis), Andreas Bouchalakis, Daniel Podence, Mohamed Camara (71' Vasilios Torosidis), Guerrero (70' Karim Ansarifard). Coach: Pedro Martins.
Goals: 23', 59' Lazaros Christodoulopoulos 0-1, 0-2, 68' Guerrero 0-3, 82' Shkelqim Demhasaj 1-3.
Referee: Kirill Levnikov (RUS)   Attendance: 6,258.

16.08.18   Linzer Stadion, Linz: LASK Linz – Besiktas JK 2-1 (1-0)
LASK Linz: Alexander Schlager, Emanuel Pogatetz, Christian Ramsebner, Gernot Trauner, Reinhold Ranftl, Maximilian Ullmann, James Holland, Thomas Goiginger (87' Yusuf Otubanjo), Peter Michorl, João Victor Santos Sá (66' Dominik Frieser), Samuel Tetteh (79' Florian Jamnig). Coach: Oliver Glasner.
Besiktas JK: Tolga Zengin, Adriano, Pepe, Caner Erkin, Gary Medel, Enzo Roco, Ryan Babel, Jeremain Lens, Tolgay Arslan (72' Gökhan Gönül), Oguzhan Özyakup (46' Ricardo Quaresma), Cyle Larin (72' Álvaro Negredo). Coach: Senol Günes.
Goals: 42' João Victor Santos Sá 1-0, 69' Dominik Frieser 2-0, 90' Álvaro Negredo 2-1.
Referee: Nikola Dabanovic (MNE)   Attendance: 13,739.
Sent off: 90+2' Álvaro Negredo.

Besiktas JK won on away goals.

16.08.18   Stadyen DASK Brestski, Brest: FK Dynamo Brest – Apollon FC Limassol 1-0 (0-0)
FK Dynamo Brest: Aleksandr Gutor, Maksim Vitus, Oleg Veretilo, Giannis Kargas, Pavel Nekhaychik, Zeljko Filipovic (76' Sergey Krivets), Oleksandr Noyok, Pavel Savitskiy (84' Pavel Sedko), Chidi Osuchukwu, Gaby Kiki, Nivaldo (64' Oleksiy Khoblenko). Coach: Marcel Licka.
Apollon FC Limassol: Bruno Vale, Valentin Roberge, Kévin Bru, Facundo Pereyra, Héctor Yuste, Giorgos Vasiliou, Esteban Sachetti (70' Mustapha Carayol), Emilio Zelaya (63' Anton Maglica), João Pedro, Fotis Papoulis (59' Sasa Markovic), Adrián Sardinero. Coach: Sofronis Avgousti.
Goal: 86' Pavel Nekhaychik 1-0.
Referee: Martin Strömbergsson (SWE)   Attendance: 8,800.

16.08.18   MAPEI Stadium – Città del Tricolore, Reggio Emilia:
            Atalanta Bergamo – Hapoel Haifa 2-0 (0-0)
Atalanta Bergamo: Pierluigi Gollini, Andrea Masiello, Berat Djimsiti, Timothy Castagne, Gianluca Mancini, "Papu" Alejandro Gómez (83' Musa Barrow), Remo Freuler (77' Luca Valzania), Mario Pasalic, Arkadiusz Reca, Matteo Pessina, Duván Zapata (86' Andreas Cornelius). Coach: Gian Piero Gasperini.
Hapoel Haifa: Ernestas Setkus, Gabriel Tamas, Nisso Kapiloto, Dor Malul, Risto Mitrevski, Hen Dilmoni (76' Gal Arel), Rasmus Sjöstedt (67' Gil Vermouth), Radu Gînsari, Almog Buzaglo (30' Maxim Plakushchenko), Guy Hadida, Thanasis Papazoglou. Coach: Nir Klinger.
Goals: 71' Duván Zapata 1-0, 90+2' Andreas Cornelius 2-0.
Referee: Frank Schneider (FRA)   Attendance: 6,546.

(Atalanta Bergamo played their home match at MAPEI Stadium – Città del Tricolore instead of their regular stadium, Stadio Atleti Azzurri d'Italia, as it wasn't given a UEFA licence to hold games)

16.08.18 St. Jakob-Park, Basel: FC Basel – Vitesse Arnhem 1-0 (1-0)
FC Basel: Jonas Omlin, Silvan Widmer, Éder Álvarez Balanta, Eray Cümart, Valentin Stocker, Serey Dié, Luca Zuffi, Fabian Frei, Raoul Petretta, Ricky van Wolfswinkel (90+3' Kevin Bua), Albian Ajeti (46' Dimitri Oberlin). Coach: Marcel Koller.
Vitesse Arnhem: Eduardo, Alexander Büttner, Maikel van der Werff, Vyacheslav Karavaev, Jake Clarke-Salter, Thulani Serero, Navarone Foor, Matús Bero (28' Rasmus Thelander), Roy Beerens (82' Mitchell van Bergen), Tim Matavz (71' Oussama Darfalou), Bryan Linssen.
Coach: Leonid Slutsky.
Goal: 30' Albian Ajeti 1-0.
Referee: Daniel Siebert (GER)   Attendance: 12,334.
Sent off: 26' Jake Clarke-Salter.

16.08.18 Brøndby Stadion, Brøndby: Brøndby IF – Spartak Subotica 2-1 (0-0)
Brøndby IF: Marvin Schwäbe, Paulus Arajuuri (66' Johan Larsson), Anthony Jung, Jens Gammelby, Joël Kabongo, Dominik Kaiser, Lasse Vigen Christensen, Josip Radosevic, Hany Mukhtar, Ante Erceg (14' Hjörtur Hermannsson), Mikkel Uhre (59' Kamil Wilczek).
Coach: Alexander Zorniger.
Spartak Subotica: Nikola Peric, Stefan Milosevic, Andrija Vukcevic, Noboru Shimura, Nemanja Tekijaski, Bojan Cecaric, Nemanja Glavcic, Milan Marcic (77' Tim Chow), David Dundjerski, Dejan Djenic, Ognjen Djuricin (68' Vladimir Torbica).
Coach: Vladimir Gacinovic.
Goals: 69' Dominik Kaiser 1-0, 80' Dejan Djenic 1-1, 90+3' Kamil Wilczek 2-1.
Referee: Hüseyin Göçek (TUR)   Attendance: 10,142.
Sent off: 11' Joël Kabongo.

16.08.18 Stadion Pecara, Sikori Brijeg: Zrinjski Mostar – PFC Ludogorets Razgrad 1-1 (0-1)
Zrinjski Mostar: Antonio Soldo, Pero Stojkic (78' Semir Pezer), Slobodan Jakovljevic, Advan Kadusic, Ognjen Todorovic, Damir Sovsic (46' Toni Jovic), Hrvoje Barisic, Frane Cirjak, Edin Rustemovic, Nemanja Bilbija, Kristijan Stanic (61' Milos Filipovic). Coach: Blaz Sliskovic.
PFC Ludogorets Razgrad: Jorge Broun, Cosmin Moti, Cicinho, Rafael Forster, Svetoslav Dyakov, Gustavo Campanharo (90' Anton Nedyalkov), Wanderson, Natanael Pimienta, Claudiu Keserü (86' Jacek Góralski), Marcelinho, "Vura" Virgil Misidjan (73' Jody Lukoki).
Coach: Paulo Autuori.
Goals: 24' Claudiu Keserü 0-1, 90+2' Nemanja Bilbija 1-1.
Referee: Bas Nijhuis (HOL)   Attendance: 3,500.

16.08.18 Stade Josy Barthel, Luxembourg: F91 Dudelange – Legia Warszawa 2-2 (2-1)
F91 Dudelange: Jonathan Joubert, Jerry Prempeh, Kevin Malget, Aniss El Hriti, Marc-André Kruska (79' Bryan Mélisse), Stélvio, Dominik Stolz (90' Danel Sinani), Edisson Jordanov, Clément Couturier, David Turpel, Patrick Stumpf (74' Milan Bisevac).
Coach: Dino Toppmöller.
Legia Warszawa: Arkadiusz Malarz, Michal Pazdan, Adam Hlousek, Dominik Nagy (69' Kasper Hämäläinen), Mateusz Wieteska, Krzysztof Maczynski (77' Eduardo da Silva), Michal Kucharczyk, Chris Philipps (46' Sebastian Szymanski), Cafú, José Kanté, Carlitos López.
Coach: Sá Pinto.
Goals: 7' Patrick Stumpf 1-0, 17' Stélvio 2-0, 33', 86' José Kanté 2-1, 2-2.
Referee: Ivaylo Stoyanov (BUL)   Attendance: 2,000.
Sent off: 90+5' Michal Kucharczyk.

(F91 Dudelange played their home match at Stade Josy Barthel, Luxembourg, instead of their regular stadium Stade Jos Nosbaum, Dudelange)

16.08.18   INEA stadion, Poznan: KKS Lech Poznan – KRC Genk 1-2 (0-2)
KKS Lech Poznan: Jasmin Buric, Thomas Rogne (29' Maciej Orlowski), Nikola Vujadinovic, Rafal Janicki, Vernon, Tomasz Cywka, Maciej Gajos (77' Darko Jevtic), Petro Tiba, Kamil Józwiak, Christian Gytkjær (73' Pawel Tomczyk), João Amaral. Coach: Ivan Djurdjevic.
KRC Genk: Danny Vukovic, Sebastien Dewaest, Jere Uronen, Joseph Aidoo, Joakim Mæhle, Pozuelo (60' Jakub Piotrowski), Ruslan Malinovskiy (74' Ibrahima Seck), Sander Berge, Leandro Trossard (60' Edon Zhegrova), Mbwana Samatta, Dieumerci N'Dongala.
Coach: Philippe Clement.
Goals: 19' Mbwana Samatta 0-1, 45+1' Leandro Trossard 0-2 (p), 50' Tomasz Cywka 1-2.
Referee: Marco Guida (ITA)   Attendance: 20,765.

16.08.18   Ljudski vrt, Maribor: NK Maribor – Glasgow Rangers FC 0-0
NK Maribor: Jasmin Handanovic, Marko Suler, Mitja Viler, Sasa Ivkovic, Denis Klinar (52' Aleks Pihler), Blaz Vrhovec, Amir Dervisevic (73' Dare Vrsic), Dino Hotic, Marcos Tavares, Jasmin Mesanovic (80' Jan Mlakar), Luka Zahovic. Coach: Darko Milanic.
Glasgow Rangers FC: Allan McGregor, James Tavernier, Connor Goldson, Nikola Katic, Scott Arfield, Ryan Jack, Andy Halliday, Oviemuno Ejaria (68' Ryan Kent), Jamie Murphy (76' Ross McCrorie), Candeias, Alfredo Morelos. Coach: Steven Gerrard.
Referee: Jonathan Lardot (BEL)   Attendance: 11,166.

16.08.18   Stadion Partizana, Beograd: Partizan Beograd – FC Nordsjælland 3-2 (3-1)
Partizan Beograd: Vladimir Stojkovic, Marc Valiente, Nemanja Miletic (I), Sasa Zdjelar, Svetozar Markovic, Goran Zakaric (80' Milan Smiljanic), Nebojsa Kosovic, Marko Jankovic (70' Atmin Djerlek), Danilo Pantic (82' Gabriel Enache), Nemanja Miletic (II), Ricardo Gomes. Coach: Zoran Mirkovic.
FC Nordsjælland: Nicolai Larsen, Karlo Bartolec, Mads Pedersen, Andreas Skovgaard, Abdel Mumin, Magnus Andersen (58' Mikkel Rygaard Jensen), Mohammed Kudus (68' Nicklas Strunck Jakobsen), Jacob Christensen, Mikkel Damsgaard, Godsway Donyoh (58' Jonathan Amon), Andreas Skov Olsen. Coach: Kasper Hjulmand.
Goals: 9' Andreas Skov Olsen 0-1, 11' Nemanja Miletic (I) 1-1, 30' Marko Jankovic 2-1, 35' Svetozar Markovic 3-1, 76' Jonathan Amon 3-2.
Referee: Kristo Tohver (EST)   Attendance: 9,372.

16.08.18   Arena Nationala, Bucuresti: Fotbal Club FCSB – Hajduk Split 2-1 (0-0)
Fotbal Club FCSB: Cristian Balgradean, Junior Maranhão, Romario Sandu Benzar, Bogdan Planic, Mihai Balasa, Filipe Teixeira, Mihai Pintilii (83' Raul Rusescu), Lucian Filip (15' Dragos Nedelcu), Harlem Gnohéré, Florin Tanase (46' Olimpiu Morutan), Dennis Man. Coach: Nicolae Dica.
Hajduk Split: Josip Posavec, André Fomitschow, Stipe Vucur, Borja López (65' Ádám Gyurcsó), Bozo Mikulic, Mijo Caktas, Hamza Barry, Josip Juranovic, Stanko Juric (56' Jairo), Mirko Ivanovski (73' Michele Sego), Ahmed Said. Coach: Zeljko Kopic.
Goals: 55' Harlem Gnohéré 1-0 (p), 82' Ahmed Said 1-1, 90+3' Harlem Gnohéré 2-1.
Referee: Juan Martínez Munuera (ESP)   Attendance: 27,410.

16.08.18   Allianz Stadion, Vienna: SK Rapid Wien – Slovan Bratslava 4-0 (1-0)
SK Rapid Wien: Richard Strebinger, Mario Sonnleitner, Marvin Potzmann, Boli Bolingoli-Mbombo, Mateo Barac, Christoph Knasmüllner, Stefan Schwab (87' Mert Müldür), Thomas Murg (90' Aleksandar Kostic), Dejan Ljubicic, Deni Alar (78' Andrei Ivan), Veton Berisha. Coach: Goran Djuricin.
Slovan Bratislava: Dominik Greif, Kornel Saláta, Mitch Apau (80' Boris Cmiljanic), Vasil Bozhikov, Ibrahim Rabiu (67' Vukan Savicevic), Nono Delgado, Kenan Bajric, "Moha" Mohammed Rharsalla, Aleksandar Cavric, Andraz Sporar, Dejan Drazic (81' Filip Holosko). Coach: Martin Sevela.
Goals: 3', 79' Christoph Knasmüllner 1-0, 2-0, 84' Thomas Murg 3-0, 90+4' Christoph Knasmüllner 4-0.
Referee: Davide Massa (ITA)   Attendance: 17,800.

16.08.18   Stadion Feyenoord, Rotterdam: Feyenoord Rotterdam – AS Trencín 1-1 (1-1)
Feyenoord Rotterdam: Kenneth Vermeer, Jan-Arie van der Heijden, Eric Botteghin, Bart Nieuwkoop (67' Lutsharel Geertruida), Tyrell Malacia (83' Wouter Burger), Jens Toornstra, Jordy Clasie, Tonny Vilhena, Robin van Persie (71' Dylan Vente), Steven Berghuis, Sam Larsson. Coach: Giovanni van Bronckhorst.
AS Trencín: Igor Semrinec, Jamie Lawrence, Lukás Skovajsa, Martin Sulek, Reuben Yem, Ashraf El Mahdioui, Abdul Zubairu (90+2' Desley Ubbink), Joey Sleegers, Antonio Mance (86' Emeka Umeh), Hamza Catakovic, Philip Azango. Coach: Ricardo Moniz.
Goals: 8' Eric Botteghin 1-0, 9' Antonio Mance 1-1.
Referee: Jakob Kehlet (DEN)   Attendance: 31,500.

16.08.18   GHELAMCO-arena, Gent: KAA Gent – Jagiellonia Bialystok 3-1 (1-0)
KAA Gent: Lovre Kalinic, Nana Asare, Igor Plastun, Sigurd Rosted, Thomas Foket, Vadis Odjidja-Ofoe, Franko Andrijasevic (67' Roman Yaremchuk), Birger Verstraete, Jean-Luc Dompé (79' Stallone Limbombe), Giorgi Chakvetadze, Taiwo Awoniyi (77' Jonathan David). Coach: Yves Vanderhaeghe.
Jagiellonia Bialystok: Marián Kelemen, Lukasz Burliga, Nemanja Mitrovic, Guilherme, Ivan Runje, Arvydas Novikovas (81' Karol Swiderski), Martin Pospísil, Przemyslaw Frankowski (85' Jakub Wójcicki), Bartosz Kwiecien (43' Cillian Sheridan), Taras Romanczuk, Roman Bezjak. Coach: Ireneusz Mamrot.
Goals: 13' Taiwo Awoniyi 1-0, 58' Martin Pospísil 1-1, 84' Roman Yaremchuk 2-1, 89' Jonathan David 3-1.
Referee: Bastian Dankert (GER)   Attendance: 16,000.

16.08.18   Stadion Rujevica, Rijeka: NK Rijeka – Sarpsborg 08 0-1 (0-0)
NK Rijeka: Simon Sluga, Roberto Puncec, Dario Zuparic, Mario Pavelic (87' Antonio Colak), Leonard Zuta, Srdan Grahovac, Domagoj Pavicic (67' Jakov Puljic), Dario Canadija, Alexander Gorgon, Héber (77' Zoran Kvrzic), Boadu Maxwell Acosty. Coach: Matjaz Kek.
Sarpsborg 08: Alexander Vasyutin, Amin Askar (75' Tobias Heintz), Joackim Jørgensen (59' Bjørn Utvik), Joachim Thomassen, Joonas Tamm, Matti Lund Nielsen, Ole Halvorsen, Jon-Helge Tveita (82' Kristoffer Larsen), Kristoffer Zachariassen, Patrick Mortensen, Rashad Muhammed. Coach: Geir Bakke.
Goal: 83' Patrick Mortensen 0-1.
Referee: Donatas Rumsas (LTU)   Attendance: 5,351.

16.08.18   Turf Moor, Burnley: Burnley FC – Istanbul Basaksehir FK 1-0 (0-0, 0-0)
Burnley FC: Joe Hart, Phil Bardsley, Stephen Ward, Kevin Long, Ben Gibson, Charlie Taylor, Aaron Lennon (58' Jóhann Gudmundsson), Ashley Westwood (82' Jack Cork), Jeffrey Hendrick, Ashley Barnes (120+2' James Tarkowski), Samuel Vokes (82' Chris Wood). Coach: Sean Dyche.
Istanbul Basaksehir FK: Mert Günok, Manuel da Costa, Gaël Clichy, Alexandru Epureanu, Júnior Caiçara, Emre Belözoglu, Mahmut Tekdemir (92' Gökhan Inler), Edin Visca, Kerim Frei (102' Stefano Napoleoni), Irfan Kahveci (109' Milos Jojic), Rijad Bajic (66' Emmanuel Adebayor). Coach: Abdullah Avci.
Goal: 97' Jack Cork 1-0.
Referee: István Kovács (ROM)   Attendance: 16,583.

Burnley FC won after extra time.

16.08.18   Stade Matmut-Atlantique, Bordeaux:
Girondins de Bordeaux – FC Mariupol 2-1 (0-0)
Girondins de Bordeaux: Benoît Costil, Igor Lewczuk, Pablo Castro, Maxime Poundjé, Otávio (89' Jaroslav Plasil), Jules Koundé, Younousse Sankharé, Lukas Lerager (62' Aurélien Tchouaméni), Zaydou Youssouf, Nicolas de Préville, François Kamano (63' Valentín Vada). Coach: Gustavo Poyet.
FC Mariupol: Evgen Galchuk, Maksim Biliy, Igor Kyryukhantsev (46' Pavel Polegenko), Besir Demiri, Joyskim Dawa (46' Sergey Yavorskiy), Igor Tyshchenko (62' Vladislav Vakula), Vyacheslav Churko, Dmytro Myshnov, Oleksandr Pikhalyonok, Ruslan Fomin, Andriy Boryachuk. Coach: Oleksandr Babych.
Goals: 54' Maxime Poundjé 1-0, 56' Younousse Sankharé 2-0, 66' Ruslan Fomin 2-1.
Referee: Andrew Dallas (SCO)   Attendance: 11,375.

16.08.18   Lerkendal Stadion, Trondheim: Rosenborg BK – Cork City FC 3-0 (2-0)
Rosenborg BK: André Hansen, Tore Reginiussen, Vegar Hedenstad (74' Erlend Reitan), Birger Meling, Besim Serbecic, Mike Jensen, Anders Trondsen (60' Anders Konradsen), Marius Lundemo, Nicklas Bendtner, Alexander Søderlund, Jonathan Levi (61' Pål Helland). Coach: Rini Coolen.
Cork City FC: Mark McNulty, Damien Delaney, Steven Beattie, Shane Griffin, Sean McLoughlin, Jimmy Keohane, Conor McCormack, Gearóid Morrissey (46' Barry McNamee), Kieran Sadlier, Garry Buckley (75' John Dunleavy), Karl Sheppard (72' Ronan Coughlin). Coach: John Caulfield.
Goals: 26' Besim Serbecic 1-0, 34' Alexander Søderlund 2-0, 58' Anders Trondsen 3-0.
Referee: Mads-Kristoffer Kristoffersen (DEN)   Attendance: 8,028.

16.08.18   Vodafone-Völlurin, Reykjavík: Valur Reykjavík – FC Sheriff Tiraspol 2-1 (1-0)
Valur Reykjavík: Anton Ari Einarsson, Birkir Sævarsson, Bjarni Eiríksson, Eidur Sigurbjörnsson, Sebastian Hedlund, Haukur Sigurdsson, Kristinn Sigurdsson, Andri Adolphsson (69' Kristinn Halldórsson), Einar Karl Ingvarsson (81' Ólafur Finsen), Patrick Pedersen, Dion Jeremy Acoff. Coach: Ólafur Jóhannesson.
FC Sheriff Tiraspol: Serghei Pascenco, Ante Kulusic, Mateo Susic, Veaceslav Posmac, Cristiano (66' Wilfried Balima), Yuri Kendysh, Gheorghe Anton, Evgheni Oancea (46' "Jô" Joálisson), Ziguy Badibanga, Al-Haji Kamara, Gerson Rodrigues (46' Rifet Kapic). Coach: Goran Sablic.
Goals: 40' Haukur Sigurdsson 1-0, 68' Ziguy Badibanga 1-1, 90+1' Kristinn Halldórsson 2-1.
Referee: Marco Fritz (GER)   Attendance: 1,224.

FC Sheriff Tiraspol won on away goals.

16.08.18   Estádio Municipal de Braga, Braga: Sporting Braga – Zorya Luhansk 2-2 (0-0)
Sporting Braga: Matheus Magalhães, Raúl Silva (38' Pablo Santos), Ricardo Esgaio, Diogo Figueiras (85' Bruno Xadas), Nuno Sequeira, Bruno Viana, Fransérgio, João Novais (79' Ricardo Ryller), Ricardo Horta, Wilson Eduardo, Dyego Sousa. Coach: Abel Ferreira.
Zorya Luhansk: Luis Felipe (68' Zauri Makharadze), Vitaliy Vernidub, Oleksandr Svatok, Oleksandr Tymchyk, Bogdan Mykhaylychenko, Dmytro Khomchenovsky, Igor Kharatin, Oleksandr Karavayev, Silas, Bohdan Lednev (46' Vladyslav Kochergin), Rafael Ratão (76' Vladyslav Kabayev). Coach: Yuriy Vernydub.
Goals: 65' João Novais 1-0, 70' Rafael Ratão 1-1, 73' Ricardo Horta 2-1, 83' Oleksandr Karavayev 2-2.
Referee: Aleksandar Stavrev (MKD)   Attendance: 12,224.

Zorya Luhansk won on away goals.

PLAY-OFF ROUND

23.08.18   Mikheil Meskhis Sakhelobis Stadioni, Tbilisi:
          Torpedo Kutaisi – PFC Ludogorets Razgrad 0-1 (0-1)
Torpedo Kutaisi: Rion Kvaskhvadze, Mamuka Kobakhidze, Giorgi Kimadze (69' Arfang Daffé), Levan Gegetchkori, Oleksandr Azatsky, Lazar Marin, Grigol Dolidze, Giorgi Kukhianidze (83' Levan Kutalia), Marek Hlinka, Mate Tsintsadze, Milos Lacny (61' Tornike Kapanadze). Coach: Kakhaber Chkhetiani.
PFC Ludogorets Razgrad: Jorge Broun, Cosmin Moti, Cicinho, Anton Nedyalkov, Svetoslav Dyakov, Gustavo Campanharo (66' Jacek Góralski), Wanderson, Natanael Pimienta, Claudiu Keserü (80' Jody Lukoki), Marcelinho (90+4' Georgi Terziev), "Vura" Virgil Misidjan.
Coach: Paulo Autuori.
Goal: 45+2' Wanderson 0-1)
Referee: Hüseyin Göçek (TUR)   Attendance: 17.869.

(Torpedo Kutaisi played their home match at Mikheil Meskhis Sakhelobis Stadioni, Tbilisi, instead of their regular stadium Ramaz Shengelias Sakhelobis Stadioni, Kutaisi)

23.08.18   Krestovsky Stadium, St. Petersburg: Zenit St. Petersburg – Molde FK 3-1 (0-1)
Zenit St. Petersburg: Andrei Lunev, Branislav Ivanovic, Aleksandr Anyukov, Igor Smolnikov (68' Anton Zabolotny), Miha Mevlja, Róbert Mak, Hernani (88' Magomed Ozdoev), Matías Kranevitter (59' Aleksandr Erokhin), Daler Kuzyaev, Artem Dzyuba, Sebastián Driussi. Coach: Sergey Semak.
Molde FK: Andreas Linde, Vegard Forren, Ruben Gabrielsen, Kristoffer Haugen, Christoffer Remmer, Petter Strand (74' Fredrik Brustad), Etzaz Hussain, Babacar Sarr, Eirik Hestad (86' Magnus Eikrem), Fredrik Aursnes, Erling Håland (78' Stian Gregersen).
Coach: Ole Gunnar Solskjær.
Goals: 42' Eirik Hestad 0-1, 71' Artem Dzyuba 1-1, 80' Anton Zabolotny 2-1, 90' Miha Mevlja 3-1.
Referee: Deniz Aytekin (GER)   Attendance: 40,677.

23.08.18   Stadión pod Dubnom, Zilina: AS Trencín – AEK Larnaca 1-1 (0-0)
AS Trencín: Igor Semrinec, Lukás Skovajsa, Martin Sulek (86' Erhan Masovic), Keston Julien, Reuben Yem, Ashraf El Mahdioui, Abdul Zubairu (84' Desley Ubbink), Joey Sleegers (80' Osman Bukari), Antonio Mance, Hamza Catakovic, Philip Azango. Coach: Ricardo Moniz.
AEK Larnaca: Toño, Mikel González, Daniel Mojsov, Truyols, Igor Carioca, Ivan Trickovski, Jorge Larena (78' Nacho Cases), Acorán, Hector Hevel, Apostolos Giannou (83' Florian Taulemesse), Tete (65' Jean Luc Assoubre). Coach: Andoni Iraola.
Goals: 55' Joey Sleegers 1-0, 60' Acorán 1-1.
Referee: Antonio Mateu Lahoz (ESP)   Attendance: 6,107.

(AS Trencín played this home match at Stadión pod Dubnom, Zilina, instead of their regular stadium, Stadión na Sihoti, Trencín, due to renovation)

23.08.18   Neo GSP Stadium, Nicosia: APOEL Nicosia – FK Astana 1-0 (0-0)
APOEL Nicosia: Boy Waterman, Carlão, Emilio N'Sue, Praxitelis Vouros, Caju, Nuno Morais, Lucas Souza, Ghayas Zahid (88' Savvas Gentsoglou), Roland Sallai, Moussa Al Taamari (74' Giorgos Efrem), Dellatorre (62' Reza Ghoochannejhad). Coach: Bruno Baltazar.
FK Astana: Nenad Eric, Antonio Rukavina, Dmitriy Shomko, Sergiy Maliy, Evgeni Postnikov, Marin Tomasov (90+1 Abzal Beysebekov), Ivan Maevski, Serikzhan Muzhikov, László Kleinheisler, Pedro Henrique (72' Baktiyor Zaynutdinov), Junior Kabananga (85' Rangelo Janga). Coach: Roman Grygorchuk.
Goal: 79' Caju 1-0.
Referee: Daniel Siebert (GER)   Attendance: 12,855.

23.08.18   Marijampoles sporto centro stadione, Marijampolé:
            FK Sūduva Marijampolé – Celtic FC 1-1 (1-1)
FK Sūduva Marijampolé: Ivan Kardum, Vaidas Slavickas, Algis Jankauskas, Vitaly Gayduchik, Andro Svrljuga, Guilherme Finkler (46' Daniel Offenbacher), Povilas Leimonas, Robertas Vézevicius (60' Julius Kasparavicius), Jovan Cadenovic, Ovidijus Verbickas (90' Giedrius Matulevicius), Rigino Cicilia. Coach: Vladimir Cheburin.
Celtic FC: Craig Gordon, Cristian Gamboa (66' Emilio Izaguirre), Jozo Simunovic (52' Mikael Lustig), Kieran Tierney, Kristoffer Ajer, Scott Brown, James Forrest, Callum McGregor, Olivier Ntcham, Moussa Dembélé, Michael Johnston (66' Leigh Griffiths).
Coach: Brendan Rodgers.
Goals: 3' Olivier Ntcham 0-1, 13' Ovidijus Verbickas 1-1.
Referee: Ivan Bebek (CRO)   Attendance: 5,100.

23.08.18   Bolshaya Sportivnaya Arena, Tiraspol: FC Sheriff Tiraspol – Qarabag FK 1-0 (1-0)
FC Sheriff Tiraspol: Serghei Pascenco, Mateo Susic, Veaceslav Posmac, Vladimir Kovacevic, Cristiano, Yuri Kendysh (88' Petru Racu), Gheorghe Anton, Rifet Kapic, Ziguy Badibanga, "Jô" Joálisson (72' Wilfried Balima), Alexandru Boiciuc (68' Al-Haji Kamara).
Coach: Goran Sablic.
Qarabag FK: Vagner, Rashad Sadygov, Maksim Medvedev, Badavi Hüseynov, Míchel, Qara Qarayev, Filip Ozobic, Simeon Slavchev (73' Ansi Agolli), Wilde Guerrier, Dzon Delarge (46' Abdellah Zoubir), Mahir Madatov. Coach: Gurban Gurbanov.
Goal: 8' Rifet Kapic 1-0.
Referee: Harald Lechner (AUT)   Attendance: 5,073.

23.08.18 Andruv stadion, Olomouc: SK Sigma Olomouc – Sevilla 0-1 (0-0)
SK Sigma Olomouc: Milos Buchta, Michal Veprek, Jan Sterba, Václav Jemelka, Martin Sladky, Jakub Plsek (85' Pavel Dvorák), David Houska, Tomás Zahradnícek (87' Martin Hála), Simon Falta, Lukás Kalvach, Martin Nespor (79' Jirí Texl). Coach: Václav Jílek.
Sevilla FC: Tomás Vaclík, Aleix Vidal (71' Jesús Navas), Guilherme Arana, Joris Gnagnon, Juan Berrocal, Éver Banega, Maxime Gonalons, Pablo Sarabia, Ibrahim Amadou (71' Sergi Gómez), Nolito (66' André Silva), Luis Muriel. Coach: Pablo Machín.
Goal: 84' Pablo Sarabia 0-1.
Referee: Bobby Madden (SCO)   Attendance: 11,709.

23.08.18 Sarpsborg Stadion, Sarpsborg: Sarpsborg 08 – Maccabi Tel Aviv 3-1 (2-1)
Sarpsborg 08: Alexander Vasyutin, Amin Askar, Joackim Jørgensen, Joachim Thomassen, Joonas Tamm, Matti Lund Nielsen, Jon-Helge Tveita, Kristoffer Zachariassen, Tobias Heintz (88' Kristoffer Larsen), Patrick Mortensen, Rashad Muhammed (80' Jørgen Larsen). Coach: Geir Bakke.
Maccabi Tel Aviv: Predrag Rajkovic, Eitan Tibi, Saborit, Elazar Dasa, Jair Amador, Dor Mikha, Roslan Barski (88' Eyal Golasa), Dan Glazer, Vidar Kjartansson (76' Itay Shechter), Aaron Schoenfeld, Omer Atzili (67' Chikeluba Ofoedu). Coach: Vladimir Ivic.
Goals: 2' Tobias Heintz 1-0, 7' Matti Lund Nielsen 2-0 (p), 13' Vidar Kjartansson 2-1 (p), 56' Patrick Mortensen 3-1 (p).
Referee: Vladislav Bezborodov (RUS)   Attendance: 6,363.

23.08.18 Swedbank Stadion, Malmö: Malmö FF – FC Midtjylland 2-2 (2-0)
Malmö FF: Johan Dahlin, Behrang Safari (64' Franz Brorsson), Rasmus Bengtsson, Lasse Nielsen, Andreas Vindheim (78' Eric Larsson), Søren Rieks, Anders Christiansen, Fouad Bachirou, Oscar Lewicki (71' Arnór Ingvi Traustason), Markus Rosenberg, Marcus Antonsson. Coach: Uwe Rösler.
FC Midtjylland: Jesper Hansen, Kian Hansen, Marc Hende, Alexander Scholz, Joel Andersson, Bubacarr Sanneh, Jakob Poulsen, Tim Sparv, Gustav Wikheim (78' Awer Mabil), Frank Onyeka (90+2' Mads Thychosen), Paul Ebere Onuachu (64' Ayo Simon Okosun). Coach: Jess Thorup.
Goals: 12' Markus Rosenberg 1-0, 24' Marcus Antonsson 2-0, 60' Gustav Wikheim 2-1, 77' Ayo Simon Okosun 2-2.
Referee: Srdan Jovanovic (SER)   Attendance: 11,487.

23.08.18 Stade Josy Barthel, Luxembourg: F91 Luxembourg – CFR Cluj 2-0 (0-0)
F91 Dudelange: Jonathan Joubert (53' Joé Frising), Tom Schnell, Jerry Prempeh, Kevin Malget, Aniss El Hriti, Marc-André Kruska, Stélvio, Dominik Stolz, Clément Couturier (88' Bryan Mélisse), David Turpel, Patrick Stumpf (65' Danel Sinani). Coach: Dino Toppmöller.
CFR Cluj: Giedrius Arlauskas, Andrei Muresan, Paulo Vinícius, Camora, Cristian Manea, Emmanuel Culio (10' Mate Males), Ovidiu Hoban, Mihai Bordeianu (71' Giuseppe De Luca), Alexandru Paun (61' Sebastian Mailat), George Tucudean, Billel Omrani.
Coach: Toni Conceição.
Goals: 67' David Turpel 1-0, 80' Danel Sinani 2-0.
Referee: Andreas Ekberg (SWE)   Attendance: 2,556.

(F91 Dudelange played their home match at Stade Josy Barthel, Luxembourg, instead of their regular stadium Stade Jos Nosbaum, Dudelange)

23.08.18   St. Jakob-Park, Basel: FC Basel – Apollon FC Limassol 3-2 (1-0)
FC Basel: Martin Hansen, Silvan Widmer, Éder Álvarez Balanta (66' Taulant Xhaka), Raoul Petretta, Eray Cümart, Serey Dié, Luca Zuffi, Fabian Frei, Aldo Kalulu (59' Kevin Bua), Ricky van Wolfswinkel, Albian Ajeti (87' Samuele Campo). Coach: Marcel Koller.
Apollon FC Limassol: Bruno Vale, Valentin Roberge, Charis Kyriakou, Kévin Bru (39' Mustapha Carayol), Héctor Yuste, Giorgos Vasiliou, Esteban Sachetti, João Pedro, Fotis Papoulis (79' Sasa Markovic), Anton Maglica (72' Emilio Zelaya), Adrián Sardinero.
Coach: Sofronis Avgousti.
Goals: 6' Ricky van Wolfswinkel 1-0, 49' Anton Maglica 1-1, 53' Fotis Papoulis 1-2, 69' Ricky van Wolfswinkel 2-2, 84' Eray Cümart 3-2.
Referee: Matej Jug (SVN)   Attendance: 10,743.

23.08.18   MAPEI Stadium – Città del Tricolore, Reggio Emilia:
               Atalanta Bergamo – FC København 0-0
Atalanta Bergamo: Pierluigi Gollini, Andrea Masiello, Rafael Tolói, Hans Hateboer (90+2' Timothy Castagne), Robin Gosens, Gianluca Mancini, "Papu" Alejandro Gómez, Marten de Roon, Remo Freuler, Mario Pasalic (46' Duván Zapata), Musa Barrow (80' Andreas Cornelius). Coach: Gian Piero Gasperini.
FC København: Jesse Joronen, Andreas Bjelland, Peter Ankersen, Nicolai Boilesen, Denis Vavro, Zeca (46' William Kvist), Viktor Fischer (80' Kenan Kodro), Nicolaj Thomsen, Robert Skov, Dame N'Doye, Pieros Sotiriou (77' Ján Gregus). Coach: Ståle Solbakken.
Referee: Pavel Královec (CZE)   Attendance: 7,680.

(Atalanta Bergamo played their home match at MAPEI Stadium – Città del Tricolore instead of their regular stadium, Stadio Atleti Azzurri d'Italia, as it wasn't given a UEFA licence to hold games)

23.08.18   Stadio Georgios Karaiskáki, Piraeus: Olympiakos Piraeus – Burnley 3-1 (1-1)
Olympiakos Piraeus: Andreas Gianniotis, Jagos Vukovic, Omar Elabdellaoui, Roderick Miranda, Kostas Tsimikas, Lazaros Christodoulopoulos (84' Karim Ansarifard), Kostas Fortounis (89' Ioannis Fetfatzidis), Andreas Bouchalakis, Daniel Podence, Mohamed Camara, Guerrero. Coach: Pedro Martins.
Burnley FC: Tom Heaton, Phil Bardsley, Stephen Ward (66' Aaron Lennon), Kevin Long, Ben Gibson, Charlie Taylor, Jack Cork, Jóhann Gudmundsson (76' Samuel Vokes), Jeffrey Hendrick, Ashley Barnes, Chris Wood (62' James Tarkowski). Coach: Sean Dyche.
Goals: 19' Kostas Fortounis 1-0, 33' Chris Wood 1-1 (p), 49' Andreas Bouchalakis 2-1, 60' Kostas Fortounis 3-1 (p).
Referee: Slavko Vincic (SVN)   Attendance: 26,010.
Sent off: 59' Ben Gibson.

23.08.18   Stadion Stozice, Ljubljana: Olimpija Ljubljana – FC Spartak Trnava 0-2 (0-2)
Olimpija Ljubljana: Aljaz Ivacic, Branko Ilic (82' Goran Brkic), Dino Stiglec, Vitalijs Maksimenko, Rok Kronaveter, Marko Putincanin, Stefan Savic, Daniel Avramovski (62' Asmir Suljic), Tomislav Tomic, Nik Kapun (62' Kingsley Boateng), Issah Abass.
Coach: Aleksandar Linta.
FC Spartak Trnava: Martin Chudy, Martin Tóth, Matús Conka, Ivan Hladík, Andrej Kadlec, Erik Grendel, Jakub Rada (71' Matej Oravec), Anton Sloboda, Lukás Gressák, Erik Jirka (86' Lukás Lupták), Marek Bakos (80' Oliver Janso). Coach: Radoslav Látal.
Goals: 23' Marek Bakos 0-1 (p), 35' Branko Ilic 0-2 (og).
Referee: Craig Pawson (ENG)   Attendance: 7,500.
Sent off: 29' Martin Tóth.

23.08.18   Stadion Partizana, Beograd: Partizan Beograd – Besiktas JK 1-1 (1-1)
Partizan Beograd: Vladimir Stojkovic, Marc Valiente, Nemanja Miletic (I), Sasa Zdjelar, Svetozar Markovic, Goran Zakaric, Nebojsa Kosovic (66' Aleksandar Scekic), Marko Jankovic (35' Djordje Ivanovic), Danilo Pantic, Nemanja Miletic (II), Ricardo Gomes (74' Nemanja Nikolic). Coach: Zoran Mirkovic.
Besiktas JK: Tolga Zengin, Adriano, Pepe (76' Enzo Roco), Caner Erkin, Gökhan Gönül, Gary Medel, Domagoj Vida, Ricardo Quaresma (79' Gökhan Töre), Necip Uysal, Tolgay Arslan (89' Güven Yalçin), Cyle Larin. Coach: Senol Günes.
Goals: 14' Ricardo Gomes 1-0, 15' Tolgay Arslan 1-1.
Referee: Ivan Kruzliak (SVK)   Attendance: 16,240.

23.08.18   Allianz Stadion, Vienna: SK Rapid Wien – Fotbal Club FCSB 3-1 (2-0)
SK Rapid Wien: Richard Strebinger, Mario Sonnleitner, Marvin Potzmann, Boli Bolingoli-Mbombo, Mateo Barac, Christoph Knasmüllner (86' Aleksandar Kostic), Stefan Schwab, Thomas Murg (89' Mert Müldür), Dejan Ljubicic, Deni Alar (68' Andrei Ivan), Veton Berisha. Coach: Goran Djuricin.
Fotbal Club FCSB: Cristian Balgradean, Alexandru Stan, Romario Sandu Benzar, Bogdan Planic, Mihai Balasa, Filipe Teixeira, Mihai Roman (I) (58' Raul Rusescu), Mihai Pintilii, Ovidiu Popescu (46' Florinel Coman), Olimpiu Morutan (46' Dennis Man), Harlem Gnohéré. Coach: Nicolae Dica.
Goals: 4' Christoph Knasmüllner 1-0, 40' Mario Sonnleitner 2-0, 47' Harlem Gnohéré 2-1, 49' Stefan Schwab 3-1.
Referee: William Collum (SCO)   Attendance: 19,300.
Sent off: 84' Veton Berisha.

23.08.18   Luminus Arena, Genk: KRC Genk – Brøndby IF 5-2 (2-0)
KRC Genk: Danny Vukovic, Sebastien Dewaest, Jere Uronen, Jhon Lucumí, Joakim Mæhle, Pozuelo, Ruslan Malinovskiy, Sander Berge, Leandro Trossard, Mbwana Samatta, Dieumerci N'Dongala (74' Joseph Paintsil). Coach: Philippe Clement.
Brøndby IF: Marvin Schwäbe, Paulus Arajuuri, Johan Larsson, Anthony Jung, Hjörtur Hermannsson, Dominik Kaiser (79' Simon Tibbling), Lasse Vigen Christensen (89' Kasper Fisker), Josip Radosevic, Hany Mukhtar, Kamil Wilczek, Ante Erceg (72' Mikkel Uhre). Coach: Alexander Zorniger.
Goals: 36' Mbwana Samatta 1-0, 45+1' Leandro Trossard 2-0 (p), 47' Hjörtur Hermannsson 2-1, 51' Kamil Wilczek 2-2, 55', 70' Mbwana Samatta 3-2, 4-2, 90+1' Leandro Trossard 5-2.
Referee: Andris Treimanis (LAT)   Attendance: 12,110.

23.08.18   Slavutych-Arena, Zaporizhya: Zorya Luhansk – RB Leipzig 0-0
Zorya Luhansk: Luis Felipe, Vitaliy Vernidub, Oleksandr Svatok, Oleksandr Tymchyk, Bogdan Mykhaylychenko, Dmytro Khomchenovskyi (59' Vladyslav Kabayev), Igor Kharatin, Oleksandr Karavayev (83' Artem Gordienko), Silas, Bohdan Lednev, Rafael Ratão (57' Vladyslav Kochergin). Coach: Yuriy Vernydub.
RB Leipzig: Yvon Mvogo, Willi Orban, Nordi Mukiele (62' Emil Forsberg), Ibrahima Konaté, Stefan Ilsanker, Diego Demme, Bruma, Konrad Laimer (80' Lukas Klostermann), Marcelo Saracchi, Timo Werner, Matheus Cunha (72' Yussuf Poulsen). Coach: Ralf Rangnick.
Referee: Benoît Bastien (FRA)   Attendance: 5,127.
Sent off: 16' Bohdan Lednev.

(Zorya Luhansk played their home match at Slavutych-Arena, Zaporizhya, instead of their regular stadium Avanhard Stadium, Luhansk, due to the war conditions in Eastern Ukraine)

23.08.18   Lerkendal Stadion, Trondheim: Rosenborg BK – KF Shkëndija 79 3-1 (3-0)
Rosenborg BK: André Hansen, Tore Reginiussen, Even Hovland, Vegar Hedenstad (78' Erlend Reitan), Birger Meling, Mike Jensen, Anders Konradsen, Marius Lundemo (74' Djordje Denic), Nicklas Bendtner, Issam Jebali, Jonathan Levi (68' Pål Helland). Coach: Rini Coolen.
KF Shkëndija 79: Kostadin Zahov, Gledi Mici, Mevlan Murati, Visar Musliu, Mevlan Adili, Armend Alimi, Ennur Totre, Besart Ibraimi, Izair Emini (78' Besmir Bojku), Valmir Nafiu (63' Remzi Selmani), Stênio Júnior. Coach: Qatip Osmani.
Goals: 11' Issam Jebali 1-0, 15' Nicklas Bendtner 2-0, 44' Jonathan Levi 3-0, 76' Stênio Júnior 3-1.
Referee: Orel Grinfeld (ISR)   Attendance: 8,767.

23.08.18   GHELAMCO-arena, Gent: KAA Gent – Girondins de Bordeaux 0-0
KAA Gent: Lovre Kalinic, Nana Asare, Igor Plastun, Sigurd Rosted, Thomas Foket, Vadis Odjidja-Ofoe, Birger Verstraete, Jean-Luc Dompé (79' Stallone Limbombe), Giorgi Chakvetadze (87' Brecht Dejaegere), Roman Yaremchuk, Taiwo Awoniyi (75' Jonathan David). Coach: Yves Vanderhaeghe.
Girondins de Bordeaux: Benoît Costil, Igor Lewczuk, Pablo Castro, Maxime Poundjé, Jules Koundé, Jaroslav Plasil, Younousse Sankharé, Lukas Lerager, Zaydou Youssouf (75' Samuel Kalu), Jimmy Briand, Nicolas de Préville (86' François Kamano). Coach: Gustavo Poyet.
Referee: Aliyar Aghayev (AZE)   Attendance: 13.239.
Sent off: 90+2' Jules Koundé.

23.08.18   Ibrox Stadium, Glasgow: Glasgow Rangers FC – FC Ufa 1-0 (1-0)
Glasgow Rangers FC: Allan McGregor, James Tavernier, Connor Goldson, Jon Flanagan, Nikola Katic, Scott Arfield, Ryan Jack, Ryan Kent (77' Glenn Middleton), Oviemuno Ejaria, Candeias (69' Kyle Lafferty), Alfredo Morelos. Coach: Steven Gerrard.
FC Ufa: Aleksandr Belenov, Bojan Jokic, Pavel Alikin, Ionut Nedelcearu, Jemal Tabidze, Azamat Zaseev (85' Ondrej Vanek), Veroljub Salatic, Ivan Paurevic, Dmitri Zhivoglyadov, Ivan Oblyakov (83' Catalin Carp), Sylvester Igboun (90+2' Vyacheslav Krotov). Coach: Sergei Tomarov.
Goal: 41' Connor Goldson 1-0.
Referee: Daniel Stefanski (POL)   Attendance: 49,338.

30.08.18   Stadion Neftyanik, Ufa: FC Ufa – Glasgow Rangers FC 1-1 (1-1)
FC Ufa: Aleksandr Belenov, Bojan Jokic, Pavel Alikin (52' Ivan Oblyakov), Ionut Nedelcearu, Jemal Tabidze, Veroljub Salatic (76' Vyacheslav Krotov), Dmitry Sysuyev, Ivan Paurevic, Ondrej Vanek, Dmitri Zhivoglyadov, Sylvester Igboun. Coach: Sergei Tomarov.
Glasgow Rangers FC: Allan McGregor, James Tavernier, Connor Goldson, Jon Flanagan, Nikola Katic, Scott Arfield (69' Andrew Halliday), Ryan Jack, Ryan Kent, Oviemuno Ejaria, Candeias (46' Kyle Lafferty), Alfredo Morelos. Coach: Steven Gerrard.
Goals: 9' Oviemuno Ejaria 0-1, 32' Dmitry Sysuyev 1-1.
Referee: Tobias Stieler (GER)   Attendance: 13,186.
Sent off: 38' Alfredo Morelos, 66' Jon Flanagan.

30.08.18   Astana Arena, Astana: FK Astana – APOEL Nicosia 1-0 (1-0, 1-0)
FK Astana: Nenad Eric, Antonio Rukavina, Marin Anicic, Dmitriy Shomko, Evgeni Postnikov, Marin Tomasov, Ivan Maevski (120+2' Yuriy Logvinenko), Serikzhan Muzhikov (53' Richard Almeyda), László Kleinheisler (99' Abzal Beysebekov), Pedro Henrique, Junior Kabananga (84' Rangelo Janga). Coach: Roman Grygorchuk.
APOEL Nicosia: Boy Waterman, Carlão, Emilio N'Sue, Praxitelis Vouros (120+1' Savvas Gentsoglou), Caju, Nuno Morais, Lucas Souza, Ghayas Zahid (64' Tomás De Vincenti), Roland Sallai, Moussa Al Taamari (84' Giorgos Efrem), Reza Ghoochannejhad (94' Dellatorre). Coach: Bruno Baltazar.
Goal: 16' Pedro Henrique 1-0 (p).
Referee: Jakob Kehlet (DEN)   Attendance: 26,000.

FK Astana won on penalties after extra time (2-1).
Penalties: Nuno Morais 1-0, Almeyda 1-1, De Vincenti missed, Anicic missed,
  Efrem missed, Pedro Henrique 1-2, Dellatorre missed, Beysebekov missed,
  Lucas Souza missed.

30.08.18   AEK Arena – Georgios Karapatakis, Larnaca: AEK Larnaca – AS Trenčín 3-0 (2-0)
AEK Larnaca: Toño, Mikel González, Daniel Mojsov, Truyols, Igor Carioca, Ivan Trickovski, Jorge Larena (84' Facundo García), Acorán, Hector Hevel, Apostolos Giannou (74' Florian Taulemesse), Tete (62' Nacho Cases). Coach: Andoni Iraola.
AS Trenčín: Igor Semrinec, Martin Sulek, Keston Julien, Reuben Yem, Jakub Paur, Desley Ubbink (73' Peter Klescík), Ashraf El Mahdioui, Joey Sleegers (62' Osman Bukari), Antonio Mance (73' Emeka Umeh), Hamza Catakovic, Philip Azango. Coach: Ricardo Moniz.
Goals: 1' Apostolos Giannou 1-0, 36' Acorán 2-0, 65' Apostolos Giannou 3-0.
Referee: Sergei Karasev (RUS)   Attendance: 4,777.

30.08.18   Telia Parken, København: FC København – Atalanta Bergamo 0-0
FC København: Jesse Joronen, Andreas Bjelland, Peter Ankersen, Nicolai Boilesen (109' William Kvist), Denis Vavro, Rasmus Falk (66' Pieros Sotiriou), Zeca, Viktor Fischer (109' Pierre Bengtsson), Nicolaj Thomsen (79' Ján Gregus), Robert Skov, Dame N'Doye. Coach: Ståle Solbakken.
Atalanta Bergamo: Pierluigi Gollini, Andrea Masiello, Rafael Tolói, José Palomino, Timothy Castagne, Robin Gosens (95' Ali Adnan), "Papu" Alejandro Gómez, Marten de Roon, Remo Freuler (90' Matteo Pessina), Mario Pasalic (57' Musa Barrow), Duván Zapata (54' Andreas Cornelius). Coach: Gian Piero Gasperini.
Referee: Anastasios Sidiropoulos (GRE)   Attendance: 18,378.

FC København won on penalties after extra time (3-4).
Penalties: de Roon 1-0, Sotiriou 1-1, Ali Adnan 2-1, Gregus 2-2, Gómez missed, 2-3 Skov,
  Masiello 3-3, N'Doye missed, Cornelius missed, Vavro 3-4.

30.08.18   Red Bull Arena, Leipzig: RB Leipzig – Zorya Luhansk 3-2 (1-1)
RB Leipzig: Yvon Mvogo, Willi Orban, Lukas Klostermann, Ibrahima Konaté (59' Emil Forsberg), Stefan Ilsanker, Kevin Kampl, Marcel Sabitzer, Konrad Laimer (79' Bruma), Yussuf Poulsen (59' Jean-Kévin Augustin), Timo Werner, Matheus Cunha.
Coach: Ralf Rangnick.
Zorya Luhansk: Luis Felipe, Vitaliy Vernidub, Artem Gordienko (68' Vladyslav Kochergin), Oleksandr Svatok, Oleksandr Tymchyk, Bogdan Mykhaylychenko, Igor Kharatin, Oleksandr Karavayev, Silas, Rafael Ratão (80' Vasiliy Prijma), Vladyslav Kabayev (69' Yevgen Cheberko). Coach: Yuriy Vernydub.
Goals: 7' Matheus Cunha 1-0, 35' Rafael Ratão 1-1, 48' Artem Gordienko 1-2, 69' Jean-Kévin Augustin 2-2, 90' Emil Forsberg 3-2 (p).
Referee: Danny Makkelie (HOL)   Attendance: 17,644.

30.08.18   Ludogorets Arena, Razgrad: PFC Ludogorets Razgrad – Torpedo Kutaisi 4-0 (2-0)
PFC Ludogorets Razgrad: Renan, Cosmin Moti, Cicinho, Anton Nedyalkov, Svetoslav Dyakov (72' Jacek Góralski), Gustavo Campanharo, Wanderson (87' Dimo Bakalov), Natanael Pimienta, Claudiu Keserü, Marcelinho, "Vura" Virgil Misidjan (70' Jody Lukoki).
Coach: Paulo Autuori.
Torpedo Kutaisi: Rion Kvaskhvadze, Mamuka Kobakhidze, Levan Gegetchkori, Oleksandr Azatsky, Lazar Marin, Grigol Dolidze (77' Giorgi Kimadze), Levan Kutalia (46' Arfang Daffé), Marek Hlinka, Mate Tsintsadze, Milos Lacny (58' Giorgi Kukhianidze), Tornike Kapanadze. Coach: Kakhaber Chkhetiani.
Goals: 6' "Vura" Virgil Misidjan 1-0, 38', 59' Gustavo Campanharo 2-0, 3-0, 62' Wanderson 4-0.
Referee: Mattias Gestranius (FIN)   Attendance: 5.340.

30.08.18   Neo GSP Stadium, Nicosia: Apollon FC Limassol – FC Basel 1-0 (0-0)
Apollon FC Limassol: Bruno Vale, Valentin Roberge, Charis Kyriakou, André Schembri (63' Adrián Sardinero), Facundo Pereyra (78' Sasa Markovic), Héctor Yuste, Giorgos Vasiliou, Esteban Sachetti, João Pedro (73' Marios Stylianou), Fotis Papoulis, Anton Maglica.
Coach: Sofronis Avgousti.
FC Basel: Martin Hansen, Silvan Widmer, Éder Álvarez Balanta, Raoul Petretta, Eray Cümart, Serey Dié, Luca Zuffi (76' Afimico Pululu), Fabian Frei, Samuele Campo (46' Albian Ajeti), Ricky van Wolfswinkel, Noah Okafor (80' Kevin Bua). Coach: Marcel Koller.
Goal: 53' Charis Kyriakou 1-0.
Referee: Ruddy Buquet (FRA)   Attendance: 4,005.

Apollon FC Limassol won on away goals.

(Apollon FC Limassol played their home match at Neo GSP Stadium, Nicosia, instead of their regular stadium, Tsirio Stadium, Limassol)

30.08.18   Aker Stadion, Molde: Molde – Zenit St. Petersburg 2-1 (0-1)
Molde FK: Andreas Linde, Vegard Forren, Ruben Gabrielsen, Kristoffer Haugen, Christoffer Remmer (90' Leke James), Petter Strand (61' Magnus Eikrem), Etzaz Hussain, Babacar Sarr, Eirik Hestad, Fredrik Aursnes (71' Pawel Cibicki), Erling Håland.
Coach: Ole Gunnar Solskjær.
Zenit St. Petersburg: Andrei Lunev, Branislav Ivanovic, Aleksandr Anyukov (86' Neto), Igor Smolnikov, Miha Mevlja, Aleksandr Erokhin, Leandro Paredes, Hernani, Daler Kuzyaev (76' Matías Kranevitter), Anton Zabolotny, Sebastián Driussi (67' Róbert Mak).
Coach: Sergey Semak.
Goals: 21' Daler Kuzyaev 0-1, 65' Eirik Hestad 1-1, 77' Erling Håland 2-1.
Referee: Carlos del Cerro Grande (ESP)   Attendance: 5,414.

30.08.18   Winner Stadium, Netanya: Maccabi Tel Aviv – Sarpsborg 08 2-1 (0-0)
Maccabi Tel Aviv: Predrag Rajkovic, Sheran Yeini, Eitan Tibi, Saborit, Elazar Dasa, Dor Mikha, Roslan Barski (87' Aaron Schoenfeld), Dan Glazer, Vidar Kjartansson (46' Itay Shechter), Eliran Atar (71' Yonatan Cohen), Omer Atzili. Coach: Vladimir Ivic.
Sarpsborg 08: Alexander Vasyutin, Amin Askar (86' Harmeet Singh), Joackim Jørgensen (89' Jørgen Horn), Joachim Thomassen, Bjørn Utvik, Matti Lund Nielsen, Ole Halvorsen, Jon-Helge Tveita, Kristoffer Zachariassen, Patrick Mortensen, Rashad Muhammed (64' Tobias Heintz). Coach: Geir Bakke.
Goals: 52' Omer Atzili 1-0 (p), 60' Eliran Atar 2-0, 81' Ole Halvorsen 2-1 (p).
Referee: Artur Soares Dias (POR)   Attendance: 10,673

(Maccabi Tel Aviv played their home match at Winner Stadium instead of their regular stadium, Bloomfield Stadium, due to renovation)

30.08.18   Tofiq Bahramov adina Respublika stadionu, Baku:
               Qarabag FK – FC Sheriff Tiraspol 3-0 (2-0)
Qarabag FK: Vagner, Rashad Sadygov, Maksim Medvedev, Badavi Hüseynov, Qara Qarayev, Filip Ozobic (82' Joshgun Diniyev), Simeon Slavchev, Wilde Guerrier, Abdellah Zoubir (80' Dzon Delarge), Innocent Emeghara, Mahir Madatov (88' Abbas Hüseynov).
Coach: Gurban Gurbanov.
FC Sheriff Tiraspol: Serghei Pascenco, Petru Racu (55' Antun Palic), Mateo Susic, Veaceslav Posmac, Vladimir Kovacevic, Cristiano, Gheorghe Anton, Rifet Kapic, Ziguy Badibanga, "Jô" Joálisson (68' Gerson Rodrigues), Alexandru Boiciuc (26' Al-Haji Kamara).
Coach: Goran Sablic.
Goals: 9' Maksim Medvedev 1-0, 42' Wilde Guerrier 2-0, 55' Filip Ozobic 3-0.
Referee: Aleksandar Stavrev (MKD)   Attendance: 21,350.

(Qarabag FK played their home match at Tofiq Bahramov adina Respublika stadionu, instead of their regular stadium Azersun Arena)

30.08.18   Stadionul Dr. Constantin Radulescu, Cluj-Napoca:
CFR Cluj – F91 Dudelange 2-3 (0-0)
CFR Cluj: Jesús Fernández, Paulo Vinícius, Camora, Ádám Lang, Cristian Manea, Mate Males, Alexandru Ionita (II), Mihai Bordeianu (54' Alexandru Paun), Sebastian Mailat (46' Robert Tambe), George Tucudean (68' Júlio Baptista), Billel Omrani. Coach: Toni Conceição.
F91 Dudelange: Joé Frising, Tom Schnell, Jerry Prempeh, Bryan Mélisse, Kevin Malget (79' Edisson Jordanov), Aniss El Hriti, Stélvio, Dominik Stolz, Clément Couturier, Danel Sinani (87' Sanel Ibrahimovic), David Turpel (90+2' Mario Pokar). Coach: Dino Toppmöller.
Goals: 51', 54' Danel Sinani 0-1, 0-2, 78' David Turpel 0-3, 85' Robert Tambe 1-3, 88' Billel Omrani 2-3.
Referee: Davide Massa (ITA)   Attendance: 12,000.

30.08.18   MCH Arena, Herning: FC Midtjylland – Malmö FF 0-2 (0-1)
FC Midtjylland: Jesper Hansen, Kian Hansen, Marc Hende, Alexander Scholz, Joel Andersson (75' Awer Mabil), Bubacarr Sanneh, Jakob Poulsen, Tim Sparv, Gustav Wikheim, Ayo Simon Okosun (56' Paul Ebere Onuachu), Frank Onyeka (56' Mayron George). Coach: Jess Thorup.
Malmö FF: Johan Dahlin, Behrang Safari (90' Franz Brorsson), Rasmus Bengtsson, Lasse Nielsen, Andreas Vindheim (80' Eric Larsson), Søren Rieks, Anders Christiansen, Fouad Bachirou, Oscar Lewicki, Markus Rosenberg, Marcus Antonsson (84' Arnór Ingvi Traustason). Coach: Uwe Rösler.
Goals: 32' Marcus Antonsson 0-1, 79' Markus Rosenberg 0-2.
Referee: Serdar Gözübüyük (HOL)   Attendance: 9,175.

30.08.18   Vodafone Stadyumu, Istanbul: Besiktas JK – Partizan Beograd 3-0 (2-0)
Besiktas JK: Utku Yuvakuran, Adriano, Pepe, Caner Erkin (87' Gökhan Töre), Gökhan Gönül, Gary Medel (77' Dorukhan Toköz), Domagoj Vida, Ricardo Quaresma, Necip Uysal (27' Oguzhan Özyakup), Tolgay Arslan, Cyle Larin. Coach: Senol Günes.
Partizan Beograd: Vladimir Stojkovic, Marc Valiente, Nemanja Miletic (I), Sasa Zdjelar, Svetozar Markovic (46' Nemanja Nikolic), Aleksandar Scekic (57' Gabriel Enache), Goran Zakaric, Danilo Pantic, Nemanja Miletic (II), Ricardo Gomes, Djordje Ivanovic (62' Seydouba Soumah). Coach: Zoran Mirkovic.
Goals: 37' Pepe 1-0, 45+1' Oguzhan Özyakup 2-0, 68' Pepe 3-0.
Referee: Ovidiu Hategan (ROM)   Attendance: 33,658.

30.08.18   Telekom Arena, Skopje: KF Shkëndija 79 – Rosenborg BK 0-2 (0-0)
KF Shkëndija 79: Kostadin Zahov, Gledi Mici (86' Shefit Shefiti), Mevlan Murati, Visar Musliu, Egzon Bejtulai, Armend Alimi, Ennur Totre (76' Besmir Bojku), Besart Ibraimi, Izair Emini, Valmir Nafiu (64' Remzi Selmani), Stênio Júnior. Coach: Qatip Osmani.
Rosenborg BK: André Hansen, Tore Reginiussen (87' Besim Serbecic), Even Hovland, Vegar Hedenstad, Birger Meling, Mike Jensen, Anders Konradsen, Marius Lundemo, Nicklas Bendtner (74' Alexander Søderlund), Issam Jebali, Jonathan Levi (62' Djordje Denic). Coach: Rini Coolen.
Goals: 67' Even Hovland 0-1, 84' Tore Reginiussen 0-2.
Referee: Aleksey Kulbakov (BLS)   Attendance: 10,950.
(Besart Ibraimi missed a penalty kick (20'), Izair Emini missed a penalty kick (48'))

(KF Shkëndija 79 played their home match at Telekom Arena, Skopje, instead of their regular stadium Ecolog Arena, Tetovo, due to renovation)

30.08.18   Arena Nationala, Bucuresti: Fotbal Club FCSB – SK Rapid Wien 2-1 (2-0)
Fotbal Club FCSB: Andrei Vlad, Alexandru Stan, Romario Sandu Benzar, Bogdan Planic, Mihai Balasa, Filipe Teixeira, Mihai Roman (I) (74' Florinel Coman), Mihai Pintilii, Lucian Filip (85' Dennis Man), Harlem Gnohéré, Florin Tanase (45' Raul Rusescu).
Coach: Nicolae Dica.
SK Rapid Wien: Richard Strebinger, Mario Sonnleitner, Marvin Potzmann, Mateo Barac, Mert Müldür (65' Stephan Auer), Christoph Knasmüllner (76' Maximilian Hofmann), Stefan Schwab, Thomas Murg (90' Manuel Martic), Dejan Ljubicic, Deni Alar, Andrei Ivan.
Coach: Goran Djuricin.
Goals: 12' Harlem Gnohéré 1-0, 45+2' Mihai Roman 2-0, 63' Mario Sonnleitner 2-1.
Referee: Michael Oliver (ENG)   Attendance: 31,274.
Sent off: 90+1' Mihai Balasa.

30.08.18   Brøndby Stadion, Brøndby: Brøndby IF – KRC Genk 2-4 (1-2)
Brøndby IF: Marvin Schwäbe, Paulus Arajuuri, Johan Larsson, Anthony Jung, Joël Kabongo, Dominik Kaiser, Lasse Vigen Christensen (79' Jens Gammelby), Josip Radosevic (46' Simon Tibbling), Hany Mukhtar, Kamil Wilczek (79' Nikolai Laursen), Ante Erceg.
Coach: Alexander Zorniger.
KRC Genk: Danny Vukovic, Sebastien Dewaest, Jere Uronen, Jhon Lucumí, Joakim Mæhle (80' Rubin Seigers), Pozuelo (70' Jakub Piotrowski), Ruslan Malinovskiy, Sander Berge, Leandro Trossard (62' Joseph Paintsil), Mbwana Samatta, Dieumerci N'Dongala.
Coach: Philippe Clement.
Goals: 15' Ruslan Malinovskiy 0-1, 33' Dieumerci N'Dongala 0-2, 34' Kamil Wilczek 1-2, 58' Johan Larsson 2-2, 66' Sebastien Dewaest 2-3, 87' Mbwana Samatta 2-4.
Referee: Gediminas Mazeika (LTU)   Attendance: 8,636.

30.08.18   Stadión Antona Malatinského, Trnava:
           FC Spartak Trnava – Olimpija Ljubljana 1-1 (1-1)
FC Spartak Trnava: Martin Chudy, Matús Conka, Ivan Hladík, Boris Godál, Andrej Kadlec, Matej Oravec, Erik Grendel (72' Oliver Janso), Jakub Rada, Vakhtang Chanturishvili (89' Lukás Lupták), Erik Jirka (90+2' Stefan Pekár), Marek Bakos. Coach: Radoslav Látal.
Olimpija Ljubljana: Aljaz Ivacic, Branko Ilic, Dino Stiglec, Vitalijs Maksimenko, Macky Frank Bagnack, Rok Kronaveter, Matic Crnic, Tomislav Tomic, Nik Kapun (74' Goran Brkic), Kingsley Boateng (69' Stefan Savic), Issah Abass (82' Asmir Suljic). Coach: Safet Hadzic.
Goals: 12' Boris Godál 1-0, 42' Nik Kapun 1-1.
Referee: Luca Banti (ITA)   Attendance: 15,642.

30.08.18   Stade Matmut-Atlantique, Bordeaux: Girondins de Bordeaux – KAA Gent 2-0 (1-0)
Girondins de Bordeaux: Benoît Costil, Igor Lewczuk, Pablo Castro, Maxime Poundjé, Sergi Palencia, Jaroslav Plasil, Lukas Lerager, Aurélien Tchouaméni, Jimmy Briand (68' Nicolas de Préville), François Kamano, Samuel Kalu (83' Zaydou Youssouf). Coach: Gustavo Poyet.
KAA Gent: Lovre Kalinic, Nana Asare, Igor Plastun, Sigurd Rosted, Thomas Foket, Vadis Odjidja-Ofoe (46' Brecht Dejaegere), Birger Verstraete, Jean-Luc Dompé (69' Giorgi Kvilitaia), Giorgi Chakvetadze, Roman Yaremchuk, Taiwo Awoniyi (63' Jonathan David).
Coach: Yves Vanderhaeghe.
Goals: 10' François Kamano 1-0, 64' Jimmy Briand 2-0 (p).
Referee: Jesús Gil Manzano (ESP)   Attendance: 35,039.

30.08.18 Turf Moor, Burnley: Burnley FC – Olympiakos Piraeus 1-1 (0-0)
Burnley FC: Tom Heaton, Phil Bardsley, Kevin Long, Ben Mee, Charlie Taylor, Aaron Lennon (75' Jack Cork), Ashley Westwood, Jeffrey Hendrick, Ashley Barnes (65' Matej Vydra), Samuel Vokes, Dwight McNeil (75' Chris Wood). Coach: Sean Dyche.
Olympiakos Piraeus: Andreas Gianniotis, Jagos Vukovic, Omar Elabdellaoui, Roderick Miranda, Kostas Tsimikas, Lazaros Christodoulopoulos, Kostas Fortounis (88' Vasilios Torosidis), Andreas Bouchalakis, Daniel Podence (90+4' Pape Cissé), Mohamed Camara, Guerrero (72' "Koka" Ahmed Hassan). Coach: Pedro Martins.
Goals: 83' Daniel Podence 0-1, 86' Matej Vydra 1-1.
Referee: Viktor Kassai (HUN)   Attendance: 15,234.

30.08.18 Celtic Park, Glasgow: Celtic FC – FK Sūduva Marijampolé 3-0 (1-0)
Celtic FC: Craig Gordon, Mikael Lustig, Dedryck Boyata, Kieran Tierney (69' Emilio Izaguirre), Kristoffer Ajer, Scott Brown, Scott Sinclair, Callum McGregor, Olivier Ntcham, Leigh Griffiths (65' Ryan Christie), Michael Johnston (78' Jonny Hayes). Coach: Brendan Rodgers.
FK Sūduva Marijampolé: Ivan Kardum, Vaidas Slavickas, Algis Jankauskas, Vitaly Gayduchik, Andro Svrljuga, Aleksandar Zivanovic, Gerson Acevedo, Daniel Offenbacher (79' Ovidijus Verbickas), Jovan Cadenovic (56' Povilas Leimonas), Sandro Gotal (73' Julius Kasparavicius), Rigino Cicilia. Coach: Vladimir Cheburin.
Goals: 27' Leigh Griffiths 1-0, 53' Callum McGregor 2-0, 61' Kristoffer Ajer 3-0.
Referee: Georgi Kabakov (BUL)   Attendance: 44,639.

30.08.18 Estadio Ramón Sánchez Pizjuán, Sevilla:
       Sevilla FC – SK Sigma Olomouc 3-0 (2-0)
Sevilla FC: Tomás Vaclík, Daniel Carriço, Aleix Vidal, Sergi Gómez, Guilherme Arana, Joris Gnagnon, Éver Banega (68' Roque Mesa), Franco Vázquez (79' Luis Muriel), Maxime Gonalons, Nolito, André Silva (65' Wissam Ben Yedder). Coach: Pablo Machín.
SK Sigma Olomouc: Milos Buchta, Michal Veprek, Roman Polom, Jan Kotouc, Martin Sladky, Jakub Plsek (58' Jirí Texl), David Houska, Tomás Zahradnícek, Simon Falta (70' Pavel Dvorák), Lukás Kalvach (60' Martin Hála), Martin Nespor. Coach: Václav Jílek.
Goals: 21' Maxime Gonalons 1-0, 26' Martin Nespor 2-0 (og), 75' Wissam Ben Yedder 3-0.
Referee: István Kovács (ROM)   Attendance: 30,311.

GROUP STAGE

GROUP A

Bayer Leverkusen	6	4	1	1	16 - 9	13
FC Zürich	6	3	1	2	7 - 6	10
AEK Larnaca	6	0	4	2	5 - 7	5
PFC Ludogorets Razgrad	6	0	4	2	5 - 7	4

GROUP B

Red Bull Salzburg	6	6	0	0	17 - 6	18
Celtic FC	6	3	0	3	6 - 8	9
RB Leipzig	6	2	1	3	9 - 8	7
Rosenborg BK	6	0	1	5	4 - 14	1

GROUP C

Zenit St. Petersburg	6	3	2	1	6 - 5	11
Slavia Praha	6	3	1	2	4 - 3	10
Girondins de Bordeaux	6	2	1	3	6 - 6	7
FC København	6	1	2	3	3 - 5	5

GROUP D

Dinamo Zagreb	6	4	2	0	11 - 3	14
Fenerbahçe	6	2	2	2	7 - 7	8
FC Spartak Trnava	6	2	1	3	4 - 7	7
RSC Anderlecht	6	0	3	3	2 - 7	3

GROUP E

Arsenal FC	6	5	1	0	12 - 2	16
Sporting CP	6	4	1	1	13 - 3	13
Vorskla Poltava	6	1	0	5	4 - 13	3
Qarabag FK	6	1	0	5	2 - 13	3

GROUP F

Real Betis Sevilla	6	3	3	0	7 - 2	12
Olympiakos Piraeus	6	3	1	2	11 - 6	10
AC Milan	6	3	1	2	12 - 9	10
F91 Dudelange	6	0	1	5	3 - 16	1

GROUP G

Villarreal CF	6	2	4	0	12 - 5	10
SK Rapid Wien	6	3	1	2	6 - 9	10
Glasgow Rangers FC	6	1	3	2	8 - 8	6
Spartak Moskva	6	1	2	3	8 - 12	5

GROUP H

Eintracht Frankfurt	6	6	0	0	17 - 5	18
Lazio Roma	6	3	0	3	9 - 11	9
Apollon FC Limassol	6	2	1	3	10 - 10	7
Olympique Marseille	6	0	1	5	6 - 16	1

GROUP I

KRC Genk	6	3	2	1	14 - 8	11
Malmö FF	6	2	3	1	7 - 6	9
Besiktas JK	6	2	1	3	9 - 11	7
Sarpsborg 08	6	1	2	3	8 - 13	5

GROUP J

Sevilla FC	6	4	0	2	18 - 6	12
FK Krasnodar	6	4	0	2	8 - 8	12
Standard Liège	6	3	1	2	7 - 9	10
Akhisar Belediyespor	6	0	1	5	4 - 14	1

GROUP K

Dinamo Kiev	6	3	2	1	10 - 7	11
Stade Rennes	6	3	0	3	7 - 8	9
FK Astana	6	2	2	2	7 - 7	8
FK Jablonec	6	1	2	3	6 - 8	5

GROUP L

Chelsea FC	6	5	1	0	12 - 3	16
BATE Borisov	6	3	0	3	9 - 9	9
MOL Vidi FC	6	2	1	3	5 - 7	7
PAOK Saloniki	6	1	0	5	5 - 12	3

The numbers 1 and 2 in each group advance to knockout phase.

GROUP A

20.09.18   Ludogorets Arena, Razgrad:
PFC Ludogorets Razgrad – Bayer Leverkusen 2-3 (2-1)
PFC Ludogorets Razgrad: Renan, Cosmin Moti, Cicinho, Anton Nedyalkov, Svetoslav Dyakov (76' Jacek Góralski), Gustavo Campanharo, Wanderson, Natanael Pimienta, Claudiu Keserü, Marcelinho (82' Juninho Brandão), Jody Lukoki. Coach: Paulo Autuori.
Bayer Leverkusen: Lukás Hrádecky, Aleksandar Dragovic, Mitchell Weiser, Wendell, Jonathan Tah, Lars Bender (72' Leon Bailey), Dominik Kohr, Kai Havertz, Isaac Kiese Thelin (90+1' Lucas Alario), Julian Brandt, Paulinho (46' Kevin Volland). Coach: Heiko Herrlich.
Goals: 8' Claudiu Keserü 1-0, 31' Marcelinho 2-0, 38' Kai Havertz 2-1, 63' I.K. Thelin 2-2, 69' Kai Havertz 2-3.
Referee: Paolo Mazzoleni (ITA)   Attendance: 8,240.

20.09.18   Neo GSP Stadium, Nicosia: AEK Larnaca – FC Zürich 0-1 (0-0)
AEK Larnaca: Toño, Mikel González, Daniel Mojsov, Thomas Ioannou, Igor Carioca (79' Jean Luc Assoubre), Ivan Trickovski, Jorge Larena (83' Facundo García), Acorán, Hector Hevel, Apostolos Giannou, Tete (64' Florian Taulemesse). Coach: Andoni Iraola.
FC Zürich: Yanick Brecher, Umaru Bangura, Pa Modou Jagne, Andreas Maxsø, Victor Pálsson, Antonio Marchesano (86' Alain Nef), Salim Khelifi (90+2' Adrian Winter), Hekuran Kryeziu, Benjamin Kololli, Kevin Rüegg, Stephen Odey (75' Assan Ceesay).
Coach: Ludovic Magnin.
Goal: 61' Benjamin Kololli 0-1 (p).
Referee: Jonathan Lardot (BEL)   Attendance: 3,173.
Sent off: 84' Pa Modou Jagne.

(AEK Larnaca played their three home matches at Neo GSP Stadium, Nicosia, instead of their regular stadium AEK Arena – Georgios Karapatakis, Larnaca)

04.10.18   Stadion Letzigrund, Zürich: FC Zürich – PFC Ludogorets Razgrad 1-0 (0-0)
FC Zürich: Yanick Brecher, Alain Nef, Umaru Bangura, Andreas Maxsø, Marco Schönbächler (71' Roberto Rodríguez), Victor Pálsson, Hekuran Kryeziu, Benjamin Kololli, Kevin Rüegg, Toni Domgjoni, Stephen Odey (82' Assan Ceesay). Coach: Ludovic Magnin.
PFC Ludogorets Razgrad: Renan, Cosmin Moti, Cicinho, Anton Nedyalkov, Svetoslav Dyakov (70' Jacek Góralski), Gustavo Campanharo, Wanderson, Natanael Pimienta, Marcelinho (79' May Mahlangu), Jody Lukoki, Juninho Brandão (71' Jakub Swierczok). Coach: Paulo Autuori.
Goal: 84' Victor Pálsson 1-0.
Referee: Juan Martínez Munuera (ESP)   Attendance: 7,092.

04.10.18   BayArena, Leverkusen: Bayer Leverkusen – AEK Larnaca 4-2 (1-1)
Bayer Leverkusen: Lukás Hrádecky, Sven Bender, Aleksandar Dragovic, Mitchell Weiser, Wendell, Lars Bender, Karim Bellarabi, Dominik Kohr (83' Tin Jedvaj), Kai Havertz (70' Julian Brandt), Kevin Volland, Leon Bailey (46' Lucas Alario). Coach: Heiko Herrlich.
AEK Larnaca: Toño, Mikel González, Daniel Mojsov, Truyols, Igor Carioca, Ivan Trickovski, Acorán, Nacho Cases (82' Jean Luc Assoubre), Joan Tomás (67' Tete), Hector Hevel, Apostolos Giannou (89' Dimitris Raspas). Coach: Andoni Iraola.
Goals: 25' Ivan Trickovski 0-1, 44' Kai Havertz 1-1, 49', 88' Lucas Alario 2-1, 3-1, 90+1' Dimitris Raspas 3-2, 90+2' Julian Brandt 4-2.
Referee: Evgen Aranovskiy (UKR)   Attendance: 23,354.

25.10.18   Stadion Letzigrund, Zürich: FC Zürich – Bayer Leverkusen 3-2 (1-0)
FC Zürich: Yanick Brecher, Umaru Bangura, Pa Modou Jagne, Andreas Maxsø, Adrian Winter (58' Salim Khelifi), Antonio Marchesano (89' Alain Nef), Hekuran Kryeziu, Benjamin Kololli (79' Roberto Rodríguez), Kevin Rüegg, Toni Domgjoni, Stephen Odey.
Coach: Ludovic Magnin.
Bayer Leverkusen: Lukás Hrádecky, Sven Bender, Aleksandar Dragovic (46' Mitchell Weiser), Wendell, Tin Jedvaj, Lars Bender, Karim Bellarabi, Dominik Kohr, Kai Havertz, Isaac Kiese Thelin (46' Kevin Volland), Leon Bailey (79' Julian Brandt).
Coach: Heiko Herrlich.
Goals: 44' Antonio Marchesano 1-0, 50', 54' Karim Bellarabi 1-1, 1-2, 59' Toni Domgjoni 2-2, 78' Stephen Odey 3-2.
Referee: Äliyar Agayev (AZE)   Attendance: 12,427.

25.10.18   Neo GSP Stadium, Nicosia: AEK Larnaca – PFC Ludogorets Razgrad 1-1 (1-1)
AEK Larnaca: Toño, Mikel González, Catalá, Truyols (72' Acorán), Thomas Ioannou, Igor Carioca, Ivan Trickovski, Jorge Larena, Hector Hevel, Apostolos Giannou (63' Florian Taulemesse), Tete (83' Jean Luc Assoubre). Coach: Andoni Iraola.
PFC Ludogorets Razgrad: Renan, Cosmin Moti, Cicinho, Anton Nedyalkov, Svetoslav Dyakov (81' May Mahlangu), Gustavo Campanharo (62' Jacek Góralski), Wanderson, Natanael Pimienta, Claudiu Keserü (84' Jakub Swierczok), Marcelinho, Jody Lukoki.
Coach: Antoni Zdravkov.
Goals: 7' Jody Lukoki 0-1, 25' Jorge Larena 1-1 (p).
Referee: Enea Jorgji (ALB)   Attendance: 2,631.

08.11.18   BayArena, Leverkusen: Bayer Leverkusen – FC Zürich 1-0 (0-0)
Bayer Leverkusen: Lukás Hrádecky, Aleksandar Dragovic, Mitchell Weiser, Wendell (74' Lars Bender), Tin Jedvaj, Charles Aránguiz (62' Paulinho), Julian Baumgartlinger, Dominik Kohr, Lucas Alario, Julian Brandt (62' Isaac Kiese Thelin), Leon Bailey. Coach: Heiko Herrlich.
FC Zürich: Yanick Brecher, Alain Nef, Umaru Bangura, Andreas Maxsø, Antonio Marchesano (69' Assan Ceesay), Salim Khelifi (55' Victor Pálsson), Hekuran Kryeziu, Benjamin Kololli, Kevin Rüegg, Toni Domgjoni, Stephen Odey. Coach: Ludovic Magnin.
Goal: 60' Tin Jedvaj 1-0.
Referee: Pawel Gil (POL)   Attendance: 16,179.

08.11.18   Ludogorets Arena, Razgrad: PFC Ludogorets Razgrad – AEK Larnaca 0-0
PFC Ludogorets Razgrad: Renan, Cosmin Moti, Cicinho, Anton Nedyalkov, Svetoslav Dyakov (66' Lucas Sasha), Gustavo Campanharo, Wanderson, Natanael Pimienta, Claudiu Keserü (76' Jakub Swierczok), Marcelinho, Jody Lukoki (86' João Paulo). Coach: Antoni Zdravkov.
AEK Larnaca: Toño, Mikel González, Catalá, Thomas Ioannou, Igor Carioca, Ivan Trickovski (87' Konstantinos Konstantinou), Acorán (81' Florian Taulemesse), Hector Hevel, Facundo García, Apostolos Giannou, Jean Luc Assoubre (71' Tete). Coach: Andoni Iraola.
Referee: Ola Hobber Nilsen (NOR)   Attendance: 4,520.

29.11.18   Stadion Letzigrund, Zürich: FC Zürich – AEK Larnaca 1-2 (0-1)
FC Zürich: Yanick Brecher, Alain Nef, Umaru Bangura, Mirlind Kryeziu, Roberto Rodríguez (73' Adrian Winter), Victor Pálsson, Antonio Marchesano (46' Bledian Krasniqi), Salim Khelifi, Fabio Dixon, Toni Domgjoni (88' Simon Sohm), Stephen Odey.
Coach: Ludovic Magnin.
AEK Larnaca: Toño, Mikel González, Truyols, Thomas Ioannou, Igor Carioca, Jorge Larena (84' Joan Tomás), Acorán (77' Jean Luc Assoubre), Hector Hevel, Facundo García, Apostolos Giannou, Florian Taulemesse (65' Ivan Trickovski). Coach: Andoni Iraola.
Goals: 38' Apostolos Giannou 0-1, 74' Salim Khelifi 1-1, 85' Ivan Trickovski 1-2.
Referee: Aleksey Eskov (RUS)   Attendance: 6,107.

29.11.18   BayArena, Leverkusen: Bayer Leverkusen – PFC Ludogorets Razgrad 1-1 (0-0)
Bayer Leverkusen: Ramazan Özcan, Aleksandar Dragovic, Mitchell Weiser, Wendell, Panagiotis Retsos (34' Julian Baumgartlinger), Charles Aránguiz (63' Lars Bender), Sam Schreck (73' Kai Havertz), Isaac Kiese Thelin, Lucas Alario, Leon Bailey, Paulinho.
Coach: Heiko Herrlich.
PFC Ludogorets Razgrad: Renan, Cosmin Moti, Cicinho, Georgi Terziev, Rafael Forster, Svetoslav Dyakov, Lucas Sasha (89' Dimo Bakalov), Wanderson, Jacek Góralski, João Paulo (63' Marcelinho), Jakub Swierczok (82' Anton Nedyalkov). Coach: Antoni Zdravkov.
Goals: 69' Marcelinho 0-1, 85' Mitchell Weiser 1-1.
Referee: Dennis Higler (HOL)   Attendance: 16,066.

13.12.18   Neo GSP Stadium, Nicosia: AEK Larnaca – Bayer Leverkusen 1-5 (1-2)
AEK Larnaca: Andreas Christodoulou, Català, Truyols, Thomas Ioannou, Igor Carioca, Acorán, Nacho Cases (46' Hector Hevel), Joan Tomás, Facundo García, Apostolos Giannou (84' Konstantinos Konstantinou), Tete (58' Ivan Trickovski). Coach: Andoni Iraola.
Bayer Leverkusen: Thorsten Kirschbaum, Aleksandar Dragovic, Mitchell Weiser, Wendell (82' Jakub Bednarczyk), Julian Baumgartlinger, Dominik Kohr, Sam Schreck, Isaac Kiese Thelin, Lucas Alario (88' Adrian Stanilewicz), Julian Brandt (46' Leon Bailey), Paulinho.
Coach: Heiko Herrlich.
Goals: 26' Català 1-0, 28' Dominik Kohr 1-1, 41' Lucas Alario 1-2 (p), 68' Dominik Kohr 1-3. 78' Paulinho 1-4, 86' Lucas Alario 1-5.
Referee: François Letexier (FRA)   Attendance: 1,584.

13.12.18   Ludogorets Arena, Razgrad: PFC Ludogorets Razgrad – FC Zürich 1-1 (1-1)
PFC Ludogorets Razgrad: Jorge Broun, Cicinho, Georgi Terziev, Rafael Forster, Anton Nedyalkov, Svetoslav Dyakov (82' Lucas Sasha), Wanderson (87' Dimo Bakalov), Natanael Pimienta, Jacek Góralski, Marcelinho, Jakub Swierczok (72' Claudiu Keserü).
Coach: Antoni Zdravkov.
FC Zürich: Andris Vanins, Umaru Bangura, Mirlind Kryeziu, Hakim Guenouche, Adrian Winter, Victor Pálsson, Salim Khelifi, Benjamin Kololli (76' Roberto Rodríguez), Fabio Dixon (46' Bledian Krasniqi), Toni Domgjoni, Stephen Odey (90' Alain Nef).
Coach: Ludovic Magnin.
Goals: 21' Rafael Forster 0-1 (og), 45+1' Jakub Swierczok 1-1.
Referee: Kirill Levnikov (RUS)   Attendance: 2,150.

GROUP B

20.09.18   Red Bull Arena, Leipzig: RB Leipzig – Red Bull Salzburg 2-3 (0-2)
RB Leipzig: Yvon Mvogo, Nordi Mukiele (46' Marcel Halstenberg), Dayot Upamecano, Ibrahima Konaté, Stefan Ilsanker, Kevin Kampl, Marcel Sabitzer, Bruma (46' Diego Demme), Konrad Laimer, Jean-Kévin Augustin (46' Yussuf Poulsen), Matheus Cunha. Coach: Ralf Rangnick.
Red Bull Salzburg: Alexander Walke, Andreas Ulmer, Stefan Lainer, André Ramalho, Marin Pongracic, Reinhold Yabo (71' Takumi Minamino), Xaver Schlager (86' Zlatko Junuzovic), Diadié Samassékou, Amadou Haïdara, Munas Dabour (84' Fredrik Gulbrandsen), Hannes Wolf. Coach: Marco Rose.
Goals: 20' Munas Dabour 0-1, 22' Amadou Haïdara 0-2, 70' Konrad Laimer 1-2, 82' Yussuf Poulsen 2-2, 89' Fredrik Gulbrandsen 2-3.
Referee: Andreas Ekberg (SWE)   Attendance: 24,057.

20.09.18   Celtic Park, Glasgow: Celtic FC – Rosenborg BK 1-0 (0-0)
Celtic FC: Craig Gordon, Mikael Lustig, Dedryck Boyata, Filip Benkovic, Kieran Tierney, Scott Brown, James Forrest (58' Michael Johnston), Callum McGregor, Tom Rogic (58' Scott Sinclair), Olivier Ntcham, Odsonne Édouard (76' Leigh Griffiths). Coach: Brendan Rodgers.
Rosenborg BK: André Hansen, Tore Reginiussen, Even Hovland, Vegar Hedenstad, Birger Meling, Mike Jensen, Anders Konradsen (45+1' Marius Lundemo), Djordje Denic, Alexander Søderlund (78' Jonathan Levi), Issam Jebali, Yann-Erik de Lanlay (69' Anders Trondsen). Coach: Rini Coolen.
Goal: 87' Leigh Griffiths 1-0.
Referee: Pawel Gil (POL)   Attendance: 47,287.

04.10.18   Lerkendal Stadion, Trondheim: Rosenborg BK – RB Leipzig 1-3 (0-1)
Rosenborg BK: André Hansen, Tore Reginiussen, Even Hovland, Vegar Hedenstad (62' Erlend Reitan), Alex Gersbach, Mike Jensen, Anders Konradsen, Djordje Denic (77' Matthías Vilhjálmsson), Alexander Søderlund, Yann-Erik de Lanlay (68' Issam Jebali), Jonathan Levi. Coach: Rini Coolen.
RB Leipzig: Yvon Mvogo, Marcel Halstenberg (74' Marcelo Saracchi), Willi Orban, Nordi Mukiele (80' Marcel Sabitzer), Ibrahima Konaté, Stefan Ilsanker, Diego Demme (64' Lukas Klostermann), Bruma, Konrad Laimer, Jean-Kévin Augustin, Matheus Cunha. Coach: Ralf Rangnick.
Goals: 12' Jean-Kévin Augustin 0-1, 54' Ibrahima Konaté 0-2, 61' Matheus Cunha 0-3, 79' Issam Jebali 1-3.
Referee: Marco Guida (ITA)   Attendance: 11,484.

04.10.18   Red Bull Arena, Salzburg: Red Bull Salzburg – Celtic FC 3-1 (0-1)
Red Bull Salzburg: Alexander Walke, Andreas Ulmer, Stefan Lainer, André Ramalho, Marin Pongracic, Xaver Schlager, Diadié Samassékou, Amadou Haïdara, Munas Dabour (85' Reinhold Yabo), Takumi Minamino (71' Zlatko Junuzovic), Hannes Wolf (79' Fredrik Gulbrandsen). Coach: Marco Rose.
Celtic FC: Craig Gordon, Mikael Lustig, Dedryck Boyata, Kieran Tierney, Jack Hendry, Youssuf Mulumbu (78' Ryan Christie), James Forrest, Callum McGregor, Olivier Ntcham, Leigh Griffiths (60' Scott Sinclair), Odsonne Édouard (82' Lewis Morgan).
Coach: Brendan Rodgers.
Goals: 2' Odsonne Édouard 0-1, 55' Munas Dabour 1-1, 61' Takumi Minamino 2-1, 73' Munas Dabour 3-1 (p).
Referee: Sergey Boyko (UKR)   Attendance: 24,085.
Sent off: 72' James Forrest.

25.10.18   Red Bull Arena, Salzburg: Red Bull Salzburg – Rosenborg BK 3-0 (1-0)
Red Bull Salzburg: Alexander Walke, Andreas Ulmer, Stefan Lainer, André Ramalho, Marin Pongracic, Zlatko Junuzovic, Diadié Samassékou (75' Xaver Schlager), Amadou Haïdara, Fredrik Gulbrandsen, Munas Dabour (72' Smail Prevljak), Hannes Wolf (82' Takumi Minamino). Coach: Marco Rose.
Rosenborg BK: André Hansen, Even Hovland, Vegar Hedenstad, Alex Gersbach, Besim Serbecic, Mike Jensen (71' Djordje Denic), Anders Konradsen, Marius Lundemo, Nicklas Bendtner (56' Matthías Vilhjálmsson), Yann-Erik de Lanlay (66' Samuel Adegbenro), Jonathan Levi. Coach: Rini Coolen.
Goals: 34' Munas Dabour 1-0, 53' Hannes Wolf 2-0, 59' Munas Dabour 3-0 (p).
Referee: Irfan Peljto (BIH)   Attendance: 20,639.

25.10.18   Red Bull Arena, Leipzig: RB Leipzig – Celtic FC 2-0 (2-0)
RB Leipzig: Yvon Mvogo, Willi Orban, Lukas Klostermann, Dayot Upamecano, Kevin Kampl (84' Erik Majetschak), Marcel Sabitzer (61' Stefan Ilsanker), Bruma, Konrad Laimer, Marcelo Saracchi, Jean-Kévin Augustin (90+1' Yussuf Poulsen), Matheus Cunha.
Coach: Ralf Rangnick.
Celtic FC: Craig Gordon, Cristian Gamboa (46' Mikael Lustig), Dedryck Boyata, Jozo Simunovic (75' Jack Hendry), Kieran Tierney, Callum McGregor, Olivier Ntcham, Ryan Christie, Lewis Morgan (71' Scott Sinclair), Kouassi Eboue, Odsonne Édouard.
Coach: Brendan Rodgers.
Goals: 31' Matheus Cunha 1-0, 35' Bruma 2-0.
Referee: Pavel Královec (CZE)   Attendance: 38,126.

08.11.18   Lerkendal Stadion, Trondheim: Rosenborg BK – Red Bull Salzburg 2-5 (0-4)
Rosenborg BK: André Hansen, Even Hovland, Birger Meling, Besim Serbecic, Erlend Reitan, Mike Jensen, Anders Konradsen, Djordje Denic (85' Matthías Vilhjálmsson), Nicklas Bendtner, Alexander Søderlund (46' Marius Lundemo), Samuel Adegbenro (75' Jonathan Levi). Coach: Rini Coolen.
Red Bull Salzburg: Alexander Walke, Andreas Ulmer, Stefan Lainer, André Ramalho, Jérôme Onguéné, Xaver Schlager (89' Christoph Leitgeb), Diadié Samassékou, Amadou Haïdara, Fredrik Gulbrandsen (85' Smail Prevljak), Munas Dabour, Takumi Minamino (78' Hannes Wolf). Coach: Marco Rose.
Goals: 6', 19' Takumi Minamino 0-1, 0-2, 37' Fredrik Gulbrandsen 0-3, 45' Takumi Minamino 0-4, 52' Samuel Adegbenro 1-4, 57' Even Hovland 1-5 (og), 62' Mike Jensen 2-5.
Referee: Aleksey Eskov (RUS)   Attendance: 12,386.

08.11.18   Celtic Park, Glasgow: Celtic FC – RB Leipzig 2-1 (1-0)
Celtic FC: Craig Gordon, Mikael Lustig, Dedryck Boyata, Filip Benkovic, Kieran Tierney, Scott Sinclair (90' Kristoffer Ajer), James Forrest (83' Youssuf Mulumbu), Callum McGregor, Tom Rogic, Ryan Christie, Odsonne Édouard. Coach: Brendan Rodgers.
RB Leipzig: Yvon Mvogo, Willi Orban, Nordi Mukiele (70' Diego Demme), Dayot Upamecano, Stefan Ilsanker (46' Kevin Kampl), Marcel Sabitzer, Bruma, Konrad Laimer, Marcelo Saracchi (16' Marcel Halstenberg), Jean-Kévin Augustin, Matheus Cunha. Coach: Ralf Rangnick.
Goals: 11' Kieran Tierney 1-0, 78' Jean-Kévin Augustin 1-1, 79' Odsonne Édouard 2-1.
Referee: Xavier Estrada Fernández (ESP)   Attendance: 56,027.

29.11.18   Red Bull Arena, Salzburg: Red Bull Salzburg – RB Leipzig 1-0 (0-0)
Red Bull Salzburg: Alexander Walke, Andreas Ulmer, Stefan Lainer, André Ramalho, Marin Pongracic, Zlatko Junuzovic, Xaver Schlager, Diadié Samassékou, Fredrik Gulbrandsen (76' Takumi Minamino), Munas Dabour (90+2' Smail Prevljak), Hannes Wolf (87' Patson Daka). Coach: Marco Rose.
RB Leipzig: Yvon Mvogo, Willi Orban, Nordi Mukiele (70' Lukas Klostermann), Dayot Upamecano, Stefan Ilsanker, Bruma, Konrad Laimer, Marcelo Saracchi (78' Marcel Halstenberg), Timo Werner, Jean-Kévin Augustin (62' Yussuf Poulsen), Matheus Cunha. Coach: Ralf Rangnick.
Goal: 74' Fredrik Gulbrandsen 1-0.
Referee: Orel Grinfeld (ISR)   Attendance: 29,520.

29.11.18   Lerkendal Stadion, Trondheim: Rosenborg BK – Celtic FC 0-1 (0-1)
Rosenborg BK: André Hansen, Tore Reginiussen, Even Hovland, Vegar Hedenstad, Birger Meling, Mike Jensen, Anders Konradsen (45+1' Djordje Denic), Anders Trondsen (66' Matthías Vilhjálmsson), Nicklas Bendtner, Yann-Erik de Lanlay, Samuel Adegbenro (78' Jonathan Levi). Coach: Rini Coolen.
Celtic FC: Craig Gordon, Mikael Lustig (66' Cristian Gamboa), Dedryck Boyata, Filip Benkovic, Kieran Tierney, Scott Sinclair, James Forrest (77' Scott Brown), Callum McGregor, Tom Rogic, Ryan Christie, Odsonne Édouard (66' Leigh Griffiths). Coach: Brendan Rodgers.
Goal: 42' Scott Sinclair 0-1.
Referee: Halis Özkahya (TUR)   Attendance: 14,061.

13.12.18   Red Bull Arena, Leipzig: RB Leipzig – Rosenborg BK 1-1 (0-0)
RB Leipzig: Yvon Mvogo, Willi Orban, Nordi Mukiele (81' Lukas Klostermann), Ibrahima Konaté, Stefan Ilsanker, Kevin Kampl (69' Marcel Sabitzer), Bruma, Konrad Laimer, Marcelo Saracchi, Jean-Kévin Augustin (46' Yussuf Poulsen), Matheus Cunha. Coach: Ralf Rangnick.
Rosenborg BK: André Hansen, Tore Reginiussen, Even Hovland, Birger Meling, Erlend Reitan, Mike Jensen, Anders Konradsen, Anders Trondsen (75' Djordje Denic), Matthías Vilhjálmsson (83' Erik Botheim), Issam Jebali (68' Pål Helland), Samuel Adegbenro. Coach: Rini Coolen.
Goals: 47' Matheus Cunha 1-0, 86' Tore Reginiussen 1-1.
Referee: Sergey Boyko (UKR)   Attendance: 16,957.

13.12.18   Celtic Park, Glasgow: Celtic FC – Red Bull Salzburg 1-2 (0-0)
Celtic FC: Craig Gordon, Mikael Lustig (21' Kristoffer Ajer), Jozo Simunovic, Filip Benkovic, Kieran Tierney, Scott Sinclair (46' Scott Brown), James Forrest, Callum McGregor, Tom Rogic, Ryan Christie (58' Olivier Ntcham), Odsonne Édouard. Coach: Brendan Rodgers.
Red Bull Salzburg: Alexander Walke, Andreas Ulmer, Stefan Lainer, André Ramalho, Jérôme Onguéné, Zlatko Junuzovic, Diadié Samassékou, Enock Mwepu (80' Christoph Leitgeb), Munas Dabour (90+1' Smail Prevljak), Takumi Minamino (74' Fredrik Gulbrandsen), Hannes Wolf. Coach: Marco Rose.
Goals: 67' Munas Dabour 0-1, 78' Fredrik Gulbrandsen 0-2, 90+5' Olivier Ntcham 1-2.
Referee: Ruddy Buquet (FRA)   Attendance: 57,578.

Olivier Ntcham missed a penalty kick (90+5').

GROUP C

20.09.18   Telia Parken, København: FC København – Zenit St. Petersburg 1-1 (0-1)
FC København: Jesse Joronen, Andreas Bjelland, Peter Ankersen, Nicolai Boilesen, Denis Vavro, Zeca, Viktor Fischer (90+3' Sotirios Papagiannopoulos), Nicolaj Thomsen (61' Rasmus Falk), Robert Skov, Dame N'Doye, Pieros Sotiriou (77' Ján Gregus). Coach: Ståle Solbakken.
Zenit St. Petersburg: Andrei Lunev, Branislav Ivanovic, Aleksandr Anyukov, Igor Smolnikov, Neto, Aleksandr Erokhin, Róbert Mak (58' Claudio Marchisio), Leandro Paredes, Daler Kuzyaev (89' Anton Zabolotny), Artem Dzyuba, Sebastián Driussi (79' Oleg Shatov). Coach: Sergey Semak.
Goals: 44' Róbert Mak 0-1, 63' Pieros Sotiriou 1-1.
Referee: Georgi Kabakov (BUL)   Attendance: 19,005.

20.09.18   Sinobo Stadium, Praha: Slavia Praha – Girondins de Bordeaux 1-0 (1-0)
Slavia Praha: Ondrej Kolár, Ondrej Kúdela, Jan Boril, Vladimír Coufal, Jaromír Husbauer, Miroslav Stoch (79' Alexandru Baluta), Michael Ngadeu-Ngadjui, Jaromír Zmrhal (83' Michal Frydrych), Tomás Soucek, Ibrahim Traoré (90+3' Jan Matousek), Stanislav Tecl.
Coach: Jindrich Trpisovsky.
Girondins de Bordeaux: Benoît Costil, Pablo Castro, Youssouf Sabaly, Sergi Palencia, Jules Koundé, Jaroslav Plasil (85' Otávio), Younousse Sankharé (70' Andreas Cornelius), Aurélien Tchouaméni, Jimmy Briand, François Kamano (60' Yann Karamoh), Samuel Kalu.
Coach: Éric Bedouet.
Goal: 35' Jaromír Zmrhal 1-0.
Referee: Bas Nijhuis (HOL)   Attendance: 16,548.

04.10.18   Stade Matmut-Atlantique, Bordeaux:
Girondins de Bordeaux – FC København 1-2 (0-1)
Girondins de Bordeaux: Benoît Costil, Pablo Castro, Maxime Poundjé, Sergi Palencia, Otávio, Jules Koundé, Younousse Sankharé, Lukas Lerager (78' Aurélien Tchouaméni), Jimmy Briand (62' Andreas Cornelius), François Kamano (63' Yann Karamoh), Samuel Kalu.
Coach: Éric Bedouet.
FC København: Stephan Andersen, Andreas Bjelland, Sotirios Papagiannopoulos (86' Denis Vavro), Peter Ankersen, Nicolai Boilesen, William Kvist (58' Robert Skov), Ján Gregus, Zeca, Nicolaj Thomsen (70' Rasmus Falk), Dame N'Doye, Pieros Sotiriou. Coach: Ståle Solbakken.
Goals: 42' Pieros Sotiriou 0-1, 84' Younousse Sankharé 1-1, 90+2' Robert Skov 1-2.
Referee: Roi Reinshreiber (ISR)   Attendance: 11,860.
Sent off: 90+3' Zeca.

François Kamano missed a penalty kick (45+4').

04.10.18   Krestovsky Stadium, St. Petersburg: Zenit St. Petersburg – Slavia Praha 1-0 (0-0)
Zenit St. Petersburg: Andrei Lunev, Branislav Ivanovic, Aleksandr Anyukov, Neto, Elmir Nabiullin (90+3' Anton Zabolotny), Aleksandr Erokhin, Róbert Mak (64' Daler Kuzyaev), Leandro Paredes, Matías Kranevitter, Artem Dzyuba, Sebastián Driussi (63' Aleksandr Kokorin). Coach: Sergey Semak.
Slavia Praha: Ondrej Kolár, Ondrej Kúdela, Jan Boril, Vladimír Coufal (83' Michal Frydrych), Josef Husbauer, Miroslav Stoch, Michael Ngadeu-Ngadjui, Jaromír Zmrhal, Tomás Soucek, Ibrahim Traoré (90' Simon Deli), Jan Matousek (53' Alexandru Baluta).
Coach: Jindrich Trpisovsky.
Goal: 80' Aleksandr Kokorin 1-0.
Referee: Hüseyin Göçek (TUR)   Attendance: 45,408.

25.10.18   Krestovsky Stadium, St. Petersburg:
Zenit St. Petersburg – Girondins de Bordeaux 2-1 (1-1)
Zenit St. Petersburg: Andrei Lunev, Branislav Ivanovic, Neto, Elmir Nabiullin, Emanuel Mammana, Aleksandr Erokhin, Róbert Mak (76' Oleg Shatov), Leandro Paredes, Daler Kuzyaev, Artem Dzyuba (86' Anton Zabolotny), Sebastián Driussi (88' Magomed Ozdoev). Coach: Sergey Semak.
Girondins de Bordeaux: Benoît Costil, Igor Lewczuk, Pablo Castro, Maxime Poundjé, Otávio, Jules Koundé, Younousse Sankharé, Aurélien Tchouaméni, Jimmy Briand (79' Nicolas de Préville), Yann Karamoh (67' Zaydou Youssouf), Samuel Kalu. Coach: Éric Bedouet.
Goals: 26' Jimmy Briand 0-1, 41' Artem Dzyuba 1-1, 85' Daler Kuzyaev 2-1.
Referee: Dr. Felix Brych (GER)   Attendance: 45,723.

Artem Dzyuba missed a penalty kick (53').

25.10.18   Telia Parken, København: FC København – Slavia Praha 0-1 (0-0)
FC København: Stephan Andersen, Pierre Bengtsson, Andreas Bjelland, Sotirios Papagiannopoulos, Peter Ankersen, Ján Gregus, Rasmus Falk (84' Denis Vavro), Viktor Fischer (71' Carlo Holse), Robert Skov (84' Kenan Kodro), Dame N'Doye, Pieros Sotiriou.
Coach: Ståle Solbakken.
Slavia Praha: Ondrej Kolár, Ondrej Kúdela, Jan Boril, Vladimír Coufal, Josef Husbauer (90+1' Simon Deli), Miroslav Stoch (86' Michal Frydrych), Michael Ngadeu-Ngadjui, Jaromír Zmrhal, Tomás Soucek, Ibrahim Traoré, Jan Matousek (72' Stanislav Tecl).
Coach: Jindrich Trpisovsky.
Goal: 46' Jan Matousek 0-1.
Referee: Luca Banti (ITA)   Attendance: 20,672.

08.11.18   Stade Matmut-Atlantique, Bordeaux:
              Girondins de Bordeaux – Zenit St. Petersburg 1-1 (1-0)
Girondins de Bordeaux: Benoît Costil, Pablo Castro, Youssouf Sabaly, Maxime Poundjé, Vukasin Jovanovic, Jaroslav Plasil (84' Nicolas de Préville), Younousse Sankharé, Lukas Lerager, Andreas Cornelius (46' Jimmy Briand), François Kamano (67' Yann Karamoh), Samuel Kalu. Coach: Éric Bedouet.
Zenit St. Petersburg: Andrei Lunev, Aleksandr Anyukov (60' Róbert Mak), Neto, Miha Mevlja, Elmir Nabiullin, Emanuel Mammana, Claudio Marchisio, Aleksandr Erokhin (65' Daler Kuzyaev), Leandro Paredes, Anton Zabolotny, Sebastián Driussi (78' Oleg Shatov). Coach: Sergey Semak.
Goals: 35' François Kamano 1-0 (p), 72' Anton Zabolotny 1-1.
Referee: Harald Lechner (AUT)   Attendance: 8,907.

08.11.18   Sinobo Stadium, Praha: Slavia Praha – FC København 0-0
Slavia Praha: Ondrej Kolár, Michal Frydrych, Jan Boril, Simon Deli, Miroslav Stoch, Jan Sykora (79' Alexandru Baluta), Michael Ngadeu-Ngadjui, Jaromír Zmrhal (79' Milan Skoda), Tomás Soucek, Ibrahim Traoré, Peter Olayinka. Coach: Jindrich Trpisovsky.
FC København: Stephan Andersen, Andreas Bjelland, Peter Ankersen, Nicolai Boilesen (35' Pierre Bengtsson), Denis Vavro, Ján Gregus, Rasmus Falk (79' Jonas Wind), Zeca, Robert Skov (64' Nicolaj Thomsen), Dame N'Doye, Pieros Sotiriou. Coach: Ståle Solbakken.
Referee: Mattias Gestranius (FIN)   Attendance: 18,702.

29.11.18   Krestovsky Stadium, St. Petersburg:
              Zenit St. Petersburg – FC København 1-0 (0-0)
Zenit St. Petersburg: Andrei Lunev, Branislav Ivanovic, Aleksandr Anyukov, Miha Mevlja, Aleksandr Erokhin (74' Claudio Marchisio), Róbert Mak, Leandro Paredes, Hernani (88' Magomed Ozdoev), Daler Kuzyaev, Artem Dzyuba, Sebastián Driussi (60' Anton Zabolotny). Coach: Sergey Semak.
FC København: Stephan Andersen, Pierre Bengtsson, Andreas Bjelland, Peter Ankersen, Denis Vavro (54' Sotirios Papagiannopoulos), Ján Gregus, Zeca, Robert Skov (78' Jonas Wind), Dame N'Doye, Pieros Sotiriou, Carlo Holse (60' Rasmus Falk). Coach: Ståle Solbakken.
Goal: 59' Róbert Mak 1-0.
Referee: Slavko Vincic (SVN)   Attendance: 45,199.

29.11.18   Stade Matmut-Atlantique, Bordeaux:
              Girondins de Bordeaux – Slavia Praha 2-0 (0-0)
Girondins de Bordeaux: Benoît Costil, Pablo Castro, Youssouf Sabaly, Sergi Palencia, Jules Koundé, Lukas Lerager, Aurélien Tchouaméni, Zaydou Youssouf (76' Younousse Sankharé), Nicolas de Préville (71' François Kamano), Andreas Cornelius, Samuel Kalu (81' Yann Karamoh). Coach: Éric Bedouet.
Slavia Praha: Ondrej Kolár, Jan Boril, Vladimír Coufal, Simon Deli, Josef Husbauer, Miroslav Stoch (77' Milan Skoda), Michael Ngadeu-Ngadjui, Jaromír Zmrhal, Tomás Soucek, Ibrahim Traoré (46' Jan Sykora), Jan Matousek (51' Peter Olayinka). Coach: Jindrich Trpisovsky.
Goals: 49' Nicolas de Préville 1-0, 90+5' Jules Koundé 2-0.
Referee: Fábio Veríssimo (POR)   Attendance: 6,311.

13.12.18 Telia Parken, København: FC København – Girondins de Bordeaux 0-1 (0-0)
FC København: Stephan Andersen, Andreas Bjelland (9' Sotirios Papagiannopoulos), Peter Ankersen, Nicolai Boilesen (62' Pierre Bengtsson), Denis Vavro, Rasmus Falk (73' Ján Gregus), Zeca, Nicolaj Thomsen, Robert Skov, Dame N'Doye, Pieros Sotiriou.
Coach: Ståle Solbakken.
Girondins de Bordeaux: Benoît Costil, Pablo Castro, Youssouf Sabaly, Maxime Poundjé, Otávio, Jules Koundé, Jaroslav Plasil, Lukas Lerager, Jimmy Briand, Nicolas de Préville (61' François Kamano), Andreas Cornelius (60' Yann Karamoh). Coach: Éric Bedouet.
Goal: 73' Jimmy Briand 0-1.
Referee: Hüseyin Göçek (TUR)   Attendance: 18,209.

13.12.18 Sinobo Stadium, Praha: Slavia Praha – Zenit St. Petersburg 2-0 (2-0)
Slavia Praha: Ondrej Kolár, Ondrej Kúdela, Jaroslav Zeleny (90+2' Alexandru Baluta), Vladimír Coufal, Josef Husbauer, Miroslav Stoch (90' Michal Frydrych), Michael Ngadeu-Ngadjui, Jaromír Zmrhal, Tomás Soucek, Milan Skoda (85' Ibrahim Traoré), Peter Olayinka.
Coach: Jindrich Trpisovsky.
Zenit St. Petersburg: Mikhail Kerzhakov, Igor Smolnikov, Neto, Miha Mevlja, Elmir Nabiullin (46' Róbert Mak), Emanuel Mammana, Claudio Marchisio, Oleg Shatov (73' Daler Kuzyaev), Hernani, Matías Kranevitter, Anton Zabolotny (46' Sebastián Driussi). Coach: Sergey Semak.
Goals: 32' Jaromír Zmrhal 1-0, 41' Miroslav Stoch 2-0.
Referee: Andrew Dallas (SCO)   Attendance: 17,748.

GROUP D

20.09.18 City Arena Trnanva, Trnava: FC Spartak Trnava – RSC Anderlecht 1-0 (0-0)
FC Spartak Trnava: Martin Chudy, Martin Tóth, Matús Conka (51' Jirí Kulhánek), Boris Godál, Andrej Kadlec, Matej Oravec, Erik Grendel, Jakub Rada, Vakhtang Chanturishvili, Erik Jirka (64' Patryk Malecki), Marek Bakos (87' Oliver Janso). Coach: Radoslav Látal.
RSC Anderlecht: Thomas Didillon, Ognjen Vranjes, Andy Najar (65' Kenny Saief), Antonio Milic, Bubacarr Sanneh, Sven Kums, Knowlegde Musona (83' Evgen Makarenko), Adrien Trebel, Ivan Santini, Landry Nany Dimata (83' Pieter Gerkens), Francis Amuzu.
Coach: Hein Vanhaezebrouck.
Goal: 79' Matej Oravec 1-0.
Referee: Kevin Clancy (SCO)   Attendance: 17,114.

20.09.18 Stadion Maksimir, Zagreb: Dinamo Zagreb – Fenerbahçe 4-1 (2-0)
Dinamo Zagreb: Dominik Livakovic, Kévin Théophile-Catherine, Emir Dilaver, Petar Stojanovic, Amir Rrahmani, Ivan Sunjic, Amer Gojak, Daniel Olmo, Mario Gavranovic (85' Mario Budimir), Mislav Orsic (76' Damian Kadzior), Izet Hajrovic (82' Tongo Doumbia).
Coach: Nenad Bjelica.
Fenerbahçe: Harun Tekin, Roman Neustädter, Ismail Köybasi, Diego Reyes, Sener Özbayrakli, Mehmet Topal, Alper Potuk (80' Islam Slimani), Aatif Chahechouhe (65' Baris Ailici), Eljif Elmas, Michael Frey, Yassine Benzia (65' Jaílson). Coach: Phillip Cocu.
Goals: 16' Ivan Sunjic 1-0, 25' Izet Hajrovic 2-0, 47' Roman Neustädter 2-1,
57' Izet Hajrovic 3-1, 60' Daniel Olmo 4-1.
Referee: Craig Pawson (ENG)   Attendance: 17,303.

04.10.18   Ülker Stadyumu Fenerbahçe Sükrü Saracoglu Spor Kompleksi, Istanbul:
Fenerbahçe – FC Spartak Trnava 2-0 (0-0)
Fenerbahçe: Harun Tekin, Martin Skrtel, Mauricio Isla, Roman Neustädter, Hasan-Ali Kaldirim, Diego Reyes (76' Ismail Köybasi), Jaílson, Eljif Elmas, André Ayew (76' Mathieu Valbuena), Islam Slimani (88' Mehmet Topal), Michael Frey. Coach: Phillip Cocu.
FC Spartak Trnava: Martin Chudy, Martin Tóth (66' Ivan Hladík), Boris Godál, Andrej Kadlec, Matej Oravec, Erik Grendel (68' Ali Ghorbani), Jakub Rada, Lukáš Gressák, Vakhtang Chanturishvili, Erik Jirka (82' Fabian Miesenböck), Marek Bakos. Coach: Radoslav Látal.
Goals: 52', 69' Islam Slimani 1-0, 2-0.
Referee: Tobias Welz (GER)   Attendance: 29,622.

04.10.18   Stade Constant Vanden Stock, Bruxelles:
RSC Anderlecht – Dinamo Zagreb 0-2 (0-1)
RSC Anderlecht: Thomas Didillon, Ognjen Vranjes, Andy Najar (66' Kenny Saief), Antonio Milic, Bubacarr Sanneh, Evgen Makarenko, Adrien Trebel, Zakaria Bakkali (89' Ryota Morioka), Ivan Santini, Landry Nany Dimata (85' Jamie Lawrence), Francis Amuzu.
Coach: Hein Vanhaezebrouck.
Dinamo Zagreb: Dominik Livakovic, Kévin Théophile-Catherine, Emir Dilaver (46' Dino Peric), Petar Stojanovic, Amir Rrahmani, Arijan Ademi, Amer Gojak, Daniel Olmo, Mislav Orsic (90' Mario Gavranovic), Izet Hajrovic (76' Ivan Sunjic), Bruno Petkovic.
Coach: Nenad Bjelica.
Goals: 19' Izet Hajrovic 0-1 (p), 68' Amer Gojak 0-2.
Referee: Vladislav Bezborodov (RUS)   Attendance: 12,137.
Sent off: 46' Ognjen Vranjes, 90+3' Kévin Théophile-Catherine.

25.10.18   Stade Constant Vanden Stock, Bruxelles: RSC Anderlecht – Fenerbahçe 2-2 (1-0)
RSC Anderlecht: Thomas Didillon, Jamie Lawrence, Bubacarr Sanneh, Sebastiaan Bornauw, Alexis Saelemaekers (86' Andy Najar), Sven Kums, Adrien Trebel, Kenny Saief, Pieter Gerkens (86' Dauda Mohammed), Zakaria Bakkali, Ivan Santini.
Coach: Hein Vanhaezebrouck.
Fenerbahçe: Harun Tekin, Martin Skrtel, Mauricio Isla, Roman Neustädter, Hasan-Ali Kaldirim, Diego Reyes, Jaílson, Eljif Elmas (86' Alper Potuk), Islam Slimani (74' André Ayew), Michael Frey, Yassine Benzia (74' Oguz Güçtekin). Coach: Phillip Cocu.
Goals: 35', 50' Zakaria Bakkali 1-0, 2-0, 53' Michael Frey 2-1, 57' Hasan-Ali Kaldirim 2-2.
Referee: Georgi Kabakov (BUL)   Attendance: 13,292.

25.10.18   City Arena Trnanva, Trnava: FC Spartak Trnava – Dinamo Zagreb 1-2 (1-0)
FC Spartak Trnava: Martin Chudy, Martin Tóth, Matús Conka, Boris Godál, Matej Oravec, Erik Grendel, Jakub Rada (82' Davit Skhirtladze), Lukáš Gressák, Vakhtang Chanturishvili, Erik Jirka (70' Patryk Malecki), Ali Ghorbani. Coach: Radoslav Látal.
Dinamo Zagreb: Dominik Livakovic, Marko Leskovic, Petar Stojanovic, Amir Rrahmani, Dino Peric, Arijan Ademi, Amer Gojak, Daniel Olmo (86' Ivan Sunjic), Mario Gavranovic (88' Bruno Petkovic), Mislav Orsic, Izet Hajrovic (74' Damian Kadzior). Coach: Nenad Bjelica.
Goals: 32' Ali Ghorbani 1-0, 64' Mario Gavranovic 1-1, 77' Mislav Orsic 1-2.
Referee: Jakob Kehlet (DEN)

Match was played behind closed doors.

08.11.18 Ülker Stadyumu Fenerbahçe Sükrü Saracoglu Spor Kompleksi, Istanbul:
Fenerbahçe – RSC Anderlecht 2-0 (0-0)
Fenerbahçe: Harun Tekin, Martin Skrtel, Roman Neustädter, Hasan-Ali Kaldirim, Sener Özbayrakli, Mathieu Valbuena (82' Ismail Köybasi), Jaílson (88' Mauricio Isla), Eljif Elmas, André Ayew, Islam Slimani, Michael Frey. Coach: Erwin Koeman.
RSC Anderlecht: Thomas Didillon, Ognjen Vranjes, Antonio Milic, Sebastiaan Bornauw (46' Bubacarr Sanneh), Alexis Saelemaekers (77' Andy Najar), Sven Kums, Evgen Makarenko, Adrien Trebel (77' Albert-Mboyo Sambi Lokonga), Pieter Gerkens, Zakaria Bakkali, Landry Nany Dimata. Coach: Hein Vanhaezebrouck.
Goals: 71' Mathieu Valbuena 1-0, 74' Michael Frey 2-0.
Referee: Andreas Ekberg (SWE)   Attendance: 32,789.
Sent off: 79' Zakaria Bakkali.

08.11.18 Stadion Maksimir, Zagreb: Dinamo Zagreb – FC Spartak Trnava 3-1 (2-0)
Dinamo Zagreb: Dominik Livakovic, Kévin Théophile-Catherine, Petar Stojanovic, Amir Rrahmani, Dino Peric, Arijan Ademi, Amer Gojak, Daniel Olmo (90' Mario Budimir), Mario Gavranovic (77' Bruno Petkovic), Mislav Orsic (82' Ivan Sunjic), Izet Hajrovic.
Coach: Nenad Bjelica.
FC Spartak Trnava: Martin Chudy, Martin Tóth, Matús Conka, Boris Godál, Andrej Kadlec (86' Filip Dangubic), Jakub Rada, Lukás Gressák, Davit Skhirtladze (83' Jirí Kulhánek), Vakhtang Chanturishvili, Erik Jirka, Ali Ghorbani (71' Patryk Malecki).
Coach: Radoslav Látal.
Goals: 22' Amer Gojak 1-0, 36' Andrej Kadlec 2-0 (og), 63' Vakhtang Chanturishvili 2-1, 79' Mislav Orsic 3-1.
Referee: Sergey Boyko (UKR)   Attendance: 18,154.

29.11.18 Stade Constant Vanden Stock, Bruxelles: RSC Anderlecht – FC Spartak Trnava 0-0
RSC Anderlecht: Thomas Didillon, Dennis Appiah, Jamie Lawrence, Bubacarr Sanneh, Sebastiaan Bornauw, Knowlegde Musona (81' Francis Amuzu), Ryota Morioka (81' Yari Verschaeren), Evgen Makarenko (81' Albert-Mboyo Sambi Lokonga), Kenny Saief, Edo Kayembe, Dauda Mohammed. Coach: Hein Vanhaezebrouck.
FC Spartak Trnava: Martin Chudy, Martin Tóth, Matej Oravec, Patryk Malecki (90+3' Oliver Janso), Erik Grendel (90' Fabian Miesenböck), Lukás Gressák, Davit Skhirtladze, Vakhtang Chanturishvili, Erik Jirka, Jirí Kulhánek, Marek Bakos (60' Ali Ghorbani).
Coach: Radoslav Látal.
Referee: Anastasios Papapetrou (GRE)   Attendance: 8,063.

29.11.18 Ülker Stadyumu Fenerbahçe Sükrü Saracoglu Spor Kompleksi, Istanbul:
Fenerbahçe – Dinamo Zagreb 0-0
Fenerbahçe: Harun Tekin, Martin Skrtel, Mauricio Isla, Roman Neustädter, Hasan-Ali Kaldirim, Mathieu Valbuena, Baris Alici, Jaílson, Eljif Elmas, Michael Frey, Yassine Benzia. Coach: Erwin Koeman.
Dinamo Zagreb: Dominik Livakovic, Kévin Théophile-Catherine, Emir Dilaver, Petar Stojanovic, Amir Rrahmani, Arijan Ademi, Amer Gojak, Daniel Olmo, Mario Gavranovic (62' Bruno Petkovic), Mislav Orsic (64' Ivan Sunjic), Izet Hajrovic (90+1' Damian Kadzior).
Coach: Nenad Bjelica.
Referee: Robert Schörgenhofer (AUT)   Attendance: 24,776.

13.12.18   City Arena Trnanva, Trnava: FC Spartak Trnava – Fenerbahçe 1-0 (1-0)
FC Spartak Trnava: Martin Chudy, Martin Tóth (64' Jirí Kulhánek), Boris Godál, Matej Oravec, Erik Grendel (81' Fabian Miesenböck), Lukás Gressák, Davit Skhirtladze, Vakhtang Chanturishvili, Erik Jirka, Marek Bakos (75' Ali Ghorbani), Kubilay Yilmaz.
Coach: Radoslav Látal.
Fenerbahçe: Harun Tekin, Martin Skrtel, Mauricio Isla, Ismail Köybasi, Diego Reyes, Sener Özbayrakli, Yigithan Güveli (82' Deniz Yilmaz), Baris Alici, Jaílson, Mahsun Çapkan (73' Muhammet Çaki), Islam Slimani. Coach: Erwin Koeman.
Goal: 41' Kubilay Yilmaz 1-0.
Referee: José María Sánchez Martínez (ESP)   Attendance: 11,413.

13.12.18   Stadion Maksimir, Zagreb: Dinamo Zagreb – RSC Anderlecht 0-0
Dinamo Zagreb: Dominik Livakovic, Marin Leovac (46' Amir Rrahmani), Kévin Théophile-Catherine, Emir Dilaver, Petar Stojanovic, Ivan Sunjic, Amer Gojak, Daniel Olmo, Mario Gavranovic (65' Bruno Petkovic), Mislav Orsic (89' Mario Situm), Izet Hajrovic.
Coach: Nenad Bjelica.
RSC Anderlecht: Frank Boeckx, Dennis Appiah, Antonio Milic (71' Alexis Saelemaeckers), Bubacarr Sanneh, Sebastiaan Bornauw (63' Hannes Delcroix), Ryota Morioka, Kenny Saief (69' Francis Amuzu), Pieter Gerkens, Zakaria Bakkali, Edo Kayembe, Ivan Santini.
Coach: Hein Vanhaezebrouck.
Referee: Sandro Schärer (SUI)   Attendance: 12,170.

GROUP E

20.09.18   Estádio José Alvalade, Lisboa: Sporting CP – Qarabag FK 2-0 (0-0)
Sporting CP: Romain Salin, Jérémy Mathieu (75' André Pinto), Sebastián Coates, Stefan Ristovski, Nemanja Gudelj, Rodrigo Battaglia, Bruno Fernandes, Nani (87' Jovane Cabral), Fredy Montero (90+2' Abdoulay Diaby), Marcos Acuña, Raphinha. Coach: José Peseiro.
Qarabag FK: Vagner, Jakub Rzezniczak, Maksim Medvedev (62' Abbas Hüseynov), Badavi Hüseynov, Qara Qarayev, Filip Ozobic, Wilde Guerrier, Joshgun Diniyev (58' Míchel), Abdellah Zoubir (68' Araz Abdullayev), Innocent Emeghara, Mahir Madatov.
Coach: Gurban Gurbanov.
Goals: 54' Raphinha 1-0, 88' Jovane Cabral 2-0.
Referee: François Letexier (FRA)   Attendance: 30,098.

20.09.18   Emirates Stadium, London: Arsenal FC – Vorskla Poltava 4-2 (1-0)
Arsenal FC: Bernd Leno, Stephan Lichtsteiner, Nacho Monreal, Sokratis Papastathopoulos, Rob Holding, Henrikh Mkhitaryan, Mohamed El Neny, Alex Iwobi (70' Emile Smith Rowe), Lucas Torreira (57' Mattéo Guendouzi), Pierre-Emerick Aubameyang (57' Mesut Özil), Danny Welbeck. Coach: Unai Emery.
Vorskla Poltava: Bogdan Shust, Volodimir Chesnakov, Igor Perduta, Artur, Ardin Dallku, Aleksandr Kobakhidze (77' Mykhaylo Sergiychuk), Pavlo Rebenok, Vyacheslav Sharpar, Dmitro Kravchenko (70' Aleksandr Sklyar), Vladyslav Kulach (75' Nicolas Careca), Yuriy Kolomoyets. Coach: Vasil Sachko.
Goals: 32' Pierre-Emerick Aubameyang 1-0, 48' Danny Welbeck 2-0,
56' Pierre-Emerick Aubameyang 3-0, 74' Mesut Özil 4-0, 77' Volodimir Chesnakov 4-1,
90+3' Vyacheslav Sharpar 4-2.
Referee: Bart Vertenten (BEL)   Attendance: 59,039.

04.10.18 Stadion Vorskla im. Oleksiya Butov'skogo, Poltava:
Vorskla Poltava – Sporting CP 1-2 (1-0)
Vorskla Poltava: Bogdan Shust, Volodimir Chesnakov, Igor Perduta, Artur, Ardin Dallku, Pavlo Rebenok, Aleksandr Sklyar, Vyacheslav Sharpar, Dmitro Kravchenko (84' Artem Gabelyuk), Vladislav Kulach (62' Mykhaylo Sergiychuk), Yuriy Kolomoyets. Coach: Vasil Sachko.
Sporting CP: Romain Salin, Jefferson, André Pinto, Sebastián Coates, Bruno Gaspar, Radosav Petrovic (70' Jovane Cabral), Bruno Fernandes, Nani, Abdoulay Diaby (70' Raphinha), Carlos Mané (58' Fredy Montero), Marcos Acuña. Coach: José Peseiro.
Goals: 10' Vladislav Kulach 1-0, 90+1' Fredy Montero 1-1, 90+3' Jovane Cabral 1-2.
Referee: Nikola Dabanovic (MNE)   Attendance: 10,082.

04.10.18 Baki Olimpiya Stadionu, Baku: Qarabag FK – Arsenal FC 0-3 (0-1)
Qarabag FK: Vagner, Ansi Agolli, Jakub Rzezniczak, Maksim Medvedev, Badavi Hüseynov, Míchel, Qara Qarayev (84' Simeon Slavchev), Filip Ozobic (67' Araz Abdullayev), Abdellah Zoubir, Innocent Emeghara, Mahir Madatov (61' Dzon Delarge). Coach: Gurban Gurbanov.
Arsenal FC: Bernd Leno, Stephan Lichtsteiner, Nacho Monreal (46' Lucas Torreira), Sokratis Papastathopoulos, Sead Kolasinac, Rob Holding, Mohamed El Neny, Alex Iwobi (71' Alexandre Lacazette), Mattéo Guendouzi, Emile Smith Rowe (65' Mesut Özil), Danny Welbeck. Coach: Unai Emery.
Goals: 4' Sokratis Papastathopoulos 0-1, 53' Emile Smith Rowe 0-2, 80' Mattéo Guendouzi 0-3.
Referee: Davide Massa (ITA)   Attendance: 63,412.

(Qarabag FK played their three home matches at Baki Olimpiya Stadionu, Baku, instead of their regular stadium Azersun Arena, Baku)

25.10.18 Baki Olimpiya Stadionu, Baku: Qarabag FK – Vorskla Poltava 0-1 (0-0)
Qarabag FK: Vagner, Rashad Sadygov, Jakub Rzezniczak, Maksim Medvedev, Míchel, Araz Abdullayev (69' Dzon Delarge), Qara Qarayev, Simeon Slavchev (58' Filip Ozobic), Wilde Guerrier, Abdellah Zoubir, Innocent Emeghara (58' Mahir Madatov).
Coach: Gurban Gurbanov.
Vorskla Poltava: Bogdan Shust, Vadim Sapay, Volodimir Chesnakov, Igor Perduta, Ardin Dallku, Najeeb Yakubu (46' Nicolas Careca), Pavlo Rebenok, Aleksandr Sklyar, Vyacheslav Sharpar, Vladislav Kulach (77' Mykhaylo Sergiychuk, 90+2' Oleksandr Chizhov), Yuriy Kolomoyets. Coach: Vasil Sachko.
Goal: 48' Vladislav Kulach 0-1.
Referee: Roi Reinshreiber (ISR)   Attendance: 22,450.

25.10.18 Estádio José Alvalade, Lisboa: Sporting CP – Arsenal FC 0-1 (0-0)
Sporting CP: Renan Ribeiro, André Pinto, Sebastián Coates, Stefan Ristovski (46' Bruno Gaspar), Radosav Petrovic, Nemanja Gudelj (71' Jovane Cabral), Rodrigo Battaglia, Bruno Fernandes, Nani (87' Abdoulay Diaby), Fredy Montero, Marcos Acuña. Coach: José Peseiro.
Arsenal FC: Bernd Leno, Stephan Lichtsteiner, Sokratis Papastathopoulos, Rob Holding, Henrikh Mkhitaryan, Aaron Ramsey, Granit Xhaka, Mohamed El Neny (58' Lucas Torreira), Mattéo Guendouzi, Pierre-Emerick Aubameyang (86' Alex Iwobi), Danny Welbeck (81' Alexandre Lacazette). Coach: Unai Emery.
Goal: 78' Danny Welbeck 0-1.
Referee: Damir Skomina (SVN)   Attendance: 40,784.

08.11.18   Stadion Vorskla im. Oleksiya Butov'skogo, Poltava:
Vorskla Poltava – Qarabag FK 0-1 (0-1)
Vorskla Poltava: Bogdan Shust, Volodimir Chesnakov, Oleksandr Chizhov, Igor Perduta, Artur, Najeeb Yakubu (55' Nicolas Careca), Pavlo Rebenok, Aleksandr Sklyar, Vyacheslav Sharpar, Vladislav Kulach, Yuriy Kolomoyets. Coach: Vasil Sachko.
Qarabag FK: Hannes Halldórsson, Rashad Sadygov, Jakub Rzeniczak, Maksim Medvedev, Míchel, Araz Abdullayev, Qara Qarayev, Simeon Slavchev, Wilde Guerrier, Abdellah Zoubir (81' Mahir Madatov), Dzon Delarge (88' Filip Ozobic). Coach: Gurban Gurbanov.
Goal: 13' Araz Abdullayev 0-1 (p).
Referee: Sandro Schärer (SUI)   Attendance: 5,479.

08.11.18   Emirates Stadium, London: Arsenal FC – Sporting CP 0-0
Arsenal FC: Petr Cech, Stephan Lichtsteiner (74' Ainsley Maitland-Niles), Sokratis Papastathopoulos, Carl Jenkinson (60' Sead Kolasinac), Rob Holding, Henrikh Mkhitaryan, Aaron Ramsey, Alex Iwobi, Mattéo Guendouzi, Emile Smith-Rowe, Danny Welbeck (30' Pierre-Emerick Aubameyang). Coach: Unai Emery.
Sporting CP: Renan Ribeiro, Jérémy Mathieu, Sebastián Coates, Bruno Gaspar, Nemanja Gudelj, Bruno Fernandes, Miguel Luís (85' Radosav Petrovic), Nani, Fredy Montero (69' Bas Dost), Abdoulay Diaby (83' Jovane Cabral), Marcos Acuña. Coach: Tiago Fernandes.
Referee: Gediminas Mazeika (LTU)   Attendance: 59,758.
Sent off: 87' Jérémy Mathieu.

29.11.18   Baki Olimpiya Stadionu, Baku: Qarabag FK – Sporting CP 1-6 (1-3)
Qarabag FK: Hannes Halldórsson, Rashad Sadygov, Jakub Rzeniczak, Maksim Medvedev, Míchel, Araz Abdullayev (82' Dzon Delarge), Qara Qarayev, Simeon Slavchev (70' Filip Ozobic), Wilde Guerrier, Abdellah Zoubir, Mahir Madatov. Coach: Gurban Gurbanov.
Sporting CP: Renan Ribeiro, Jefferson, André Pinto, Sebastián Coates, Bruno Gaspar (74' Thierry Correia), Nemanja Gudelj, Bruno Fernandes, Wendel, Nani (79' Carlos Mané), Bas Dost (71' Jovane Cabral), Abdoulay Diaby. Coach: Marcel Keizer.
Goals: 5' Bas Dost 0-1 (p), 14' Abdellah Zoubir 1-1, 20' Bruno Fernandes 1-2, 33' Nani 1-3, 65' Abdoulay Diaby 1-4, 75' Bruno Fernandes 1-5, 82' Abdoulay Diaby 1-6.
Referee: Petr Ardeleánu (CZE)   Attendance: 5,416.

29.11.18   NSK Olimpijs'kyj, Kiev: Vorskla Poltava – Arsenal FC 0-3 (0-3)
Vorskla Poltava: Bogdan Shust, Vadim Sapay (36' Nicolas Careca), Volodimir Chesnakov, Igor Perduta, Artur, Ardin Dallku, Pavlo Rebenok (85' Taras Sakiv), Aleksandr Sklyar, Vyacheslav Sharpar, Vladislav Kulach (71' Ibrahiim Kane), Yuriy Kolomoyets.
Coach: Vasil Sachko.
Arsenal FC: Petr Cech, Stephan Lichtsteiner, Carl Jenkinson, Rob Holding (60' Zech Medley), Aaron Ramsey (68' Bukayo Saka), Mohamed El Neny, Ainsley Maitland-Niles, Joseph Willock, Mattéo Guendouzi (76' Charlie Gilmour), Emile Smith-Rowe, Edward Nketiah.
Coach: Unai Emery.
Goals: 11' Emile Smith-Rowe 0-1, 27' Aaron Ramsey 0-2 (p), 41' Joseph Willock 0-3.
Referee: Bartosz Frankowski (POL)   Attendance: 7,751.

(Vorskla Poltava played this match at NSK Olimpijs'kyj, Kiev, instead of their regular stadium Stadion Vorskla im. Oleksiya Butov'skogo, Poltava, due to martial law being declared in parts of Ukraine).

13.12.18   Estádio José Alvalade, Lisboa: Sporting CP – Vorskla Poltava 3-0 (3-0)
Sporting CP: Romain Salin, André Pinto, Sebastián Coates, Stefan Ristovski (64' Thierry Correia), Radosav Petrovic, Bruno Fernandes (73' Bruno Paz), Miguel Luís, Fredy Montero (59' Pedro Marques), Carlos Mané, Marcos Acuña, Jovane Cabral. Coach: Marcel Keizer.
Vorskla Poltava: Oleksandr Tkachenko, Volodimir Chesnakov, Oleksandr Chizhov, Igor Perduta, Artur (77' Ibrahiim Kane), Ardin Dallku (46' Yuriy Kolomoyets), Taras Sakiv, Pavlo Rebenok, Aleksandr Sklyar, Artem Gabelyuk, Nicolas Careca (67' Mykhaylo Sergiychuk). Coach: Vasil Sachko.
Goals: 17' Fredy Montero 1-0, 35' Miguel Luís 2-0, 44' Ardin Dallku 3-0 (og).
Referee: Manuel Schüttengruber (AUT)   Attendance: 25,504.

13.12.18   Emirates Stadium, London: Arsenal FC – Qarabag FK 1-0 (1-0)
Arsenal FC: Emiliano Martínez, Sokratis Papastathopoulos, Laurent Koscielny (72' Nacho Monreal), Carl Jenkinson, Mesut Özil (83' Charlie Gilmour), Mohamed El Neny, Ainsley Maitland-Niles, Joseph Willock, Bukayo Saka, Alexandre Lacazette (63' Zech Medley), Edward Nketiah. Coach: Unai Emery.
Qarabag FK: Vagner, Rashad Sadygov, Jakub Rzezniczak (85' Filip Ozobic), Maksim Medvedev, Badavi Hüseynov, Míchel (61' Araz Abdullayev), Qara Qarayev, Simeon Slavchev, Wilde Guerrier, Abdellah Zoubir, Mahir Madatov (75' Dani Quintana). Coach: Gurban Gurbanov.
Goal: 17' Alexandre Lacazette 1-0.
Referee: Jens Maae (DEN)   Attendance: 58,101.

GROUP F

20.09.18   Stade Josy Barthel, Luxembourg: F91 Dudelange – AC Milan 0-1 (0-0)
F91 Dudelange: Joé Frising, Tom Schnell, Jerry Prempeh, Kevin Malget (84' Edisson Jordanov), Aniss El Hriti (80' Bryan Mélisse), Marc-André Kruska, Stélvio (75' Patrick Stumpf), Dominik Stolz, Clément Couturier, Danel Sinani, David Turpel. Coach: Dino Toppmöller.
AC Milan: Pepe Reina, Ignazio Abate, Alessio Romagnoli, Mattia Caldara, Andrea Bertolacci (70' Franck Kessié), Tiemoué Bakayoko, Samu Castillejo, Diego Laxalt, José Mauri (80' Hakan Çalhanoglu), Gonzalo Higuaín, Fabio Borini (88' Alen Halilovic). Coach: Gennaro Gattuso.
Goal: 59' Gonzalo Higuaín 0-1.
Referee: Srdan Jovanovic (SER)   Attendance: 7,983.

(F91 Dudelange played their three home matches at Stade Josy Barthel, Lucembourg, instead of their regular stadium Stade Jos Nosbaum, Dudelange)

20.09.18   Stadio Georgios Karaiskáki, Piraeus: Olympiakos Piraeus – Real Betis Sevilla 0-0
Olympiakos Piraeus: Andreas Gianniotis, Jagos Vukovic, Omar Elabdellaoui, Yassine Meryah, Kostas Tsimikas, Ionnias Fetfatzidis (71' Lazaros Christodoulopoulos), Kostas Fortounis, Andreas Bouchalakis (35' Bibras Natcho), Daniel Podence (80' Vasilios Torosidis), Mohamed Camara, "Koka" Ahmed Hassan. Coach: Pedro Martins.
Real Betis Sevilla: Joel Robles, Barragán, Sidnei, Aïssa Mandi, Joaquín (80' Antonio Sanabria), Andrés Guardado, Javi García, Giovani Lo Celso (83' Takashi Inui), Sergio León (72' Canales), Cristian Tello, Loren Morón. Coach: Quique Setién.
Referee: Daniel Stefanski (POL)   Attendance: 28,650.
Sent off: 73' Kostas Tsimikas.

04.10.18   Estadio Benito Villamarín, Sevilla: Real Betis Sevilla – F91 Dudelange 3-0 (0-0)
Real Betis Sevilla: Joel Robles, Barragán, Sidnei, Bartra, Andrés Guardado (61' Giovani Lo Celso), Javi García, Takashi Inui (72' Joaquín), William Carvalho, Sergio León (82' Wilfrid Kaptoum), Cristian Tello, Antonio Sanabria. Coach: Quique Setién.
F91 Dudelange: Joé Frising, Tom Schnell, Jerry Prempeh, Bryan Mélisse (66' Patrick Stumpf), Aniss El Hriti, Marc-André Kruska, Dominik Stolz (76' Levan Kenia), Edisson Jordanov, Clément Couturier, Danel Sinani (82' Mario Pokar), David Turpel. Coach: Dino Toppmöller.
Goals: 56' Antonio Sanabria 1-0, 80' Giovani Lo Celso 2-0, 88' Cristian Tello 3-0.
Referee: Andrew Dallas (SCO)   Attendance: 40,133.

04.10.18   Stadio Giuseppe Meazza, Milano: AC Milan – Olympiakos Piraeus 3-1 (0-1)
AC Milan: Pepe Reina, Cristián Zapata, Ricardo Rodríguez, Alessio Romagnoli, Davide Calabria, Lucas Biglia, Giacomo Bonaventura (54' Hakan Çalhanoglu), Tiemoué Bakayoko, Samu Castillejo (54' Patrick Cutrone), Gonzalo Higuaín, Suso (80' Fabio Borini).
Coach: Gennaro Gattuso.
Olympiakos Piraeus: José Sá, Vasilios Torosidis (77' Yassine Meryah), Roderick Miranda, Leonardo Koutris, Pape Cissé, Yaya Touré (83' Kostas Fortounis), Bibras Natcho, Guilherme, Ionnias Fetfatzidis, Matías Nahuel (72' Daniel Podence), Guerrero. Coach: Pedro Martins.
Goals: 14' Guerrero 0-1, 70' Patrick Cutrone 1-1, 76' Gonzalo Higuaín 2-1,
79' Patrick Cutrone 3-1.
Referee: Bobby Madden (SCO)   Attendance: 22,294.

25.10.18   Stadio Giuseppe Meazza, Milano: AC Milan – Real Betis Sevilla 1-2 (0-1)
AC Milan: Pepe Reina, Cristián Zapata, Alessio Romagnoli, Davide Calabria, Lucas Biglia (80' Andrea Bertolacci), Giacomo Bonaventura, Tiemoué Bakayoko (46' Suso), Samu Castillejo, Diego Laxalt, Gonzalo Higuaín, Fabio Borini (46' Patrick Cutrone).
Coach: Gennaro Gattuso.
Real Betis Sevilla: Pau López, Barragán, Sidnei, Aïssa Mandi, Bartra, Junior Firpo, Canales, William Carvalho (90+2' Zouhair Feddal), Giovani Lo Celso, Sergio León (67' Cristian Tello), Antonio Sanabria (79' Loren Morón). Coach: Quique Setién.
Goals: 30' Antonio Sanabria 0-1, 55' Giovani Lo Celso 0-2, 83' Patrick Cutrone 1-2.
Referee: Bas Nijhuis (HOL)   Attendance: 22,405.
Sent off: 90+4' Samu Castillejo.

25.10.18   Stade Josy Barthel, Luxembourg: F91 Dudelange – Olympiakos Piraeus 0-2 (0-0)
F91 Dudelange: Landry Bonnefoi, Milan Bisevac, Tom Schnell, Jerry Prempeh, Aniss El Hriti (74' Levan Kenia), Marc-André Kruska, Stélvio (51' Danel Sinani), Dominik Stolz (65' Bryan Mélisse), Edisson Jordanov, Clément Couturier, David Turpel. Coach: Dino Toppmöller.
Olympiakos Piraeus: José Sá, Vasilios Torosidis (69' Omar Elabdellaoui), Jagos Vukovic, Leonardo Koutris, Pape Cissé, Kostas Fortounis, Andreas Bouchalakis, Daniel Podence, Matías Nahuel (78' Bibras Natcho), Mohamed Camara, Guerrero (18' Lazaros Christodoulopoulos). Coach: Pedro Martins.
Goals: 66' Vasilios Torosidis 0-1, 81' Edisson Jordanov 0-2 (og).
Referee: Hüseyin Göçek (TUR)   Attendance: 7,500.

08.11.18   Estadio Benito Villamarín, Sevilla: Real Betis Sevilla – AC Milan 1-1 (1-0)
Real Betis Sevilla: Pau López, Aïssa Mandi, Bartra, Zouhair Feddal, Junior Firpo, Joaquín (67' Andrés Guardado), Canales, William Carvalho, Giovani Lo Celso, Cristian Tello, Antonio Sanabria (74' Loren Morón). Coach: Quique Setién.
AC Milan: Pepe Reina, Cristián Zapata, Mateo Musacchio (83' Alessio Romagnoli), Ricardo Rodríguez, Hakan Çalhanoglu (89' Andrea Bertolacci), Tiemoué Bakayoko, Diego Laxalt (76' Ignazio Abate), Franck Kessié, Fabio Borini, Suso, Patrick Cutrone. Coach: Gennaro Gattuso.
Goals: 12' Giovani Lo Celso 1-0, 62' Suso 1-1.
Referee: Craig Pawson (ENG)   Attendance: 45,647.

08.11.18   Stadio Georgios Karaiskáki, Piraeus:
            Olympiakos Piraeus – F91 Dudelange 5-1 (4-0)
Olympiakos Piraeus: José Sá, Vasilios Torosidis, Roderick Miranda, Kostas Tsimikas, Pape Cissé, Lazaros Christodoulopoulos, Bibras Natcho (62' Yaya Touré), Kostas Fortounis (57' "Koka" Ahmed Hassan), Daniel Podence, Matías Nahuel (34' Ioannis Fetfatzidis), Mohamed Camara. Coach: Pedro Martins.
F91 Dudelange: Landry Bonnefoi, Milan Bisevac, Tom Schnell, Jerry Prempeh, Bryan Mélisse, Marc-André Kruska (60' Leon Jensen), Dominik Stolz (85' Patrick Stumpf), Edisson Jordanov, Clément Couturier, Danel Sinani, David Turpel (74' Nicolas Perez).
Coach: Dino Toppmöller.
Goals: 6' Vasilios Torosidis 1-0, 15' Kostas Fortounis 2-0, 26' Lazaros Christodoulopoulos 3-0, 36' Kostas Fortounis 4-0, 69' Danel Sinani 4-1, 71' "Koka" Ahmed Hassan 5-1.
Referee: Petr Ardeleánu (CZE)   Attendance: 24,032.

29.11.18   Stadio Giuseppe Meazza, Milano: AC Milan – F91 Dudelange 5-2 (1-1)
AC Milan: Pepe Reina, Cristián Zapata, Stefan Simic, Davide Calabria, Andrea Bertolacci (58' José Mauri), Hakan Çalhanoglu, Tiemoué Bakayoko, Diego Laxalt, Alen Halilovic (52' Suso), Gonzalo Higuaín, Patrick Cutrone (80' Fabio Borini). Coach: Gennaro Gattuso.
F91 Dudelange: Landry Bonnefoi, Tom Schnell, Jerry Prempeh, Bryan Mélisse, Marc-André Kruska, Stélvio (75' Mario Pokar), Dominik Stolz (80' Levan Kenia), Edisson Jordanov, Clément Couturier, Danel Sinani (87' Nicolas Perez), David Turpel. Coach: Dino Toppmöller.
Goals: 21' P. Cutrone 1-0, 39' Dominik Stolz 1-1, 49' David Turpel 1-2, 66' Stélvio 2-2 (og), 70' Hakan Çalhanoglu 3-2, 77' Tom Schnell 4-2 (og), 80' Fabio Borini 5-2.
Referee: Vladislav Bezborodov (RUS)   Attendance: 15,521.

29.11.18   Estadio Benito Villamarín, Sevilla:
            Real Betis Sevilla – Olympiakos Piraeus 1-0 (1-0)
Real Betis Sevilla: Joel Robles, Sidnei, Aïssa Mandi, Bartra (74' Javi García), Junior Firpo, Canales, William Carvalho, Giovani Lo Celso, Sergio León (63' Takashi Inui), Cristian Tello (83' Barragán), Antonio Sanabria. Coach: Quique Setién.
Olympiakos Piraeus: José Sá, Jagos Vukovic, Omar Elabdellaoui, Kostas Tsimikas, Pape Cissé, Guilherme (81' Bibras Natcho), Kostas Fortounis, Andreas Bouchalakis (58' Guerrero), Daniel Podence, Matías Nahuel (72' Marius Vrushaj), Mohamed Camara.
Coach: Pedro Martins.
Goal: 39' Canales 1-0.
Referee: Sergey Karasev (RUS)   Attendance: 37,722.

Sergio León missed a penalty kick (18').

13.12.18   Stade Josy Barthel, Luxembourg: F91 Dudelange – Real Betis Sevilla 0-0
F91 Dudelange: Landry Bonnefoi, Tom Schnell, Jerry Prempeh, Aniss El Hriti, Stélvio, Levan Kenia (71' Kevin Malget), Dominik Stolz, Edisson Jordanov, Clément Couturier (82' Bryan Mélisse), Danel Sinani (89' Leon Jensen), David Turpel. Coach: Dino Toppmöller.
Real Betis Sevilla: Joel Robles, Sidnei, Zouhair Feddal, Joaquín (75' Ryad Boudebouz), Javi García, Takashi Inui, William Carvalho (74' Bartra), Wilfrid Kaptoum, Francis Guerrero, Cristian Tello, Loren Morón (70' Sergio León). Coach: Quique Setién.
Referee: Peter Královec (CZE)   Attendance: 4,931.

13.12.18   Stadio Georgios Karaiskáki, Piraeus: Olympiakos Piraeus – AC Milan 3-1 (0-0)
Olympiakos Piraeus: José Sá, Jagos Vukovic, Omar Elabdellaoui, Leonardo Koutris, Pape Cissé, Guilherme, Ioannis Fetfatzidis (69' Bibras Natcho), Kostas Fortounis, Daniel Podence (85' Andreas Bouchalakis), Mohamed Camara (79' Vasilios Torosidis), Guerrero.
Coach: Pedro Martins.
AC Milan: Pepe Reina, Cristián Zapata, Ignazio Abate, Ricardo Rodríguez (85' Alen Halilovic), Davide Calabria, Hakan Çalhanoglu, Tiemoué Bakayoko, Samu Castillejo, Franck Kessié, Gonzalo Higuaín, Patrick Cutrone (78' Diego Laxalt). Coach: Gennaro Gattuso.
Goals: 60' Pape Cissé 1-0, 70' Cristián Zapata 2-0 (og), 72' Cristián Zapata 2-1, 81' Kostas Fortounis 3-1 (p).
Referee: Benoît Bastien (FRA)   Attendance: 31,010.

GROUP G

20.09.18   Estadio de la Cerámica, Villarreal: Villarreal CF – Glasgow Rangers 2-2 (1-0)
Villarreal CF: Andrés Fernández, Daniele Bonera, Víctor Ruíz, Ramiro Funes Mori (67' Gerard Moreno), Miguelón Llambrich, Santi Cazorla, Alfonso Pedraza, Pablo Fornals, Carlos Bacca, Nicola Sansone (79' Samuel Chukwueze), Karl Toko Ekambi (60' Trigueros).
Coach: Javi Calleja.
Glasgow Rangers FC: Allan McGregor, James Tavernier, Connor Goldson, Borna Barisic (85' Graham Dorrans), Joe Worrall, Scott Arfield, Andrew Halliday, Ryan Kent, Lassana Coulibaly (70' Glenn Middleton), Kyle Lafferty, Candeias (77' Ross McCrorie). Coach: Steven Gerrard.
Goals: 1' Carlos Bacca 1-0, 67' Scott Arfield 1-1, 69' Gerard Moreno 2-1, 76' Kyle Lafferty 2-2.
Referee: István Kovács (ROM)   Attendance: 15,982.

20.09.18   Allianz Stadion, Vienna: SK Rapid Wien – Spartak Moskwa 2-0 (0-0)
SK Rapid Wien: Richard Strebinger, Mario Sonnleitner, Marvin Potzmann, Mateo Barac, Mert Müldür, Christoph Knasmüllner (86' Manuel Martic), Stefan Schwab, Thomas Murg, Dejan Ljubicic, Deni Alar (71' Andrija Pavlovic), Andrei Ivan (76' Veton Berisha).
Coach: Goran Djuricin.
Spartak Moskva: Aleksandr Maksimenko, Salvatore Bocchetti, Georgi Dzhikiya, Nikolai Rasskazov, Lorenzo Melgarejo, Fernando, Roman Zobnin, Artiom Timofeev (82' Mikhail Ignatov), Aleksandr Lomovitski (73' Aleksandr Samedov), Zé Luís, Pedro Rocha (73' Ivelin Popov). Coach: Massimo Carrera.
Goals: 50' Artiom Timofeev 1-0 (og), 68' Thomas Murg 2-0.

Referee: Alain Bieri (SUI)   Attendance: 21,400.
04.10.18   Otkrytiye Arena, Moskva: Spartak Moskva – Villarreal CF 3-3 (1-1)
Spartak Moskva: Aleksandr Maksimenko, Salvatore Bocchetti, Georgi Dzhikiya, Nikolai Rasskazov, Dmitriy Kombarov (90' Artiom Timofeev), Lorenzo Melgarejo, Fernando, Roman Zobnin, Aleksandr Lomovitski (80' Aleksandr Tashaev), Mikhail Ignatov (69' Sofiane Hanni), Zé Luís. Coach: Massimo Carrera.
Villarreal CF: Andrés Fernández, Daniele Bonera, Mario Gaspar, Víctor Ruíz, Ramiro Funes Mori, Trigueros, Alfonso Pedraza, Pablo Fornals, Samuel Chukwueze (71' Santi Cazorla), Nicola Sansone (61' Gerard Moreno), Karl Toko Ekambi (77' Miguel Layún).
Coach: Javi Calleja.
Goals: 13' Karl Toko Ekambi 0-1, 34' Zé Luís 1-1 (p), 49' Pablo Fornals 1-2, 82' Zé Luís 2-2, 85' Lorenzo Melgarejo 3-2, 90+6' Santi Cazorla 3-3 (p).
Referee: Daniel Siebert (GER)   Attendance: 21,264.

04.10.18   Ibrox Stadium, Glasgow: Glasgow Rangers FC – SK Rapid Wien 3-1 (1-1)
Glasgow Rangers FC: Allan McGregor, James Tavernier, Connor Goldson, Jon Flanagan, Joe Worrall, Scott Arfield, Ryan Kent (90' Andrew Halliday), Ovie Ejaria, Lassana Coulibaly, Candeias, Alfredo Morelos (90+5' Glenn Middleton). Coach: Steven Gerrard.
SK Rapid Wien: Richard Strebinger, Mario Sonnleitner, Marvin Potzmann, Mateo Barac (33' Christopher Dibon), Mert Müldür, Stefan Schwab, Thomas Murg, Dejan Ljubicic, Veton Berisha (72' Boli Bolingoli-Mbombo), Andrija Pavlovic, Andrei Ivan (58' Deni Alar). Coach: Dietmar Kühbauer.
Goals: 42' Veton Berisha 0-1, 44' Alfredo Morelos 1-1, 84' James Tavernier 2-1 (p), 90+4' Alfredo Morelos 3-1.
Referee: Ruddy Buquet (FRA)   Attendance: 47,534.

25.10.18   Ibrox Stadium, Glasgow: Glasgow Rangers FC – Spartak Moskva 0-0
Glasgow Rangers FC: Allan McGregor, James Tavernier, Connor Goldson, Jon Flanagan, Joe Worrall, Ryan Jack (68' Eros Grezda), Ryan Kent, Ovie Ejaria, Lassana Coulibaly, Candeias (86' Glenn Middleton), Alfredo Morelos. Coach: Steven Gerrard.
Spartak Moskva: Aleksandr Maksimenko, Salvatore Bocchetti, Georgi Dzhikiya, Nikolai Rasskazov, Lorenzo Melgarejo, Fernando, Roman Zobnin, Aleksandr Tashaev (46' Sofiane Hanni), Aleksandr Lomovitski (46' Roman Eremenko), Mikhail Ignatov (84' Ivelin Popov), Zé Luís. Coach: Raúl Riancho.
Referee: Kevin Blom (HOL)   Attendance: 49,068.

25.10.18   Estadio de la Cerámica, Villarreal: Villarreal CF – SK Rapid Wien 5-0 (3-0)
Villarreal CF: Andrés Fernández, Jaume Costa, Miguel Layún, Ramiro Funes Mori, Álvaro González, Miguelón Llambrich, Trigueros, Pablo Fornals (65' Samuel Chukwueze), Santiago Cáseres (78' Santi Cazorla), Karl Toko Ekambi, Dani Raba (70' Gerard Moreno).
Coach: Javi Calleja.
SK Rapid Wien: Richard Strebinger, Mario Sonnleitner, Marvin Potzmann (46' Andrei Ivan), Boli Bolingoli-Mbombo, Mateo Barac, Mert Müldür, Stefan Schwab, Thomas Murg (77' Christoph Knasmüllner), Dejan Ljubicic, Deni Alar, Veton Berisha (60' Manuel Thurnwald). Coach: Dietmar Kühbauer.
Goals: 26' Pablo Fornals 1-0, 30' Karl Toko Ekambi 2-0, 45' Mateo Barac 3-0 (og), 63' Dani Raba 4-0, 85' Gerard Moreno 5-0.
Referee: Halis Özkahya (TUR)   Attendance: 14,158.
Sent off: 79' Jaume Costa.

08.11.18   Otkrytiye Arena, Moskva: Spartak Moskva – Glasgow Rangers FC 4-3 (2-3)
Spartak Moskva: Aleksandr Maksimenko, Salvatore Bocchetti, Ilya Kutepov, Nikolai Rasskazov, Roman Eremenko (60' Denis Glushakov), Ivelin Popov (71' Artiom Timofeev), Lorenzo Melgarejo, Fernando, Sofiane Hanni, Roman Zobnin, Luiz Adriano (82' Zé Luís). Coach: Raúl Riancho.
Glasgow Rangers FC: Allan McGregor, James Tavernier, Connor Goldson, Jon Flanagan (82' Andy Halliday), Nikola Katic, Scott Arfield, Ovie Ejaria (90+4' Gareth McAuley), Lassana Coulibaly (82' Eros Grezda), Candeias, Alfredo Morelos, Glenn Middleton. Coach: Steven Gerrard.
Goals: 5' Roman Eremenko 0-1 (og), 22' Lorenzo Melgarejo 1-1, 27' Candeias 1-2, 35' C. Goldson 2-2, 41' Glenn Middleton 2-3, 58' Luiz Adriano 3-3, 59' Sofiane Hanni 4-3.
Referee: Ivan Bebek (CRO)   Attendance: 22,296.

08.11.18   Allianz Stadion, Vienna: SK Rapid Wien – Villarreal CF 0-0
SK Rapid Wien: Richard Strebinger, Mario Sonnleitner, Christopher Dibon (75' Boli Bolingoli-Mbombo), Marvin Potzmann, Mert Müldür, Stefan Schwab, Thomas Murg (46' Christoph Knasmüllner), Dejan Ljubicic, Veton Berisha, Andrija Pavlovic (90+2' Manuel Martic), Andrei Ivan. Coach: Dietmar Kühbauer.
Villarreal CF: Andrés Fernández, Daniele Bonera (46' Ramiro Funes Mori), Mario Gaspar, Víctor Ruíz, Miguel Layún (61' Karl Toko Ekambi), Santi Cazorla, Alfonso Pedraza, Santiago Cáseres, Nicola Sansone, Gerard Moreno, Dani Raba (76' Pablo Fornals). Coach: Javi Calleja.
Referee: Srdan Jovanovic (SER)   Attendance: 22,100.

29.11.18   Otkrytiye Arena, Moskva: Spartak Moskva – SK Rapid Wien 1-2 (1-0)
Spartak Moskva: Artem Rebrov, Andrey Eshchenko, Ilya Kutepov, Georgi Dzhikiya, Dmitriy Kombarov, Denis Glushakov, Lorenzo Melgarejo (81' Ivelin Popov), Sofiane Hanni (72' Aleksandr Samedov), Artiom Timofeev, Luiz Adriano, Zé Luís. Coach: Oleg Kononov.
SK Rapid Wien: Richard Strebinger, Marvin Potzmann, Maximilian Hofmann, Boli Bolingoli-Mbombo, Mateo Barac, Mert Müldür, Christoph Knasmüllner, Manuel Martic, Dejan Ljubicic (64' Stefan Schwab), Deni Alar (64' Philipp Schobesberger), Veton Berisha (81' Manuel Thurnwald). Coach: Dietmar Kühbauer.
Goals: 20' Zé Luís 1-0, 80' Mert Müldür 1-1, 90+1' Philipp Schobesberger 1-2.
Referee: Pawel Gil (POL)   Attendance: 20,739.

29.11.18   Ibrox Stadium, Glasgow: Glasgow Rangers FC – Villarreal CF 0-0
Glasgow Rangers FC: Allan McGregor, James Tavernier, Connor Goldson, Jon Flanagan, Joe Worrall, Scott Arfield, Ryan Jack, Lassana Coulibaly (90+2' Ross McCrorie), Candeias, Alfredo Morelos (79' Kyle Lafferty), Glenn Middleton. Coach: Steven Gerrard.
Villarreal CF: Andrés Fernández, Mario Gaspar, Jaume Costa, Ramiro Funes Mori, Álvaro González, Trigueros (62' Santi Cazorla), Manu Morlanes, Pablo Fornals (74' Samuel Chukwueze), Santiago Cáseres, Carlos Bacca (63' Gerard Moreno), Karl Toko Ekambi. Coach: Javi Calleja.
Referee: Matej Jug (SVN)   Attendance: 50,171.
Sent off: 44' Candeias.

13.12.18 Estadio de la Cerámica, Villarreal: Villarreal CF – Spartak Moskva 2-0 (1-0)
Villarreal CF: Andrés Fernández, Mario Gaspar, Jaume Costa, Víctor Ruíz, Álvaro González, Javi Fuego, Pablo Fornals, Samuel Chukwueze (80' Santi Cazorla), Santiago Cáseres, Gerard Moreno (77' Alfonso Pedraza), Karl Toko Ekambi (72' Carlos Bacca). Coach: Luis García.
Spartak Moskva: Aleksandr Maksimenko, Ilya Kutepov, Georgi Dzhikiya, Nikolai Rasskazov, Denis Glushakov, Ivelin Popov, Lorenzo Melgarejo, Sofiane Hanni (67' Pedro Rocha), Aleksandr Lomovitski (55' Aleksandr Tashaev), Luiz Adriano (74' Jano Ananidze), Zé Luís. Coach: Oleg Kononov.
Goals: 11' Samuel Chukwueze 1-0, 48' Karl Toko Ekambi 2-0.
Referee: Andris Treimanis (LAT)   Attendance: 12,903.
Sent off: 90' Jaume Costa.

13.12.18 Allianz Stadion, Vienna: SK Rapid Wien – Glasgow Rangers FC 1-0 (0-0)
SK Rapid Wien: Richard Strebinger, Stephan Auer, Maximilian Hofmann, Boli Bolingoli-Mbombo, Mateo Barac, Mert Müldür, Stefan Schwab, Thomas Murg (46' Christoph Knasmüllner), Manuel Martic (78' Dejan Ljubicic), Veton Berisha, Andrei Ivan (62' Philipp Schobesberger). Coach: Dietmar Kühbauer.
Glasgow Rangers FC: Allan McGregor, Gareth McAuley, James Tavernier, Connor Goldson, Borna Barisic, Ross McCrorie, Scott Arfield, Ryan Jack (79' Kyle Lafferty), Lassana Coulibaly (71' Eros Grezda), Alfredo Morelos, Glenn Middleton. Coach: Steven Gerrard.
Goal: 84' Dejan Ljubicic 1-0.
Referee: Paolo Mazzoleni (ITA)   Attendance: 23,850.

GROUP H

20.09.18 Orange Vélodrome, Marseille: Olympique Marseille – Eintracht Frankfurt 1-2 (1-0)
Olympique Marseille: Yohann Pelé, Adil Rami (7' Luiz Gustavo), Duje Caleta-Car, Boubacar Kamara, Dimitri Payet, Kevin Strootman, Bouna Sarr, Lucas Ocampos (72' Nemanja Radonjic), Maxime Lopez, Valère Germain, Florian Thauvin (84' Kostas Mitroglou). Coach: Rudi García.
Eintracht Frankfurt: Kevin Trapp, David Abraham, Jetro Willems, Danny da Costa, Evan Obite N'Dicka, Jonathan de Guzmán (62' Simon Falette), Makoto Hasebe, Filip Kostic, Lucas Torró, Mijat Gacinovic (46' Nicolai Müller), Sébastien Haller (75' Luka Jovic). Coach: Adi Hütter.
Goals: 3' Lucas Ocampos 1-0, 52' Lucas Torró 1-1, 89' Luka Jovic 1-2.
Referee: Matej Jug (SVN)
Sent off: 59' Jetro Willems.

Match was played behind closed doors.

20.09.18 Stadio Olimpico, Roma: Lazio Roma – Apollon FC Limassol 2-1 (1-0)
Lazio Roma: Silvio Proto, Dusan Basta, Martín Cáceres, Francesco Acerbi, Riza Durmisi, Bastos, Milan Badelj (61' Lucas Leiva), Luis Alberto (62' Ciro Immobile), Sergej Milinkovic-Savic (73' Senad Lulic), Alessandro Murgia, Felipe Caicedo. Coach: Simone Inzaghi.
Apollon FC Limassol: Bruno Vale, Valentin Roberge, Charis Kyriakou (46' Sasa Markovic), André Schembri, Facundo Pereyra (69' Emilio Zelayà), Héctor Yuste, Giorgos Vasiliou, Esteban Sachetti, João Pedro, Fotis Papoulis, Anton Maglica (46' Mustapha Carayol). Coach: Sofronis Avgousti.
Goals: 14' Luis Alberto 1-0, 84' Ciro Immobile 2-0 (p), 87' Emilio Zelaya 2-1.
Referee: Aliyar Agayev (AZE)   Attendance: 11,898.

04.10.18   Neo GSP Stadium, Nicosia: Apollon FC Limassol – Olympique Marseille 2-2 (0-0)
Apollon FC Limassol: Bruno Vale, Valentin Roberge, Kévin Bru, Richard Soumah, Facundo Pereyra, Héctor Yuste (11' Sasa Markovic), Mustapha Carayol (65' Anton Maglica), Esteban Sachetti, Emilio Zelaya, João Pedro, Adrián Sardinero (54' Fotis Papoulis).
Coach: Sofronis Avgousti.
Olympique Marseille: Yohann Pelé, Hiroki Sakai (46' Bouna Sarr), Jordan Amavi, Duje Caleta-Car, Boubacar Kamara, Dimitri Payet, Luiz Gustavo (75' Grégory Sertic), Kevin Strootman, Maxime Lopez, Kostas Mitroglou (46' Valère Germain), Nemanja Radonjic.
Coach: Rudi García.
Goals: 50' Dimitri Payet 0-1, 67' Luiz Gustavo 0-2, 74' Sasa Markovic 1-2, 90' Emilio Zelaya 2-2.
Referee: Harald Lechner (AUT)   Attendance: 3,031.

(Apollon FC Limassol played their three home match at Neo GSP Stadium, Nicosia, instead of their regular stadium, Tsirio Stadium, Limassol)

04.10.18   Commerzbank-Arena, Frankfurt am Main:
           Eintracht Frankfurt – Lazio Roma 4-1 (2-1)
Eintracht Frankfurt: Kevin Trapp, Marco Russ, Simon Falette, Danny da Costa, Jonathan de Guzmán (87' Marc Stendera), Makoto Hasebe, Filip Kostic (78' Taleb Tawatha), Lucas Torró, Mijat Gacinovic, Sébastien Haller, Luka Jovic (67' Ante Rebic). Coach: Adi Hütter.
Lazio Roma: Silvio Proto, Dusan Basta, Francesco Acerbi, Riza Durmisi (18' Senad Lulic), Wallace, Luiz Felipe, Lucas Leiva (76' Luis Alberto), Marco Parolo, Joaquín Correa, Sergej Milinkovic-Savic (84' Valon Berisha), Ciro Immobile. Coach: Simone Inzaghi.
Goals: 4' Danny da Costa 1-0, 23' Marco Parolo 1-1, 28' Filip Kostic 2-1. 52' Luka Jovic 3-1, 90+4' Danny da Costa 4-1.
Referee: Serdar Gözübüyük (HOL)   Attendance: 47,000.
Sent off: 45+3' Dusan Basta, 58' Joaquín Correa.

25.10.18   Commerzbank-Arena, Frankfurt am Main:
           Eintracht Frankfurt – Apollon FC Limassol 2-0 (2-0)
Eintracht Frankfurt: Frederik Rønnow, David Abraham (68' Marco Russ), Danny da Costa (57' Jetro Willems), Evan Obite N'Dicka, Jonathan de Guzmán, Makoto Hasebe, Gelson Fernandes, Filip Kostic, Mijat Gacinovic, Sébastien Haller, Ante Rebic (82' Luka Jovic).
Coach: Adi Hütter.
Apollon FC Limassol: Bruno Vale, Valentin Roberge, Chambos Kyriakou, Facundo Pereyra (46' Emilio Zelaya), Mustapha Carayol (46' André Schembri), Giorgos Vasiliou, Sasa Markovic, Esteban Sachetti, João Pedro, Fotis Papoulis, Anton Maglica (67' Marios Stylianou). Coach: Sofronis Avgousti.
Goals: 13' Filip Kostic 1-0, 32' Sébastien Haller 2-0.
Referee: Sergey Ivanov (RUS)   Attendance: 47,000.

25.10.18   Orange Vélodrome, Marseille: Olympique Marseille – Lazio Roma 1-3 (0-1)
Olympique Marseille: Steve Mandanda, Adil Rami, Hiroki Sakai, Jordan Amavi (80' Bouna Sarr), Boubacar Kamara, Dimitri Payet, Luiz Gustavo, Kevin Strootman, Lucas Ocampos, Morgan Sanson (66' Clinton N'Jie), Kostas Mitroglou (66' Valère Germain).
Coach: Rudi García.
Lazio Roma: Thomas Strakosha, Stefan Radu, Martín Cáceres, Francesco Acerbi, Wallace, Lucas Leiva (48' Adam Marusic), Senad Lulic (62' Valon Berisha), Marco Parolo, Sergej Milinkovic-Savic, Felipe Caicedo (74' Danilo Cataldi), Ciro Immobile.
Coach: Simone Inzaghi.
Goals: 10' Wallace 0-1, 59' Felipe Caicedo 0-2, 86' Dimitri Payet 1-2, 90' Adam Marusic 1-3.
Referee: Jesús Gil Manzano (ESP)   Attendance: 31,930.

08.11.18   Neo GSP Stadium, Nicosia: Apollon FC Limassol – Eintracht Frankfurt 2-3 (0-1)
Apollon FC Limassol: Tasos Kissas, Valentin Roberge, Chambos Kyriakou, Dylan Ouédraogo, André Schembri (68' David Faupala), Giorgos Vasiliou (61' João Pedro), Sasa Markovic, Marios Stylianou, Esteban Sachetti, Anton Maglica (46' Emilio Zelaya), Adrián Sardinero.
Coach: Sofronis Avgousti.
Eintracht Frankfurt: Kevin Trapp, David Abraham, Jetro Willems, Danny da Costa, Evan Obite N'Dicka, Makoto Hasebe, Gelson Fernandes (77' Jonathan de Guzmán), Mijat Gacinovic, Marc Stendera, Sébastien Haller (66' Ante Rebic), Luka Jovic (85' Nicolai Müller).
Coach: Adi Hütter.
Goals: 17' Luka Jovic 0-1, 55' Sébastien Haller 0-2, 58' Mijat Gacinovic 0-3, 71', 90+4' Emilio Zelaya 1-3, 2-3 (p).
Referee: Tiago Martins (POR)   Attendance: 6,888.
Sent off: 81' Marc Stendera.

Sofronis Avgousti sent to the stands (37').

08.11.18   Stadio Olimpico, Roma: Lazio Roma – Olympique Marseille 2-1 (1-0)
Lazio Roma: Thomas Strakosha, Francesco Acerbi, Riza Durmisi, Adam Marusic, Wallace (57' Bastos), Luiz Felipe, Marco Parolo, Valon Berisha (70' Sergej Milinkovic-Savic), Joaquín Correa (82' Luis Alberto), Danilo Cataldi, Ciro Immobile. Coach: Simone Inzaghi.
Olympique Marseille: Yohann Pelé, Adil Rami (79' Bouna Sarr), Hiroki Sakai, Duje Caleta-Car, Luiz Gustavo, Kevin Strootman, Lucas Ocampos, Morgan Sanson (69' Dimitri Payet), Maxime Lopez, Florian Thauvin (82' Kostas Mitroglou), Clinton N'Jie. Coach: Rudi García.
Goals: 45+1' Marco Parolo 1-0, 55' Joaquín Correa 2-0, 60' Florian Thauvin 2-1.
Referee: Vladislav Bezborodov (RUS)   Attendance: 14,705.

29.11.18   Commerzbank-Arena, Frankfurt am Main:
          Eintracht Frankfurt – Olympique Marseille 4-0 (2-0)
Eintracht Frankfurt: Kevin Trapp, Marco Russ, Taleb Tawatha (64' Filip Kostic), Jetro Willems, Simon Falette, Danny da Costa, Makoto Hasebe, Gelson Fernandes, Mijat Gacinovic, Sébastien Haller (73' Ante Rebic), Luka Jovic (80' Nicolai Müller). Coach: Adi Hütter.
Olympique Marseille: Yohann Pelé, Tomás Hubocan, Jordan Amavi, Duje Caleta-Car, Boubacar Kamara, Luiz Gustavo, Bouna Sarr (80' Christopher Rocchia), Maxime Lopez (61' Rolando), Kostas Mitroglou, Valère Germain (64' Florian Chabrolle), Nemanja Radonjic.
Coach: Rudi García.
Goals: 2' Luka Jovic 1-0, 17' Luiz Gustavo 2-0 (og), 62' Bouna Sarr 3-0 (og), 67' Luka Jovic 4-0.
Referee: John Beaton (SCO)   Attendance: 47,000.

29.11.18   Neo GSP Stadium, Nicosia: Apollon FC Limassol – Lazio Roma 2-0 (1-0)
Apollon FC Limassol: Bruno Vale, Valentin Roberge, Dylan Ouédraogo, Richard Soumah, André Schembri (66' Fotis Papoulis), Sasa Markovic, Esteban Sachetti, Danilo Spoljaric, João Pedro, Adrián Sardinero (78' Emilio Zelaya), David Faupala (66' Anton Maglica).
Coach: Sofronis Avgousti.
Lazio Roma: Silvio Proto, Martín Cáceres, Francesco Acerbi, Riza Durmisi, Bastos (60' Senad Lulic), Luiz Felipe, Valon Berisha, Joaquín Correa, Danilo Cataldi, Alessandro Murgia (60' Alessandro Rossi), Felipe Caicedo (85' Nicolò Armini). Coach: Simone Inzaghi.
Goals: 31' David Faupala 1-0, 82' Sasa Markovic 2-0.
Referee: Roi Reinshreiber (ISR)   Attendance: 1,131.

13.12.18   Orange Vélodrome, Marseille:
Olympique Marseille – Apollon FC Limassol 1-3 (1-2)
Olympique Marseille: Florian Escales, Adil Rami, Hiroki Sakai, Duje Caleta-Car, Boubacar Kamara, Dimitri Payet (76' Clinton N'Jie), Luiz Gustavo, Kevin Strootman (59' Bouna Sarr), Lucas Ocampos, Maxime Lopez, Florian Thauvin (62' Nemanja Radonjic).
Coach: Rudi García.
Apollon FC Limassol: Bruno Vale, Valentin Roberge, Chambos Kyriakou, Dylan Ouédraogo, Kévin Bru (46' Fotis Papoulis), André Schembri (59' David Faupala), Giorgos Vasiliou, Sasa Markovic, Marios Stylianou, Anton Maglica (71' Richard Soumah), Adrián Sardinero.
Coach: Sofronis Avgousti.
Goals: 8' Anton Maglica 0-1 (p), 11' Florian Thauvin 1-1, 30' Anton Maglica 1-2, 56' Marios Stylianou 1-3.
Referee: Radu Petrescu (ROM)   Attendance: 9,274.
Sent off: 7' Boubacar Kamara, 90+3' Lucas Ocampos.

13.12.18   Stadio Olimpico, Roma: Lazio Roma – Eintracht Frankfurt 1-2 (0-0)
Lazio Roma: Silvio Proto, Martín Cáceres (75' Senad Lulic), Francesco Acerbi, Riza Durmisi, Bastos, Luiz Felipe, Valon Berisha (75' Alessandro Rossi), Luis Alberto, Joaquín Correa, Danilo Cataldi, Alessandro Murgia. Coach: Simone Inzaghi.
Eintracht Frankfurt: Frederik Rønnow, Marco Russ, Taleb Tawatha, Jetro Willems, Simon Falette, Danny da Costa, Makoto Hasebe (32' Evan Obite N'Dicka), Gelson Fernandes, Nicolai Müller (79' Luka Jovic), Mijat Gacinovic (88' Marc Stendera), Sébastien Haller.
Coach: Adi Hütter.
Goals: 56' Joaquín Correa 1-0, 65' Mijat Gacinovic 1-1, 71' Sébastien Haller 1-2.
Referee: Halil Umut Meler (TUR)   Attendance: 18,252.

GROUP I

20.09.18   Vodafone Stadyumu, Istanbul: Besiktas JK – Sarpsborg 08 3-1 (0-0)
Besiktas JK: Loris Karius, Pepe, Caner Erkin, Gökhan Gönül (85' Necip Uysal), Gary Medel, Enzo Roco, Jeremain Lens, Gökhan Töre (46' Ryan Babel), Oguzhan Özyakup, Adem Ljajic (78' Tolgay Arslan), Cyle Larin. Coach: Senol Günes.
Sarpsborg 08: Alexander Vasyutin, Jørgen Horn, Amin Askar, Joachim Thomassen, Joonas Tamm, Matti Lund Nielsen (86' Gaute Vetti), Ole Halvorsen (70' Harmeet Singh), Kristoffer Zachariassen, Tobias Heintz, Patrick Mortensen, Rashad Muhammed (81' Jørgen Larsen).
Coach: Geir Bakke.
Goals: 51' Ryan Babel 1-0, 69' Enzo Roco 2-0, 82' Jeremain Lens 3-0, 90+4' Kristoffer Zachariassen 3-1.
Referee: Tamás Bognár (HUN)   Attendance: 24,955.

20.09.18 Luminus Arena, Genk: KRC Genk – Malmö FF 2-0 (1-0)
KRC Genk: Danny Vukovic, Sebastien Dewaest, Jere Uronen, Joseph Aidoo, Joakim Mæhle, Pozuelo (76' Ibrahima Seck), Ruslan Malinovskiy, Sander Berge, Leandro Trossard, Mbwana Samatta (86' Marcus Ingvartsen), Dieumerci N'Dongala (72' Joseph Paintsil).
Coach: Philippe Clement.
Malmö FF: Johan Dahlin, Behrang Safari (80' Egzon Binaku), Rasmus Bengtsson, Lasse Nielsen, Andreas Vindheim, Søren Rieks, Anders Christiansen (86' Romain Gall), Fouad Bachirou, Oscar Lewicki, Markus Rosenberg, Marcus Antonsson (55' Arnór Ingvi Traustason). Coach: Uwe Rösler.
Goals: 37' Leandro Trossard 1-0, 71' Mbwana Samatta 2-0.
Referee: Aleksey Eskov (RUS)   Attendance: 11,590.

04.10.18 Swedbank Stadion, Malmö: Malmö FF – Besiktas JK 2-0 (0-0)
Malmö FF: Johan Dahlin, Behrang Safari, Rasmus Bengtsson, Lasse Nielsen (90+2' Franz Brorsson), Andreas Vindheim, Søren Rieks, Anders Christiansen (72' Bonke Innocent), Fouad Bachirou, Arnór Ingvi Traustason (85' Marcus Antonsson), Oscar Lewicki, Markus Rosenberg. Coach: Uwe Rösler.
Besiktas JK: Loris Karius, Pepe, Caner Erkin, Gökhan Gönül (82' Oguzhan Özyakup), Gary Medel, Domagoj Vida, Jeremain Lens, Necip Uysal, Gökhan Töre (59' Ryan Babel), Vágner Love, Adem Ljajic (70' Ricardo Quaresma). Coach: Senol Günes.
Goals: 53' Caner Erkin 1-0 (og), 76' Markus Rosenberg 2-0 (p).
Referee: Aleksandar Stavrev (MKD)   Attendance: 17,174.

04.10.18 Sarpsborg Stadion, Sarpsborg: Sarpsborg 08 – KRC Genk 3-1 (1-0)
Sarpsborg 08: Alexander Vasyutin, Amin Askar, Joackim Jørgensen, Joachim Thomassen, Joonas Tamm, Matti Lund Nielsen, Ole Halvorsen (73' Tobias Heintz), Jon-Helge Tveita, Kristoffer Zachariassen, Patrick Mortensen, Rashad Muhammed (82' Harmeet Singh). Coach: Geir Bakke.
KRC Genk: Danny Vukovic, Sebastien Dewaest, Bojan Nastic (46' Jere Uronen), Jhon Lucumí, Joakim Mæhle, Pozuelo, Ruslan Malinovskiy (66' Bryan Heynen), Sander Berge, Leandro Trossard, Mbwana Samatta, Dieumerci N'Dongala (46' Joseph Paintsil).
Coach: Philippe Clement.
Goals: 6' Patrick Mortensen 1-0. 49' Leandro Trossard 1-1, 54' Kristoffer Zachariassen 2-1, 63' Patrick Mortensen 3-1.
Referee: Ivan Bebek (CRO)   Attendance: 7,885.

25.10.18 Sarpsborg Stadion, Sarpsborg: Sarpsborg 08 – Malmö FF 1-1 (0-0)
Sarpsborg 08: Alexander Vasyutin, Jørgen Horn, Amin Askar (85' Jørgen Larsen), Joachim Thomassen, Joonas Tamm, Matti Lund Nielsen (87' Harmeet Singh), Ole Halvorsen, Jon-Helge Tveita, Kristoffer Zachariassen, Patrick Mortensen, Rashad Muhammed (77' Tobias Heintz). Coach: Geir Bakke.
Malmö FF: Johan Dahlin, Behrang Safari, Rasmus Bengtsson (57' Franz Brorsson), Lasse Nielsen, Andreas Vindheim, Søren Rieks, Anders Christiansen (83' Bonke Innocent), Fouad Bachirou, Arnór Ingvi Traustason, Oscar Lewicki (65' Marcus Antonsson), Markus Rosenberg. Coach: Uwe Rösler.
Goals: 79' Andreas Vindheim 0-1, 87' Ole Halvorsen 1-1.
Referee: Pawel Raczkowski (POL)   Attendance: 8,022.

25.10.18   Vodafone Stadyumu, Istanbul: Besiktas JK – KRC Genk 2-4 (0-1)
Besiktas JK: Loris Karius, Caner Erkin (85' Mustafa Pektemek), Gökhan Gönül, Gary Medel, Domagoj Vida, Jeremain Lens, Ricardo Quaresma, Necip Uysal, Tolgay Arslan (27' Enzo Roco), Oguzhan Özyakup, Cyle Larin (46' Vágner Love). Coach: Senol Günes.
KRC Genk: Danny Vukovic, Sebastien Dewaest, Jere Uronen, Jhon Lucumí, Joakim Mæhle, Pozuelo (80' Ibrahima Seck), Ruslan Malinovskiy, Bryan Heynen, Mbwana Samatta (87' Zinho Gano), Dieumerci N'Dongala, Joseph Paintsil (75' Jakub Piotrowski).
Coach: Philippe Clement.
Goals: 23', 70' Mbwana Samatta 0-1, 0-2, 74' Vágner Love 1-2,
81' Dieumerci N'Dongala 1-3, 83' Jakub Piotrowski 1-4, 86' Vágner Love 2-4.
Referee: Daniel Stefanski (POL)   Attendance: 25,209.

08.11.18   Swedbank Stadion, Malmö: Malmö FF – Sarpsborg 08 1-1 (0-0)
Malmö FF: Johan Dahlin, Behrang Safari (86' Romain Gall), Rasmus Bengtsson, Lasse Nielsen, Andreas Vindheim (61' Eric Larsson), Søren Rieks, Anders Christiansen, Fouad Bachirou, Arnór Ingvi Traustason, Markus Rosenberg, Marcus Antonsson (79' Carlos Strandberg). Coach: Uwe Rösler.
Sarpsborg 08: Alexander Vasyutin, Jørgen Horn, Amin Askar, Joachim Thomassen, Joonas Tamm, Matti Lund Nielsen, Ole Halvorsen, Jon-Helge Tveita, Gaute Vetti (90+1' Joackim Jørgensen), Patrick Mortensen, Rashad Muhammed (73' Tobias Heintz). Coach: Geir Bakke.
Goals: 63' Patrick Mortensen 0-1, 67' Marcus Antonsson 1-1.
Referee: Miroslav Zelinka (CZE)   Attendance: 17,601.

08.11.18   Luminus Arena, Genk: KRC Genk – Besiktas JK 1-1 (0-1)
KRC Genk: Danny Vukovic, Sebastien Dewaest, Jere Uronen, Joseph Aidoo, Joakim Mæhle, Pozuelo, Ruslan Malinovskiy (60' Sander Berge), Bryan Heynen, Mbwana Samatta, Dieumerci N'Dongala (89' Marcus Ingvartsen), Joseph Paintsil (66' Ivan Fiolic).
Coach: Philippe Clement.
Besiktas JK: Tolga Zengin, Pepe, Caner Erkin, Gary Medel, Domagoj Vida, Dorukhan Toköz (73' Adem Ljajic), Jeremain Lens (12' Mustafa Pektemek), Ricardo Quaresma, Necip Uysal, Oguzhan Özyakup (90' Vágner Love), Ryan Babel. Coach: Senol Günes.
Goals: 16' Ricardo Quaresma 0-1, 87' Sander Berge 1-1.
Referee: Tobias Stieler (GER)   Attendance: 14,292.

29.11.18   Sarpsborg Stadion, Sarpsborg: Sarpsborg 08 – Besiktas JK 2-3 (2-0)
Sarpsborg 08: Alexander Vasyutin, Jørgen Horn, Joachim Thomassen, Joonas Tamm (50' Joackim Jørgensen), Matti Lund Nielsen, Ole Halvorsen, Jon-Helge Tveita, Kristoffer Zachariassen, Tobias Heintz (68' Amin Askar), Patrick Mortensen, Rashad Muhammed (85' Jørgen Larsen). Coach: Geir Bakke.
Besiktas JK: Loris Karius, Adriano (78' Fatih Aksoy), Caner Erkin, Domagoj Vida, Dorukhan Toköz, Jeremain Lens (90+2' Erdem Seçgin), Necip Uysal, Oguzhan Özyakup, Adem Ljajic, Mustafa Pektemek, Cyle Larin (58' Vágner Love). Coach: Senol Günes.
Goals: 1' Rashad Muhammed 1-0, 6' Tobias Heintz 2-0, 62' Jeremain Lens 2-1,
66' Vágner Love 2-2, 90' Jeremain Lens 2-3.
Referee: Harald Lechner (AUT)   Attendance: 8,022.

118

29.11.18   Swedbank Stadion, Malmö: Malmö FF – KRC Genk 2-2 (0-1)
Malmö FF: Johan Dahlin, Behrang Safari (81' Franz Brorsson), Rasmus Bengtsson, Lasse Nielsen, Andreas Vindheim, Søren Rieks, Anders Christiansen (82' Romain Gall), Fouad Bachirou, Arnór Ingvi Traustason (54' Marcus Antonsson), Oscar Lewicki, Markus Rosenberg. Coach: Uwe Rösler.
KRC Genk: Danny Vukovic, Sebastien Dewaest, Jere Uronen, Joseph Aidoo, Joakim Mæhle, Pozuelo (86' Bryan Heynen), Ruslan Malinovskiy, Sander Berge, Leandro Trossard, Mbwana Samatta (73' Zinho Gano), Joseph Paintsil (54' Dieumerci N'Dongala).
Coach: Philippe Clement.
Goals: 42' Pozuelo 0-1, 53' Joseph Paintsil 0-2, 65' Oscar Lewicki 1-2, 67' Marcus Antonsson 2-2.
Referee: Srdjan Jovanovic (SER)   Attendance: 16,117.

13.12.18   Vodafone Stadyumu, Istanbul: Besiktas JK – Malmö FF 0-1 (0-0)
Besiktas JK: Loris Karius, Adriano, Gary Medel, Domagoj Vida, Dorukhan Toköz, Ricardo Quaresma, Necip Uysal, Oguzhan Özyakup (60' Gökhan Töre), Vágner Love (72' Cyle Larin), Adem Ljajic, Mustafa Pektemek (78' Fatih Aksoy). Coach: Senol Günes.
Malmö FF: Johan Dahlin, Behrang Safari (55' Franz Brorsson), Rasmus Bengtsson, Lasse Nielsen, Andreas Vindheim, Søren Rieks (80' Eric Larsson), Fouad Bachirou, Arnór Ingvi Traustason (75' Anders Christiansen), Oscar Lewicki, Markus Rosenberg, Marcus Antonsson. Coach: Uwe Rösler.
Goal: 51' Marcus Antonsson 0-1.
Referee: Luca Banti (ITA)   Attendance: 24,955.
Sent off: 65' Ricardo Quaresma.

13.12.18   Luminus Arena, Genk: KRC Genk – Sarpsborg 08 4-0 (2-0)
KRC Genk: Danny Vukovic, Sebastien Dewaest, Jere Uronen (75' Bojan Nastic), Joseph Aidoo, Joakim Mæhle, Pozuelo (65' Ruslan Malinovskiy), Ibrahima Seck, Sander Berge, Leandro Trossard (80' Dieumerci N'Dongala), Zinho Gano, Joseph Paintsil.
Coach: Philippe Clement.
Sarpsborg 08: Alexander Vasyutin, Jørgen Horn, Joachim Thomassen (56' Amin Askar), Joonas Tamm, Matti Lund Nielsen, Ole Halvorsen (82' Kristoffer Larsen), Jon-Helge Tveita, Kristoffer Zachariassen, Tobias Heintz, Patrick Mortensen, Rashad Muhammed (62' Jørgen Larsen). Coach: Geir Bakke.
Goals: 3' Zinho Gano 1-0, 5' Joseph Paintsil 2-0, 64' Sander Berge 3-0, 67' Joseph Aidoo 4-0.
Referee: István Kovács (ROM)   Attendance: 12,240.

GROUP J

20.09.18   Estadio Ramón Sánchez Pizjuán, Sevilla: Sevilla FC – Standard Liège 5-1 (2-1)
Sevilla FC: Tomás Vaclík, Simon Kjær, Daniel Carriço, Sergi Gómez, Guilherme Arana, Jesús Navas (80' Nolito), Éver Banega, Franco Vázquez (76' Pablo Sarabia), Ibrahim Amadou (15' Roque Mesa), Wissam Ben Yedder, Quincy Promes. Coach: Pablo Machín.
Standard Liège: Guillermo Ochoa, Luis Cavanda, Kostas Laifis, Collins Fai, Zinho Vanheusden, Christian Luyindama Nekadio, Mehdi Carcela-González (78' Uche Agbo), Gojko Cimirot, Razvan Marin, Moussa Djenepo (62' Maxime Lestienne), Orlando Sá (62' Renaud Emond). Coach: Michel Preud'homme.
Goals: 8' Éver Banega 1-0, 39' Moussa Djenepo 1-1, 41' Franco Vázquez 2-1, 49', 70' Wissam Ben Yedder 3-1, 4-1, 74' Éver Banega 5-1 (p).
Referee: Gediminas Mazeika (LTU)   Attendance: 30,003.

20.09.18   Spor Toto Akhisar Belediye Stadi, Akhisar:
Akhisar Belediyespor – FK Krasnodar 0-1 (0-1)
Akhisar Belediyespor: Fatih Öztürk, Avdija Vrsajevic, Kadir Keles (81' Onur Ayik), Mustafa Yumlu, Caner Osmanpasa, Serginho, Güray Vural, Abdoulwhaid Sissoko, Josué (60' Bilal Kisa), Adrien Regattin (60' Elvis Manu), Evgen Seleznyov. Coach: Cem Kavcak.
FK Krasnodar: Stanislav Kritsyuk, Aleksandr Martynovich, Uros Spajic, Cristian Ramírez, Pavel Mamaev (69' Mauricio Pereyra), Charles Kaboré, Dmitriy Stotskiy, Yuri Gazinskiy, Victor Claesson, Ari (84' Sergey Petrov), Wamberto (79' Christian Cueva).
Coach: Murad Musaev.
Goal: 26' Victor Claesson 0-1.
Referee: Ville Nevalainen (FIN)   Attendance: 6,555.

04.10.18   Stadion FK Krasnodar, Krasnodar: FK Krasnodar – Sevilla FC 2-1 (0-1)
FK Krasnodar: Stanislav Kritsyuk, Aleksandr Martynovich, Uros Spajic, Cristian Ramírez, Pavel Mamaev (74' Magomed Suleymanov), Charles Kaboré (69' Mauricio Pereyra), Christian Cueva, Yuri Gazinskiy, Sergey Petrov, Victor Claesson, Wamberto (84' Tornike Okriashvili).
Coach: Murad Musaev.
Sevilla FC: Tomás Vaclík, Simon Kjær, Sergi Gómez, Guilherme Arana, Joris Gnagnon, Jesús Navas, Éver Banega, Roque Mesa, Nolito (76' Franco Vázquez), Luis Muriel (61' André Silva), Quincy Promes (77' Wissam Ben Yedder). Coach: Pablo Machín.
Goals: 43' Charles Kaboré 0-1 (og), 72' Mauricio Pereyra 1-1, 88' Tornike Okriashvili 2-1.
Referee: Martin Strömbergsson (SWE)   Attendance: 31,346.

04.10.18   Stade Maurice Dufrasne, Liège: Standard Liège – Akhisar Belediyespor 2-1 (2-1)
Standard Liège: Guillermo Ochoa, Sébastien Pocognoli, Luis Cavanda, Kostas Laifis, Christian Luyindama Nekadio, Mehdi Carcela-González, Gojko Cimirot, Razvan Marin, Uche Agbo (76' Paul M'Poku), Moussa Djenepo, Renaud Emond (83' Orlando Sá).
Coach: Michel Preud'homme.
Akhisar Belediyespor: Fatih Öztürk, Miguel Lopes, Mustafa Yumlu, Caner Osmanpasa, Bilal Kisa (40' Abdoulwhaid Sissoko), Güray Vural, Josué, Aykut Çeviker, Hélder Barbosa, Evgen Seleznyov (80' Elvis Manu), Onur Ayik (72' Adrien Regattin). Coach: Cihat Arslan.
Goals: 17' Renaud Emond 1-0, 32' Onur Ayik 1-1, 40' Moussa Djenepo 2-1.
Referee: Manuel Schüttengruber (AUT)   Attendance: 8,233.
Sent off: 82' Mustafa Yumlu.

25.10.18   Stade Maurice Dufrasne, Liège: Standard Liège – FK Krasnodar 2-1 (0-1)
Standard Liège: Guillermo Ochoa, Sébastien Pocognoli, Luis Cavanda, Kostas Laifis, Collins Fai (78' Maxime Lestienne), Christian Luyindama Nekadio, Mehdi Carcela-González, Gojko Cimirot, Razvan Marin, Uche Agbo (46' Moussa Djenepo), Renaud Emond (84' Samuel Bastien). Coach: Michel Preud'homme.
FK Krasnodar: Andrey Sinitsyn, Aleksandr Martynovich, Uros Spajic, Cristian Ramírez, Charles Kaboré, Mauricio Pereyra (77' Christian Cueva), Yuri Gazinskiy, Sergey Petrov, Victor Claesson, Ari (76' Ivan Ignatyev), Wamberto (80' Magomed Suleymanov).
Coach: Murad Musaev.
Goals: 39' Ari 0-1, 47' Renaud Emond 1-1, 90+3' Kostas Laifis 2-1.
Referee: Marco Guida (ITA)   Attendance: 8,393.

25.10.18   Estadio Ramón Sánchez Pizjuán, Sevilla:
Sevilla FC – Akhisar Belediyespor 6-0 (3-0)
<u>Sevilla FC:</u> Tomás Vaclík, Gabriel Mercado, Daniel Carriço (59' Ibrahim Amadou), Aleix Vidal, Sergi Gómez, Jesús Navas (54' Nolito), Franco Vázquez, Pablo Sarabia (54' Guilherme Arana), Roque Mesa, Luis Muriel, Quincy Promes. Coach: Pablo Machín.
<u>Akhisar Belediyespor:</u> Milan Lukac, Miguel Lopes, Kadir Keles (46' Hélder Barbosa), Dany Nounkeu, Caner Osmanpasa, Güray Vural, Abdoulwhaid Sissoko, Josué (77' Eray Ataseven), Adrien Regattin, Aykut Çeviker, Evgen Seleznyov (63' Onur Ayik). Coach: Cihat Arslan.
<u>Goals:</u> 7' Roque Mesa 1-0, 9' Pablo Sarabia 2-0 (p), 35' Milan Lukac 3-0 (og), 50' Luis Muriel 4-0, 60' Quincy Promes 5-0, 67' Gabriel Mercado 6-0.
<u>Referee:</u> Kevin Clancy (SCO)   Attendance: 29,720.

08.11.18   Stadion FK Krasnodar, Krasnodar: FK Krasnodar – Standard Liège 2-1 (0-1)
<u>FK Krasnodar:</u> Matvei Safonov, Aleksandr Martynovich, Uros Spajic, Charles Kaboré (73' Magomed Suleymanov), Christian Cueva (46' Mauricio Pereyra), Dmitriy Stotskiy, Yuri Gazinskiy, Sergey Petrov, Victor Claesson (66' Ivan Ignatyev), Ari, Wamberto.
Coach: Murad Musaev.
<u>Standard Liège:</u> Guillermo Ochoa, Kostas Laifis, Collins Fai, Zinho Vanheusden, Christian Luyindama Nekadio, Mehdi Carcela-González, Maxime Lestienne (83' Samuel Bastien), Gojko Cimirot, Razvan Marin (89' Paul M'Poku), Moussa Djenepo (89' Orlando Sá), Renaud Emond. Coach: Michel Preud'homme.
<u>Goals:</u> 19' Mehdi Carcela-González 0-1, 79' Magomed Suleymanov 1-1, 82' Wamberto 2-1.
<u>Referee:</u> Aleksandar Stavrev (MKD)   Atteandance: 21,526.

08.11.18   Spor Toto Akhisar Belediye Stadi, Akhisar:
Akhisar Belediyespor – Sevilla FC 2-3 (0-2)
<u>Akhisar Belediyespor:</u> Milan Lukac, Avdija Vrsajevic, Miguel Lopes, Caner Osmanpasa (46' Kadir Keles), Güray Vural, Abdoulwhaid Sissoko, Josué, Aykut Çeviker, Eray Ataseven (72' Onur Ayik), Hélder Barbosa (88' Bilal Kisa), Elvis Manu. Coach: Cihat Arslan.
<u>Sevilla FC:</u> Tomás Vaclík, Sergio Escudero, Aleix Vidal, Sergi Gómez, Joris Gnagnon, Éver Banega, Franco Vázquez, Ibrahim Amadou, Nolito (64' Roque Mesa), Luis Muriel (74' Pablo Sarabia), Quincy Promes (88' Daniel Carriço). Coach: Pablo Machín.
<u>Goals:</u> 12' Nolito 0-1, 38' Luis Muriel 0-2, 52' Elvis Manu 1-2, 78' Onur Ayik 2-2, 87' Éver Banega 2-3 (p).
<u>Referee:</u> Benoît Millot (FRA)   Attendance: 6,430.
<u>Sent off:</u> 56' Sergi Gómez.

Güray Vural missed a penalty kick (57').

29.11.18   Stadion FK Krasnodar, Krasnodar: FK Krasnodar – Akhisar Belediyespor 2-1 (0-1)
<u>FK Krasnodar:</u> Matvei Safonov, Aleksandr Martynovich, Uros Spajic, Cristian Ramírez, Charles Kaboré, Christian Cueva (70' Magomed Suleymanov), Dmitriy Stotskiy (46' Ivan Ignatyev), Yuri Gazinskiy, Sergey Petrov, Ari (72' Mauricio Pereyra), Wamberto.
Coach: Murad Musaev.
<u>Akhisar Belediyespor:</u> Milan Lukac, Avdija Vrsajevic, Miguel Lopes, Caner Osmanpasa, Serginho (84' Kadir Keles), Güray Vural, Abdoulwhaid Sissoko, Adrien Regattin, Aykut Çeviker (72' Eray Ataseven), Hélder Barbosa, Elvis Manu (42' Onur Ayik).
Coach: Cihat Arslan.
<u>Goals:</u> 24' Serginho 0-1, 49' Yuri Gazinskiy 1-1, 57' Ari 2-1.
<u>Referee:</u> Ivaylo Stoyanov (BUL)   Attendance: 11,008.

29.11.18 Stade Maurice Dufrasne, Liège: Standard Liège – Sevilla FC 1-0 (0-0)
Standard Liège: Guillermo Ochoa, Kostas Laifis, Collins Fai, Zinho Vanheusden, Christian Luyindama Nekadio, Mehdi Carcela-González (85' Maxime Lestienne), Gojko Cimirot, Paul M'Poku (43' Razvan Marin), Samuel Bastien, Moussa Djenepo, Renaud Emond (65' Orlando Sá). Coach: Michel Preud'homme.
Sevilla FC: Tomás Vaclík, Simon Kjær, Gabriel Mercado, Daniel Carriço, Aleix Vidal (52' Pablo Sarabia), Guilherme Arana (85' Luis Muriel), Éver Banega, Franco Vázquez (76' André Silva), Roque Mesa, Wissam Ben Yedder, Quincy Promes. Coach: Pablo Machín.
Goal: 62' Moussa Djenepo 1-0.
Referee: Daniel Siebert (GER)   Attendance: 12,882.
Sent off: 68' Pablo Sarabia.

13.12.18 Estadio Ramón Sánchez Pizjuán, Sevilla: Sevilla FC – FK Krasnodar 3-0 (2-0)
Sevilla FC: Tomás Vaclík, Gabriel Mercado, Daniel Carriço, Sergio Escudero, Sergi Gómez, Éver Banega (70' Ibrahim Amadou), Franco Vázquez, Roque Mesa, Wissam Ben Yedder (72' Jesús Navas), Quincy Promes, André Silva (77' Luis Muriel). Coach: Pablo Machín.
FK Krasnodar: Stanislav Kritsyuk, Jón Fjóluson, Aleksandr Martynovich, Cristian Ramírez, Charles Kaboré, Mauricio Pereyra (51' Dmitriy Stotskiy), Yuri Gazinskiy, Sergey Petrov, Victor Claesson, Wamberto (77' Roman Shishkin), Ivan Ignatyev (61' Christian Cueva). Coach: Murad Musaev.
Goals: 5', 10' Wissam Ben Yedder 1-0, 2-0, 49' Éver Banega 3-0 (p).
Referee: Daniel Stefanski (POL)   Attendance: 34,114.
Sent off: 48' Cristian Ramírez.

13.12.18 Spor Toto Akhisar Belediye Stadi, Akhisar:
Akhisar Belediyespor – Standard Liège 0-0
Akhisar Belediyespor: Milan Lukac, Avdija Vrsajevic, Kadir Keles, Caner Osmanpasa, Serginho (17' Eray Ataseven), Abdoulwhaid Sissoko, Josué, Adrien Regattin (71' Onur Ayik), Aykut Çeviker, Hélder Barbosa (90+2' Bilal Kisa), Elvis Manu. Coach: Cihat Arslan.
Standard Liège: Guillermo Ochoa, Milos Kosanovic, Collins Fai, Zinho Vanheusden, Christian Luyindama Nekadio, Mehdi Carcela-González, Maxime Lestienne, Razvan Marin, Uche Agbo (60' Paul M'Poku), Samuel Bastien (83' Renaud Emond), Orlando Sá (83' Obbi Oularé). Coach: Michel Preud'homme.
Referee: Ádám Farkas (HUN)   Attendance: 2,674.

GROUP K

20.09.18 Roazhon Park, Rennes: Stade Rennes – FK Jablonec 2-1 (1-0)
Stade Rennes: Tomás Koubek, Damien Da Silva, Mexer, Hamari Traoré, Jérémy Gelin (65' Hatem Ben Arfa), Ramy Bensebaini, Clément Grenier, Benjamin André, Theoson Siebatcheu, Romain Del Castillo (61' M'Baye Niang), Ismaïli Sarr (75' Benjamin Bourigeaud). Coach: Sabri Lamouchi.
FK Jablonec: Vlastimil Hrubý, Tomás Holes, Matej Hanousek, David Hovorka, David Lischka, Tomás Hübschman, Jakub Povazanec, Michal Trávník, Lukás Masopust (77' Vojtech Kubista), Martin Dolezal (46' Jan Chramosta), Vladimir Jovovic (88' Tomás Brecka). Coach: Petr Rada.
Goals: 31' Ismaïli Sarr 1-0, 54' Michal Trávník 1-1, 90+1' Hatem Ben Arfa 2-1 (p).
Referee: Ole Hobber Nilsen (NOR)   Attendance: 20,628.

20.09.18   NSK Olimpijs'kyj, Kiev: Dinamo Kiev – FK Astana 2-2 (2-1)
Dinamo Kiev: Denis Boyko, Josip Pivaric, Tamás Kádár, Tomasz Kedziora, Mykyta Burda, Sergiy Sydorchuk, Denys Garmash (79' Mikkel Duelund), Vitaliy Buyalskiy (90+3' Volodymyr Shepeliev), Benjamin Verbic, Viktor Tsygankov (90+1' Mikola Morozyuk), Nazariy Rusyn. Coach: Aleksandr Khatskevich.
FK Astana: Nenad Eric, Antonio Rukavina, Marin Anicic, Dmitriy Shomko, Evgeni Postnikov, Marin Tomasov (88' Roman Murtazaev), Ivan Maevski, Richard Almeyda (80' Serikzhan Muzhikov), László Kleinheisler, Pedro Henrique, Junior Kabananga (82' Rangelo Janga). Coach: Roman Grygorchuk.
Goals: 11' Viktor Tsygankov 1-0, 21' Marin Anicic 1-1, 45+1' Denys Garmash 2-1, 90+5' Roman Murtazaev 2-2.
Referee: Halis Özkahya (TUR)   Attendance: 21,783.

04.10.18   Astana Arena, Astana: FK Astana – Stade Rennes 2-0 (0-0)
FK Astana: Nenad Eric, Antonio Rukavina, Marin Anicic, Dmitriy Shomko, Evgeni Postnikov, Marin Tomasov, Ivan Maevski, Richard Almeyda (63' Serikzhan Muzhikov), Pedro Henrique, Junior Kabananga (72' Rangelo Janga), Baktiyor Zaynutdinov (75' Yuriy Logvinenko). Coach: Roman Grygorchuk.
Stade Rennes: Abdoulaye Diallo, Ludovic Baal (28' Ramy Bensebaini), Damien Da Silva, Medhi Zeffane, Jérémy Gelin, Clément Grenier, Benjamin André, Benjamin Bourigeaud, Denis Poha (77' Jakob Johansson), James Lea Siliki (69' Romain Del Castillo), M'Baye Niang. Coach: Sabri Lamouchi.
Goals: 64' Baktiyor Zaynutdinov 1-0, 90+1' Marin Tomasov 2-0.
Referee: Mattias Gestranius (FIN)   Attendance: 25,302.

04.10.18   Stadion Strelnice, Jablonec nad Nisou: FK Jablonec – Dinamo Kiev 2-2 (1-2)
FK Jablonec: Vlastimil Hrubý, Tomás Holes, Matej Hanousek, David Hovorka, David Lischka, Tomás Hübschman, Jakub Povazanec, Michal Trávník, Lukás Masopust (86' Vojtech Kubista), Jan Chramosta (78' Davis Ikaunieks), Vladimir Jovovic (90+2' Eduard Sobol). Coach: Petr Rada.
Dinamo Kiev: Denis Boyko, Mikola Morozyuk, Josip Pivaric, Tamás Kádár, Tomasz Kedziora, Mykyta Burda, Sergiy Sydorchuk, Denys Garmash, Vitaliy Buyalskiy (79' Volodymyr Shepeliev), Viktor Tsygankov, Artem Besedin. Coach: Aleksandr Khatskevich.
Goals: 8' Viktor Tsygankov 0-1, 14' Denys Garmash 0-2, 33' David Hovorka 1-2, 81' Michal Trávník 2-2.
Referee: Sébastien Delferière (BEL)   Attendance: 5,077.

25.10.18   Stadion Strelnice, Jablonec nad Nisou: FK Jablonec – FK Astana 1-1 (1-1)
FK Jablonec: Vlastimil Hrubý, Tomás Holes, Matej Hanousek, David Hovorka, David Lischka, Tomás Hübschman, Jakub Povazanec, Michal Trávník (90+1' Vojtech Kubista), Lukás Masopust, Jan Chramosta (57' Davis Ikaunieks), Vladimir Jovovic (87' Rafael Acosta). Coach: Petr Rada.
FK Astana: Nenad Eric, Antonio Rukavina, Marin Anicic, Evgeni Postnikov, Marin Tomasov, Ivan Maevski, Richard Almeyda (90' Roman Murtazaev), László Kleinheisler, Pedro Henrique (46' Serikzhan Muzhikov), Junior Kabananga (74' Rangelo Janga), Baktiyor Zaynutdinov. Coach: Roman Grygorchuk.
Goals: 4' Jakub Povazanec 1-0, 11' Pedro Henrique 1-1.
Referee: Robert Schörgenhofer (AUT)   Attendance: 4,909.

25.10.18   Roazhon Park, Rennes: Stade Rennes – Dinamo Kiev 1-2 (1-1)
Stade Rennes: Abdoulaye Diallo, Damien Da Silva, Hamari Traoré, Jérémy Gelin, Ramy Bensebaini, Jakob Johansson (90' James Lea Siliki), Clément Grenier, Benjamin André, M'Baye Niang (74' Hatem Ben Arfa), Romain Del Castillo (61' Benjamin Bourigeaud), Ismaïla Sarr. Coach: Sabri Lamouchi.
Dinamo Kiev: Denis Boyko, Mikola Morozyuk (80' Tchê Tchê), Tamás Kádár, Tomasz Kedziora, Mykyta Burda, Sidcley, Vitali Mykolenko, Denys Garmash (68' Sergiy Sydorchuk), Vitaliy Buyalskiy, Benjamin Verbic (74' Vladyslav Supriaha), Volodymyr Shepeliev.
Coach: Aleksandr Khatskevich.
Goals: 21' Tomasz Kedziora 0-1, 41' Clément Grenier 1-1, 89' Vitaliy Buyalskiy 1-2.
Referee: Tamás Bognár (HUN)   Attendance: 28,001.
Sent off: 94' Volodymyr Shepeliev.

08.11.18   Astana Arena, Astana: FK Astana – FK Jablonec 2-1 (1-1)
FK Astana: Nenad Eric, Antonio Rukavina, Marin Anicic, Evgeni Postnikov, Marin Tomasov, Ivan Maevski, Richard Almeyda (71' Serikzhan Muzhikov), László Kleinheisler, Pedro Henrique (80' Roman Murtazaev), Junior Kabananga (61' Rangelo Janga), Baktiyor Zaynutdinov. Coach: Roman Grygorchuk.
FK Jablonec: Vlastimil Hrubý, Eduard Sobol (72' Milos Kratochvíl), Tomás Holes, Matej Hanousek, David Hovorka, David Lischka, Tomás Hübschman, Jakub Povazanec, Michal Trávník, Martin Dolezal, Vladimir Jovovic (89' Vojtech Kubista). Coach: Petr Rada.
Goals: 18' Pedro Henrique 1-0, 41' Baktiyor Zaynutdinov 1-1 (og), 88' Evgeni Postnikov 2-1.
Referee: István Vad (II) (HUN)   Attendance: 20,092.

08.11.18   NSK Olimpijs'kyj, Kiev: Dinamo Kiev – Stade Rennes 3-1 (1-0)
Dinamo Kiev: Denis Boyko, Tamás Kádár, Tomasz Kedziora, Mykyta Burda, Sidcley, Vitali Mykolenko, Vitaliy Buyalskiy, Tchê Tchê (83' Sergiy Sydorchuk), Benjamin Verbic (90' Vladyslav Supriaha), Viktor Tsygankov, Mykola Shaparenko (90+2' Mikkel Duelund).
Coach: Aleksandr Khatskevich.
Stade Rennes: Tomás Koubek, Damien Da Silva, Medhi Zeffane, Hamari Traoré (46' M'Baye Niang), Ramy Bensebaini, Gerzino Nyamsi (74' Jérémy Gelin), Hatem Ben Arfa, Benjamin Bourigeaud, Denis Poha, James Lea Siliki, Ismaïla Sarr (71' Theoson Siebatcheu).
Coach: Sabri Lamouchi.
Goals: 13' Benjamin Verbic 1-0, 68' Vitali Mykolenko 2-0, 72' Mykola Shaparenko 3-0, 89' Theoson Siebatcheu 3-1.
Referee: John Beaton (SCO)   Attendance: 24,402.

29.11.18   Astana Arena, Astana: FK Astana – Dinamo Kiev 0-1 (0-1)
FK Astana: Nenad Eric, Antonio Rukavina, Marin Anicic, Evgeni Postnikov, Marin Tomasov, Ivan Maevski, Richard Almeyda (58' Serikzhan Muzhikov), László Kleinheisler, Junior Kabananga (62' Rangelo Janga), Roman Murtazaev, Baktiyor Zaynutdinov (76' Dmitriy Shomko). Coach: Roman Grygorchuk.
Dinamo Kiev: Denis Boyko, Tamás Kádár, Tomasz Kedziora, Mykyta Burda, Sidcley, Vitali Mykolenko, Tchê Tchê, Benjamin Verbic (76' Sergiy Sydorchuk), Viktor Tsygankov (84' Mikola Morozyuk), Mykola Shaparenko (64' Denys Garmash), Volodymyr Shepeliev.
Coach: Aleksandr Khatskevich.
Goal: 29' Benjamin Verbic 0-1.
Referee: Ivan Bebek (CRO)   Attendance: 26,508.

29.11.18 Stadion Strelnice, Jablonec nad Nisou: FK Jablonec – Stade Rennes 0-1 (0-0)
FK Jablonec: Vlastimil Hrubý, Eduard Sobol (63' Milos Kratochvíl), Tomás Holes, Vojtech Kubista, Matej Hanousek, David Hovorka, David Lischka, Tomás Hübschman (82' Jan Chramosta), Jakub Povazanec, Michal Trávník, Martin Dolezal. Coach: Petr Rada.
Stade Rennes: Tomás Koubek, Damien Da Silva, Mexer, Medhi Zeffane, Hamari Traoré, Jakob Johansson, Clément Grenier (77' Hatem Ben Arfa), Benjamin André, Benjamin Bourigeaud (63' M'Baye Niang), James Lea Siliki, Ismaïla Sarr (89' Adrien Hunou). Coach: Sabri Lamouchi.
Goal: 55' Clément Grenier 0-1.
Referee: Tiago Martins (POR)   Attendance: 4,712.

13.12.18 Roazhon Park, Rennes: Stade Rennes – FK Astana 2-0 (0-0)
Stade Rennes: Abdoulaye Diallo, Damien Da Silva, Mexer, Hamari Traoré, Ramy Bensebaini, Hatem Ben Arfa (90+2' Adrien Hunou), Clément Grenier, Benjamin André, Benjamin Bourigeaud (82' M'Baye Niang), Theoson Siebatcheu (75' Jakob Johansson), Ismaïla Sarr. Coach: Julien Stephane.
FK Astana: Nenad Eric, Antonio Rukavina, Marin Anicic, Evgeni Postnikov, Marin Tomasov, Ivan Maevski, Richard Almeyda (46' Abzal Beysebekov), László Kleinheisler (86' Dmitriy Shomko), Pedro Henrique (81' Roman Murtazaev), Junior Kabananga, Baktiyor Zaynutdinov. Coach: Roman Grygorchuk.
Goals: 68', 73' Ismaïla Sarr 1-0, 2-0.
Referee: Serdar Gözübüyük (HOL)   Attendance: 24,535.

Benjamin Bourigeaud missed a penalty kick (67').

13.12.18 NSK Olimpijs'kyj, Kiev: Dinamo Kiev – FK Jablonec 0-1 (0-1)
Dinamo Kiev: Georgiy Bushchan, Tamás Kádár, Tomasz Kedziora, Mykyta Burda, Vitali Mykolenko, Sergiy Sydorchuk, Benjamin Verbic, Viktor Tsygankov, Mykola Shaparenko (60' Heorhii Tsitaishvili), Volodymyr Shepeliev, Artem Besedin (66' Mikkel Duelund, 76' Oleksandr Andrievsky). Coach: Aleksandr Khatskevich.
FK Jablonec: Vlastimil Hrubý, Tomás Holes, Matej Hanousek, David Hovorka, David Lischka, Tomás Hübschman, Michal Trávník, Milos Kratochvíl (89' Tomás Brecka), Martin Dolezal, Jan Chramosta (70 Rafael Acosta), Vladimir Jovovic (79' Eduard Sobol). Coach: Petr Rada.
Goal: 10' Martin Dolezal 0-1.
Referee: Vilhjálmur Alvar Thórarinsson (ISL)   Attendance: 11,300.

GROUP L

20.09.18 Stadio Toumba, Thessaloniki: PAOK Saloniki – Chelsea FC 0-1 (0-1)
PAOK Saloniki: Alexandros Paschalakis, Fernando Varela, Evgen Khacheridi, Alin Tosca, Pontus Wernbloom, Vieirinha, Omar El Kaddouri, Maurício, Evgen Shakhov (69' Aleksandar Prijovic), Dimitrios Pelkas (62' Amr Warda), Léo Jabá (82' Diego Biseswar). Coach: Razvan Lucescu.
Chelsea FC: Kepa, Marcos Alonso (66' Azpilicueta), Antonio Rüdiger, Davide Zappacosta, Andreas Christensen, Ross Barkley, Jorginho (65' Cesc Fàbregas), N'Golo Kanté, Willian, Pedro, Álvaro Morata (81' Olivier Giroud). Coach: Maurizio Sarri.
Goals: 7' Willian 0-1.
Referee: Alberto Undiano Mallenco (ESP)   Attendance: 24,310.

20.09.18   Groupama Aréna, Budapest: MOL Vidi FC – BATE Borisov 0-2 (0-1)
MOL Vidi FC: Tomás Tujvel, Roland Juhász, Attila Fiola (64' Armin Hodzic), Loïc Négo, Paulo Vinícius, Stopira, Anel Hadzic, Georgi Milanov (76' Szilveszter Hangya), István Kovács, Boban Nikolov (78' Zsombor Berecz), Marko Scepovic. Coach: Marko Nikolic.
BATE Borisov: Denis Scherbitski, Egor Filipenko, Denis Polyakov, Nemanja Milunovic, Aleksander Filipovic, Igor Stasevich (88' Maksim Volodko), Dmitriy Baga, Stanislav Dragun, Mirko Ivanic (67' Mikhail Gordeychuk), Jasse Tuominen (61' Maksim Skavysh), Evgeni Yablonski. Coach: Aleksei Baga.
Goals: 27' Jasse Tuominen 0-1, 85' Egor Filipenka 0-2.
Referee: Mads-Kristoffer Kristoffersen (DEN)   Attendance: 14,726.
Sent off: 90+5' Aleksander Filipovic.

(MOL Vidi FC played their three home matches at Groupama Arena, Budapest, instead of their regular stadium MOL Aréna Sóstó, Székesfehérvár, due to delays with the construction of their new stadium)

04.10.18   Borisov Arena, Borisov: BATE Borisov – PAOK Saloniki 1-4 (0-3)
BATE Borisov: Denis Scherbitski, Egor Filipenko, Denis Polyakov, Maksim Volodko, Aleksey Rios, Igor Stasevich (77' Mikhail Gordeychuk), Dmitriy Baga, Stanislav Dragun (71' Aliaksandr Hleb), Mirko Ivanic, Jasse Tuominen (59' Maksim Skavysh), Evgeni Yablonski. Coach: Aleksei Baga.
PAOK Saloniki: Alexandros Paschalakis, Léo Matos, José Ángel Crespo, Fernando Varela, Alin Tosca, Maurício, Cañas, Dimitrios Pelkas, Aleksandar Prijovic (76' Chuba Akpom), Dimitris Limnios (70' Diego Biseswar), Léo Jabá (86' Vieirinha). Coach: Razvan Lucescu.
Goals: 6' Aleksandar Prijovic 0-1, 11', 17' Léo Jabá 0-2, 0-3, 61' José Ángel Crespo 1-3 (og), 73' Dimitrios Pelkas 1-4.
Referee: Robert Schörgenhofer (AUT)   Attendance: 10,527.

04.10.18   Stamford Bridge, London: Chelsea FC – MOL Vidi FC 1-0 (0-0)
Chelsea FC: Kepa, Gary Cahill, Emerson, Davide Zappacosta, Andreas Christensen, Cesc Fàbregas, Mateo Kovacic, Ruben Loftus-Cheek (66' Ross Barkley), Willian (74' Victor Moses), Pedro (54' Eden Hazard), Álvaro Morata. Coach: Maurizio Sarri.
MOL Vidi FC: Tomás Tujvel, Roland Juhász, Attila Fiola, Loïc Négo, Paulo Vinícius, Stopira, Szabolcs Huszti (77' István Kovács), Anel Hadzic (83' Máté Pátkai), Georgi Milanov (83' Armin Hodzic), Boban Nikolov, Marko Scepovic. Coach: Marko Nikolic.
Goal: 70' Álvaro Morata 1-0.
Referee: Miroslav Zelinka (CZE)   Attendance: 39.925.

25.10.18   Stamford Bridge, London: Chelsea FC – BATE Borisov 3-1 (2-0)
Chelsea FC: Kepa, Gary Cahill, Emerson, Davide Zappacosta, Andreas Christensen, Cesc Fàbregas, Mateo Kovacic (77' N'Goto Kanté), Ruben Loftus-Cheek, Willian (57' Victor Moses), Olivier Giroud, Pedro (60' Callum Hudson-Odoi). Coach: Maurizio Sarri.
BATE Borisov: Denis Scherbitski, Egor Filipenko, Maksim Volodko, Aleksander Filipovic, Aliaksandr Hleb (59' Mirko Ivanic), Aleksey Rios, Igor Stasevich, Dmitriy Baga (76' Evgeni Yablonski), Stanislav Dragun, Maksim Skavysh, Nikolay Signevich (71' Jasse Tuominen). Coach: Aleksei Baga.
Goals: 2', 8', 54' Ruben Loftus-Cheek 1-0, 2-0, 3-0, 80' Aleksey Rios 3-1.
Referee: Paolo Mazzoleni (ITA)   Attendance: 39,799.

25.10.18 Stadio Toumba, Thessaloniki: PAOK Saloniki – MOL Vidi FC 0-2 (0-2)
PAOK Saloniki: Alexandros Paschalakis, Léo Matos, José Ángel Crespo, Fernando Varela, Alin Tosca, Omar El Kaddouri, Evgen Shakhov (52' Aleksandar Prijovic), Cañas, Dimitrios Pelkas, Nikolaos Karelis (66' Diego Biseswar), Dimitris Limnios (46' Amr Warda).
Coach: Razvan Lucescu.
MOL Vidi FC: Ádám Kovácsik, Roland Juhász, Attila Fiola, Loïc Négo, Paulo Vinícius, Stopira, Szabolcs Huszti (73' István Kovács), Anel Hadzic, Máté Pátkai, Georgi Milanov (79' Boban Nikolov), Marko Scepovic (65' Armin Hodzic). Coach: Marko Nikolic.
Goals: 12' Szabolcs Huszti 0-1, 45' Stopira 0-2.
Referee: Yevhen Aranovskyi (UKR)   Attendance: 15,118.

08.11.18 Borisov Arena, Borisov: BATE Borisov – Chelsea FC 0-1 (0-0)
BATE Borisov: Denis Scherbitski, Egor Filipenko, Aleksander Filipovic, Aliaksandr Hleb (81' Evgeniy Berezkin), Aleksey Rios, Igor Stasevich, Dmitriy Baga, Stanislav Dragun, Zakhar Volkov, Maksim Skavysh (76' Hervaine Moukam), Nikolay Signevich (73' Jasse Tuominen). Coach: Aleksei Baga.
Chelsea FC: Kepa, Gary Cahill, Emerson, Davide Zappacosta, Andreas Christensen, Ross Barkley, Jorginho, Ruben Loftus-Cheek (64' Mateo Kovacic), Eden Hazard (62' Willian), Olivier Giroud, Pedro (85' Callum Hudson-Odoi). Coach: Maurizio Sarri.
Goal: 53' Olivier Giroud 0-1.
Referee: Nikola Dabanovic (MNE)   Attendance: 13,141.

08.11.18 Groupama Aréna, Budapest: MOL Vidi FC – PAOK Saloniki 1-0 (0-0)
MOL Vidi FC: Ádám Kovácsik, Roland Juhász, Attila Fiola, Loïc Négo, Paulo Vinícius, Stopira, Szabolcs Huszti (66' István Kovács), Anel Hadzic, Máté Pátkai, Georgi Milanov (58' Boban Nikolov), Marko Scepovic (77' Armin Hodzic). Coach: Marko Nikolic.
PAOK Saloniki: Alexandros Paschalakis, Léo Matos, José Ángel Crespo, Fernando Varela, Alin Tosca, Pontus Wernbloom, Omar El Kaddouri (63' Chuba Akpom), Evgen Shakhov, Aleksandar Prijovic, Dimitris Limnios (60' Diego Biseswar), Léo Jabá (71' Amr Warda). Coach: Razvan Lucescu.
Goal: 50' Georgi Milanov 1-0.
Referee: Ali Palabiyik (TUR)   Attendance: 17,208.

29.11.18 Borisov Arena, Borisov: BATE Borisov – MOL Vidi FC 2-0 (1-0)
BATE Borisov: Denis Scherbitski, Egor Filipenko (46' Denis Polyakov), Aleksander Filipovic, Aliaksandr Hleb (66' Maksim Skavysh), Aleksey Rios, Igor Stasevich (90' Mikhail Gordeychuk), Dmitriy Baga, Stanislav Dragun, Mirko Ivanic, Zakhar Volkov, Nikolay Signevich. Coach: Aleksei Baga.
MOL Vidi FC: Ádám Kovácsik, Roland Juhász, Attila Fiola, Loïc Négo (67' István Kovács), Paulo Vinícius, Stopira, Szabolcs Huszti (74' Boban Nikolov), Anel Hadzic, Máté Pátkai (64' Armin Hodzic), Georgi Milanov, Marko Scepovic. Coach: Marko Nikolic.
Goals: 22' Nikolay Signevich 1-0, 85' Mirko Ivanic 2-0.
Referee: Carlos del Cerro Grande (ESP)   Attendance: 8,963.

29.11.18   Stamford Bridge, London: Chelsea FC – PAOK Saloniki 4-0 (2-0)
Chelsea FC: Kepa, Gary Cahill, Emerson, Davide Zappacosta (63' Ethan Ampadu), Andreas Christensen, Cesc Fàbregas, Ross Barkley, Ruben Loftus-Cheek, Olivier Giroud (75' Álvaro Morata), Pedro (66' Willian), Callum Hudson-Odoi. Coach: Maurizio Sarri.
PAOK Saloniki: Alexandros Paschalakis, Léo Matos, José Ángel Crespo, Evgen Khacheridi, Pontus Wernbloom, Vieirinha, Omar El Kaddouri (76' Fernando Varela), Maurício (78' Dimitrios Pelkas), Evgen Shakhov, Aleksandar Prijovic (46' Amr Warda), Léo Jabá. Coach: Razvan Lucescu.
Goals: 27', 37' Olivier Giroud 1-0, 2-0, 60' Callum Hudson-Odoi 3-0, 78' Álvaro Morata 4-0.
Referee: Kristo Tohver (EST)   Attendance: 33,933.
Sent off: 7' Evgen Khacheridi.

13.12.18   Stadio Toumba, Thessaloniki: PAOK Saloniki – BATE Borisov 1-3 (0-3)
PAOK Saloniki: Alexandros Paschalakis, Léo Matos, José Ángel Crespo, Fernando Varela, Vieirinha (46' Alin Tosca), Maurício, Cañas, Dimitrios Pelkas (55' Chuba Akpom), Aleksandar Prijovic, Dimitris Limnios (46' Amr Warda), Léo Jabá. Coach: Razvan Lucescu.
BATE Borisov: Denis Scherbitski, Denis Polyakov, Aleksander Filipovic, Aleksey Rios, Igor Stasevich, Dmitriy Baga, Stanislav Dragun (88' Evgeni Yablonski), Mirko Ivanic, Zakhar Volkov, Maksim Skavysh (83' Mikhail Gordeychuk), Nikolay Signevich.
Coach: Aleksei Baga.
Goals: 18' Maksim Skavysh 0-1, 42', 45+1' Nikolay Signevich 0-2 (p), 0-3,
59' Aleksandar Prijovic 1-3.
Referee: Tobias Welz (GER)   Attendance: 13,483.
Sent off: 61' Nikolay Signevich.

13.12.18   Groupama Aréna, Budapest: MOL Vidi FC – Chelsea FC 2-2 (1-1)
MOL Vidi FC: Ádam Kovácsik, Roland Juhász, Attila Fiola, Loïc Négo, Paulo Vinícius, Stopira, Szabolcs Huszti (81' Armin Hodzic), Anel Hadzic (85' Máté Pátkai), Georgi Milanov (81' István Kovács), Boban Nikolov, Marko Scepovic. Coach: Marko Nikolic.
Chelsea FC: Willy Caballero, Emerson, Davide Zappacosta, Andreas Christensen, Ethan Ampadu, Cesc Fàbregas, Ross Barkley, Ruben Loftus-Cheek, Willian (56' Pedro), Álvaro Morata (45+1' Olivier Giroud), Callum Hudson-Odoi. Coach: Maurizio Sarri.
Goals: 30' Willian 0-1, 32' Ethan Ampadu 1-1 (og), 56' Loïc Négo 2-1,
75' Olivier Giroud 2-2.
Referee: Aleksandar Stavrev (MKD)   Attendance: 19,242.

KNOCKOUT PHASE
ROUND OF 32

SSC Napoli, Valencia CF, Internazionale, SL Benfica, FC Viktoria Plzen, Club Brugge KV, Shakhtar Donetsk, Galatasaray entered the UEFA Europa League as the group stage third-placed teams from the UEFA Champions League.

12.02.19   Ülker Stadyumu Fenerbahçe Sükrü Saracoglu Spor Kompleksi, Istanbul: Fenerbahçe – Zenit St.Petersburg 1-0 (1-0)
Fenerbahçe: Harun Tekin, Martin Skrtel, Mauricio Isla, Victor Moses (84' Alper Potuk), Hasan-Ali Kaldirim, Sadik Çiftpinar, Mathieu Valbuena (90+2' Roman Neustädter), Mehmet Topal, Jaílson, Eljif Elmas (72' André Ayew), Islam Slimani. Coach: Ersun Yanal.
Zenit St. Petersburg: Andrei Lunev, Branislav Ivanovic, Aleksandr Anyukov, Yaroslav Rakitskiy, Elmir Nabiullin (61' Igor Smolnikov), Róbert Mak (85' Claudio Marchisio), Hernani, Wilmar Barrios, Matías Kranevitter, Artem Dzyuba, Sebastián Driussi (74' Sardar Azmoun). Coach: Sergey Semak.
Goal: 21' Islam Slimani 1-0.
Referee: Ruddy Buquet (FRA)   Attendance: 36,572.

Róbert Mak missed a penalty kick (44').

The Fenerbahçe v Zenit St.Petersburg match was scheduled on 12 February in order to avoid a scheduling conflict with the Galatasaray v SL Benfica match, in the same city.

14.02.19   Allianz Stadion, Vienna: SK Rapid Wien – Internazionale 0-1 (0-1)
SK Rapid Wien: Richard Strebinger, Mario Sonnleitner, Marvin Potzmann, Maximilian Hofmann, Boli Bolingoli-Mbombo, Manuel Thurnwald (53' Philipp Schobesberger), Stefan Schwab, Srdan Grahovac (64' Christoph Knasmüllner), Dejan Ljubicic, Veton Berisha (82' Thomas Murg), Andrei Ivan. Coach: Dietmar Kühbauer.
Internazionale: Samir Handanovic, João Miranda, Kwadwo Asamoah, Stefan de Vrij, Cédric Soares, Ivan Perisic, Radja Nainggolan (83' Danilo D'Ambrosio), Borja Valero, Matías Vecino, Matteo Politano (78' Antonio Candreva), Lautaro Martínez. Coach: Luciano Spalletti.
Goal: 39' Lautaro Martínez 0-1 (p).
Referee: Tobias Stieler (GER)   Attendance: 23,850.

14.02.19   Sinobo Stadium, Praha: Slavia Praha – KRC Genk 0-0
Slavia Praha: Ondrej Kolár, Ondrej Kúdela, Jan Boril, Vladimír Coufal, Josef Husbauer (77' Alex Král), Miroslav Stoch, Michael Ngadeu-Ngadjui, Jaromír Zmrhal (60' Peter Olayinka), Petr Sevcík, Tomás Soucek, Milan Skoda (76' Mick van Buren). Coach: Jindrich Trpisovsky.
KRC Genk: Danny Vukovic, Sebastien Dewaest, Joseph Aidoo, Joakim Mæhle, Ruslan Malinovskiy, Ivan Fiolic (57' Pozuelo), Casper De Norre, Bryan Heynen, Leandro Trossard (87' Jakub Piotrowski), Mbwane Samatta, Dieumerci N'Dongala (69' Joseph Paintsil). Coach: Philippe Clement.
Referee: Andris Treimanis (LAT)   Attendance: 18,125.

14.02.19   Stadion FK Krasnodar, Krasnodar: FK Krasnodar – Bayer Leverkusen 0-0
FK Krasnodar: Stanislav Kritsyuk, Aleksandr Martynovich, Sergey Petrov, Uros Spajic, Charles Kaboré, Mauricio Pereyra (80' Artem Golubev), Dmitriy Stotskiy, Victor Claesson, Kristoffer Olsson (71' Magomed Suleymanov), Wamberto, Ivan Ignatyev.
Coach: Murad Musaev.
Bayer Leverkusen: Lukás Hradecky, Sven Bender (83' Aleksandar Dragovic), Mitchell Weiser, Wendell, Jonathan Tah, Charles Aránguiz, Karim Bellarabi, Kai Havertz, Kevin Volland, Julian Brandt, Leon Bailey (80' Lucas Alario). Coach: Peter Bosz.
Referee: Davide Massa (ITA)   Attendance: 34,827.

14.02.19   Roazhon Park, Rennes: Stade Rennes – Real Betis Sevilla 3-3 (3-1)
Stade Rennes: Tomás Koubek, Damien Da Silva, Mexer, Medhi Zeffane, Hamari Traoré, Hatem Ben Arfa, Clément Grenier (69' Jérémy Gelin), Benjamin André, Adrien Hunou (80' Ramy Bensebaini), M'Baye Niang, Ismaïla Sarr (49' Benjamin Bourigeaud).
Coach: Julien Stéphane.
Real Betis Sevilla: Joel Robles, Sidnei, Aïssa Mandi, Junior Firpo (27' Diego Lainez), Joaquín (84' Barragán), Andrés Guardado, Javi García, Canales, William Carvalho, Giovani Lo Celso, Loren Morón (72' Jesé). Coach: Quique Setién.
Goals: 2' Adrien Hunou 1-0, 10' Javi García 2-0 (og), 32' Giovani Lo Celso 2-1, 45+3' Hatem Ben Arfa 3-1 (p), 62' Sidnei 3-2, 90' Diego Lainez 3-3.
Referee: Anastasios Sidiropoulos (GRE)   Attendance: 28,656.

14.02.19   Stadio Georgios Karaiskáki, Piraeus: Olympiakos Piraeus – Dynamo Kyiv 2-2 (2-1)
Olympiakos Piraeus: José Sá, Jagos Vukovic, Yassine Meryah, KostasTsimikas, Pape Cissé, Guilherme, Kostas Fortounis (69' Bibras Natcho), Daniel Podence (81' Lazaros Christodoulopoulos), Mohamed Camara, Koka Ahmed Hassan, Gil Dias (86' Georgios Masouras). Coach: Pedro Martins.
Dynamo Kyiv: Denis Boyko, Tomasz Kedziora, Mykyta Burda, Artem Shabanov, Vitali Mykolenko, Vitaliy Buyalskiy, Benjamin Verbic, Viktor Tsygankov, Mykola Shaparenko (82' Denys Garmash), Volodymyr Shepelev, Fran Sol (82' Nazariy Rusyn).
Coach: Aleksandr Khatskevich.
Goals: 9' Koka Ahmed Hassan 1-0, 27' Vitaliy Buyalskiy 1-1, 40' Gil Dias 2-1, 89' Benjamin Verbic 2-2.
Referee: Craig Pawson (ENG)   Attendance: 31,020.

14.02.19   Stadio Olimpico, Roma: Lazio Roma – Sevilla FC 0-1 (0-1)
Lazio Roma: Thomas Strakosha, Stefan Radu, Francesco Acerbi, Bastos (57' Luiz Felipe), Adam Marusic, Lucas Leiva, Senad Lulic, Marco Parolo (46' Danilo Cataldi), Luis Alberto (44' Riza Durmisi), Joaquín Correa, Felipe Caicedo. Coach: Simone Inzaghi.
Sevilla FC: Tomáš Vaclík, Simon Kjær, Gabriel Mercado, Sergio Escudero (75' Quincy Promes), Sergi Gómez, Jesús Navas, Éver Banega, Franco Vázquez, Pablo Sarabia (83' Ibrahim Amadou), Wissam Ben Yedder (72' Munir), André Silva. Coach: Pablo Machín.
Goal: 22' Wissam Ben Yedder 0-1.
Referee: Slavko Vincic (SVN)   Attendance: 19,766.

14-02-19   Borisov Arena, Borisov: BATE Borisov – Arsenal FC 1-0 (1-0)
BATE Borisov: Denis Scherbitski, Egor Filipenko, Aleksander Filipovic, Aliaksandr Hleb (58' Evgeniy Berezkin), Aleksey Rios, Igor Stasevich, Dmitriy Baga, Stanislav Dragun, Zakhar Volkov, Nemanja Milic (69' Bojan Dubajic), Maksim Skavysh (80' Hervaine Moukam).
Coach: Aleksei Baga.
Arsenal FC: Petr Cech, Nacho Monreal, Laurent Koscielny, Shkodran Mustafi, Sead Kolasinac (74' Denis Suárez), Henrikh Mkhitaryan, Granit Xhaka (69' Lucas Torreira), Alex Iwobi, Ainsley Maitland-Niles (68' Pierre-Emerick Aubameyang), Mattéo Guendouzi, Alexandre Lacazette. Coach: Unai Emery.
Goal: 45' Stanislav Dragun 1-0.
Referee: Srdan Jovanovic (SER)   Attendance: 12,527.
Sent off: 85' Alexandre Lacazette.

14.02.19   Türk Telekom Stadyumu, Istanbul: Galatasaray – SL Benfica 1-2 (0-1)
Galatasaray: Fernando Muslera, Yuto Nagatomo, Martin Linnes (73' Mariano), Marcão Teixeira, Christian Luyindama Nekadio, Sofiane Féghouli, Fernando, Younès Belhanda, Papa Alioune "Badou" N'Diaye (73' Sinan Gümüs), Mbaye Diagne, Henry Onyekuru.
Coach: Fatih Terim.
SL Benfica: Odisseas Vlachodimos, Sébastien Corchia, Rúben Dias, Yuri Ribeiro, Francisco Ferreira "Ferro", Eduardo Salvio (48' Gabriel), Franco Cervi (81' Filip Krovinovic), Gedson Fernandes (87' Andreas Samaris), Florentino Luís, Haris Seferovic, João Félix.
Coach: Bruno Lage.
Goals: 27' Eduardo Salvio 0-1 (p), 54' Christian Luyindama Nekadio 1-1, 64' Haris Seferovic 1-2.
Referee: Jesús Gil Manzano (ESP)   Attendance: 42,722.

14.02.19   Doosan Aréna, Plzen: FC Viktoria Plzen – Dinamo Zagreb 2-1 (0-1)
FC Viktoria Plzen: Matús Kozácik, Roman Hubník, Ludek Pernica, Milan Havel, Tomás Horava, Jan Kovarík, Ales Cermák (46' Roman Procházka), Patrik Hrosovsky, Joel Kayamba, Ubong Moses Ekpai (70' Milan Petrzela), Jean-David Beauguel (81' Tomás Chory).
Coach: Pavel Vrba.
Dinamo Zagreb: Dominik Livakovic, Marin Leovac, Kévin Théophile-Catherine, Emir Dilaver, Petar Stojanovic, Arijan Ademi, Amer Gojak, Daniel Olmo, Mislav Orsic (76' Iyayi Atiemwen), Mario Situm (64' Nikola Moro), Bruno Petkovic. Coach: Nenad Bjelica.
Goals: 41' Daniel Olmo 0-1, 54', 83' Ludek Pernica 1-1, 2-1.
Referee: Serdar Gözübüyük (HOL)   Attendance: 9,731.

14.02.19   Jan Breydel Stadium, Brugge: Club Brugge KV – Red Bull Salzburg 2-1 (0-1)
Club Brugge KV: Ethan Horvath, Stefano Denswil, Brandon Mechele, Dion Cools (46' Krépin Diatta), Ruud Vormer, Mats Rits, Hans Vanaken, Sofyan Amrabat (46' Benoît Poulain), Siebe Schrijvers (79' Loïs Openda), Wesley, Emmanuel Dennis Bonaventure. Coach: Ivan Leko.
Red Bull Salzburg: Alexander Walke, Andreas Ulmer, Stefan Lainer, André Ramalho, Marin Pongracic, Zlatko Junuzovic, Xaver Schlager (76' Enock Mwepu), Diadié Samassékou, Fredrik Gulbrandsen (85' Takumi Minamino), Munas Dabour, Hannes Wolf (89' Patson Daka).
Coach: Marco Rose.
Goals: 17' Zlatko Junuzovic 0-1, 64' Stefano Denswil 1-1, 81' Wesley 2-1.
Referee: Georgi Kabakov (BUL)   Attendance: 16,457.

14.02.19   Stadion Letzigrund, Zürich: FC Zürich – SSC Napoli 1-3 (0-2)
FC Zürich: Yanick Brecher, Alain Nef, Umaru Bangura, Joel Untersee, Andreas Maxsø, Levan Kharabadze, Adrian Winter (67' Assan Ceesay), Hekuran Kryeziu, Benjamin Kololli, Toni Domgjoni (46' Antonio Marchesano), Stephen Odey (80' Salim Khelifi).
Coach: Ludovic Magnin.
SSC Napoli: Alex Meret, Nikola Maksimovic, Kalidou Koulibaly, Kévin Malcuit, Faouzi Ghoulam (76' Sebastiano Luperto), Allan (59' Amadou Diawara), Piotr Zielinski, Fabián Ruiz, José Callejón, Lorenzo Insigne (68' Adam Ounas), Arkadiusz Milik. Coach: Carlo Ancelotti.
Goals: 12' Lorenzo Insigne 0-1, 21' José Callejón 0-2, 77' Piotr Zielinski 0-3, 83' Benjamin Kololli 1-3 (p).
Referee: Milorad Mazic (SER)   Attendance: 24,000.

14.02.19   Swedbank Stadion, Malmö: Malmö FF – Chelsea FC 1-2 (0-1)
Malmö FF: Johan Dahlin, Behrang Safari, Rasmus Bengtsson, Lasse Nielsen, Andreas Vindheim, Søren Rieks, Anders Christiansen (82' Romain Gall), Fouad Bachirou, Arnór Ingvi Traustason (70' Oscar Lewicki), Markus Rosenberg, Marcus Antonsson (70' Carlos Strandberg). Coach: Uwe Rösler.
Chelsea FC: Kepa, David Luiz, Azpilicueta, Emerson, Andreas Christensen, Ross Barkley, Mateo Kovacic, Jorginho (74' N'Golo Kanté), Willian (71' Eden Hazard), Olivier Giroud, Pedro (84' Callum Hudson-Odoi). Coach: Maurizio Sarri.
Goals: 30' Ross Barkley 0-1, 58' Olivier Giroud 0-2, 80' Anders Christiansen 1-2.
Referee: Aleksei Kulbakov (BLS)   Attendance: 20,312.

14.02.19   Oblasny SportKomplex Metalist, Kharkiv:
            Shakhtak Donetsk – Eintracht Frankfurt 2-2 (1-1)
Shakhtar Donetsk: Andriy Pyatov, Sergiy Krivtsov, Ismaily, Bogdan Butko, Davit Khotcholava, Marlos (69' Manor Solomon), Taras Stepanenko, Taison, Alan Patrick, Viktor Kovalenko (81' Maksym Malyshev), Júnior Moraes (90' Sergiy Bolbat).
Coach: Paulo Fonseca.
Eintracht Frankfurt: Kevin Trapp, Martin Hinteregger, Danny da Costa, Evan Obite N'Dicka, Makoto Hasebe, Gelson Fernandes (82' Jonathan de Guzmán), Sebastian Rode (46' Jetro Willems), Filip Kostic, Mijat Gacinovic, Ante Rebic, Luka Jovic. Coach: Adi Hütter.
Goals: 7' Martin Hinteregger 0-1, 10' Marlos 1-1 (p), 50' Filip Kostic 1-2, 67' Taison 2-2.
Referee: Anthony Taylor (ENG)   Attendance: 13,059.
Sent off: 11' Taras Stepanenko.

(Shakhtar Donetsk played their home match at Oblasny SportKomplex Metalist, Kharkiv, instead of their regular stadium Donbass Arena, Donetsk, due to the war conditions in Eastern Ukraine)

14.02.19   Celtic Park, Glasgow: Celtic FC – Valencia CF 0-2 (0-1)
Celtic FC: Scott Bain, Emilio Izaguirre, Dedryck Boyata, Jozo Simunovic, Jeremy Toljan, Scott Brown, Scott Sinclair (59' Timothy Weah), James Forrest, Callum McGregor, Ryan Christie (59' Odsonne Édouard), Oliver Burke. Coach: Brendan Rodgers.
Valencia CF: Neto, Ezequiel Garay, Cristiano Piccini (78' Kevin Gamiero), Mouctar Daikhaby, Toni Lato, Daniel Wass, Dani Parejo (46' Francis Coquelin), Denis Cheryshev (64' Gonçalo Guedes), Geoffrey Kondogbia, Carlos Soler, Rubén Sobrino. Coach: Marcelino.
Goals: 42' Denis Cheryshev 0-1, 49' Rubén Sobrino 0-2.
Referee: Ovidiu Hategan (ROM)   Attendance: 57,430.

14-02-19   Estádio José Alvalade, Lisboa: Sporting CP – Villarreal CF 0-1 (0-1)
Sporting CP: Romain Salin, André Pinto, Sebastián Coates, Bruno Gaspar (27' Stefan Ristovski), Radosav Petrovic (69' Wendel), Bruno Fernandes, Miguel Luís, Bas Dost, Marcos Acuña, Raphinha, Jovane Cabral (69' Luiz Phellype). Coach: Marcel Keizer.
Villarreal CF: Andrés Fernández, Mario Gaspar, Víctor Ruíz, Ramiro Funes Mori, Álvaro González, Javi Fuego, Trigueros (63' Santiago Cáseres), Alfonso Pedraza, Pablo Fornals (80' Vicente Iborra), Samuel Chukwueze (74' Dani Raba), Carlos Bacca. Coach: Javi Calleja.
Goal: 3' Alfonso Pedraza 0-1.
Referee: Clément Turpin (FRA)   Attendance: 27,134.
Sent off: 76' Marcos Acuña.

20.02.19   Estadio Ramón Sánchez Pizjuán, Sevilla: Sevilla FC – Lazio Roma 2-0 (1-0)
Sevilla FC: Tomás Vaclík, Simon Kjær, Gabriel Mercado, Sergio Escudero (6' Quincy Promes), Sergi Gómez, Jesús Navas, Franco Vázquez, Pablo Sarabia, Roque Mesa (82' Marko Rog), Wissam Ben Yedder, André Silva (64' Ibrahim Amadou). Coach: Pablo Machín.
Lazio Roma: Thomas Strakosha, Stefan Radu, Francesco Acerbi, Patric (49' Joaquín Correa), Adam Marusic, Senad Lulic, Milan Badelj (76' Riza Durmisi), Danilo Cataldi, Sergej Milinkovic-Savic (56' Rômulo), Felipe Caicedo, Ciro Immobile. Coach: Simone Inzaghi.
Goals: 20' Wissam Ben Yedder 1-0, 78' Pablo Sarabia 2-0.
Referee: Anthony Taylor (ENG)   Attendance: 34,521.
Sent off: 60' Franco Vázquez, 71' Adam Marusic.

The Sevilla FC v Lazio Roma match was scheduled on 20 February in order to avoid a scheduling conflict with the Real Betis Sevilla v Stade Rennes match, in the same city.

21.02.19   Stadion Maksimir, Zagreb: Dinamo Zagreb – FC Viktoria Plzen 3-0 (2-0)
Dinamo Zagreb: Dominik Livakovic, Marin Leovac, Kévin Théophile-Catherine, Emir Dilaver, Sadegh Moharrami, Arijan Ademi, Ivan Sunjic, Daniel Olmo, Mislav Orsic (88' Amer Gojak), Izet Hajrovic (68' Nikola Moro), Bruno Petkovic (90+2' Komnen Andric).
Coach: Nenad Bjelica.
FC Viktoria Plzen: Matús Kozácik, David Limbersky, Ludek Pernica, Milan Havel (74' Radim Rezník), Milan Petrzela, Tomás Horava (57' Marek Bakos), Roman Procházka, Jan Kovarík, Patrik Hrosovsky, Joel Kayamba, Jean-David Beauguel (67' Tomás Chory).
Coach: Pavel Vrba.
Goals: 15' Mislav Orsic 1-0, 34' Emir Dilaver 2-0, 73' Bruno Petkovic 3-0.
Referee: István Kovács (ROM)   Attendance: 25,860.
Sent off: 86' David Limbersky.

21-02-19   Red Bull Arena, Wals-Siezenheim: Red Bull Salzburg – Club Brugge KV 4-0 (3-0)
Red Bull Salzburg: Alexander Walke, Andreas Ulmer, Stefan Lainer, Jérôme Onguéné, Marin Pongracic (77' Albert Vallci), Zlatko Junuzovic (71' Enock Mwepu), Xaver Schlager, Diadié Samassékou, Munas Dabour, Patson Daka, Hannes Wolf (63' Takumi Minamino).
Coach: Marco Rose.
Club Brugge KV: Ethan Horvath, Benoît Poulain, Stefano Denswil, Brandon Mechele, Ruud Vormer, Mats Rits, Hans Vanaken, Sofyan Amrabat (63' Krépin Diatta), Siebe Schrijvers (69' Loïs Openda), Wesley (84' Jelle Vossen), Emmanuel Dennis Bonaventure. Coach: Ivan Leko.
Goals: 17' Xaver Schlager 1-0, 29', 43' Patson Daka 2-0, 3-0, 90+4' Munas Dabour 4-0.
Referee: Daniel Siebert (GER)   Attendance: 24,717.

Munas Dabour missed a penalty kick (11').

21.02.19   Stadio San Paolo, Napoli: SSC Napoli – FC Zürich 2-0 (1-0)
SSC Napoli: Alex Meret, Vlad Chiriches (56' Sebastiano Luperto), Kalidou Koulibaly, Elseid Hysaj, Faouzi Ghoulam, Piotr Zielinski (66' Allan), Adam Ounas (77' Arkadiusz Milik), Amadou Diawara, Dries Mertens, Simone Verdi, Lorenzo Insigne. Coach: Carlo Ancelotti.
FC Zürich: Yanick Brecher, Umaru Bangura, Mirlind Kryeziu, Marco Schönbächler (65' Bledian Krasniqi), Adrian Winter, Salim Khelifi, Benjamin Kololli (82' Levan Kharabadze), Toni Domgjoni, Simon Sohm, Assan Ceesay, Stephen Odey (60' Lavdim Zumberi).
Coach: Ludovic Magnin.
Goals: 43' Simone Verdi 1-0, 75' Adam Ounas 2-0.
Referee: Anastasios Sidiropoulos (GRE)   Attendance: 17,579.

21.02.19   Commerzbank-Arena, Frankfurt am Main:
Eintracht Frankfurt – Shakhtar Donetsk 4-1 (2-0)
Eintracht Frankfurt: Kevin Trapp, David Abraham, Martin Hinteregger, Danny da Costa, Evan Obite N'Dicka, Makoto Hasebe, Sebastian Rode (74' Jetro Willems), Filip Kostic, Mijat Gacinovic (90+1' Jonathan de Guzmán), Sébastien Haller, Luka Jovic (71' Ante Rebic).
Coach: Adi Hütter.
Shakhtar Donetsk: Andriy Pyatov, Ismaily, Bogdan Butko (66' Sergiy Bolbat), Davit Khotcholava, Mykola Matviyenko, Marlos, Taison, Alan Patrick, Viktor Kovalenko (80' Olarenwaju Kayode), Manor Solomon (46' Maycon), Júnior Moraes. Coach: Paulo Fonseca.
Goals: 23' Luka Jovic 1-0, 27' Sébastien Haller 2-0 (p), 64' Júnior Moraes 2-1, 80' Sébastien Haller 3-1, 88' Ante Rebic 4-2.
Referee: Antonio Mateu Lahoz (ESP)   Attendance: 47,000.

21.02.19   Estadio de Mestalla, Valencia: Valencia CF – Celtic FC 1-0 (0-0)
Valencia CF: Neto, Ezequiel Garay (23' Francis Coquelin), Mouctar Daikhaby, Toni Lato, Daniel Wass (76' Lee Kang-In), Dani Parejo, Gonçalo Guedes, Carlos Soler, Ferrán Torres, Rubén Sobrino (68' Kevin Gamiero), Santi Mina. Coach: Marcelino.
Celtic FC: Scott Bain, Dedryck Boyata, Jozo Simunovic, Jeremy Toljan, Kristoffer Ajer, Scott Brown, Jonny Hayes, James Forrest (63' Odsonne Édouard), Callum McGregor, Ryan Christie, Oliver Burke (73' Michael Johnston). Coach: Brendan Rodgers.
Goal: 70' Kevin Gamiero 1-0.
Referee: Deniz Aytekin (GER)   Attendance: 36,619.
Sent off: 37' Jeremy Toljan.

21.02.19   Gazprom Arena, St.Petersburg: Zenit St.Petersburg – Fenerbahçe 3-1 (2-1)
Zenit St. Petersburg: Andrei Lunev, Branislav Ivanovic, Aleksandr Anyukov, Igor Smolnikov, Yaroslav Rakitskiy, Magomed Ozdoev, Hernani (56' Róbert Mak), Wilmar Barrios, Artem Dzyuba (88' Leon Musaev), Sardar Azmoun (80' Anton Zabolotny), Sebastián Driussi.
Coach: Sergey Semak.
Fenerbahçe: Harun Tekin, Martin Skrtel, Victor Moses, Hasan-Ali Kaldirim (67' Ismail Köybasi), Sener Özbayrakli, Sadik Çiftpinar, Mehmet Topal, Alper Potuk (46' Tolgay Arslan), Jaílson (80' Islam Slimani), Eljif Elmas, André Ayew. Coach: Ersun Yanal.
Goals: 4' Magomed Ozdoev 1-0, 37' Sardar Azmoun 2-0, 43' Mehmet Topal 2-1, 76' Sardar Azmoun 3-1.
Referee: Michael Oliver (ENG)   Attendance: 50,448.

21.02.19   Estadio de la Cerámica, Villarreal: Villarreal CF – Sporting CP 1-1 (0-1)
Villarreal CF: Andrés Fernández, Mario Gaspar, Víctor Ruíz, Ramiro Funes Mori, Miguelón Llambrich (71' Santi Cazorla), Javi Fuego (63' Vicente Iborra), Trigueros, Alfonso Pedraza, Pablo Fornals, Gerard Moreno, Dani Raba (57' Karl Toko Ekambi). Coach: Javi Calleja.
Sporting CP: Romain Salin, Jefferson, Sebastián Coates, Stefan Ristovski (83' Luiz Phellype), Tiago Ilori, Cristian Borja, Nemanja Gudelj, Bruno Fernandes, Wendel, Bas Dost, Abdoulay Diaby (77' Raphinha). Coach: Marcel Keizer.
Goals: 45+1' Bruno Fernandes 0-1, 80' Pablo Fornals 1-1.
Referee: Pavel Královec (CZE)   Attendance: 14,098.
Sent off: 50' Jefferson.

21.02.19   Emirates Stadium, London: Arsenal FC – BATE Borisov 3-0 (2-0)
Arsenal FC: Petr Cech, Stephan Lichtsteiner, Nacho Monreal, Laurent Koscielny (56' Sokratis Papastathopoulos), Shkodran Mustafi, Mesut Özil, Henrikh Mkhitaryan (78' Denis Suárez), Granit Xhaka, Alex Iwobi, Mattéo Guendouzi (64' Lucas Torreira), Pierre-Emerick Aubameyang. Coach: Unai Emery.
BATE Borisov: Denis Scherbitski, Egor Filipenko, Aleksander Filipovic, Aleksey Rios, Igor Stasevich, Dmitriy Baga (58' Aliaksandr Hleb), Stanislav Dragun (64' Evgeniy Berezkin), Slobodan Simovic, Zakhar Volkov, Nemanja Milic, Maksim Skavysh (72' Bojan Dubajic). Coach: Aleksei Baga.
Goals: 4' Zakhar Volkov 1-0 (og), 39' Shkodran Mustafi 2-0,
60' Sokratis Papastathopoulos 3-0.
Referee: Alberto Undiano Mallenco (ESP)   Attendance: 58,812.

21.02.19   Stadio Giuseppe Meazza, Milano: Internazionale – SK Rapid Wien 4-0 (2-0)
Internazionale: Samir Handanovic, Kwadwo Asamoah, Andrea Ranocchia, Cédric Soares, Milan Skriniar (77' João Miranda), Ivan Perisic, Antonio Candreva, Radja Nainggolan, Matías Vecino, Marcelo Brozovic (62' Borja Valero), Lautaro Martínez (66' Matteo Politano). Coach: Luciano Spalletti.
SK Rapid Wien: Richard Strebinger, Mario Sonnleitner, Marvin Potzmann, Maximilian Hofmann, Boli Bolingoli-Mbombo (75' Philipp Schobesberger), Christoph Knasmüllner (64' Stefan Schwab), Srdan Grahovac, Thomas Murg, Dejan Ljubicic, Andrija Pavlovic, Andrei Ivan (64' Mert Müldür). Coach: Dietmar Kühbauer.
Goals: 11' Matías Vecino 1-0, 18' Andrea Ranocchia (18'), 80' Ivan Perisic 3-0,
87' Matteo Politano 4-0.
Referee: Artur Soares Dias (POR)   Attendance: 32,158.

21.02.19   Luminus Arena, Genk: KRC Genk – Slavia Praha 1-4 (1-1)
KRC Genk: Danny Vukovic (58' Nordin Jackers), Sebastien Dewaest, Jhon Lucumí, Joakim Mæhle, Pozuelo, Ruslan Malinovskiy, Casper De Norre (56' Jere Uronen), Bryan Heynen (29' Dries Wouters), Leandro Trossard, Mbwane Samatta, Junya Ito. Coach: Philippe Clement.
Slavia Praha: Ondrej Kolár, Ondrej Kúdela, Jan Boril, Vladimír Coufal, Simon Deli, Alex Král, Jaromír Zmrhal, Lukás Masopust (65' Peter Olayinka), Tomás Soucek, Ibrahim Traoré (63' Miroslav Stoch), Milan Skoda (75' Mick van Buren). Coach: Jindrich Trpisovsky.
Goals: 10' Leandro Trossard 1-0, 23' Vladimír Coufal 1-1, 54' Ibrahim Traoré 1-2,
64', 69' Milan Skoda 1-3, 1-4.
Referee: Bobby Madden (SCO)   Attendance: 13,688.

21.02.19   BayArena, Leverkusen: Bayer Leverkusen – FK Krasnodar 1-1 (0-0)
Bayer Leverkusen: Lukás Hradecky, Aleksandar Dragovic (86' Isaac Kiese Thelin), Mitchell Weiser, Wendell, Jonathan Tah, Charles Aránguiz, Kai Havertz (66' Julian Baumgartlinger), Kevin Volland, Lucas Alario, Julian Brandt, Leon Bailey. Coach: Peter Bosz.
FK Krasnodar: Matvei Safonov, Aleksandr Martynovich, Sergey Petrov, Uros Spajic, Cristian Ramírez, Charles Kaboré, Mauricio Pereyra, Victor Claesson (78' Dmitriy Stotskiy), Kristoffer Olsson (61' Yuri Gazinskiy), Wamberto, Ivan Ignatyev (70' Magomed Suleymanov). Coach: Murad Musaev.
Goals: 84' Magomed Suleymanov 0-1, 87' Charles Aránguiz 1-1.
Referee: Gedimanas Mazeika (LTU)   Attendance: 16,084.

FK Krasnodar won on away goals.

21.02.19   Stamford Bridge, London: Chelsea FC – Malmö FF 3-0 (0-0)
Chelsea FC: Willy Caballero, Azpilicueta (79' Ethan Ampadu), Emerson, Antonio Rüdiger, Andreas Christensen, Ross Barkley (76' Jorginho), Mateo Kovacic, N'Golo Kanté (76' Ruben Loftus-Cheek), Willian, Olivier Giroud, Callum Hudson-Odoi. Coach: Maurizio Sarri.
Malmö FF: Johan Dahlin, Behrang Safari, Rasmus Bengtsson, Lasse Nielsen, Andreas Vindheim, Søren Rieks, Anders Christiansen (72' Oscar Lewicki), Fouad Bachirou, Arnór Ingvi Traustason (72' Romain Gall), Markus Rosenberg (62' Carlos Strandberg), Marcus Antonsson. Coach: Uwe Rösler.
Goals: 55' Olivier Giroud 1-0, 74' Ross Barkley 2-0, 84' Callum Hudson-Odoi 3-0.
Referee: Orel Grinfeld (ISR)   Attendance: 39,813.
Sent off: 73' Rasmus Bengtsson.

21.02.19   Estadio Benito Villamarín, Sevilla: Real Betis Sevilla – Stade Rennes 1-3 (1-2)
Real Betis Sevilla: Joel Robles, Sidnei, Aïssa Mandi, Bartra, Joaquín (89' Emerson), Andrés Guardado (78' Diego Lainez), Canales, William Carvalho, Giovani Lo Celso, Jesé (69' Sergio León), Loren Morón. Coach: Quique Setién.
Stade Rennes: Tomáš Koubek, Damien Da Silva, Mexer, Hamari Traoré, Ramy Bensebaini (78' Medhi Zeffane), Hatem Ben Arfa, Clément Grenier, Benjamin Bourigeaud (75' Jérémy Gelin), Adrien Hunou (84' Romain Del Castillo), M'Baye Niang, Ismaïla Sarr.
Coach: Julien Stéphane.
Goals: 22' Ramy Bensebaini 0-1, 30' Adrien Hunou 0-1, 41' Giovani Lo Celso 1-2, 90+4' M'Baye Niang 1-3.
Referee: Viktor Kassai (HUN)   Attendance: 43,623.

21.02.19   NSK Olimpiyskiy Stadium, Kiev: Dynamo Kyiv – Olympiakos Piraeus 1-0 (1-0)
Dynamo Kyiv: Denis Boyko, Tomasz Kedziora, Mykyta Burda, Artem Shabanov, Vitali Mykolenko, Vitaliy Buyalskiy, Benjamin Verbic (90+2' Yevhenii Smyrnyi), Viktor Tsygankov, Mykola Shaparenko (76' Denys Garmash), Volodymyr Shepelev, Fran Sol (90+2' Nazariy Rusyn). Coach: Aleksandr Khatskevich.
Olympiakos Piraeus: José Sá, Vasilios Torosidis, Yassine Meryah, KostasTsimikas, Pape Cissé, Guilherme, Kostas Fortounis (65' Guerrero), Andreas Bouchalakis (65' Bibras Natcho), Daniel Podence, Koka Ahmed Hassan, Gil Dias (46' Georgios Masouras).
Coach: Pedro Martins.
Goal: 32' Fran Sol 1-0.
Referee: Ivan Kruzliak (SVK)   Attendance: 48,902.

21.02.19   Estádio do Sport Lisboa e Benfica, Lisboa: SL Benfica – Galatasaray 0-0
SL Benfica: Odisseas Vlachodimos, André Almeida, Álex Grimaldo, Rúben Dias, Francisco Ferreira "Ferro", Pizzi (83' Gabriel), Franco Cervi (59' Rafa Silva), Gedson Fernandes, Florentino Luís, Haris Seferovic, João Félix (76' Jonas). Coach: Bruno Lage.
Galatasaray: Fernando Muslera, Mariano, Yuto Nagatomo, Marcão Teixeira, Christian Luyindama Nekadio, Ryan Donk (78' Sinan Gümüs), Sofiane Féghouli (84' Emre Akbaba), Younès Belhanda, Papa Alioune "Badou" N'Diaye, Mbaye Diagne, Henry Onyekuru (83' Yunus Akgün). Coach: Fatih Terim.
Referee: Ovidiu Hategan (ROM)   Attendance: 49,545.

ROUND OF 16

07.03.19   Commerzbank-Arena, Frankfurt am Main: Eintracht Frankfurt – Internazionale 0-0
Eintracht Frankfurt: Kevin Trapp, Martin Hinteregger, Danny da Costa, Evan Obite N'Dicka, Makoto Hasebe, Gelson Fernandes, Sebastian Rode (77' Jetro Willems), Filip Kostic, Mijat Gacinovic, Sébastien Haller (80' Gonçalo Paciência), Luka Jovic. Coach: Adi Hütter.
Internazionale: Samir Handanovic, Kwadwo Asamoah, Stefan de Vrij, Danilo D'Ambrosio, Milan Skriniar, Ivan Perisic (59' Antonio Candreva), Borja Valero (80' Cédric Soares), Matías Vecino, Marcelo Brozovic, Matteo Politano, Lautaro Martínez. Coach: Luciano Spalletti.
Referee: William Collum (SCO)   Attendance: 48,000.

Marcelo Brozovic missed a penalty kick (22').
Coach Adi Hütter sent to the stands (54').

07.03.19   Stadion Maksimir, Zagreb: Dinamo Zagreb – SL Benfica 1-0 (1-0)
Dinamo Zagreb: Dominik Livakovic, Marin Leovac, Kévin Théophile-Catherine, Emir Dilaver, Petar Stojanovic, Ivan Sunjic, Amer Gojak (78' Nikola Moro), Daniel Olmo, Mislav Orsic, Damian Kadzior (84' Mario Situm), Bruno Petkovic (89' Mario Gavranovic).
Coach: Nenad Bjelica.
SL Benfica: Odisseas Vlachodimos, Sébastien Corchia, Álex Grimaldo, Rúben Dias, Francisco Ferreira "Ferro", Gabriel, Filip Krovinovic, Gedson Fernandes (71' Andrija Zivkovic), Florentino Luís (58' Rafa Silva), Haris Seferovic (35' Franco Cervi), João Félix.
Coach: Bruno Lage.
Goal: 38' Bruno Petkovic 1-0 (p).
Referee: Michael Oliver (ENG)   Attendance: 29,704.

07.03.19   Estadio Ramón Sánchez Pizjuán, Sevilla: Sevilla FC – Slavia Praha 2-2 (2-2)
Sevilla FC: Tomás Vaclík (45+1' Juan Soriano), Simon Kjær, Gabriel Mercado, Sergi Gómez, Max Wöber (46' Roque Mesa), Jesús Navas, Éver Banega (76' Quincy Promes), Pablo Sarabia, Marko Rog, Wissam Ben Yedder, Munir. Coach: Pablo Machín.
Slavia Praha: Ondrej Kolár, Ondrej Kúdela, Jan Boril, Vladimír Coufal, Simon Deli, Alex Král (79' Michael Ngadeu-Ngadjui), Miroslav Stoch, Jaromír Zmrhal (73' Milan Skoda), Lukás Masopust (60' Peter Olayinka), Tomás Soucek, Ibrahim Traoré. Coach: Jindrich Trpisovsky.
Goals: 1' Wissam Ben Yedder 1-0, 25' Miroslav Stoch 1-1, 28' Munir 2-1, 39' Alex Král 2-2.
Referee: Ruddy Buquet (FRA)   Attendance: 30.698.

07.03.19   Roazhon Park, Rennes: Stade Rennes – Arsenal FC 3-1 (1-1)
Stade Rennes: Tomás Koubek, Damien Da Silva, Mexer, Medhi Zeffane, Ramy Bensebaini, Hatem Ben Arfa, Clément Grenier (90+1' Jérémy Gelin), Benjamin André, Benjamin Bourigeaud (73' James Lea Siliki), Adrien Hunou, Ismaïla Sarr. Coach: Julien Stéphane.
Arsenal FC: Petr Cech, Nacho Monreal, Sokratis Papastathopoulos, Laurent Koscielny, Shkodran Mustafi, Mesut Özil (70' Aaron Ramsey), Henrikh Mkhitaryan, Granit Xhaka, Alex Iwobi (53' Mattéo Guendouzi), Lucas Torreira, Pierre-Emerick Aubameyang (79' Sead Kolasinac). Coach: Unai Emery.
Goals: 4' Alex Iwobi 0-1, 42' Benjamin Bourigeaud 1-1, 65' Nacho Monreal 2-1 (og), 88' Ismaïla Sarr 3-1.
Referee: Ivan Kruzliak (SVK)   Attendance: 29,771.
Sent off: 41' Sokratis Papastathopoulos.

07.03.19   Gazprom Arena, St.Petersburg, St.Petersburg:
            Zenit St. Petersburg – Villarreal CF 1-3 (1-1)
Zenit St. Petersburg: Andrei Lunev, Branislav Ivanovic, Igor Smolnikov, Yaroslav Rakitskiy, Róbert Mak (72' Oleg Shatov), Magomed Ozdoev (88' Anton Zabolotny), Wilmar Barrios, Daler Kuzyaev, Artem Dzyuba, Sardar Azmoun (75' Hernani), Sebastián Driussi.
Coach: Sergey Semak.
Villarreal CF: Andrés Fernández, Jaume Costa, Víctor Ruíz, Ramiro Funes Mori, Álvaro González, Miguelón Llambrich, Vicente Iborra, Manu Morlanes (72' Santiago Cáseres), Pablo Fornals (78' Santi Cazorla), Samuel Chukwueze, Gerard Moreno (85' Carlos Bacca).
Coach: Javi Calleja.
Goals: 33' Vicente Iborra 0-1, 35' Sardar Azmoun 1-1, 64' Gerard Moreno 1-2, 71' Manu Morlanes 1-3.
Referee: Gianluca Rocchi (ITA)   Attendance: 51,826.

07.03.19   Stamford Bridge, London: Chelsea FC – Dynamo Kyiv 3-0 (1-0)
Chelsea FC: Kepa, David Luiz, Marcos Alonso, Davide Zappacosta, Andreas Christensen, Ross Barkley (62' Ruben Loftus-Cheek), Mateo Kovacic, Jorginho (62' N'Golo Kanté), Willian (78' Callum Hudson-Odoi), Olivier Giroud, Pedro. Coach: Maurizio Sarri.
Dynamo Kyiv: Denis Boyko, Tomasz Kedziora, Mykyta Burda, Artem Shabanov, Vitali Mykolenko, Sergiy Sydorchuk, Vitaliy Buyalskiy (71' Sidcley), Viktor Tsygankov, Mykola Shaparenko, Volodymyr Shepelev, Nazariy Rusyn (66' Denys Garmash).
Coach: Aleksandr Khatskevich.
Goals: 17' Pedro 1-0, 65' Willian 2-0, 90' Callum Hudson-Odoi 3-0.
Referee: Slavko Vincic (SVN)   Attendance: 37,280.

07.03.19   Stadio San Paolo, Napoli: SSC Napoli – Red Bull Salzburg 3-0 (2-0)
SSC Napoli: Alex Meret, Nikola Maksimovic, Mário Rui, Kalidou Koulibaly, Elseid Hysaj, Allan, Piotr Zielinski (66' Amadou Diawara), Fabián Ruiz, Dries Mertens (72' Lorenzo Insigne), José Callejón, Arkadiusz Milik (81' Adam Ounas). Coach: Carlo Ancelotti.
Red Bull Salzburg: Alexander Walke, Andreas Ulmer, Stefan Lainer, André Ramalho, Jérôme Onguéné, Zlatko Junuzovic (62' Enock Mwepu), Xaver Schlager, Diadié Samassékou, Munas Dabour (76' Takumi Minamino), Patson Daka (62' Fredrik Gulbrandsen), Hannes Wolf.
Coach: Marco Rose.
Goals: 10' Arkadiusz Milik 1-0, 18' Fabián Ruiz 2-0, 58' Jérôme Onguéné 3-0 (og).
Referee: Aleksei Kulbakov (BLS)   Attendance: 32,579.

07.03.19   Estadio de Mestalla, Valencia: Valencia CF – FK Krasnodar 2-1 (2-0)
Valencia CF: Neto, Gabriel Paulista, Cristiano Piccini, Mouctar Daikhaby, Toni Lato, Dani Parejo, Francis Coquelin, Gonçalo Guedes (70' Denis Cheryshev), Carlos Soler, Kevin Gamiero (79' Rubén Sobrino), Rodrigo (63' Santi Mina). Coach: Marcelino.
FK Krasnodar: Matvei Safonov, Aleksandr Martynovich, Sergey Petrov, Uros Spajic, Cristian Ramírez, Charles Kaboré, Dmitriy Stotskiy (55' Ari), Yuri Gazinskiy (89' Artem Golubev), Victor Claesson, Kristoffer Olsson, Wamberto (80' Magomed Suleymanov).
Coach: Murad Musaev.
Goals: 12', 24' Rodrigo 1-0, 2-0, 63' Victor Claesson 2-1.
Referee: Orel Grinfeld (ISR)   Attendance: 36,274.

14.03.19   NSK Olimpiyskiy Stadium, Kiev: Dynamo Kyiv – Chelsea FC 0-5 (0-3)
Dynamo Kyiv: Denis Boyko, Tamás Kádár, Tomasz Kedziora, Mykyta Burda, Sidcley (81' Yevhenii Smyrnyi), Vitali Mykolenko, Sergiy Sydorchuk (65' Tchê Tchê), Denys Garmash, Viktor Tsygankov, Mykola Shaparenko, Volodymyr Shepelev (87' Oleksandr Andrievsky).
Coach: Aleksandr Khatskevich.
Chelsea FC: Kepa, Marcos Alonso, Antonio Rüdiger, Davide Zappacosta (69' Azpilicueta), Andreas Christensen, Mateo Kovacic, N'Golo Kanté (65' Jorginho), Ruben Loftus-Cheek, Willian (74' Pedro), Olivier Giroud, Callum Hudson-Odoi. Coach: Maurizio Sarri.
Goals: 5', 33' Olivier Giroud 0-1, 0-2, 45+1' Marcos Alonso 0-3, 59' Olivier Giroud 0-4, 78' Callum Hudson-Odoi 0-5.
Referee: Tobias Stieler (GER)   Attendance: 64,830.

14.03.19   Red Bull Arena, Wals-Siezenheim: Red Bull Salzburg – SSC Napoli 3-1 (1-1)
Red Bull Salzburg: Alexander Walke, Andreas Ulmer, Stefan Lainer, André Ramalho, Jérôme Onguéné, Diadié Samassékou, Dominik Szoboszlai (74' Christoph Leitgeb), Enock Mwepu (59' Fredrik Gulbrandsen), Munas Dabour, Takumi Minamino (86' Erling Håland), Hannes Wolf. Coach: Marco Rose.
SSC Napoli: Alex Meret, Vlad Chiriches (78' Kévin Malcuit), Mário Rui, Elseid Hysaj, Sebastiano Luperto, Allan, Piotr Zielinski (74' Amadou Diawara), Fabián Ruiz, Dries Mertens (88' Amin Younes), José Callejón, Arkadiusz Milik. Coach: Carlo Ancelotti.
Goals: 14' Arkadiusz Milik 0-1, 25' Munas Dabour 1-1, 65' Fredrik Gulbrandsen 2-1, 90+2' Christoph Leitgeb 3-1.
Referee: Carlos del Cerro Grande (ESP)   Attendancce: 29,520.

14.03.19   Stadion FK Krasnodar, Krasnodar: FK Krasnodar – Valencia CF 1-1 (0-0)
FK Krasnodar: Matvei Safonov, Jón Fjóluson, Sergey Petrov (75' Magomed Suleymanov), Uros Spajic, Cristian Ramírez, Mauricio Pereyra (90+1' Ivan Taranov), Yuri Gazinskiy, Victor Claesson, Kristoffer Olsson, Wamberto, Ari (30' Dmitriy Stotskiy). Coach: Murad Musaev.
Valencia CF: Neto, Gabriel Paulista, José Gayà, Mouctar Daikhaby, Daniel Wass, Francis Coquelin, Denis Cheryshev, Geoffrey Kondogbia, Carlos Soler (88' Kevin Gamiero), Rubén Sobrino (58' Rodrigo), Santi Mina (70' Gonçalo Guedes). Coach: Marcelino.
Goals: 85' Magomed Suleymanov 1-0, 90+3' Gonçalo Guedes 1-1.
Referee: Anthony Taylor (ENG)   Attendance: 35,074.

14.03.19   Stadio Giuseppe Meazza, Milano: Internazionale – Eintracht Frankfurt 0-1 (0-1)
Internazionale: Samir Handanovic, Stefan de Vrij, Danilo D'Ambrosio, Cédric Soares (62' Andrea Ranocchia), Milan Skriniar, Ivan Perisic, Antonio Candreva, Borja Valero (73' Sebastiano Esposito), Matías Vecino, Matteo Politano (80' Davide Merola), Keita Baldé. Coach: Luciano Spalletti.
Eintracht Frankfurt: Kevin Trapp, Martin Hinteregger, Jetro Willems (73' Marc Stendera), Danny da Costa, Evan Obite N'Dicka, Makoto Hasebe, Sebastian Rode (89' Gonçalo Paciência), Filip Kostic, Mijat Gacinovic (59' Jonathan de Guzmán), Sébastien Haller, Luka Jovic. Coach: Adi Hütter.
Goal: 6' Luka Jovic 0-1.
Referee: Ovidiu Hategan (ROM)   Attendance: 49,866.

14.03.19   Estádio do Sport Lisboa e Benfica, Lisboa:
SL Benfica – Dinamo Zagreb 3-0 (0-0, 1-0)
SL Benfica: Odisseas Vlachodimos, André Almeida, Rúben Dias, Yuri Ribeiro (46' Álex Grimaldo), Francisco Ferreira "Ferro", Ljubomir Fejsa, Pizzi (119' Gedson Fernandes), Gabriel, Andrija Zivkovic (46' Jonas), Rafa Silva, João Filipe "Jota" (62' João Félix). Coach: Bruno Lage.
Dinamo Zagreb: Dominik Livakovic, Kévin Théophile-Catherine, Emir Dilaver, Petar Stojanovic, Amir Rrahmani, Amer Gojak (98' Iyayi Atiemwen), Nikola Moro, Daniel Olmo, Mislav Orsic (109' Dino Peric), Damian Kadzior (75' Mario Situm), Bruno Petkovic (86' Mario Gavranovic). Coach: Nenad Bjelica.
Goals: 71' Jonas 1-0, 94' Francisco Ferreira "Ferro" 2-0, 105' Álex Grimaldo 3-0.
Referee: Deniz Aytekin (GER)   Attendance: 47,808.
Sent off: 104' Petar Stojanovic.

SL Benfica won after extra time.

14.03.19   Sinobo Stadium, Praha: Slavia Praha – Sevilla FC 4-3 (1-1, 2-2)
Slavia Praha: Ondrej Kolár, Ondrej Kúdela, Jan Boril, Simon Deli, Alex Král (105 Michal Frydrych), Miroslav Stoch (93' Mick van Buren), Michael Ngadeu-Ngadjui, Lukás Masopust (90+2' Jaromír Zmrhal), Tomás Soucek, Ibrahim Traoré, Milan Skoda (77' Peter Olayinka). Coach: Jindrich Trpisovsky.
Sevilla FC: Tomás Vaclík, Simon Kjær, Daniel Carriço, Sergi Gómez, Jesús Navas, Éver Banega, Pablo Sarabia (80' André Silva), Roque Mesa (74' Maxime Gonalons), Wissam Ben Yedder (104' Marko Rog), Quincy Promes, Munir (90' Franco Vázquez). Coach: Pablo Machín.
Goals: 15' Michael Ngadeu-Ngadjui 1-0, 44' Wissam Ben Yedder 1-1 (p), 47' Tomás Soucek 2-1 (p), 54' Munir 2-2, 98' Franco Vázquez 2-3, 102' Mick van Buren 3-3, 119' Ibrahim Traoré 4-3.
Referee: Aleksei Kulbakov (BLS)   Attendance: 19,020.

Slavia Praha won after extra time.

14.03.19 Emirates Stadium, London: Arsenal FC – Stade Rennes 3-0 (2-0)
Arsenal FC: Petr Cech, Nacho Monreal, Laurent Koscielny, Shkodran Mustafi, Sead Kolasinac, Mesut Özil (70' Henrikh Mkhitaryan), Aaron Ramsey (87' Lucas Torreira), Granit Xhaka, Ainsley Maitland-Niles, Pierre-Emerick Aubameyang, Alexandre Lacazette (70' Alex Iwobi). Coach: Unai Emery.
Stade Rennes: Tomás Koubek, Damien Da Silva, Mexer, Hamari Traoré, Ramy Bensebaini, Hatem Ben Arfa, Clément Grenier (70' Adrien Hunou), Benjamin André (79' James Lea Siliki), Benjamin Bourigeaud, M'Baye Niang, Ismaïla Sarr. Coach: Julien Stéphane.
Goals: 5' Pierre-Emerick Aubameyang 1-0, 15' Ainsley Maitland-Niles 2-0, 72' Pierre-Emerick Aubameyang 3-0.
Referee: Andris Treimanis (LAT)   Attendance: 59,453.

14.03.19 Estadio de la Cerámica, Villarreal: Villarréal CF – Zenit St.Petersburg 2-1 (1-0)
Villarreal CF: Andrés Fernández, Mario Gaspar, Jaume Costa, Víctor Ruíz, Ramiro Funes Mori (77' Miguelón Llambrich), Álvaro González, Vicente Iborra (70' Santi Cazorla), Pablo Fornals, Santiago Cáseres (46' Manu Morlanes), Carlos Bacca, Gerard Moreno.
Coach: Javi Calleja.
Zenit St. Petersburg: Andrei Lunev (64' Mikhail Kerzhakov), Branislav Ivanovic, Igor Smolnikov, Yaroslav Rakitskiy, Emanuel Mammana, Oleg Shatov, Magomed Ozdoev, Hernani, Wilmar Barrios (46' Matías Kranevitter), Sardar Azmoun (71' Róbert Mak), Sebastián Driussi. Coach: Sergey Semak.
Goals: 29' Gerard Moreno 1-0, 47' Carlos Bacca 2-0, 90+1' Branislav Ivanovic 2-1.
Referee: Artur Soares Dias (POR)   Attendance: 14,027.

QUARTER-FINALS

11.04.19 Emirates Stadium, London: Arsenal FC – SSC Napoli 2-0 (2-0)
Arsenal FC: Petr Cech, Nacho Monreal, Sokratis Papastathopoulos, Laurent Koscielny, Sead Kolasinac, Mesut Özil (67' Henrikh Mkhitaryan), Aaron Ramsey, Ainsley Maitland-Niles, Lucas Torreira (77' Mohamed El Neny), Pierre-Emerick Aubameyang, Alexandre Lacazette (67' Alex Iwobi). Coach: Unai Emery.
SSC Napoli: Alex Meret, Nikola Maksimovic, Mário Rui, Kalidou Koulibaly, Elseid Hysaj, Allan, Piotr Zielinski, Fabián Ruiz (82' Adam Ounas), Dries Mertens (66' Arkadiusz Milik), José Callejón, Lorenzo Insigne (82' Amin Younes). Coach: Carlo Ancelotti.
Goals: 14' Aaron Ramsey 1-0, 25' Kalidou Koulibaly 2-0 (og).
Referee: Alberto Undiano Mallenco (ESP)   Attendance: 59,738.

11.04.19   Estadio de la Cerámica, Villarreal: Villarreal CF – Valencia CF 1-3 (1-1)
Villarreal CF: Andrés Fernández, Mario Gaspar (80' Alfonso Pedraza), Víctor Ruíz, Álvaro González, Xavi Quintillà, Santi Cazorla, Vicente Iborra (67' Carlos Bacca), Pablo Fornals, Samuel Chukwueze, Santiago Cáseres (72' Manu Morlanes), Gerard Moreno.
Coach: Javi Calleja.
Valencia CF: Neto, Ezequiel Garay, Facundo Roncaglia (58' Cristiano Piccini), Gabriel Paulista, José Gayà, Daniel Wass, Dani Parejo, Gonçalo Guedes, Ferrán Torres (61' Francis Coquelin), Kevin Gamiero (69' Denis Cheryshev), Rodrigo. Coach: Marcelino.
Goals: 6' Gonçalo Guedes 0-1, 36' Santi Cazorla 1-1 (p), 90' Daniel Wass 1-2, 90+3' Gonçalo Guedes 1-3.
Referee: Michael Oliver (ENG)   Attendance: 17,605.

Dani Parejo misses a penalty kick (6').

11.04.19   Estádio do Sport Lisboa e Befica, Lisboa:
   SL Benfica – Eintracht Frankfurt 4-2 (2-1)
SL Benfica: Odisseas Vlachodimos, Sébastien Corchia (66' Pizzi), Jardel, Álex Grimaldo, Rúben Dias, Ljubomir Fejsa, Andreas Samaris (85' Andrija Zivkovic), Rafa Silva (60' Haris Seferovic), Franco Cervi, Gedson Fernandes, João Félix. Coach: Bruno Lage.
Eintracht Frankfurt: Kevin Trapp, David Abraham, Martin Hinteregger, Danny da Costa, Evan Obite N'Dicka, Makoto Hasebe, Gelson Fernandes, Sebastian Rode (85' Mijat Gacinovic), Filip Kostic, Ante Rebic (68' Gonçalo Paciência), Luka Jovic (60' Jonathan de Guzmán). Coach: Adi Hütter.
Goals: 21' João Félix 1-0 (p), 40' Luka Jovic 1-1, 43' João Félix 2-1, 50' Rúben Dias 3-1, 54' João Félix 4-1, 72' Gonçalo Paciência 4-2.
Referee: Anthony Taylor (ENG)   Attendance: 54.175.
Sent off: 20' Evan Obite N'Dicka.

11.04.19   Sinobo Stadium, Praha: Slavia Praha – Chelsea FC 0-1 (0-0)
Slavia Praha: Ondrej Kolár, Jan Boril, Vladimír Coufal, Simon Deli, Alex Král, Miroslav Stoch (64' Jaromír Zmrhal), Michael Ngadeu-Ngadjui, Lukás Masopust (74' Josef Husbauer), Petr Sevcík, Ibrahim Traoré, Peter Olayinka (82' Mick van Buren).
Coach: Jindrich Trpisovsky.
Chelsea FC: Kepa, Azpilicueta, Marcos Alonso, Antonio Rüdiger, Andreas Christensen, Ross Barkley (75' Ruben Loftus-Cheek), Mateo Kovacic (68' N'Golo Kanté), Jorginho, Willian, Olivier Giroud, Pedro (59' Eden Hazard). Coach: Maurizio Sarri.
Goal: 86' Marcos Alonso 0-1.
Referee: Felix Zwayer (GER)   Attendance: 17,484.

18.04.19   Stadio San Paolo, Napoli: SSC Napoli – Arsenal FC 0-1 (0-1)
SSC Napoli: Alex Meret, Vlad Chiriches, Nikola Maksimovic (46' Dries Mertens), Kalidou Koulibaly, Faouzi Ghoulam (71' Mário Rui), Allan, Piotr Zielinski, Fabián Ruiz, José Callejón, Lorenzo Insigne (61' Amin Younes), Arkadiusz Milik. Coach: Carlo Ancelotti.
Arsenal FC: Petr Cech, Nacho Monreal, Sokratis Papastathopoulos, Laurent Koscielny, Sead Kolasinac, Aaron Ramsey (34' Henrikh Mkhitaryan), Granit Xhaka (61' Mohamed El Neny), Ainsley Maitland-Niles, Lucas Torreira, Pierre-Emerick Aubameyang, Alexandre Lacazette (68' Alex Iwobi). Coach: Unai Emery.
Goal: 36' Alexandre Lacazette 0-1.
Referee: Ovidiu Hategan (ROM)   Attendance: 39,438.

18.04.19   Estadio de Mestalla, Valencia: Valencia CF – Villarreal CF 2-0 (1-0)
Valencia CF: Neto, Facundo Roncaglia, Mouctar Diakhaby, Toni Lato, Daniel Wass, Dani Parejo (62' Francis Coquelin), Gonçalo Guedes (68' Lee Kang-In), Carlos Soler (46' Gabriel Paulista), Ferrán Torres, Kevin Gameiro, Santi Mina. Coach: Marcelino.
Villarreal CF: Andrés Fernández, Jaume Costa, Víctor Ruíz, Ramiro Funes Mori, Trigueros (74' Javi Fuego), Manu Morlanes, Alfonso Pedraza, Santiago Cáseres (64' Pablo Fornals), Andrei Ratiu, Gerard Moreno, Dani Raba (46' Samuel Chukwueze). Coach: Javi Calleja.
Goals: 13' Toni Lato 1-0, 54' Dani Parejo 2-0.
Referee: William Collum (SCO)   Attendance: 26,403.

18.04.19   PSD Bank Arena, Frankfurt am Main: Eintracht Frankfurt – SL Benfica 2-0 (1-0)
Eintracht Frankfurt: Kevin Trapp, David Abraham, Simon Falette (90+2' Jetro Willems), Danny da Costa, Makoto Hasebe, Gelson Fernandes, Sebastian Rode (86' Lucas Torró), Filip Kostic, Mijat Gacinovic, Ante Rebic, Luka Jovic (76' Gonçalo Paciência). Coach: Adi Hütter.
SL Benfica: Odisseas Vlachodimos, André Almeida (79' Jonas), Jardel, Álex Grimaldo, Rúben Dias, Ljubomir Fejsa, Andreas Samaris (70' Pizzi), Rafa Silva (72' Eduardo Salvio), Gedson Fernandes, Haris Seferovic, João Félix. Coach: Bruno Lage.
Goals: 37' Filip Kostic 1-0, 67' Sebastian Rode 2-0.
Referee: Daniele Orsato (ITA)   Attendance: 48,000.

Coach Bruno Lage sent to the stands (38').

Eintracht Frankfurt won on away goals.

18.04.19   Stamford Bridge, London: Chelsea FC – Slavia Praha 4-3 (4-1)
Chelsea FC: Kepa, David Luiz, Azpilicueta, Emerson, Andreas Christensen, Ross Barkley (70' Jorginho), Mateo Kovacic, N'Golo Kanté, Eden Hazard (65' Willian), Olivier Giroud, Pedro (87' Callum Hudson-Odoi). Coach: Maurizio Sarri.
Slavia Praha: Ondrej Kolár, Ondrej Kúdela, Jan Boril, Simon Deli, Alex Král, Michael Ngadeu-Ngadjui, Jaromír Zmrhal (85' Milan Skoda), Lukás Masopust (52' Peter Olayinka), Petr Sevcík (78' Miroslav Stoch), Tomás Soucek, Ibrahim Traoré. Coach: Jindrich Trpisovsky.
Goals: 5' Pedro 1-0, 9' Simon Deli 2-0 (og), 17' Olivier Giroud 3-0, 25' Tomás Soucek 3-1, 27' Pedro 4-1, 51', 54' Petr Sevcík 4-2, 4-3.
Referee: Damir Skomina (SVN)   Attendance: 38,326.

SEMI-FINALS

02.05.19   Emirates Stadium, London: Arsenal FC – Valencia CF 3-1 (2-1)
Arsenal FC: Petr Cech, Sokratis Papastathopoulos, Laurent Koscielny (82' Nacho Monreal), Shkodran Mustafi, Sead Kolasinac, Mesut Özil (75' Henrikh Mkhitaryan), Granit Xhaka, Ainsley Maitland-Niles, Mattéo Guendouzi (58' Lucas Torreira), Pierre-Emerick Aubameyang, Alexandre Lacazette. Coach: Unai Emery.
Valencia CF: Neto, Ezequiel Garay, Facundo Roncaglia, Gabriel Paulista, Cristiano Piccini, José Gayá, Mouctar Diakhaby (YC31), Dani Parejo (YC70), Gonçalo Guedes (71' Kevin Gameiro), Carlos Soler (71' Daniel Wass), Rodrigo (88' Santi Mina). Coach: Marcelino.
Goals: 11' Mouctar Diakhaby 0-1, 18', 26' Alexandre Lacazette 1-1, 2-1, 90+1' Pierre-Emerick Aubameyang 3-1.
Referee: Clément Turpin (FRA)   Attendance: 58,969.

02.05.19   PSD Bank Arena, Frankfurt am Main: Eintracht Frankfurt – Chelsea FC 1-1 (1-1)
Eintracht Frankfurt: Kevin Trapp, David Abraham, Martin Hinteregger, Simon Falette, Danny da Costa, Makoto Hasebe (YC58), Gelson Fernandes (YC61) (73' Gonçalo Paciência), Sebastian Rode, Filip Kostic, Mijat Gacinovic (90+2' Jetro Willems), Luka Jovic.
Coach: Adi Hütter.
Chelsea FC: Kepa, David Luiz, Azpilicueta, Emerson, Andreas Christensen (YC19), Jorginho, N'Golo Kanté, Ruben Loftus-Cheek (83' Mateo Kovacic), Willian (61' Eden Hazard), Olivier Giroud, Pedro. Coach: Maurizio Sarri.
Goals: 23' Luka Jovic 1-0, 45' Pedro 1-1.
Referee: Carlos del Cerro Grande (ESP)   Attendance: 48,000.

09.05.19   Estadio de Mestalla, Valencia: Valencia CF – Arsenal FC 2-4 (1-1)
Valencia CF: Neto, Ezequiel Garay (YC38), Gabriel Paulista (YC90+2), Cristiano Piccini (56' Carlos Soler), José Gayá (YC43), Daniel Wass, Dani Parejo, Francis Coquelin, Gonçalo Guedes (71' Ferrán Torres), Kevin Gameiro, Rodrigo (72' Santi Mina). Coach: Marcelino.
Arsenal FC: Petr Cech, Nacho Monreal, Sokratis Papastathopoulos, Laurent Koscielny, Sead Kolasinac (71' Shkodran Mustafi), Mesut Özil (YC62) (62' Henrikh Mkhitaryan), Granit Xhaka, Ainsley Maitland-Niles, Lucas Torreira (80' Mattéo Guendouzi), Pierre-Emerick Aubameyang, Alexandre Lacazette (YC90+2). Coach: Unai Emery.
Goals: 11' Kevin Gameiro 1-0, 17' Pierre-Emerick Aubameyang 1-1,
50' Alexandre Lacazette 1-2, 58' Kevin Gameiro 2-2,
69', 88' Pierre-Emerick Aubameyang 2-3, 2-4.
Referee: Danny Makkelie (HOL)   Attendance: 44,481.

09.05.19   Stamford Bridge, London: Chelsea FC – Eintracht Frankfurt 1-1 (1-0, 1-1)
Chelsea FC: Kepa, David Luiz, Azpilicueta (YC82), Emerson, Andreas Christensen (74' Davide Zappacosta (YC120+1)), Mateo Kovacic (YC52), Jorginho, Ruben Loftus-Cheek (86' Ross Barkley), Willian (62' Pedro), Eden Hazard, Olivier Giroud (96' Gonzalo Higuaín). Coach: Maurizio Sarri.
Eintracht Frankfurt: Kevin Trapp, David Abraham (YC90), Martin Hinteregger, Simon Falette (YC38), Danny da Costa, Makoto Hasebe, Sebastian Rode (YC40) (70' Jonathan de Guzmán (YC90+1)), Filip Kostic, Mijat Gacinovic (118' Gonçalo Paciência), Ante Rebic (90+3' Sébastien Haller), Luka Jovic. Coach: Adi Hütter.
Goals: 28' Ruben Loftus-Cheek 1-0, 49' Luka Jovic 1-1.
Referee: Ovidiu Hategan (ROM)   Attendance: 36,070.

Chelsea FC won on penalties after extra time (4-3).
Penalties: Haller 0-1, Barkley 1-1, Jovic 1-2, Azpilicueta missed, De Guzmán 1-3,
           Jorginho 2-3, Hinteregger missed, David Luiz 3-3, Gonçalo Paciência missed,
           Hazard 4-3.

FINAL

29.05.19 Baki Olimpiya Stadionu, Baku (AZE): Chelsea FC – Arsenal FC 4-1 (0-0)
Chelsea FC: Kepa, David Luiz, Azpilicueta, Emerson, Andreas Christensen (YC68), Mateo Kovacic (76' Ross Barkley), Jorginho, N'Golo Kanté, Eden Hazard (89' Davide Zappacosta), Olivier Giroud, Pedro (71' Willian). Coach: Maurizio Sarri.
Arsenal FC: Petr Cech, Nacho Monreal (66' Mattéo Guendouzi), Sokratis Papastathopoulos, Laurent Koscielny, Sead Kolasinac, Mesut Özil (77' Joseph Willock), Granit Xhaka, Ainsley Maitland-Niles, Lucas Torreira (67' Alex Iwobi), Pierre-Emerick Aubameyang, Alexandre Lacazette. Coach: Unai Emery.
Goals: 49' Olivier Giroud 1-0, 60' Pedro 2-0, 65' Eden Hazard 3-0 (p), 69' Alex Iwobi 3-1, 72' Eden Hazard 4-1.
Referee: Gianluca Rocchi (ITA)   Attendance: 51,370.

UEFA EUROPA LEAGUE 2019-2020

PRELIMINARY ROUND

27.06.19   Stade Parc des Sports, Differdange:
Progrès Niederkorn – Cardiff Metropolitan University 1-0 (0-0)
Progrès Niederkorn: Sebastian Flauss, Tom Laterza (78' Ricky Borges), Ben Vogel, Metin Karayer, Tim Hall, Aldin Skenderovic, Yann Matias Marques, Sébastien Thill, Belmin Muratovic, Mayron De Almeida, Issa Bah (60' Florik Shala). Coach: Roland Vrabec.
Cardiff Metropolitan University: Will Fuller, Kyle McCarthy, Emlyn Lewis, Bradley Woolridge, Dylan Rees, Joel Edwards, Charlie Corsby (63' Rhydian Morgan), Will Evans (85' Tim Parker), Chris Baker, Dan Spencer (75' Jordan Lam), Eliot Evans.
Coach: Christian Edwards.
Goal: 62' Mayron De Almeida 1-0.
Referee: Luis Teixeira (POR)   Attendance: 1,984.

Progrès Niederkorn played their home match at Stade Parc des Sports, Differdange, instead of theire regular stadium Stade Jos Haupert, Niederkorn which does not meet UEFA requirements.

27.06.19   Cardiff International Sports Stadium, Cardiff:
Barry Town United – Cliftonville FC 0-0
Barry Town United: Mike Lewis, Luke Cummings, Luke Cooper, Chris Hugh, Jack Compton (72' Drew Fahiya), Clayton Green, Robbie Patten (72' Troy Greening), Evan Press, Kayne McLaggon, Jonathan Hood, Jordan Cotterill (82' Tom Fry). Coach: Gavin Chesterfield.
Cliftonville FC: Richard Brush, Garry Breen, Liam Bagnall, Conor McMenamin (83' Ryan Curran), Joe Gorman, Levi Ives, Conor McDermott (90+6' Thomas Maguire), Chris Curran, Aaron Harkin, Ronan Doherty (79' Joe Gormley), Rory Donnelly.
Coach: Paddy McLaughlin.
Referee: Jason Barcelo (GIB)   Attendance: 2,106.

Barry Town United played their home match at Cardiff International Sports Stadium, Cardiff, instead of their regular stadium Jenner Park Stadium, Barry which does not meet UEFA requirements.

27.06.19   Estadi Comunal d'Andorra la Vella, Andorra la Vella:
UE Sant Julià – Europa FC 3-2 (1-1)
UE Sant Julià: Ferran Pol, Toni Lao, Soualio Bakayoko, Nicolae Vasile, Pedro Muñoz, Jonny, Sénah Mango, Miguel Luque, Loïc Malatini (80' Walter Balufo), Fousseyni Cissé, Joel Méndez (72' Quentin Leite Pereira). Coach: Emiliano González.
Europa FC: Javi Muñoz, Sergio Sánchez, Rahim Ayew, Olmo González, Diego Portilla, Velasco (84' Jayce Mascarenhas-Olivero), Juampe Rico, Liam Walker, Mustapha Yahaya, Marco Rosa (67' Andre Tjay de Barr), Adrián Gallardo (77' Manu Dimas).
Coach: Rafael Escobar.
Goals: 4' Adrián Gallardo 0-1, 44' Joel Méndez 1-1, 46' Sénah Mango 1-2 (og), 64' Joel Méndez 2-2, 90+3' Pedro Muñoz 3-2.
Referee: Dragan Petrovic (BIH)   Attendance: 300.
Sent off: 75' Fousseyni Cissé.

27.06.19   Gundadalur, Tórshavn: KÍ Klaksvík – SP Tre Fiori 5-1 (2-0)
KÍ Klaksvík: Kristian Joensen, Jesper Brinck, Ísak Simonsen, Deni Pavlovic, Semir Hadzibulic (85' Darius Lewis), Patrik Johannesen (76' Torbjørn Grytten), Jákup Andreasen, Jóannes Bjartalíd, Simen Sandmæl, Jóannes Danielsen, Jonn Johannesen (70' Boris Dosljak). Coach: Mikkjal Thomassen.
SP Tre Fiori: Aldo Simoncini, Enea Righetti, Leandro Carubini, Alessandro D'Addario, Claudio Cuzzilla (62' Joel Apezteguía Hijuelos), Mattia Costantini, Luca Angelini (46' Nicolo Bacchiocchi), Manolo Pestrin (75' Andrea Tamagnini), Daniele Compagno, Martin Lago Ramiro, Andrea Compagno. Coach: Matteo Cecchetti.
Goals: 9' Patrik Johannesen 1-0, 37' Simen Sandmæl 2-0, 56' Jonn Johannesen 3-0, 73', 83' Jóannes Bjartalíd 4-0, 5-0, 90+3' Andrea Compagno 5-1.
Referee: Robert Jenkins (WAL)   Attendance: 575.

KÍ Klaksvík played their home match at Gundadalur, Tórshavn, instead of their regular stadium Vid Djúpumyrar, Klaksvík which does not meet UEFA requierements.

27.06.19   Stadio Olimpico di Serravalle, Serravalle: SP La Fiorita – UE Engordany 0-1 (0-1)
SP La Fiorita: Gianluca Vivan, Samuele Olivi, Roberto Di Maio, Marco Gasperoni, Riccardo Mezzadri, Simone Loiodice, Armando Amati (72' Damiano Tommasi), Nicolás Castro, Andrea Bracaletti, Danilo Rinaldi (83' José Hirsch), Fabrizio Castellazzi (60' Mirco Vassallo). Coach: Juri Tamburini.
UE Engordany: Jesús Coca, Miguel Ruiz, Rafael Brito, Aarón Sánchez, Deivis De Jesús Soares, Mario Spano, Sébastien Aguéro, Nikola Zugic (83' Jorge Sebastián Varela), Hamza Bouharma, Míguel Laborda (75' Fábio Serra Alves), Sebastián Gómez (70' Marc Ferré). Coach: Filipe Busto.
Goal: 31' Aarón Sánchez 0-1.
Referee: Christophe Pires Martins (LUX)   Attendance: 302.
Sent off: 87' Mirco Vassallo, 87' Deivis De Jesús Soares.

27.06.19   The Showgrounds, Ballymena: Ballymena United – NSÍ Runavík 2-0 (0-0)
Ballymena United: Ross Glendinning, Tony Kane, Jim Ervin, Steven McCullough, Scot Whiteside, Kofi Balmer, Jude Winchester (86' Ryan Harpur), Declan Carville, Leroy Millar, Cathair Friel (79' Ryan Mayse), Adam Lecky. Coach: David Jeffrey.
NSÍ Runavík: Tórdur Thomsen, Oddur Højgaard, Pól Justinussen, Jóhan Davidsen, Bárdur Jógvansson-Hansen, Per Langgaard (68' Betuel Hansen), Pætur Hentze, Peder Nersveen, Petur Knudsen, Klæmint Olsen, Búi Egilsson (70' Jann Benjaminsen). Coach: Gudjón Thórdarson.
Goals: 49' Leroy Millar 1-0, 55' Jude Winchester 2-0.
Referee: Athanasios Tzilos (GRE)   Attendance: 2,270.

27.06.19   Stadiumi Fadil Vokrri, Pristina: Prishtina KF – St.Joseph's FC 1-1 (1-1)
Prishtina KF: Visar Bekaj, Armend Dallku, Armend Thaçi, Leotrim Bekteshi, Abdul Bashiru, Diar Miftaraj, Kreshnik Uka (67' Meriton Korenica), Gauthier Mankenda, Endrit Krasniqi, Ergyn Ahmeti (78' Qendrim Zyba), Alban Shillova (49' Laurit Boshnjaku). Coach: Mirel Josa.
St.Joseph's FC: Fran Mateo, Federico Villar, Pecci, Mauri Torres, Iván Lobato, Ezequiel Rojas, Domingo Ferrer (84' Andrew Hernandez), Juanma González, Pedrito, Juanfri Peña (89' Daniel Guerrero), Boro (76' Ernesto Cornejo). Coach: Raúl Procopio.
Goals: 28' Armend Dallku 1-0 (p), 31' Juanfri Peña 1-1.
Referee: Helgi Mikael Jónasson (ISL)   Attendance: 4,000.

02.07.19   Victoria Stadium, Gibraltar: St.Joseph's FC – Prishtina KF 2-0 (0-0)
St.Joseph's FC: Fran Mateo, Federico Villar, Pecci, Mauri Torres, Iván Lobato, Ezequiel Rojas, Domingo Ferrer (70' Ernesto Cornejo), Juanma González (84' Andrew Hernandez), Pedrito (87' Francisco Cano), Juanfri Peña, Boro. Coach: Raúl Procopio.
Prishtina KF: Visar Bekaj, Armend Dallku, Armend Thaçi, Leotrim Bekteshi, Abdul Bashiru, Diar Miftaraj, Kreshnik Uka (52' Ahmet Haliti), Gauthier Mankenda, Laurit Boshnjaku (76' Meriton Korenica), Endrit Krasniqi, Ergyn Ahmeti (56' Khalid Abdul Basit).
Coach: Mirel Josa.
Goals: 75' Federico Villar 1-0, 80' Juanfri Peña 2-0.
Referee: Luca Barbeno (SMR)   Attendance: 500.
Sent off: 48' Armend Dallku, 48' Leotrim Bekteshi, 90+3' Ezequiel Rojas.

04.07.19   Cardiff International Sports Stadium, Cardiff:
            Cardiff Metropolitan University – Progrès Niederkorn 2-1 (1-0)
Cardiff Metropolitan University: Will Fuller, Kyle McCarthy, Emlyn Lewis, Bradley Woolridge, Dylan Rees, Joel Edwards, Charlie Corsby (77' Dion Phillips), Will Evans, Chris Baker, Eliot Evans (56' Mael Davies), Jordan Lam (61' Tim Parker).
Coach: Christian Edwards.
Progrès Niederkorn: Sebastian Flauss, Tom Laterza, Ben Vogel, Metin Karayer, Tim Hall, Aldin Skenderovic, Yann Matias Marques (70 Yannick Bastos), Sébastien Thill, Belmin Muratovic (88' Adrien Ferino), Mayron De Almeida, Issa Bah (85' Filipe Correira Santos).
Coach: Roland Vrabec.
Goals: 2' Jordan Lam 1-0, 67' Dylan Rees 2-0 (p) / 73 Mayron De Almeida 2-1.
Referee: Loukas Sotiriou (CYP)   Attendance: 1,316.

Progrès Niederkorn won on away goals.

Cardiff Metropolitan University played their home match at Cardiff International Sports Stadium, Cardiff, instead of their regular stadium Cyncoed Campus, Cardiff which does not meet UEFA requirements.

04.07.19   Estadi Comunal d'Andorra la Vella, Andorra la Vella:
            UE Engordany – SP La Fiorita 2-1 (1-0)
UE Engordany: Jesús Coca, Miguel Ruiz, Rafael Brito, Aarón Sánchez, Mario Spano, Sébastien Aguéro, Nikola Zugic (76' Marc Ferré), Hamza Bouharma, Míguel Laborda (56' Morgan Lafont), Sebastián Gómez, Fábio Serra Alves (86' Jorge Sebastián Varela).
Coach: Filipe Busto.
SP La Fiorita: Gianluca Vivan, Samuele Olivi, Roberto Di Maio, Marco Gasperoni, Riccardo Mezzadri, Luca Righini, José Hirsch (87' Alessandro Guidi), Simone Loiodice (63' Armando Amati), Nicolás Castro, Andrea Bracaletti (74' Fabrizio Castellazzi), Danilo Rinaldi.
Coach: Juri Tamburini.
Goals: 17' Nikola Zugic 1-0, 84' Marco Gasperoni 2-1 (og) / 78' Jesús Coca 1-1 (og).
Referee: Alexandru Tean (MOL)   Attendance: 428.

04.07.19 Svangaskard, Toftir: NSÍ Runavík – Ballymena United 0-0
NSÍ Runavík: Tórdur Thomsen, Oddur Højgaard, Pól Justinussen, Jóhan Davidsen, Bárdur Jógvansson-Hansen, Pætur Hentze (85' Óli Olsen), Jann Mortensen (64' Øssur Dalbúd), Peder Nersveen, Petur Knudsen, Jann Benjaminsen (74' Búi Egilsson), Klæmint Olsen.
Coach: Gudjón Thórdarson.
Ballymena United: Ross Glendinning, Tony Kane (84' Andrew Burns), Jim Ervin, Steven McCullough, Scot Whiteside, Kofi Balmer, Jude Winchester (90+2' Ryan Harpur), Declan Carville, Leroy Millar, Cathair Friel, Adam Lecky. Coach: David Jeffrey.
Referee: Besfort Kasumi (KOS) Attendance: 553.

NSÍ Runavík played their home match at Svangaskard, Toftir, instead of their regular stadium Vid Løkin, Runavík which does not meet UEFA requierements.

04.07.19 Victoria Stadium, Gibraltar: Europa FC – UE Sant Julià 4-0 (1-0)
Europa FC: Dayle Coleing, Sergio Sánchez, Rahim Ayew (79' Ethan Jolley), Olmo González, Diego Portilla (61' Jayce Mascarenhas-Olivero), Juampe Rico, Liam Walker, Mustapha Yahaya, Marco Rosa, Andre Tjay de Barr, Adrián Gallardo (70' Velasco).
Coach: Rafael Escobar.
UE Sant Julià: Anthony Kasparian, Toni Lao, Soualio Bakayoko (57' Walter Balufo), Nicolae Vasile, Pedro Muñoz, Jonny, Sénah Mango, Miguel Luque, Quentin Leite Pereira (62' Luis Blanco), Loïc Malatini, Joel Méndez. Coach: Emiliano González.
Goals: 38' Adrián Gallardo 1-0, 48' Andre Tjay de Barr 2-0, 78' Liam Walker 3-0, 90+2' Juampe Rico 4-0.
Referee: Matthew De Gabriele (MLT) Attendance: 1,075.
Sent off: 83' Jonny.

04.07.19 Stadio Olimpico di Serravalle, Serravalle: SP Tre Fiori – KÍ Klaksvík 0-4 (0-3)
SP Tre Fiori: Aldo Simoncini, Enea Righetti, Leandro Carubini (77' Eduardo Marconi), Alessandro D'Addario, Claudio Cuzzilla (66' Nicola Della Valle), Mattia Costantini, Luca Angelini (52' Manolo Pestrin), Daniele Compagno, Joel Apezteguía Hijuelos, Martin Lago Ramiro, Andrea Compagno. Coach: Matteo Cecchetti.
KÍ Klaksvík: Kristian Joensen, Jesper Brinck, Ísak Simonsen, Deni Pavlovic (79' Ólavur Niclasen), Semir Hadzibulic, Patrik Johannesen (57' Páll Klettskard), Jákup Andreasen, Jóannes Bjartalíd, Simen Sandmæl, Jóannes Danielsen, Jonn Johannesen (46' Magnus Stamnestrø). Coach: Mikkjal Thomassen.
Goals: 29' Jóannes Bjartalíd 0-1 (p), 33' Jonn Johannesen 0-2, 45+2' Patrik Johannesen 0-3, 75' Jóannes Danielsen 0-4.
Referee: Novak Simovic (SRB) Attendance: 177.

04.07.19 Solitude, Belfast: Cliftonville FC – Barry Town United 4-0 (2-0)
Cliftonville FC: Richard Brush, Garry Breen, Liam Bagnall, Conor McMenamin (85' Ronan Wilson), Joe Gorman, Levi Ives, Conor McDermott, Chris Curran, Ronan Doherty, Rory Donnelly (86' Thomas Maguire), Joe Gormley (85' Jamie Harney).
Coach: Paddy McLaughlin.
Barry Town United: Mike Lewis, Paul Morgan, Luke Cooper, Chris Hugh, Troy Greening, Clayton Green, Robbie Patten (73' Tom Fry), Evan Press, Kayne McLaggon, Jonathan Hood (79' Sam Snaith), Jordan Cotterill (64' Jack Compton). Coach: Gavin Chesterfield.
Goals: 25' Conor McMenamin 1-0, 44' Joe Gormley 2-0, 82' Conor McDermott 3-0, 84' Rory Donnelly 4-0.
Referee: Fyodor Zammit (MLT) Attendance: 1,946.

FIRST QUALIFYING ROUND

09.07.19   Victoria Stadium, Gibraltar: St.Joseph's FC – Glasgow Rangers FC 0-4 (0-0)
St.Joseph's FC: Fran Mateo, Federico Villar, Pecci (70' Andrew Hernandez), Mauri Torres, Iván Lobato, Daniel Guererro, Domingo Ferrer (70' Ryan Casciaro), Pedrito (76' Sykes Garro), Juanfri Peña, Ernesto Cornejo, Boro. Coach: Raúl Procopio.
Glasgow Rangers FC: Allan McGregor, James Tavernier, Connor Goldson, Borna Barisic, Nikola Katic, Steven Davis, Ryan Jack (62' Joe Aribo), Sheyi Ojo, Glen Kamara, Jordan Jones (71' Greg Stewart), Jermain Defoe (63' Alfredo Morelos). Coach: Steven Gerrard.
Goals: 50 Ryan Jack 0-1, 56' Sheyi Ojo 0-2, 68' Connor Goldson 0-3, 77' Alfredo Morelos 0-4.
Referee: Nejc Kajtazovic (SVN)   Attendance: 2,050.

09.07.19   MFA Centenary Stadium, Ta'Qali: Gzira United – Hajduk Split 0-2 (0-1)
Gzira United: Justin Haber, Arthur Henrique, Rodolfo Soares, Fernando Barbosa, Nicky Muscat (83' Sacha Borg), Hamed Koné, Gianmarco Conti (72' Andrew Cohen), Juan Corbalan, Zachary Scerri, Jefferson, Ridwaru Adeyemo (62' Elvis Sakyi). Coach: Giovanni Tedesco.
Hajduk Split: Tomislav Duka, Oleksandr Svatok (75' Stefan Simic), Ardian Ismajli, Domagoj Bradaric (61' Ivan Dolcek), Ádám Gyurcsó (67' Francesco Tahiraj), Hamza Barry, Bassel Jradi, Stanko Juric, Darko Nejasmic, Jairo, Ivan Delic. Coach: Sinia Orescanin.
Goals: 44' Ádám Gyurcsó 0-1, 90+6' Ivan Dolcek 0-2.
Referee: Gal Leibovitz (ISR)   Attendance: 683.

09.07.19   Stadion Bâlgarska Armija, Sofia: CSKA Sofia – OFK Titograd 4-0 (1-0)
CSKA Sofia: Vytautas Cerniauskas, Plamen Galabov, Stoycho Atanasov, Nuno Tomás, Geferson (80' Petar Zanev), Graham Carey (60' Kristiyan Malinov), Rúben Pinto, Tiago Rodrigues, Diego Fabbrini, Ali Sowe, Evandro (73' Janio Bikel). Coach: Dobromir Mitov.
OFK Titograd: Sasa Ivanovic, Radule Zivkovic (86' Ognjen Gasevic), Ivan Novovic, Marko Roganovic (65' Slobodan Perisic), Balsa Banovic, Ajanah-Chinedu Chukwujekwu, Mirko Raicevic, Jovan Nikolic, Vojin Pavlovic (78' Milos Brnovic), Radomir Djalovic, Mendy Mamadou. Coach: Dragoljub Djuretic.
Goals: 40' Evandro 1-0, 53' Tiago Rodrigues 2-0, 55' Geferson 3-0, 72' Kristiyan Malinov 4-0.
Referee: Luis Godinho (POR)   Attendance: 8,500.

10.07.19   Stade de la Frontière, Esch-sur-Alzette: Jeunesse d'Esch – Tobol Kustanai 0-0
Jeunesse d'Esch: Kévin Sommer, Arsène Menèssou, Alessandro Fiorani, Emmanuel Lapierre (78' Clayton De Sousa Moreira), Johannes Steinbach, Halim Meddour, Yannick Makota (61' Frederick Kyereh), Milos Todorovic, Luca Duriatti, David Soares De Sousa (72' Brandon Soares Rosa), Almir Klica. Coach: Nicolas Huysman.
Tobol Kustanai: Emil Balayev, Viktor Dmitrenko, Fernander Kassaï, Jaba Kankava, Azat Nurgaliev, Artūras Zulpa, Nika Kvekveskiri, Nikita Bocharov, Ruslan Valiullin, Mikhail Gordeychuk (59' Bauyrzhan Turysbek), Senin Sebai (60' Maxim Fedin).
Coach: Vladimir Gazzaev.
Referee: Eldorjan Hamiti (ALB)   Attendance: 1,384.

11.07.19   Gyumri City Stadium, Gyumri: Pyunik Yerevan FC – KF Shkupi 3-3 (1-2)
Pyunik Yerevan FC: Andrija Dragojevic, Antonio Stankov, Maksim Zhestokov, Kristi Marku, Armen Manucharyan, Karlen Mkrtchyan, Sergiy Shevchuk, Artem Simonyan (46' Edgar Manucharyan), Stanislav Efimov, Erik Vardanyan, Artur Miranyan.
Coach: Aleksandr Tarkhanov.
KF Shkupi: Thulio, Muharem Bajrami, Bojan Gjorgievski, Darko Ilieski, Mevlan Adili, Sabit Bilalli, Fatih Ismaili, Lamine Diack (53' Fatjon Jusufi), Marin Jurina, Serginho (83' Besart Krivanjeva), Oumar Goudiaby (69' Artan Veliu). Coach: Recai Sahinler.
Goals: 4' Erik Vardanyan 1-0 (p), 26' Muharem Bajrami 1-1, 43' Darko Ilieski 1-2, 60' Muharem Bajrami 1-3, 80' Maksim Zhestokov 2-3, 85' Edgar Manucharyan 3-3.
Referee: Luca Barbeno (SMR)   Attendance: 2,050.

Pyunik Yerevan FC played their home match at Gyumri City Stadium, Gyumri, instead ot heir regular stadium Vazgen Sargsyan Republican Stadium, Yerevan.

11.07.19   Stadion Qajimuqan Muñaytpasov, Shymkent:
         FK Ordabasy – Torpedo Kutaisi 1-0 (0-0)
FK Ordabasy: Dmytro Nepogodov, Pablo Fontanello, Sergiy Maliy, Mardan Tolebek (56' Ziguy Badibanga), Temirlan Yerlanov, Abdoulaye Diakhaté, May Mahlangu, Timur Dosmagambetov, Mirzad Mehanovic (67' Aleksey Shchetkin), João Paulo, Toktar Zhangylyshbay (73' Marat Bystrov). Coach: Kakhaber Tskhadadze.
Torpedo Kutaisi: Roin Kvaskhvadze, Davit Khurtsilava, Vazha Tabatadze, Tsotne Nadaraia, Anri Chichinadze, Vakhtang Nebieridze, Mate Tsintsadze, Papuna Poniava (86' Tsotne Mosiashvili), Temur Chogadze (69' Otar Kobakhidze), Tornike Kapanadze (78' Tamaz Tsetskhladze), Zaza Tsitskishvili. Coach: Kakhaber Chkhetiani.
Goal: 67' Temirlan Yerlanov 1-0.
Referee: Roomer Tarajev (EST)   Attendance: 15,900.

11.07.19   Olimpiskā centra Ventspils Stadionā, Ventspils:
         FK Ventspils – KF Teuta Durrës 3-0 (1-0)
FK Ventspils: Konstantin Machnovskiy, Jean Alcénat (84' Ingars Stuglis), Abdoul Mamah, Giorgi Mchedlishvili, Hélio Batista, João Ananias (40' Pavel Osipov), Jevgenijs Kazacoks, Daniils Ulimbasevs, Tosin Aiyegun, Mykhaylo Sergiychuk (66' Kaspars Svārups), Lucas Villela. Coach: Igor Klosovs.
KF Teuta Durrës: Isli Hidi, Renato Arapi, Rustem Hoxha, Alexandros Kouros, Fabjan Beqja (62' Arlind Kalaja), Gerhard Progni, Blagoja Todorovski (85' Darko Nikac), Albano Aleksi, Lancinet Sidibe, Sherif Kallaku, Tomislav Busic. Coach: Shpëtim Kuçi.
Goals: 5' Mykhaylo Sergiychuk 1-0, 78' Daniils Ulimbasevs 2-0, 88' Tosin Aiyegun 3-0.
Referee: Daniyar Sakhi (KAZ)   Attendance: 1,730.

11.07.19   FFA Academy Stadium, Yerevan: FC Alashkert – Makedonija GP 3-1 (1-0)
FC Alashkert: Ognjen Cancarevic, Hrayr Mkoyan, Gagik Dagbashyan, Hayk Ishkhanyan, Taron Voskanyan, Artak Grigoryan, Danilo Sekulic, Gustavo Marmentini dos Santos (71' Tiago Cametá), Vahagn Hayrapetyan, Uros Nenadovic (89' Mihran Manasyan), Nikita Tankov (85' Tiago Galvão). Coach: Abraham Khashmanyan.
Makedonija GP: Marko Jovanovski, Filip Misevski (69' Esmin Licina), Fernando Augusto, Bianor, Bobi Bozinovski, Dejan Tanturovski, Robson, Kristijan Filipovski, Hristijan Pecov, Alen Jasaroski, Padu (89' Luka Trajkoski). Coach: Bobi Stojkoski.
Goals: 16' Nikita Tankov 1-0, 52' Alen Jasaroski 1-1, 66' Danilo Sekulic 2-1, 82' Bianor 3-1 (og).
Referee: Nathan Verboomen (BEL)   Attendance: 1,285.

FC Alashkert played their home match at FFA Academy Stadium, Yerevan, instead of their regular Alashkert Stadium, Yerevan.

11.07.19   Stadiumi Laçi, Laçi: KF Laçi – Hapoel Be'er Sheva 1-1 (1-0)
KF Laçi: Gentian Selmani, Aleksandar Ignjatovic, David Domgjoni, Eglentin Gjoni, Abdurraman Fangaj, Ardit Deliu, Regi Lushkja, Juljan Shehu, Teco, Kyrian Nwabueze (82' Elvi Berisha), Redon Xhixha (87' Ndricim Shtubina). Coach: Sulejman Starova.
Hapoel Be'er Sheva: Ernestas Setkus, Miguel Vítor, Ben Bitton, Loai Taha, Sean Goldberg, Eden Shamir, Naor Sabag (87' Tomer Yosefi), Jimmy Marín, Ben Sahar (77' José Carrillo), Nigel Hasselbaink, Niv Zrihan (71' Gal Levi). Coach: Barak Bakhar.
Goals: 3' Kyrian Nwabueze 1-0, 78' Gal Levi 1-1.
Referee: Loukas Sotiriou (CYP)   Attendance: 1,400.

11.07.19   Rakvere Linnastaadion, Rakvere:
          JK Narva Trans – FK Buducnost Podgorica 0-2 (0-1)
JK Narva Trans: Marko Meerits, Roman Nesterovski, Tanel Tamberg, Joseph Saliste (86' Aleksei Stepanov), Irie Elysée, Dmitri Proshin, Denis Polyakov, Artjom Skinjov, Aleksandr Zakarlyuka, Nikita Mihhailov (87' Viktor Plotnikov), Eric McWoods (82' Eduard Golovljov). Coach: Andrey Semin.
FC Buducnost Podgorica: Milos Dragojevic, Dejan Boljevic, Luka Mirkovic, Slavko Damjanovic, Stefan Milic, Drasko Bozovic (88' Vasilije Terzic), Milos Mijic, Milos Vucic, Dusan Bakic (70' Dusan Stoiljkovic), Igor Ivanovic, Mihailo Perovic (76' Aleksandar Vujacic). Coach: Branko Brnovic.
Goals: 12' Igor Ivanovic 0-1, 88' Milos Mijic 0-2.
Referee: Sergey Tsinkevich (BLS)   Attendance: 319.

JK Narva Trans played their home match at Rakvere Linnastaadion, Rakvere, instead of their regular stadium Narva Kreenholmi Stadium, Narva.

11.07.19 AEK Arena – George Karapatakis, Larnaca:
AEK Larnaca – CS Petrocub Hîncesti 1-0 (1-0)
AEK Larnaca: Toño, Mikel González, Daniel Mojsov (85' Nacho Cases), Truyols, Thomas Ioannou (46' Tete), Ivan Trickovski, Lluis Sastre, Hector Hevel (68' Acorán), Raúl Ruiz, Apostolos Giannou, Florian Taulemesse. Coach: Imanol Idiakez.
CS Petrocub Hîncesti: Cristian Avram, Maxim Potîrniche, Ion Jardan, Victor Mudrac, Andrei Cojocari, Alexandru Bejan (70' Iaser Turcan), Dan Taras (62' Vlad Slivca), Jessie Guera Djou, Jacques Onana Ndzomo, Donalio Melachio Douanla, Alexandr Dedov (10' Vadim Gulceac). Coach: Lilian Popescu.
Goal: 4' Hector Hevel 1-0.
Referee: Michal Ocenás (SVK)   Attendance: 3,561.

11.07.19 Savon Sanomat Areena, Kuopio: Kuopion PS – FK Vitebsk 2-0 (0-0)
Kuopion PS: Otso Virtanen, Babacar Diallo, Luis Murillo, Kalle Taimi, Vinko Soldo, Petteri Pennanen, Reuben Ayarna, Ville Saxman, Ilmari Niskanen (72' Saku Savolainen), Issa Thiaw (77' Tommi Jyry), Rangel (86' Ariel Ngueukam). Coach: Jani Honkavaara.
FK Vitebsk: Dmitri Gushchenko, Akaki Khubutia, Oleg Karamushka, Mikhail Kozlov, Maranhão, Daniil Chalov, Artem Stargorodskiy (59' Anton Matveenko), Artem Skitov, Maksim Feshchuk, Nikolai Zolotov, Kirill Pechenin. Coach: Sergey Yasinsky.
Goals: 61' Luis Murillo 1-0, 74' Rangel 2-0.
Referee: Danilo Grujic (SRB)   Attendance: 2,560.

11.07.19 A. Le Coq Arena, Tallinn: FC Flora Tallinn – Radnicki Nis 2-0 (0-0)
FC Flora Tallinn: Matvei Igonen, Gert Kams, Märten Kuusk, Henrik Pürg, Henri Järvelaid, Konstantin Vassiljev, Mikhel Ainsalu, Martin Miller, Vladislavs Kreida, Frank Liivak, Erik Sorga (73' Mark Lepik). Coach: Jürgen Henn.
Radnicki Nis: Nikola Petrovic, Aleksandar Todorovski, Stefan Djordjevic, Ivan Ostojic, Lazar Djordjevic, Taras Bondarenko, Nemanja Tomic (63' Veljko Batrovic), Dejan Meleg (78' Sasa Stojanovic), Ryota Noma, Erik Jirka, Milan Bojovic (70' Milan Makaric).
Coach: Simo Krunic.
Goals: 75' Mark Lepik 1-0, 89' Konstantin Vassiljev 2-0.
Referee: Alexandru Tean (MOL)   Attendance: 1,250.

11.07.19 Bayil Arena, Baku: Sabail FK – CS Universitatea Craiova 2-3 (1-1)
Sabail FK: Daniel Bozinovski, Erico, Elvin Yunuszade, Ürfan Abbasov, Mickael Essien (59' Dylan Duventru), Shahriyar Rahimov (84' Eltun Yagublu), Rahid Amirquliyev, Bilal Hamdi (72' Fahmin Muradbayli), Eugeniu Cociuc, Agabala Ramazanov, Mirabdulla Abbasov. Coach: Aftandil Hadzhiyev.
CS Universitatea Craiova: Mirko Pigliacelli, Renato Kelic, Ivan Martic, Nicusor Bancu, Stephane Acka, Alexandru Mateiu, Bogdan Vatajelu (90' Stefan Baiaram), Kamer Qaka, Cristian Barbut (73' Alexandru Ionita), Antoni Ivanov, Mihai Roman (II) (68' Carlos Fortes). Coach: Corneliu Papura.
Goals: 13' Alexandru Mateiu 0-1, 33' Agabala Ramazanov 1-1, 51' Nicusor Bancu 1-2, 67' Mihai Roman (II) 1-3, 82' Agabala Ramazanov 2-3.
Referee: Fyodor Zammit (MLT)   Attendance: 2,550.

11.07.19   Vilniaus LFF stadionas, Vilnius: FK Riteriai – KÍ Klaksvík 1-1 (0-0)
FK Riteriai: Tomas Svedkauskas, Valdemars Borovskis, Justinas Janusevskis, Ricardas Sveikauskas, Aleksandr Levsinas, Valentin Jeriomenko, Tomas Dombrauskis, Artsem Hurenka, Dovydas Virksas (75' Dominyk Kodz), Donatas Kazlauskas, Teremas Moffi.
Coach: Aurelijus Skarbalius.
KÍ Klaksvík: Kristian Joensen, Jesper Brinck, Ísak Simonsen, Deni Pavlovic, Semir Hadzibulic, Boris Dosljak, Patrik Johannesen (89' Páll Klettskard), Jákup Andreasen, Jóannes Bjartalíd (86' Torbjørn Grytten), Simen Sandmæl (90+1' Jonn Johannesen), Jóannes Danielsen. Coach: Mikkjal Thomassen.
Goals: 46' Valdemars Borovskis 1-0, 56' Jákup Andreasen 1-1.
Referee: Bram Van Driessche (BEL)   Attendance: 1,480.

11.07.19   MFA Centenary Stadium, Ta'Qali: Balzan FC – NK Domzale 3-4 (2-1)
Balzan FC: Kristijan Naumovski, Steven Bezzina, Aleksandar Kosoric, Ivan Bozovic, Uros Ljubomirac (82' Andrija Majdevac), Paul Fenech, Nenad Sljivic, Stefan Dimic, Ricardo Correa (86' Lydon Micallef), Alfred Effiong (69' Arthur Faría), Stephen Pisani.
Coach: Jacques Scerri.
NK Domzale: Grega Sorcan, Gaber Dobrovoljc, Gregor Sikosek, Tilen Klemencic, Senijad Ibricic, Amedej Vetrih, Josip Corluka, Adam Gnezda Cerin, Matej Podlogar (76' Ziga Repas), Slobodan Vuk (83' Dario Kolobaric), Tonci Mujan (64' Mattias Käit). Coach: Simon Rozman.
Goals: 5' Senijad Ibricic 0-1 (p), 34' Ricardo Correa 1-1, 38' Uros Ljubomirac 2-1, 49' Slobodan Vuk 2-2, 56' Alfred Effiong 3-2, 61' Gregor Sikosek 3-3, 76' Matej Podlogar 3-4.
Referee: Aleksey Matyunin (RUS)   Attendance: 389.

11.07.19   Futbalovy Stadión MFK Ruzomberok, Ruzomberok:
           MFK Ruzomberok – Levski Sofia 0-2 (0-1)
MFK Ruzomberok: Ivan Krajcírik, Ján Maslo, Matej Curma, Michal Jonec, Alexander Mojzis, Tihomir Kostadinov, Kristi Qose, Dalibor Takác (69' Marek Zsigmund), Adam Brenkus (59' Filip Hasek), Peter Gál-Andrezly, Stefan Gerec (79' Ondrej Novotny). Coach: Ján Haspra.
Levski Sofia: Milan Mijatovic, Zhivko Milanov, Nuno Reis, Ivan Goranov, Giannis Kargas, Martin Raynov, Davide Mariani (90+1' Franco Mazurek), Khaly Thiam, Paulinho, Iliya Yurukov (88' Zdravko Dimitrov), Stanislav Ivanov (90+3' Iliya Dimitrov).
Coach: Petar Hubchev.
Goals: 36' Davide Mariani 0-1, 51' Paulinho 0-2.
Referee: Petri Viljanen (FIN)   Attendance: 3,695.

11.07.19   Swedbank Stadion, Malmö: Malmö FF – Ballymena United 7-0 (3-0)
Malmö FF: Johan Dahlin, Behrang Safari, Lasse Nielsen, Franz Brorsson, Søren Rieks, Fouad Bachirou (69' Bonke Innocent), Oscar Lewicki, Erdal Rakip, Markus Rosenberg (59' Marcus Antonsson), Guillermo Molins, Jo Inge Berget (59' Eric Larsson). Coach: Uwe Rösler.
Ballymena United: Ross Glendinning, Tony Kane, Jim Ervin, Steven McCullough, Scot Whiteside, Kofi Balmer, Andy McGrory, Jude Winchester (75' Shane McGinty), Declan Carville (51' Andrew Burns), Leroy Millar, Adam Lecky (72' Cathair Friel).
Coach: David Jeffrey.
Goals: 31', 33' Markus Rosenberg 1-0, 2-0, 44' Erdal Rakip 3-0, 46' Franz Brorsson 4-0, 48' Markus Rosenberg 5-0, 54' Guillermo Molins 6-0, 74' Erdal Rakip 7-0.
Referee: Igor Pajac (CRO)   Attendance: 8,667.

11.07.19   Gradski Stadion, Banja Luka: Radnik Bijeljina – Spartak Trnava 2-0 (1-0)
Radnik Bijeljina: Dalibor Kozic, Milos Simonovic, Slavisa Radovic, Velibor Djuric, Pavle Susic, Nikola Popara, Ivan Subert, Nedim Mekic (86' Vladimir Bradonjic), Dejan Maksimovic (79' Milos Plavsic), Demir Peco, Seid Zukic (66' Jovan Motika). Coach: Mladen Zizovic.
Spartak Trnava: Dobrivoj Rusov, Matús Turna (55' Filip Orsula), Bogdan Mitrea, Jozef Menich, Lucas Lovat, Marko Tesija, Emir Halilovic, Matej Jakúbek (55' Alex Sobczyk), Filip Dangubic (79' Marko Kelemen), Kristián Mihálek, Rafael Tavares. Coach: Ricardo Chéu.
Goals: 34' Nedim Mekic 1-0, 48' Velibor Djuric 2-0.
Referee: Volen Chinkov (BUL)   Attendance: 1,500.

Radnik Bijejina played their home match at Gradski Stadion, Banja Luka, instead of their regular stadium Gradski stadion, Bijeljina.

11.07.19   Brann Stadion, Bergen: SK Brann – Shamrock Rovers 2-2 (2-1)
SK Brann: Håkon Opdal, Taijo Teniste, Bismar Acosta, Ruben Kristiansen, Christian Rismark, Fredrik Haugen, Kristoffer Løkberg (68' Petter Strand), Amer Ordagic (74' Ruben Jenssen), Veton Berisha, Gilli Rólantsson Sørensen, Gilbert Koomson (82' Daouda Bamba).
Coach: Lars Nilsen.
Shamrock Rovers: Alan Mannus, Joey O'Brien, Sean Kavanagh, Roberto Lopes, Ethan Boyle, Lee Grace, Ronan Finn (77' Aaron McEneff), Greg Bolger, Jack Byrne, Trevor Clarke (66' Dylan Watts), Aaron Greene (65' Graham Cummins). Coach: Stephen Bradley.
Goals: 12 Taijo Teniste 1-0, 34' Amer Ordagic 1-1 (og), 36' Veton Berisha 2-1 (p), 90+4' Roberto Lopes 2-2.
Referee: Juxhin Xhaja (ALB)   Attendance: 4,560.

11.07.19   Boris Paichadze Dinamo Arena, Tbilisi: Dinamo Tbilisi – UE Engordany 6-0 (2-0)
Dinamo Tbilisi: José Perales, Gudzha Rukhaia, Giorgi Kimadze, Víctor Mongil, Davit Kobouri, Nika Ninua, Levan Kutalia, Giorgi Kukhianidze (76' Bakar Kardava), Giorgi Papava (57' Giorgi Zaria), Nodar Kavtaradze, Levan Shengelia (63' Arfang Daffé).
Coach: Félix Vicente Miranda.
UE Engordany: Jesús Coca, Jorge Sebastián Varela, Rafael Brito, Deivis De Jesus Soares, Mario Spano, Sébastien Aguéro, Hamza Bouharma, Míguel Laborda (71' Edu Peppe), Sebastián Gómez (90+3' Brian Mengual Maneiro), Fábio Serra Alves, Morgan Lafont (85' Rodrigo Guida). Coach: Filipe Busto.
Goals: 6' Nika Ninua 1-0, 21' Giorgi Kukhianidze 2-0, 61' Nodar Kavtaradze 3-0, 69' Levani Kutalia 4-0 (p), 71' Giorgi Kukhianidze 5-0, 80' Giorgi Zaria 6-0.
Referee: Morten Krogh (DEN)   Attendance: 3,680.

11.07.19   Marijampolés sporto centro stadione, Marijampolé:
          Kauno Zalgiris – Apollon Limassol 0-2 (0-1)
Kauno Zalgiris: Deividas Mikelionis, "Rudi" Rudinilson Silva (58' Edvinas Kloniūnas), Rimvydas Sadauskas, Karolis Silkaitis, Pijus Sirvys (78' Philip Otele), Dominykas Galkevicius, Yuriy Bushman, Martynas Dapkus, Daniel Romanovskij, Deividas Sesplaukis (65' Linas Pilibaitis), João Figueiredo. Coach: Mindaugas Cepas.
Apollon Limassol: Joël Mall, Vahid Selimovic (46' Attila Szalai), Ioannis Pittas, Vincent Bessat, Héctor Yuste, Sasa Markovic, Esteban Sachetti, Emilio Zelaya, João Pedro, Fotios Papoulis (64' Serge Gakpé), Adrián Sardinero (79' Diego Aguirre). Coach: Sofronis Avgousti.
Goals: 14' Ioannis Pittas 0-1, 90' Emilio Zelaya 0-2 (p).
Referee: Admir Sehovic (BIH)   Attendance: 717.

Kauno Zalgiris played their home match at Sūduva Stadium, Marijampolé, insteadof their temporary stadium SM Tauras Stadium, Kaunas which does not meet UEFA requirements.

11.07.19   Sammy Ofer Stadium, Haifa: Maccabi Haifa – NS Mura 2-0 (0-0)
Maccabi Haifa: Guy Haimov, Rami Gershon, Ernest Mabouka, Ayed Habashi, Ofri Arad (86'
Allyson), Yuval Ashkenazi, Yosef Raz Meir, Neta Lavi, Maxim Plakushchenko (51'
Mohammed Awaed), Dolev Haziza, Yarden Shua (72' Mohammad Abu Fani).
Coach: Marco Balbul.
NS Mura: Matko Obradovic, Klemen Sturm, Zan Karnicnik (74' Timo Horvat), Aleksandar
Boskovic, Matic Marusko, Ziga Kous, Alen Kozar, Jon Sporn, Amadej Marosa (73' Andrija
Bubnjar), Luka Bobicanec (79' Kai Cipot), Luka Susnjara. Coach: Ante Simundza.
Goals: 64' Yuval Ashkenazi 1-0, 68' Mohammed Awaed 2-0.
Referee: Manfredas Lukjancukas (LTU)   Attendance: 16,127.

11.07.19   Nagyerdei Stadion, Debrecen: Debreceni VSC – FK Kukësi 3-0 (0-0)
Debreceni VSC: Sándor Nagy, János Ferenczi, Csaba Szatmári, Bence Pávkovics, Dániel
Tözsér, Nikola Trujic (88' Richárd Csösz), Kevin Varga, Attila Haris, Erik Kusnyír (89' Ákos
Kinyik), Tamás Takács (52' Haruna Garba), Márk Szécsi. Coach: András Herczeg.
FK Kukësi: Stivi Frashëri, Ardijan Cuculi, Olsi Teqja, Tome Kitanovski, Simon Rrumbullaku,
Valdet Rama, Eduart Rroca (76' Emiljano Musta), Besar Musolli, Vesel Limaj, Valon Ethemi
(71' Arbër Çyrbja), Vasil Shkurti. Coach: Ernest Gjoka.
Goals: 54' Haruna Garba 1-0, 77', 83' Kevin Varga 2-0, 3-0.
Referee: Sebastian Gishamer (AUT)   Attendance: 10,250.

11.07.19   Stadions Daugava, Liepāja: FK Liepāja – Dinamo Minsk 1-1 (1-0)
FK Liepāja: Valentins Ralkevics, Vadims Zulevs, Deniss Ivanovs, Seydina Keita, Jānis
Ikaunieks, Raivis Jurkovskis, Amâncio Fortes (82' Danu Spataru), Leonel Strumia, Kristers
Tobers, Richard Friday, Dodô. Coach: Aleksandrs Starkovs.
Dinamo Minsk: Maksim Plotnikov, Andrei Zaleski, Aleksey Gavrilovich, Aleksandr Chizh,
Seidu Yahaya, Dinko Trebotic, Nikita Kaplenko, Vladislav Lyakh (46' Georgi Tigiev), Nikita
Demchenko (72' Dmytro Bilonog), Kehinde Fatai, Yegor Zubovich (79' Kirill Vergeychik).
Coach: Sergei Gurenko.
Goals: 12' Jānis Ikaunieks 1-0 (p), 88' Nikita Kaplenko 1-1.
Referee: António Carvalho Nobre (POR)   Attendance: 3,793.

11.07.19   Seaview, Belfast: Crusaders FC – B36 Tórshavn 2-0 (1-0)
Crusaders FC: Sean O'Neill, Billy Joe Burns, Howard Beverland, Chris Hegarty, Michael
Ruddy, Declan Caddell (63' Rory Hale), Philip Lowry, Jordan Forsythe (90+9' Gary
Thompson), Paul Heatley (78' David Cushley), Ross Clarke, Jordan Owens.
Coach: Stephen Baxter.
B36 Tórshavn: Hans Jørgensen, Erling Jacobsen, Alex Mellemgaard, Jónas Næs, Eli Nielsen,
Árni Frederiksberg, Benjamin Heinesen (60' Stefan Radosavljevic), Andrias Eriksen, Michal
Przybylski (90+1' Hannes Agnarsson), Magnus Holm Jacobsen, Lukasz Cieslewicz (90+7'
Brian Jacobsen). Coach: Jákub á Borg.
Goals: 33' Chris Hegarty 1-0, 79' Philip Lowry 2-0.
Referee: Yigal Frid (ISR)   Attendance: 1,112.

Jordan Owens missed a penalty kick (2').

11.07.19 Brøndby Stadion, Brøndby: Brøndby IF – FC Inter Turku 4-1 (1-1)
Brøndby IF: Marvin Schwäbe, Paulus Arajuuri, Anthony Jung, Hjörtur Hermannsson, Dominik Kaiser (90+1' Tobias Børkeeiet), Lasse Vigen Christensen (64' Kasper Fisker), Josip Radosevic, Simon Tibbling (83' Jesper Lindstrøm), Simon Hedlund, Kamil Wilczek, Kevin Mensah. Coach: Niels Frederiksen.
FC Inter Turku: Henrik Moisander, Niko Markkula, Luciano Balbi, Juuso Hämäläinen, Miro Tenho, Daan Klinkenberg, Álvaro Muñiz, Aleksi Paananen (81' Elias Mastokangas), Timo Furuholm, Mika Ojala (75' Mikko Kuningas), Filip Valencic. Coach: José Riveiro.
Goals: 5' Kamil Wilczek 1-0, 2-0 Timo Furuholm 1-1, 67' Kamil Wilczek 2-1, 71' Simon Tibbling 3-1, 78' Kasper Fisker 4-1.
Referee: Kristoffer Karlsson (SWE)   Attendance: 10,296.

11.07.19   Aker Stadion, Molde: Molde FK – KR Reykjavík 7-1 (4-0)
Molde FK: Álex Craninx, Vegard Forren, Kristoffer Haraldseid, Kristoffer Haugen, Martin Bjørnbak, Magnus Eikrem (82' Mattias Moström), Etzaz Hussain, Eirik Hestad, Fredrik Aursnes (70' Fredrik Sjølstad), Ohi Omoijuanfo, Leke James (75' Erling Knudtzon). Coach: Erling Moe.
KR Reykjavik: Beitir Ólafsson, Arnór Adalsteinsson, Skúli Jón Fridgeirsson, Kristinn Jónsson, Finnur Tómas Pálmason (46' Gunnar Gunnarsson), Pálmi Pálmason, Arnthór Ingi Kristinsson (78' Ægir Jónasson), Pablo Punyed, Óskar Hauksson, Kennie Chopart, Tobias Thomsen (86' Björgvin Stefánsson). Coach: Rúnar Kristinsson.
Goals: 7' Leke James 1-0, 29' Fredrik Aursnes 2-0, 31' Leke James 3-0, 41' Leke James 4-0, 63' Vegard Forren 5-0, 66' Etzaz Hussain 6-0, 71' Tobias Thomsen 6-1, 90+3' Ohi Omoijuanfo 7-1.
Referee: Aleksandrs Golubevs (LAT)   Attendance: 3,756.

11.07.19   Tose Proeski Arena, Skopje: Akademija Pandev – Zrinjski Mostar 0-3 (0-2)
Akademija Pandev: Dusan Cubrakovic, Tomislav Iliev, Dime Dimov, Ljupco Doriev, David Atanasovski, Georgi Stoilov, Stefan Kostov, Daniel Milovanovikj (78' Kristijan Velinovski), Goran Tomovski, Sasko Pandev (68' Mario Krstovski), Kristijan Stojkovski (66' Riste Temelkov). Coach: Jugoslav Trencovski.
Zrinjski Mostar: Ivan Brkic, Tomislav Barbaric, Dario Rugasevic, Slobodan Jakovljevic, Advan Kadusic, Ivan Curjuric, Damir Sovsic (76' Semir Pezer), Edin Rustemovic, Miljan Govedarica, Stanisa Mandic (83' Marko Bencun), Irfan Hadzic (66' Ivan Lendric). Coach: Hari Vukas.
Goals: 12' Irfan Hadzic 0-1, 28' Stanisa Mandic 0-2, 55' Miljan Govedarica 0-3.
Referee: Kai Erik Steen (NOR)   Attendance: 1,562.

Akademija Pandev played their home match at Tose Proeski Arena, Skopje, instead of their regular stadium Stadion Kukus, Strumica which does not meet UEFA requirements.

11.07.19   Stadyen Budaunik Stroitel, Soligorsk:
            Shakhtyor Soligorsk – Hibernians FC 1-0 (0-0)
Shakhtyor Soligorsk: Andrey Klimovich, Sergey Matvejchik, Igor Burko, Nikola Antic, Aleksandr Sachivko, Yuri Kovalev, Július Szöke, Valeriy Gromyko, Max Ebong Ngome (46' Mykyta Tatarkov), Elis Bakaj, Vladimir Khvashchinskiy (46' Nikolai Yanush). Coach: Sergey Tashuev.
Hibernians FC: Marko Jovicic, Andrei Agius, Márcio Silveira, Ferdinando Apap, Timothy Tabone, Bjorn Kristensen, Dunstan Vella, Jake Grech (74' Jens Wemmer), Leonardo Nanni (89' David Xuereb), Joseph Mbong, Terence Groothusen. Coach: Stefano Sanderra.
Goal: 69' Valeriy Gromyko 1-0.
Referee: Jovan Kaludjerovic (MNE)   Attendance: 3,048.

11.07.19   Stadionul Zimbru, Chisinau: Speranta Nisporeni – Neftçi PFK Baku 0-3 (0-2)
Speranta Nisporeni: Daniil Avdyushkin, Oliver Fula, Bruno Barbosa, Stefan Efros, Mihail Bolun, Fabrice Eloundou, Ichaka Tiehi, Felipe Ponce, Dayron Mosquera (46' Ion Dragan), Alisher Mirzoev (87' Ruslan Chelari), Maxim Iurcu (79' Constantin Sandu).
Coach: Cristian Efros.
Neftçi PFK Baku: Salahat Agayev, Kyrylo Petrov, Mamadou Mbodj, Anton Krivotsyuk, Omar Buludov, Vangelis Platellas (69' Rahman Hadzhiyev), Emin Makhmudov, Mamadou Kane, Steeven Joseph-Monrose (87' Ismayil Zülfügarli), Rauf Aliyev, Dário Júnior da Silva (80' Namiq Alasgarov). Coach: Roberto Bordin.
Goals: 16' Emin Makhmudov 0-1 (p), 36' Steeven Joseph-Monrose 0-2, 76' Rahman Hadzhiyev 0-3.
Referee: Tim Marshall (NIR)   Attendance: 1,370.

Speranta Nisporeni played their home match at Stadionul Zimbru, Chisinau, instead of their regular stadium Stadionul Eliade, Nisporeni which does not meet UEFA requirements.

11.07.19   Stade Émile Mayrisch, Esch-sur-Alzette:
           CS Fola Esch – Chikhura Sachkhere 1-2 (1-0)
CS Fola Esch: Emanuel Cabral, Billy Bernard, Julien Klein, Cédric Sacras, Veldin Muharemovic, Dejvid Sinani (89' Jean Sylvio Ouassiero), Gérard Mersch, Bruno Freire, Gauthier Caron (75' Achraf Drif), Ken Corral (86' Zachary Hadji), Moussa Seydi.
Coach: Jeff Strasser.
Chikhura Sachkhere: Dino Hamzic, Davit Maisashvili, Lasha Chikvaidze, Revaz Chiteishvili, Oleg Mamasakhlisi, Besik Dekanoidze (90' Shota Kashia), Irakli Lekvtadze (75' Giorgi Pantsulaia), Giorgi Koripadze, Teimuraz Markozashvili, Rati Ardazishvili (65' Demur Chikhladze), Mikheil Sardalishvili. Coach: Soso Pruidze.
Goals: 22' Dejvid Sinani 1-0 (p), 59' Mikheil Sardalishvili 1-1, 86' Giorgi Koripadze 1-2 (p).
Referee: Rauf Jabbarov (AZE)   Attendance: 1,087.

11.07.19   Stadion Stozice, Ljubljana: Olimpija Ljubljana – FK Rīgas Futbola skola 2-3 (0-0)
Olimpija Ljubljana: Nejc Vidmar, Denis Sme, Macky Frank Bagnack, Eric Boakye, Marko Putincanin (72' Luka Menalo), Asmir Suljic, Stefan Savic, Tomislav Tomic, Endri Çekiçi, Rok Kidric (63' Ante Vukusic), Mario Jurcevic. Coach: Safet Hadzic.
FK Rīgas Futbola skola: Kaspers Ikstens, Vitalijs Jagodinskis, Edvinas Girdvainis, Vladislavs Sorokins, Tomás Simkovic (77' Tin Vukmanic), Takayuki Seto, Slavko Blagojevic, Andrejs Ciganiks (64' Alain Cedric Kouadio), Andrija Kaludjerovic (71' Glebs Kluskins), Roberts Savalnieks, Darko Lemajic. Coach: Valdas Dambrauskas.
Goals: 52' Darko Lemajic 0-1 (p), 81' Eric Boakye 1-1, 88' Glebs Kluskins 1-2, 90' Luka Menalo 2-2, 90+3' Tin Vukmanic 2-3.
Referee: Urs Schnyder (SUI)   Attendance: 4,200.

11.07.19 Corbett Sports Stadium, Rhyl:
Connah's Quay Nomads FC – Kilmarnock FC 1-2 (0-0)
Connah's Quay Nomads FC: Lewis Brass, George Horan, Danny Holmes, John Disney, Callum Roberts, Danny Harrison, Jay Owen, Michael Bakare, Callum Morris, Declan Poole, Michael Wilde. Coach: Andy Morrison.
Kilmarnock FC: Jamie MacDonald, Kirk Broadfoot, Stephen O'Donnell, Stuart Findlay, Greg Taylor, Chris Burke, Alan Power, Gary Dicker, Dominic Thomas (78' Greg Kiltie), Rory McKenzie (64' Mohamed El Makrini), Eamonn Brophy. Coach: Angelo Alessio.
Goals: 75' Greg Taylor 1-0 (og), 82' Eamonn Brophy 1-1 (p), 90+2' Stuart Findlay 1-2.
Referee: Erik Lambrechts (BEL)   Attendance: 1,410.

Connah's Quay Nomads FC played their home match at Corbett Sports Stadium, Rhyl, instead of their regular stadium Deeside Stadium, Connah's Quay which does not meet UEFA requirements.

11.07.19 Victoria Stadium, Gibraltar: Europa FC – Legia Warszawa 0-0
Europa FC: Dayle Coleing, Sergio Sánchez, Rahim Ayew, Olmo González, Ethan Jolley, Velasco (82' Manu Dimas), Álex Quillo (59' Marco Rosa), Juampe Rico, Liam Walker, Mustapha Yahaya, Andre Tjay de Barr (88' Adrián Gallardo). Coach: Rafael Escobar.
Legia Warszawa: Radoslaw Majecki, Artur Jedrzejczyk, William Rémy, Dominik Nagy (76' Salvador Agra), Mateusz Wieteska, Arvydas Novikovas, Marko Vesovic, André Martins, Valeriane Gvilia, Carlitos López, Vamara Sanogo (45+2' Sandro Kulenovic).
Coach: Aleksandar Vukovic.
Referee: Alex Troleis (FRO)   Attendance: 787.

11.07.19 MOL Aréna, Dunajská Streda:
DAC Dunajská Streda – KS Cracovia Kraków 1-1 (1-1)
DAC Dunajská Streda: Martin Jedlicka, Éric Davis (60' César Blackman), Lubomír Satka, Dominik Kruzliak, Zsolt Kalmár, Kristián Kostrna, Kristopher Vida (71' Abdulrahman Taiwo), Máté Vida, Lukás Cmelík (76' Eric Ramírez), Connor Ronan, Marko Divkovic.
Coach: Peter Hyballa.
KS Cracovia Kraków: Michal Peskovic, Cornel Rapa, Niko Datkovic, Michal Helik, Kamil Pestka (46' Diego Ferraresso), Janusz Gol, Damian Dabrowski (84' Milan Dimun), Sergiu Hanca, Bojan Cecaric (62' Mateusz Wdowiak), Pelle van Amersfoort, "Rafa" Rafael Lopes.
Coach: Michal Probierz.
Goals: 40' Dominik Kruzliak 0-1 (og), 44' Marko Divkovic 1-1.
Referee: Rade Obrenovic (SVN)   Attendance: 9,860.

11.07.19 Stadionul Marin Anastasovici, Giurgiu:
            Fotbal Club FCSB – FC Milsami Orhei 2-0 (1-0)
Fotbal Club FCSB: Andrei Daniel Vlad, Bogdan Planic, Claudiu Belu, Iulian Cristea, Mihai Roman (I), Dragos Nedelcu, Razvan Oaida (62' Lucian Filip), Adrian Ioan Hora, Florin Tanase, Florinel Coman (90+5' Cristián Dumitru), Dennis Man (79' Ovidiu Popescu).
Coach: Bogdan Andone.
FC Milsami Orhei: Anatolii Chirinciuc, Vadim Bolohan, Vasile Jardan, Artur Craciun, Alexandru Antoniuc, Alexandru Onica, Gheorghe Andronic, Andrei Rusnac, Victor Stîna (85' Maxim Antoniuc), Sergiu Platica, Sergiu Nazar (60' Veaceslav Zagaevschii).
Coach: Veaceslav Rusnac.
Goals: 12', 56' Florin Tanase 1-0, 2-0.
Referee: Kristoffer Hagenes (NOR)   Attendance: 4,824.
Sent off: 73' Lucian Filip.

Fotbal Club FCSB played their home match at Stadionul Marin Anastasovici, Giurgiu, instead of their regular stadium Arena Nationala, Bucharest.

11.07.19 Stadion na Banovom brdu, Beograd:
            FK Cukaricki-Stankom – FC Banants Erevan 3-0 (1-0)
FK Cukaricki-Stankom: Nemanja Belic, Miroslav Bogosavac, Darko Puskaric, Nikola Cirkovic, Luka Stojanovic (72' Aleksandar Djordjevic), Luka Lukovic (53' Veljko Birmancevic), Marko Docic, Stefan Kovac, Stefan Sapic, Slobodan Tedic, Milutin Vidosavljevic (82' Bojica Nikcevic). Coach: Aleksander Veselinovic.
FC Banants Erevan: Aram Ayrapetyan, Vahagn Ayvazyan, Andranik Voskanyan, Edward Kpodo, Narek Petrosyan, Aram Bareghamyan, Artak Dashyan (72' Hakob Hakobyan), Pape Camara, Igor Stanojevic, Evgeni Kobzar (68' Karen Melkonyan), Aleksandar Glisic (87' Semen Sinyavskiy). Coach: Ilshat Faizulin.
Goals: 43' Slobodan Tedic 1-0, 80' Stefan Kovac 2-0, 90+2' Slobodan Tedic 3-0.
Referee: Ívar Orri Kristjánsson (ISL)   Attendance: 1,203.

11.07.19 Stadion Pod Goricom, Podgorica: FK Zeta Golubovci – MOL Vidi FC 1-5 (1-3)
FK Zeta Golubovci: Zoran Akovic, Djordjije Vukcevic, Nemanja Sekulic, Balsa Goranovic, Zvonko Ceklic, Armin Bosnjak, Goran Milojko, Stefan Vukcevic (60' Alex Yamoah), Amel Tuzovic, Srdjan Krstovic (76' Lazar Lambulic), Ivan Vukcevic (90+3' Matija Lambulic).
Coach: Dejan Roganovic.
MOL Vidi FC: Ádam Kovácsik, Roland Juhász, Attila Fiola, Loïc Négo, Stopira, Anel Hadzic, Máté Pátkai (61' Ivan Petryak), Ákos Elek, Georgi Milanov (64' Szabolcs Huszti), Boban Nikolov, Marko Scepovic (80' Márkó Futács). Coach: Marko Nikolic.
Goals: 3', 12' Loïc Négo 0-1, 0-2, 17' Balsa Goranovic 1-2, 23' Loïc Négo 1-3, 86' Roland Juhász 1-4, 90+3' Szabolcs Huszti 1-5.
Referee: Georgi Vadachkoria (GEO)   Attendance: 965.

FK Zeta Golubovci played their home match at Stadion Pod Goricom, Podgorica, instead of their regular stadium Stadion Tresnjica, Golubovci which does not meet UEFA requirements.

11.07.19   Solitude, Belfast: Cliftonville FC – FK Haugesund 0-1 (0-1)
Cliftonville FC: Richard Brush, Garry Breen, Liam Bagnall, Conor McMenamin, Joe Gorman (87' Thomas Maguire), Levi Ives, Conor McDermott, Chris Curran (67' Ryan Curran), Ronan Doherty, Rory Donnelly, Joe Gormley. Coach: Paddy McLaughlin.
FK Haugesund: Helge Sandvik, Doug Bergqvist, Mikkel Desler, Benjamin Tiedemann Hansen, Christian Grindheim (46' Kevin Krygård), Sondre Tronstad, Torbjørn Kallavåg, Niklas Sandberg, Bruno Leite, Martin Samuelsen (82' Fredrik Knudsen), Ibrahima Koné (33' Kristoffer Velde). Coach: Jostein Grindhaug.
Goal: 42' Christian Grindheim 0-1.
Referee: Laurent Kopriwa (LUX)   Attendance: 1,342.
Sent off: 79' Torbjørn Kallavåg.

11.07.19   Richmond Park, Dublin: St Patrick's Athletic – IFK Norrköping 0-2 (0-0)
St Patrick's Athletic: Brendan Clarke, Ian Bermingham, Simon Madden, Kevin Toner, Lee Desmond, Ciaran Kelly, Conor Clifford (83' Jake Walker), Cian Coleman (64' Rhys McCabe), Jamie Lennon, Gary Shaw (64' Dean Clarke), Michael Drennan. Coach: Harry Kenny.
IFK Norrköping: Isak Pettersson, Lars Gerson, Kasper Larsen, Filip Dagerstål, Rasmus Lauritsen, Gudmundur Thórarinsson (75' Sead Haksabanovic), Simon Thern, Alexander Fransson, Christoffer Nyman (69' Kalle Holmberg), Simon Skrabb (86' Egzon Binaku), Jordan Larsson. Coach: Jens Gustafsson.
Goals: 55' Simon Thern 0-1, 85' Lee Desmond 0-2 (og).
Referee: Lionel Tschudi (SUI)   Attendance: 2,389.

11.07.19   Pittodrie Stadium, Aberdeen: Aberdeen FC – Rovaniemi PS 2-1 (1-0)
Aberdeen FC: Joe Lewis, Andrew Considine, Shay Logan, Michael Devlin, Scott McKenna, Niall McGinn (82' James Wilson), Lewis Ferguson, Ryan Hedges (61' Dean Campbell), Scott Wright (74' Connor McLennan), Sam Cosgrove, Jon Gallagher. Coach: Derek McInnes.
Rovaniemi PS: Antonio Reguero, Taye Taïwo, Mohamadou Sissoko, Atte Sihvonen, Juho Hyvärinen, Kalle Katz, Eetu Muinonen (57' Tarik Kada), Sergio Llamas (76' Tommi Jäntti), Lucas Lingman, Aleksandr Kokko (65' Niklas Jokelainen), Youness Rahimi.
Coach: Pasi Tuutti.
Goals: 36' Niall McGinn 1-0. 48' Sam Cosgrove 2-0, 90+3' Niklas Jokelainen 2-1.
Referee: Kaspar Sjöberg (SWE)   Attendance: 14,377.

11.07.19   Turner's Cross, Cork: Cork City – Progrès Niederkorn 0-2 (0-2)
Cork City: Mark McNulty, Colm Horgan (24' Mark O'Sullivan), Dan Casey, Conor McCarthy, Ronan Hurley, Sean McLoughlin, Conor McCormack, Gearóid Morrissey, Garry Buckley (61' Gary Boylan), Karl Sheppard, Joel Coustrain (80' Darragh Crowley).
Coaches: John Cotter & Frank Kelleher.
Progrès Niederkorn: Sebastian Flauss, Tom Laterza, Ben Vogel, Metin Karayer, Tim Hall, Aldin Skenderovic, Sébastien Thill (88' Adrien Ferino), Christian Silaj, Belmin Muratovic (71' Jacky Mmaee), Mayron De Almeida, Kempes Tekiela (90+3' Yann Matias Marques).
Coach: Roland Vrabec.
Goals: 11' Belmin Muratovic 0-1, 21' Mayron De Almeida 0-2 (p).
Referee: Aleksandrs Anufrijevs (LAT)   Attendance: 3,137.

11.07.19   Illovszky Rudolf Stadion, Budapest: Budapest Honvéd – FK Zalgiris 3-1 (1-0)
Budapest Honvéd: Rubi Levkovic, Ivan Lovric, Djordje Kamber, Bence Batik, Nikolasz Kovács, Tibor Heffler, Tonci Kukoc (74' Eke Uzoma), Dániel Gazdag, Bence Banó-Szabó (83' Dávid Kálnoki-Kis), David N'Gog (70' Dominik Cipf), Amadou Moutari.
Coach: Giuseppe Sannino.
FK Zalgiris: Martin Berkovec, Donovan Slijngard, Klemen Bolha, Rolandas Baravykas (67' Matas Vareika), Saulius Mikoliūnas (72' Karolis Uzéla), Liviu Antal, Víctor Pérez (88' Domantas Simkus), Modestas Vorobjovas, Marko Tomic, Tomislav Kis, Pau Morer.
Coach: Marek Zub.
Goals: 32' Bence Banó-Szabó 1-0, 55' David N'Gog 2-0, 69' Dániel Gazdag 3-0 (p), 90+2' Karolis Uzéla 3-1.
Referee: Boris Marhefka (SVK)   Attendance: 3,622.

Dániel Gazdag missed a penalty kick (85').

Budapest Honvéd played their home match at Illovszky Rudolf Stadion, Budapest, instead of their regular stadium Bozsik Stadion, Budapest, due to reconstruction.

11.07.19   Stadion Pecara, Siroki Brijeg: Siroki Brijeg – FK Kairat 1-2 (1-1)
Siroki Brijeg: Martin Zlomislic, Josip Kvesic, Dino Coric, Bernardo Matic, Dominik Kovacic, Mario Babic (57' Alen Jurilj), Ivan Enin, Mato Stanic (68' Boze Vukoja), Mateo Maric, Drazen Bagaric, Toni Jovic (79' Zvonimir Vukoja). Coach: Goce Sedloski.
FK Kairat: Stas Pokatilov, Eldos Akhmetov, Gafurzhan Suyombaev, Dino Mikanovic, Rade Dugalic, Aybol Abiken (56' Islambek Kuat), Bauyrzhan Islamkhan (76' Sergey Keiler), Georgiy Zhukov, Konrad Wrzesinski, Ramazan Orazov (64' Nebojsa Kosovic), Aderinsola Eseola. Coach: Aleksey Shpilevski.
Goals: 29' Aderinsola Eseola 0-1, 34' Ivan Enin 1-1, 58' Aderinsola Eseola 1-2.
Referee: Sebastian Coltescu (ROM)   Attendance: 2,436.

11.07.19   Kópavogsvöllur, Kópavogur: Breidablik – FC Vaduz 0-0
Breidablik: Gunnleifur Gunnleifsson, Damir Muminovic, Elfar Helgason, Arnar Geirsson, Gudjón Lydsson, Andri Yeoman, Höskuldur Gunnlaugsson (83' Brynjólfur Darri Willumsson), Viktor Örn Margeirsson, Gísli Eyjólfsson (63' Aron Bjarnason), Kolbeinn Thórdarson (73' Viktor Einarsson), Thomas Mikkelsen. Coach: Ágúst Gylfason.
FC Vaduz: Benjamin Büchel, Denis Simani, Yannick Schmid, Berkay Sülüngöz, Gianni Antoniazzi, Cédric Gasser (76' Gabriel Lüchinger), Milan Gajic, Boris Prokopic, Sandro Wieser, Dominik Schwizer, Tunahan Çiçek (61' Mohamed Coulibaly). Coach: Mario Frick.
Referee: Nikola Popov (BUL)   Attendance: 1,153.

11.07.19   Samsung völlurinn, Gardabær: UMF Stjarnan – FCI Levadia Tallinn 2-1 (1-0)
UMF Stjarnan: Haraldur Björnsson, Jósef Kristinn Jósefsson (46' Ævar Jóhannesson), Brynjar Gudjónsson, Daníel Laxdal, Jóhann Laxdal, Martin Rauschenberg Brorsen, Thorsteinn Már Ragnarsson, Heidar Ægisson (61' Eyjólfur Hédinsson), Alex Thór Hauksson, Gudmundur Hafsteinsson (90+1' Baldur Sigurdsson), Hilmar Árni Halldórsson.
Coach: Rúnar Sigmundsson.
FCI Levadia Tallinn: Sergei Lepmets, Markus Jürgenson, Dmitri Kruglov (71' Igor Dudarev), Maksim Podholjuzin, Evgeniy Osipov, Marek Kaljumäe, Mark Roosnupp (40' Kirill Nesterov), Rasmus Peetson (79' Pavel Marin), Aime Marcelin Gando, Nikita Andreev, João Morelli. Coach: Aleksandar Rogic.
Goals: 15', 74' Thorsteinn Már Ragnarsson 1-0, 2-0, 79' Nikita Andreev 2-1.
Referee: Denis Scherbakov (BLS)   Attendance: 876.

16.07.19   Banants Stadion, Yerevan: FC Banants Erevan – FK Cukaricki-Stankom 0-5 (0-2)
FC Banants Erevan: Aram Ayrapetyan, Vahagn Ayvazyan, Andranik Voskanyan, Edward Kpodo, Narek Petrosyan, Aram Bareghamyan (60' Evgeni Kobzar), Artak Dashyan, Pape Camara, Igor Stanojevic (46' Hakob Hakobyan), Karen Melkonyan, Aleksandar Glisic (73' Semen Sinyavskiy). Coach: Ilshat Faizulin.
FK Cukaricki-Stankom: Nemanja Belic, Miroslav Bogosavac, Darko Puskaric (73' Dimitrije Kamenovic), Nikola Cirkovic, Luka Stojanovic, Luka Lukovic, Marko Docic (59' Aleksandar Djordjevic), Stefan Kovac, Stefan Sapic, Slobodan Tedic (53' Veljko Birmancevic), Milutin Vidosavljevic. Coach: Aleksander Veselinovic.
Goals: 3' Luka Stojanovic 0-1, 31' Slobodan Tedic 0-2, 49' Luka Lukovic 0-3, 71' Veljko Birmancevic 0-4, 75' Luka Stojanovic 0-5 (p).
Referee: Ioannis Papadopoulos (GRE)   Attendance: 2,100.

16.07.19   Svangaskard, Toftir: KÍ Klaksvík – FK Riteriai 0-0
KÍ Klaksvík: Kristian Joensen, Jesper Brinck, Ísak Simonsen, Deni Pavlovic, Semir Hadzibulic, Boris Dosljak, Patrik Johannesen (90+4' Páll Klettskard), Jákup Andreasen, Jóannes Bjartalíd (84' Jonn Johannesen), Simen Sandmæl (90+2' Torbjørn Grytten), Jóannes Danielsen. Coach: Mikkjal Thomassen.
FK Riteriai: Tomas Svedkauskas, Valdemars Borovskis, Justinas Janusevskis, Ricardas Sveikauskas, Aleksandr Levsinas, Valentin Jeriomenko (59' Lajo Traore), Tomas Dombrauskis, Artem Hurenka, Dovydas Virksas (62' Dominyk Kodz), Donatas Kazlauskas, Teremas Moffi. Coach: Aurelijus Skarbalius.
Referee: Yaroslav Kozyk (UKR)   Attendance: 980.

KÍ Klaksvík won on away goals.

KÍ Klaksvík played their home match at Svangaskard, Toftir, instead of their regular stadium Vid Djúpumyrar, Klaksvík which did not meet UEFA requirements.

16.07.19   Stadion Pod Goricom, Podgorica: OFK Titograd – CSKA Sofia 0-0
OFK Titograd: Sasa Ivanovic, Radule Zivkovic (65' Marko Milickovic), Ivan Novovic, Marko Roganovic, Balsa Banovic, Ajanah-Chinedu Chukwujekwu, Mirko Raicevic (74' Milos Brnovic), Jovan Nikolic, Vojin Pavlovic, Radomir Djalovic, Mendy Mamadou (86' Ognjen Gasevic). Coach: Dragoljub Djuretic.
CSKA Sofia: Vytautas Cerniauskas, Nikolay Bodurov, Kristiyan Malinov, Plamen Galabov, Geferson, Valentin Antov (67' Rúben Pinto), Graham Carey (82' Ali Sowe), Janio Bikel, Diego Fabbrini (60' Mitko Mitkov), Tony Watt, Evandro. Coach: Dobromir Mitov.
Referee: Vasilis Dimitriou (CYP)   Attendance: 969.

OFK Titograd played their home match at Stadion Pod Goricom, Podgorica, instead of their regular stadium Mladost Stadium, Podgorica which did not meet UEFA requirements.

17.07.19   Boris Paichadze Dinamo Arena, Tbilisi:
Chikhura Sachkhere – CS Fola Esch 2-1 (1-0)
Chikhura Sachkhere: Dino Hamzic, Shota Kashia (76' Revaz Chiteishvili), Davit Maisashvili, Lasha Chikvaidze, Oleg Mamasakhlisi, Besik Dekanoidze (63' Irakli Lekvtadze), Giorgi Koripadze, Rati Ardazishvili (67' Mikheil Ergemlidze), Demur Chikhladze, Giorgi Pantsulaia, Mikheil Sardalishvili. Coach: Soso Pruidze.
CS Fola Esch: Emanuel Cabral, Billy Bernard, Julien Klein, Cédric Sacras, Veldin Muharemovic, Dejvid Sinani, Gérard Mersch (68' Jean Sylvio Ouassiero), Bruno Freire (75' Zachary Hadji), Gauthier Caron (46' Achraf Drif), Ken Corral, Moussa Seydi.
Coach: Jeff Strasser.
Goals: 25' Rati Ardazishvili 1-0, 73' Mikheil Sardalishvili 2-0, 89' Dejvid Sinani 2-1 (p).
Referee: Dragan Petrovic (BIH)   Attendance: 1,458.
Sent off: 32' Veldin Muharemovic.

Chikhura Sachkhere played their home match at Boris Paichadze Dinamo Arena, Tbilisi, instead of their regular stadium Central Stadium, Sachkhere which did not meet UEFA requirements.

18.07.19   Astana Arena, Nur-Sultan: Tobol Kustanai – Jeunesse d'Esch 1-1 (1-0)
Tobol Kustanai: Emil Balayev, Viktor Dmitrenko, Fernander Kassaï, Dmitry Miroshnichenko (62' Ruslan Valiullin), Jaba Kankava, Azat Nurgaliev (82' Mikhail Gordeychuk), Artūras Zulpa, Nika Kvekveskiri, Nikita Bocharov, Bauyrzhan Turysbek (67' Maxim Fedin), Senin Sebai. Coach: Vladimir Gazzaev.
Jeunesse d'Esch: Kévin Sommer, Arsène Menèssou, Alessandro Fiorani, Emmanuel Lapierre, Johannes Steinbach, Halim Meddour, Milos Todorovic, Luca Duriatti, David Soares De Sousa (79' Clayton De Sousa Moreira), Mehmet Arslan (72' Yannick Makota), Almir Klica.
Coach: Nicolas Huysman.
Goals: 22' Halim Meddour 1-0 (og), 59' Mehmet Arslan 1-1 (p).
Referee: Emmanouil Skoulas (GRE)   Attendance: 2,500.

Jeunesse d'Esch won on away goals.

Tobol Kustanai played their home match at Astana Arena, Nur-Sultan, instead of their regular stadium Kostanay Central Stadium, Kostanay.

18.07.19   Trening centar Petar Milosevski, Skopje: Makedonija GP – FC Alashkert 0-3 (0-1)
Makedonija GP: Marko Jovanovski, Fernando Augusto (51' Ermadin Adem), Bianor, Bobi Bozinovski, Dejan Tanturovski, Esmin Licina, Robson, Kristijan Filipovski (66' Filip Misevski), Hristijan Pecov, Alen Jasaroski, Padu (46' Benjamin Demir).
Coaches: Aleksandar Tanevski & Bobi Stojkoski.
FC Alashkert: Ognjen Cancarevic, Hrayr Mkoyan, Gagik Dagbashyan, Hayk Ishkhanyan, Taron Voskanyan, Tiago Cametá, Artak Grigoryan (61' Tiago Galvão), Danilo Sekulic (77' Sargis Shahinyan), Vahagn Hayrapetyan, Uros Nenadovic, Nikita Tankov (72' Artur Avagimian). Coach: Abraham Khashmanyan.
Goals: 21' Uros Nenadovic 0-1, 68' Tiago Galvão 0-2, 74' Taron Voskanyan 0-3.
Referee: Christophe Pires Martins (LUX)   Attendance: 656.

Makedonija GP played their home match at Trening centar Petar Milosevski, Skopje, instead of their regular stadium Gjorce Petrov Stadium, Skopje.

18.07.19   Ortaliq Stadion, Almaty: FK Kairat – Siroki Brijeg 2-1 (0-0)
FK Kairat: Stas Pokatilov, Eldos Akhmetov, Gafurzhan Suyombaev, Dino Mikanovic, Rade Dugalic, Aybol Abiken (46' Ramazan Orazov), Islambek Kuat, Bauyrzhan Islamkhan, Georgiy Zhukov, Aderinsola Eseola (79' Márton Eppel), Yerkebulan Seidakhmet (71' Konrad Wrzesinski). Coach: Aleksey Shpilevski.
Siroki Brijeg: Martin Zlomislic, Josip Kvesic, Dino Coric, Bernardo Matic, Dominik Kovacic, Petar Franjic, Mario Babic (57' Stipe Juric), Ivan Enin, Mateo Maric (46' Mato Stanic), Drazen Bagaric, Toni Jovic (65' Alen Jurilj). Coach: Goce Sedloski.
Goals: 90' Drazen Bagaric 0-1 (p), 90+2' Ramazan Orazov 1-1, 90+3' Islambek Kuat 2-1.
Referee: Denys Shurman (UKR)   Attendance: 18,500.

18.07.19   Stadiumi Niko Dovana, Durrës: KF Teuta Durrës – FK Ventspils 1-0 (0-0)
KF Teuta Durrës: Isli Hidi, Renato Arapi, Rustem Hoxha, Alexandros Kouros, Fabjan Beqja (76' Lorenco Vila), Albano Aleksi (57' Gerhard Progni), Lancinet Sidibe (71' Tefik Osmani), Florent Avdyli, Sherif Kallaku, Tomislav Busic, Darko Nikac. Coach: Shpëtim Kuçi.
FK Ventspils: Konstantin Machnovskiy, Jean Alcénat, Abdoul Mamah, Giorgi Mchedlishvili, Hélio Batista, Pavel Osipov, Jevgenijs Kazacoks, Tosin Aiyegun, Kaspars Svārups, Mykhaylo Sergiychuk (85' Raens Tālbergs), Lucas Villela (90+3' Abdullahi Alfa). Coach: Igor Klosovs.
Goal: 48' Sherif Kallaku 1-0.
Referee: Erez Papir (ISR)   Attendance: 575.

18.07.19   Veritas Stadion, Turku: FC Inter Turku – Brøndby IF 2-0 (0-0)
FC Inter Turku: Henrik Moisander, Niko Markkula, Luciano Balbi (86' Mikko Kuningas), Juuso Hämäläinen, Miro Tenho, Arttu Hoskonen (70' Daan Klinkenberg), Álvaro Muñiz, Aleksi Paananen, Niilo Mäenpää (76' Albion Ademi), Timo Furuholm, Filip Valencic.
Coach: José Riveiro.
Brøndby IF: Marvin Schwäbe, Anthony Jung, Hjörtur Hermannsson, Jens Gammelby, Kasper Fisker (90' Paulus Arajuuri), Dominik Kaiser, Simon Tibbling, Simon Hedlund, Tobias Børkeeiet (58' Josip Radosevic), Kevin Mensah, Mikael Uhre (59' Kamil Wilczek).
Coach: Niels Frederiksen.
Goals: 52' Niko Markkula 1-0, 56' Filip Valencic 2-0.
Referee: Keith Kennedy (NIR)   Attendance: 3,711.

18.07.19   Daugava Stadionā, Riga: FK Rīgas Futbols skola – Olimpija Ljubljana 0-2 (0-1)
FK Rīgas Futbola skola: Kaspers Ikstens, Vitalijs Jagodinskis, Edvinas Girdvainis, Vladislavs Sorokins, Tomás Simkovic (87' Alans Sinelnikovs), Takayuki Seto, Slavko Blagojevic, Tin Vukmanic (73' Andrejs Ciganiks), Roberts Savalnieks, Darko Lemajic, Alain Cedric Kouadio (64' Andrija Kaludjerovic). Coach: Valdas Dambrauskas.
Olimpija Ljubljana: Nejc Vidmar, Vitalijs Maksimenko, Macky Frank Bagnack, Eric Boakye, Goran Brkic (74' Marko Putincanin), Asmir Suljic (67' Stefan Savic), Tomislav Tomic (90+5' Vitja Valencic), Endri Çekiçi, Ante Vukusic, Mario Jurcevic, Luka Menalo.
Coach: Safet Hadzic.
Goals: 45+1' Endri Çekiçi 0-1, 90+2' Stefan Savic 0-2.
Referee: Peter Kjærgaard-Andersen (DEN)   Attendance: 3,652.

FK Rīgas Futbola skola played their home match at Daugava Stadionā, Riga, instead of their regular stadium Stadions Arkadija, Riga which did not meet UEFA requirements.

18.07.19   A. Le Coq Arena, Tallinn:
   FCI Levadia Tallinn – UMF Stjarnan 3-2 (1-1, 2-1) (a.e.t.)
FCI Levadia Tallinn: Sergei Lepmets, Dmitri Kruglov, Maksim Podholjuzin, Evgeniy Osipov, Igor Dudarev (71' Markus Jürgenson), Kirill Nesterov (80' Pavel Marin), Marek Kaljumäe, Rasmus Peetson (76' Érick Moreno), Aime Marcelin Gando, Nikita Andreev (116' Artjom Komlov), João Morelli. Coach: Aleksandar Rogic.
UMF Stjarnan: Haraldur Björnsson, Jósef Kristinn Jósefsson (49' Ævar Jóhannesson), Brynjar Gudjónsson, Daníel Laxdal (93' Gudjón Baldvinsson), Jóhann Laxdal, Martin Rauschenberg Brorsen, Thorsteinn Már Ragnarsson (80' Baldur Sigurdsson), Heidar Ægisson, Alex Thór Hauksson, Gudmundur Hafsteinsson (60' Eyjólfur Hédinsson), Hilmar Árni Halldórsson.
Coach: Rúnar Sigmundsson.
Goals: 17' Evgeniy Osipov 1-0, 25' Thorsteinn Már Ragnarsson 1-1, 89' Evgeniy Osipov 2-1, 105' Dmitri Kruglov 3-1 (p), 120+3' Brynjar Gudjónsson 3-2.
Referee: Besfort Kasumi (KOS)   Attendance: 1,446.

UMF Stjarnan won on away goals.

18.07.19   Rovaniemen Keskuskenttä, Rovaniemi: Rovaniemi PS – Aberdeen FC 1-2 (1-1)
Rovaniemi PS: Antonio Reguero, Taye Taïwo, Mohamadou Sissoko, Atte Sihvonen, Juho Hyvärinen, Kalle Katz, Eetu Muinonen (81' Tommi Jäntti), Agnaldo Moraes (68' Youness Rahimi), Lucas Lingman, Tarik Kada, Aleksandr Kokko (66' Niklas Jokelainen).
Coach: Pasi Tuutti.
Aberdeen FC: Joe Lewis, Andrew Considine, Shay Logan, Ash Taylor, Scott McKenna, Niall McGinn (87' Scott Wright), Lewis Ferguson, Dean Campbell, Ryan Hedges, Sam Cosgrove (66' Curtis Main), Jon Gallagher. Coach: Derek McInnes.
Goals: 2' Tarik Kada 1-0, 27' Sam Cosgrove 1-1 (p), 90+4' Lewis Ferguson 1-2.
Referee: Ümit Öztürk (TUR)   Attendance: 2,000.

18.07.19   Stadionul Ion Oblemenci, Craiova: CS Universitatea Craiova – Sabail FK 3-2 (1-0)
CS Universitatea Craiova: Mirko Pigliacelli, Renato Kelic (76' Florin Gardos), Ivan Martic, Tiago Ferreira, Nicusor Bancu, Alexandru Mateiu, Bogdan Vatajelu, Kamer Qaka (70' Vasile Constantin), Cristian Barbut, Alexandru Cicâldau (57' Antoni Ivanov), Carlos Fortes.
Coach: Corneliu Papura.
Sabail FK: Daniel Bozinovski, Erico, Elvin Yunuszade, Ürfan Abbasov (87' Eltun Yagublu), Shahriyar Rahimov, Rahid Amirquliyev, Bilal Hamdi (58' Fahmin Muradbayli), Vüqar Baybalayev, Eugeniu Cociuc, Agabala Ramazanov, Mirabdulla Abbasov (58' Dylan Duventru). Coach: Aftandil Hadzhiyev.
Goals: 28' Alexandru Cicâldau 1-0, 54' Bogdan Vatajelu 2-0, 67' Agabala Ramazanov 2-1, 69' Dylan Duventru 2-2, 90' Carlos Fortes 3-2.
Referee: Helgi Mikael Jónasson (ISL)   Attendance: 15,763.

18.07.19   Stadyen Dynama, Minsk: Dinamo Minsk – FK Liepāja 1-2 (0-1)
Dinamo Minsk: Maksim Plotnikov, Andrei Zaleski (79' Nikita Demchenko), Aleksey Gavrilovich, Maksim Shvetsov, Georgi Tigiev (74' Aleksandr Ksenofontov), Aleksandr Chizh, Seidu Yahaya, Dinko Trebotic, Dmytro Bilonog, Kehinde Fatai, Yegor Zubovich (62' Kirill Vergeychik). Coach: Sergei Gurenko.
FK Liepāja: Valentins Ralkevics, Vadims Zulevs, Deniss Ivanovs, Seydina Keita, Raivis Jurkovskis, Amâncio Fortes, Leonel Strumia, Kristers Tobers, Richard Friday (77' Vüqar Asgarov), Dodô, Danu Spataru (76' Mārtins Kigurs). Coach: Aleksandrs Starkovs.
Goals: 10' Danu Spataru 0-1, 70' Dodô 0-2, 90+1' Valentins Ralkevics 1-2 (og).
Referee: Nick Walsh (SCO)   Attendance: 6,705.

18.07.19 Vivacom Arena – Georgi Asparuhov Stadium, Sofia:
Levski Sofia – MFK Ruzomberok 2-0 (1-0)
Levski Sofia: Milan Mijatovic, Zhivko Milanov, Nuno Reis, Ivan Goranov, Giannis Kargas, Martin Raynov (78' Deni Alar), Davide Mariani, Khaly Thiam, Stanislav Kostov (58' Zdravko Dimitrov), Paulinho (72' Iliya Yurukov), Stanislav Ivanov. Coach: Petar Hubchev.
MFK Ruzomberok: Ivan Krajcírik, Ján Maslo, Matej Curma, Michal Jonec, Alexander Mojzis, Filip Twardzik (74' Ondrej Novotny), Tihomir Kostadinov (70' Filip Hasek), Kristi Qose, Dalibor Takác (67' Adam Brenkus), Peter Gál-Andrezly, Stefan Gerec. Coach: Ján Haspra.
Goals: 33' Davide Mariani 1-0, 90+2' Deni Alar 2-0.
Referee: Veaceslav Banari (MOL)   Attendance: 17,250.

18.07.19 Vilniaus LFF stadionas, Vilnius: FK Zalgiris – Budapest Honvéd 1-1 (1-0)
FK Zalgiris: Martin Berkovec, Donovan Slijngard, Klemen Bolha, Rolandas Baravykas (89' Domantas Simkus), Saulius Mikoliūnas, Liviu Antal, Víctor Pérez, Modestas Vorobjovas, Marko Tomic (66' Matas Vareika), Tomislav Kis, Pau Morer. Coach: Marek Zub.
Budapest Honvéd: Rubi Levkovic, Ivan Lovric, Djordje Kamber, Dávid Kálnoki-Kis (57' Eke Uzoma), Bence Batik, Tonci Kukoc, Barna Kesztyűs (78' Mark Hegedüs), Dániel Gazdag, Bence Banó-Szabó, David N'Gog, Amadou Moutari (70' Vladyslav Kulach).
Coach: Giuseppe Sannino.
Goals: 18' Liviu Antal 1-0, 62' Djordje Kamber 1-1.
Referee: Rohit Saggi (NOR)   Attendance: 3,725.

18.07.19 Rheinpark Stadion, Vaduz: FC Vaduz – Breidablik 2-1 (0-0)
FC Vaduz: Benjamin Büchel, Denis Simani, Yannick Schmid, Berkay Sülüngöz, Gianni Antoniazzi, Cédric Gasser (76' Maximilian Göppel), Milan Gajic, Boris Prokopic, Dominik Schwizer, Mohamed Coulibaly (79' Noah Frick), Tunahan Çiçek (85' Aron Sele).
Coach: Mario Frick.
Breidablik: Gunnleifur Gunnleifsson, Damir Muminovic, Elfar Helgason, Arnar Geirsson (79' Thórir Gudjónsson), Gudjón Lydsson (66' Gísli Eyjólfsson), Andri Yeoman, Höskuldur Gunnlaugsson, Viktor Örn Margeirsson, Kolbeinn Thórdarson, Thomas Mikkelsen, Alexander Sigurdarson (73' Aron Bjarnason). Coach: Ágúst Gylfason.
Goals: 57' Mohamed Coulibaly 1-0, 79' Dominik Schwizer 2-0, 90+3' Höskuldur Gunnlaugsson 2-1.
Referee: Genc Nuza (KOS)   Attendance: 837.

18.07.19 Mikheil Meskhis sakhelobis Stadioni, Tbilisi:
Torpedo Kutaisi – FK Ordabasy 0-2 (0-0)
Torpedo Kutaisi: Roin Kvaskhvadze, Davit Khurtsilava, Vazha Tabatadze (80' Davit Ionanidze), Tsotne Nadaraia, Anri Chichinadze, Vakhtang Nebieridze, Grigol Dolidze (59' Zaza Tsitskishvili), Mate Tsintsadze, Papuna Poniava, Tornike Kapanadze (61' Temur Chogadze), Otar Kobakhidze. Coach: Kakhaber Chkhetiani.
FK Ordabasy: Dmytro Nepogodov, Pablo Fontanello, Sergiy Maliy, Temirlan Yerlanov, Marat Bystrov, Kyrylo Kovalchuk (72' Mirzad Mehanovic), Abdoulaye Diakhaté, May Mahlangu, Timur Dosmagambetov, João Paulo (86' Samat Shamshi), Aleksey Shchetkin (62' Ziguy Badibanga). Coach: Kakhaber Tskhadadze.
Goals: 81' Mirzad Mehanovic 0-1, 90+4' Ziguy Badibanga 0-2.
Referee: Aristotelis Diamantopoulos (GRE)   Attendance: 3,753.

Torpedo Kutaisi played their home match at Mikheil Meskhis sakhelobis Stadioni, Tbilisi, instead of their regular stadium Ramaz Shengelia Stadium, Kutaisi.

18.07.19   Neo GSP Stadium, Nicosia: Apollon Limassol – Kauno Zalgiris 4-0 (2-0)
Apollon Limassol: Joël Mall, Attila Szalai, Ioannis Pittas (56' Serge Gakpé), Dylan Ouédraogo, Facundo Pereyra, Giorgos Vasiliou, Sasa Markovic (69' Chambos Kyriakou), Diego Aguirre (56' Giannis Gianniotas), Esteban Sachetti, Emilio Zelaya, João Pedro.
Coach: Sofronis Avgousti.
Kauno Zalgiris: Deividas Mikelionis, Arūnas Klimavicius, "Rudi" Rudinilson Silva (60' Edvinas Kloniūnas), Karolis Silkaitis, Pijus Sirvys, Linas Pilibaitis, Dominykas Galkevicius, Yuriy Bushman, Martynas Dapkus (46' Rimvydas Sadauskas), Rokas Krusnauskas (70' Benas Anisas), João Figueiredo. Coach: Mindaugas Cepas.
Goals: 5', 43', 60' Emilio Zelaya 1-0, 2-0 (p), 3-0 (p), 83' Attila Szalai 4-0.
Referee: Vladimir Moskalev (RUS)   Attendance: 1,427.

Apollon Limassol played their home match at Neo GSP Stadium, Nicosia, instead of their regular stadium Tsirio Stadium, Limassol.

18.07.19   Stadion Cracovii im. Józefa Piłsudskiego, Kraków:
             KS Cracovia Kraków – DAC Dunajská Streda 2-2 (1-0, 1-1) (a.e.t.)
KS Cracovia Kraków: Michal Peskovic, Cornel Rapa, Diego Ferraresso, David Jablonsky, Michal Helik, Janusz Gol, Damian Dabrowski (72' Milan Dimun), Sergiu Hanca (95' Filip Piszczek), Bojan Cecaric (106' Rubio), Pelle van Amersfoort, "Rafa" Rafael Lopes (84' Mateusz Wdowiak). Coach: Michal Probierz.
DAC Dunajská Streda: Martin Jedlicka, Éric Davis, Lubomír Satka, Kristián Kostrna, Dominik Kruzliak, Zsolt Kalmár (105' Abdulrahman Taiwo), Máté Vida, Lukás Cmelík (24' César Blackman), Connor Ronan, Eric Ramírez (98' Kristopher Vida), Marko Divkovic (120' Danilo Beskorovainyi). Coach: Peter Hyballa.
Goals: 2' "Rafa" Rafael Lopes 1-0, 47' Connor Ronan 1-1, 94' Eric Ramírez 1-2, 120+2' Filip Piszczek 2-2.
Referee: Athanasios Tzilos (GRE)   Attendance: 13,255.

DAC Dunajská Streda won on away goals.

18.07.19   Haugesund Stadion, Haugesund: FK Haugesund – Cliftonville FC 5-1 (3-1)
FK Haugesund: Helge Sandvik, Doug Bergqvist, Mikkel Desler, Benjamin Tiedemann Hansen, Sondre Tronstad, Niklas Sandberg, Bruno Leite, Kristoffer Velde, Anthony Ikedi, Martin Samuelsen (72' Eric Ndayisenga), Ibrahima Koné (61' Kevin Krygård).
Coach: Jostein Grindhaug.
Cliftonville FC: Richard Brush, Garry Breen, Liam Bagnall (61' Ryan Curran), Conor McMenamin, Joe Gorman, Levi Ives, Conor McDermott, Chris Curran, Ronan Doherty (80' Ronan Wilson), Rory Donnelly, Joe Gormley (70' Thomas Maguire).
Coach: Paddy McLaughlin.
Goals: 5' Kristoffer Velde 1-0, 17' Conor McMenamin 1-1, 36' Niklas Sandberg 2-1, 45+1' Ibrahima Koné 3-1, 52' Bruno Leite 4-1, 68' Kristoffer Velde 5-1.
Referee: Mario Zebec (CRO)   Attendance: 2,633.

18.07.19   Complexul Sportiv Raional, Orhei:
FC Milsami Orhei – Fotbal Club FCSB 1-2 (0-2)
FC Milsami Orhei: Anatolii Chirinciuc, Vadim Bolohan, Vasile Jardan, Artur Craciun, Alexandru Antoniuc, Alexandru Onica, Gheorghe Andronic, Andrei Rusnac (81' Sergiu Nazar), Victor Stîna (67' Veaceslav Zagaevschii), Maxim Antoniuc, Sergiu Platica.
Coach: Veaceslav Rusnac.
Fotbal Club FCSB: Andrei Daniel Vlad, Bogdan Planic, Claudiu Belu, Iulian Cristea, Mihai Roman (I), Dragos Nedelcu, Razvan Oaida, Florin Tanase (72' Ovidiu Popescu), Florinel Coman (58' Adrian Ioan Hora), Dennis Man (64' Robert Ion), Cristián Dumitru.
Coach: Bogdan Andone.
Goals: 4' Cristián Dumitru 0-1, 42' Razvan Oaida 0-2, 47' Vadim Bolohan 1-2.
Referee: Timotheos Christofi (CYP)   Attendance: 3,000.

18.07.19   Stadion Bijeli Brijeg, Mostar: Zrinjski Mostar – Akademija Pandev 3-0 (0-0)
Zrinjski Mostar: Ivan Brkic, Dario Rugasevic, Slobodan Jakovljevic, Tomislav Barisic, Renato Gojkovic, Ivan Curjuric, Frane Cirjak (59' Damir Sovsic), Edin Rustemovic (79' Semir Pezer), Stanisa Mandic, Kristijan Stanic (46' Miljan Govedarica), Ivan Lendric. Coach: Hari Vukas.
Akademija Pandev: Marko Alchevski (65' David Denkovski), Tomislav Iliev, Dime Dimov, Ljupco Doriev, Mihail Manevski, Riste Temelkov, Gjorgji Tanusev (67' Sasko Pandev), Georgi Stoilov, Stefan Kostov, Daniel Milovanovikj, Mario Krstovski (75' Vane Jovanov).
Coach: Jugoslav Trencovski.
Goals: 50' Stanisa Mandic 1-0, 79' Miljan Govedarica 2-0, 90+2' Renato Gojkovic 3-0.
Referee: Ondrej Pechanec (CZE)   Attendance: 2,500.

18.07.19   Stadionul Zimbru, Chisinau: CS Petrocub Hîncesti – AEK Larnaca 0-1 (0-0)
CS Petrocub Hîncesti: Cristian Avram, Maxim Potîrniche, Ion Jardan (60' Vadim Gulceac), Victor Mudrac, Vlad Slivca, Andrei Cojocari, Alexandru Bejan (82' Arcadie Rusu), Dan Taras (70' Vladimir Bogdanovic), Vladimir Ambros, Jessie Guera Djou, Jacques Onana Ndzomo.
Coach: Lilian Popescu.
AEK Larnaca: Toño, Mikel González, Daniel Mojsov, Truyols, Ivan Trickovski, Lluis Sastre, Acorán (77' Raúl Ruiz), Nacho Cases, Hector Hevel (90' Jean Luc Assoubre), Apostolos Giannou (83' Florian Taulemesse), Tete. Coach: Imanol Idiakez.
Goal: 90+2' Maxim Potîrniche 0-1 (og).
Referee: Novak Simovic (SRB)   Attendance: 5,316.

CS Petrocub Hîncesti played their home match at Stadionul Zimbru, Chisinau, instead of their regular stadium Stadionul Municipal, Hîncesti which did not meet UEFA requirements.

18.07.19   Bakcell Arena, Baku: Neftçi PFK Baku – Speranta Nisporeni 6-0 (4-0)
Neftçi PFK Baku: Salahat Agayev, Vojislav Stankovic, Kyrylo Petrov, Anton Krivotsyuk, Omar Buludov, Vangelis Platellas (54' Rahman Hadzhiyev), Emin Makhmudov, Mamadou Kane (54' Soni Mustivar), Steeven Joseph-Monrose, Rauf Aliyev, Dário Júnior da Silva (71' Ismayil Zülfùgarli). Coach: Roberto Bordin.
Speranta Nisporeni: Denis Macogonenco, Ion Arabadji, Óliver Fula, Bruno Barbosa, Stefan Efros, Mihail Bolun, Fabrice Eloundou (68' Luis Ferney Ríos), Felipe Ponce, Constantin Sandu (55' Ion Dragan), Ruslan Chelari (78' Dayron Mosquera), Maxim Iurcu.
Coach: Cristian Efros.
Goals: 18' Vangelis Platellas 1-0, 24' Emin Makhmudov 2-0 (p), 40' Vangelis Platellas 3-0, 42' Dário Júnior da Silva 4-0, 67' Steeven Joseph-Monrose 5-0, 78' Ismayil Zülfùgarli 6-0.
Referee: Julian Weinberger (AUT)   Attendance: 6,500.

18.07.19 Estadi Comunal d'Andorra la Vella, Andorra la Vella:
UE Engordany – Dinamo Tbilisi 0-1 (0-0)
UE Engordany: Gerardo Rubio, Miguel Ruiz, Rafael Brito (89' Jorge Sebastián Varela), Deivis De Jesus Soares, Mario Spano, Marc Ferré, Sébastien Aguéro, Hamza Bouharma, Sebastián Gómez (87' Edu Peppe), Fábio Serra Alves, Morgan Lafont (72' Míguel Laborda).
Coach: Filipe Busto.
Dinamo Tbilisi: José Perales, Gudzha Rukhaia, Oleksandr Kaplienko, Davit Kobouri, Abdel Jalil Medioub, Levan Kutalia, Mychailo Shyshka (60' Nika Ninua), Arfang Daffé, Bakar Kardava, Akaki Shulaia (55' Nodar Kavtaradze), Giorgi Zaria (74' Giorgi Kukhianidze).
Coach: Félix Vicente Miranda.
Goal: 81' Abdel Jalil Medioub 0-1.
Referee: Balász Berke (HUN)   Attendance: 408.

18.07.19 Yaakov Turner Toto Stadium, Beer Sheva: Hapoel Be'er Sheva – KF Laçi 1-0 (0-0)
Hapoel Be'er Sheva: Ernestas Setkus, Miguel Vítor, Ben Bitton, Loai Taha, Sean Goldberg, Ramzi Safouri (74' Niv Zrihan), Eden Shamir, Naor Sabag, Jimmy Marín, Nigel Hasselbaink (85' Marwan Kabha), José Carrillo (59' Ben Sahar). Coach: Barak Bakhar.
KF Laçi: Gentian Selmani, Aleksandar Ignjatovic, David Domgjoni, Eglentin Gjoni, Abdurraman Fangaj (86' Rudolf Turkaj), Ardit Deliu, Regi Lushkja, Juljan Shehu, Teco (74' Elvi Berisha), Kyrian Nwabueze, Redon Xhixha. Coach: Sulejman Starova.
Goal: 69' Naor Sabag 1-0.
Referee: Tihomir Pejin (CRO)   Attendance: 10,980.

18.07.19 Stade Parc des Sports, Differdange: Progrès Niederkorn – Cork City 1-2 (0-1)
Progrès Niederkorn: Sebastian Flauss, Ben Vogel, Metin Karayer, Tim Hall, Aldin Skenderovic, Yann Matias Marques, Sébastien Thill (90+1' Adrien Ferino), Christian Silaj, Belmin Muratovic (66' Issa Bah), Mayron De Almeida, Kempes Tekiela (85' Florik Shala).
Coach: Roland Vrabec.
Cork City: Mark McNulty, Colm Horgan, Conor McCarthy, Ronan Hurley (90+6' Kevin O'Connor), Sean McLoughlin, Conor McCormack, Gearóid Morrissey, Garry Buckley, Karl Sheppard, Joel Coustrain (88' Dan Casey), Daire O'Connor (82' Shane Griffin).
Coach: Frank Kelleher.
Goals: 3' Garry Buckley 0-1, 47' Conor McCarthy 0-2, 68' Issa Bah 1-2.
Referee: Matthew De Gabriele (MLT)   Attendance: 1,927.

Progrès Niederkorn played their home match at Stade Parc des Sports, Differdange, instead of their regular stadium, Stade Jos Haupert, Niederkorn.

18.07.19 Stadion Poljud, Split: Hajduk Split – Gzira United 1-3 (1-0)
Hajduk Split: Tomislav Duka, Borja López, Josip Basic, Oleksandr Svatok, Ivan Dolcek (58' Josip Juranovic), Hamza Barry, Bassel Jradi, Dino Besirovic (81' Anthony Kalik), Francesco Tahiraj (59' Stanko Juric), Jairo, Ivan Delic. Coach: Sinia Orescanin.
Gzira United: Justin Haber, Arthur Henrique, Rodolfo Soares (77' Zachary Scerri), Fernando Barbosa, Nicky Muscat, Andrew Cohen (86' Amadou Samb), Hamed Koné, Gianmarco Conti, Juan Corbalan, Elvis Sakyi (66' Sacha Borg), Jefferson. Coach: Giovanni Tedesco.
Goals: 7' Bassel Jradi 1-0, 57 Jefferson 1-1, 69', 90+6' Hamed Koné 1-2, 1-3.
Referee: Nikolas Neokleous (CYP)   Attendance: 18,236.

Gzira United won on away goals.

18.07.19 Mestni Stadion Fazanerija, Murska Sobota: NS Mura – Maccabi Haifa 2-3 (1-2)
NS Mura: Matko Obradovic, Klemen Sturm, Klemen Pucko, Aleksandar Boskovic, Matic Marusko, Alen Kozar (46' Marin Karamarko), Jon Sporn (82' Ziga Laci), Timo Horvat (45+2' Andrija Bubnjar), Amadej Marosa, Luka Bobicanec, Luka Susnjara. Coach: Ante Simundza.
Maccabi Haifa: Guy Haimov, Rami Gershon, Ernest Mabouka, Ayed Habashi, Ofri Arad, Ikouwem Utin, Yuval Ashkenazi (77' Yanic Wildschut), Neta Lavi, Dolev Haziza (45+3' Mohammad Abu Fani), Mohammed Awaed (68' Nikita Rukavytsya), Yarden Shua. Coach: Marco Balbul.
Goals: 6' Luka Bobicanec 1-0, 31' Mohammed Awaed 1-1, 35', 76' Yuval Ashkenazi 1-2, 1-3, 81' Jon Sporn 2-3.
Referee: Tomasz Musial (POL)   Attendance: 3,950.

18.07.19 Elbasan Arena, Elbasan: FK Kukësi – Debreceni VSC 1-1 (1-0)
FK Kukësi: Stivi Frashëri, Ardijan Cuculi (61' Bruno Lulaj), Olsi Teqja, Tome Kitanovski, Simon Rrumbullaku, Valdet Rama, Eduart Rroca, Besar Musolli, Vesel Limaj (73' Emiljano Musta), Valon Ethemi (84' Arbër Çyrbja), Vasil Sjkurti. Coach: Ernest Gjoka.
Debreceni VSC: Sándor Nagy, János Ferenczi, Csaba Szatmári, Bence Pávkovics, Erik Kusnyír, Dániel Tözsér, Nikola Trujic (82' Richárd Csösz), Kevin Varga, Attila Haris (90' Alex Damásdi), Márk Szécsi, Daniel Zsóri (66' Haruna Garba). Coach: András Herczeg.
Goals: 17' Valon Ethemi 1-0, 58' Csaba Szatmári 1-1.
Referee: Stanislav Todorov (BUL)   Attendance: 547.

FK Kukësi played their home match at Elbasan Arena, Elbasan, instead of their regular stadium Stadiumi Zeqir Ymeri, Kukës.

18.07.19 Östgötaporten, Norrköping: IFK Norrköping – St Patrick's Athletic 2-1 (1-0)
IFK Norrköping: Isak Pettersson, Lars Gerson, Kasper Larsen, Filip Dagerstål, Rasmus Lauritsen, Gudmundur Thórarinsson, Simon Thern, Alexander Fransson (88' Andreas Blomqvist), Christoffer Nyman (73' Kalle Holmberg), Simon Skrabb (63' Egzon Binaku), Jordan Larsson. Coach: Jens Gustafsson.
St Patrick's Athletic: Brendan Clarke, Ian Bermingham, Simon Madden, Kevin Toner, Lee Desmond, Ciaran Kelly, Conor Clifford, Cian Coleman (64' Darragh Markey), Jamie Lennon (73' Rhys McCabe), Gary Shaw (52' Dean Clarke), Michael Drennan. Coach: Harry Kenny.
Goals: 36' Jordan Larsson 1-0, 72' Conor Clifford 1-1, 85' Kalle Holmberg 2-1.
Referee: Dejan Jakimovski (MCD)   Attendance: 5,925.
Sent off: 89' Ciaran Kelly.

18.07.19 Gundadalur, Tórshavn: B36 Tórshavn – Crusaders FC 2-3 (1-2)
B36 Tórshavn: Hans Jørgensen, Erling Jacobsen (62' Michal Przybylski), Jónas Næs (83' Gilli Samuelsen), Bjarni Petersen, Eli Nielsen, Árni Frederiksberg, Andrias Eriksen, Magnus Holm Jacobsen, Hugin Samuelsen (72' Hannes Agnarsson), Stefan Radosavljevic, Lukasz Cieslewicz. Coach: Jákub á Borg.
Crusaders FC: Sean O'Neill, Billy Joe Burns, Howard Beverland, Chris Hegarty, Michael Ruddy, Declan Caddell (65' Rory Hale), Philip Lowry, Jordan Forsythe (86' Gary Thompson), Paul Heatley, Ross Clarke, Jordan Owens (83' David Cushley). Coach: Stephen Baxter.
Goals: 3' Jordan Forsythe 0-1, 28' Paul Heatley 0-2, 37' Hugin Samuelsen 1-2, 51' Lukasz Cieslewicz 2-2, 68' Paul Heatley 2-3.
Referee: Milovan Milacic (MNE)   Attendance: 1,422.

18.07.19   MFA Centenary Stadium, Ta'Qali: Hibernians FC – Shakhtyor Soligorsk 0-1 (0-0)
Hibernians FC: Marko Jovicic, Andrei Agius, Márcio Silveira (67' Jens Wemmer), Ferdinando Apap, Timothy Tabone, Bjorn Kristensen, Dunstan Vella, Jake Grech (80' Matthew Farrugia), Leonardo Nanni, Joseph Mbong (80' Connor Zammit), Terence Groothusen.
Coach: Stefano Sanderra.
Shakhtyor Soligorsk: Andrey Klimovich, Pavel Rybak, Sergey Matvejchik, Nikola Antic, Aleksandr Sachivko, Aleksandr Selyava, Yuri Kovalev, Július Szöke, Valeriy Gromyko (78' Igor Burko), Max Ebong Ngome (64' Mykyta Tatarkov), Elis Bakaj (82' Nikolai Yanush).
Coach: Sergey Tashuev.
Goal: 65' Mykyta Tatarkov 0-1.
Referee: Furkat Atazhanov (KAZ)   Attendance: 608.
Sent off: 33' Aleksandr Selyava, 73' Ferdinando Apap.

18.07.19   Puskás Akadémia Pancho Aréna, Felcsút: MOL Vidi FC – FK Zeta Golubovci 0-0
MOL Vidi FC: Ádam Kovácsik, Roland Juhász, Loïc Négo, Stopira, Szabolcs Huszti, Anel Hadzic, Máté Pátkai (64' Georgi Milanov), Ákos Elek, István Kovács, Ivan Petryak (79' Armin Hodzic), Marko Scepovic (80' Márkó Futács). Coach: Marko Nikolic.
FK Zeta Golubovci: Zoran Akovic, Djordjije Vukcevic, Nemanja Sekulic, Balsa Goranovic, Zvonko Ceklic, Armin Bosnjak (89' Davor Kontic), Goran Milojko, Stefan Vukcevic (65' Jovan Baosic), Amel Tuzovic, Srdjan Krstovic, Ivan Vukcevic (83' Matija Lambulic).
Coach: Dejan Roganovic.
Referee: Paul McLaughlin (IRL)   Attendance: 2,148.
Sent off: 74' Djordjije Vukcevic.

MOL Vidi FC played their home match at Puskás Akadémia Pancho Aréna, Felcsút, instead of their regular stadium MOL Aréna Sóstó, Székesfehérvár.

18.07.19   Stadyen Central'ny Vitsyebski, Vitebsk: FK Vitebsk – Kuopion PS 1-1 (1-0)
FK Vitebsk: Dmitri Gushchenko, Akaki Khubutia (65' Vladislav Fedosov), Oleg Karamushka, Anton Matveenko (85' Vladislav Ryzhkov), Mikhail Kozlov, Maranhão, Artem Stargorodskiy (76' Sergey Volkov), Artem Skitov, Maksim Feshchuk, Nikolai Zolotov, Kirill Pechenin.
Coach: Sergey Yasinsky.
Kuopion PS: Otso Virtanen, Babacar Diallo, Luis Murillo, Luc Tabi Manga (79' Kalle Taimi), Vinko Soldo, Petteri Pennanen, Reuben Ayarna, Ville Saxman, Ilmari Niskanen (90+2' Saku Savolainen), Issa Thiaw, Rangel (82' Ariel Ngueukam). Coach: Jani Honkavaara.
Goals: 27' Artem Stargorodskiy 1-0, 53' Babacar Diallo 1-1.
Referee: Hugo Miguel (POR)   Attendance: 4,780.

18.07.19   Tose Proeski Arena, Skopje: KF Shkupi – Pyunik Yerevan FC 1-2 (0-2)
KF Shkupi: Thulio, Muharem Bajrami, Bojan Gjorgievski, Darko Ilieski, Mevlan Adili, Sabit Bilalli, Fatih Ismaili (60' Besart Krivanjeva), Lamine Diack (69' Fatjon Jusufi), Marin Jurina, Serginho, Oumar Goudiaby (46' Artan Veliu). Coach: Recai Sahinler.
Pyunik Yerevan FC: Andrija Dragojevic, Artak Yedigaryan, Antonio Stankov, Maksim Zhestokov, Kristi Marku, Armen Manucharyan, Karlen Mkrtchyan, Sergiy Shevchuk, Artem Simonyan (67' Steven Alfred), Erik Vardanyan, Artur Miranyan.
Coach: Aleksandr Tarkhanov.
Goals: 7' Artak Yedigaryan 0-1, 31' Artur Miranyan 0-2, 82' Marin Jurina 1-2.
Referee: Vitaliy Romanov (UKR)   Attendance: 8,045.
Sent off: 86' Serginho.

KF Shkupi played their home match at Tose Proeski Arena, Skopje, instead of their regular stadium Cair Stadium, Skopje which did not meet UEFA requirements.

18.07.19 The Showgrounds, Ballymena: Ballymena United – Malmö FF 0-4 (0-1)
Ballymena United: Ross Glendinning, Andrew Burns, Jonathan Addis (75' Joshua Kelly), Steven McCullough, Kofi Balmer, Ryan Harpur (70' Ross Lavery), Andy McGrory, Shane McGinty, Leroy Millar, Ryan Mayse, Adam Lecky (71' Cathair Friel). Coach: David Jeffrey.
Malmö FF: Dusan Melichárek, Behrang Safari, Lasse Nielsen, Franz Brorsson, Oscar Lewicki (68' Søren Rieks), Erdal Rakip (74' Anders Christiansen), Romain Gall, Bonke Innocent, Guillermo Molins (61' Tim Prica), Jo Inge Berget, Marcus Antonsson. Coach: Uwe Rösler.
Goals: 27' Behrang Safari 0-1, 52' Guillermo Molins 0-2, 68' Erdal Rakip 0-3, 79' Romain Gall 0-4 (p).
Referee: Oskari Hämäläinen (FIN)   Attendance: 1,736.

18.07.19 City Arena Trnava, Trnava: Spartak Trnava – Radnik Bijeljina 2-0 (1-0, 2-0) (a.e.t.)
Spartak Trnava: Dobrivoj Rusov, Bogdan Mitrea, Timotej Záhumensky, Lucas Lovat, Ivan Mesík, Marko Tesija, Emir Halilovic (93' Matús Turna), Filip Dangubic (64' Marko Kelemen), Rafael Tavares (77' Matej Jakúbek), Filip Orsula (80' Kristián Mihálek), Alex Sobczyk. Coach: Ricardo Chéu.
Radnik Bijeljina: Dalibor Kozic, Milos Simonovic, Slavisa Radovic, Velibor Djuric (88' Vladimir Bradonjic), Pavle Susic (61' Alem Merajic), Nikola Popara, Ivan Subert, Nedim Mekic, Dejan Maksimovic (99' Milos Plavsic), Demir Peco, Seid Zukic (54' Jovan Motika). Coach: Mladen Zizovic.
Goals: 10' Alex Sobczyk 1-0, 87' Kristián Mihálek 2-0.
Referee: Rahim Hasanov (AZE)   Attendance: 4,222.
Sent off: 108' Bogdan Mitrea.

Spartak Trnava won on penalties after extra time (3-2).
Penalties: Tesija 1-0, Merajic 1-1, Sobczyk 2-1, Motika missed, Záhumensky missed, Mekic 2-2, Lucas Lovat missed, Plavsic missed, Jakúbek 3-2, Popara missed.

18.07.19 Rugby Park, Kilmarnock: Kilmarnock FC – Connah's Quay Nomads FC 0-2 (0-0)
Kilmarnock FC: Jamie MacDonald, Kirk Broadfoot, Stephen O'Donnell, Stuart Findlay, Greg Taylor, Chris Burke (82' Innes Cameron), Mohamed El Makrini (87' Dominic Thomas), Alan Power, Gary Dicker, Rory McKenzie, Eamonn Brophy. Coach: Angelo Alessio.
Connah's Quay Nomads FC: Lewis Brass, George Horan, Danny Holmes, John Disney, Callum Roberts (83' Priestley Farquharson), Jay Owen, Callum Morris, Ryan Wignall, Declan Poole, Michael Wilde, Michael Bakare (70' Jamie Insall). Coach: Andy Morrison.
Goals: 50' Ryan Wignall 0-1, 80' Callum Morris 0-2 (p).
Referee: Ferenc Karakó (HUN)   Attendance: 8,306.
Sent off: 79' Stuart Findlay, 85' Ryan Wignall.

18.07.19 Gradski Stadion Cair, Nis: Radnicki Nis – FC Flora Tallinn 2-2 (0-0)
Radnicki Nis: Marko Knezevic, Aleksandar Todorovski, Stefan Djordjevic, Ivan Ostojic, Lazar Djordjevic, Taras Bondarenko, Sasa Stojanovic, Nemanja Tomic, Veljko Batrovic (59' Dejan Meleg), Erik Jirka (73' Nikola Cumic), Milan Bojovic (59' Stefan Mihajlovic).
Coach: Simo Krunic.
FC Flora Tallinn: Matvei Igonen, Gert Kams, Märten Kuusk, Henrik Pürg, Henri Järvelaid, Konstantin Vassiljev, Mikhel Ainsalu, Martin Miller (66' Vlasiy Sinyavskiy), Vladislavs Kreida, Frank Liivak, Erik Sorga (78' Mark Lepik). Coach: Jürgen Henn.
Goals: 68' Stefan Mihajlovic 1-0, 80' Henrik Pürg 1-1, 84' Nikola Cumic 2-1, 90+3' Mark Lepik 2-2.
Referee: Zbynek Proske (CZE)   Attendance: 4,329.

18.07.19   Sportni Park, Domzale: NK Domzale – Balzan FC 1-0 (1-0)
NK Domzale: Grega Sorcan, Gaber Dobrovoljc, Gregor Sikosek, Tilen Klemencic, Senijad Ibricic, Josip Corluka, Mattias Käit (46' Ziga Repas), Adam Gnezda Cerin, Matej Podlogar (80' Sven Karic), Slobodan Vuk (66' Shamar Nicholson), Tonci Mujan.
Coach: Simon Rozman.
Balzan FC: Kristijan Naumovski, Steven Bezzina, Aleksandar Kosoric, Ivan Bozovic, Uros Ljubomirac (75' Andrija Majdevac), Augustine Loof, Paul Fenech (59' Arthur Faría), Nenad Sljivic, Stefan Dimic (62' Ricardo Correa), Alfred Effiong, Stephen Pisani.
Coach: Jacques Scerri.
Goal: 21' Slobodan Vuk 1-0.
Referee: Marcel Bîrsan (ROM)   Attendance: 1,648.

18.07.19   Stadion Pod Goricom, Podgorica:
             FC Buducnost Podgorica – JK Narva Trans 4-1 (1-1)
FC Buducnost Podgorica: Milos Dragojevic, Dejan Boljevic, Luka Mirkovic, Slavko Damjanovic, Stefan Milic, Drasko Bozovic (68' Milos Raickovic), Milos Mijic, Milos Vucic, Dusan Bakic, Igor Ivanovic (32' Dusan Stoiljkovic), Mihailo Perovic (77' Dejan Zarubica).
Coach: Branko Brnovic.
JK Narva Trans: Marko Meerits, Roman Nesterovski, Tanel Tamberg, Joseph Saliste, Irie Elysée, Denis Polyakov, German Slein (44' Eric McWoods), Artjom Skinjov, Aleksandr Zakarlyuka (78' Dmitri Proshin), Eduard Golovljov (63' Viktor Plotnikov), Nikita Mihhailov.
Coach: Andrey Semin.
Goals: 2' Milos Vucic 1-0, 39' Eduard Golovljov 1-1, 49' Dusan Bakic 2-1,
56' Mihailo Perovic 3-1, 78' Dejan Zarubica 4-1.
Referee: Stefan Apostolov (BUL)   Attendance: 1,700.

18.07.19   Ibrox Stadium, Glasgow: Glasgow Rangers FC – St Joseph's FC 6-0 (2-0)
Glasgow Rangers FC: Wesley Foderingham, Connor Goldson, Matt Polster, George Edmundson, Andy Halliday, Greg Stewart, Glen Kamara, Greg Docherty (67' Josh McPake), Joe Aribo, Alfredo Morelos (67' Jermain Defoe), Jake Hastie (58' Scott Arfield).
Coach: Steven Gerrard.
St.Joseph's FC: Jamie Robba, Federico Villar, Mauri Torres, Jaime Serra, Daniel Guererro, Domingo Ferrer (79' Sykes Garro), Andrew Hernandez, Pedrito (72' José Reyes), Juanfri Peña, Ernesto Cornejo (69' Evan Green), Boro. Coach: Raúl Procopio.
Goals: 3' Joe Aribo 1-0, 45+1', 57', 66' Alfredo Morelos 2-0, 3-0 (p), 4-0,
77', 86' Jermain Defoe 5-0, 6-0.
Referee: Christopher Jäger (AUT)   Attendance: 45,718.

18.07.19   Tallaght Stadium, Dublin: Shamrock Rovers – SK Brann 2-1 (0-0)
Shamrock Rovers: Alan Mannus, Joey O'Brien, Sean Kavanagh, Roberto Lopes, Ethan Boyle, Lee Grace, Ronan Finn (80' Gary O'Neill), Greg Bolger, Jack Byrne, Dylan Watts (63' Aaron McEneff), Graham Cummins (75' Daniel Carr). Coach: Stephen Bradley.
SK Brann: Håkon Opdal, Taijo Teniste (84' Azar Karadas), Bismar Acosta, Ruben Kristiansen, Christian Rismark, Fredrik Haugen, Amer Ordagic, Petter Strand (84' Ruben Jenssen), Veton Berisha, Gilli Rólantsson Sørensen, Gilbert Koomson (46' Daouda Bamba).
Coach: Lars Nilsen.
Goals: 57' Daouda Bamba 0-1, 76' Jack Byrne 1-1, 87' Gary O'Neill 2-1.
Referee: Kári Jóannesarson á Høvdanum (FRO)   Attendance: 5,135.

18.07.19 Stadion Miejski Legii Warszawa im. Marszalka Józefa Pilsudskiego, Warszawa: Legia Warszawa – Europa FC 3-0 (2-0)
Legia Warszawa: Radoslaw Majecki, Artur Jedrzejczyk, William Rémy, Mateusz Wieteska, Arvydas Novikovas, Marko Vesovic, André Martins (70' Tomasz Jodlowiec), Dominik Nagy (46' Salvador Agra), Valeriane Gvilia, Carlitos López, Sandro Kulenovic (63' Jaroslaw Niezgoda). Coach: Aleksandar Vukovic.
Europa FC: Dayle Coleing, Sergio Sánchez, Rahim Ayew, Olmo González, Jayce Mascarenhas-Olivero, Álex Quillo (61' Marco Rosa), Juampe Rico, Liam Walker, Mustapha Yahaya, Adrián Gallardo (68' Manu Dimas), Andre Tjay de Barr (55' Velasco).
Coach: Rafael Escobar.
Goals: 7' Carlitos López 1-0, 13' Sandro Kulenovic 2-0, 60' Carlitos López 3-0.
Referee: Robert Jenkins (WAL)   Attendance: 14,839.
Sent off: 54' Sergio Sánchez.

18.07.19 Alvogenvöllurinn, Reykavík: KR Reykjavík – Molde FK 0-0
KR Reykjavik: Beitir Ólafsson, Gunnar Gunnarsson, Arnór Adalsteinsson (46' Aron Jósepsson), Skúli Jón Fridgeirsson, Ástbjörn Thórdarson, Pálmi Pálmason (71' Atli Sigurjónsson), Finnur Margiersson (78' Kristinn Jónsson), Pablo Punyed, Kennie Chopart, Björgvin Stefånsson, Ægir Jónasson. Coach: Rúnar Kristinsson.
Molde FK: Álex Craninx, Vegard Forren, Ruben Gabrielsen, Kristoffer Haraldseid, Kristoffer Haugen, Etzaz Hussain, Fredrik Aursnes (71' Eirik Hestad), Martin Ellingsen, Erling Knudtzon (82' Leke James), Mattias Moström, Ohi Omoijuanfo (62' Mathis Bolly). Coach: Erling Moe.
Referee: Ian McNabb (NIR)   Attendance: 355.

SECOND QUALIFYING ROUND

Bye: FK Sarajevo.

23.07.19 FFA Academy Stadium, Yerevan: FC Ararat-Armenia – Lincoln Red Imps 2-0 (2-0)
FC Ararat-Armenia: Stefan Cupic, Rochdi Achenteh, Dmitri Guzj, Ângelo Meneses, Georgi Pashov, Armen Ambartsumyan (84' Gor Malakyan), Kódjo Alphonse, Petros Avetisyan, Anton Kobyalko (70' Louis Ogana), Furdjel Narsingh, Mailson (62' Zakaria Sanogo).
Coach: Vardan Minasyan.
Lincoln Red Imps: Lolo Soler, Marcos Pérez, Joseph Chipolina, Oli (46' Federico Cataruozzolo), Bernardo Lopes, Roy Chipolina, Sergio Molina (53' Jesús Toscano), Borja Gil, Anthony Hernandez, James Coombes (62' Falu Aranda), Kike Gómez. Coach: Víctor Afonso.
Goals: 31' Anton Kobyalko 1-0, 45+2' Kódjo Alphonse 2-0.
Referee: Trustin Farrugia Cann (MLT)   Attendance: 1,500.
Sent off: 49' Marcos Pérez.

23.07.19 Gundadalur, Tórshavn: HB Tórshavn – Linfield FC 2-2 (1-1)
HB Tórshavn: Teitur Gestsson, Brynjar Hlödversson (85' Daniel Johansen), Jógvan Davidsen, Lasse Andersen, Símun Samuelsen, Magnus Egilsson, Hørdur Askham, Tróndur Jensen, Adrian Justinussen (78' Pætur Petersen), Sebastian Pingel (70' Dan í Soylu), Ari Olsen.
Coach: Heimir Gudjónsson.
Linfield FC: Rohan Ferguson, Chris Casement, Matthew Clarke, Mark Stafford, Niall Quinn (83' Joel Cooper), Jamie Mulgrew, Jimmy Callacher, Daniel Kearns (81' Shayne Lavery), Bastien Héry, Andrew Waterworth, Jordan Stewart (77' Kirk Millar). Coach: David Healy.
Goals: 2' Andrew Waterworth 0-1, 37' Adrian Justinussen 1-1 (p), 88' Andrew Waterworth 1-2 (p), 89' Pætur Petersen 2-2.
Referee: Ádám Farkas (HUN)   Attendance: 751.

23.07.19 Tose Proeski Arena, Skopje: KF Shkëndija 79 – F91 Dudelange 1-2 (1-0)
KF Shkëndija 79: Bekim Redjepi, Gledi Mici (76' Omar Imeri), Mevlan Murati, Visar Musliu, Egzon Bejtulai, Armend Alimi, Zeni Husmani (60' Ennur Totre), Agim Ibraimi, Alves, Stênio Júnior, Marjan Radeski (62' Besart Ibraimi). Coach: Qatip Osmani.
F91 Dudelange: Tim Kips, Tom Schnell, Ricardo Delgado, Mehdi Kirch, Mohamed Bouchouari, Mario Pokar, Dominik Stolz, Mickaël Garos (80' Charles Morren), Sabir Bougrine (46' Antoine Bernier), Danel Sinani, Bertino Cabral Barbosa (64' Adel Bettaieb). Coach: Henri Bossi.
Goals: 8' Agim Ibraimi 1-0 (p), 64' Adel Bettaieb 1-1, 69' Danel Sinani 1-2 (p).
Referee: Tore Hansen (NOR)   Attendance: 2,602.

KF Shkëndija 79 played their home match at Tose Proeski Arena, Skopje, instead of their regular stadium Ecolog Arena, Tetovo which was undergoing renovation.

23.07.19 Estadi Comunal d'Andorra la Vella, Andorra la Vella:
FC Santa Coloma – FK Astana 0-0
FC Santa Coloma: Eloy Casals, Moisés San Nicolás, Enric Pi (58' Jordi Aláez), Marc Rebés, Chus Rubio (83' Aleix Cistero), Andreu Ramos, Juanma Miranda, Chus Sosa, Pedro Santos, André Azevedo, Diego Nájero (73' Nicolás Medina). Coach: Marc Rodríguez Rebull.
FK Astana: Nenad Eric, Antonio Rukavina, Yuriy Logvinenko, Marin Anicic, Evgeny Postnikov, Luka Simunovic, Rúnar Sigurjónsson (64' Ndombe Mubele), Marin Tomasov, Ivan Maevski, Roman Murtazaev, Dorin Rotariu (82' Serikzhan Muzhikov).
Coach: Roman Grygorchuk.
Referee: Robert Hennessy (IRL)   Attendance: 382.

23.07.19 Stadio Olimpico di Serravalle, Serravalle:
SP Tre Penne – FK Sūdova Marijampolé 0-5 (0-2)
SP Tre Penne: Mattia Migani, Mirko Palazzi, Andrea Rossi, Christofer Genestreti, Nicola Gai, Enrico Cibelli, Michael Ballistini (69' Alex Gasperoni), Luca Patregnani, Stefano Fraternali, Luca Ceccaroli (59' Matteo Semprini), Luca Sorrentino (78' Giovanni Casolla).
Coach: Stefano Ceci.
FK Sūdova Marijampolé: Ivan Kardum, Algis Jankauskas, Andro Svrljuga, Aleksandar Zivanovic, Semir Kerla, Jovan Cadjenovic, Ovidijus Verbickas, Giedrius Matulevicius (76' Povilas Leimonas), Josip Tadic (84' Tosaint Ricketts), Mihret Topcagic, Paulius Golubickas (60' Eligijus Jankasukas). Coach: Vladimir Cheburin.
Goals: 9' Giedrius Matulevicius 0-1, 20' Mihret Topcagic 0-2, 66' Andro Svrljuga 0-3, 81' Josip Tadic 0-4, 90+1' Tosaint Ricketts 0-5.
Referee: Krzysztof Jakubik (POL)   Attendance: 354.

24.07.19 Národny Futbalovy Stadión, Bratislava: Slovan Bratislava – KF Feronikeli 2-1 (1-0)
Slovan Bratislava: Dominik Greif, Vasil Bozhikov, Artem Sukhotskiy, Myenty Abena, Marin Ljubicic, Dávid Holman (67' Dávid Strelec), Nono Delgado (86' Joeri de Kamps), Kenan Bajric, "Moha" Mohammed Rharsalla, Andraz Sporar, Rafael Ratão (70' Erik Daniel).
Coach: Vladimir Radenkovic.
KF Feronikeli: Florian Smakiqi, Lapidar Lladrovci, Arber Prekazi, Perparim Islami, Jean Carioca (76' Mevlan Zeka), Yll Hoxha, Argjend Malaj (82' Besmir Bojku), Albert Dabiqaj, Kastriot Rexha, Astrit Fazliu, Mendurim Hoti (90+4' Jetmir Topalli).
Coach: Zekirija Ramadani.
Goals: 9' Nono Delgado 1-0, 62' Andraz Sporar 2-0 (p), 67' Mendurim Hoti 2-1.
Referee: Ioannis Papadopoulos (GRE)   Attendance: 7,150.

25.07.19 Gyumri City Stadium, Gyumri: Pyunik Yerevan FC – FK Jablonec 2-1 (2-0)
Pyunik Yerevan FC: Andrija Dragojevic, Artak Yedigaryan, Antonio Stankov, Maksim Zhestokov, Kristi Marku, Armen Manucharyan, Sergiy Shevchuk, Artem Simonyan (66' Steven Alfred), Stanislav Efimov, Erik Vardanyan, Artur Miranyan (81' Aleksandr Galimov). Coach: Aleksandr Tarkhanov.
FK Jablonec: Jan Hanus, Jakub Jugas, Tomás Brecka, Libor Holík, Tomás Hübschman, Jakub Povazanez, Jan Sykora, Milos Kratochvíl (90+2' Tomás Pilík), Jan Matousek (86' Jan Chramosta), Martin Dolezal, Vladimir Jovovic (28' Rafael Acosta). Coach: Petr Rada.
Goals: 6', 30' Artur Miranyan 1-0, 2-0, 53' Martin Dolezal 2-1.
Referee: Fedayri San (SUI)   Attendance: 1,940.

Pyunik Yerevan FC played their home match at Gyumri City Stadium, Gyumri, instead of their regular stadium Vazgen Sargsyan Republic Stadium, Yerevan.

25.07.19 Olimpiska centra Ventspils Stadionā, Ventspils:
FK Ventspils – Gzira United 4-0 (1-0)
FK Ventspils: Konstantin Machnovskiy, Jean Alcénat, Abdoul Mamah, Giorgi Mchedlishvili, Hélio Batista, Guga Palavandishvili, Jevgenijs Kazacoks (79' Ingars Stuglis), Tosin Aiyegun, Kaspars Svārups (73' Pavel Osipov), Mykhaylo Sergiychuk (89' Bekkhan Aliev), Lucas Villela. Coach: Igor Klosovs.
Gzira United: Justin Haber, Arthur Henrique, Rodolfo Soares, Fernando Barbosa, Nicky Muscat, Andrew Cohen, Hamed Koné, Gianmarco Conti, Juan Corbalan, Zachary Scerri (80' Elvis Sakyi), Jefferson. Coach: Giovanni Tedesco.
Goals: 41' Kaspars Svārups 1-0, 50' Hélio Batista 2-0, 83' Ingars Stuglis 3-0, 87' Tosin Aiyegun 4-0.
Referee: Dimitar Meckarovski (MCD)   Attendance: 2,196.

25.07.19 Qäbälä Sähär stadionu, Qabala: Gabala FK – Dinamo Tbilisi 0-2 (0-1)
Gabala FK: Anar Nazirov, Rasim Ramaldanov, Ivica Zunic, Yusif Nabiyev, Merab Gigauri, Amin Seydiyev, Qismat Aliyev (85' Asif Mammadov), Clésio, Fernán Ferreiro, Davit Volkovi (61' Rovlan Muradov), Ulvu Isgandarov (77' Christian Kouakou). Coach: Zaur Hasimov.
Dinamo Tbilisi: José Perales, Giorgi Kimadze, Víctor Mongil, Nodar Iashvili, Davit Kobouri, Nika Ninua, Levan Kutalia, Giorgi Kukhianidze (65' Bakar Kardava), Giorgi Papava, Nodar Kavtaradze (74' Arfang Daffé), Levan Shengelia (86' Kwame Karikari).
Coach: Félix Vicente Miranda.
Goals: 41' Levan Kutalia 0-1, 87' Arfang Daffé 0-2.
Referee: Nick Walsh (SCO)   Attendance: 2,800.

25.07.19 Stadiumi Selman Stërmasi, Tiranë:
FK Partizani Tirana – FC Sheriff Tiraspol 0-1 (0-1)
FK Partizani Tirana: Alban Hoxha (I), Egzon Belica, Enea Bitri, Libanot Ibrahimi, Esin Hakaj, Bruno Telushi (71' Aristóteles Romero), William Cordeiro, Ron Broja, Esat Mala, Eraldo Çinari (51' Jasir Asani), Theophilus Solomon (57' Joseph Ekuban). Coach: Franco Lerda.
FC Sheriff Tiraspol: Zvonimir Mikulic, Artem Hordienko (86' Jaroslaw Jach), Ousmane N'Diaye, Mateo Muzek, Cristiano, Wilfried Balima, Jury Kendysh (90+4' Antun Palic), Gheorghe Anton, Liridon Latifi (48' Maxim Cojocaru (I)), Gabrijel Boban, Robert Tambe. Coach: Zoran Zekic.
Goal: 24' Robert Tambe 0-1.
Referee: Kirill Levnikov (RUS)   Attendance: 1,750.

25.07.19   AEK Arena – Georgios Karapatakis, Larnaca:
　　　　　AEK Larnaca – Levski Sofia 3-0 (0-0)
AEK Larnaca: Toño, Mikel González, Daniel Mojsov, Truyols, Ivan Trickovski (87' Matija Spoljaric), Lluis Sastre, Acorán, Nacho Cases, Hector Hevel (76' Jean Luc Assoubre), Raúl Ruiz, Apostolos Giannou (78' Florian Taulemesse). Coach: Imanol Idiakez.
Levski Sofia: Milan Mijatovic, Zhivko Milanov, Nuno Reis, Ivan Goranov, Giannis Kargas (46' Iliya Yurukov), Martin Raynov, Davide Mariani, Khaly Thiam, Deni Alar (46' Nasiru Mohammed), Paulinho, Stanislav Ivanov (83' Zdravko Dimitrov). Coach: Petar Hubchev.
Goals: 67' Apostolos Giannou 1-0, 70' Raúl Ruiz 2-0, 75' Hector Hevel 3-0.
Referee: Tiago Martins (POR)　　Attendance: 3,177.
Sent off: 45+2' Zhivko Milanov.

25.07.19   Stadion Galgenwaard, Utrecht: FC Utrecht – Zrinjski Mostar 1-1 (0-1)
FC Utrecht: David Jensen, Willem Janssen, Emil Bergström, Leon Guwara, Sean Klaiber, Adam Maher, Sander van de Streek (80' Urby Emanuelson), Simon Gustafson, Justin Lonwijk (57' Nick Venema), Vaclav Cerny (62' Patrick Joosten), Gyrano Kerk.
Coach: John van den Brom.
Zrinjski Mostar: Ivan Brkic, Mario Ticinovic (57' Stanisa Mandic), Tomislav Barbaric, Dario Rugasevic, Slobodan Jakovljevic (66' Renato Gojkovic), Advan Kadusic, Damir Sovsic, Frane Cirjak, Edin Rustemovic, Miljan Govedarica, Irfan Hadzic (62' Ivan Lendric).
Coach: Hari Vukas.
Goals: 34' Miljan Govedarica 0-1, 61' Gyrano Kerk 1-1.
Referee: Aleksei Eskov (RUS)　　Attendance: 17,221.

25.07.19   Boris Paichadze Dinamo Arena, Tbilisi:
　　　　　Chikhura Sachkhere – Aberdeen FC 1-1 (1-0)
Chikhura Sachkhere: Dino Hamzic, Shota Kashia, Davit Maisashvili, Lasha Chikvaidze, Revaz Chiteishvili (74' Demur Chikhladze), Oleg Mamasakhlisi, Besik Dekanoidze, Irakli Lekvtadze (76' Giorgi Pantsulaia), Giorgi Koripadze, Mikheil Sardalishvili, Mikheil Ergemlidze.
Coach: Soso Pruidze.
Aberdeen FC: Joe Lewis, Andrew Considine, Shay Logan, Ash Taylor (18' Craig Bryson), Scott McKenna, Funso Ojo, Lewis Ferguson, Niall McGinn, Ryan Hedges, Sam Cosgrove, Jon Gallagher (82' James Wilson). Coach: Derek McInnes.
Goals: 41' Giorgi Koripadze 1-0 (p), 68' Sam Cosgrove 1-1 (p).
Referee: Horatiu Fesnic (ROM)　　Attendance: 3,218.

Chikhura Sachkhere played their home match at Boris Paichadze Dinamo Arena, Tbilisi, instead of their regular stadium Central Stadium, Sachkhere which did not meet UEFA requirements.

25.07.19 ETO Park, Györ: Budapest Honvéd – CS Universitatea Craiova 0-0
Budapest Honvéd: Rubi Levkovic, Ivan Lovric (75' MacDonald Niba Ngwa), Djordje Kamber, Bence Batik, Eke Uzoma, Tonci Kukoc, Barna Kesztyüs, Dániel Gazdag, Bence Banó-Szabó, David N'Gog (81' Dominik Cipf), Amadou Moutari (65' Vladyslav Kulach).
Coach: Giuseppe Sannino.
CS Universitatea Craiova: Mirko Pigliacelli, Renato Kelic, Ivan Martic, Nicusor Bancu, Stephane Acka, Alexandru Mateiu, Bogdan Vatajelu, Kamer Qaka (65' Antoni Ivanov), Cristian Barbut, Alexandru Cicâldau (90+1' Vasile Constantin), Carlos Fortes (46' Mihai Roman (II)). Coach: Corneliu Papura.
Referee: Kevin Clancy (SCO)   Attendance: 2,720.

Budapest Honvéd played their home match at ETO Park, Györ, instead of their regular stadium Bozsik Stadion, Budapest, due to reconstruction.

25.07.19 Haugesund Stadion, Haugesund: FK Haugesund – SK Sturm Graz 2-0 (0-0)
FK Haugesund: Helge Sandvik, Doug Bergqvist, Mikkel Desler, Benjamin Tiedemann Hansen, Sondre Tronstad, Thore Baardsen Pedersen, Niklas Sandberg, Bruno Leite, Kristoffer Velde (90+3' Eric Ndayisenga), Kevin Krygård, Ibrahima Koné (76' Martin Samuelsen).
Coach: Jostein Grindhaug.
SK Sturm Graz: Jörg Siebenhandl, Thomas Schrammel, Anastasios Avlonitis, Emanuel Sakic (71' Fabian Koch), Lukas Spendlhofer, Jakob Jantscher, Juan Domínguez, Ivan Ljubic, Otar Kiteishvili, Philipp Hosiner (71' Emeka Eze), Markus Pink (65' Michael John Lema).
Coach: Nestor El Maestro.
Goals: 51' Kevin Krygård 1-0, 64' Niklas Sandberg 2-0.
Referee: Donatas Rumsas (LTU)   Attendance: 3,501.

25.07.19 Stadion Energa Gdansk, Gdansk: Lechia Gdansk – Brøndby IF 2-1 (1-0)
Lechia Gdansk: Dusan Kuciak, Blazej Augustyn, Zarko Udovicic, Filip Mladenovic, Michal Nalepa, Daniel Lukasik, Lukás Haraslín (79' Slawomir Peszko), Patryk Lipski (83' Tomasz Makowski), Jaroslaw Kubicki, Karol Fila, Flávio Paixão (74' Artur Sobiech).
Coach: Piotr Stokowiec.
Brøndby IF: Marvin Schwäbe, Paulus Arajuuri, Anthony Jung, Hjörtur Hermannsson, Dominik Kaiser, Lasse Vigen Christensen, Josip Radosevic, Simon Tibbling (75' Kasper Fisker), Simon Hedlund, Kamil Wilczek, Kevin Mensah (81' Jens Gammelby). Coach: Niels Frederiksen.
Goals: 26' Flávio Paixão 1-0 (p), 59' Simon Hedlund 1-1, 63' Patryk Lipski 2-1.
Referee: John Beaton (SCO)   Attendance: 25,875.

25.07.19 Aker Stadion, Molde: Molde FK – FK Cukaricki-Stankom 0-0
Molde FK: Álex Craninx, Vegard Forren, Kristoffer Haraldseid, Kristoffer Haugen, Martin Bjørnbak, Magnus Eikrem (77' Fredrik Sjølstad), Etzaz Hussain, Eirik Hestad, Fredrik Aursnes, Ohi Omoijuanfo, Leke James (66' Mathis Bolly). Coach: Erling Moe.
FK Cukaricki-Stankom: Nemanja Belic, Miroslav Bogosavac, Darko Puskaric, Nikola Cirkovic, Luka Stojanovic (62' Veljko Birmancevic), Marko Docic, Samuel Owusu, Stefan Kovac (84' Kosta Aleksic), Stefan Sapic, Aleksandar Djordjevic, Slobodan Tedic.
Coach: Aleksander Veselinovic.
Referee: Donald Robertson (SCO)   Attendance: 3,198.
Sent off: 90+5' Veljko Birmancevic.

25.07.19   Stadion Arsenal, Tula: Arsenal Tula – Neftçi PFK Baku 0-1 (0-1)
Arsenal Tula: Mikhail Levashov, Kirill Kombarov, Gia Grigalava, Maxim Belyaev, Víctor Álvarez, Igor Gorbatenko, Sergey Tkachev, Goran Causic, Daniil Lesovoy, Alexandru Tudorie (46' Evgeniy Lutsenko), Lameck Banda (46' Georgi Kostadinov).
Coach: Igor Cherevchenko.
Neftçi PFK Baku: Salahat Agayev, Vojislav Stankovic, Kyrylo Petrov, Anton Krivotsyuk, Omar Buludov, Soni Mustivar, Emin Makhmudov (88' Vangelis Platellas), Mamadou Kane, Steeven Joseph-Monrose, Rauf Aliyev, Dário Júnior da Silva (73' Namiq Alasgarov).
Coach: Roberto Bordin.
Goal: 45+1' Dário Júnior da Silva 0-1.
Referee: Enea Jorgji (ALB)   Attendance: 16,720.

25.07.19   Yeni Malatya Stadyumu, Malatya: Yeni Malatyaspor – Olimpija Ljubljana 2-2 (1-1)
Yeni Malatyaspor: Fabien Farnolle, Issam Chebake, Arturo Mina, Teenage Hadebe, Murat Yildirim, Mitchell Donald (64' Guilherme), Nuri Aydin (62' Ahmed Ildiz), Erkan Kas, Thievy Bifouma, Adis Jahovic, Moryké Fofana (75' Berk Yildiz). Coach: Sergen Yalçın.
Olimpija Ljubljana: Nejc Vidmar, Miral Samardzic, Macky Frank Bagnack, Eric Boakye, Goran Brkic (70' Marko Putincanin), Asmir Suljic (73' Luka Menalo), Stefan Savic, Tomislav Tomic, Endri Çekiçi, Ante Vukusic (90+4' Haris Kadric), Mario Jurcevic.
Coach: Safet Hadzic.
Goals: 13' Ante Vukusic 0-1, 20' Arturo Mina 1-1, 66' Adis Jahovic 2-1 (p), 74' Stefan Savic 2-2.
Referee: João Pinheiro (POR)   Attendance: 9,146.

25.07.19   A. Le Coq Arena, Tallinn: FC Flora Tallinn – Eintracht Frankfurt 1-2 (1-1)
FC Flora Tallinn: Matvei Igonen, Gert Kams, Märten Kuusk, Henrik Pürg, Henri Järvelaid, Konstantin Vassiljev, Mikhel Ainsalu, Martin Miller (76' Vlasiy Sinyavskiy), Vladislavs Kreida, Frank Liivak (86' Rauno Alliku), Erik Sorga (82' Mark Lepik). Coach: Jürgen Henn.
Eintracht Frankfurt: Felix Wiedwald, David Abraham, Danny da Costa (88' Timothy Chandler), Evan Obite N'Dicka, Makoto Hasebe, Filip Kostic, Lucas Torró, Mijat Gacinovic (64' Daichi Kamada), Dominik Kohr, Gonçalo Paciência (64' Dejan Joveljic), Ante Rebic.
Coach: Adi Hütter.
Goals: 24' Lucas Torró 0-1, 34' Mikhel Ainsalu 1-1, 71' Dejan Joveljic 1-2.
Referee: Ali Palabiyik (TUR)   Attendance: 8,500.

25.07.19   Adidas Aréna, Mladá Boleslav: FK Mladá Boleslav – FK Ordabasy 1-1 (1-1)
FK Mladá Boleslav: Jan Seda, Daniel Pudil, Laco Takács, Antonín Krapka (62' Lukáš Budínsky), Marco Tulio, Marek Matejovsky, Jakub Fulnek (75' Pavel Bucha), Michal Hubínek, Tomáš Ladra, Muris Mesanovic (63' Tomás Wágner), Nikolay Komlichenko.
Coach: Jozef Weber.
FK Ordabasy: Dmytro Nepogodov, Pablo Fontanello, Sergiy Maliy, Temirlan Yerlanov, Marat Bystrov, Abdoulaye Diakhaté, May Mahlangu, Timur Dosmagambetov, Mirzad Mehanovic (72' Kyrylo Kovalchuk), João Paulo (46' Aleksey Shchetkin), Ziguy Badibanga (87' Samat Shamshi). Coach: Kakhaber Tskhadadze.
Goals: 21' Mirzad Mehanovic 0-1, 45+2' Nikolay Komlichenko 1-1.
Referee: Sergey Tsinkevich (BLS)   Attendance: 3,721.

25.07.19   FFA Academy Stadium, Yerevan: FC Alashkert – Fotbal Club FCSB 0-3 (0-0)
FC Alashkert: Ognjen Cancarevic, Hrayr Mkoyan, Gagik Dagbashyan, Hayk Ishkhanyan, Taron Voskanyan, Tiago Cametá, Artak Grigoryan, Danilo Sekulic (65' Gustavo Marmentini Santos), Vahagn Hayrapetyan, Uros Nenadovic (72' Vardan Poghosyan), Nikita Tankov (55' Gegam Kadimyan). Coach: Abraham Khashmanyan.
Fotbal Club FCSB: Andrei Daniel Vlad, Bogdan Planic, Iulian Cristea, Lucian Filip, Ionut Vîna, Ovidiu Popescu, Dragos Nedelcu, Adrian Ioan Hora (46' Razvan Oaida), Florin Tanase, Florinel Coman (90+1' Ovidiu Perianu), Dennis Man (77' Diogo Salomão).
Coach: Bogdan Andone.
Goals: 60' Florin Tanase 0-1, 68' Iulian Cristea 0-2, 82' Florinel Coman 0-3.
Referee: Robert Harvey (IRL)   Attendance: 1,420.

FC Alashkert played their home match at FFA Academy Stadium, Yerevan, instead of their regular Alashkert Stadium, Yerevan.

25.07.19   Stadyen Budaunik Stroitel, Soligorsk: Shakhtyor Soligorsk – Esbjerg fB 2-0 (1-0)
Shakhtyor Soligorsk: Andrey Klimovich, Pavel Rybak, Sergey Matvejchik (52' Igor Burko), Nikola Antic, Aleksandr Sachivko, Yuri Kovalev, Július Szöke, Valeriy Gromyko (86' Nikolai Yanush), Max Ebong Ngome, Elis Bakaj, Mykyta Tatarkov (46' Sergey Balanovich).
Coach: Sergey Tashuev.
Esbjerg fB: Jeppe Højbjerg, Markus Halsti (69' Rudolph Austin), Jesper Lauridsen, Viktor Tranberg, Daniel Anyembe, Joni Kauko (46' Jacob Sørensen), Lasha Parunashvili, Mark Brink, Patrick Egelund, Pyry Soiri (69' Mathias Kristensen), Adrian Petre.
Coach: John Lammers.
Goals: 5' Elis Bakaj 1-0, 55' Pavel Rybak 2-0.
Referee: Mete Kalkavan (TUR)   Attendance: 3,050.

25.07.19   Yaakov Turner Toto Stadium, Beer Sheva:
            Hapoel Be'er Sheva – FK Kairat 2-0 (1-0)
Hapoel Be'er Sheva: Ernestas Setkus, Miguel Vítor, Ben Bitton, Loai Taha, Sean Goldberg, Marwan Kabha, Ramzi Safouri (54' Ben Sahar), Eden Shamir, David Keltjens (87' Naor Sabag), Jimmy Marín, Nigel Hasselbaink (78' Niv Zrihan). Coach: Barak Bakhar.
FK Kairat: Stas Pokatilov, Eldos Akhmetov, Gafurzhan Suyombaev, Dino Mikanovic, Rade Dugalic, Aybol Abiken (76' Ramazan Orazov), Islambek Kuat, Bauyrzhan Islamkhan (67' Márton Eppel), Georgiy Zhukov, Konrad Wrzesinski (67' Yerkebulan Seidakhmet), Aderinsola Eseola. Coach: Aleksey Shpilevski.
Goals: 10' Ramzi Safouri 1-0 (p), 2-0 Eden Shamir (63).
Referee: Ricardo de Burgos Bengoetxea (ESP)   Attendance: 8,167.

25.07.19   Stadion Balgarska Armija, Sofia: CSKA Sofia – NK Osijek 1-0 (0-0)
CSKA Sofia: Vytautas Cerniauskas, Nikolay Bodurov, Petar Zanev (78' Graham Carey), Kristiyan Malinov, Nuno Tomás, Geferson, Tiago Rodrigues, Janio Bikel, Diego Fabbrini (63' Valentin Antov), Ali Sowe, Evandro (82' Bozhidar Chorbadzhiyski).
Coach: Ljubomir Petrovic.
NK Osijek: Ivica Ivusic, Tomislav Sorsa, Mile Skoric, Ante Majstorovic, Mihael Zaper (90+4' Marko Dugandzic), László Kleinheisler (83' Dmytro Lyopa), Petar Bockaj, Marin Pilj (78' Vedran Jugovic), Bosko Sutalo, Mirko Maric, Antonio Mance. Coach: Dino Skender.
Goal: 53' Evandro 1-0.
Referee: Paolo Valeri (ITA)   Attendance: 7,500.

25.07.19 Stadion Lokomotiv, Plovdiv: Lokomotiv Plovdiv – Spartak Trnava 2-0 (1-0)
Lokomotiv Plovdiv: Martin Lukov, Milos Petrovic, Josip Tomasevic, Stephen Eze, Dimitar Iliev, Momchil Tsvetanov, Parvizchon Umarbaev (90+5' Edin Bahtic), Petar Vitanov, Birsent Karagaren (77' David Malembana), Alen Ozbolt (79' Georgi Iliev), Ante Aralica.
Coach: Bruno Akrapovic.
Spartak Trnava: Dobrivoj Rusov, Timotej Záhumensky, Jozef Menich, Lucas Lovat, Ivan Mesík, Marko Tesija, Emir Halilovic, Filip Dangubic (69' Marko Kelemen), Rafael Tavares (80' Matús Turna), Filip Orsula, Gino van Kessel (56' Matej Jakúbek). Coach: Ricardo Chéu.
Goals: 39', 61' Dimitar Iliev 1-0 (p), 2-0 (p).
Referee: Timotheos Christofi (CYP)   Attendance: 5,900.

25.07.19 Corbett Sports Stadium, Rhyl:
   Connah's Quay Nomads FC – Partizan Beograd 0-1 (0-0)
Connah's Quay Nomads FC: Lewis Brass, George Horan, Danny Holmes, John Disney, Callum Roberts, Jay Owen, Callum Morris, Declan Poole, Michael Wilde, Nathan Woolfe (58' Michael Bakare), Jamie Insall (73' Priestley Farquharson). Coach: Andy Morrison.
Partizan Beograd: Vladimir Stojkovic, Bojan Ostojic, Nemanja Miletic (I), Sasa Zdjelar, Slobodan Urosevic, Strahinja Pavlovic, Zoran Tosic, Aleksandar Scekic, Seydouba Soumah, Umar Sadiq (46' Ognjen Ozegovic), Djordje Ivanovic (73' Filip Stevanovic).
Coach: Savo Milosevic.
Goal: 62' Aleksandar Scekic 0-1.
Referee: Michal Ocenás (SVK)   Attendance: 829.

Connah's Quay Nomads FC played their home match at Corbett Sports Stadium, Rhyl, instead of their regular stadium Deeside Stadium, Connah's Quay which does not meet UEFA requirements.

25.07.19 Stadion Miejski, Gliwice: Piast Gliwice – Riga FC 3-2 (0-1)
Piast Gliwice: Frantisek Plach, Uros Korun, Mikkel Kirkeskov, Jakub Czerwinski, Marcin Pietrowski, Tom Hateley, Gerard Badía (62' Martin Konczkowski), Patryk Dziczek, Joel Valencia (74' Patryk Sokolowski), Piotr Parzyszek (87' Dominik Steczyk), Jorge Félix.
Coach: Waldemar Fornalik.
Riga FC: Roberts Ozols, Georgios Valerianos, Stefan Panic, Olegs Laizāns, Ritvars Rugins, Vyacheslav Sharpar, Tomislav Saric, Felipe Brisola (43' Aleksejs Visnakovs), Deniss Rakels (80' Joël Bopesu), Elvis Stuglis, Roman Debelko (84' Kamil Bilinski).
Coach: Mihails Konevs.
Goals: 22' Roman Debelko 0-1, 66' Jakub Czerwinski 1-1, 82', 85' Jorge Félix 2-1, 3-1, 86' Uros Korun 3-2 (og).
Referee: Manuel Schüttengruber (AUT)   Attendance: 5,100.

25.07.19 Östgötaporten, Norrköping: IFK Norrköping – FK Liepāja 2-0 (1-0)
IFK Norrköping: Isak Pettersson, Lars Gerson, Kasper Larsen, Filip Dagerstål, Rasmus Lauritsen, Gudmundur Thórarinsson, Simon Thern, Alexander Fransson (72' Sead Haksabanovic), Christoffer Nyman (89' Henrik Castegren), Simon Skrabb, Kalle Holmberg (86' Andreas Blomqvist). Coach: Jens Gustafsson.
FK Liepāja: Valentins Ralkevics, Vadims Zulevs, Deniss Ivanovs, Seydina Keita, Raivis Jurkovskis, Amâncio Fortes, Leonel Strumia, Kristers Tobers, Mārtins Kigurs (81' Cristián Torres), Richard Friday (72' Danu Spataru), Dodô. Coach: Aleksandrs Starkovs.
Goals: 1' Simon Thern 1-0, 80' Sead Haksabanovic 2-0.
Referee: Hüseyin Göçek (TUR)   Attendance: 5,440.

25.07.19   Puskás Akadémia Pancho Aréna, Felcsút: MOL Vidi FC – FC Vaduz 1-0 (1-0)
MOL Vidi FC: Ádám Kovácsik, Roland Juhász, Attila Fiola, Loïc Négo, Stopira, Szabolcs Huszti (57' Ivan Petryak), Anel Hadzic, Ákos Elek (46' Máté Pátkai), Georgi Milanov, Boban Nikolov, Marko Scepovic (87' Márkó Futács). Coach: Marko Nikolic.
FC Vaduz: Benjamin Büchel, Denis Simani, Pius Dorn, Yannick Schmid, Berkay Sülüngöz, Gianni Antoniazzi (84' Maximilian Göppel), Boris Prokopic (71' Milan Gajic), Sandro Wieser, Dominik Schwizer, Manuel Sutter (66' Mohamed Coulibaly), Tunahan Çiçek.
Coach: Mario Frick.
Goal: 5' Stopira 1-0.
Referee: Kai Erik Steen (NOR)   Attendance: 2,224.

MOL Vidi FC played their home match at Puskás Akadémia Pancho Aréna, Felcsút, instead of their regular stadium MOL Aréna Sóstó, Székesfehérvár.

25.07.19   Swissporarena, Luzern: FC Luzern – KÍ Klaksvík 1-0 (0-0)
FC Luzern: Marius Müller, Lazar Cirkovic, Otar Kakabadze, Marvin Schulz, Stefan Knezevic, Silvan Sidler, Idriz Voca, Christian Schneuwly, Pascal Schürpf, Shkelqim Demhasaj (55' Francesco Margiotta), Eric Tia (55' Blessing Eleke). Coach: Thomas Häberli.
KÍ Klaksvík: Kristian Joensen, Jesper Brinck, Ísak Simonsen, Deni Pavlovic, Semir Hadzibulic (82' Steinbjørn Olsen), Patrik Johannesen, Jákup Andreasen, Jóannes Bjartalíd (72' Boris Dosljak), Simen Sandmæl, Jóannes Danielsen, Páll Klettskard (66' Torbjørn Grytten).
Coach: Mikkjal Thomassen.
Goal: 90+3' Christian Schneuwly 1-0.
Referee: Halis Özkahya (TUR)   Attendance: 6,344.

25.07.19   MOL Aréna, Dunajská Streda: DAC Dunajská Streda – Atromitos FC 1-2 (1-2)
DAC Dunajská Streda: Martin Jedlicka, Éric Davis (74' César Blackman), Kristián Kostrna, Dominik Kruzliak, Matej Oravec, Zsolt Kalmár, Máté Vida, Lukás Cmelík (61' Dominik Veselovsky), Connor Ronan (30' Kristopher Vida), Eric Ramírez, Marko Divkovic.
Coach: Peter Hyballa.
Atromitos FC: Balász Megyeri, Madson, Dimitrios Goutas, Spyros Risvanis, Alexandros Katranis, Javier Umbides, Kyriakos Kivrakidis (39' Spyridon Natsos), Charilaos Charisis, Georgios Manousos, Apostolos Vellios (74' Tal Kahila), Clarck N'Sikulu (61' Farley Rosa).
Coach: Yannis Anastasiou.
Goals: 20' Javier Umbides 0-1, 35' Kristopher Vida 1-1, 43' Georgios Manousos 1-2.
Referee: Bastian Dankert (GER)   Attendance: 9,980.

25.07.19   GHELAMCO-arena, Gent: KAA Gent – FC Viitorul Constanta 6-3 (5-1)
KAA Gent: Thomas Kaminski, Nana Asare, Mikael Lustig, Igor Plastun, Sigurd Rosted (70' Milad Mohammadi), Vadis Odjidja-Ofoe, Brecht Dejaegere (62' Alessio Castro-Montes), Elisha Owusu, Yuya Kubo (62' Giorgi Beridze), Roman Yaremchuk, Jonathan David.
Coach: Jess Thorup.
FC Viitorul Constanta: Árpád Tordai, Sebastian Mladen, Paul Iacob (46' Virgil Ghita), Bradley de Nooijer, Vlad Achim, Bogdan Tîru, Andrei Artean, Lyes Houri, Alexandru Matan (72' Andreas Calcan), Gabriel Iancu, George Ganea (62' Denis Dragus). Coach: Gheorghe Hagi.
Goals: 4' Nana Asare 1-0, 13' Brecht Dejaegere 2-0, 21' Sebastian Mladen 2-1, 35' Yuya Kubo 3-1, 42' Roman Yaremchuk 4-1 (p), 45' Yuya Kubo 5-1, 50' Roman Yaremchuk 6-1, 56', 61' Bogdan Tîru 6-2, 6-3.
Referee: Aleksandar Stavrev (MCD)   Attendance: 13,398.

25.07.19 Stadio Harilaou Kleánthis Vikelídis Stadium, Thessaloniki:
Aris Saloniki – AEL Limassol 0-0
Aris Saloniki: Julián Cuesta, Daniel Sundgren, Mihály Korhut, Lindsay Rose, Fran Vélez, Nicolas Diguiny, Migjen Basha (74' Lucas Sasha), Javier Matilla, Ioannis Fetfatzidis (65' Daniel Larsson), Martín Tonso (84' Nicolás Martínez), Brown Ideye.
Coach: Savvas Pantelidis.
AEL Limassol: Vózinha, Nils Teixeira, Dossa Júnior (80' Ivan Carlos), Boris Godál, André Teixeira, Christos Wheeler (88' Andreas Avraam), Adnan Aganovic, Marko Adamovic (62' Gevorg Ghazaryan), Jon Gaztañaga, Davor Zdravkovski, Rubén Jurado. Coach: Dusan Kerkez.
Referee: Stuart Attwell (ENG)   Attendance: 17,488.

25.07.19 Stade Josy Barthel, Luxembourg: Jeunesse d'Esch – Vitória de Guimarães 0-1 (0-0)
Jeunesse d'Esch: Kévin Sommer, Arsène Menèssou, Alessandro Fiorani, Emmanuel Lapierre, Johannes Steinbach, Halim Meddour, Milos Todorovic, Luca Duriatti, David Soares De Sousa (70' Yannick Makota), Valentin Kouamé, Almir Klica (78' Mehmet Arslan).
Coach: Nicolas Huysman.
Vitória de Guimarães: João Miguel Silva, Víctor García, Pedrão, Rafa Soares, Edmond Tapsoba, João Carlos Teixeira (62' Pêpê Rodrigues), Rochinha (84' João Correia), Almoatasembellah Ali Mohamed (88' Mikel Agu), Joseph Amoah, Alexandre Guedes, Davidson. Coach: Ivo Vieira.
Goal: 90+4' Joseph Amoah 0-1.
Referee: Bojan Pandzic (SWE)   Attendance: 3,617.

Jeunesse d'Esch played their home match at Stade Josy Barthel, Luxembourg, instead of their regular stadium Stade de la Frontière, Esch-sur-Alzette which did not meet UEFA requirements.

25.07.19   AFAS Stadion, Alkmaar: AZ Alkmaar – BK Häcken 0-0
AZ Alkmaar: Marco Bizot, Ron Vlaar, Stijn Wuytens (59' Yukinari Sugawara), Jonas Svensson, Owen Wijndal, Fredrik Midtsjø (77' Pantelis Hatzidiakos), Teun Koopmeiners, Guus Til, Albert Gudmundsson (58' Oussama Idrissi), Myron Boadu, Calvin Stengs.
Coach: Arne Slot.
BK Häcken: Peter Abrahamsson, Joona Toivio, Óskar Sverrisson, Elohor Ekpolo (87' Adam Andersson), Gustav Berggren, Rasmus Lindgren, Erik Friberg, Ahmed Yasin, Daleho Irandust (71' Juhani Ojala), Viktor Lundberg, Paulinho (77' Alexander Faltsetas). Coach: Andreas Alm.
Referee: Serhiy Boyko (UKR)   Attendance: 11,492.

25.07.19   Sportni Park, Domzale: NK Domzale – Malmö FF 2-2 (1-1)
NK Domzale: Grega Sorcan, Gaber Dobrovoljc, Gregor Sikosek, Tilen Klemencic, Senijad Ibricic (90+2' Branko Ilic), Josip Corluka, Mattias Käit, Adam Gnezda Cerin, Slobodan Vuk (37' Matej Podlogar), Tonci Mujan (89' Sven Karic), Shamar Nicholson.
Coach: Simon Rozman.
Malmö FF: Johan Dahlin, Behrang Safari, Rasmus Bengtsson, Lasse Nielsen (80' Franz Brorsson), Søren Rieks (68' Jonas Knudsen), Anders Christiansen, Fouad Bachirou, Oscar Lewicki, Markus Rosenberg, Jo Inge Berget, Marcus Antonsson (77' Guillermo Molins).
Coach: Uwe Rösler.
Goals: 37' Shamar Nicholson 1-0, 42' Rasmus Bengtsson 1-1, 48' Adam Gnezda Cerin 2-1, 52' Marcus Antonsson 2-2.
Referee: Michael Fabbri (ITA)   Attendance: 2,043.

25.07.19   Ibrox Stadium, Glasgow: Glasgow Rangers FC – Progrès Niederkorn 2-0 (1-0)
Glasgow Rangers FC: Allan McGregor, James Tavernier, Connor Goldson, George Edmundson, Steven Davis, Scott Arfield (66' Jordan Jones), Ryan Jack, Andy Halliday, Sheyi Ojo (81' Greg Stewart), Joe Aribo, Alfredo Morelos (75' Jermain Defoe).
Coach: Steven Gerrard.
Progrès Niederkorn: Sebastian Flauss, Tom Laterza, Adrien Ferino, Ben Vogel, Metin Karayer, Tim Hall, Aldin Skenderovic (33' Yann Matias Marques), Christian Silaj, Belmin Muratovic (46' Jacky Mmaee), Mayron De Almeida, Kempes Tekiela (80' Emmanuel Françoise).
Coach: Roland Vrabec.
Goals: 20' Joe Aribo 1-0, 54' Sheyi Ojo 2-0.
Referee: Espen Eskås (NOR)   Attendance: 43,629.
Sent off: 88' Tom Laterza.

25.07.19   Stadion Pod Goricom, Podgorica:
           FC Buducnost Podgorica – Zorya Luhansk 1-3 (0-2)
FC Buducnost Podgorica: Milos Dragojevic, Dejan Boljevic, Luka Mirkovic (77' Ivan Bojovic), Slavko Damjanovic, Stefan Milic, Drasko Bozovic (46' Milos Raickovic), Milos Mijic, Milos Vucic, Dusan Bakic (46' Dejan Zarubica), Mihailo Perovic, Dusan Stoiljkovic.
Coach: Branko Brnovic.
Zorya Luhansk: Nikita Shevchenko, Vitaliy Vernidub, Oleksandr Tymchyk, Artem Gromov (80' Levan Arveladze), Dmytro Khomchenovsky, Vladen Yurchenko (64' Maksym Lunyov), Dmitriy Ivanisenya, Bogdan Mykhaylychenko (85' Joel Abu Hanna), Yevgen Cheberko, Vladyslav Kochergin, Pylyp Budkovsky. Coach: Viktor Skripnik.
Goals: 15', 19' Artem Gromov 0-1, 0-2, 60' Mihailo Perovic 1-2, 82' Levan Arveladze 1-3.
Referee: Massimiliano Irrati (ITA)   Attendance: 5,500.

25.07.19   Stade de la Meinau, Strasbourg: RC Strasbourg – Maccabi Haifa 3-1 (1-1)
RC Strasbourg: Matz Sels, Lamine Koné, Lionel Carole, Alexander Djiku, Ismaël Aaneba (46' Adrien Thomasson), Mohamed Simakan, Jonas Martin, Jean Ricner Bellegarde (77' Kévin Lucien Zohi), Youssouf Fofana, Nuno Da Costa (84' Dimitri Liénard), Ludovic Ajorque.
Coach: Thierry Laurey.
Maccabi Haifa: Guy Haimov, Rami Gershon, Ernest Mabouka, Ayed Habashi, Ofri Arad, Yuval Ashkenazi, Yosef Raz Meir, Neta Lavi, Maxim Plakuschenko (67' Dolev Haziza), Nikita Rukavytsya (89' Allyson), Yarden Shua (50' Sun Menachem). Coach: Marco Balbul.
Goals: 39' Maxim Plakuschenko 0-1, 45' Ludovic Ajorque 1-1 (p), 47' Adrien Thomasson 2-1, 61' Jonas Martin 3-1.
Referee: Kevin Blom (HOL)   Attendance: 20,137.
Sent off: 44' Ayed Habashi.

25.07.19   Molineux Stadium, Wolverhampton:
           Wolverhampton Wanderers – Crusaders FC 2-0 (1-0)
Wolverhampton Wanderers: Rui Patrício, Ryan Bennett, Willy Boly, Conor Coady, Jonny Castro (64' Rúben Vinagre), João Moutinho, Leander Dendoncker, Rúben Neves (58' Raúl Jiménez), Diogo Jota, Morgan Gibbs-White (85' Romain Saïss), Adama Traoré.
Coach: Nuno Espírito Santo.
Crusaders FC: Sean O'Neill, Sean Ward, Billy Joe Burns, Chris Hegarty, Declan Caddell (67' Gary Thompson), Philip Lowry, Jordan Forsythe, Paul Heatley, Ross Clarke (61' Jordan Owens), Jarlath O'Rourke, Rory Hale (82' David Cushley). Coach: Stephen Baxter.
Goals: 37' Diogo Jota 1-0, 90+3' Rúben Vinagre 2-0.
Referee: Kristoffer Karlsson (SWE)   Attendance: 29,708.

25.07.19   Vodafone-Völlurin, Reykjavík:
   Valur Reykjavík – PFC Ludogorets Razgrad 1-1 (1-0)
Valur Reykjavík: Anton Ari Einarsson, Birkir Sævarsson, Eidur Sigurbjörnsson, Orri Ómarsson, Sebastian Hedlund, Kaj Leo í Bartalsstovu, Einar Karl Ingvarsson (67' Kristinn Sigurdsson), Lasse Petry, Kristinn Halldórsson (71' Bjarni Eiríksson), Ívar Jónsson, Patrick Pedersen (88' Birnir Snær Ingason). Coach: Ólafur Jóhannesson.
PFC Ludogorets Razgrad: Plamen Iliev, Cicinho (88' Jody Lukoki), Georgi Terziev, Rafael Forster, Anton Nedyalkov, Anicet Andrianantenaina, Jacek Góralski, Stéphane Badji (70' Jakub Swierczok), Claudiu Keserü, Mavis Tchibota (61' Wanderson), Jorginho.
Coach: Stoicho Stoev.
Goals: 11' Lasse Petry 1-0, 90+2' Anicet Andrianantenaina 1-1.
Referee: Georgios Kominis (GRE)   Attendance: 802.

25.07.19   Stadio Giuseppe Moccagatta, Alessandria: Torino FC – Debreceni VSC 3-0 (2-0)
Torino FC: Salvatore Sirigu, Lorenzo De Silvestri, Cristian Ansaldi, Nicolas N'Koulou, Armando Izzo, Bremer, Soualiho Meïté, Daniele Baselli, Iago Falqué (75' Sasa Lukic), Andrea Belotti, Álex Berenguer (80' Simone Zaza). Coach: Walter Mazzarri.
Debreceni VSC: Sándor Nagy, János Ferenczi, Ákos Kinyik (74' Erik Kusnyír), Csaba Szatmári, Bence Pávkovics, Dániel Tözsér, Nikola Trujic, Kevin Varga (86' Ádám Pintér), Attila Haris, Márk Szécsi, Dániel Zsóri (46' Haruna Garba). Coach: András Herczeg.
Goals: 20' Andrea Belotti 1-0 (p), 42' Cristian Ansaldi 2-0, 90+3' Simone Zaza 3-0.
Referee: Jens Maae (DEN)   Attendance: 4,376.

Torino FC played their home match at Stadio Giuseppe Moccagatta, Alessandria, instead of their regular stadium Stadio Olimpico Grande Torino, Torino.

25.07.19   Stadion Miejski Legii Warszawa im. Marszalka Józefa Pilsudskiego, Warszawa:
   Legia Warszawa – Kuopion PS 1-0 (1-0)
Legia Warszawa: Radoslaw Majecki, Artur Jedrzejczyk, Luís Rocha (81' Pawel Stolarski), Mateusz Wieteska, Arvydas Novikovas, Marko Vesovic, André Martins, Dominik Nagy (61' Luquinhas), Valeriane Gvilia (73' Domagoj Antolic), Carlitos López, Sandro Kulenovic.
Coach: Aleksandar Vukovic.
Kuopion PS: Otso Virtanen, Babacar Diallo, Luis Murillo, Luc Tabi Manga (65' Saku Savolainen), Vinko Soldo, Petteri Pennanen, Reuben Ayarna, Ville Saxman, Ilmari Niskanen, Issa Thiaw (74' Ariel Ngueukam), Rangel (80' Tommi Jyry). Coach: Jani Honkavaara.
Goal: 9' Mateusz Wieteska 1-0.
Referee: Ivan Bebek (CRO)   Attendance: 11,678.

25.07.19   RCDE Stadium, Cornella de Llobregat: RCD Espanyol – UMF Stjarnan 4-0 (0-0)
RCD Espanyol: Diego López, Javi López, Naldo, Lluís López, Adrià Pedrosa (74' Dídac Vilà), Granero (54' Lei Wu), Víctor Sánchez (54' Marc Roca), Sergi Darder, Melendo, Facundo Ferreyra, Borja Iglesias. Coach: David Gallego.
UMF Stjarnan: Haraldur Björnsson, Brynjar Gudjónsson, Daníel Laxdal (64' Thorri Geir Rúnarsson), Jóhann Laxdal, Martin Rauschenberg Brorsen, Eyjólfur Hédinsson, Thorsteinn Már Ragnarsson, Heidar Ægisson, Alex Thór Hauksson (82' Sölvi Gudbjargarson), Gudmundur Hafsteinsson (46' Gudjón Baldvinsson), Hilmar Árni Halldórsson.
Coach: Rúnar Sigmundsson.
Goals: 49', 57' Facundo Ferreyra 1-0, 2-0, 60', 68' Borja Iglesias 3-0, 4-0.
Referee: Alain Durieux (LUX)   Attendance: 19,122.

25.07.19 Tallaght Stadium, Dublin: Shamrock Rovers – Apollon Limassol 2-1 (1-1)
Shamrock Rovers: Alan Mannus, Joey O'Brien, Sean Kavanagh, Roberto Lopes, Ethan Boyle, Lee Grace, Ronan Finn (77' Gary O'Neill), Greg Bolger, Aaron McEneff (85' Dylan Watts), Jack Byrne, Daniel Carr (64' Aaron Greene). Coach: Stephen Bradley.
Apollon Limassol: Joël Mall, Attila Szalai, Ioannis Pittas (61' Serge Gakpé), Vincent Bessat, Héctor Yuste, Sasa Markovic, Esteban Sachetti, Emilio Zelaya (81' Facundo Pereyra), João Pedro, Fotios Papoulis (72' Diego Aguirre), Giannis Gianniotas. Coach: Sofronis Avgousti.
Goals: 5' Fotios Papoulis 0-1, 14' Lee Grace 1-1, 58' Roberto Lopes 2-1.
Referee: Stephan Klossner (SUI)   Attendance: 5,396.
Sent off: 83' Esteban Sachetti.

30.07.19 Marijampolés sporto centro stadione, Marijampolé:
    FK Sūduva Marijampolé – SP Tre Penne 5-0 (3-0)
FK Sūdova Marijampolé: Ivan Kardum, Algis Jankauskas, Andro Svrljuga, Aleksandar Zivanovic, Semir Kerla, Jovan Cadjenovic, Ovidijus Verbickas, Giedrius Matulevicius (77' Povilas Leimonas), Josip Tadic (81' Sandro Gotal), Mihret Topcagic (64' Tosaint Ricketts), Paulius Golubickas. Coach: Vladimir Cheburin.
SP Tre Penne: Mattia Migani, Mirko Palazzi, Andrea Rossi, Alex Gasperoni, Nicola Chiaruzzi, Enrico Cibelli, Stefano Fraternali, Matteo Semprini (87' Giacomo Zafferani), Francesco Perrotta (90+3' Simone Nanni), Luca Ceccaroli (90+2' Andrea Zanotti), Luca Sorrentino. Coach: Stefano Ceci.
Goals: 14' Josip Tadic 1-0, 17' Semir Kerla 2-0, 39', 55' Mihret Topcagic 3-0, 4-0, 89' Sandro Gotal 5-0.
Referee: Artyom Kuchin (KAZ)   Attendance: 1,850.

30.07.19 Victoria Stadium, Gibraltar: Lincoln Red Imps – FC Ararat-Armenia 1-2 (0-1)
Lincoln Red Imps: Lolo Soler, Joseph Chipolina, Bernardo Lopes, Jesús Toscano, Roy Chipolina (67' Ethan Britto), Federico Cataruozzolo (46' Sergio Molina), Borja Gil, Gato, Falu Aranda, Anthony Hernandez, Kike Gómez (27' James Coombes). Coach: Víctor Afonso.
FC Ararat-Armenia: Stefan Cupic, Rochdi Achenteh, Dmitri Guzj, Ângelo Meneses, Georgi Pashov (59' Artur Danielyan), Ilja Antonov, Kódjo Alphonse (77' Gor Malakyan), Petros Avetisyan, Furdjel Narsingh, Louis Ogana, Zakaria Sanogo (63' Alex Júnior Christian). Coach: Vardan Minasyan.
Goals: 45+1', 58' Louis Ogana 0-1, 0-2, 74' Anthony Hernandez 1-2.
Referee: Alexandre Boucaut (BEL)   Attendance: 684.

30.07.19 Stade Josy Barthel, Luxembourg: F91 Dudelange – KF Shkëndija 79 1-1 (0-0)
F91 Dudelange: Tim Kips, Tom Schnell, Ricardo Delgado, Mehdi Kirch, Mohamed Bouchouari, Mario Pokar (90' Mickaël Garos), Dominik Stolz, Charles Morren, Danel Sinani, Adel Bettaieb (63' Laurent Pomponi), Antoine Bernier (84' Omar Natami).
Coach: Emilio Ferrera.
KF Shkëndija 79: Kostadin Zahov, Gledi Mici, Mevlan Murati (83' Konstantin Cheshmedzhiev), Visar Musliu, Egzon Bejtulai, Armend Alimi, Zeni Husmani, Besart Ibraimi (77' Omar Imeri), Agim Ibraimi, Juan Felipe Alves (66' Valjmir Nafiu), Marjan Radeski.
Coach: Qatip Osmani.
Goals: 78' Ricardo Delgado 1-0, 90+2' Agim Ibraimi 1-1.
Referee: Iwan Arwel Griffith (WAL)   Attendance: 1,022.
Sent off: 84' Visar Musliu, 90+4' Valjmir Nafiu, 90+5' Agim Ibraimi.

F91 Dudelange played their home match at Stade Josy Barthel, Luxembourg, instead of their regular stadium Stade Jos Nosbaum, Dudelange.

30.07.19   Stadiumi Fadil Vokrri, Pristina: KF Feronikeli – Slovan Bratislava 0-2 (0-1)
KF Feronikeli: Florian Smakiqi, Lapidar Lladrovci, Arber Prekazi, Perparim Islami (68' Jetmir Topalli), Jean Carioca, Yll Hoxha, Albert Dabiqaj, Kastriot Rexha, Besmir Bojku (60' Mevlan Zeka), Astrit Fazliu, Mendurim Hoti (76' Milos Krkotic).
Coaches: Zekirija Ramadani & Dejan Vukicevic.
Slovan Bratislava: Dominik Greif, Vasil Bozhikov, Vernon, Jurij Medvedev, Myenty Abena, Dávid Holman (66' Nono Delgado), Joeri de Kamps, Erik Daniel (72' Rafael Ratão), Kenan Bajric (83' Dávid Strelec), "Moha" Mohammed Rharsalla, Andraz Sporar. Coach: Ján Kozák.
Goals: 19' Vernon 0-1, 54' Dávid Holman 0-2.
Referee: Yigal Frid (ISR)   Attendance: 5,250.
Sent off: 88' Mevlan Zeka.

KF Feronikeli played their home match at Stadiumi Fadil Vokrri, Pristina, instead of their regular stadium Rexhep Rexhepi Stadium, Drenas which did not meet UEFA requirements.

31.07.19   Stadion na Banovom brdu, Beograd: FK Cukaricki-Stankom – Molde FK 1-3 (0-2)
FK Cukaricki-Stankom: Nemanja Belic, Miroslav Bogosavac, Darko Puskaric, Nikola Cirkovic, Luka Stojanovic (46' Milutin Vidosavljevic), Marko Docic, Samuel Owusu, Stefan Kovac (81' Kosta Aleksic), Stefan Sapic, Aleksandar Djordjevic (70' Asmir Kajevic), Slobodan Tedic. Coach: Aleksander Veselinovic.
Molde FK: Álex Craninx, Vegard Forren, Kristoffer Haraldseid, Kristoffer Haugen, Martin Bjørnbak, Magnus Eikrem (79' Martin Ellingsen), Etzaz Hussain, Eirik Hestad, Fredrik Aursnes, Ohi Omoijuanfo (70' Erling Knudtzon), Leke James (87' Mathis Bolly).
Coach: Erling Moe.
Goals: 4' Ohi Omoijuanfo 0-1, 38' Magnus Eikrem 0-2, 78' Erling Knudtzon 0-3, 82' Asmir Kajevic 1-3.
Referee: Mykola Balakin (UKR)   Attendance: 3,014.

01.08.19   Astana Arena, Astana: FK Astana – FC Santa Coloma 4-1 (1-1)
FK Astana: Nenad Eric, Antonio Rukavina, Yuriy Logvinenko, Marin Anicic, Dmitriy Shomko, Evgeny Postnikov, Rúnar Sigurjónsson (63' Roman Murtazaev), Ivan Maevski, Rangelo Janga (89' Yuriy Pertsukh), Dorin Rotariu, Ndombe Mubele (60' Marin Tomasov). Coach: Roman Grygorchuk.
FC Santa Coloma: Eloy Casals, Moisés San Nicolás, Enric Pi, Marc Rebés, Andreu Ramos (74' Nicolás Medina), Juanma Miranda, Chus Sosa (78' Diego Nájero), Pedro Santos, Jordi Aláez (80' Albert Mercadé), Aleix Cistero, André Azevedo. Coach: Marc Rodríguez Rebull.
Goals: 7' Enric Pi 0-1, 24' Rúnar Sigurjónsson 1-1 (p), 73', 79',
90+4' Marin Tomasov 2-1, 3-1, 4-1.
Referee: Giorgi Kruashvili (GEO)   Attendance: 16,103.

01.08.19   Stadion Qajimuqan Muñaytpasov, Shymkent:
           FK Ordabasy – FK Mladá Boleslav 2-3 (1-2)
FK Ordabasy: Dmytro Nepogodov, Pablo Fontanello, Sergiy Maliy (46' João Paulo), Temirlan Yerlanov, Marat Bystrov, Abdoulaye Diakhaté, May Mahlangu (59' Kyrylo Kovalchuk), Timur Dosmagambetov, Mirzad Mehanovic, Ziguy Badibanga, Aleksey Shchetkin (72' Toktar Zhangylyshbay). Coach: Kakhaber Tskhadadze.
FK Mladá Boleslav: Jan Seda, Daniel Pudil, Laco Takács, Antonín Krapka, Marco Tulio, Marek Matejovsky, Michal Hubínek, Tomás Ladra (66' Jakub Fulnek), Pavel Bucha (83' Jonas Auer), Muris Mesanovic (90+3' Jakub Klíma), Nikolay Komlichenko. Coach: Jozef Weber.
Goals: 8' Marek Matejovsky 0-1, 33' Nikolay Komlichenko 0-2 (p), 45' Aleksey Shchetkin 1-2, 47' Muris Mesanovic 1-3, 56' Abdoulaye Diakhaté 2-3 (p).
Referee: Mads-Kristoffer Kristoffersen (DEN)   Attendance: 17,000.

01.08.19   Ortaliq Stadion, Almaty: FK Kairat – Hapoel Be'er Sheva 1-1 (1-0)
FK Kairat: Stas Pokatilov, Eldos Akhmetov, Gafurzhan Suyombaev, Dino Mikanovic, Rade Dugalic (66' Márton Eppel), Aybol Abiken, Islambek Kuat, Bauyrzhan Islamkhan (83' Konrad Wrzesinski), Georgiy Zhukov, Aderinsola Eseola, Yerkebulan Seidakhmet (66' Ramazan Orazov). Coach: Aleksey Shpilevski.
Hapoel Be'er Sheva: Ernestas Setkus, Miguel Vítor (46' Amit Biton), Ben Bitton, Loai Taha, Sean Goldberg, Marwan Kabha, Ramzi Safouri (67' Ben Sahar), Eden Shamir, David Keltjens, Jimmy Marín, Nigel Hasselbaink (75' Niv Zrihan). Coach: Barak Bakhar.
Goals: 40', 63' Rade Dugalic 1-0, 1-1 (og).
Referee: Ola Hobber Nilsen (NOR)   Attendance: 23,000.
Sent off: 55' Eldos Akhmetov, 88' Vladimir Plotnikov (*not used sub*), 90+6' Gafurzhan Suyombaev.

01.08.19   Stadionul Central, Ovidiu: FC Viitorul Constanta – KAA Gent 2-1 (0-1)
FC Viitorul Constanta: Catalin Cabuz, Sebastian Mladen, Virgil Ghita, Bradley de Nooijer, Vlad Achim, Bogdan Tîru, Andrei Artean (62' Eric de Oliveira), Lyes Houri, Alexandru Matan (55' Steliano Filip), Gabriel Iancu, George Ganea (73' Andreas Calcan). Coach: Gheorghe Hagi.
KAA Gent: Thomas Kaminski, Nana Asare, Mikael Lustig, Igor Plastun, Michael Ngadeu-Ngadjui, Vadis Odjidja-Ofoe, Brecht Dejaegere (57' Louis Verstraete), Elisha Owusu, Yuya Kubo (59' Roman Bezus), Roman Yaremchuk (88' Mamadou Sylla), Jonathan David. Coach: Jess Thorup.
Goals: 38' Roman Yaremchuk 0-1, 47', 61' Gabriel Iancu 1-1 (p), 2-1 (p).
Referee: José Luis Munuera Montero (ESP)   Attendance: 4,088.

01.08.19   Savon Sanomat Areena, Kuopio: Kuopion PS – Legia Warszawa 0-0
Kuopion PS: Otso Virtanen, Babacar Diallo, Luis Murillo, Luc Tabi Manga, Vinko Soldo, Petteri Pennanen, Reuben Ayarna, Ville Saxman (76' Ats Purje), Ilmari Niskanen, Issa Thiaw (89' Ariel Ngueukam), Rangel. Coach: Jani Honkavaara.
Legia Warszawa: Radoslaw Majecki, Artur Jedrzejczyk, William Rémy (66' Igor Lewczuk), Luís Rocha, Arvydas Novikovas, Marko Vesovic, André Martins, Dominik Nagy (90+1' Tomasz Jodlowiec), Valeriane Gvilia, Carlitos López (61' Domagoj Antolic), Sandro Kulenovic. Coach: Aleksandar Vukovic.
Referee: Lawrence Visser (BEL)   Attendance: 3,200.

01.08.19   Slavutych-Arena, Zaporizhia: Zorya Luhansk – FC Buducnost Podgorica 1-0 (1-0)
Zorya Luhansk: Zauri Makharadze, Vitaliy Vernidub, Oleksandr Tymchyk (64' Nikita Kamenyuka), Joel Abu Hanna, Artem Gromov (61' Vladyslav Kabayev), Dmytro Khomchenovsky, Dmitriy Ivanisenya, Yevgen Cheberko, Vladyslav Kochergin (68' Igor Chaykovskiy), Bohdan Lednev, Maksym Lunyov. Coach: Viktor Skripnik.
FC Buducnost Podgorica: Milos Dragojevic, Dejan Boljevic, Luka Mirkovic, Nikola Djuric, Stefan Milic, Drasko Bozovic, Petar Grbic (53' Milos Raickovic), Milos Mijic, Vasilije Terzic, Mihailo Perovic (37' Bojan Roganovic), Dusan Stoiljkovic (75' Dejan Zarubica). Coach: Branko Brnovic.
Goal: 32' Artem Gromov 1-0.
Referee: Neil Doyle (IRL)   Attendance: 6,158.
Sent off: 33' Nikola Djuric, 34' Drasko Bozovic.

Zorya Luhansk played their home match at Slavutych-Arena, Zaporizhia, Instead of their regular stadium Avanhard Stadium, Luhansk, due to the war conditions in Eastern Ukraine.

01.08.19   Stadionul Ion Oblemenco, Craiova:
           CS Universitatea Craiova – Budapest Honvéd 0-0 (a.e.t.)
CS Universitatea Craiova: Mirko Pigliacelli, Renato Kelic, Ivan Martic (13' Marius Briceag), Nicusor Bancu, Stephane Acka, Alexandru Mateiu, Bogdan Vatajelu (63' Alexandru Ionita), Cristian Barbut, Antoni Ivanov (75' Kamer Qaka), Alexandru Cicâldau, Mihai Roman (II) (94' Carlos Fortes). Coach: Corneliu Papura.
Budapest Honvéd: Rubi Levkovic (40' Attila Berla), Ivan Lovric, Djordje Kamber, Bence Batik, Patrick George Ikenne-King, Federico Moretti (73' Eke Uzoma), Tonci Kukoc (92' MacDonald Niba Ngwa), Barna Kesztyüs, Bence Banó-Szabó, Vladyslav Kulach (78' David N'Gog), Amadou Moutari. Coach: Giuseppe Sannino.
Referee: Arnold Hunter (NIR)   Attendance: 22,134.

CS Universitatea Craiova won on penalties after extra (3-1).
Penalties: Kamber missed, Ionita 0-1, Batik missed, Carlos Fortes 0-2, N'Gog 1-2, Cicaldau 1-3, Banó-Szabó missed.

01.08.19   Stadions Skonto, Riga: Riga FC – Piast Gliwice 2-1 (1-1)
Riga FC: Roberts Ozols, Georgios Valerianos, Herdi Prenga, Stefan Panic, Aleksejs Visnakovs (67' Deniss Rakels), Vyacheslav Sharpar (61' Olegs Laizāns), Felipe Brisola, Roger, Armands Pētersons, Elvis Stuglis, Roman Debelko (80' Kamil Bilinski). Coach: Mihails Konevs.
Piast Gliwice: Frantisek Plach, Uros Korun, Batosz Rymaniak, Mikkel Kirkeskov, Jakub Czerwinski, Martin Konczkowski, Tom Hateley (86' Aleksander Jagiello), Gerard Badía (69' Patryk Sokolowski), Patryk Dziczek, Piotr Parzyszek (58' Dominik Steczyk), Jorge Félix. Coach: Waldemar Fornalik.
Goals: 20' Jorge Félix 0-1, 26' Armands Pētersons 1-1, 83' Kamil Bilinski 2-1.
Referee: Eitan Shmuelevich (ISR)   Attendance: 3,541.

Riga FC won on away goals.

01.08.19   Vivacom Arena – Georgi Asparuhov, Sofia: Levski Sofia – AEK Larnaca 0-4 (0-2)
Levski Sofia: Milan Mijatovic, Nuno Reis, Ivan Goranov, Diyan Ivanov, Martin Raynov, Khaly Thiam (5' Iliya Yurukov), Ivaylo Naydenov, Stanislav Kostov (52' Franco Mazurek), Paulinho, Nigel Robertha, Stanislav Ivanov (68' Zdravko Dimitrov). Coach: Petar Hubchev.
AEK Larnaca: Toño, Mikel González, Daniel Mojsov, Truyols (70' Simranjit Thandi), Ivan Trickovski, Lluis Sastre, Acorán, Nacho Cases (75' Florian Taulemesse), Hector Hevel, Raúl Ruiz (54' Tete), Apostolos Giannou. Coach: Imanol Idiakez.
Goals: 8', 29', 75', 82' Ivan Trickovski 0-1 (p), 0-2, 0-3, 0-4.
Referee: Glenn Nyberg (SWE)   Attendance: 550.

01.08.19   Nagyerdei Stadion, Debrecen: Debreceni VSC – Torino FC 1-4 (0-2)
Debreceni VSC: Sándor Nagy, János Ferenczi, Csaba Szatmári, Bence Pávkovics, Erik Kusnyír, Dániel Tözsér, Nikola Trujic (90' Richárd Csösz), Kevin Varga (63' Dániel Zsóri), Attila Haris, Márk Szécsi, Haruna Garba (80' Temitope Adeniji). Coach: András Herczeg.
Torino FC: Salvatore Sirigu, Lorenzo De Silvestri, Cristian Ansaldi, Nicolas N'Koulou, Armando Izzo (83' Wilfried Singo), Bremer, Soualiho Meïté, Daniele Baselli (45' Tomás Rincón), Simone Zaza, Andrea Belotti (76' Vincenzo Millico), Álex Berenguer.
Coach: Walter Mazzarri.
Goals: 25' Simone Zaza 0-1, 32' Armando Izzo 0-2, 52' Haruna Garba 1-2, 69' Andrea Belotti 1-3, 90+2' Vincenzo Millico 1-4.
Referee: Fran Jovic (CRO)   Attendance: 15,350.

01.08.19 Bravida Arena, Göteborg: BK Häcken – AZ Alkmaar 0-3 (0-1)
BK Häcken: Peter Abrahamsson, Joona Toivio, Óskar Sverrisson, Elohor Ekpolo (75' Adam Andersson), Rasmus Lindgren, Erik Friberg (85' Gustav Berggren), Ahmed Yasin, Alexander Faltsetas, Daleho Irandust, Paulinho (65' Ali Youssef), Kwame Kizito. Coach: Andreas Alm.
AZ Alkmaar: Marco Bizot, Ron Vlaar, Stijn Wuytens, Pantelis Hatzidiakos, Owen Wijndal, Fredrik Midtsjø, Teun Koopmeiners, Guus Til (73' Jordy Clasie), Oussama Idrissi (68' Thomas Ouwejan), Myron Boadu (79' Ferdy Druijf), Calvin Stengs. Coach: Arne Slot.
Goals: 42' Myron Boadu 0-1, 56' Calvin Stengs 0-2, 67' Oussama Idrissi 0-3.
Referee: Frank Schneider (FRA)   Attendance: 3,845.

01.08.19 Bolshaya Sportivnaya Arenan, Tiraspol:
FC Sheriff Tiraspol – FK Partizani Tirana 1-1 (0-1)
FC Sheriff Tiraspol: Zvonimir Mikulic, Artem Hordienko (46' Veaceslav Posmac), Ousmane N'Diaye, Mateo Muzek, Cristiano, Wilfried Balima, Jury Kendysh, Gheorghe Anton, Liridon Latifi (84' Jaroslaw Jach), Gabrijel Boban (90+3' Maxim Cojocaru (I)), Robert Tambe. Coach: Zoran Zekic.
FK Partizani Tirana: Alban Hoxha (I), Egzon Belica, Lorenc Trashi (79' Eraldo Çinari), Deian Boldor, Enea Bitri, Bruno Telushi, William Cordeiro (87' Jurgen Bardhi), Ron Broja, Esat Mala, Jasir Asani (70' Brian Brown), Theophilus Solomon. Coach: Franco Lerda.
Goals: 29' Jasir Asani 0-1, 63' Ousmane N'Diaye 1-1.
Referee: Igor Pajac (CRO)   Attendance: 5,248.

01.08.19 Stadions Daugava, Liepāja: FK Liepāja – IFK Norrköping 0-1 (0-0)
FK Liepāja: Valentins Ralkevics, Vadims Zulevs (82' Vügar Asgarov), Deniss Ivanovs, Seydina Keita, Raivis Jurkovskis, Amâncio Fortes, Leonel Strumia, Kristers Tobers, Mārtins Kigurs (70' Raivis Vilumsons), Richard Friday (68' Danu Spataru), Dodô. Coach: Aleksandrs Starkovs.
IFK Norrköping: Isak Pettersson, Lars Gerson, Kasper Larsen, Filip Dagerstål, Rasmus Lauritsen, Gudmundur Thórarinsson (90+2' Henrik Castegren), Simon Thern (77' Andreas Blomqvist), Alexander Fransson, Christoffer Nyman, Simon Skrabb, Kalle Holmberg (56' Sead Haksabanovic). Coach: Jens Gustafsson.
Goal: 89' Sead Haksabanovic 0-1.
Referee: Marius Avram (ROM)   Attendance: 4,174.

01.08.19 Swedbank Stadion, Malmö: Malmö FF – NK Domzale 3-2 (2-2)
Malmö FF: Dusan Melichárek, Behrang Safari, Rasmus Bengtsson, Lasse Nielsen (46' Eric Larsson), Søren Rieks, Anders Christiansen, Fouad Bachirou, Oscar Lewicki, Markus Rosenberg, Jo Inge Berget (88' Franz Brorsson), Marcus Antonsson (87' Guillermo Molins). Coach: Uwe Rösler.
NK Domzale: Grega Sorcan, Gaber Dobrovoljc, Gregor Sikosek (84' Matej Podlogar), Tilen Klemencic, Sven Karic, Senijad Ibricic, Josip Corluka (88' Branko Ilic), Mattias Käit, Adam Gnezda Cerin, Tonci Mujan (59' Slobodan Vuk), Shamar Nicholson. Coach: Simon Rozman.
Goals: 12' Shamar Nicholson 0-1, 21' Oscar Lewicki 1-1, 32' Markus Rosenberg 2-1, 45+1' Sven Karic 2-2. 83' Rasmus Bengtsson 3-2.
Referee: Amaury Delerue (FRA)   Attendance: 12,348.

01.08.19 Rheinpark Stadion, Vaduz: FC Vaduz – MOL Vidi FC 2-0 (0-0, 1-0) (a.e.t.)
FC Vaduz: Benjamin Büchel, Maximilian Göppel, Pius Dorn, Yannick Schmid, Berkay Sülüngöz, Gianni Antoniazzi, Milan Gajic, Sandro Wieser (82' Boris Prokopic), Dominik Schwizer (114' Jens Hofer), Manuel Sutter (115' Noah Frick), Tunahan Çiçek (72' Mohamed Coulibaly). Coach: Mario Frick.
MOL Vidi FC: Ádam Kovácsik, Roland Juhász, Attila Fiola (46' Ivan Petryak), Loïc Négo, Stopira, Szabolcs Huszti (103' Armin Hodzic), Máté Pátkai, Ákos Elek, Georgi Milanov (64' István Kovács), Boban Nikolov, Marko Scepovic (83' Márkó Futács). Coach: Marko Nikolic.
Goals: 61' Milan Gajic 1-0 (p), 100' Mohamed Coulibaly 2-0.
Referee: Manfredas Lukjancukas (LTU)   Attendance: 1,253.
Sent off: 107' Gianni Antoniazzi.

FC Vaduz won after extra time.

01.08.19 Bakcell Arena, Baku: Neftçi PFK Baku – Arsenal Tula 3-0 (0-0)
Neftçi PFK Baku: Salahat Agayev, Vojislav Stankovic, Kyrylo Petrov, Anton Krivotsyuk, Omar Buludov, Soni Mustivar, Emin Makhmudov (62' Namiq Alasgarov), Mamadou Kane, Steeven Joseph-Monrose, Rauf Aliyev (77' Mamadou Mbodj), Dário Júnior da Silva (90+1' Rhman Hadzhiyev). Coach: Roberto Bordin.
Arsenal Tula: Mikhail Levashov, Kirill Kombarov (72' Lameck Banda), Gia Grigalava, Maxim Belyaev, Víctor Álvarez, Igor Gorbatenko, Sergey Tkachev, Georgi Kostadinov (80' Alexandru Tudorie), Goran Causic, Daniil Lesovoy, Evgeniy Lutsenko.
Coach: Igor Cherevchenko.
Goals: 49' Rauf Aliyev 1-0, 89' Dário Júnior da Silva 2-0 (p), 90+3' Mamadou Mbodj 3-0.
Referee: Alan Mario Sant (MLT)   Attendance: 9,000.

01.08.19 Boris Paichadze Dinamo Arena, Tbilisi: Dinamo Tbilisi – Gabala FK 3-0 (0-0)
Dinamo Tbilisi: José Perales, Giorgi Kimadze, Víctor Mongil, Nodar Iashvili (36' Gudzha Rukhaia), Davit Kobouri, Nika Ninua, Levan Kutalia (78' Kwame Karikari), Giorgi Kukhianidze, Giorgi Papava, Nodar Kavtaradze (69' Arfang Daffé), Levan Shengelia.
Coach: Félix Vicente Miranda.
Gabala FK: Anar Nazirov, Rasim Ramaldanov, Ivica Zunic (40' Sadig Quliyev), Asif Mammadov, Merab Gigauri, Amin Seydiyev, Qismat Aliyev, Christian Kouakou (81' Roman Hüseynov), Clésio, Fernán Ferreiro (72' Ulvu Isgandarov), Davit Volkovi.
Coach: Zaur Hasimov.
Goals: 68', 88' Levan Shengelia 1-0, 2-0, 90+3' Kwame Karikari 3-0.
Referee: Petri Viljanen (FIN)   Attendance: 8,153.

01.08.19 Svangaskard, Toftir: KÍ Klaksvík – FC Luzern 0-1 (0-1)
KÍ Klaksvík: Kristian Joensen, Jesper Brinck, Ísak Simonsen, Deni Pavlovic, Semir Hadzibulic (80' Torbjørn Grytten), Patrik Johannesen, Jákup Andreasen, Jóannes Bjartalíd, Simen Sandmæl (80' Jonn Johannesen), Jóannes Danielsen, Páll Klettskard.
Coach: Mikkjal Thomassen.
FC Luzern: Marius Müller, Christian Schwegler, Simon Grether, Lucas Alves "Lucão", Marvin Schulz (68' Remo Arnold), Stefan Knezevic, Idriz Voca, Pascal Schürpf (62' Otar Kakabadze), Tsiy William Ndenge, Shkelqim Demhasaj (83' Francesco Margiotta), Blessing Eleke.
Coach: Thomas Häberli.
Goal: 34' Idriz Voca 0-1.
Referee: Martin Strömbergsson (SWE)   Attendance: 1,229.

KÍ Klaksvík played their home match at Svangaskard, Toftir, instead of their regular stadium Vid Djúpumyar, Klaksvík which did not meet UEFA requirements.

01.08.19   Stadion pod Bijelim Brijegom, Mostar:
Zrinjski Mostar – FC Utrecht 2-1 (0-1, 1-1) (a.e.t.)
Zrinjski Mostar: Ivan Brkic, Tomislav Barbaric, Dario Rugasevic, Slobodan Jakovljevic, Advan Kadusic, Damir Sovsic, Frane Cirjak (59' Ivan Curjuric), Edin Rustemovic (78' Semir Pezer), Miljan Govedarica (87' Mario Ticinovic), Stanisa Mandic, Irfan Hadzic (103' Ivan Lendric). Coach: Hari Vukas.
FC Utrecht: David Jensen, Willem Janssen, Emil Bergström, Leon Guwara, Sean Klaiber (87' Giovanni Troupée), Adam Maher, Sander van de Streek, Simon Gustafson, Justin Lonwijk (80' Joris van Overeem), Vaclav Cerny (66' Issah Abass), Gyrano Kerk (105' Urby Emanuelson). Coach: John van den Brom.
Goals: 45+1' Simon Gustafson 0-1, 65' Irfan Hadzic 1-1, 111' Stanisa Mandic 2-1.
Referee: Antti Munukka (FIN)   Attendance: 5,984.

Zrinjski Mostar won after extra time.

01.08.19   Stadio Peristeriou, Athens: Atromitos FC – DAC Dunajská Streda 3-2 (2-0)
Atromitos FC: Balász Megyeri, Madson, Dimitrios Goutas, Spyros Risvanis, Alexandros Katranis, Javier Umbides (86' Spyridon Natsos), Kyriakos Kivrakidis, Charilaos Charisis, Georgios Manousos, Apostolos Vellios (60' Tal Kahila), Clarck N'Sikulu (70' Farley Rosa). Coach: Yannis Anastasiou.
DAC Dunajská Streda: Martin Jedlicka, Kristián Kostrna, Dominik Kruzliak, César Blackman (76' Marko Divkovic), Matej Oravec (62' Dominik Veselovsky), Zsolt Kalmár, Máté Vida, Lukás Cmelík (46' Kristopher Vida), Connor Ronan, Eric Ramírez, Abdulrahman Taiwo. Coach: Peter Hyballa.
Goals: 22' Alexandros Katranis 1-0, 28' Georgios Manousos 2-0 (p), 53' Eric Ramírez 2-1, 72' Zsolt Kalmár 2-2 (p), 76' Spyros Risvanis 3-2.
Referee: Mohammed Al-Hakim (SWE)   Attendance: 2,450.

01.08.19   Stadion Strelnice, Jablonec nad Nisou: FK Jablonec – Pyunik Yerevan FC 0-0
FK Jablonec: Jan Hanus, Jakub Jugas, Tomás Brecka, Libor Holík, Tomás Hübschman, Jakub Povazanez, Jan Sykora, Milos Kratochvíl (54' Jan Krob), Jan Matousek (76' Tomás Pilík), Martin Dolezal, Vladimir Jovovic (66' Jan Chramosta). Coach: Petr Rada.
Pyunik Yerevan FC: Andrija Dragojevic, Artak Yedigaryan (32' Artem Simonyan), Antonio Stankov, Maksim Zhestokov, Kristi Marku, Armen Manucharyan, Karlen Mkrtchyan, Sergiy Shevchuk, Stanislav Efimov, Erik Vardanyan, Artur Miranyan (90+2' Steven Alfred). Coach: Aleksandr Tarkhanov.
Referee: Sergey Lapochkin (RUS)   Attendance: 3,675.
Sent off: 87' Erik Vardanyan, 88' Tomás Brecka.

01.08.19   Sammy Ofer Stadium, Haifa: Maccabi Haifa – RC Strasbourg 2-1 (2-1)
Maccabi Haifa: Guy Haimov, Rami Gershon, Sun Menachem, Ofri Arad, Yuval Ashkenazi, Yosef Raz Meir, Allyson, Neta Lavi, Maxim Plakuschenko (72' Mohammed Abu Fani), Nikita Rukavytsya (63' Dolev Haziza), Yarden Shua (67' Muhamad Awad). Coach: Marco Balbul.
RC Strasbourg: Matz Sels (46' Bingourou Kamara), Lamine Koné, Stefan Mitrovic, Lionel Carole, Alexander Djiku, Mohamed Simakan, Jonas Martin, Dimitri Liénard, Adrien Thomasson (72' Nuno Da Costa), Youssouf Fofana, Ludovic Ajorque (86' Ibrahima Sissoko). Coach: Thierry Laurey.
Goals: 17' Ludovic Ajorque 0-1, 25' Yarden Shua 1-1, 40' Nikita Rukavytsya 2-1.
Referee: Maurizio Mariani (ITA)   Attendance: 23,038.

01.08.19 AEK Arena – Georgios Karapatakis, Larnaca:
 AEL Limassol – Aris Saloniki 0-1 (0-1)
AEL Limassol: Vózinha, Nils Teixeira (65' Jarchinio Antonia), Boris Godál, André Teixeira, Christos Wheeler (52' Andreas Avraam), Adnan Aganovic, Marko Adamovic, Jon Gaztañaga, Davor Zdravkovski, Gevorg Ghazaryan, Rubén Jurado (52' Ivan Carlos).
Coach: Dusan Kerkez.
Aris Saloniki: Julián Cuesta, Daniel Sundgren, Mihály Korhut, Lindsay Rose, Fran Vélez, Nicolas Diguiny, Migjen Basha, Javier Matilla, Ioannis Fetfatzidis (68' Lucas Sasha), Daniel Larsson (61' Martín Tonso), Brown Ideye (86' Nicolás Martínez). Coach: Savvas Pantelidis.
Goal: 14' Nicolas Diguiny 0-1 (p).
Referee: Jorge de Sousa (POR)   Attendance: 3,346.
Sent off: 83' Boris Godál.

AEL Limassol played their home match at AEK Arena – Georgios Karapatakis, Larnaca, instead of their regular stadium Tsirio Stadium, Limassol.

01.08.19 Neo GSP Stadium, Nicosia:
 Apollon Limassol – Shamrock Rovers 3-1 (1-0, 2-1) (a.e.t.)
Apollon Limassol: Joël Mall, Charis Kyriakou (105' Facundo Pereyra), Héctor Yuste, Sasa Markovic, Diego Aguirre, Roger Tamba M'Pinda (58' Attila Szalai), Serge Gakpé (77' Adrián Sardinero), Emilio Zelaya, João Pedro, Fotios Papoulis, Giannis Gianniotas (90' Ioannis Pittas). Coach: Sofronis Avgousti.
Shamrock Rovers: Alan Mannus, Joey O'Brien (83' Dylan Watts), Sean Kavanagh, Roberto Lopes, Ethan Boyle, Lee Grace, Ronan Finn (86' Daniel Carr), Greg Bolger (105' Thomas Oluwya), Aaron McEneff (75' Gary O'Neill), Jack Byrne, Aaron Greene.
Coach: Stephen Bradley.
Goals: 18' Emilio Zelaya 1-0, 64' Attila Szalai 2-0, 69' Aaron Greene 2-1,
102' Adrián Sardinero 3-1.
Referee: Michael Tykgaard (DEN)   Attendance: 2,987.
Sent off: 67' Fotios Papoulis, 92' Lee Grace.

Apollon Limassol won after extra time.

Apollon Limassol played their home match at Neo GSP Stadium, Nicosia, instead of their regular stadium Tsirio Stadium, Limassol.

01.08.19 Ludogorets Arena, Razgrad: PFC Ludogorets Razgrad – Valur Reykjavík 4-0 (2-0)
PFC Ludogorets Razgrad: Plamen Iliev, Georgi Terziev, Rafael Forster, Jordan Ikoko, Anton Nedyalkov, Anicet Andrianantenaina, Jacek Góralski, Dan Biton, Claudiu Keserü (79' Jakub Swierczok), Mavis Tchibota (64' Wanderson), Jorginho (84' Jody Lukoki).
Coach: Stoicho Stoev.
Valur Reykjavík: Hannes Halldórsson (46' Anton Ari Einarsson), Birkir Sævarsson, Eidur Sigurbjörnsson, Sebastian Hedlund, Haukur Sigurdsson, Kristinn Sigurdsson (66' Ólafur Finsen), Kaj Leo í Bartalsstovu, Lasse Petry (72' Orri Ómarsson), Kristinn Halldórsson, Ívar Jónsson, Patrick Pedersen. Coach: Ólafur Jóhannesson.
Goals: 7' Sebastian Hedlund 1-0 (og), 24' Jordan Ikoko 2-0,
82', 84' Jakub Swierczok 3-0, 4-0.
Referee: Pavel Orel (CZE)   Attendance: 4,120.

01.08.19   Brøndby Stadion, Brøndby: Brøndby IF – Lechia Gdansk 4-1 (1-0, 2-1) (a.e.t.)
Brøndby IF: Marvin Schwäbe, Paulus Arajuuri, Anthony Jung, Hjörtur Hermannsson, Dominik Kaiser, Lasse Vigen Christensen (78' Tobias Børkeeiet), Josip Radosevic, Simon Tibbling (70' Mikael Uhre), Simon Hedlund (90' Jesper Lindstrøm), Kamil Wilczek, Kevin Mensah (119' Jens Gammelby). Coach: Niels Frederiksen.
Lechia Gdansk: Dusan Kuciak, Blazej Augustyn, Zarko Udovicic (57' Slawomir Peszko), Filip Mladenovic, Michal Nalepa, Daniel Lukasik (57' Maciej Gajos), Lukás Haraslín (97' Rafal Wolski), Patryk Lipski, Tomasz Makowski, Karol Fila, Flávio Paixão (97' Artur Sobiech). Coach: Piotr Stokowiec.
Goals: 15' Paulus Arajuuri 1-0, 53' Kamil Wilczek 2-0, 67' Flávio Paixão 2-1, 94', 118' Jesper Lindstrøm 3-1, 4-1.
Referee: Miroslav Zelinka (CZE)   Attendance: 16,426.

Brøndby IF won after extra time.

01.08.19   Stade Josy Barthel, Luxembourg: Progrès Niedercorn – Glasgow Rangers FC 0-0
Progrès Niederkorn: Sebastian Flauss, Adrien Ferino, Ben Vogel, Metin Karayer, Tim Hall, Yann Matias Marques, Emmanuel Françoise (84' Kempes Tekiela), Sébastien Thill (64' Florik Shala), Christian Silaj, Mayron De Almeida, Jacky Mmaee (70' Issa Bah). Coach: Roland Vrabec.
Glasgow Rangers FC: Allan McGregor, James Tavernier, Connor Goldson, Borna Barisic (46' Andy Halliday), Nikola Katic, Scott Arfield (76' Greg Docherty), Ryan Jack, Glen Kamara, Joe Aribo, Jermain Defoe (76' Alfredo Morelos), Sheyi Ojo. Coach: Steven Gerrard.
Referee: Ivaylo Stoyanov (BUL)   Attendance: 3,867.

Progrès Niederkorn played their home match at Stade Josy Barthel, Luxembourg, instead of their regular stadium, Stade Jos Haupert, Niederkorn.

01.08.19   Blue Water Arena, Esbjerg: Esbjerg fB – Shakhtyor Soligorsk 0-0
Esbjerg fB: Jeppe Højbjerg, Rudolph Austin (63' Mark Brink), Jesper Lauridsen, Viktor Tranberg, Daniel Anyembe, Joni Kauko, Lasha Parunashvili, Nicklas Røjkjær (63' Yury Yakovenko), Jacob Sørensen, Pyry Soiri (72' Mathias Kristensen), Adrian Petre. Coach: John Lammers.
Shakhtyor Soligorsk: Andrey Klimovich, Pavel Rybak, Sergey Matvejchik, Igor Burko (77' Mykyta Tatarkov), Nikola Antic, Sergey Balanovich (83' Nikolai Yanush), Aleksandr Sachivko, Yuri Kovalev, Július Szöke, Max Ebong Ngome, Elis Bakaj (88' Vladimir Khvashchinskiy). Coach: Sergey Tashuev.
Referee: Duje Strukan (CRO)   Attendance: 4,517.
Sent off: 90' Július Szöke.

01.08.19   Stadion Stozice, Ljubljana: Olimpija Ljubljana – Yeni Malatyaspor 0-1 (0-0)
Olimpija Ljubljana: Nejc Vidmar, Miral Samardzic, Macky Frank Bagnack, Eric Boakye, Marko Putincanin (87' Goran Brkic), Asmir Suljic (16' Luka Menalo), Stefan Savic (68' Vitja Valencic), Tomislav Tomic, Endri Çekiçi, Ante Vukusic, Mario Jurcevic. Coach: Safet Hadzic.
Yeni Malatyaspor: Fabien Farnolle, Erkan Kas (69' Eren Tozlu), Mustafa Akbas, Issam Chebake, Arturo Mina, Murat Yildirim (61' Guilherme), Robin Yalçin, Rahman Bugra Çagiran, Adis Jahovic, Thievy Bifouma, Moryké Fofana (61' Gökhan Töre). Coach: Sergen Yalçin.
Goal: 77' Adis Jahovic 0-1.
Referee: Filip Glova (SVK)   Attendance: 7,812.
Sent off: 38' Endri Çekiçi.

01.08.19   MFA Centenary Stadium, Ta'Qali: Gzira United – FK Ventspils 2-2 (1-0)
Gzira United: Justin Haber, Arthur Henrique, Rodolfo Soares, Fernando Barbosa, Nicky Muscat, Andrew Cohen, Hamed Koné, Gianmarco Conti, Juan Corbalan, Amadou Samb (80' Zachary Scerri), Jefferson. Coach: Giovanni Tedesco.
FK Ventspils: Konstantin Machnovskiy, Jean Alcénat, Abdoul Mamah, Giorgi Mchedlishvili, Hélio Batista, Pavel Osipov (55' Lucas Villela), Eduards Tīdenbergs (69' Mykhaylo Sergiychuk), Jevgenijs Kazacoks, Abdullahi Alfa (44' Guga Palavandishvili), Tosin Aiyegun, Kaspars Svārups. Coach: Igor Klosovs.
Goals: 15' Jefferson 1-0, 72' Jevgenijs Kazacoks 1-1, 79' Mykhaylo Sergiychuk 1-2, 90+3' Jefferson 2-2.
Referee: Thorvaldur Árnason (ISL)   Attendance: 332.
Sent off: 90+4' Amadou Samb, Konstantin Machnovskiy.

01.08.19   Merkur Arena, Graz: SK Sturm Graz – FK Haugesund 2-1 (1-0)
SK Sturm Graz: Jörg Siebenhandl, Thomas Schrammel, Anastasios Avlonitis, Emanuel Sakic, Lukas Spendlhofer, Jakob Jantscher, Philipp Huspek (75' Michael John Lema), Juan Domínguez, Thorsten Röcher (27' Philipp Hosiner), Ivan Ljubic (76' Christoph Leitgeb), Otar Kiteishvili. Coach: Nestor El Maestro.
FK Haugesund: Helge Sandvik, Doug Bergqvist, Mikkel Desler, Benjamin Tiedemann Hansen, Sondre Tronstad, Thore Baardsen Pedersen, Niklas Sandberg (46' Torbjørn Kallevåg), Bruno Leite (79' Joakim Nilsen), Kristoffer Velde, Kevin Krygård, Ibrahima Koné (90+3' Fredrik Knudsen). Coach: Jostein Grindhaug.
Goals: 15' Niklas Sandberg 1-0 (og), 48' Ivan Ljubic 2-0, 68' Kevin Krygård 2-1.
Referee: Juri Frischer (EST)   Attendance: 2,000.

01.08.19   Commerzbank-Arena, Frankfurt am Main:
            Eintracht Frankfurt – FC Flora Tallinn 2-1 (1-1)
Eintracht Frankfurt: Felix Wiedwald, Makoto Hasebe, Danny da Costa (86' Erik Durm), Almamy Touré, Evan Obite N'Dicka, Filip Kostic, Lucas Torró, Dominik Kohr (75' Gelson Fernandes), Daichi Kamada, Gonçalo Paciência, Dejan Joveljic (67' Mijat Gacinovic). Coach: Adi Hütter.
FC Flora Tallinn: Matvei Igonen, Gert Kams, Märten Kuusk, Henrik Pürg, Henri Järvelaid, Konstantin Vassiljev, Mihkel Ainsalu, Vlasiy Sinyavskiy, Vladislavs Kreida (78' Markus Poom), Frank Liivak (60' Rauno Alliku), Erik Sorga (70' Mark Lepik). Coach: Jürgen Henn.
Goals: 37' Gonçalo Paciência 1-0, 40' Vlasiy Sinyavskiy 1-1, 54' Gonçalo Paciência 2-1 (p).
Referee: Jørgen Daugbjerg Burchardt (DEN)   Attendance: 48,000.

01.08.19   Stadionul Marin Anastasovici, Giurgiu: Fotbal Club FCSB – FC Alashkert 2-3 (1-3)
Fotbal Club FCSB: Andrei Daniel Vlad, Alexandru Stan (46' Diogo Salomão), Mihai Balasa, Claudiu Belu, Iulian Cristea, Thierry Moutinho (24' Florinel Coman), Lucian Filip, Ionut Vîna, Ovidiu Popescu, Razvan Oaida, Florin Tanase (82' Bogdan Planic). Coach: Bogdan Andone.
FC Alashkert: Ognjen Cancarevic, Hrayr Mkoyan, Gagik Dagbashyan, Hayk Ishkhanyan, Taron Voskanyan, Tiago Cametá, Artak Grigoryan, Thiago Galvão (68' Nikita Tankov), Gustavo Marmentini Santos, Vahagn Hayrapetyan (68' Sargis Shahinyan), Uros Nenadovic (75' Gegam Kadimyan). Coach: Abraham Khashmanyan.
Goals: 10' Florin Tanase 1-0 (p), 24', 28' Gustavo Marmentini Santos 1-1, 1-2 (p), 45' Thiago Galvão 1-3, 59' Florinel Coman 2-3.
Referee: Peter Kralovic (SVK)   Attendance: 1,828.
Sent off: 27' Mihai Balasa, 63' Gustavo Marmentini Santos.

Fotbal Club FCSB played their home match at Stadionul Marin Anastasovici, Giurgiu, instead of their regular stadium Arena Nationala, Bucurest.

01.08.19   Windsor Park, Belfast: Linfield FC – HB Tórshavn 1-0 (1-0)
Linfield FC: Rohan Ferguson, Chris Casement, Mark Stafford, Niall Quinn, Jamie Mulgrew, Jimmy Callacher, Daniel Kearns (71' Shayne Lavery), Bastien Héry, Joel Cooper, Andrew Waterworth, Jordan Stewart (75' Kirk Millar). Coach: David Healy.
HB Tórshavn: Bjarti Vitalis Mørk, Brynjar Hlödversson (61' Dan í Soylu), Jógvan Davidsen, Lasse Andersen, Símun Samuelsen, Magnus Egilsson, René Joensen (75' Pætur Petersen), Hørdur Askham, Tróndur Jensen, Adrian Justinussen, Sebastian Pingel (61' Ari Olsen). Coach: Heimir Gudjónsson.
Goal: 20' Andrew Waterworth 1-0 (p).
Referee: Halil Umut Meler (TUR)

Match was played behind closed doors.

01.08.19   Stadion Gradski vrt, Osijek: NK Osijek – CSKA Sofia 1-0 (1-0, 1-0) (a.e.t.)
NK Osijek: Ivica Ivusic, Tomislav Sorsa, Mile Skoric, Ante Majstorovic, Mihael Zaper (91' Benedik Mioc), László Kleinheisler (46' Dmytro Lyopa), Petar Bockaj, Marin Pilj, Bosko Sutalo, Mirko Maric, Antonio Mance (106' Luka Marin). Coach: Dino Skender.
CSKA Sofia: Vytautas Cerniauskas, Nikolay Bodurov, Petar Zanev (64' Ivan Turitsov), Kristiyan Malinov (80' Graham Carey), Raúl Albentosa, Nuno Tomás, Geferson, Tiago Rodrigues, Janio Bikel, Diego Fabbrini (104' Tony Watt), Ali Sowe.
Coach: Ljubomir Petrovic.
Goal: 28' Ante Majstorovic 1-0.
Referee: Robert Schörgenhofer (AUT)   Attendance: 7,214.

CSKA Sofia won on penalties after extra time (4-3).
Penalties: Lyopa 1-0, Tiago Rodrigues 1-1, Bockaj missed, Carey 1-2, Skoric missed, Geferson missed, Pilj 2-2, Bodurov 2-3, Maric 3-3, Sowe 3-4.

01.08.19   Pittodrie Stadium, Aberdeen: Aberdeen FC – Chikhura Sachkhere 5-0 (2-0)
Aberdeen FC: Joe Lewis, Andrew Considine, Shay Logan, Gregory Leigh (67' Dean Campbell), Scott McKenna, Funso Ojo, Lewis Ferguson, Niall McGinn (62' Scott Wright), Ryan Hedges, Sam Cosgrove (82' Bruce Anderson), Jon Gallagher. Coach: Derek McInnes.
Chikhura Sachkhere: Dino Hamzic, Shota Kashia, Davit Maisashvili, Lasha Chikvaidze, Revaz Chiteishvili (52' Teimurazi Markozashvili), Oleg Mamasakhlisi, Besik Dekanoidze (52' Giorgi Pantsulaia), Irakli Lekvtadze, Giorgi Koripadze, Mikheil Sardalishvili, Mikheil Ergemlidze (72' Demur Chikhladze). Coach: Soso Pruidze.
Goals: 9', 20' Sam Cosgrove 1-0, 2-0, 58' Gregory Leigh 3-0, 65' Scott Wright 4-0, 80' Sam Cosgrove 5-0.
Referee: Rade Obrenovic (SVN)   Attendance: 15,167.

01.08.19 City Arena Trnava, Trnava: Spartak Trnava – Lokomotiv Plovdiv 3-1 (1-0)
Spartak Trnava: Dobrivoj Rusov, João Diogo, Bogdan Mitrea, Timotej Záhumensky, Lucas Lovat, Ivan Mesík, Marko Tesija, Emir Halilovic (82' Marko Kelemen), Filip Dangubic (82' Matej Jakúbek), Rafael Tavares, Alex Sobczyk (72' Gino van Kessel). Coach: Ricardo Chéu.
Lokomotiv Plovdiv: Martin Lukov, Milos Petrovic, David Malembana, Josip Tomasevic, Stephen Eze, Dimitar Iliev, Momchil Tsvetanov, Petar Vitanov (57' Parvizchon Umarbaev), Birsent Karagaren, Alen Ozbolt (89' Wiris), Ante Aralica (72' Georgi Iliev).
Coach: Bruno Akrapovic.
Goals: 16' Filip Dangubic 1-0, 53' Bogdan Mitrea 2-0 (p), 71' Rafael Tavares 3-0, 74' Alen Ozbolt 3-1.
Referee: Erik Lambrechts (BEL)   Attendance: 6,702.
Sent off: 35' Timotej Záhumensky.

Lokomotiv Plovdiv won on away goals.

01.08.19 Seaview, Belfast: Crusaders FC – Wolverhampton Wanderers 1-4 (1-3)
Crusaders FC: Sean O'Neill, Sean Ward, Billy Joe Burns, Chris Hegarty, Philip Lowry, Jordan Forsythe, Paul Heatley, Ross Clarke (78' Declan Caddell), Jarlath O'Rourke, Rory Hale (83' Gary Thompson), Jordan Owens (80' David Cushley). Coach: Stephen Baxter.
Wolverhampton Wanderers: Rui Patrício, Ryan Bennett, Willy Boly, Conor Coady, Jonny Castro, João Moutinho, Leander Dendoncker, Rúben Neves (68' Romain Saïss), Raúl Jiménez (55' Morgan Gibbs-White), Adama Traoré, Diogo Jota (68' Rúben Vinagre).
Coach: Nuno Espírito Santo.
Goals: 13' Ryan Bennett 1-0 (og), 15' Raúl Jiménez 1-1, 38' Ryan Bennett 1-2, 45' Raúl Jiménez 1-3, 77' Jordan Forsythe 1-4 (og).
Referee: Nejc Kajtazovic (SVN)   Attendance: 2,700.

01.08.19 Estádio Dom Afonso Henriques, Guimarães:
            Vitória de Guimarães – Jeunesse d'Esch 4-0 (1-0)
Vitória de Guimarães: João Miguel Silva, Pedrão, Rafa Soares, Falaye Sacko, Edmond Tapsoba, Rochinha (71' João Correia), Pêpê Rodrigues, Almoatasembellah Ali Mohamed (60' João Carlos Teixeira), Joseph Amoah, Alexandre Guedes (83' João Pedro), Davidson.
Coach: Ivo Vieira.
Jeunesse d'Esch: Kévin Sommer, Arsène Menèssou, Alessandro Fiorani, Emmanuel Lapierre, Johannes Steinbach, Halim Meddour, Yannick Makota, Milos Todorovic, Luca Duriatti (68' David Soares De Sousa), Mehmet Arslan (76' Andrea Deidda), Valentin Kouamé (68' Almir Klica). Coach: Nicolas Huysman.
Goals: 14' Edmond Tapsoba 1-0, 63' Alexandre Guedes 2-0, 88' Edmond Tapsoba 3-0 (p), 90+3' João Carlos Teixeira 4-0.
Referee: Vitali Meshkov (RUS)   Attendance: 16,352.

01.08.19   Stadion Partizana, Beograd:
Partizan Beograd – Connah's Quay Nomads FC 3-0 (0-0)
Partizan Beograd: Vladimir Stojkovic, Rajko Brezancic (73' Slobodan Urosevic), Bojan Ostojic, Nemanja Miletic (I), Strahinja Pavlovic, Zoran Tosic (63' Ognjen Ozegovic), Aleksandar Scekic, Seydouba Soumah, Sasa Zdjelar, Umar Sadiq, Djordje Ivanovic (46' Filip Stevanovic). Coach: Savo Milosevic.
Connah's Quay Nomads FC: Lewis Brass, George Horan, Danny Holmes, John Disney, Callum Roberts, Danny Harrison (63' Ryan Wignall), Jay Owen, Callum Morris, Declan Poole, Michael Wilde (74' Priestley Farquharson), Jamie Insall (81' Michael Bakare).
Coach: Andy Morrison.
Goals: 54' Zoran Tosic 1-0, 70' Ognjen Ozegovic 2-0, 73' Filip Stevanovic 3-0.
Referee: Luis Godinho (POR)   Attendance: 8,200.

01.08.19   Samsung völlurinn, Gardabær: UMF Stjarnan – RCD Espanyol 1-3 (0-1)
UMF Stjarnan: Haraldur Björnsson, Daníel Laxdal, Jóhann Laxdal, Martin Rauschenberg Brorsen, Eyjólfur Hédinsson, Thorsteinn Már Ragnarsson (69' Gudmundur Hafsteinsson), Thorri Geir Rúnarsson (69' Baldur Sigurdsson), Heidar Ægisson, Alex Thór Hauksson, Sölvi Gudbjargarson, Hilmar Árni Halldórsson (65' Nimo Gribenco). Coach: Rúnar Sigmundsson.
RCD Espanyol: Diego López, Bernardo Espinosa, Dídac Vilà, Javi López, Naldo, Adrià Pedrosa (70' Javi Puado), Víctor Sánchez (65' Iturraspe), Marc Roca, Melendo, Facundo Ferreyra, Borja Iglesias (65' Lei Wu). Coach: David Gallego.
Goals: 5' Adrià Pedrosa 0-1, 52' Borja Iglesias 0-2, 79' Facundo Ferreyra 0-3, 87' Baldur Sigurdsson 1-3.
Referee: Dumitri Muntean (MOL)   Attendance: 1,020.

Hilmar Árni Halldórsson missed a penalty kick (19').

THIRD QUALIFYING ROUND

06.08.19   Vazgen Sargsyan anvan Hanrapetakan Marzadasht, Yerevan:
FC Ararat-Armenia – FC Saburtalo Tbilisi 1-2 (1-0)
FC Ararat-Armenia: Stefan Cupic, Rochdi Achenteh, Dmitri Guzj, Ângelo Meneses, Georgi Pashov, Gor Malakyan (57' Ilja Antonov), Kódjo Alphonse, Petros Avetisyan (78' Zakaria Sanogo), Anton Kobyalko (71' Louis Ogana), Furdjel Narsingh, Mailson.
Coach: Vardan Minasyan.
FC Saburtalo Tbilisi: Omar Migineishvili, Giorgi Rekhviashvili, Luka Lakvekheliani, Levan Kakubava, Giorgi Diasamidze, Sandro Altunashvili, Nikoloz Mali, Alwyn Tera (71' Levan Kenia), Giorgi Gabedava, Ognjen Rolovic (57' Gagi Margvelashvili), Giorgi Kokhreidze (84' Dachi Tsnobiladze). Coach: Giorgi Chiabrishvili.
Goals: 31' Anton Kobyalko 1-0, 72' Sandro Altunashvili 1-1, 76' Levan Kenia 1-2.
Referee: Alain Bieri (SUI)   Attendance: 10,500.

FC Ararat-Armenia played their home match at Vazgen Sargsyan anvan Hanrapetakan Marzadasht, Yerevan, instead of their regular stadium Yerevan Football Academy Stadium, Yereven which did not meet UEFA requirements.

06.08.19   Daugavas Stadionā, Riga: Riga FC – HJK Helsinki 1-1 (0-1)
Riga FC: Roberts Ozols, Georgios Valerianos, Herdi Prenga, Stefan Panic, Tomislav Saric (76'
Vyacheslav Sharpar), Felipe Brisola, Roger (74' Aleksejs Visnakovs), Armands Pētersons,
Elvis Stuglis, Roman Debelko (61' Kamil Bilinski), Vladislavs Fjodorovs.
Coach: Mihails Konevs.
HJK Helsinki: Maksim Rudakov, Rafinha (58' Henri Toivomäki), Nikolai Alho, Daniel
O'Shaughnessy, Faith Obilor, William Parra, Riku Riski, Kaan Kairinen, Sebastian Dahlström,
Evans Mensah (67' Petteri Forsell), Tim Väyrynen (89' Erfan Zeneli). Coach: Toni Koskela.
Goals: 7' Tim Väyrynen 0-1, 81' Kamil Bilinski 1-1.
Referee: Kirill Levnikov (RUS)   Attendance: 3,468.

Riga FC played their home match at Daugava Stadium, Riga, instead of their regular stadium Skonto Stadium, Riga.

06.08.19   Stadion Pod Godgom, Podgorica: FK Sutjeska Niksic – Linfield FC 1-2 (1-1)
FK Sutjeska Niksic: Vladan Giljen, Darko Bulatovic, Aleksandar Sofranac, Bojan Ciger,
Marko Cetkovic, Damir Kojasevic, Branislav Jankovic, Marko Vucic (83' Miljan
Vlaisavljevic), Nemanja Nedic, Novica Erakovic (68' Vladan Bubanja), Bojan Bozovic (46'
Stefan Nikolic). Coach: Nikola Rakojevic.
Linfield FC: Rohan Ferguson, Chris Casement, Ryan McGivern, Matthew Clarke, Mark
Stafford, Niall Quinn, Jamie Mulgrew, Kirk Millar (87' Jordan Stewart), Bastien Héry (90+3'
Daniel Kearns), Stephen Fallon (84' Andrew Mitchell), Shayne Lavery. Coach: David Healy.
Goals: 11' Damir Kojasevic 1-0, 38', 65' Kirk Millar 1-1, 1-2.
Referee: Alan Mario Sant (MLT)   Attendance: 3,850.

FK Sutjeska Niksic played their home match at Stadion Pod Goricom, Podgorica, instead of their regular stadium Stadion kraj Bistrice, Niksic which did not meet UEFA requirements.

07.08.19   Národny Futbalovy Stadión, Bratislava: Slovan Bratislava – Dundalk FC 1-0 (0-0)
Slovan Bratislava: Dominik Greif, Vasil Bozhikov, Vernon, Jurij Medvedev, Myenty Abena,
Marin Ljubicic, Dávid Holman, Joeri de Kamps, "Moha" Mohammed Rharsalla (77' Erik
Daniel), Andraz Sporar (80' Aleksandar Cavric), Rafael Ratão (67' Dejan Drazic).
Coach: Ján Kozák.
Dundalk FC: Gary Rogers, Dane Massey, Andrew Boyle, Sean Gannon, Daniel Cleary, Chris
Shields, Sean Murray (70' Patrick McEleney), John Mountney, Jamie McGrath, Patrick Hoban
(87' Cameron Dummigan), Michael Duffy (88' Daniel Kelly). Coach: Vinny Perth.
Goal: 86' Dávid Holman 1-0.
Referee: Frank Schneider (FRA)   Attendance: 9,980.

08.08.19   Astana Arena, Nur-Sultan: FK Astana – Valletta FC 5-1 (3-0)
FK Astana: Nenad Eric, Antonio Rukavina, Yuriy Logvinenko, Dmitriy Shomko, Evgeny
Postnikov, Luka Simunovic, Rúnar Sigurjónsson, Marin Tomasov, Ivan Maevski (63' Yuriy
Pertsukh), Dorin Rotariu (87' Roman Murtazaev), Ndombe Mubele (63' Rangelo Janga).
Coach: Roman Grygorchuk.
Valletta FC: Henry Bonello, Joseph Zerafa, Ryan Camilleri, Jean Borg, Douglas Packer (78'
Matteo Piciollo), Rowen Muscat, Kyrian Nwoko (61' Shaun Dimech), Enmy Peña, Kevin
Tulimieri (61' Nicholas Pulis), Yuri, Mario Fontanella. Coach: Darren Abdilla.
Goals: 8' Rúnar Sigurjónsson 1-0, 15' Yuriy Logvinenko 2-0, 35' Marin Tomasov 3-0,
57' Rúnar Sigurjónsson 4-0, 67' Mario Fontanella 4-1, 80' Rangelo Janga 5-1.
Referee: Vladislav Bezborodov (RUS)   Attendance: 18,707.

08.08.19   AEK Arena – George Karapatakis, Larnaca: AEK Larnaca – KAA Gent 1-1 (0-1)
AEK Larnaca: Toño, Mikel González, Daniel Mojsov, Truyols (48' Raúl Ruiz), Ivan Trickovski, Lluis Sastre, Acorán (82' Florian Taulemesse), Nacho Cases, Hector Hevel, Apostolos Giannou, Tete (71' Jean Luc Assoubre). Coach: Imanol Idiakez.
KAA Gent: Thomas Kaminski, Nana Asare, Mikael Lustig, Igor Plastun, Michael Ngadeu-Ngadjui, Vadis Odjidja-Ofoe, Brecht Dejaegere (57' Louis Verstraete), Elisha Owusu, Yuya Kubo (78' Alessio Castro-Montes), Roman Yaremchuk (62' Laurent Depoitre), Jonathan David. Coach: Jess Thorup.
Goals: 26' Roman Yaremchuk 0-1, 88' Ivan Trickovski 1-1.
Referee: Svein Oddvar Moen (NOR)   Attendance: 3,360.

08.08.19   Vazgen Sargsyan anvan Hanrapetakan Marzadasht, Yerevan:
Pyunik Yerevan FC – Wolverhampton Wanderers 0-4 (0-2)
Pyunik Yerevan FC: Andrija Dragojevic, Antonio Stankov, Maksim Zhestokov, Kristi Marku, Armen Manucharyan, Karlen Mkrtchyan, Sergiy Shevchuk, Artem Simonyan, Stanislav Efimov (55' Marko Burzanovic), Denis Mahmudov (63' Steven Alfred), Artur Miranyan.
Coach: Aleksandr Tarkhanov.
Wolverhampton Wanderers: Rui Patrício, Ryan Bennett, Willy Boly, Matt Doherty (63' Patrick Cutrone), Conor Coady, Rúben Vinagre, João Moutinho, Romain Saïss, Leander Dendoncker, Raúl Jiménez (71' Rúben Neves), Diogo Jota (63' Jonny Castro).
Coach: Nuno Espírito Santo.
Goals: 29' Matt Doherty 0-1, 42', 46' Raúl Jiménez 0-2, 0-3, 90+1' Rúben Neves 0-4 (p).
Referee: Michael Fabbri (ITA)   Attendance: 13,050.

08.08.19   Generali Arena, Praha: AC Sparta Praha – Trabzonspor 2-2 (1-0)
AC Sparta Praha: Florin Nita, Lukás Stetina, Costa Nhamoinesu, Matej Hanousek, Michal Trávník (87' David Moberg-Karlsson), Guélor Kanga, Martin Hasek, Srdjan Plavsic (90' Dávid Hancko), Michal Sácek, Ladislav Krejcí, Benjamin Tetteh (79' Libor Kozák).
Coach: Václav Jílek.
Trabzonspor: Ugurcan Çakir, João Pereira, Filip Novák, Majid Hosseini, Hüseyin Türkmen, John Obi Mikel (46' Alexander Sørloth), José Sosa, Abdülkadir Parmak, Abdülkadir Ömür (76' Donis Avdijaj), Anthony Nwakaeme, Caleb Ekuban (90+3' Dogan Erdogan).
Coach: Ünal Karaman.
Goals: 16' Costa Nhamoinesu 1-0, 68' Guélor Kanga 2-0, 84' Caleb Ekuban 2-1, 89' Alexander Sørloth 2-2.
Referee: José Luis Munuera Montero (ESP)

Match was played behind closed doors.

08.08.19   Stadionul Ion Oblemenco, Craiova:
CS Universitatea Craiova – AEK Athens 0-2 (0-0)
CS Universitatea Craiova: Mirko Pigliacelli, Renato Kelic, Marius Briceag, Nicusor Bancu, Stephane Acka, Alexandru Mateiu, Bogdan Vatajelu, Cristian Barbut (73' Alexandru Ionita), Antoni Ivanov (66' Kamer Qaka), Alexandru Cicâldau, Mihai Roman (II) (73' Carlos Fortes).
Coach: Corneliu Papura.
AEK Athens: Vasilios Barkas, Niklas Hult, Ognjen Vranjes, Paulinho, Efstratios Svarnas, David Simão (82' Nenad Krsticic), Petros Mandalos, André Simões, Chico Geraldes, Viktor Klonaridis (39' Marko Livaja), Daniele Verde (64' Nélson Oliveira). Coach: Miguel Cardoso.
Goals: 60' Petros Mandalos 0-1, 85' Marko Livaja 0-2.
Referee: Dennis Higler (HOL)   Attendance: 2,530.

08.08.19   Brøndby Stadion, Brøndby: Brøndby IF – Sporting Braga 2-4 (1-2)
Brøndby IF: Marvin Schwäbe, Paulus Arajuuri, Anthony Jung, Hjörtur Hermannsson, Kasper Fisker (58' Simon Tibbling), Dominik Kaiser, Josip Radosevic, Simon Hedlund, Kamil Wilczek, Kevin Mensah, Mikael Uhre (67' Jesper Lindstrøm). Coach: Niels Frederiksen.
Sporting Braga: Matheus Magalhães, Ricardo Esgaio, Nuno Sequeira, Pablo Santos, Bruno Viana, Fransérgio (68' João Novais), João Palhinha, André Horta, Wilson Eduardo (70' Murilo), Paulinho (81' Ahmed Hassan Mahgoug "Koka"), Ricardo Horta. Coach: Sá Pinto.
Goals: 15' Dominik Kaiser 1-0, 18' Paulinho 1-1, 20' André Horta 1-2, 50' Dominik Kaiser 2-2, 90+2' Ricardo Horta 2-3, 90+4' Hjörtur Hermannsson 2-4 (og).
Referee: Tamás Bognár (HUN)   Attendance: 15,642.

08.08.19   Daugavas Stadionā, Riga: FK Ventspils – Vitória de Guimarães 0-3 (0-1)
FK Ventspils: Vjaceslavs Kudrjavcevs, Jean Alcénat, Abdoul Mamah, Giorgi Mchedlishvili (74' Raens Tālbergs), Hélio Batista, Guga Palavandishvili (66' Pavel Osipov), Jevgenijs Kazacoks, Tosin Aiyegun, Kaspars Svārups, Mykhaylo Sergiychuk (54' Daniils Ulimbasevs), Lucas Villela. Coach: Igor Klosovs.
Vitória de Guimarães: João Miguel Silva, Florent Hanin, Pedrão, Falaye Sacko, Edmond Tapsoba, Rochinha (75' André Almeida), Pêpê Rodrigues, Almoatasembellah Ali Mohamed, Joseph Amoah, Alexandre Guedes (79' João Carlos Teixeira), Davidson (85' Lucas Soares). Coach: Ivo Vieira.
Goals: 30' Davidson 0-1, 50' Pêpê Rodrigues 0-2, 80' Joseph Amoah 0-3.
Referee: Filip Glova (SVK)   Attendance: 472.

FK Ventspils played their home match at Daugavas Stadionā, Riga, instead of their regular stadium Ventspils Olimpiskais Stadions, Ventspils.

08.08.19   Bolshaya Sportivnaya Arena, Tiraspol: FC Sheriff Tiraspol – AIK Solna 1-2 (0-2)
FC Sheriff Tiraspol: Zvonimir Mikulic, Andrej Lukic, Mateo Muzek, Cristiano, Ariel Borysiuk, Wilfried Balima (76' Maxim Cojocaru (I)), Jury Kendysh, Gheorghe Anton (46' Artem Hordienko), Liridon Latifi (87' Jaroslaw Jach), Gabrijel Boban, Robert Tambe. Coach: Zoran Zekic.
AIK Solna: Oscar Linnér, Per Karlsson, Robert Lundström (90+1' Heradi Rashidi), Karol Mets, Sebastian Larsson, Panajotis Dimitriadis (73' Rasmus Lindkvist), Enoch Adu, Anton Salétros, Tarik Elyounoussi, Kolbeinn Sigthórsson (76' Nabil Bahoui), Henok Goitom. Coach: Rikard Norling.
Goals: 12' Andrej Lukic 0-1 (og), 14' Kolbeinn Sigthórsson 0-2, 56' Jury Kendysh 1-2 (p).
Referee: Kevin Clancy (SCO)   Attendance: 6,341.

08.08.19   Haugesund Stadion, Haugesund: FK Haugesund – PSV Eindhoven 0-1 (0-1)
FK Haugesund: Helge Sandvik, Doug Bergqvist, Mikkel Desler, Benjamin Tiedemann Hansen, Sondre Tronstad, Thore Baardsen Pedersen, Niklas Sandberg, Bruno Leite (74' Joakim Nilsen), Kristoffer Velde, Shuaibu Ibrahim (57' Ibrahima Koné), Kevin Krygård (71' Christian Grindheim). Coach: Jostein Grindhaug.
PSV Eindhoven: Jeroen Zoet, Nick Viergever, Timo Baumgartl, Denzel Dumfries, Gastón Pereiro (59' Cody Gakpo), Érick Gutiérrez (89' Jorrit Hendrix), Michal Sadílek, Pablo Rosario, Bruma (79' Hirving Lozano), Steven Bergwijn, Donyell Malen. Coach: Mark van Bommel.
Goal: 24' Steven Bergwijn 0-1 (p).
Referee: Matej Jug (SVN)   Attendance: 5,150.

08.08.19   Aker Stadion, Molde: Molde FK – Aris Saloniki 3-0 (2-0)
Molde FK: Álex Craninx, Ruben Gabrielsen, Kristoffer Haraldseid, Kristoffer Haugen, Martin Bjørnbak, Magnus Eikrem, Etzaz Hussain (75' Martin Ellingsen), Eirik Hestad (90+3' Mattias Mostrøm), Fredrik Aursnes, Ohi Omoijuanfo (85' Erling Knudtzon), Leke James.
Coach: Erling Moe.
Aris Saloniki: Julián Cuesta, Daniel Sundgren, Mihály Korhut, Lindsay Rose, Fran Vélez, Nicolas Diguiny, Migjen Basha (69' Georgios Delizisis), Javier Matilla, Lucas Sasha, Martín Tonso (75' Ioannis Fetfatzidis), Brown Ideye (81' Daniel Larsson). Coach: Savvas Pantelidis.
Goals: 27' Magnus Eikrem 1-0, 32' Eirik Hestad 2-0, 87' Martin Ellingsen 3-0.
Referee: Maurizio Mariani (ITA)   Attendance: 3,953.
Sent off: 64' Fran Vélez.

08.08.19   Stadion Chornomorets, Odessa: FK Mariupol – AZ Alkmaar 0-0
FC Mariupol: Rustam Khudzhamov, Pavel Polegenko, Sergiy Chobotenko, Oleksii Bykov, Valeriy Fedorchuk, Igor Tyshchenko (86' Igor Kyryukhantsev), Vyacheslav Churko, Dmytro Myshnov, Sergiy Gorbunov (76' Joyskim Dawa), Maksym Chekh (63' Vyacheslav Tankovskiy), Vladislav Vakula. Coach: Oleksandr Babych.
AZ Alkmaar: Marco Bizot, Ron Vlaar, Stijn Wuytens (73' Jordy Clasie), Jonas Svensson (80' Yukinari Sugawara), Thomas Ouwejan, Owen Wijndal, Fredrik Midtsjø (86' Albert Gudmundsson), Teun Koopmeiners, Oussama Idrissi, Myron Boadu, Calvin Stengs.
Coach: Arne Slot.
Referee: Michael Tykgaard (DEN)   Attendance: 4,426.

FK Mariupol played their home match at Stadion Chronomorets, Odessa, instead of their regular stadium Volodymyr Boiko Stadium, Mariupol, due to the war conditions in Eastern Ukraine.

08.08.19   Stockhorn Arena, Thun: FC Thun – Spartak Moskva 2-3 (0-2)
FC Thun: Guillaume Faivre, Stefan Glarner, Nikki Havenaar, Miguel Rodrigues, Sven Joss (77' Dennis Salanovic), Roy Gelmi, Miguel Castroman, Basil Stillhart, Nias Hefti, Simone Rapp, Ridge Munsy (46' Matteo Tosetti). Coach: Marc Schneider.
Spartak Moskva: Aleksandr Maksimenko, Georgi Dzhikiya, Samuel Gigot, Ayrton, Nikolai Rasskazov, Jano Ananidze (60' André Schürrle), Roman Zobnin, Reziuan Mirzov (72' Aleksandr Tashaev), Ayaz Guliev, Zelimkhan Bakaev (87' Lorenzo Melgarejo), Ezequiel Ponce. Coach: Oleg Kononov.
Goals: 22' Ezequiel Ponce 0-1, 29' Zelimkhan Bakaev 0-2, 52' Nias Hefti 1-2, 59' Simone Rapp 2-2, 73' Zelimkhan Bakaev 2-3.
Referee: Irfan Peljto (BIH)   Attendance: 6,150.

André Schürrle missed a penalty kick (66').

08.08.19   Swedbank Stadion, Malmö: Malmö FF – Zrinjski Mostar 3-0 (1-0)
Malmö FF: Johan Dahlin, Behrang Safari, Rasmus Bengtsson, Eric Larsson, Søren Rieks, Anders Christiansen (82' Bonke Innocent), Fouad Bachirou, Oscar Lewicki, Markus Rosenberg, Guillermo Molins (78' Marcus Antonsson), Jo Inge Berget (78' Franz Brorsson).
Coach: Uwe Rösler.
Zrinjski Mostar: Ivan Brkic, Tomislav Barbaric, Dario Rugasevic (79' Mario Ticinovic), Slobodan Jakovljevic, Advan Kadusic, Damir Sovsic (61' Damir Zlomislic), Frane Cirjak, Edin Rustemovic, Miljan Govedarica, Stanisa Mandic, Irfan Hadzic (67' Ivan Lendric).
Coach: Hari Vukas.
Goals: 36' Rasmus Bengtsson 1-0, 66' Anders Christiansen 2-0, 74' Søren Rieks 3-0.
Referee: Stuart Attwell (ENG)   Attendance: 14,103.

08.08.19   Bakcell Arena, Baku: Neftçi PFK Baku – Bnei Yehuda Tel Aviv 2-2 (1-2)
Neftçi PFK Baku: Salahat Agayev, Vojislav Stankovic (87' Mamadou Mbodj), Kyrylo Petrov, Anton Krivotsyuk, Omar Buludov, Soni Mustivar, Vangelis Platelas (80' Bagaliy Dabo), Emin Makhmudov, Steeven Joseph-Monrose, Rauf Aliyev (73' Namiq Alasgarov), Dário Júnior da Silva. Coach: Roberto Bordin.
Bnei Yehuda Tel Aviv: Emilijus Zubas, Dan Mori, Alban Pnishi, Shay Mazor (89' Paz Ben Ari), Daniel Felscher, Amir Rustom, Tamabi Sages, Ismaila Soro, Mohammad Ghadir (69' Ariel Matan Lazmi), Dor Jan (84' Dor Kochav), Avishay Cohen. Coach: Yossi Abukasis.
Goals: 26' Tamabi Sages 0-1, 36' Mohammad Ghadir 0-2, 43' Steeven Joseph-Monrose 1-2, 90+7' Namiq Alasgarov 2-2.
Referee: Karim Abed (FRA)   Attendance: 10,000.

08.08.19   Winner Stadium, Netanya: Maccabi Tel Aviv – FC Sūduva Marijampolė 1-2 (0-1)
Maccabi Tel Aviv: Andreas Gianniotis, Saborit, Shahar Piven-Bachtiar, Jair Amador, Maor Kandil, Dor Mikha, Dor Peretz, Dan Glazer (81' Avi Rikan), Nick Blackman (63' Eliran Atar), Itay Shechter (46' Chikeluba Ofoedu), Yonatan Cohen. Coach: Vladimir Ivic.
FK Sūdova Marijampolė: Ivan Kardum, Algis Jankauskas, Andro Svrljuga, Aleksandar Zivanovic, Semir Kerla, Jovan Cadjenovic, Ovidijus Verbickas, Giedrius Matulevicius (75' Povilas Leimonas), Josip Tadic (70' Eligijus Jankauskas), Mihret Topcagic (86' Robertas Vėzevicius), Paulius Golubickas. Coach: Vladimir Cheburin.
Goals: 37' Semir Kerla 0-1, 76' Eligijus Jankauskas 0-2, 84' Chikeluba Ofoedu 1-2.
Referee: Neil Doyle (IRL)   Attendance: 8,512.

Maccabi Tel Aviv played their home match at Netanya Stadium, Netanya, instead of their regular stadium Bloomfield Stadium, Tel Aviv which was undergoing renovation.

08.08.19   Ludogorets Arena, Razgrad: PFC Ludogorets Razgrad – The New Saints 5-0 (3-0)
PFC Ludogorets Razgrad: Plamen Iliev, Cosmin Moti, Rafael Forster, Jordan Ikoko, Anton Nedyalkov, Anicet Andriantenaina (61' Stéphane Badji), Jacek Góralski, Dan Biton (77' Jakub Swierczok), Claudiu Keserü, Jody Lukoki, Mavis Tchibota (70' Wanderson).
Coach: Stoicho Stoev.
The New Saints: Paul Harrison, Simon Spender (69' Kane Lewis), Christopher Marriott, Keston Davies (46' Blaine Hudson), Ryan Harrington, Aeron Edwards, Jon Routledge, Daniel Redmond, Ryan Brobbel, Jamie Mullan, Dean Ebbe (61' Greg Draper). Coach: Scott Ruscoe.
Goals: 10' Ryan Harrington 1-0 (og), 28' Mavis Tchibota 2-0, 43' Jody Lukoki 3-0, 65' Claudiu Keserü 4-0, 76' Cosmin Moti 5-0.
Referee: Marius Avram (ROM)   Attendance: 4,120.

Cosmin Moti missed a penalty kick (76').

08.08.19 Stade Roi Baudouin, Brussels:
Royal Antwerp FC – FC Viktoria Plzen 1-0 (1-0)
Royal Antwerp FC: Sinan Bolat, Simen Juklerød, Buta, Abdoulaye Seck, Júnior Pius (26' Dylan Batubinsika), Faris Haroun, Lior Refaelov (87' Amara Baby), Geoffry Hairemans (61' Didier Lamkel Zé), Alexis De Sart, Dieumerci Mbokani, Ivo Rodrigues. Coach: László Bölöni.
FC Viktoria Plzen: Ales Hruska, Radim Rezník, David Limbersky, Jakub Brabec, Lukás Hejda (46' Tomás Horava), Jan Kovarík (68' Joel Kayamba), Jan Kopic, Patrik Hrosovsky, Lukás Kalvach, Dominik Janosek, Michal Krmencík (84' Tomás Chory). Coach: Pavel Vrba.
Goals: 29' Ivo Rodrigues 1-0.
Referee: Jens Maae (DEN)   Attendance: 15,734.

Royal Antwerp FC played their home match at Stade Roi Baudouin, Brussels, instead of their regular stadium Bosuilstadion, Antwerp, which does not meet UEFA requirements.

08.08.19 Stadion Lokomotiv, Plovdiv: Lokomotiv Plovdiv – RC Strasbourg 0-1 (0-1)
Lokomotiv Plovdiv: Martin Lukov, Milos Petrovic, Josip Tomasevic, Stephen Eze, Dimitar Iliev, Momchil Tsvetanov, Parvizchon Umarbaev (67' Wiris), Petar Vitanov (83' Georgi Iliev), Birsent Karagaren, Alen Ozbolt (67' David Malembana), Ante Aralica.
Coach: Bruno Akrapovic.
RC Strasbourg: Matz Sels, Lamine Koné, Stefan Mitrovic, Abdallah N'Dour, Alexander Djiku, Mohamed Simakan, Jonas Martin, Ibrahima Sissoko, Jean Ricner Bellegarde (83' Kévin Lucien Zohi), Youssouf Fofana (65' Kenny Lala), Nuno Da Costa (76' Ludovic Ajorque).
Coach: Thierry Laurey.
Goal: 11' Stefan Mitrovic 0-1.
Referee: João Pedro Pinheiro (POR)   Attendance: 7,600.
Sent off: 11' Josip Tomasevic.

08.08.19 De Kuip, Rotterdam: Feyenoord Rotterdam – Dinamo Tbilisi 4-0 (1-0)
Feyenoord Rotterdam: Kenneth Vermeer, Jan-Arie van der Heijden, Eric Botteghin, Ridgeciano Haps, Bart Nieuwkoop (46' Lutsharel Geertruida), Leroy Fer, Renato Tapia (77' Wouter Burger), Orkun Kökçü, Steven Berghuis, Sam Larsson, Luis Sinisterra (72' Luciano Narsingh). Coach: Jaap Stam.
Dinamo Tbilisi: José Perales, Gudzha Rukhaia, Giorgi Kimadze, Víctor Mongil, Davit Kobouri, Nika Ninua, Levan Kutalia, Giorgi Kukhianidze (77' Bakar Kardava), Giorgi Papava, Nodar Kavtaradze (86' Kwame Karikari), Levan Shengelia (46' Akaki Shulaia).
Coach: Félix Vicente Miranda.
Goals: 43' Luis Sinisterra 1-0, 82' Davit Kobouri 2-0 (og), 85' Steven Berghuis 3-0 (p), 88' Luciano Narsingh 4-0.
Referee: Serhiy Boyko (UKR)   Attendance: 36,500.
Sent off: 79' Akaki Shulaia.

08.08.19 Stadion Vasil Levski, Sofia: CSKA Sofia – Zorya Luhansk 1-1 (1-1)
CSKA Sofia: Vytautas Cerniauskas, Petar Zanev, Kristiyan Malinov, Raúl Albentosa, Nuno Tomás, Geferson (77' Viv Solomon-Otabor), Ivan Turitsov (62' Diego Fabbrini), Tiago Rodrigues, Janio Bikel, Ali Sowe, Evandro (82' Graham Carey). Coach: Ljubomir Petrovic.
Zorya Luhansk: Mykyta Shevchenko, Vitaliy Vernidub, Dmitriy Ivanisenya (70' Levan Arveladze), Oleksandr Tymchyk, Joel Abu Hanna, Dmytro Khomchenovsky, Vladlen Yurchenko (65' Nazariy Rusyn), Bogdan Mykhaylichenko, Vladyslav Kochergin, Pylyp Budkovsky, Maksym Lunyov (65' Bohdan Lednev). Coach: Viktor Skripnik.
Goals: 13' Evandro 1-0, 45+1' Vladlen Yurchenko 1-1 (p).
Referee: Sandro Schärer (SUI)   Attendance: 15,310.

CSKA Sofia played their home match at Stadion Vasil Levski, Sofia, instead of their regular stadium Balgarska Armia Stadium, Sofia.

08.08.19 Stadion Bilino Polje, Zenica: FK Sarajevo – BATE Borisov 1-2 (0-1)
FK Sarajevo: Vladan Kovacevic, Bojan Letic, Darko Lazic, Besim Serbecic, Andrej Djokanovic (58' Alen Mustafic), Nebojsa Gavric (87' Gedeon Guzina), Anel Hebibovic, Haris Handzic, Krste Velkoski, Slobodan Milanovic (74' Aladin Sisic), Benjamin Tatar. Coach: Husref Musemic.
BATE Borisov: Anton Chichkan, Aleksander Filipovic, Aleksey Rios, Igor Stasevich, Dmitriy Baga (89' Evgeniy Berezkin), Stanislav Dragun, Slobodan Simovic, Hervaine Moukam (73' Jasse Tuominen), Evgeni Yablonski, Zakhar Volkov, Maksim Skavysh (90+1' Bojan Dubajic). Coach: Aleksei Baga.
Goals: 19' Dmitriy Baga 0-1, 71' Hervaine Moukam 0-2 (p), 79' Haris Handzic 1-2.
Referee: Alexander Boucaut (BEL)   Attendance: 7,124.

FK Sarajevo played their home match at Stadion Bilino Polje, Zenica, instead of their regular stadium Kosevo City Stadium, Sarajevo.

08.08.19 Stade Josy Barthel, Luxembourg: F91 Dudelange – JK Nõmme Kalju 3-1 (2-1)
F91 Dudelange: Tim Kips, Tom Schnell, Ricardo Delgado, Mehdi Kirch (90+1' Thibaut Lesquoy), Mohamed Bouchouari, Mario Pokar, Ryan Klapp, Dominik Stolz (85' Omar Natami), Charles Morren, Danel Sinani, Antoine Bernier. Coach: Emilio Ferrera.
JK Nõmme Kalju: Pavel Londak, Aleksandr Kulinits, Maximiliano Uggè, Vladimir Avilov, Deniss Tjapkin, Andriy Markovych, Sander Puri, Igor Subbotin (73' Robert Kirss), Réginald Mbu-Alidor, Kasper Paur (60' Max Mata), Peeter Klein (85' Vladyslav Khomutov). Coach: Roman Kozhukhovskyi.
Goals: 28', 30' Dominik Stolz 1-0, 2-0, 41' Sander Puri 2-1, 75' Dominik Stolz 3-1.
Referee: Fábio Veríssimo (POR)   Attendance: 1,239.
Sent off: 90' Robert Kirss.

F91 Dudelange played their home match at Stade Josy Barthel, Luxembourg, instead of their regular stadium, Stade Jos Nosbaum, Dudelange.

08.08.19 Östgötaporten, Norrköping: IFK Norrköping – Hapoel Be'er Sheva 1-1 (0-0)
IFK Norrköping: Isak Pettersson, Lars Gerson, Kasper Larsen, Filip Dagerstål, Rasmus Lauritsen, Simon Thern, Alexander Fransson, Sead Haksabanovic, Maic Sema (69' Kalle Holmberg), Christoffer Nyman, Simon Skrabb (85' Gudmundur Thórarinsson).
Coach: Jens Gustafsson.
Hapoel Be'er Sheva: Ernestas Setkus, Ben Bitton, Loai Taha, Sean Goldberg, Amit Biton, Marwan Kabha, Ramzi Safouri (90' Jimmy Marín), Eden Shamir, David Keltjens, Nigel Hasselbaink (82' Ben Sahar), José Carrillo (76' Niv Zrihan). Coach: Barak Bakhar.
Goals: 51' Maic Sema 1-0, 55' Eden Shamir 1-1.
Referee: Pol van Boekel (HOL)   Attendance: 6,479.

08.08.19   MCH Arena, Herning: FC Midtjylland – Glasgow Rangers FC 2-4 (0-1)
FC Midtjylland: Jesper Hansen, Erik Sviatchenko, Alexander Scholz, Joel Andersson, Rasmus Nicolaisen (73' Awer Mabil), Tim Sparv (58' Júnior Brumado), Gustav Wikheim (58' Mikael Anderson), Evander, Frank Onyeka, Jens-Lys Cajuste, Sory Kaba. Coach: Kenneth Andersen.
Glasgow Rangers FC: Allan McGregor, James Tavernier, Connor Goldson, John Flanagan, Nikola Katic, Scott Arfield (82' Greg Docherty), Ryan Jack, Glen Kamara, Joe Aribo, Jordan Jones (82' Sheyi Ojo), Alfredo Morelos. Coach: Steven Gerrard.
Goals: 43' Alfredo Morelos 0-1, 52' Joe Aribo 0-2, 56' Nikola Katic 0-3, 58' Frank Onyeka 1-3, 63' Sory Kaba 2-3, 70' Scott Arfield 2-4.
Referee: Kristo Tohver (EST)   Attendance: 9,322.

08.08.19   Stadion Rujevica, Rijeka: HNK Rijeka – Aberdeen FC 2-0 (0-0)
NK Rijeka: Andrej Prskalo, Ivan Tomecak (75' Momcilo Raspopovic), Roberto Puncec, Dario Zuparic, Zoran Kvrzic, Luka Capan (85' Dani Iglesias), Tibor Halilovic, Stipe Loncar, Ivan Lepinjica, Antonio Colak, Boadu Maxwell Acosty (64' Robert Muric). Coach: Igor Biscan.
Aberdeen FC: Joe Lewis, Andrew Considine, Shay Logan, Gregory Leigh, Scott McKenna, Funso Ojo, Lewis Ferguson, Niall McGinn (76' Dean Campbell), Ryan Hedges (86' Curtis Main), Sam Cosgrove, Jon Gallagher (76' Scott Wright). Coach: Derek McInnes.
Goals: 62' Antonio Colak 1-0 (p), 88' Robert Muric 2-0.
Referee: Ricardo de Burgos Bengoetxea (ESP)   Attendance: 6,452.

08.08.19   Generali Arena, Vienna: Austria Wien – Apollon Limassol 1-2 (1-1)
Austria Wien: Ivan Lucic, Michael Madl, Florian Klein, Christoph Martschinko, Maudo, Alexander Grünwald, Thomas Ebner (79' Manprit Sarkaria), James Jeggo (58' Christoph Monschein), Tarkan Serbest, Dominik Prokop, Bright Edomwonyi (68' Dominik Fitz). Coach: Christian Ilzer.
Apollon Limassol: Joël Mall, Charis Kyriakou, Attila Szalai, Facundo Pereyra (75' Emilio N'Sue), Héctor Yuste, Sasa Markovic, Diego Aguirre (85' Giorgos Vasiliou), Serge Gakpé, João Pedro, Adrián Sardinero, Giannis Gianniotas (63' Ioannis Pittas).
Coach: Sofronis Avgousti.
Goals: 14' Sasa Markovic 0-1 (p), 41' Florian Klein 1-1 (p), 50' Serge Gakpé 1-2.
Referee: Massimoliano Irrati (ITA)   Attendance: 8,165.
Sent off: 90+2' Michael Madl.

08.08.19   Rheinpark Stadion,Vaduz: FC Vaduz – Eintracht Frankfurt 0-5 (0-3)
FC Vaduz: Benjamin Büchel, Denis Simani, Maximilian Göppel, Pius Dorn, Yannick Schmid, Berkay Sülüngöz, Boris Prokopic, Sandro Wieser (75' Aron Sele), Mohamed Coulibaly, Manuel Sutter (46' Dominik Schwizer), Tunahan Çiçek (66' Noah Frick). Coach: Mario Frick.
Eintracht Frankfurt: Felix Wiedwald, Makoto Hasebe, David Abraham, Martin Hinteregger, Danny da Costa, Gelson Fernandes (66' Jonathan de Guzmán), Filip Kostic, Mijat Gacinovic, Dominik Kohr, Daichi Kamada (73' Ante Rebic), Gonçalo Paciência (73' Dejan Joveljic). Coach: Adi Hütter.
Goals: 11', 27' Filip Kostic 0-1, 0-2, 40' Dominik Kohr 0-3, 53' Gonçalo Paciência 0-4, 63' Mijat Gacinovic 0-5.
Referee: Paul Tierney (ENG)   Attendance: 5,908.

08.08.19   Stadionul Marin Anastasovici, Giurgiu:
Fotbal Club FCSB – FK Mladá Boleslav 0-0
Fotbal Club FCSB: Andrei Daniel Vlad, Valentin Cretu, Aristides Soiledis, Bogdan Planic, Iulian Cristea, Lucian Filip (32' Ionut Pantîru), Ionut Vîna, Ovidiu Popescu (46' Thierry Moutinho), Razvan Oaida, Florin Tanase (80' Lukasz Gikiewicz), Florinel Coman. Coach: Vergil Andronache.
FK Mladá Boleslav: Jan Seda, Daniel Pudil, Laco Takács, Antonín Krapka, Marco Tulio, Marek Matejovsky (75' Lukás Budínsky), Michal Hubínek, Tomás Ladra (65' Jakub Fulnek), Pavel Bucha, Muris Mesanovic (88' Jonas Auer), Nikolay Komlichenko. Coach: Jozef Weber.
Referee: Adrien Jaccottet (SUI)   Attendance: 2,315.

Fotbal Club FCSB played their home match at Stadionul Marin Anastasovici, Giurgiu, instead of their regular stadium Arena Nationala, Bucurest.

08.08.19   Stadio Olimpico Grande Torino, Torino: Torino FC – Shakhtyor Soligorsk 5-0 (2-0)
Torino FC: Salvatore Sirigu, Lorenzo De Silvestri, Cristian Ansaldi, Nicolas N'Koulou (85' Wilfried Singo), Armando Izzo (46' Kevin Bonifazi), Bremer, Soualiho Meïté, Daniele Baselli, Simone Zaza, Andrea Belotti, Álex Berenguer (77' Tomás Rincón). Coach: Walter Mazzarri.
Shakhtyor Soligorsk: Andrey Klimovich, Pavel Rybak, Sergey Matvejchik, Igor Burko, Nikola Antic, Sergey Balanovich (73' Vladimir Khvashchinskiy), Aleksandr Sachivko, Yuri Kovalev, Ruslan Khadarkevich (66' Nikolai Yanush), Max Ebong Ngome, Elis Bakaj (77' Eduards Visnakovs). Coach: Sergey Tashuev.
Goals: 2' Andrea Belotti 1-0, 15' Armando Izzo 2-0, 63' Andrea Belotti 3-0 (p), 72' Lorenzo De Silvestri 4-0, 76' Kevin Bonifazi 5-0.
Referee: Daniel Stefanski (POL)   Attendance: 15,977.

08.08.19   Stadion Miejski Legii Warszawa im. Marszalka Józefa Pilsudskiego, Warszawa:
Legia Warszawa – Atromitos FC 0-0
Legia Warszawa: Radoslaw Majecki, Artur Jedrzejczyk, Igor Lewczuk, Luís Rocha, Arvydas Novikovas, Marko Vesovic, Domagoj Antolic, André Martins, Valeriane Gvilia, Luquinhas, Sandro Kulenovic (65' Carlitos López). Coach: Aleksandar Vukovic.
Atromitos FC: Balász Megyeri, Madson, Tal Kahila, Dimitrios Goutas, Spyros Risvanis, Alexandros Katranis, Javier Umbides (61' Farley Rosa), Charilaos Charisis (72' Roland Ugrai), Spyridon Natsos, Georgios Manousos (83' João Talocha), Apostolos Vellios. Coach: Yannis Anastasiou.
Referee: Manuel Schüttengruber (AUT)   Attendance: 15,093.

08.08.19   Stadion Partizana, Beograd: Partizan Beograd – Yeni Malatyaspor 3-1 (1-0)
Partizan Beograd: Vladimir Stojkovic, Bojan Ostojic (79' Igor Vujacic), Nemanja Miletic (I), Slobodan Urosevic, Strahinja Pavlovic, Zoran Tosic, Aleksandar Scekic, Seydouba Soumah, Sasa Zdjelar, Umar Sadiq (84' Ognjen Ozegovic), Filip Stevanovic (46' Takuma Asano).
Coach: Savo Milosevic.
Yeni Malatyaspor: Fabien Farnolle, Erkan Kas, Mustafa Akbas, Issam Chebake, Arturo Mina, Robin Yalçin, Rahman Bugra Çagiran (56' Guilherme), Ghilane Chalali (71' Murat Yildirim), Adis Jahovic, Thievy Bifouma (46' Gökhan Töre), Moryké Fofana. Coach: Sergen Yalçin.
Goals: 4' Umar Sadiq 1-0, 67' Takuma Asano 2-0, 83' Issam Chebake 2-1, 90' Seydouba Soumah 3-1 (p).
Referee: Sergey Ivanov (RUS)   Attendance: 13,442.

08.08.19   Swissporarena, Luzern: FC Luzern – RCD Espanyol 0-3 (0-1)
FC Luzern: Marius Müller, Christian Schwegler, Lazar Cirkovic, Otar Kakabadze, Lucas Alves "Lucão", Marvin Schulz, Silvan Sidler (61' Ibrahima Ndiaye), Idriz Voca, Tsiy William Ndenge, Shkelqim Demhasaj (78' Francesco Margiotta), Blessing Eleke (89' Eric Tia).
Coach: Thomas Häberli.
RCD Espanyol: Diego López, Dídac Vilà, Javi López, Naldo, Lluís López, Adrià Pedrosa (67' Matías Vargas), Víctor Sánchez, Marc Roca (61' Sergi Darder), Melendo, Facundo Ferreyra (71' Lei Wu), Borja Iglesias. Coach: David Gallego.
Goals: 28' Facundo Ferreyra 0-1, 59' Dídac Vilà 0-2, 89' Matías Vargas 0-3.
Referee: Fran Jovic (CRO)   Attendance: 9,191.

13.08.19   A. Le Coq Arena, Tallinn: JK Nõmme Kalju – F91 Dudelange 0-1 (0-0)
JK Nõmme Kalju: Pavel Londak, Aleksandr Kulinits, Maximiliano Uggè, Vladimir Avilov, Deniss Tjapkin, Andriy Markovych, Sander Puri (78' Aleksandr Volkov), Igor Subbotin (65' Max Mata), Kasper Paur (55' Réginald Mbu-Alidor), Vladyslav Khomutov, Peeter Klein.
Coach: Roman Kozhukhovskyi.
F91 Dudelange: Tim Kips, Tom Schnell, Ricardo Delgado, Mehdi Kirch, Mohamed Bouchouari, Mario Pokar (78' Sabir Bougrine), Ryan Klapp (78' Mickaël Garos), Dominik Stolz, Charles Morren, Danel Sinani (88' Corenthyn Lavie), Antoine Bernier.
Coach: Emilio Ferrera.
Goal: 56' Danel Sinani 0-1.
Referee: Sergey Lapochkin (RUS)   Attendance: 1,202.
Sent off: 34' Vladyslav Khomutov.

JK Nõmme Kalju played their home match at A. Le Coq Arena, Tallinn, instead of their regular stadium Hiiu Stadium, Tallinn which did not meet UEFA requirements.

13.08.19   Windsor Park, Belfast: Linfield FC – FK Sutjeska Niksic 3-2 (2-1)
Linfield FC: Rohan Ferguson, Chris Casement, Ryan McGivern, Matthew Clarke, Mark Stafford, Niall Quinn (76' Jordan Stewart), Jamie Mulgrew, Kirk Millar (67' Joel Cooper), Bastien Héry, Stephen Fallon, Shayne Lavery (79' Andrew Waterworth). Coach: David Healy.
FK Sutjeska Niksic: Vladan Giljen, Darko Bulatovic, Aleksandar Sofranac, Bojan Ciger, Marko Cetkovic, Damir Kojasevic, Milovan Petrovikj, Miljan Vlaisavljevic (63' Marko Vucic), Nemanja Nedic, Novica Erakovic (85' Stefan Nikolic), Bojan Bozovic (73' Bozo Markovic). Coach: Nikola Rakojevic.
Goals: 7' Mark Stafford 1-0, 15' Bojan Bozovic 1-1, 18' Shayne Lavery 2-1, 61' Bojan Bozovic 2-2, 76' Matthew Clarke 3-2.
Referee: Miroslav Zelinka (CZE)   Attendance: 3,639.
Sent off: 36' Aleksandar Sofranac.

13.08.19 Tallaght Stadium, Dublin: Dundalk FC – Slovan Bratislava 1-3 (0-2)
Dundalk FC: Gary Rogers, Dane Massey, Andrew Boyle, Sean Gannon, Daniel Cleary (46' Sean Hoare), Chris Shields, Sean Murray (46' Patrick McEleney), John Mountney, Jamie McGrath (79' Georgie Kelly), Patrick Hoban, Michael Duffy. Coach: Vinny Perth.
Slovan Bratislava: Dominik Greif, Vasil Bozhikov, Vernon, Jurij Medvedev (65' Mitch Apau), Myenty Abena, Marin Ljubicic, Dávid Holman, Joeri de Kamps, Aleksandar Cavric (61' Erik Daniel), Andraz Sporar, Rafael Ratão (85' Artem Sukhotsky). Coach: Ján Kozák.
Goals: 12' Rafael Ratão 0-1, 33' Aleksandar Cavric 0-2, 70' Michael Duffy 1-2, 90+3' Erik Daniel 1-3.
Referee: Robert Schörgenhofer (AUT) Attendance: 4,199.

Dundalk FC played their home match at Tallaght Stadium, Dublin, instead of their regular stadium Oriel Park, Dundalk which did not meet UEFA requirements.

14.08.19 Mikheil Meskhis sakhelobis Stadioni, Tbilisi:
          FC Saburtalo Tbilisi – FC Ararat-Armenia 0-2 (0-1)
FC Saburtalo Tbilisi: Omar Migineishvili, Giorgi Rekhviashvili, Gagi Margvelashvili, Luka Lakvekheliani, Levan Kakubava (69' Tornike Gorgiashvili), Giorgi Diasamidze (58' Levan Kenia), Sandro Altunashvili, Nikoloz Mali, Alwyn Tera, Giorgi Gabedava (60' Ognjen Rolovic), Giorgi Kokhreidze. Coach: Giorgi Chiabrishvili.
FC Ararat-Armenia: Dmitriy Abakumov, Rochdi Achenteh, Dmitri Guzj, Ângelo Meneses, Georgi Pashov, Gor Malakyan (70' Ilja Antonov), Armen Ambartsumyan (57' Petros Avetisyan), Kódjo Alphonse, Anton Kobyalko (80' Aleksandar Damcevski), Furdjel Narsingh, Mailson. Coach: Vardan Minasyan.
Goals: 10' Anton Kobyalko 0-1, 67' Petros Avetisyan 0-2 (p).
Referee: Mykola Balakin (UKR) Attendance: 14,904.

14.08.19 Estádio Dom Afonso Henriques, Guimarães:
          Vitória de Guimarães – FK Ventspils 6-0 (1-0)
Vitória de Guimarães: João Miguel Silva, Florent Hanin, Pedrão, Falaye Sacko, Edmond Tapsoba, Rochinha, Pêpê Rodrigues, Almoatasembellah Ali Mohamed, Joseph Amoah (7' André Almeida), Alexandre Guedes (63' João Pedro), Davidson (76' João Carlos Teixeira). Coach: Ivo Vieira.
FK Ventspils: Vjaceslavs Kudrjavcevs, Jean Alcénat (52' Pavel Osipov), Abdoul Mamah, Giorgi Mchedlishvili, Hélio Batista, Rashid Obuobi (58' Daniils Ulimbasevs), Guga Palavandishvili, Ingars Stuglis (35' Kaspars Svārups), Tosin Aiyegun, Mykhaylo Sergiychuk, Lucas Villela. Coach: Igor Klosovs.
Goals: 28' Davidson 1-0, 48', 58' Rochinha 2-0, 3-0, 79' João Carlos Teixeira 4-0, 80' João Pedro 5-0, 86' Pêpê Rodrigues 6-0.
Referee: Halil Umut Meler (TUR) Attendance: 12,741.

14.08.19 Stadio Peristeriou, Athens: Atromitos FC – Legia Warszawa 0-2 (0-1)
Atromitos FC: Balász Megyeri, Madson (69' Javier Umbides), Tal Kahila (58' Roland Ugrai), Dimitrios Goutas, Spyros Risvanis, Alexandros Katranis, Farley Rosa, Charilaos Charisis, Spyridon Natsos, Georgios Manousos, Apostolos Vellios (84' Clarck N'Sikulu). Coach: Yannis Anastasiou.
Legia Warszawa: Radoslaw Majecki, Artur Jedrzejczyk, Igor Lewczuk, Luís Rocha (62' Mateusz Wieteska), Pawel Stolarski, Marko Vesovic (68' Dominik Nagy), André Martins, Cafú, Valeriane Gvilia, Luquinhas (77' Carlitos López), Sandro Kulenovic. Coach: Aleksandar Vukovic.
Goals: 29' Pawel Stolarski 0-1, 51' Valeriane Gvilia 0-2.
Referee: Bas Nijhuis (HOL) Attendance: 2,019.

15.08.19   Telia 5G -areena, Helsinki: HJK Helsinki – Riga FC 2-2 (1-0)
HJK Helsinki: Maksim Rudakov, Rafinha (81' Ivan Tarasov), Nikolai Alho (77' Henri Toivomäki), Daniel O'Shaughnessy, Faith Obilor, William Parra, Riku Riski, Petteri Forsell, Kaan Kairinen (71' Sebastian Dahlström), Evans Mensah, Tim Väyrynen.
Coach: Toni Koskela.
Riga FC: Roberts Ozols, Georgios Valerianos, Herdi Prenga, Stefan Panic, Antonijs Cernomordijs, Tomislav Saric (56' Olegs Laizāns), Felipe Brisola, Roger (90+2' Ritvars Rugins), Armands Pētersons, Roman Debelko, Vladislavs Fjodorovs (60' Deniss Rakels).
Coach: Mihails Konevs.
Goals: 5' Petteri Forsell 1-0, 62' Roman Debelko 1-1, 69' Tim Väyrynen 2-1, 80' Roman Debelko 2-2.
Referee: Mohammed Al-Hakim (SWE)   Attendance: 6,847.

Riga FC won on away goals.

15.08.19   Boris Paichadze Dinamo Arena, Tbilisi:
               Dinamo Tbilisi – Feyenoord Rotterdam 1-1 (0-0)
Dinamo Tbilisi: José Perales, Gudzha Rukhaia, Giorgi Kimadze (80' Irakli Azarov), Víctor Mongil, Davit Kobouri (37' Mychailo Shyshka), Nika Ninua, Abdel Jalil Medioub, Giorgi Papava, Nodar Kavtaradze (69' Nodar Iashvili), Bakar Kardava, Levan Shengelia.
Coach: Félix Vicente Miranda.
Feyenoord Rotterdam: Kenneth Vermeer, Jan-Arie van der Heijden, Eric Botteghin (70' Liam Kelly), Ridgeciano Haps (70' Tyrell Malacia), Lutsharel Geertruida, Renato Tapia, Orkun Kökçü, Wouter Burger, Luciano Narsingh, Steven Berghuis (79' Naoufal Bannis), Sam Larsson. Coach: Jaap Stam.
Goals: 52' Levan Shengelia 1-0, 57' Eric Botteghin 1-1.
Referee: Sascha Stegemann (GER)

Match was played behind closed doors.

15.08.19   Otkrytie Arena, Moskva: Spartak Moskva – FC Thun 2-1 (0-1)
Spartak Moskva: Aleksandr Maksimenko, Andrey Eshchenko, Georgi Dzhikiya, Samuel Gigot, Ayrton, André Schürrle (88' Jano Ananidze), Roman Zobnin, Reziuan Mirzov (70' Lorenzo Melgarejo), Ayaz Guliev, Zelimkhan Bakaev (77' Georgi Melkadze), Ezequiel Ponce.
Coach: Oleg Kononov.
FC Thun: Guillaume Faivre, Stefan Glarner, Nikki Havenaar, Nicola Sutter (79' Dennis Salanovic), Sven Joss (71' Ridge Munsy), Chris Kablan, Miguel Castroman, Basil Stillhart, Kenan Fatkic (63' Roy Gelmi), Nias Hefti, Simone Rapp. Coach: Marc Schneider.
Goals: 7' Stefan Glarner 0-1, 52' Ezequiel Ponce 1-1, 58' André Schürrle 2-1.
Referee: Srdjan Jovanovic (SRB)   Attendance: 33,076.

15.08.19   Marijampolės sporto centro stadione, Marijampolė:
FK Sūduva Marijampolė – Maccabi Tel Aviv 2-1 (2-0)
FK Sūdova Marijampolė: Ivan Kardum, Algis Jankauskas, Andro Svrljuga, Aleksandar Zivanovic, Semir Kerla, Jovan Cadjenovic, Ovidijus Verbickas (68' Ivan Hladík), Giedrius Matulevicius (79' Renan Oliveira), Josip Tadic (73' Eligijus Jankauskas), Mihret Topcagic, Paulius Golubickas. Coach: Vladimir Cheburin.
Maccabi Tel Aviv: Andreas Gianniotis, Saborit (77' Dor Peretz), Geraldes, Shahar Piven-Bachtiar, Jair Amador, Avi Rikan (58' Matan Hozez), Dor Mikha, Dan Glazer, Itay Shechter (46' Nick Blackman), Chikeluba Ofoedu, Yonatan Cohen. Coach: Vladimir Ivic.
Goals: 12' Mihret Topcagic 1-0, 45+1' Andro Svrljuga 2-0, 86' Nick Blackman 2-1.
Referee: Tore Hansen (NOR)   Attendance: 5,337.
Sent off: 90+4' Yonatan Cohen.

15.08.19   Borisov Arena, Borisov: BATE Borisov – FK Sarajevo 0-0
BATE Borisov: Anton Chichkan, Aleksander Filipovic, Aleksey Rios, Igor Stasevich, Dmitriy Baga, Stanislav Dragun (90+2' Evgeniy Berezkin), Slobodan Simovic, Hervaine Moukam (68' Jasse Tuominen), Evgeni Yablonski, Zakhar Volkov, Maksim Skavysh (79' Bojan Dubajic). Coach: Aleksei Baga.
FK Sarajevo: Vladan Kovacevic, Bojan Letic, Darko Lazic, Besim Serbecic, Andrej Djokanovic (33' Alen Mustafic), Nebojsa Gavric (73' Slobodan Milanovic), Anel Hebibovic, Aladin Sisic, Haris Handzic, Krste Velkoski, Benjamin Tatar (53' Mersudin Ahmetovic). Coach: Husref Musemic.
Referee: Kevin Blom (HOL)   Attendance: 11,876.

15.08.19   Friends Arena, Solna: AIK Solna – FC Sheriff Tiraspol 1-1 (0-0)
AIK Solna: Oscar Linnér, Per Karlsson, Robert Lundström, Rasmus Lindkvist, Karol Mets, Daniel Granli, Sebastian Larsson, Enoch Adu, Anton Salétros (59' Nabil Bahoui), Tarik Elyounoussi (90+1' Panajotis Dimitriadis), Henok Goitom. Coach: Rikard Norling.
FC Sheriff Tiraspol: Zvonimir Mikulic, Ousmane N'Diaye, Matej Palcic (67' Artem Hordienko), Andrej Lukic, Mateo Muzek (90' Jaroslaw Jach), Cristiano, Ariel Borysiuk, Jury Kendysh, Liridon Latifi, Gabrijel Boban, Robert Tambe (80' Wilfried Balima).
Coach: Zoran Zekic.
Goals: 61' Nabil Bahoui 1-0, 86' Gabrijel Boban 1-1.
Referee: Roi Reinshreiber (ISR)   Attendance: 13,122.

15.08.19   Stadyen Dynama, Minsk: Shakhtyor Soligorsk – Torino FC 1-1 (0-0)
Shakhtyor Soligorsk: Andrey Klimovich, Pavel Rybak (67' Igor Burko), Sergey Matvejchik, Nikola Antic, Sergey Balanovich (84' Darko Bodul), Aleskandr Selyava, Yuri Kovalev, Ruslan Khadarkevich, Július Szöke, Max Ebong Ngome, Elis Bakaj (76' Nikolai Yanush).
Coach: Sergey Tashuev.
Torino FC: Salvatore Sirigu, Lorenzo De Silvestri, Cristian Ansaldi (62' Ola Aina), Nicolas N'Koulou, Kevin Bonifazi (83' Wilfried Singo), Bremer, Tomás Rincón, Soualiho Meïté, Sasa Lukic, Simone Zaza, Andrea Belotti (76' Vincenzo Millico). Coach: Walter Mazzarri.
Goals: 80' Simone Zaza 0-1, 90+1' Nikolai Yanush 1-1 (p).
Referee: Radu Petrescu (ROM)   Attendance: 6,154.

15.08.19   Neo GSP Stadium, Nicosia: Apollon Limassol – Austria Wien 3-1 (1-1)
Apollon Limassol: Joël Mall, Charis Kyriakou (75' Emilio N'Sue), Attila Szalai, Facundo Pereyra (66' Ioannis Pittas), Héctor Yuste, Sasa Markovic, Diego Aguirre, Serge Gakpé (83' Emilio Zelaya), João Pedro, Adrián Sardinero, Giannis Gianniotas. Coach: Sofronis Avgousti.
Austria Wien: Ivan Lucic, Florian Klein, Stephan Zwierschitz, Christoph Martschinko, Johannes Handl, Maudo, Alexander Grünwald, Maximilian Sax (63' Bright Edomwonyi), Vesel Demaku, Christoph Monschein (71' Benedikt Pichler), Dominik Fitz (63' James Jeggo). Coach: Christian Ilzer.
Goals: 18' Maudo 0-1, 45+2' Serge Gakpé 1-1 (p), 55' Johannes Handl 2-1 (og), 67' Giannis Gianniotas 3-1.
Goals: Pawel Gil (POL)   Attendance: 2,750.

Apollon Limassol played their home match at Neo GSP Stadium, Nicosia, instead of their regular stadium Tsirio Stadium, Limassol.

15.08.19   Lokotrans Aréna, Mladá Boleslav:
FK Mladá Boleslav – Fotbal Club FCSB 0-1 (0-0)
FK Mladá Boleslav: Jan Seda, Daniel Pudil, Laco Takács, Antonín Krapka, Marco Tulio (46' Jakub Fulnek), Marek Matejovsky, Michal Hubínek (90+2' Jirí Klíma), Tomás Ladra, Pavel Bucha, Muris Mesanovic, Tomás Wágner (70' Ewerton). Coach: Jozef Weber.
Fotbal Club FCSB: Andrei Daniel Vlad, Valentin Cretu, Aristides Soiledis, Bogdan Planic, Iulian Cristea, Thierry Moutinho (63' Ionut Pantîru), Ionut Vîna, Ovidiu Popescu, Razvan Oaida, Florin Tanase, Florinel Coman. Coach: Vergil Andronache.
Goal: 90+1' Ionut Pantîru 0-1.
Referee: Jonathan Lardot (BEL)   Attendance: 4,695.
Sent off: 75' Antonín Krapka.

15.08.19   Yeni Malatya Stadyumu, Malatya: Yeni Malatyaspor – Partizan Beograd 1-0 (1-0)
Yeni Malatyaspor: Fabien Farnolle, Erkan Kas, Mustafa Akbas, Issam Chebake (10' Rahman Bugra Çagiran), Arturo Mina, Murat Yildirim, Gökhan Töre, Guilherme (74' Eren Tozlu), Ghilane Chalali, Adis Jahovic, Thievy Bifouma (68' Moryké Fofana). Coach: Sergen Yalçin.
Partizan Beograd: Vladimir Stojkovic, Bojan Ostojic, Nemanja Miletic (I), Slobodan Urosevic, Strahinja Pavlovic, Zoran Tosic (71' Aleksandar Lutovac), Aleksandar Seekic, Seydouba Soumah (82' Lazar Pavlovic), Sasa Zdjelar, Takuma Asano, Umar Sadiq (90+6' Ognjen Ozegovic). Coach: Savo Milosevic.
Goal: 7' Adis Jahovic 1-0.
Referee: Chris Kavanagh (ENG)   Attendance: 14,665.

15.08.19   Stadion Pecara, Sikori Brijeg: Zrinjski Mostar – Malmö FF 1-0 (0-0)
Zrinjski Mostar: Ivan Brkic, Mario Ticinovic (72' Marko Bencun), Tomislav Barbaric, Slobodan Jakovljevic, Advan Kadusic, Ivan Curjuric (81' Frane Cirjak), Damir Sovsic, Edin Rustemovic, Miljan Govedarica, Stanisa Mandic (65' Pero Stojkic), Ivan Lendric. Coach: Hari Vukas.
Malmö FF: Johan Dahlin, Behrang Safari, Rasmus Bengtsson, Eric Larsson, Lasse Nielsen, Jonas Knudsen, Anders Christiansen (68' Arnór Ingvi Traustason), Fouad Bachirou, Oscar Lewicki, Markus Rosenberg (87' Romain Gall), Marcus Antonsson (6' Guillermo Molins). Coach: Uwe Rösler.
Goal: 90+1' Damir Sovsic 1-0 (p).
Referee: Artyom Kuchin (KAZ)   Attendance: 4,509.

Zrinjski Mostar played their home match at Stadion Pecara, Siroki Brijeg, instead of their regular stadium Stadion pod Bijelim Brijegom, Mostar.

15.08.19   Slavutych-Arena, Zaporizhia: Zorya Luhansk – CSKA Sofia 1-0 (0-0)
Zorya Luhansk: Mykyta Shevchenko, Vitaliy Vernidub, Dmitriy Ivanisenya, Oleksandr Tymchyk, Joel Abu Hanna (4' Yevgen Cheberko), Dmyto Khomchenovsky, Vladlen Yurchenko (46' Bohdan Lednev), Bogdan Mykhaylichenko, Vladyslav Kochergin, Pylyp Budkovsky (90+4' Vladyslav Kabayev), Nazariy Rusyn. Coach: Viktor Skripnik.
CSKA Sofia: Vytautas Cerniauskas, Petar Zanev, Kristiyan Malinov (82' Diego Fabbrini), Raúl Albentosa, Nuno Tomás, Geferson (87' Tony Watt), Ivan Turitsov, Tiago Rodrigues, Janio Bikel, Ali Sowe, Evandro (56' Mitko Mitkov). Coach: Ljubomir Petrovic.
Goal: 89' Nazariy Rusyn 1-0.
Referee: Amaury Delerue (FRA)   Attendance: 7,857.
Sent off: 22' Ivan Turitsov, 90' Nazariy Rusyn.

Zorya Luhansk played their home match at Slavutych-Arena, Zaporizhia, instead of their regular stadium Avanhard Stadium, Luhansk, due to the war conditions in Eastern Ukraine.

15.08.19   HaMoshava Stadium, Petah Tikva:
             Bnei Yehuda Tel Aviv – Neftçi PFK Baku 2-1 (1-0)
Bnei Yehuda Tel Aviv: Emilijus Zubas, Dan Mori, Alban Pnishi, Shay Mazor (74' Shimshon Tza'adon), Daniel Felscher, Amir Rustom, Tamabi Sages, Ismaila Soro, Mohammad Ghadir (78' Ariel Matan Lazmi), Dor Jan (88' Ben Shimoni), Avishay Cohen. Coach: Yossi Abukasis.
Neftçi PFK Baku: Salahat Agayev, Kyrylo Petrov, Mamadou Mbodj, Anton Krivotsyuk, Omar Buludov (63' Bagaliy Dabo), Soni Mustivar, Emin Makhmudov, Mamadou Kane (46' Rahman Hadzhiyev), Steeven Joseph-Monrose, Rauf Aliyev, Dário Júnior da Silva (81' Vangelis Platelas). Coach: Roberto Bordin.
Goals: 15' Dor Jan 1-0, 66' Tamabi Sages 2-0, 90+3' Emin Makhmudov 2-1 (p).
Referee: Daniele Doveri (ITA)   Attendance: 4,000.

Bnei Yehuda Tel Aviv played their home match at HaMoshava Stadium, Petah Tikva, instead of their regular stadium Bloomfield Stadium, Tel Aviv which is undergoing renovation.

15.08.19   Racecourse Ground, Wrexham:
             The New Saints – PFC Ludogorets Razgrad 0-4 (0-2)
The New Saints: Paul Harrison, Christopher Marriott, Blaine Hudson, Keston Davies, Kane Lewis, Ryan Harrington, Aeron Edwards, Daniel Redmond, Ryan Brobbel (78' Adrian Cieslewicz), Jamie Mullan (74' Billy Whitehouse), Dean Ebbe (68' Kurtis Byrne). Coach: Scott Ruscoe.
PFC Ludogorets Razgrad: Renan, Stanislav Manolev, Dragos Grigore, Cicinho, Rafael Forster, Svetoslav Dyakov, Wanderson, Jacek Góralski (68' Dan Biton), Stéphane Badji, Jody Lukoki (75' Mavis Tchibota), Jakub Swierczok (81' Claudiu Keserü). Coach: Stoicho Stoev.
Goals: 36' Jakub Swierczok 0-1, 42' Jody Lukoki 0-2, 77' Jakub Swierczok 0-3, 90+2' Dan Biton 0-4.
Referee: Kristo Tohver (EST)   Attendance: 712.

The New Saints played their home match at Racecource Ground, Wrexham, instead of their regular stadium Park Hill, Oswestry due to UEFA regulations.

15.08.19 Yaakov Turner Toto Stadium, Beersheva:
Hapoel Be'er Sheva – IFK Norrköping 3-1 (0-0)
Hapoel Be'er Sheva: Ernestas Setkus, Ben Bitton, Loai Taha, Sean Goldberg, Amit Biton, Marwan Kabha, Ramzi Safouri (84' Jimmy Marín), Eden Shamir, David Keltjens, Ben Sahar (60' Niv Zrihan), Nigel Hasselbaink (78' José Carrillo). Coach: Barak Bakhar.
IFK Norrköping: Isak Pettersson, Lars Gerson, Kasper Larsen, Filip Dagerstål, Rasmus Lauritsen, Gudmundur Thórarinsson, Simon Thern, Alexander Fransson, Sead Haksabanovic (78' Egzon Binaku), Christoffer Nyman (88' Kalle Holmberg), Simon Skrabb (78' Henrik Castegren). Coach: Jens Gustafsson.
Goals: 67' Niv Zrihan 1-0, 72' Nigel Hasselbaink 2-0, 82' Rasmus Lauritsen 2-1, 90+4' Niv Zrihan 3-1.
Referee: Anastasios Papapetrou (GRE)   Attendance: 10,088.

15.08.19 Medical Park Stadyumu, Trabzon: Trabzonspor – AC Sparta Praha 2-1 (1-0)
Trabzonspor: Ugurcan Çakir, João Pereira, Filip Novák, Majid Hosseini, Hüseyin Türkmen, José Sosa, Abdülkadir Parmak (84' Dogan Erdogan), Abdülkadir Ömür (90+9' Yusuf Sari), Anthony Nwakaeme, Alexander Sørloth (79' John Obi Mikel), Caleb Ekuban.
Coach: Ünal Karaman.
AC Sparta Praha: Florin Nita, Costa Nhamoinesu (61' Dávid Hancko), Uros Radakovic (67' Libor Kozák), Matej Hanousek, Guélor Kanga, Martin Hasek (76' Georges Mandjeck), Srdjan Plavsic, Michal Sácek, Ladislav Krejcí, Benjamin Tetteh, Adam Hlozek. Coach: Václav Jílek.
Goals: 11' Alexander Sørloth 1-0, 78' Adam Hlozek 1-1. 90+8' Filip Novák 2-1.
Referee: Jakob Kehlet (DEN)   Attendance: 34,462.
Sent off: 88' Srdjan Plavsic.

15.08.19 Ta'Qali National Stadium, Ta'Qali: Valletta FC – FK Astana 0-4 (0-2)
Valletta FC: Yenez Cini, Joseph Zerafa (54' Eslit Sala), Ryan Camilleri, Jean Borg, Douglas Packer, Rowen Muscat, Enmy Peña, Matteo Piciollo (62' Shaun Dimech), Kevin Tulimieri (62' Nicholas Pulis), Yuri, Mario Fontanella. Coach: Darren Abdilla.
FK Astana: Nenad Eric, Antonio Rukavina, Dmitriy Shomko (80' Abzal Beysebekov), Evgeny Postnikov, Luka Simunovic, Rúnar Sigurjónsson (68' Zarko Tomasevic), Marin Tomasov, Ivan Maevski, Serikzhan Muzhikov (76' Rangelo Janga), Roman Murtazaev, Dorin Rotariu. Coach: Roman Grygorchuk.
Goals: 25' Roman Murtazaev 0-1, 37' Marin Tomasov 0-2, 68' Roman Murtazaev 0-3, 89' Marin Tomasov 0-4.
Referee: Stephan Klossner (SUI)   Attendance: 595.

15.08.19 Doosan Aréna, Plzen: Viktoria Plzen – Royal Antwerp FC 2-1 (0-0, 1-0) (a.e.t.)
FC Viktoria Plzen: Ales Hruska, David Limbersky, Jakub Brabec, Lukás Hejda, Milan Havel (114' Radim Reznik), Tomás Horava, Jan Kopic, Patrik Hrosovsky, Lukás Kalvach (75' Tomás Chory), Joel Kayamba (107' Adam Hlousek), Michal Krmencík (102' Ondrej Mihálik). Coach: Pavel Vrba.
Royal Antwerp FC: Sinan Bolat, Simen Juklerød, Dylan Batubinsika, Buta, Abdoulaye Seck, Faris Haroun, Lior Refaelov, Geoffry Hairemans (94' Amara Baby), Alexis De Sart (106' Sander Coopman), Ivo Rodrigues (84' Didier Lamkel Zé), Jonathan Bolingi (45' Dieumerci Mbokani). Coach: László Bölöni.
Goals: 81', 97' Michal Krmencík 1-0, 2-0, 113' Dieumerci Mbokani 2-1.
Referee: Davide Massa (ITA)   Attendance: 9,717.
Sent off: 101' Abdoulaye Seck.

Royal Antwerp FC won after extra time on away goals.

15.08.19 Olympiako Stadio Spyros Louis, Athens:
AEK Athens – CS Universitatea Craiova 1-1 (1-0)
AEK Athens: Vasilios Barkas, Ognjen Vranjes, Paulinho, Hélder Lopes, Efstratios Svarnas, Nenad Krsticic (58' David Simão), Petros Mandalos, André Simões (83' Konstantinos Galanopoulos), Chico Geraldes, Nélson Oliveira, Marko Livaja (58' Daniele Verde). Coach: Miguel Cardoso.
CS Universitatea Craiova: Mirko Pigliacelli, Renato Kelic, Ivan Martic, Nicusor Bancu, Stephane Acka, Alexandru Mateiu, Cristian Barbut, Antoni Ivanov (80' Vasile Constantin), Alexandru Cicâldau, Valentin Mihaila (55' Bogdan Vatajelu), Mihai Roman (II) (64' Carlos Fortes). Coach: Corneliu Papura.
Goals: 26' Petros Mandalos 1-0, 63' Antoni Ivanov 1-1.
Referee: Jérôme Brisard (FRA)

Match was played behind closed doors.

15.08.19 Philips Stadion, Eindhoven: PSV Eindhoven – FK Haugesund 0-0
PSV Eindhoven: Jeroen Zoet, Nick Viergever, Timo Baumgartl, Denzel Dumfries (46' Jordan Teze), Érick Gutiérrez, Michal Sadílek, Pablo Rosario, Bruma (59' Mohammed Ihattaren), Steven Bergwijn, Donyell Malen, Cody Gakpo. Coach: Mark van Bommel.
FK Haugesund: Helge Sandvik, Doug Bergqvist, Mikkel Desler, Benjamin Tiedemann Hansen, Sondre Tronstad, Thore Baardsen Pedersen, Niklas Sandberg, Bruno Leite (85' Joakim Nilsen), Kristoffer Velde, Kevin Krygård (75' Christian Grindheim), Ibrahima Koné (70' Martin Samuelsen). Coach: Jostein Grindhaug.
Referee: Juan Martínez Munuera (ESP)   Attendance: 22,759.

15.08.19 Stadio Harilaou Kleánthis Vikelídis, Thessaloniki:
Aris Saloniki – Molde FK 3-1 (2-0, 3-0) (a.e.t.)
Aris Saloniki: Julián Cuesta, Daniel Sundgren, Mihály Korhut (104' Migjen Basha), Lindsay Rose, Georgios Delizisis, Nicolas Diguiny, Javier Matilla, Ioannis Fetfatzidis (79' Hamza Younès), Lucas Sasha, Daniel Larsson (64' Nicolás Martínez), Brown Ideye (102' Martín Tonso). Coach: Savvas Pantelidis.
Molde FK: Álex Craninx, Ruben Gabrielsen, Kristoffer Haraldseid, Kristoffer Haugen (55' Vegard Forren), Martin Bjørnbak, Magnus Eikrem (75' Martin Ellingsen), Etzaz Hussain, Eirik Hestad (99' Erling Knudtzon), Fredrik Aursnes, Ohi Omoijuanfo (88' Mathis Bolly), Leke James. Coach: Erling Moe.
Goals: 25' Javier Matilla 1-0, 37' Georgios Delizisis 2-0, 84' Nicolas Diguiny 3-0, 105+1' Mathis Bolly 3-1.
Referee: Robert Harvey (IRL)   Attendance: 12,821.

Molde FK won after extra time.

15.08.19 Stade de la Meinau, Strasbourg: RC Strasbourg – Lokomotiv Plovdiv 1-0 (1-0)
RC Strasbourg: Matz Sels, Lamine Koné, Stefan Mitrovic, Lionel Carole, Abdallah N'Dour, Mohamed Simakan (83' Jonas Martin), Benjamin Corgnet (77' Kenny Lala), Dimitri Liénard, Ibrahima Sissoko, Nuno Da Costa (65' Ludovic Ajorque), Kévin Lucien Zohi.
Coach: Thierry Laurey.
Lokomotiv Plovdiv: Martin Lukov, Milos Petrovic, David Malembana, Stephen Eze, Dimitar Iliev, Momchil Tsvetanov, Parvizchon Umarbaev (77' Georgi Iliev), Petar Vitanov (63' Wiris), Birsent Karagaren (83' Eliton Pardinho Junior), Alen Ozbolt, Ante Aralica.
Coach: Bruno Akrapovic.
Goal: 8' Kévin Lucien Zohi 1-0.
Referee: John Beaton (SCO)   Attendance: 19,109.

15.08.19   Cars Jeans Stadion, The Hague: AZ Alkmaar – FK Mariupol 4-0 (2-0)
AZ Alkmaar: Marco Bizot, Ron Vlaar (80' Pantelis Hatzidiakos), Stijn Wuytens (75' Jordy Clasie), Jonas Svensson, Thomas Ouwejan, Owen Wijndal, Fredrik Midtsjø, Teun Koopmeiners, Oussama Idrissi, Myron Boadu (69' Ferdy Druijf), Calvin Stengs. Coach: Arne Slot.
FC Mariupol: Rustam Khudzhamov, Sergey Yavorskiy, Pavel Polegenko, Igor Kyryukhantsev, Sergiy Chobotenko, Oleksii Bykov (46' Viktor Korniienko), Valeriy Fedorchuk, Vyacheslav Tankovskiy, Vyacheslav Churko (69' Dmytro Topalov), Dmytro Myshnov (83' Oleksii Kashchuk), Vladislav Vakula. Coach: Oleksandr Babych.
Goals: 20' Calvin Stengs 1-0, 44' Thomas Ouwejan 2-0, 62' Stijn Wuytens 3-0, 90' Sergey Yavorskiy 4-0 (og).
Referee: Bartosz Frankowski (POL)   Attendance: 8,018.

AZ Alkmaar played their home match at Cars Jeans Stadion, The Hague, instead of their regular stadium AFAS Stadion, Alkmaar, due to a roof collapse on 10th August 2019 at the AFAS Stadion.

15.08.19   GHELAMCO-arena, Gent: KAA Gent – AEK Larnaca 3-0 (0-0)
KAA Gent: Thomas Kaminski, Nana Asare, Mikael Lustig, Igor Plastun, Michael Ngadeu-Ngadjui, Vadis Odjidja-Ofoe, Brecht Dejaegere, Elisha Owusu, Laurent Depoitre (81' Alessio Castro-Montes), Roman Yaremchuk (87' Louis Verstraete), Jonathan David. Coach: Jess Thorup.
AEK Larnaca: Toño, Mikel González, Daniel Mojsov, Truyols (73' Raúl Ruiz), Ivan Trickovski, Lluis Sastre, Acorán, Nacho Cases (83' Jean Luc Assoubre), Hector Hevel, Apostolos Giannou, Tete (73' Florian Taulemesse). Coach: Imanol Idiakez.
Goals: 64' Laurent Depoitre 1-0, 90+3', 90+6' Jonathan David 2-0, 3-0.
Referee: Martin Strömbergsson (SWE)   Attendance: 15,533.

15.08.19   Commerzbank-Arena, Frankfurt am Main:
              Eintracht Frankfurt – FC Vaduz 1-0 (1-0)
Eintracht Frankfurt: Kevin Trapp, Marco Russ (37' Martin Hinteregger), Timothy Chandler, Erik Durm, Almamy Touré, Evan Obite N'Dicka, Jonathan de Guzmán, Sebastian Rode (72' Daichi Kamada), Lucas Torró, Mijat Gacinovic (66' Gonçalo Paciência), Dejan Joveljic. Coach: Adi Hütter.
FC Vaduz: Benjamin Büchel, Denis Simani, Maximilian Göppel, Pius Dorn, Yannick Schmid, Berkay Sülüngöz, Boris Prokopic (74' Noah Frick), Sandro Wieser, Mohamed Coulibaly, Manuel Sutter (66' Dominik Schwizer), Tunahan Çiçek (80' Nicolae Milinceanu). Coach: Mario Frick.
Goal: 31' Jonathan de Guzmán 1-0.
Referee: Nikola Dabanovic (MNE)   Attendance: 48,000.

15.08.19   Estádio Municipal de Braga, Braga: Sporting Braga – Brøndby IF 3-1 (2-0)
Sporting Braga: Matheus Magalhães, Ricardo Esgaio, Pablo Santos (71' Vítor Tormena), Caju, Bruno Viana, João Novais, João Palhinha, André Horta (59' Bruno Xadas), Wilson Eduardo (67' Francisco Trincão), Paulinho, Murilo. Coach: Sá Pinto.
Brøndby IF: Marvin Schwäbe, Paulus Arajuuri, Anthony Jung, Hjörtur Hermannsson, Jens Gammelby, Dominik Kaiser (46' Kasper Fisker), Josip Radosevic, Simon Hedlund (73' Peter Bjur), Tobias Børkeeiet, Jesper Lindstrøm, Kamil Wilczek (46' Ante Erceg). Coach: Niels Frederiksen.
Goals: 19' João Palhinha 1-0, 41' André Horta 2-0, 66' Paulinho 3-0, 85' Peter Bjur 3-1.
Referee: Aleksei Eskov (RUS)   Attendance: 11,964.

15.08.19   Molineux Stadium, Wolverhampton:
Wolverhampton Wanderers – Pyunik Yerevan FC 4-0 (0-0)
Wolverhampton Wanderers: John Rudy, Conor Coady, Vallejo, Rúben Vinagre, Max Kilman, João Moutinho (52' Leander Dendoncker), Romain Saïss, Morgan Gibbs-White, Adama Traoré, Patrick Cutrone (72' Raúl Jiménez), Pedro Neto (72' Diogo Jota).
Coach: Nuno Espírito Santo.
Pyunik Yerevan FC: Andrija Dragojevic, Antonio Stankov, Maksim Zhestokov, Armen Manucharyan, Anton Belov, Karlen Mkrtchyan, Sergiy Shevchuk (75' Denis Mahmudov), Artem Simonyan (71' Artak Yedigaryan), Stanislav Efimov (46' Aleksandr Galimov), Erik Vardanyan, Artur Miranyan. Coach: Aleksandr Tarkhanov.
Goals: 54' Pedro Neto 1-0, 58' Morgan Gibbs-White 2-0, 64' Rúben Vinagre 3-0, 87' Diogo Jota 4-0.
Referee: Donatas Rumsas (LTU)   Attendance: 29,391.

15.08.19   Ibrox Stadium, Glasgow: Glasgow Rangers FC – FC Midtjylland 3-1 (2-0)
Glasgow Rangers FC: Allan McGregor, James Tavernier, Connor Goldson, John Flanagan, Nikola Katic, Steven Davis, Scott Arfield, Ryan Jack (69' Greg Docherty), Glen Kamara, Sheyi Ojo (69' Jordan Jones), Alfredo Morelos (81' Jermain Defoe). Coach: Steven Gerrard.
FC Midtjylland: Jesper Hansen, Erik Sviatchenko, Alexander Scholz, Joel Andersson, Rasmus Nicolaisen, Gustav Wikheim, Evander, Mikael Anderson (69' Tim Sparv), Frank Onyeka, Jens-Lys Cajuste (46' Awer Mabil), Sory Kaba (82' Artem Dovbyk).
Coach: Kenneth Andersen.
Goals: 14' Alfredo Morelos 1-0, 39' Sheyi Ojo 2-0, 49' Alfredo Morelos 3-0, 72' Evander 3-1.
Referee: Marco Di Bello (ITA)   Attendance: 47,184.

15.08.19   Pittodrie Stadium, Aberdeen: Aberdeen FC – HNK Rijeka 0-2 (0-2)
Aberdeen FC: Joe Lewis, Andrew Considine, Shay Logan, Gregory Leigh, Scott McKenna, Funso Ojo, Lewis Ferguson, Niall McGinn (35' Dean Campbell), Ryan Hedges (75' James Wilson), Sam Cosgrove (53' Curtis Main), Jon Gallagher. Coach: Derek McInnes.
NK Rijeka: Andrej Prskalo, Roberto Puncec, Dario Zuparic, Momcilo Raspopovic, Zoran Kvrzic, Luka Capan, Tibor Halilovic (83' Dani Iglesias), Stipe Loncar (75' Robert Muric), Ivan Lepinjica, Antonio Colak, Boadu Maxwell Acosty (82' Matej Vuk). Coach: Igor Biscan.
Goals: 10' Stipe Loncar 0-1, 32' Antonio Colak 0-2.
Referee: Harald Lechner (AUT)   Attendance: 15,246.
Sent off: 20' Funso Ojo.

15.08.19   RCDE Stadium, Cornella de Llobregat: RCD Espanyol – FC Luzern 3-0 (3-0)
RCD Espanyol: Diego López, Bernardo Espinosa, Dídac Vilà, Lluís López, Pipa Ávila, Granero, Iturraspe, Sergi Darder (52' Pol Lozano), Matías Vargas (56' Nico Melamed Ribaudo), Lei Wu, Víctor Campuzano (56' Javi Puado). Coach: David Gallego.
FC Luzern: Marius Müller, Christian Schwegler (74' Shkelqim Demhasaj), Lazar Cirkovic, Otar Kakabadze, Lucas Alves "Lucão", Idriz Voca, Remo Arnold, Tsiy William Ndenge, Francesco Margiotta, Blessing Eleke (62' Pascal Schürpf), Ibrahima Ndiaye (65' Silvan Sidler). Coach: Thomas Häberli.
Goals: 3' Lei Wu 1-0, 27', 38' Víctor Campuzano 2-0, 3-0.
Referee: Jorge de Sousa (POR)   Attendance: 13,214.

PLAY-OFF ROUND

22.08.19 Astana Arena, Nur-Sultan: FK Astana – BATE Borisov 3-0 (2-0)
FK Astana: Nenad Eric, Antonio Rukavina, Yuriy Logvinenko, Dmitriy Shomko, Evgeny Postnikov, Luka Simunovic, Rúnar Sigurjónsson, Marin Tomasov (82' Rangelo Janga), Ivan Maevski, Dorin Rotariu, Ndombe Mubele (46' Roman Murtazaev).
Coach: Roman Grygorchuk.
BATE Borisov: Anton Chichkan, Aleksander Filipovic, Aleksey Rios, Igor Stasevich, Dmitriy Baga (61' Willum Thór Willumsson), Stanislav Dragun, Slobodan Simovic, Hervaine Moukam (54' Jasse Tuominen), Evgeni Yablonski, Zakhar Volkov, Maksim Skavysh (79' Anton Saroka). Coach: Aleksei Baga.
Goals: 23' Marin Tomasov 1-0, 44' Yuriy Logvinenko 2-0, 52' Rúnar Sigurjónsson 3-0 (p).
Referee: Serhiy Boyko (UKR)   Attendance: 24,369.

22.08.19 Vazgen Sargsyan anvan Hanrapetakan Marzadasht, Yerevan:
 FC Ararat-Armenia – F91 Dudelange 2-1 (1-0)
FC Ararat-Armenia: Dmitriy Abakumov, Rochdi Achenteh, Ângelo Meneses, Aleksandar Damcevski, Georgi Pashov, Gor Malakyan (82' Ilja Antonov), Kódjo Alphonse, Petros Avetisyan (56' Armen Ambartsumyan), Anton Kobyalko (75' Louis Ogana), Furdjel Narsingh, Mailson. Coach: Vardan Minasyan.
F91 Dudelange: Jonathan Joubert, Tom Schnell, Ricardo Delgado, Mehdi Kirch, Mohamed Bouchouari, Mario Pokar, Ryan Klapp (78' Mickaël Garos), Dominik Stolz (54' Omar Natami), Charles Morren, Danel Sinani (90+2' Mehdi Ouamri), Antoine Bernier.
Coach: Emilio Ferrera.
Goals: 22' Mailson 1-0, 68' Danel Sinani 1-1, 90+3' Ilja Antonov 2-1.
Referee: Harald Lechner (AUT)   Attendance: 11,000.

FC Ararat-Armenia played their home match at Vazgen Sargsyan anvan Hanrapetakan Marzadasht, Yerevan, instead of their regular stadium Yerevan Football Academy Stadium, Yereven which did not meet UEFA requirements.

22.08.19 Marijampolės sporto centro stadione, Marijampolė:
 FK Sūduva – Ferencvárosi TC 0-0
FK Sūdova Marijampolė: Ivan Kardum, Algis Jankauskas, Andro Svrljuga, Aleksandar Zivanovic, Semir Kerla, Ivan Hladík, Renan Oliveira (78' Eligijus Jankauskas), Ovidijus Verbickas, Giedrius Matulevicius, Josip Tadic (69' Sandro Gotal), Mihret Topcagic (90+2' Robertas Vėzevicius). Coach: Vladimir Cheburin.
Ferencvárosi TC: Dénes Dibusz, Gergö Lovrencsics, Marcel Heister, Miha Blazic, Lasha Dvali, Michal Skvarka (76' Roland Varga), Dávid Sigér, Igor Kharatin, Oleksandr Zubkov, Tokmac Nguen (87' Lukács Böle), Franck Boli (67' Tamás Priskin). Coach: Serhiy Rebrov.
Referee: Manuel Schüttengruber (AUT)   Attendance: 5,741.

22.08.19 Swedbank Stadion, Malmö: Malmö FF – Bnei Yehuda Tel Aviv 3-0 (2-0)
Malmö FF: Johan Dahlin, Behrang Safari, Rasmus Bengtsson, Eric Larsson, Felix Beijmo (67'
Lasse Nielsen), Søren Rieks (82' Jonas Knudsen), Anders Christiansen, Fouad Bachirou, Arnór
Ingvi Traustason (60' Guillermo Molins), Oscar Lewicki, Markus Rosenberg.
Coach: Uwe Rösler.
Bnei Yehuda Tel Aviv: Emilijus Zubas, Dan Mori, Alban Pnishi, Shay Mazor, Daniel Felscher,
Matan Baltaksa, Tamabi Sages, Ismaila Soro (85' Shimshon Tza'adon), Mohammad Ghadir
(67' Dor Elo), Dor Jan (73' Ariel Matan Lazmi), Avishay Cohen. Coach: Yossi Abukasis.
Goals: 36' Markus Rosenberg 1-0, 40' Rasmus Bengtsson 2-0, 47' Oscar Lewicki 3-0.
Referee: Pawel Raczkowski (POL)   Attendance: 13,956.

22.08.19 Ludogorets Arena, Razgrad: PFC Ludogorets Razgrad – NK Maribor 0-0
PFC Ludogorets Razgrad: Plamen Iliev, Cosmin Moti, Cicinho, Rafael Forster, Anton
Nedyalkov, Anicet Andrianantenaina (78' Jakub Swierczok), Wanderson (72' Mavis
Tchibota), Stéphane Badji, Dan Biton (65' Marcelinho), Claudiu Keserü, Jorginho.
Coach: Stoicho Stoev.
NK Maribor: Kenan Piric, Mitja Viler, Martin Milec, Sasa Ivkovic, Spiro Pericic, Rok
Kronaveter (65' Marcos Tavares), Blaz Vrhovec, Alexandru Cretu, Rudi Pozeg Vancas (80'
Jasmin Mesanovic), Dino Hotic, Luka Zahovic (65' Martin Kramaric). Coach: Darko Milanic.
Referee: Jakob Kehlet (DEN)   Attendance: 6,230.
Sent off: 57' Dino Hotic.

22.08.19 De Kuip, Rotterdam: Feyenoord Rotterdam – Hapoel Be'er Sheva 3-0 (1-0)
Feyenoord Rotterdam: Kenneth Vermeer, Eric Botteghin, Edgar Ié, Ridgeciano Haps, Rick
Karsdorp, Leroy Fer (88' Wouter Burger), Renato Tapia, Orkun Kökçü, Luciano Narsingh,
Steven Berghuis, Sam Larsson (73' Luis Sinisterra). Coach: Jaap Stam.
Hapoel Be'er Sheva: Ernestas Setkus, Miguel Vítor (81' Naor Sabag), Ben Bitton, Loai Taha,
Sean Goldberg, Marwan Kabha, Ramzi Safouri, Eden Shamir, David Keltjens (68' Jimmy
Marín), Nigel Hasselbaink, Niv Zrihan (64' Ben Sahar). Coach: Barak Bakhar.
Goals: 33' Sam Larsson 1-0, 56', 78' Leroy Fer 2-0, 3-0.
Referee: Andris Treimanis (LAT)   Attendance: 35,000.

22.08.19 Telia Parken, København: FC København – Riga FC 3-1 (1-1)
FC København: Sten Grytebust, Pierre Bengtsson, Sotirios Papagiannopoulos, Karlo Bartolec,
Victor Nelsson, Rasmus Falk (79' Mohammed Daramy), Zeca, Viktor Fischer, Jens Stage,
Pieros Soteriou, Carlo Holse (46' Michael Santos). Coach: Ståle Solbakken.
Riga FC: Roberts Ozols, Stefan Panic, Antonijs Cernomordijs, Vladimirs Kamess, Ritvars
Rugins, Vyacheslav Sharpar, Felipe Brisola (68' Olegs Laizāns), Roger (68' Deniss Rakels),
Armands Pētersons, Elvis Stuglis, Vladislavs Fjodorovs (84' Aleksejs Visnakovs).
Coach: Mihails Konevs.
Goals: 18' Viktor Fischer 1-0, 41' Vladimirs Kamess 1-1, 62' Pieros Sotiriou 2-1 (p),
90+3' Mohammed Daramy 3-1.
Referee: Bas Nijhuis (HOL)   Attendance: 13,930.

22.08.19   Olympiako Stadio Spyros Louis, Athens: AEK Athens – Trabzonspor 1-3 (1-2)
AEK Athens: Vasilios Barkas, Ognjen Vranjes, Paulinho, Hélder Lopes, Efstratios Svarnas, David Simão (63' Nenad Krsticic), Petros Mandalos, André Simões, Nélson Oliveira (84' Giorgos Giakoumakis), Marko Livaja, Daniele Verde (65' Chico Geraldes).
Coach: Miguel Cardoso.
Trabzonspor: Ugurcan Çakir, João Pereira, Filip Novák, Majid Hosseini, Hüseyin Türkmen, José Sosa, Abdülkadir Parmak, Abdülkadir Ömür, Anthony Nwakaeme (72' Donis Avdijaj), Alexander Sørloth (77' Dogan Erdogan), Caleb Ekuban (90+2' Yusuf Sari).
Coach: Ünal Karaman.
Goals: 4' Marko Livaja 1-0, 29', 44', 70' Caleb Ekuban 1-1, 1-2, 1-3.
Referee: Daniel Siebert (GER)   Attendanace: 141.

José Sosa missed a penalty kick (24').

22.08.19   Stadion Miejski Legii Warszawa im. Marszalka Józefa Pilsudskiego, Warszawa:
       Legia Warszawa – Glasgow Rangers FC 0-0
Legia Warszawa: Radoslaw Majecki, Artur Jedrzejczyk, Igor Lewczuk, Luís Rocha, Pawel Stolarski, Marko Vesovic (84' Dominik Nagy), André Martins, Cafú (71' Domagoj Antolic), Valeriane Gvilia, Luquinhas, Sandro Kulenovic. Coach: Aleksandar Vukovic.
Glasgow Rangers FC: Allan McGregor, James Tavernier, Connor Goldson, John Flanagan, Nikola Katic, Steven Davis, Scott Arfield (87' Glen Kamara), Ryan Jack, Joe Aribo, Sheyi Ojo, Alfredo Morelos (87' Jermain Defoe). Coach: Steven Gerrard.
Referee: Benoît Bastien (FRA)   Attendance: 26,665.

22.08.19   Stadionul Marin Anastasovici, Giurgiu:
       Fotbal Club FCSB – Vitória de Guimarães 0-0
Fotbal Club FCSB: Cristian Balgradean, Valentin Cretu, Aristides Soiledis, Bogdan Planic, Ionut Pantîru, Mihai Roman (I) (46' Adrian Popa), Mihai Pintilii (66' Razvan Oaida), Ionut Vîna (60' Harlem Gnohéré), Ovidiu Popescu, Florin Tanase, Florinel Coman.
Coach: Vergil Andronache.
Vitória de Guimarães: Douglas Jesus, Florent Hanin, Valeriy Bondarenko, Falaye Sacko, Edmond Tapsoba, Rochinha (66' Rafa Soares), Pêpê Rodrigues, Almoatasembellah Ali Mohamed, André Almeida (62' Denis Poha), Davidson, Bruno Duarte (76' Alexandre Guedes). Coach: Ivo Vieira.
Referee: Matej Jug (SVN)   Attendance: 4,518.

Fotbal Club FCSB played their home match at Stadionul Marin Anastasovici, Giurgiu, instead of their regular stadium Arena Nationala, Bucurest.

22.08.19   GHELAMCO-arena, Gent: KAA Gent – HNK Rijeka 2-1 (0-1)
KAA Gent: Thomas Kaminski, Nana Asare, Mikael Lustig, Igor Plastun, Michael Ngadeu-Ngadjui, Vadis Odjidja-Ofoe, Brecht Dejaegere (63' Roman Bezus), Elisha Owusu, Laurent Depoitre, Roman Yaremchuk (83' Louis Verstraete), Jonathan David (89' Yuya Kubo).
Coach: Jess Thorup.
NK Rijeka: Andrej Prskalo, Roberto Puncec, Dario Zuparic, Momcilo Raspopovic, Zoran Kvrzic (69' Darko Velkovski), Luka Capan, Tibor Halilovic, Stipe Loncar, Ivan Lepinjica, Antonio Colak (86' Jakov Puljic), Boadu Maxwell Acosty (79' Dani Iglesias).
Coach: Igor Biscan.
Goals: 39' Tibor Halilovic 0-1, 57', 71' Laurent Depoitre 1-1, 2-1.
Referee: Daniel Stefanski (POL)   Attendance: 12,198.

22.08.19 Philips Stadion, Eindhoven: PSV Eindhoven – Apollon Limassol 3-0 (0-0)
PSV Eindhoven: Jeroen Zoet, Nick Viergever, Timo Baumgartl, Olivier Boscagli (90' Toni Lato), Denzel Dumfries, Érick Gutiérrez, Pablo Rosario, Mohammed Ihattaren (81' Kostas Mitroglou), Steven Bergwijn, Donyell Malen, Cody Gakpo (84' Jorrit Hendrix).
Coach: Mark van Bommel.
Apollon Limassol: Joël Mall, Charis Kyriakou, Héctor Yuste, Sasa Markovic, Diego Aguirre, Esteban Sachetti, Serge Gakpé (76' Ioannis Pittas), Emilio Zelaya, João Pedro, Adrián Sardinero (67' Fotios Papoulis), Giannis Gianniotas (62' Facundo Pereyra).
Coach: Sofronis Avgousti.
Goals: 47' Mohammed Ihattaren 1-0, 56' Cody Gakpo 2-0, 61' Denzel Dumfries 3-0.
Referee: Aleksei Kulbakov (BLS) Attendance: 17,500.

22.08.19 Stade de la Meinau, Strasbourg: RC Strasbourg – Eintracht Frankfurt 1-0 (1-0)
RC Strasbourg: Matz Sels, Lamine Koné, Stefan Mitrovic, Lionel Carole, Kenny Lala, Alexander Djiku, Jonas Martin, Dimitri Liénard, Adrien Thomasson (77' Lebo Mothiba), Ludovic Ajorque (86' Mohamed Simakan), Kévin Lucien Zohi (64' Ibrahima Sissoko).
Coach: Thierry Laurey.
Eintracht Frankfurt: Kevin Trapp, Makoto Hasebe, David Abraham, Martin Hinteregger, Danny da Costa, Gelson Fernandes (78' Dominik Kohr), Filip Kostic, Lucas Torró, Mijat Gacinovic (46' Sebastian Rode), Daichi Kamada, Ante Rebic (46' Gonçalo Paciência).
Coach: Adi Hütter.
Goal: 33' Kévin Lucien Zohi 1-0.
Referee: Ivan Kruzliak (SVK) Attendance: 21,708.

22.08.19 De Grolsch Veste, Enschede: AZ Alkmaar – Royal Antwerp FC 1-1 (0-1)
AZ Alkmaar: Marco Bizot, Ron Vlaar, Jonas Svensson (76' Bjørn Johnsen), Pantelis Hatzidiakos (68' Yukinari Sugawara), Thomas Ouwejan (60' Albert Gudmundsson), Owen Wijndal, Fredrik Midtsjø, Teun Koopmeiners, Oussama Idrissi, Myron Boadu, Calvin Stengs.
Coach: Arne Slot.
Royal Antwerp FC: Sinan Bolat, Ritchie De Laet, Simen Juklerød, Dylan Batubinsika, Buta, Faris Haroun, Lior Refaelov (75' Dino Arslanagic), Martin Hongla, Dieumerci Mbokani, Ivo Rodrigues (66' Geoffry Hairemans), Didier Lamkel Zé (90+4' Alexis De Sart).
Coach: László Bölöni.
Goals: 38' Dylan Batubinsika 0-1, 82' Myron Boadu 1-1.
Referee: Srdjan Jovanovic (SRB) Attendance: 4,014.
Sent off: 73' Buta.

AZ Alkmaar played their home match at De Grolsch Veste, Enschede, instead of their regular stadium AFAS Stadion, Alkmaar, due to a roof collapse on 10 August 2019 at the AFAS Stadion.

22.08.19 Celtic Park, Glasgow: Celtic FC – AIK Solna 2-0 (0-0)
Celtic FC: Craig Gordon, Jozo Simunovic, Christopher Jullien, Boli Bolingoli Mbombo, Kristoffer Ajer, Scott Brown, James Forrest (82' Olivier Ntcham), Callum McGregor, Ryan Christie, Odsonne Édouard (85' Vakoun Bayo), Michael Johnston (82' Lewis Morgan).
Coach: Neil Lennon.
AIK Solna: Oscar Linnér, Per Karlsson, Robert Lundström (87' Heradi Rashidi), Rasmus Lindkvist, Karol Mets, Daniel Granli, Sebastian Larsson, Nabil Bahoui (70' Anton Salétros), Enoch Adu, Kolbeinn Sigthórsson (72' Chinedu Obasi), Henok Goitom.
Coach: Rikard Norling.
Goals: 48' James Forrest 1-0, 73' Odsonne Édouard 2-0.
Referee: Tamás Bognár (HUN) Attendance: 40,885.

22.08.19 Windsor Park, Belfast: Linfield FC – Qarabag FK 3-2 (2-1)
Linfield FC: Rohan Ferguson, Chris Casement, Matthew Clarke, Mark Stafford, Niall Quinn, Jamie Mulgrew, Jimmy Callacher, Andrew Mitchell, Bastien Héry, Joel Cooper (90+1' Kirk Millar), Shayne Lavery (80' Andrew Waterworth). Coach: David Healy.
Qarabag FK: Vagner, Rashad Sadygov, Maksim Medvedev, Qara Qarayev, Faycal Rherras, Abbas Hüseynov, Míchel, Jaime Romero, Dani Quintana (67' Magaye Gueye), Abdellah Zoubir, Mahir Emreli. Coach: Gurban Gurbanov.
Goals: 15' Faycal Rherras 0-1, 40' Mark Stafford 1-1, 45+1', 75' Shayne Lavery 2-1, 3-1, 90+3' Magaye Gueye 3-2 (p).
Referee: Sandro Schärer (SUI)   Attendance: 4,633.

22.08.19 Estádio Municipal de Braga, Braga: Sporting Braga – Spartak Moskva 1-0 (0-0)
Sporting Braga: Matheus Magalhães, Ricardo Esgaio, Nuno Sequeira, Pablo Santos (64' Vítor Tormena), Bruno Viana, Fransérgio (46' João Novais), João Palhinha, André Horta (85' Murilo), Wilson Eduardo, Paulinho, Ricardo Horta. Coach: Sá Pinto.
Spartak Moskva: Aleksandr Maksimenko, Andrey Eshchenko, Georgi Dzhikiya, Samuel Gigot, Ayrton, André Schürrle, Roman Zobnin, Reziuan Mirzov (63' Lorenzo Melgarejo), Ayaz Guliev (85' Nail Umyarov), Zelimkhan Bakaev, Ezequiel Ponce. Coach: Oleg Kononov.
Goal: 74' Ricardo Horta 1-0.
Referee: Xavier Estrada Fernández (ESP)   Attendance: 11,667.

22.08.19 Národny Futbalovy Stadión, Bratislava:
           Slovan Bratislava – PAOK Saloniki 1-0 (0-0)
Slovan Bratislava: Dominik Greif, Vasil Bozhikov, Vernon, Jurij Medvedev, Myenty Abena, Marin Ljubicic, Dávid Holman, Joeri de Kamps (77' Nono Delgado), "Moha" Mohammed Rharsalla (87' Erik Daniel), Aleksandar Cavric (54' Rafael Ratão), Andraz Sporar. Coach: Ján Kozák.
PAOK Saloniki: Alexandros Paschalakis, Léo Matos, José Ángel Crespo, Fernando Varela, Dimitris Giannoulis, Diego Biseswar (80' Miroslav Stoch), Omar El Kaddouri, Dimitrios Pelkas (66' Karol Swiderski), Anderson Esiti (76' Douglas Augusto), Chuba Akpom, Léo Jabá. Coach: Abel Ferreira.
Goal: 90+4' Myenty Abena 1-0.
Referee: Ivan Bebek (CRO)   Attendance: 20,233.

22.08.19 Stadio Olimpico Grande Torino, Torino:
           Torino FC – Wolverhampton Wanderers 2-3 (0-1)
Torino FC: Salvatore Sirigu, Lorenzo De Silvestri, Cristian Ansaldi (71' Ola Aina), Nicolas N'Koulou, Armando Izzo, Bremer, Soualiho Meïté (64' Tomás Rincón), Daniele Baselli, Simone Zaza, Andrea Belotti, Álex Berenguer (59' Sasa Lukic). Coach: Walter Mazzarri.
Wolverhampton Wanderers: Rui Patrício, Willy Boly, Conor Coady, Vallejo, Rúben Vinagre, João Moutinho, Romain Saïss, Leander Dendoncker, Raúl Jiménez (76' Patrick Cutrone), Adama Traoré (64' Jonny Castro), Diogo Jota (69' Pedro Neto). Coach: Nuno Espírito Santo.
Goals: 43' Bremer 0-1 (og), 59' Diogo Jota 0-2, 61' Lorenzo De Silvestri 1-2, 72' Raúl Jiménez 1-3, 89' Andrea Belotti 2-3 (p).
Referee: Artur Soares Dias (POR)   Attendance: 24,091.

22.08.19   RCDE Stadium, Cornella de Llobregat: RCD Espanyol – Zorya Luhansk 3-1 (0-1)
RCD Espanyol: Diego López, Dídac Vilà (46' Víctor Sánchez), Javi López, Lluís López, Fernando Calero, Granero, Iturraspe (20' Marc Roca), Sergi Darder, Facundo Ferreyra, Lei Wu, Javi Puado (71' Matías Vargas). Coach: David Gallego.
Zorya Luhansk: Mykyta Shevchenko, Dmitriy Ivanisenya (90+1' Levan Arveladze), Oleksandr Tymchyk, Joel Abu Hanna (79' Maksim Biliy), Artem Gromov, Bogdan Mykhaylichenko, Yevgen Cheberko, Vladyslav Kochergin, Bohdan Lednev, Vladyslav Kabayev, Maksym Lunyov (64' Vladlen Yurchenko). Coach: Viktor Skripnik.
Goals: 38' Vladyslav Kochergin 0-1, 58' Facundo Ferreyra 1-1, 79' Javi López 2-1, 81' Matías Vargas 3-1.
Referee: Tobias Stieler (GER)   Attendance: 13,686.

Granero missed a penalty kick (76').

22.08.19   Stadion Partizana, Beograd: Partizan Beograd – Molde FK 2-1 (1-1)
Partizan Beograd: Vladimir Stojkovic, Nemanja Miletic (I), Igor Vujacic, Slobodan Urosevic, Strahinja Pavlovic, Zoran Tosic, Aleksandar Scekic, Seydouba Soumah (73' Bibras Natcho), Sasa Zdjelar, Umar Sadiq (46' Ognjen Ozegovic), Filip Stevanovic (62' Takuma Asano). Coach: Savo Milosevic.
Molde FK: Álex Craninx, Vegard Forren, Ruben Gabrielsen, Kristoffer Haraldseid, Martin Bjørnbak, Magnus Eikrem (69' Martin Ellingsen), Etzaz Hussain, Eirik Hestad, Fredrik Aursnes, Erling Knudtzon (33' Mathis Bolly, 85' Mattias Mostrøm), Leke James.
Coach: Erling Moe.
Goals: 44' Mathis Bolly 0-1, 45+1' Seydouba Soumah 1-1, 84' Zoran Tosic 2-1.
Referee: Viktor Kassai (HUN)   Attendance: 3,157.

29.08.19   Tofiq Bahramov adina Respublika stadionu, Baku:
          Qarabag FK – Linfield FC 2-1 (1-0)
Qarabag FK: Vagner, Rashad Sadygov, Maksim Medvedev, Ailton, Rahil Mammadov, Míchel (90+1' Dani Quintana), Jaime Romero, Richard Almeyda, Abdellah Zoubir (90+1' Araz Abdullayev), Magaye Gueye (85' Qara Qarayev), Mahir Emreli. Coach: Gurban Gurbanov.
Linfield FC: Rohan Ferguson, Chris Casement, Matthew Clarke, Mark Stafford, Niall Quinn (78' Kirk Millar), Jamie Mulgrew, Jimmy Callacher, Bastien Héry, Stephen Fallon (78' Andrew Waterworth), Joel Cooper (81' Jordan Stewart), Shayne Lavery. Coach: David Healy.
Goals: 6' Jaime Romero 1-0, 88' Abdellah Zoubir 2-0, 90+3' Shayne Lavery 2-1.
Referee: Sergey Ivanov (RUS)   Attendance: 18,349.

Qarabag FK won on away goals.

Qarabag FK played their home match at Tofiq Bahramov adina Respublika stadionu, Baku, instead of their regular stadium Azersun Arena, Baku

29.08.19   Stadions Skonto, Riga: Riga FC – FC København 1-0 (0-0)
Riga FC: Roberts Ozols, Georgios Valerianos, Herdi Prenga, Stefan Panic, Antonijs Cernomordijs, Vladimirs Kamess, Vyacheslav Sharpar (66' Olegs Laizāns), Felipe Brisola, Roger (67' Deniss Rakels), Armands Pētersons (84' Miroslav Slavov), Roman Debelko.
Coach: Mihails Konevs.
FC København: Sten Grytebust, Pierre Bengtsson, Sotirios Papagiannopoulos, Karlo Bartolec, Victor Nelsson, Rasmus Falk (79' Andreas Bjelland), Zeca, Viktor Fischer (71' Michael Santos), Nikolaj Thomsen (85' Guillermo Varela), Jens Stage, Pieros Soteriou.
Coach: Ståle Solbakken.
Goal: 75' Felipe Brisola 1-0.
Referee: Pawel Gil (POL)   Attendance: 7,055.
Sent off: 90+4' Georgios Valerianos.

29.08.19   Friends Arena, Solna: AIK Solna – Celtic FC 1-4 (1-2)
AIK Solna: Oscar Linnér, Per Karlsson, Robert Lundström (79' Heradi Rashidi), Karol Mets, Daniel Granli, Sebastian Larsson, Nabil Bahoui (62' Balil Hussein), Enoch Adu, Anton Salétros, Kolbeinn Sigthórsson (62' Henok Goitom), Chinedu Obasi. Coach: Rikard Norling.
Celtic FC: Craig Gordon, Christopher Jullien, Boli Bolingoli Mbombo, Kristoffer Ajer (15' Anthony Ralston), Scott Brown, Nir Bitton, James Forrest, Callum McGregor, Ryan Christie, Odsonne Édouard (76' Vakoun Bayo), Michael Johnston (70' Lewis Morgan).
Coach: Neil Lennon.
Goals: 17' James Forrest 0-1, 33' Sebastian Larsson 1-1 (p), 34' Michael Johnston 1-2, 87' Christopher Jullien 1-3, 90+3' Lewis Morgan 1-4.
Referee: Nikola Dabanovic (MNE)   Attendance: 28,410.

29.08.19   Stadio Toumbas, Thessaloniki: PAOK Saloniki – Slovan Bratislava 3-2 (0-1)
PAOK Saloniki: Alexandros Paschalakis, José Ángel Crespo, Fernando Varela, Rodrigo Alves, Dimitris Giannoulis, Diego Biseswar, Omar El Kaddouri (31' Douglas Augusto), Dimitrios Pelkas (46' Karol Swiderski), Anderson Esiti (64' Josip Misic), Chuba Akpom, Dimitris Limnios. Coach: Abel Ferreira.
Slovan Bratislava: Dominik Greif, Vasil Bozhikov, Vernon, Jurij Medvedev, Myenty Abena, Ibrahim Rabiu (68' Nono Delgado), Dávid Holman (88' Rafael Ratão), Joeri de Kamps, Kenan Bajric, "Moha" Mohammed Rharsalla (78' Artem Sukhotsky), Andraz Sporar.
Coach: Ján Kozák.
Goals: 38' Jurij Medvedev 0-1, 49' Dimitris Limnios 1-1, 50' Karol Swiderski 2-1, 62' Vernon 2-2, 87' Dimitris Giannoulis 3-2.
Referee: Andreas Ekberg (SWE)   Attendance: 20,776.

Slovan Bratislava won on away goals.

29.08.19   Borisov Arena, Borisov: BATE Borisov – FK Astana 2-0 (1-0)
BATE Borisov: Anton Chichkan, Boris Kopitovic, Aleksander Filipovic, Aleksey Rios, Igor Stasevich, Dmitriy Baga (74' Willum Thór Willumsson), Stanislav Dragun, Evgeni Yablonski, Zakhar Volkov, Maksim Skavysh (79' Jasse Tuominen), Anton Saroka (57' Hervaine Moukam). Coach: Aleksei Baga.
FK Astana: Nenad Eric, Antonio Rukavina, Yuriy Logvinenko (87' Zarko Tomasevic), Dmitriy Shomko, Evgeny Postnikov, Luka Simunovic, Rúnar Sigurjónsson, Marin Tomasov (90+3' Abzal Beysebekov), Ivan Maevski, Roman Murtazaev (71' Rangelo Janga), Dorin Rotariu. Coach: Roman Grygorchuk.
Goals: 6' Maksim Skavysh 1-0, 85' Evgeni Yablonski 2-0.
Referee: Robert Madden (SCO)   Attendance: 10,701.

29.08.19   Neo GSP Stadium, Nicosia: Apollon Limassol – PSV Eindhoven 0-4 (0-0)
Apollon Limassol: Joël Mall, Charis Kyriakou (61' Adrián Sardinero), Attila Szalai, Héctor Yuste, Sasa Markovic, Diego Aguirre, Serge Gakpé, Emilio Zelaya, João Pedro, Fotios Papoulis (69' Ioannis Pittas), Giannis Gianniotas (77' Roger Tamba M'Pinda).
Coach: Sofronis Avgousti.
PSV Eindhoven: Jeroen Zoet, Nick Viergever, Timo Baumgartl (81' Daniel Schwaab), Olivier Boscagli, Denzel Dumfries, Jorrit Hendrix (74' Kostas Mitroglou), Érick Gutiérrez, Pablo Rosario, Mohammed Ihattaren, Donyell Malen, Cody Gakpo (77' Amar Catic).
Coach: Mark van Bommel.
Goals: 73' Mohammed Ihattaren 0-1, 76' Kostas Mitroglou 0-2, 79', 90+4' Donyell Malen 0-3, 0-4.
Referee: William Collum (SCO)   Attendance: 2,004.

Apollon Limassol played their home match at Neo GSP Stadium, Nicosia, instead of their regular stadium Tsirio Stadium, Limassol.

29.08.19   Slavutych-Arena, Zaporizhia: Zorya Luhansk – RCD Espanyol 2-2 (0-1)
Zorya Luhansk: Mykyta Shevchenko, Dmitriy Ivanisenya, Oleksandr Tymchyk, Joel Abu Hanna, Artem Gromov (58' Nazariy Rusyn), Dmytro Khomchenovsky, Bogdan Mykhaylichenko, Yevgen Cheberko, Vladyslav Kochergin, Bohdan Lednev (68' Vladlen Yurchenko), Pylyp Budkovsky (82' Vladyslav Kabayev). Coach: Viktor Skripnik.
RCD Espanyol: Diego López, Dídac Vilà, Javi López, Lluís López, Fernando Calero, Granero, Sergi Darder (66' Víctor Sánchez), Marc Roca, Matías Vargas (77' Víctor Campuzano), Melendo, Facundo Ferreyra (73' Lei Wu). Coach: David Gallego.
Goals: 34' Facundo Ferreyra 0-1, 54' Bohdan Lednev 1-1, 62' Matías Vargas 1-2, 78' Nazariy Rusyn 2-2.
Referee: Radu Petrescu (ROM)   Attendance: 10,181.

Zorya Luhansk played their home match at Slavutych-Arena, Zaporizhia, instead of their regular stadium Avanhard Stadium, Luhansk, due to the war conditions in Eastern Ukraine.

29.08.19   Aker Stadion, Molde: Molde FK – Partizan Beograd 1-1 (0-0)
Molde FK: Álex Craninx, Vegard Forren, Ruben Gabrielsen, Kristoffer Haraldseid, Kristoffer Haugen (84' Erling Knudtzon), Magnus Eikrem, Etzaz Hussain, Eirik Hestad, Fredrik Aursnes, Mathis Bolly (59' Ohi Omoijuanfo), Leke James. Coach: Erling Moe.
Partizan Beograd: Vladimir Stojkovic, Bojan Ostojic, Nemanja Miletic (I), Slobodan Urosevic, Strahinja Pavlovic, Zoran Tosic (83' Aleksandar Lutovac), Aleksandar Scekic, Seydouba Soumah (66' Bibras Natcho), Sasa Zdjelar, Takuma Asano, Umar Sadiq (68' Ognjen Ozegovic). Coach: Savo Milosevic.
Goals: 72' Leke James 1-0, 80' Nemanja Miletic (I) 1-1.
Referee: Ruddy Buquet (FRA)   Attendance: 7,102.

29.08.19   HaMoshava Stadium, Petah Tikva: Bnei Yehuda Tel Aviv – Malmö FF 0-1 (0-1)
Bnei Yehuda Tel Aviv: Emilijus Zubas, Dan Mori, Alban Pnishi (46' Matan Baltaksa), Shimshon Tza'adon, Shay Mazor, Daniel Felscher, Amir Rustom, Ariel Matan Lazmi, Ismaila Soro (46' Tamabi Sages), Dor Jan (62' Amit Zaneti), Avishay Cohen. Coach: Yossi Abukasis.
Malmö FF: Johan Dahlin, Behrang Safari, Rasmus Bengtsson (46' Felix Beijmo), Eric Larsson, Lasse Nielsen, Jonas Knudsen, Anders Christiansen (70' Marcus Antonsson), Oscar Lewicki (62' Fouad Bachirou), Romain Gall, Bonke Innocent, Guillermo Molins.
Coach: Uwe Rösler.
Goal: 7' Guillermo Molins 0-1.
Referee: Serdar Gözübüyük (HOL)   Attendance: 900.

Bnei Yehuda Tel Aviv played their home match at HaMoshava Stadium, Petah Tikva, instead of their regular stadium Bloomfield Stadium, Tel Aviv which is undergoing renovation.

29.08.19   Otkrytie Arena, Moskva: Spartak Moskva – Sporting Braga 1-2 (0-2)
Spartak Moskva: Aleksandr Maksimenko, Andrey Eshchenko, Georgi Dzhikiya, Samuel Gigot, Ayrton, André Schürrle, Roman Zobnin (75' Nail Umyarov), Reziuan Mirzov (46' Soltmurad Bakaev), Ayaz Guliev, Zelimkhan Bakaev, Ezequiel Ponce (62' Jano Ananidze).
Coach: Oleg Kononov.
Sporting Braga: Matheus Magalhães, Ricardo Esgaio, Nuno Sequeira, Bruno Viana, Vítor Tormena (39' Lucas "Ferrugem" Cunha), João Novais (76' Fransérgio), João Palhinha, André Horta, Wilson Eduardo (24' Galeno), Paulinho, Ricardo Horta. Coach: Sá Pinto.
Goals: 42', 45+3' Ricardo Horta 0-1, 0-2, 89' Zelimkhan Bakaev 1-2.
Referee: Davide Massa (ITA)   Attendance: 38,176.

29.08.19   Medical Park Stadyumu, Trabzon: Trabzonspor – AEK Athens 0-2 (0-2)
Trabzonspor: Ugurcan Çakir, João Pereira, Filip Novák, Gastón Campi, Ivanildo Fernandes, John Obi Mikel (36' Alexander Sørloth), José Sosa, Abdülkadir Parmak, Abdülkadir Ömür (44' Yusuf Sari, 83' Dogan Erdogan), Anthony Nwakaeme, Caleb Ekuban.
Coach: Ünal Karaman.
AEK Athens: Vasilios Barkas, Dmytro Chygrynskiy, Ognjen Vranjes, Michalis Bakakis, Hélder Lopes, Marios Oikonomou (88' Viktor Klonaridis), Petros Mandalos (81' Giorgos Giakoumakis), André Simões, Konstantinos Galanopoulos (58' Nenad Krsticic), Nélson Oliveira, Marko Livaja. Coach: Nikolaos Kostenoglou.
Goals: 24' Marko Livaja 0-1, 30' Petros Mandalos 0-2 (p).
Referee: Michael Oliver (ENG)   Attendance: 30,490.
Sent off: 90+3' Hélder Lopes.

Trabzonspor won on away goals.

29.08.19 Yaakov Turner Toto Stadium, Beersheva:
Hapoel Be'er Sheva – Feyenoord Rotterdam 0-3 (0-0)
Hapoel Be'er Sheva: Ernestas Setkus, Miguel Vítor (50' Tomer Yosefi), Ben Bitton, Loai Taha, Sean Goldberg (45+2' David Keltjens), Hanan Maman, Marwan Kabha, Ramzi Safouri, Naor Sabag, Jimmy Marín, Ben Sahar (64' Eden Shamir). Coach: Barak Bakhar.
Feyenoord Rotterdam: Kenneth Vermeer, Eric Botteghin, Edgar Ié, Ridgeciano Haps (77' Tyrell Malacia), Rick Karsdorp, Leroy Fer (70' Naoufal Bannis), Renato Tapia, Orkun Kökçü (59' Wouter Burger), Luciano Narsingh, Steven Berghuis, Sam Larsson. Coach: Jaap Stam.
Goals: 46' Orkun Kökçü 0-1, 52' Steven Berghuis 0-2, 61' Wouter Burger 0-3.
Referee: Gediminas Mazeika (LTU)   Attendance: 9,107.
Sent off: 42' Hanan Maman.

Naoufal Bannis missed a penalty kick (81').

29.08.19 Stade Roi Baudouin, Brussels:
Royal Antwerp FC – AZ Alkmaar 1-4 (0-0, 1-1) (a.e.t.)
Royal Antwerp FC: Sinan Bolat, Ritchie De Laet (104' Robbe Quirynen), Simen Juklerød, Dylan Batubinsika, Abdoulaye Seck, Faris Haroun, Lior Refaelov (80' Dino Arslanagic), Alexis De Sart (99' Amara Baby), Dieumerci Mbokani, Ivo Rodrigues (71' Martin Hongla), Didier Lamkel Zé. Coach: László Bölöni.
AZ Alkmaar: Marco Bizot, Ron Vlaar, Stijn Wuytens (53' Yukinari Sugawara), Jonas Svensson (67' Ferdy Druijf), Thomas Ouwejan (46' Albert Gudmundsson), Owen Wijndal, Fredrik Midtsjø, Teun Koopmeiners, Oussama Idrissi, Myron Boadu (111' Jordy Clasie), Calvin Stengs. Coach: Arne Slot.
Goals: 73' Didier Lamkel Zé 1-0, 90' Calvin Stengs 1-1, 96' Ferdy Druijf 1-2, 102' Teun Koopmeiners 1-3 (p), 113' Albert Gudmundsson 1-4.
Referee: Anastasios Sidiropoulos (GRE)   Attendance: 19,786.
Sent off: 35' Dieumerci Mbokani, 74' Didier Lamkel Zé.

AZ Alkmaar won after extra time.

29.08.19 Groupama Aréna, Budapest: Ferencvárosi TC – FK Sūduva Marijampolė 4-2 (2-1)
Ferencvárosi TC: Dénes Dibusz, Gergő Lovrencsics, Marcel Heister, Miha Blazic, Lasha Dvali, Dávid Sigér (71' Danylo Ignatenko), Igor Kharatin, Oleksandr Zubkov, Roland Varga (68' Isael), Tokmac Nguen, Franck Boli (80' Nikolay Signevich). Coach: Serhiy Rebrov.
FK Sūduva Marijampolė: Ivan Kardum, Algis Jankauskas, Andro Svrljuga, Aleksandar Zivanovic, Semir Kerla, Ivan Hladík, Jovan Cadjenovic, Ovidijus Verbickas (71' Eligijus Jankauskas), Giedrius Matulevicius (88' Robertas Vėzevicius), Josip Tadic (46' Paulius Golubickas), Mihret Topcagic. Coach: Vladimir Cheburin.
Goals: 11' Ovidijus Verbickas 0-1, 36' Roland Varga 1-1 (p), 45+1' Franck Boli 2-1, 64' Mihret Topcagic 2-2, 66' Tokmac Nguen 3-2, 90+6' Nikolay Signevich 4-2 (p).
Referee: Marco Guida (ITA)   Attendance: 18,567.

29.08.19   Stade Josy Barthel, Luxembourg:
F91 Dudelange – FC Ararat-Armenia 2-1 (0-1, 2-1) (a.e.t.)
F91 Dudelange: Jonathan Joubert, Tom Schnell, Ricardo Delgado (90' Kobe Cools), Mehdi Kirch, Mohamed Bouchouari, Mario Pokar (99' Sabir Bougrine), Ryan Klapp (69' Omar Natami), Dominik Stolz (110' Corenthyn Lavie), Charles Morren, Danel Sinani, Antoine Bernier. Coach: Emilio Ferrera.
FC Ararat-Armenia: Dmitriy Abakumov, Rochdi Achenteh, Dmitri Guzj, Ângelo Meneses, Georgi Pashov, Gor Malakyan (56' Petros Avetisyan), Armen Ambartsumyan (84' Ilja Antonov), Kódjo Alphonse, Anton Kobyalko (75' Louis Ogana), Furdjel Narsingh (105' Zakaria Sanogo), Mailson. Coach: Vardan Minasyan.
Goals: 24' Mailson 0-1, 48', 71' Danel Sinani 1-1 (p), 2-1.
Referee: Aleksandar Stavrev (MCD)   Attendance: 2,874.

Anton Kobyalko missed a penalty kick (21').

F91 Dudelange won on penalties after extra time (5-4).
Penalties: Lavie 1-0, Avetisyan missed, Morren missed, Alphonse 1-1, Bougrine 2-1, Mailson 2-2, Natami 3-2, Ângelo Meneses 3-3, Sinani 4-3, Louis Ogana 4-4, Schnell 5-4, Pashov missed.

F91 Dudelange played their home match at Stade Josy Barthel, Luxembourg, instead of their regular stadium, Stade Jos Nosbaum, Dudelange.

29.08.19   Stadion HNK Rijeka, Rijeka: HNK Rijeka – KAA Gent 1-1 (1-1)
NK Rijeka: Andrej Prskalo, Ivan Tomecak, Roberto Puncec, Dario Zuparic, Momcilo Raspopovic, Luka Capan (71' Robert Muric), Tibor Halilovic (77' Alexander Gorgon), Stipe Loncar, Ivan Lepinjica, Antonio Colak (19' Jakov Puljic), Boadu Maxwell Acosty. Coach: Igor Biscan.
KAA Gent: Thomas Kaminski, Nana Asare, Mikael Lustig, Igor Plastun, Michael Ngadeu-Ngadjui, Vadis Odjidja-Ofoe, Sven Kums (78' Alessio Castro-Montes), Brecht Dejaegere, Elisha Owusu, Laurent Depoitre (81' Giorgi Kvilitaia), Jonathan David. Coach: Jess Thorup.
Goals: 32' Jakov Puljic 1-0, 33' Igor Plastun 1-1.
Referee: François Letexier (FRA)   Attendance: 7,562.

29.08.19   Ljudski vrt, Maribor: NK Maribor – PFC Ludogorets Razgrad 2-2 (0-2)
NK Maribor: Kenan Piric, Mitja Viler, Martin Milec (46' Denis Klinar), Sasa Ivkovic, Spiro Pericic, Rok Kronaveter (60' Marcos Tavares), Blaz Vrhovec, Alexandru Cretu (86' Andrej Kotnik), Rudi Pozeg Vancas, Jasmin Mesanovic, Luka Zahovic. Coach: Darko Milanic.
PFC Ludogorets Razgrad: Plamen Iliev, Cosmin Moti, Cicinho, Rafael Forster, Anton Nedyalkov, Anicet Andrianantenaina, Wanderson, Stéphane Badji, Claudiu Keserü (69' Svetoslav Dyakov), Marcelinho (85' Jakub Swierczok), Jorginho (90' Dragos Grigore). Coach: Stanislav Genchev.
Goals: 17' Marcelinho 0-1, 26' Claudiu Keserü 0-2 (p), 65' Marcos Tavares 1-2, 72' Rudi Pozeg Vancas 2-2.
Referee: Craig Pawson (ENG)   Attendance: 9,016.

PFC Ludogorets Razgrad won on away goals.

29.08.19   Commerzbank-Arena, Frankfurt am Main:
Eintracht Frankfurt – RC Strasbourg 3-0 (1-0)
Eintracht Frankfurt: Kevin Trapp, Makoto Hasebe, Martin Hinteregger, Danny da Costa, Almamy Touré, Sebastian Rode (90' Dejan Joveljic), Filip Kostic, Dominik Kohr (75' Gelson Fernandes), Daichi Kamada, Gonçalo Paciência (83' Mijat Gacinovic), Ante Rebic.
Coach: Adi Hütter.
RC Strasbourg: Matz Sels, Lamine Koné (69' Nuno Da Costa), Stefan Mitrovic, Lionel Carole, Kenny Lala, Alexander Djiku, Jonas Martin, Dimitri Liénard, Adrien Thomasson (88' Jean Ricner Bellegarde), Ludovic Ajorque (88' Lebo Mothiba), Kévin Lucien Zohi.
Coach: Thierry Laurey.
Goals: 27' Stefan Mitrovic 1-0 (og), 60' Filip Kostic 2-0, 66' Danny da Costa 3-0.
Referee: Orel Grinfeld (ISR)   Attendance: 47,000.
Sent off: 44' Ante Rebic, 55' Dimitri Liénard.

29.08.19   Molineux Stadium, Wolverhampton:
Wolverhampton Wanderers – Torino FC 2-1 (1-0)
Wolverhampton Wanderers: Rui Patrício, Willy Boly, Conor Coady, Jonny Castro, Vallejo, João Moutinho (90' Rúben Neves), Romain Saïss, Leander Dendoncker, Raúl Jiménez (90+2' Pedro Neto), Adama Traoré, Diogo Jota (81' Patrick Cutrone). Coach: Nuno Espírito Santo.
Torino FC: Salvatore Sirigu, Lorenzo De Silvestri, Armando Izzo, Ola Aina (70' Álex Berenguer), Kevin Bonifazi, Bremer, Tomás Rincón (72' Soualiho Meïté), Daniele Baselli, Sasa Lukic, Simone Zaza (82' Vincenzo Millico), Andrea Belotti. Coach: Walter Mazzarri.
Goals: 30' Raúl Jiménez 1-0, 58' Andrea Belotti 1-1, 59' Leander Dendoncker 2-1.
Referee: Jesús Gil Manzano (ESP)   Attendance: 29,222.

29.08.19   Ibrox Stadium, Glasgow: Glasgow Rangers FC – Legia Warszawa 1-0 (0-0)
Glasgow Rangers FC: Allan McGregor, James Tavernier, Connor Goldson, Borna Barisic (64' John Flanagan), Nikola Katic, Steven Davis, Scott Arfield (72' Jordan Jones), Ryan Jack, Joe Aribo, Sheyi Ojo (90+5' Glen Kamara), Alfredo Morelos. Coach: Steven Gerrard.
Legia Warszawa: Radoslaw Majecki, Artur Jedrzejczyk, Igor Lewczuk, Luís Rocha, Pawel Stolarski (73' Dominik Nagy), Marko Vesovic, André Martins, Cafú, Valeriane Gvilia, Luquinhas, Sandro Kulenovic (56' Jaroslaw Niezgoda). Coach: Aleksandar Vukovic.
Goal: 90+1' Alfredo Morelos 1-0.
Referee: Slavko Vincic (SVN)   Attendance: 45,463.

29.08.19   Estádio Dom Afonso Henriques, Guimarães:
Vitória de Guimarães – Fotbal Club FCSB 1-0 (0-0)
Vitória de Guimarães: Douglas Jesus, Florent Hanin, Valeriy Bondarenko, Falaye Sacko, Edmond Tapsoba, Rochinha, Pêpê Rodrigues (74' João Carlos Teixeira), Denis Poha, Almoatasembellah Ali Mohamed, Davidson (86' Rafa Soares), Bruno Duarte (78' André Pereira). Coach: Ivo Vieira.
Fotbal Club FCSB: Cristian Balgradean, Valentin Cretu (27' Mihai Roman (I)), Aristides Soiledis (72' Thierry Moutinho), Bogdan Planic, Iulian Cristea, Ionut Pantîru, Mihai Pintilii (46' Harlem Gnohéré), Ionut Vîna, Ovidiu Popescu, Florin Tanase, Florinel Coman.
Coach: Bogdan Vintila.
Goal: 53' Edmond Tapsoba 1-0 (p).
Referee: Irfan Peljto (BIH)   Attendance: 18,352.

GROUP STAGE

GROUP A

Sevilla FC	6	5	0	1	14 -	3	15
APOEL Nicosia	6	3	1	2	10 -	8	10
Qarabag FK	6	1	2	3	8 -	11	5
F91 Dudelange	6	1	1	4	8 -	18	4

GROUP B

Malmö FF	6	3	2	1	8 -	6	11
FK København	6	2	3	1	5 -	4	9
Dynamo Kyiv	6	1	4	1	7 -	7	7
FC Lugano	6	0	3	3	2 -	5	3

GROUP C

FC Basel	6	4	1	1	12 -	4	13
Getafe CF	6	4	0	2	8 -	4	12
FK Krasnodar	6	3	0	3	7 -	11	9
Trabzonspor	6	0	1	5	3 -	11	1

GROUP D

LASK Linz	6	4	1	1	11 -	4	13
Sporting CP	6	4	0	2	11 -	7	12
PSV Eindhoven	6	2	2	2	9 -	12	8
Rosenborg BK	6	0	1	5	3 -	11	1

GROUP E

Celtic FC	6	4	1	1	10 -	6	13
CFR Cluj	6	4	0	2	6 -	4	12
Lazio Roma	6	2	0	4	6 -	9	6
Stade Rennes	6	1	1	4	5 -	8	4

GROUP F

Arsenal FC	6	3	2	1	14 -	7	11
Eintracht Frankfurt	6	3	0	3	8 -	10	9
Standard Liège	6	2	2	2	8 -	10	8
Vitória de Guimarães	6	1	2	3	7 -	10	5

GROUP G

FC Porto	6	3	1	2	8 - 9	10
Glasgow Rangers FC	6	2	3	1	8 - 6	9
BSC Young Boys	6	2	2	2	8 - 7	8
Feyenoord Rotterdam	6	1	2	3	7 - 9	5

GROUP H

RCD Espanyol	6	3	2	1	12 - 4	11
PFC Ludogorets Razgrad	6	2	2	2	10 - 10	8
Ferencvárosi TC	6	1	4	1	5 - 7	7
CSKA Moscow	6	1	2	3	3 - 9	5

GROUP I

KAA Gent	6	3	3	0	11 - 7	12
VfL Wolfsburg	6	3	2	1	9 - 7	11
AS Saint-Étienne	6	0	4	2	6 - 8	4
FC Oleksandriya	6	0	3	3	6 - 10	3

GROUP J

Istanbul Basaksehir FK	6	3	1	2	7 - 9	10
AS Roma	6	2	3	1	12 - 6	9
Borussia Mönchengladbach	6	2	2	2	6 - 9	8
Wolfsberger AC	6	1	2	3	7 - 8	5

GROUP K

Sporting Braga	6	4	2	0	15 - 9	14
Wolverhampton Wanderers	6	4	1	1	11 - 5	13
Slovan Bratislava	6	1	1	4	10 - 13	4
Besiktas JK	6	1	0	5	6 - 15	3

GROUP L

Manchester United	6	4	1	1	10 - 2	13
AZ Alkmaar	6	2	3	1	15 - 8	9
Partizan Beograd	6	2	2	2	10 - 10	8
FK Astana	6	1	0	5	4 - 19	3

The top two teams in each group advanced to the knockout phase.

GROUP A

19.09.19 Tofiq Bahramov adina Respublika stadionu, Baku:
Qarabag FK – Sevilla FC 0-3 (0-0)
Qarabag FK: Asmir Begovic, Maksim Medvedev, Qara Qarayev (85' Ismayil Ibrahimli), Badavi Hüseynov, Ailton, Abbas Hüseynov, Míchel, Jaime Romero (77' Dani Quintana), Richard Almeyda, Abdellah Zoubir, Magaye Gueye (67' Araz Abdullayev).
Coach: Gurban Gurbanov.
Sevilla FC: Tomás Vaclík, Escudero, Diego Carlos, Jules Koundé, Franco Vázquez, Nemanja Gudelj, Óliver Torres (86' Munas Dabour), Joan Jordán (58' Rony Lopes), Javier Hernández (72' Éver Banega), Munir, Alejandro Pozo. Coach: Lopetegui.
Goals: 62' Javier Hernández 0-1, 78' Munir 0-2, 85' Óliver Torres 0-3.
Referee: Yevhen Aranovskyi (UKR)   Attendance: 30,826.

Qarabag FK played their home matches at Tofiq Bahramov adina Respublika stadionu, Baku, instead of their regular stadium Azersun Arena, Baku

19.09.19 Neo GSP Stadium, Nicosia: APOEL Nicosia – F91 Dudelange 3-4 (0-1)
APOEL Nicosia: Vid Belec, Giorgios Merkis, Nicholas Ioannou, Dragan Mihajlovic, Savvas Gentsoglou, Antonio Jakolis (46' Moussa Al Taamari), Uros Matic, Tomás De Vincenti (76' Giorgos Efrem), Lucas Souza (46' Joãozinho), Roman Bezjak, Andrija Pavlovic.
Coach: Thomas Doll.
F91 Dudelange: Jonathan Joubert, Tom Schnell, Mehdi Kirch (63' Thibaut Lesquoy), Mohamed Bouchouari, Mario Pokar, Dominik Stolz (90+3' Kobe Cools), Mickaël Garos, Charles Morren, Danel Sinani, Antoine Bernier, Laurent Mendy (67' Corenthyn Lavie).
Coaches: Emilio Ferrera & Bertrand Crasson.
Goals: 36' Danel Sinani 0-1, 51' Antoine Bernier 0-2, 54' Andrija Pavlovic 1-2, 56' Tomás De Vincenti 2-2 (p), 58' Andrija Pavlovic 3-2, 72' Dominik Stolz 3-3, 82' Danel Sinani 3-4.
Referee: Dumitri Muntean (MOL)   Attendance: 9,313.

03.10.19 Stade Josy Barthel, Luxembourg: F91 Dudelange – Qarabag FK 1-4 (0-3)
F91 Dudelange: Jonathan Joubert, Tom Schnell, Thibaut Lesquoy, Mohamed Bouchouari, Mario Pokar (72' Kobe Cools), Ryan Klapp (56' Corenthyn Lavie), Mickaël Garos, Sabir Bougrine, Danel Sinani, Antoine Bernier, Laurent Mendy (67' Charles Morren).
Coaches: Emilio Ferrera & Bertrand Crasson.
Qarabag FK: Asmir Begovic, Rashad Sadyqov, Maksim Medvedev, Qara Qarayev (60' Simeon Slavchev, Badavi Hüseynov, Ailton, Míchel (72' Magaye Gueye), Dani Quintana (81' Araz Abdullayev), Richard Almeyda, Abdellah Zoubir, Mahir Emreli.
Coach: Gurban Gurbanov.
Goals: 11' Abdellah Zoubir 0-1, 30' Míchel 0-2, 37' Richard Almeyda 0-3 (p), 69' Dani Quintana 0-4, 90' Antoine Bernier 1-4.
Referee: John Beaton (SCO)   Attendance: 3,005.
Sent off: 62' Mickaël Garos.

F91 Dudelange played their home matches at Stade Josy Barthel, Luxembourg, instead of their regular stadium, Stade Jos Nosbaum, Dudelange.

03.10.19   Estadio Ramón Sánchez Pizjuán, Sevilla: Sevilla FC – APOEL Nicosia 1-0 (1-0)
Sevilla FC: Yassine Bounou, Escudero, Sergi Gómez, Jules Koundé, Franco Vázquez, Nemanja Gudelj, Joan Jordán, Javier Hernández (79' Munas Dabour), Rony Lopes (72' Éver Banega), Munir (61' Bryan Gil), Alejandro Pozo. Coach: Lopetegui.
APOEL Nicosia: Vid Belec, Vujadin Savic, Giorgios Merkis, Nicholas Ioannou, Dragan Mihajlovic, Savvas Gentsoglou (80' Giorgos Efrem), Antonio Jakolis, Uros Matic, Lucas Souza, Moussa Al Taamari (83' Stathis Aloneftis), Andrija Pavlovic (66' Linus Hallenius). Coach: Thomas Doll.
Goal: 17' Javier Hernández 1-0.
Referee: Bas Nijhuis (HOL)   Attendance: 30,008.

24.10.19   Tofiq Bahramov adina Respublika stadionu, Baku:
            Qarabağ FK – APOEL Nicosia 2-2 (1-2)
Qarabağ FK: Asmir Begovic, Rashad Sadyqov, Maksim Medvedev, Qara Qarayev, Badavi Hüseynov, Ailton, Míchel, Dani Quintana, Richard Almeyda, Abdellah Zoubir, Magaye Gueye (46' Mahir Emreli). Coach: Gurban Gurbanov.
APOEL Nicosia: Vid Belec, Vujadin Savic, Giorgios Merkis, Praxitelis Vouros, Nicholas Ioannou (67' Antonio Jakolis), Dragan Mihajlovic, Savvas Gentsoglou, Uros Matic, Lucas Souza, Linus Hallenius (76' Roman Bezjak), Andrija Pavlovic (85' Alef).
Coach: Thomas Doll.
Goals: 13' Dani Quintana 1-0, 29' Maksim Medvedev 1-1 (og), 45' Linus Hallenius 1-2, 58' Ailton 2-2.
Referee: Filip Glova (SVK)   Attendance: 30,824.

24.10.19   Estadio Ramón Sánchez Pizjuán, Sevilla: Sevilla FC – F91 Dudelange 3-0 (0-0)
Sevilla FC: Yassine Bounou, Escudero, Sergi Gómez (70' Diego Carlos), Jules Koundé, Franco Vázquez, Nemanja Gudelj, Óliver Torres, Luuk de Jong (52' Munir), Munas Dabour, Rony Lopes (60' Bryan Gil), Alejandro Pozo. Coach: Lopetegui.
F91 Dudelange: Jonathan Joubert, Tom Schnell, Thibaut Lesquoy, Kobe Cools, Mohamed Bouchouari, Dominick Stolz (79' Adel Bettaieb), Corenthyn Lavie, Charles Morren, Sabir Bougrine (81' Omar Natami), Danel Sinani, Antoine Bernier (76' Ryan Klapp).
Coaches: Emilio Ferrera & Bertrand Crasson.
Goals: 48', 75' Franco Vázquez 1-0, 2-0, 78' Munir 3-0.
Referee: Anastasios Papapetrou (GRE)   Attendance: 26,165.

07.11.19   Stade Josy Barthel, Luxembourg: F91 Dudelange – Sevilla FC 2-5 (0-4)
F91 Dudelange: Jonathan Joubert, Mehdi Kirch, Kobe Cools, Mohamed Bouchouari, Ryan Klapp (46' Bertino Cabral Barbosa), Dominick Stolz (86' Corenthyn Lavie), Mickaël Garos, Charles Morren, Sabir Bougrine (46' Tom Schnell), Danel Sinani, Antoine Bernier.
Coaches: Emilio Ferrera & Bertrand Crasson.
Sevilla FC: Yassine Bounou, Escudero, Sergi Gómez, Nemanja Gudelj, Óliver Torres (51' Franco Vázquez), Joan Jordán (61' Fernando), Nolito (51' Luuk de Jong), Munas Dabour, Rony Lopes, Munir, Alejandro Pozo. Coach: Lopetegui.
Goals: 17' Munas Dabour 0-1, 27', 33' Munir 0-2, 0-3, 36' Munas Dabour 0-4, 67' Munir 0-5, 69', 80' Danel Sinani 1-5, 2-5.
Referee: Vilhjálmur Thórarinsson (ISL)   Attendance: 2.848.

07.11.19   Neo GSP Stadium, Nicosia: APOEL Nicosia – Qarabag FK 2-1 (0-1)
APOEL Nicosia: Vid Belec, Vujadin Savic, Joãozinho (46' Moussa Al Tamari), Praxitelis Vouros, Nicholas Ioannou, Dragan Mihajlovic, Savvas Gentsoglou (59' Roman Bezjak), Uros Matic, Lucas Souza, Linus Hallenius (75' Giorgos Efrem), Andrija Pavlovic.
Coach: Thomas Doll.
Qarabag FK: Asmir Begovic, Rashad Sadyqov, Maksim Medvedev, Qara Qarayev, Badavi Hüseynov, Ailton, Míchel (83' Abbas Hüseynov), Dani Quintana (16' Magaye Gueye, 76' Jaime Romero), Araz Abdullayev, Richard Almeyda, Abdellah Zoubir.
Coach: Gurban Gurbanov.
Goals: 10' Maksim Medvedev 0-1, 59' Lucas Souza 1-1, 88' Nicholas Ioannou 2-1.
Referee: Manuel Schüttengruber (AUT)   Attendance: 9,432.

28.11.19   Estadio Ramón Sánchez Pizjuán, Sevilla: Sevilla FC – Qarabag FK 2-0 (0-0)
Sevilla FC: Yassine Bounou, Daniel Carriço, Escudero, Sergi Gómez, Nemanja Gudelj, Óliver Torres (68' José Mena), Javier Hernández (62' Franco Vázquez), Munas Dabour, Rony Lopes (54' Bryan Gil), Munir, Alejandro Pozo. Coach: Lopetegui.
Qarabag FK: Asmir Begovic, Maksim Medvedev, Qara Qarayev, Badavi Hüseynov, Ailton, Abbas Hüseynov (69' Araz Abdullayev), Rahil Mammadov, Míchel (84' Dani Quintana), Jaime Romero (70' Mahir Emreli), Richard Almeyda, Abdellah Zoubir.
Coach: Gurban Gurbanov.
Goals: 61' Bryan Gil 10, 90+2' Munas Dabour 2-0.
Referee: Mohammed Al-Hakim (SWE)   Attendance: 19,803.

28.11.19   Stade Josy Barthel, Luxembourg: F91 Dudelange – APOEL Nicosia 0-2 (0-2)
F91 Dudelange: Jonathan Joubert, Tom Schnell, Thibaut Lesquoy, Kobe Cools, Mohamed Bouchouari (61' Adel Bettaieb), Dominick Stolz (77' Mario Pokar), Mickaël Garos, Charles Morren, Sabir Bougrine (54' Corenthyn Lavie), Danel Sinani, Antoine Bernier.
Coaches: Emilio Ferrera & Bertrand Crasson.
APOEL Nicosia: Vid Belec, Vujadin Savic, Giorgios Merkis, Praxitelis Vouros, Nicholas Ioannou (66' Antonio Jakolis), Dragan Mihajlovic, Savvas Gentsoglou (46' Alef), Uros Matic, Lucas Souza, Moussa Al Tamari, Linus Hallenius (84' Tomás De Vincenti).
Coach: Thomas Doll.
Goals: 12' Uros Matic 0-1 (p), 43' Giorgios Merkis 0-2.
Referee: Gianluca Rocchi (ITA)   Attendance: 2,912.
Sent off: 83' Praxitelis Vouros, 90' Danel Sinani.

12.12.19   Tofiq Bahramov adina Respublika stadionu, Baku:
Qarabag FK – F91 Dudelange 1-1 (0-0)
Qarabag FK: Sahrudin Mahammadaliyev, Rashad Sadyqov, Maksim Medvedev, Qara Qarayev, Badavi Hüseynov, Ailton, Míchel, Dani Quintana (64' Jaime Romero), Abdellah Zoubir, Ismayil Ibrahimli (50' Richard Almeyda), Mahir Emreli (75' Magaye Gueye).
Coach: Gurban Gurbanov.
F91 Dudelange: Jonathan Joubert, Tom Schnell, Thibaut Lesquoy, Kobe Cools, Mohamed Bouchouari, Dominick Stolz, Mickaël Garos, Charles Morren, Sabir Bougrine (84' Mario Pokar), Adel Bettaieb (86' Laurent Mendy), Antoine Bernier (78' Ryan Klapp).
Coaches: Emilio Ferrera & Bertrand Crasson.
Goals: 63' Sabir Bougrine 0-1, 90+1' Magaye Gueye 1-1.
Referee: Kristo Tohver (EST)   Attendance: 5,823
Sent off: 46' Qara Qarayev.

12.12.19 Neo GSP Stadium, Nicosia: APOEL Nicosia – Sevilla FC 1-0 (0-0)
APOEL Nicosia: Vid Belec, Vujadin Savic, Giorgios Merkis, Nicholas Ioannou, Dragan Mihajlovic, Antonio Jakolis (79' Andreas Makris), Uros Matic, Lucas Souza, Alef, Moussa Al Tamari (90+1' Giorgos Efrem), Andrija Pavlovic (70' Tomás De Vincenti).
Coach: Loukas Hatziloukas.
Sevilla FC: Yassine Bounou, Escudero, Sergi Gómez, Nemanja Gudelj, Lucas Ocampos, Joan Jordán (46' Óliver Torres), Genaro Rodríguez, Javier Hernández (46' Munas Dabour), Rony Lopes, Alejandro Pozo, Bryan Gil (68' José Mena). Coach: Lopetegui.
Goal: 61' Vujadin Savic 1-0.
Referee: Nikola Dabanovic (MNE)   Attendance: 5,608.

Munas Dabour missed a penalty kick (57').

GROUP B

19.09.19 NSK Olimpiyskiy Stadium, Kiev: Dynamo Kyiv – Malmö FF 1-0 (0-0)
Dynamo Kyiv: Denis Boyko, Tamás Kádár, Tomasz Kedziora, Artem Shabanov, Vitali Mykolenko, Sergiy Sydorchuk, Vitaliy Buyalskiy, Benjamin Verbic, Viktor Tsygankov (90+1' Oleksandr Karavayev), Volodymyr Shepelev, Gerson Rodrigues (73' Artem Besedin).
Coach: Aleksey Mikhaylichenko.
Malmö FF: Johan Dahlin, Behrang Safari, Rasmus Bengtsson, Lasse Nielsen, Felix Beijmo (57' Eric Larsson), Søren Rieks, Anders Christiansen (73' Marcus Antonsson), Fouad Bachirou, Arnór Ingvi Traustason (86' Romain Gall), Oscar Lewicki, Markus Rosenberg.
Coach: Uwe Rösler.
Goal: 84' Vitaliy Buyalskiy 1-0.
Referee: Aleksandar Stavrev (MCD)   Attendance: 17,159.

19.09.19 Telia Parken, København: FC København – FC Lugano 1-0 (0-0)
FC København: Kalle Johnsson, Pierre Bengtsson, Sotirios Papagiannopoulos, Guillermo Varela, Victor Nelsson, Rasmus Falk (79' Pep Biel Mas), Zeca, Viktor Fischer (79' Bryan Oviedo), Jens Stage, Pieros Soteriou, Michael Santos (77' Mohammed Daramy).
Coach: Ståle Solbakken.
FC Lugano: Noam Baumann, Mijat Maric, Fabio Daprelà, Numa Lavanchy, Ákos Kecskés, Eloge Yao (70' Filip Holender), Jonathan Sabbatini, Bálint Vécsei (82' Nicola Dalmonte), Olivier Custodio, Mattia Bottani (49' Marco Aratore), Carlinhos. Coach: Fabio Celestini.
Goal: 50' Michael Santos 1-0.
Referee: Fábio Veríssimo (POR)   Attendance: 18,240.

03.10.19 Kybunpark, St.Gallen: FC Lugano – Dynamo Kyiv 0-0
FC Lugano: Noam Baumann, Mijat Maric, Fabio Daprelà, Numa Lavanchy, Eloge Yao, Marco Aratore (64' Nicola Dalmonte), Jonathan Sabbatini, Bálint Vécsei, Sandi Lovric (71' Olivier Custodio), Alexander Gerndt (78' Filip Holender), Carlinhos. Coach: Fabio Celestini.
Dynamo Kyiv: Georgiy Bushchan, Tamás Kádár, Tomasz Kedziora, Artem Shabanov, Vitali Mykolenko, Sergiy Sydorchuk, Vitaliy Buyalskiy, Benjamin Verbic (88' Carlos de Pena), Viktor Tsygankov, Volodymyr Shepelev (84' Denys Garmash), Gerson Rodrigues (70' Artem Besedin). Coach: Aleksey Mikhaylichenko.
Referee: Karim Abed (FRA)   Attendance: 1,281.

FC Lugano played their home matches at Kybunpark, St.Gallen, instead of their regular home stadium Cornaredo Stadium, Lugano, as it did not meet UEFA requirements.

03.10.19 Swedbank Stadion, Malmö: Malmö FF – FC København 1-1 (0-1)
Malmö FF: Johan Dahlin, Behrang Safari, Rasmus Bengtsson, Lasse Nielsen, Søren Rieks (46'
Eric Larsson), Anders Christiansen (58' Arnór Ingvi Traustason), Fouad Bachirou, Oscar
Lewicki, Markus Rosenberg, Jo Inge Berget, Marcus Antonsson (78' Guillermo Molins).
Coach: Uwe Rösler.
FC København: Kalle Johnsson, Pierre Bengtsson, Andreas Bjelland, Guillermo Varela, Victor
Nelsson, Rasmus Falk (85' Karlo Bartolec), Zeca, Viktor Fischer (70' Carlo Holse), Jens
Stage, Pieros Soteriou, Michael Santos (86' Mohammed Daramy). Coach: Ståle Solbakken.
Goals: 45+5' Lasse Nielsen 0-1 (og), 55' Markus Rosenberg 1-1.
Referee: Deniz Aytekin (GER)   Attendance: 19,884.

24.10.19 Swedbank Stadion, Malmö: Malmö FF – FC Lugano 2-1 (2-0)
Malmö FF: Johan Dahlin, Eric Larsson, Lasse Nielsen, Jonas Knudsen (85' Behrang Safari),
Søren Rieks, Fouad Bachirou, Arnór Ingvi Traustason, Oscar Lewicki, Bonke Innocent (68'
Rasmus Bengtsson), Guillermo Molins (77' Markus Rosenberg), Jo Inge Berget.
Coach: Uwe Rösler.
FC Lugano: Noam Baumann, Mijat Maric, Fabio Daprelà, Eloge Yao (60' Marco Aratore),
Linus Obexer (79' Filip Holender), Jonathan Sabbatini, Olivier Custodio, Sandi Lovric,
Alexander Gerndt, Mattia Bottani (81' Francisco Rodriguez), Carlinhos.
Coach: Fabio Celestini.
Goals: 13' Jo Inge Berget 1-0 (p), 32' Guillermo Molins 2-0, 50' Alexander Gerndt 2-1.
Referee: Rob Harvey (IRL)   Attendance: 16,789.

24.10.19 NSK Olimpiyskiy Stadium, Kiev: Dynamo Kyiv – FC København 1-1 (0-1)
Dynamo Kyiv: Georgiy Bushchan, Tomasz Kedziora, Artem Shabanov, Denys Popov, Vitali
Mykolenko, Sergiy Sydorchuk, Benjamin Verbic, Carlos de Pena (80' Denys Garmash), Viktor
Tsygankov, Volodymyr Shepelev, Artem Besedin. Coach: Aleksey Mikhaylichenko.
FC København: Kalle Johnsson, Bryan Oviedo, Sotirios Papagiannopoulos, Karlo Bartolec,
Victor Nelsson, Rasmus Falk (87' Guillermo Varela), Zeca, Viktor Fischer (75' Nicolaj
Thomsen), Jens Stage, Pieros Soteriou, Michael Santos (89' Nicklas Bendtner).
Coach: Ståle Solbakken.
Goals: 2' Pieros Soteriou 0-1, 53' Artem Shabanov 1-1.
Referee: Halil Umut Meler (TUR)   Attendance: 21,202.

07.11.19 Kybunpark, St.Gallen: FC Lugano – Malmö FF 0-0
FC Lugano: Noam Baumann, Mijat Maric, Fabio Daprelà, Numa Lavanchy, Eloge Yao, Marco
Aratore, Bálint Vécsei, Olivier Custodio, Mattia Bottani (57' Alexander Gerndt), Filip
Holender (81' Sandi Lovric), Carlinhos. Coach: Maurizio Jacobacci.
Malmö FF: Johan Dahlin, Behrang Safari (69' Jonas Knudsen), Rasmus Bengtsson, Lasse
Nielsen, Felix Beijmo (64' Guillermo Molins), Søren Rieks, Fouad Bachirou, Arnór Ingvi
Traustason, Oscar Lewicki (30' Bonke Innocent), Markus Rosenberg, Jo Inge Berget.
Coach: Uwe Rösler.
Referee: Giorgi Kruashvili (GEO)   Attendance: 1,875.

07.11.19   Telia Parken, København: FC København – Dynamo Kyiv 1-1 (1-0)
FC København: Kalle Johnsson, Pierre Bengtsson (69' Karlo Bartolec), Sotirios Papagiannopoulos, Guillermo Varela, Victor Nelsson, Rasmus Falk (55' Mohammed Daramy), Zeca, Viktor Fischer (82' Nicolaj Thomsen), Jens Stage, Pieros Soteriou, Michael Santos.
Coach: Ståle Solbakken.
Dynamo Kyiv: Georgiy Bushchan, Tomasz Kedziora, Artem Shabanov, Denys Popov, Vitali Mykolenko, Sergiy Sydorchuk, Benjamin Verbic (89' Carlos de Pena), Oleksandr Karavayev, Viktor Tsygankov, Volodymyr Shepelev, Artem Besedin. Coach: Aleksey Mikhaylichenko.
Goals: 4' Jens Stage 1-0, 70' Benjamin Verbic 1-1.
Referee: Tamás Bognár (HUN)   Attendance: 23,166.

Viktor Tsygankov missed a penalty kick (14').

28.11.19   Swedbank Stadion, Malmö: Malmö FF – Dynamo Kyiv 4-3 (1-2)
Malmö FF: Johan Dahlin, Behrang Safari (90+7' Jonas Knudsen), Rasmus Bengtsson, Eric Larsson (79' Guillermo Molins), Lasse Nielsen, Søren Rieks, Fouad Bachirou, Arnór Ingvi Traustason, Bonke Innocent (46' Erdal Rakip), Markus Rosenberg, Jo Inge Berget.
Coach: Uwe Rösler.
Dynamo Kyiv: Georgiy Bushchan, Tamás Kádár, Tomasz Kedziora, Artem Shabanov, Vitali Mykolenko, Sergiy Sydorchuk, Vitaly Buyalskiy (89' Denys Garmash), Benjamin Verbic (82' Oleksandr Karavayev), Viktor Tsygankov, Volodymyr Shepelev (71' Mykola Shaparenko), Artem Besedin. Coach: Aleksey Mikhaylichenko.
Goals: 2' Rasmus Bengtsson 1-0, 18' Vitali Mykolenko 1-1, 39' Viktor Tsygankov 1-2, 48' Markus Rosenberg 2-2, 57' Erdal Rakip 3-2, 77' Benjamin Verbic 3-3, 90+6' Markus Rosenberg 4-3.
Referee: Pavel Královec (CZE)   Attendance: 19,224.
Sent off: 65' Sergiy Sydorchuk

28.11.19   Kybunpark, St.Gallen: FC Lugano – FC København 0-1 (0-1)
FC Lugano: Noam Baumann, Fabio Daprelà, Numa Lavanchy, Ákos Kecskés, Linus Obexer, Marco Aratore (70' Franklin Sasere), Olivier Custodio, Sandi Lovric, Stefano Guidotti (76' Miroslav Covilo), Mattia Bottani, Carlinhos (62' Nicola Dalmonte).
Coach: Maurizio Jacobacci.
FC København: Kalle Johnsson, Pierre Bengtsson, Andreas Bjelland, Sotirios Papagiannopoulos, Karlo Bartolec, Victor Nelsson, Zeca, Nicolaj Thomsen (79' Robert Mudrazija), Pep Biel Mas (74' Rasmus Falk), Pieros Soteriou, Michael Santos (86' Guillermo Varela). Coach: Ståle Solbakken.
Goal: 27' Nicolaj Thomsen 0-1.
Referee: Aleksei Eskov (RUS)   Attendance: 1,281.

12.12.19   NSK Olimpiyskiy Stadium, Kiev: Dynamo Kyiv – FC Lugano 1-1 (0-1)
Dynamo Kyiv: Georgiy Bushchan, Tamás Kádár, Tomasz Kedziora (64' Heorhii Tsitaishvili), Denys Popov, Vitali Mykolenko, Vitaly Buyalskiy, Oleksandr Karavayev, Carlos de Pena (77' Denys Garmash), Viktor Tsygankov, Volodymyr Shepelev, Artem Besedin (81' Fran Sol).
Coach: Aleksey Mikhaylichenko.
FC Lugano: David Da Costa, Fabio Daprelà, Fulvio Sulmoni, Eloge Yao, Linus Obexer, Marco Aratore, Olivier Custodio, Sandi Lovric (84' Domen Crnigoj), Stefano Guidotti (55' Bálint Vécsei), Filip Holender, Nicola Dalmonte (64' Mijat Maric). Coach: Maurizio Jacobacci.
Goals: 45' Marco Aratore 0-1, 90+4' Viktor Tsygankov 1-1.
Referee: Aliyar Agayev (AZE)   Attendance: 15,774.

12.12.19   Telia Parken, København: FC København – Malmö FF 0-1 (0-0)
FC København: Kalle Johnsson, Pierre Bengtsson, Andreas Bjelland, Sotirios Papagiannopoulos, Guillermo Varela (84' Karlo Bartolec), Rasmus Falk, Viktor Fischer, Nicolaj Thomsen (80' Michael Santos), Robert Mudrazija (46' Carlo Holse), Dame N'Doye, Pieros Soteriou. Coach: Ståle Solbakken.
Malmö FF: Johan Dahlin, Behrang Safari (60' Jonas Knudsen), Rasmus Bengtsson, Eric Larsson, Lasse Nielsen, Søren Rieks, Anders Christiansen (80' Oscar Lewicki), Arnór Ingvi Traustason, Erdal Rakip (68' Guillermo Molins), Bonke Innocent, Markus Rosenberg. Coach: Uwe Rösler.
Goal: 77' Sotirios Papagiannopoulos 0-1 (og).
Referee: Davide Massa (ITA)   Attendance: 32,941.

GROUP C

19.09.19   Coliseum Alfonso Pérez, Getafe: Getafe CF – Trabzonspor 1-0 (1-0)
Getafe CF: Leandro Chichizola, Allan Nyom, Bruno, Raúl García, Djené Dakonam, Fayçal Fajr, Portillo, David Timor (90+1' Mauro Arambarri), Kenedy (77' Cucurella), Ángel, Enric Gallego (68' Mata). Coach: José Bordalás.
Trabzonspor: Ugurcan Çakir, João Pereira, Filip Novák, Gastón Campi, Majid Hosseini, John Obi Mikel, José Sosa, Dogan Erdogan (59' Abdülkadir Parmak), Donis Avdijaj (46' Daniel Sturridge), Anthony Nwakaeme (83' Firatcan Üzüm), Alexander Sørloth. Coach: Ünal Karaman.
Goal: 18' Ángel 1-0.
Referee: Matej Jug (SVN)   Attendance: 5,786.

19.09.19   St. Jakob-Park, Basel: FC Basel – FK Krasnodar 5-0 (2-0)
FC Basel: Jonas Omlin, Silvan Widmer, Omar Alderete, Raoul Petretta, Eray Cömart, Valentin Stocker (58' Noah Okafor), Luca Zuffi (79' Samuele Campo), Fabian Frei, Taulant Xhaka, Kevin Bua, Arthur Cabral (66' Blas Riveros). Coach: Marcel Koller.
FK Krasnodar: Matvei Safonov, Aleksandr Martynovich, Sergey Petrov, Uros Spajic, Cristian Ramírez, Ruslan Kambolov (46' Daniil Utkin), Tonny Vilhena, Kristoffer Olsson (60' Younes Namli), Wamberto, Magomed Suleymanov, Ivan Ignatyev (67' Marcus Berg). Coach: Sergey Matveev.
Goals: 9', 40' Kevin Bua 1-0, 2-0, 52' Luca Zuffi 3-0, 54' Tonny Vilhena 4-0 (og), 79' Noah Okafor 5-0.
Referee: Mattias Gestranius (FIN)   Attendance: 14,127.

03.10.19   Stadion FK Krasnodar, Krasnodar: FK Krasnodar – Getafe CF 1-2 (0-1)
FK Krasnodar: Matvei Safonov, Jón Fjóluson (46' Ari), Aleksandr Martynovich, Sergey Petrov, Uros Spajic, Cristian Ramírez, Tonny Vilhena, Kristoffer Olsson (74' Daniil Utkin), Younes Namli (70' Manuel Fernandes), Marcus Berg, Magomed Suleymanov. Coach: Sergey Matveev.
Getafe CF: Leandro Chichizola, Allan Nyom, Leandro Cabrera, Bruno, Raúl García, Fayçal Fajr, Portillo (72' Jason), David Timor, Kenedy (76' Cucurella), Ángel (84' Nemanja Maksimovic), Enric Gallego. Coach: José Bordalás.
Goals: 36', 61' Ángel 0-1, 0-2, 69' Ari 1-2.
Referee: Ivan Bebek (CRO)   Attendance: 20,035.
Sent off: 81' David Timor.

03.10.19 Medical Park Stadyumu, Trabzon: Trabzonspor – FC Basel 2-2 (1-1)
Trabzonspor: Ugurcan Çakir, Filip Novák, Gastón Campi, Majid Hosseini, Hüseyin Türkmen, John Obi Mikel, Dogan Erdogan, Donis Avdijaj (46' Anthony Nwakaeme), Abdülkadir Parmak, Daniel Sturridge (81' Kâmil Çörekçi), Alexander Sørloth (65' José Sosa).
Coach: Ünal Karaman.
FC Basel: Jonas Omlin, Silvan Widmer, Omar Alderete, Raoul Petretta, Eray Cömart, Valentin Stocker, Luca Zuffi (65' Noah Okafor), Fabian Frei, Taulant Xhaka, Kevin Bua, Kemal Ademi (70' Arthur Cabral). Coach: Marcel Koller.
Goals: 20' Silvan Widmer 0-1, 26' Abdülkadir Parmak 1-1, 78' José Sosa 2-1, 80' Noah Okafor 2-2.
Referee: Marco Di Bello (ITA)   Attendance: 23,867.

24.10.19 Medical Park Stadyumu, Trabzon: Trabzonspor – FK Krasnodar 0-2 (0-0)
Trabzonspor: Ugurcan Çakir, João Pereira, Filip Novák, Kâmil Çörekçi (68' Dogan Erdogan), Gastón Campi (83' Ahmet Canbaz), Ivanildo Fernandes, José Sosa, Abdülkadir Parmak (72' Donis Avdijaj), Anthony Nwakaeme, Alexander Sørloth, Yusuf Sari. Coach: Ünal Karaman.
FK Krasnodar: Matvei Safonov, Aleksandr Martynovich, Sergey Petrov, Uros Spajic, Cristian Ramírez, Ruslan Kambolov (76' Jón Fjóluson), Dmitriy Stotskiy (62' Manuel Fernandes), Tonny Vilhena, Kristoffer Olsson, Marcus Berg (71' Ari), Magomed Suleymanov.
Coach: Sergey Matveev.
Goals: 49' Marcus Berg 0-1, 90+2' Tonny Vilhena 0-2.
Referee: Harald Lechner (AUT)   Attendance: 26,405.

24.10.19 Coliseum Alfonso Pérez, Getafe: Getafe CF – FC Basel 0-1 (0-1)
Getafe CF: Leandro Chichizola, Allan Nyom, Bruno (14' Leandro Cabrera), Raúl García, Djené Dakonam, Fayçal Fajr, Portillo (57' Jason), Kenedy, Nemanja Maksimovic, Ángel, Jorge Molina (71' Cucurella). Coach: José Bordalás.
FC Basel: Djordje Nikolic, Silvan Widmer, Omar Alderete, Raoul Petretta, Eray Cömart, Valentin Stocker (90+3' Afimico Pululu), Luca Zuffi, Fabian Frei, Taulant Xhaka, Kevin Bua, Kemal Ademi (69' Arthur Cabral). Coach: Marcel Koller.
Goal: 18' Fabian Frei 0-1.
Referee: Jérôme Brisard (FRA)   Attendance: 6,213.
Sent off: 73' Kevin Bua.

07.11.19 Stadion FK Krasnodar, Krasnodar: FK Krasnodar – Trabzonspor 3-1 (2-0)
FK Krasnodar: Stanislav Kritsyuk, Aleksandr Martynovich, Sergey Petrov, Uros Spajic, Cristian Ramírez, Manuel Fernandes (63' Daniil Utkin), Dmitriy Stotskiy, Tonny Vilhena, Kristoffer Olsson (77' Ruslan Kambolov), Ari (66' Ivan Ignatyev), Magomed Suleymanov.
Coach: Sergey Matveev.
Trabzonspor: Erce Kardesler, Kâmil Çörekçi (87' Yusuf Sari), Gastón Campi, Majid Hosseini, Ivanildo Fernandes, Abdurahim Dursun, Serkan Asan, Dogan Erdogan, Donis Avdijaj (65' Anthony Nwakaeme), Ahmet Canbaz, Muhammet Akpinar (72' Alexander Sørloth).
Coach: Ünal Karaman.
Goals: 27' SerkanAsan 1-0 (og), 34' Manuel Fernandes 2-0, 90+3' Ivan Ignatyev 3-0, 90+4' Anthony Nwakaeme 3-1.
Referee: Benoît Bastien (FRA)   Attendance: 21,669.

240

07.11.19   St. Jakob-Park, Basel: FC Basel – Getafe CF 2-1 (1-1)
FC Basel: Jonas Omlin, Silvan Widmer, Omar Alderete, Raoul Petretta, Eray Cömart, Blas Riveros, Luca Zuffi, Fabian Frei, Taulant Xhaka (64' Samuele Campo), Edon Zhegrova (88' Afimico Pululu), Arthur Cabral (73' Kemal Ademi). Coach: Marcel Koller.
Getafe CF: Leandro Chichizola, Bruno, Raúl García, Mathías Olivera, Fayçal Fajr (79' Ángel), Portillo, David Timor (68' Allan Nyom), Nemanja Maksimovic, Mata, Enric Gallego, Hugo Duro (68' Kenedy). Coach: José Bordalás.
Goals: 8' Arthur Cabral 1-0, 45' Mata 1-1 (p), 60' Fabian Frei 2-1.
Referee: Serhiy Boyko (UKR)   Attendance: 26,298.

28.11.19   Medical Park Stadyumu, Trabzon: Trabzonspor – Getafe CF 0-1 (0-0)
Trabzonspor: Erce Kardesler, Majid Hosseini (70' Gastón Campi), Ivanildo Fernandes, Abdurahim Dursun, Serkan Asan, Dogan Erdogan, Donis Avdijaj (59' Behlül Aydin), Abdülkadir Parmak, Firatcan Üzüm, Kerem Baykus (89' Kâmil Çörekçi), Muhammet Akpinar. Coach: Ünal Karaman.
Getafe CF: Leandro Chichizola, Allan Nyom, Bruno, Djené Dakonam, Mathías Olivera, Fayçal Fajr, Portillo, Kenedy (86' Cucurella), Mauro Arambarri, Jorge Molina (62' Ángel), Mata (73' David Timor). Coach: José Bordalás.
Goal: 50' Mata 0-1.
Referee: Andris Treimanis (LAT)   Attendance: 11,465.

28.11.19   Stadion FK Krasnodar, Krasnodar: FK Krasnodar – FC Basel 1-0 (0-0)
FK Krasnodar: Stanislav Kritsyuk, Aleksandr Martynovich, Sergey Petrov, Uros Spajic, Cristian Ramírez, Yuri Gazinskiy (83' Ruslan Kambolov), Tonny Vilhena, Kristoffer Olsson (73' Daniil Utkin), Wamberto, Ari, Magomed Suleymanov (57' Younes Namli). Coach: Sergey Matveev.
FC Basel: Jonas Omlin, Emil Bergström, Silvan Widmer, Omar Alderete, Eray Cömart, Blas Riveros, Valentin Stocker (86' Afimico Pululu), Fabian Frei, Samuele Campo, Kemal Ademi (68' Arthur Cabral), Noah Okafor (85' Kevin Bua). Coach: Marcel Koller.
Goal: 72' Ari 1-0 (p).
Referee: Bobby Madden (SCO)   Attendance: 22,826.
Sent off: 90+5' Ari.

12.12.19   Coliseum Alfonso Pérez, Getafe: Getafe CF – FK Krasnodar 3-0 (0-0)
Getafe CF: David Soria, Allan Nyom, Damián Suárez, Leandro Cabrera, Djené Dakonam, Cucurella, Jason (68' Kenedy), Nemanja Maksimovic, Mauro Arambarri (82' David Timor), Ángel (73' Jorge Molina), Mata. Coach: José Bordalás.
FK Krasnodar: Stanislav Kritsyuk, Aleksandr Martynovich, Sergey Petrov, Uros Spajic, Cristian Ramírez (75' Dmitriy Skopintsev), Yuri Gazinskiy, Tonny Vilhena, Wamberto, Marcus Berg, Magomed Suleymanov (62' Younes Namli), Ivan Ignatyev (69' Daniil Utkin). Coach: Sergey Matveev.
Goals: 76' Leandro Cabrera 1-0, 78' Jorge Molina 2-0, 86' Kenedy 3-0.
Referee: Daniel Siebert (GER)   Attendance: 9,389.
Sent off: 88' Aleksandr Martynovich.

12.12.19 St. Jakob-Park, Basel: FC Basel – Trabzonspor 2-0 (1-0)
FC Basel: Jonas Omlin, Silvan Widmer, Omar Alderete, Raoul Petretta, Eray Cömart, Valentin Stocker, Luca Zuffi (78' Samuele Campo), Fabian Frei, Taulant Xhaka, Arthur Cabral (71' Kemal Ademi), Afimico Pululu (65' Noah Okafor). Coach: Marcel Koller.
Trabzonspor: Erce Kardesler, Majid Hosseini (71' Gastón Campi), Ivanildo Fernandes, Abdurahim Dursun, Serkan Asan, Ogenyi Onazi (51' Muhammet Akpinar), Dogan Erdogan, Donis Avdijaj, Abdülkadir Parmak, Firatcan Üzüm, Caleb Ekuban (78' Kerem Baykus). Coach: Ünal Karaman.
Goals: 21' Silvan Widmer 1-0, 72' Valentin Stocker 2-0.
Referee: Aleksandar Stavrev (MCD)   Attendance: 17,921.

GROUP D

19.09.19 Philips Stadion, Eindhoven: PSV Eindhoven – Sporting CP 3-2 (2-1)
PSV Eindhoven: Jeroen Zoet, Nick Viergever, Timo Baumgartl, Olivier Boscagli, Denzel Dumfries, Jorrit Hendrix, Pablo Rosario, Mohammed Ihattaren (64' Cody Gakpo), Bruma (78' Ritsu Doan), Steven Bergwijn, Donyell Malen (84' Michal Sadílek). Coach: Mark van Bommel.
Sporting CP: Renan Ribeiro, Neto, Sebastián Coates, Valentin Rosier, Bruno Fernandes, Miguel Luís (80' Pedro Mendes), Idrissa Doumbia, Wendel (90+1' Rafael Camacho), Yannick Bolasie, Marcos Acuña, Luciano Vietto (64' Jovane Cabral). Coach: Leonel Pontes.
Goals: 19' Donyell Malen 1-0, 25' Sebastián Coates 2-0 (og), 38' Bruno Fernandes 2-1 (p), 48' Timo Baumgartl 3-1, 82' Pedro Mendes 3-2.
Referee: Ivan Kruzliak (SVK)   Attendance: 30,000.

19.09.19 Linzer Stadion, Linz: LASK Linz – Rosenborg BK 1-0 (1-0)
LASK Linz: Alexander Schlager, Petar Filipovic, Reinhold Ranftl, Markus Wostry, Philipp Wiesinger, James Holland, Thomas Goiginger (80' Marko Raguz), Peter Michorl, René Renner (57' Marvin Potzmann), Samuel Tetteh (40' Dominik Frieser), Klauss. Coach: Valérien Ismaël.
Rosenborg BK: André Hansen, Tore Reginiussen, Even Hovland, Vegar Hedenstad, Birger Meling, Mike Jensen, Anders Konradsen (87' Gjermund Åsen), Marius Lundemo (73' Anders Trondsen), Alexander Søderlund, Bjørn Johnsen (73' Emil Ceide), Samuel Adegbenro. Coach: Eirik Horneland.
Goal: 45+3' James Holland 1-0.
Referee: Donatas Rumsas (LTU)   Attendance: 12,179.

LASK Linz played their home matches at Linzer Stadion, Linz, instead of their regular home stadium Waldstadion, Pasching.

03.10.19 Lerkendal Stadion, Trondheim: Rosenborg BK – PSV Eindhoven 1-4 (0-3)
Rosenborg BK: André Hansen, Even Hovland, Gustav Valsvik, Birger Meling, Mike Jensen, Gjermund Åsen, Anders Trondsen (79' Edvard Tagseth), Marius Lundemo (62' Anders Konradsen), Bjørn Johnsen (59' Alexander Søderlund), Samuel Adegbenro, Babajide Akintola. Coach: Eirik Horneland.
PSV Eindhoven: Robbin Ruiter, Nick Viergever, Timo Baumgartl, Denzel Dumfries, Jorrit Hendrix (72' Érick Gutiérrez), Michal Sadílek, Ritsu Doan (82' Bruma), Pablo Rosario, Mohammed Ihattaren (80' Kostas Mitroglou), Steven Bergwijn, Donyell Malen. Coach: Mark van Bommel.
Goals: 14' Pablo Rosario 0-1, 38' Birger Meling 0-2 (og), 41' Donyell Malen 0-3, 70' Samuel Adegbenro 1-3, 79' Donyell Malen 1-4.
Referee: Halil Umut Meler (TUR)   Attendance: 10,296.

03.10.19   Estádio José Alvalade, Lisboa: Sporting CP – LASK Linz 2-1 (0-1)
Sporting CP: Renan Ribeiro, Jérémy Mathieu, Neto (46' Luciano Vietto), Sebastián Coates, Bruno Fernandes, Miguel Luís, Idrissa Doumbia, Wendel (58' Eduardo Henrique), Yannick Bolasie, Marcos Acuña (73' Cristian Borja), Luiz Phellype. Coach: Emanuel Ferro.
LASK Linz: Alexander Schlager, Petar Filipovic, Gernot Trauner, Marvin Potzmann (72' René Renner), Reinhold Ranftl, Philipp Wiesinger, James Holland, Thomas Goiginger, Peter Michorl, Dominik Frieser (80' Thomas Sabitzer), Marko Raguz (55' Klauss).
Coach: Valérien Ismaël.
Goals: 16' Marko Raguz 0-1, 58' Luiz Phellype 1-1, 63' Bruno Fernandes 2-1.
Referee: Alain Durieux (LUX)   Attendance: 31,225.

24.10.19   Estádio José Alvalade, Lisboa: Sporting CP – Rosenborg BK 1-0 (0-0)
Sporting CP: Renan Ribeiro, Jérémy Mathieu, Sebastián Coates, Valentin Rosier, Bruno Fernandes, Idrissa Doumbia, Wendel (88' Eduardo Henrique), Yannick Bolasie, Marcos Acuña, Luciano Vietto (85' Cristian Borja), Luiz Phellype (64' Pedro Mendes).
Coach: Emanuel Ferro.
Rosenborg BK: André Hansen, Tore Reginiussen, Even Hovland, Vegar Hedenstad, Birger Meling, Mike Jensen, Gjermund Åsen (81' Pål André Helland), Marius Lundemo, Alexander Søderlund, Samuel Adegbenro (81' Bjørn Johnsen), Babajide Akintola (76' Anders Konradsen). Coach: Eirik Horneland.
Goal: 70' Yannick Bolasie 1-0.
Referee: Lawrence Visser (BEL)   Attendance: 27,671.

24.10.19   Philips Stadion, Eindhoven: PSV Eindhoven – LASK Linz 0-0
PSV Eindhoven: Jeroen Zoet, Daniel Schwaab, Nick Viergever, Denzel Dumfries, Érick Gutiérrez, Michal Sadílek, Ritsu Doan (74' Bruma), Pablo Rosario, Mohammed Ihattaren (84' Ryan Thomas), Steven Bergwijn, Cody Gakpo (84' Kostas Mitroglou).
Coach: Mark van Bommel.
LASK Linz: Alexander Schlager, Petar Filipovic, Gernot Trauner, Marvin Potzmann, Reinhold Ranftl, Philipp Wiesinger, James Holland, Thomas Goiginger, Peter Michorl, Dominik Frieser (59' Samuel Tetteh), Marko Raguz (71' Klauss). Coach: Valérien Ismaël.
Referee: Chris Kavanagh (ENG)   Attendance: 29,000.

07.11.19   Lerkendal Stadion, Trondheim: Rosenborg BK – Sporting CP 0-2 (0-2)
Rosenborg BK: André Hansen, Tore Reginiussen, Even Hovland, Vegar Hedenstad, Birger Meling, Mike Jensen, Gjermund Åsen, Anders Trondsen (78' Pål André Helland), Marius Lundemo, Alexander Søderlund, Samuel Adegbenro (77' Bjørn Johnsen).
Coach: Eirik Horneland.
Sporting CP: Renan Ribeiro, Neto, Sebastián Coates, Tiago Ilori, Cristian Borja, Valentin Rosier, Eduardo Henrique, Bruno Fernandes (90' Pedro Mendes), Idrissa Doumbia (86' Rodrigo Fernandes), Yannick Bolasie (73' Rafael Camacho), Luciano Vietto.
Coach: Emanuel Ferro.
Goals: 16' Sebastián Coates 0-1, 38' Bruno Fernandes 0-2.
Referee: Kevin Clancy (SCO)   Attendance: 11,018.

07.11.19   Linzer Stadion, Linz: LASK Linz – PSV Eindhoven 4-1 (0-1)
LASK Linz: Alexander Schlager, Petar Filipovic, Gernot Trauner, Marvin Potzmann, Reinhold Ranftl (81' René Renner), Philipp Wiesinger, James Holland, Thomas Goiginger, Peter Michorl, Dominik Frieser (61' Klauss), Marko Raguz (69' Samuel Tetteh).
Coach: Valérien Ismaël.
PSV Eindhoven: Jeroen Zoet, Daniel Schwaab, Nick Viergever, Denzel Dumfries, Érick Gutiérrez, Michal Sadílek, Ritsu Doan (64' Amar Catic), Pablo Rosario, Mohammed Ihattaren, Bruma, Cody Gakpo. Coach: Mark van Bommel.
Goals: 5' Daniel Schwaab 0-1, 56' Reinhold Ranftl 1-1, 60' Dominik Frieser (2-1), 78', 82' Klauss 3-1, 4-1.
Referee: Radu Petrescu (ROM)   Attendance: 12,658.

28.11.19   Estádio José Alvalade, Lisboa: Sporting CP – PSV Eindhoven 4-0 (3-0)
Sporting CP: Luís Maximiano, Jérémy Mathieu (73' Neto), Tiago Ilori, Valentin Rosier, Bruno Fernandes, Idrissa Doumbia, Wendel (80' Rafael Camacho), Yannick Bolasie, Marcos Acuña, Luciano Vietto, Luiz Phellype (67' Jesé). Coach: Emanuel Ferro.
PSV Eindhoven: Lars Unnerstall, Nick Viergever, Timo Baumgartl, Denzel Dumfries, Jorrit Hendrix, Michal Sadílek, Pablo Rosario (46' Gastón Pereiro), Mohammed Ihattaren, Bruma (46' Cody Gakpo), Steven Bergwijn (79' Ryan Thomas), Donyell Malen.
Coach: Mark van Bommel.
Goals: 9' Luiz Phellype 1-0, 16' Bruno Fernandes 2-0, 43' Jérémy Mathieu 3-0, 64' Bruno Fernandes 4-0 (p).
Referee: Orel Grinfeld (ISR)   Attendance: 30,146

28.11.19   Lerkendal Stadion, Trondheim: Rosenborg BK – LASK Linz 1-2 (1-1)
Rosenborg BK: André Hansen, Even Hovland, Vegar Hedenstad, Gustav Valsvik, Birger Meling, Mike Jensen, Anders Trondsen, Marius Lundemo (77' Mikael Johnsen), Bjørn Johnsen (67' Erik Botheim), Samuel Adegbenro (67' Gjermund Åsen), Babajide Akintola.
Coach: Eirik Horneland.
LASK Linz: Alexander Schlager, Petar Filipovic, Gernot Trauner, Marvin Potzmann, Reinhold Ranftl, Philipp Wiesinger, James Holland, Thomas Goiginger (88' René Renner), Peter Michorl, Dominik Frieser (71' Samuel Tetteh), Klauss (71' Marko Raguz).
Coach: Valérien Ismaël.
Goals: 20' Thomas Goiginger 0-1, 45' Bjørn Johnsen 1-1, 54' Dominik Frieser 1-2.
Referee: Giorgi Kruashvili (GEO)   Attendance: 9,775.

12.12.19   Philips Stadion, Eindhoven: PSV Eindhoven – Rosenborg BK 1-1 (0-1)
PSV Eindhoven: Lars Unnerstall, Daniel Schwaab, Nick Viergever, Olivier Boscagli, Denzel Dumfries, Ryan Thomas (61' Pablo Rosario), Érick Gutiérrez, Mohammed Ihattaren (70' Gastón Pereiro), Bruma, Steven Bergwijn (46' Donyell Malen), Cody Gakpo.
Coach: Mark van Bommel.
Rosenborg BK: Arild Østbø, Tore Reginiussen, Even Hovland, Vegar Hedenstad, Birger Meling, Mike Jensen, Anders Trondsen, Edvard Tagseth (46' Marius Lundemo), Pål André Helland (75' Erik Botheim), Alexander Søderlund, Samuel Adegbenro (81' Emil Ceide).
Coach: Eirik Horneland.
Goals: 22' Pål André Helland 0-1, 63' Mohammed Ihattaren 1-1.
Referee: Vitali Meshkov (RUS)   Attendance: 24,000.

12.12.19 Linzer Stadion, Linz: LASK Linz – Sporting CP 3-0 (2-0)
LASK Linz: Alexander Schlager, Petar Filipovic (88' Emanuel Pogatetz), Gernot Trauner, Marvin Potzmann, Reinhold Ranftl, Philipp Wiesinger, James Holland, Thomas Goiginger, Peter Michorl, Dominik Frieser (64' Samuel Tetteh), Klauss (71' Marko Raguz).
Coach: Valérien Ismaël.
Sporting CP: Renan Ribeiro, Sebastián Coates, Tiago Ilori, Cristian Borja, Valentin Rosier, Eduardo Henrique, Miguel Luís (71' Luiz Phellype), Rafael Camacho, Rodrigo Fernandes (37' Luís Maximiano *goalkeeper*), Jesé (46' Idrissa Doumbia), Pedro Mendes.
Coach: Emanuel Ferro.
Goals: 23' Gernot Trauner 1-0, 38' Klauss 2-0 (p), 90+3' Marko Raguz 3-0.
Referee: William Collum (SCO)   Attendance: 11,627.
Sent off: 34' Renan Ribeiro.

GROUP E

19.09.19 Roazhon Park, Rennes: Stade Rennes – Celtic FC 1-1 (1-0)
Stade Rennes: Edouard Mendy, Jérémy Morel, Damien Da Silva, Hamari Traoré, Joris Gnagnon, Clément Grenier (88' Theoson Siebatcheu), Jonas Martin (72' Eduardo Camavinga), Flavien Tait (72' Romain Del Castillo), Benjamin Bourigeaud, M'Baye Niang, Raphinha.
Coach: Julien Stéphane.
Celtic FC: Fraser Forster, Hatem Abd Elhamed, Christopher Jullien, Boli Bolingoli Mbombo (69' Jonny Hayes), Kristoffer Ajer, Scott Brown, James Forrest, Callum McGregor, Mohamed Elyounoussi (57' Olivier Ntcham), Ryan Christie, Odsonne Édouard (84' Vakoun Bayo).
Coach: Neil Lennon.
Goals: 38' M'Baye Niang 1-0 (p), 59' Ryan Christie 1-1 (p).
Referee: José María Sánchez Martínez (ESP)   Attendance: 27,026.
Sent off: 90+2' Vakoun Bayo.

19.09.19 Stadionul Dr. Constantin Radulescu, Cluj-Napoca:
         CFR Cluj – Lazio Roma 2-1 (1-1)
CFR Cluj: Giedrius Arlauskis, Camora, Mike Cestor, Andrei Peteleu, Kévin Boli, Andrei Burca, Ciprian Deac (90' Catalin Golofca), Damjan Djokovic, Mihai Bordeianu, Alexandru Paun (84' Emmanuel Culio), Lacina Traoré (46' Billel Omrani). Coach: Dan Petrescu.
Lazio Roma: Thomas Strakosha, Francesco Acerbi, Bastos (80' Bobby Adekanye), Denis Vavro, Lucas Leiva, Valon Berisha (67' Danilo Cataldi), Joaquín Correa, Manuel Lazzari, Sergej Milinkovic-Savic, Felipe Caicedo, Jony (80' Senad Lulic). Coach: Simone Inzaghi.
Goals: 25' Bastos 0-1, 41' Ciprian Deac 1-1 (p), 75' Billel Omrani 2-1.
Referee: Daniel Stefanski (POL)   Attendance: 9,222.

03.10.19 Stadio Olimpico, Roma: Lazio Roma – Stade Rennes 2-1 (0-0)
Lazio Roma: Thomas Strakosha, Francesco Acerbi, Bastos, Denis Vavro, Senad Lulic (82' Jony), Marco Parolo, Valon Berisha (53' Luis Alberto), Manuel Lazzari, Danilo Cataldi (53' Sergej Milinkovic-Savic), Felipe Caicedo, Ciro Immobile. Coach: Simone Inzaghi.
Stade Rennes: Edouard Mendy, Jérémy Morel, Damien Da Silva, Hamari Traoré, Souleyman Doumbia (82' Adrien Hunou), Joris Gnagnon, Clément Grenier, Jonas Martin, Flavien Tait (76' Raphinha), Eduardo Camavinga (71' Benjamin Bourigeaud), M'Baye Niang.
Coach: Julien Stéphane.
Goals: 55' Jérémy Morel 0-1, 63' Sergej Milinkovic-Savic 1-1, 75' Ciro Immobile 2-1.
Referee: Serhiy Boyko (UKR)   Attendance: 13,072.

03.10.19   Celtic Park, Glasgow: Celtic FC – CFR Cluj 2-0 (1-0)
Celtic FC: Fraser Forster, Hatem Abd Elhamed, Christopher Jullien, Boli Bolingoli Mbombo, Kristoffer Ajer, Scott Brown, James Forrest (86' Jonny Hayes), Callum McGregor, Mohamed Elyounoussi, Ryan Christie (90' Olivier Ntcham), Odsonne Édouard. Coach: Neil Lennon.
CFR Cluj: Giedrius Arlauskis, Mateo Susic, Camora, Kévin Boli, Andrei Burca, Ciprian Deac, Damjan Djokovic (81' Catalin Golofca), Mihai Bordeianu, Luís Aurélio (57' Emmanuel Culio), Mário Rondón (70' Alexandru Paun), Billel Omrani. Coach: Dan Petrescu.
Goals: 20' Odsonne Édouard 1-0, 59' Mohamed Elyounoussi 2-0.
Referee: Daniel Siebert (GER)   Attendance: 56,172.

24.10.19   Celtic Park, Glasgow: Celtic FC – Lazio Roma 2-1 (0-1)
Celtic FC: Fraser Forster, Hatem Abd Elhamed (83' Nir Bitton), Christopher Jullien, Boli Bolingoli Mbombo (85' Jonny Hayes), Kristoffer Ajer, Scott Brown, James Forrest, Callum McGregor, Mohamed Elyounoussi (66' Tom Rogic), Ryan Christie, Odsonne Édouard. Coach: Neil Lennon.
Lazio Roma: Thomas Strakosha, Francesco Acerbi, Bastos, Denis Vavro, Lucas Leiva, Marco Parolo, Joaquín Correa (73' Ciro Immobile), Manuel Lazzari, Sergej Milinkovic-Savic, Felipe Caicedo (85' Danilo Cataldi), Jony (69' Senad Lulic). Coach: Simone Inzaghi.
Goals: 40' Manuel Lazzari 0-1, 67' Ryan Christie 1-1, 89' Christopher Jullien 2-1.
Referee: Ivan Bebek (CRO)   Attendance: 56,172.

24.10.19   Roazhon Park, Rennes: Stade Rennes – CFR Cluj 0-1 (0-1)
Stade Rennes: Edouard Mendy, Jérémy Morel, Hamari Traoré, Joris Gnagnon, Benjamin Bourigeaud, Adrien Hunou, Faitout Maouassa (75' James Lea Siliki), Eduardo Camavinga, M'Baye Niang, Romain Del Castillo (8' Pépé Bonet Kapambu *goalkeeper*), Raphinha (80' Theoson Siebatcheu). Coach: Julien Stéphane.
CFR Cluj: Giedrius Arlauskis, Mateo Susic, Camora, Kévin Boli, Andrei Burca, Emmanuel Culio, Ciprian Deac, Damjan Djokovic (70' Alexandru Paun), Mihai Bordeianu (66' Ovidiu Hoban), Lacina Traoré (84' Mike Cestor), Billel Omrani. Coach: Dan Petrescu.
Goal: 9' Ciprian Deac 0-1.
Referee: Aleksei Eskov (RUS)   Attendance: 27,330.
Sent off: 5' Edouard Mendy, 46' Eduardo Camavinga, 82' Mateo Susic.

M'Baye Niang missed a penalty kick (28').

07.11.19   Stadio Olimpico, Roma: Lazio Roma – Celtic FC 1-2 (1-1)
Lazio Roma: Thomas Strakosha, Francesco Acerbi, Denis Vavro (82' Valon Berisha), Luiz Felipe, Lucas Leiva (58' Luis Alberto), Marco Parolo, Manuel Lazzari, Sergej Milinkovic-Savic, Felipe Caicedo, Ciro Immobile, Jony (58' Senad Lulic). Coach: Simone Inzaghi.
Celtic FC: Fraser Forster, Hatem Abd Elhamed (83' Nir Bitton), Christopher Jullien, Kristoffer Ajer, Scott Brown, Jonny Hayes, James Forrest (89' Moritz Bauer), Callum McGregor, Mohamed Elyounoussi, Ryan Christie (77' Olivier Ntcham), Odsonne Édouard. Coach: Neil Lennon.
Goals: 7' Ciro Immobile 1-0, 38' James Forrest 1-1, 90+5' Olivier Ntcham 1-2.
Referee: Tobias Stieler (GER)   Attendance: 26,155.

07.11.19   Stadionul Dr. Constantin Radulescu, Cluj-Napoca:
CFR Cluj – Stade Rennes 1-0 (0-0)
CFR Cluj: Giedrius Arlauskis, Camora, Ionut Andrei Peteleu (74' Ovidiu Hoban), Kévin Boli, Andrei Burca, Emmanuel Culio, Ciprian Deac (89' Alexandru Paun), Damjan Djokovic, Mihai Bordeianu, Lacina Traoré (71' Mário Rondón), Billel Omrani. Coach: Dan Petrescu.
Stade Rennes: Romain Salin, Damien Da Silva, Hamari Traoré, Joris Gnagnon, Clément Grenier, Benjamin Bourigeaud (84' Rafik Guitane), Adrien Hunou (66' Yann Gboho), Faitout Maouassa, M'Baye Niang, Romain Del Castillo (66' Theoson Siebatcheu), Raphinha. Coach: Julien Stéphane.
Goal: 87' Mário Rondón 1-0.
Referee: Tiago Martins (POR)   Attendance: 11,067.
Sent off: 90' Mário Rondón.

28.11.19   Celtic Park, Glasgow: Celtic FC – Stade Rennes 3-1 (2-0)
Celtic FC: Fraser Forster, Christopher Jullien, Moritz Bauer, Kristoffer Ajer, Greg Taylor, Scott Brown (76' Nir Bitton), James Forrest (67' Mikey Johnston), Callum McGregor, Olivier Ntcham, Ryan Christie (79' Leigh Griffiths), Lewis Morgan. Coach: Neil Lennon.
Stade Rennes: Edouard Mendy, Joris Gnagnon, Gerzino Nyamsi, Sacha Boey, Flavien Tait (80' Yann Gboho), Benjamin Bourigeaud, James Lea Siliki, Faitout Maouassa, Rafik Guitane (65' Lucas Da Cunha), Theoson Siebatcheu, Romain Del Castillo (74' Adrien Hunou). Coach: Julien Stéphane.
Goals: 22' Lewis Morgan 1-0, 45+1' Ryan Christie 2-0, 74' Mikey Johnson 3-0, 89' Adrien Hunou 3-1.
Referee: Espen Eskås (NOR)   Attendance: 56,172.

28.11.19   Stadio Olimpico, Roma: Lazio Roma – CFR Cluj 1-0 (1-0)
Lazio Roma: Silvio Proto, Francesco Acerbi, Bastos, Denis Vavro, Marco Parolo, Luis Alberto (80' Patric), Joaquín Correa, Manuel Lazzari, Danilo Cataldi, Jony (75' Senad Lulic), Bobby Adekanye (65' Felipe Caicedo). Coach: Simone Inzaghi.
CFR Cluj: Giedrius Arlauskis, Camora, Mike Cestor, Ionut Andrei Peteleu (73' Mateo Susic), Kévin Boli, Andrei Burca, Emmanuel Culio, Damjan Djokovic, Mihai Bordeianu (62' Ciprian Deac), Alexandru Paun (65' Lacina Traoré), Billel Omrani. Coach: Dan Petrescu.
Goal: 24' Joaquín Correa 1-0
Referee: Ali Palabiyik (TUR)   Attendance: 7,604.

12.12.19   Roazhon Park, Rennes: Stade Rennes – Lazio Roma 2-0 (1-0)
Stade Rennes: Romain Salin, Souleyman Doumbia, Joris Gnagnon, Gerzino Nyamsi, Sacha Boey, Clément Grenier, Flavien Tait, James Lea Siliki (74' Eduardo Camavinga), Lucas Da Cunha (77' Romain Del Castillo), Yann Gboho, Theoson Siebatcheu (70' M'Baye Niang). Coach: Julien Stéphane.
Lazio Roma: Silvio Proto, Francesco Acerbi, Bastos, Denis Vavro (74' Luca Falbo), Marco Parolo, Luis Alberto (59' Valon Berisha), Manuel Lazzari, Danilo Cataldi, Felipe Caicedo, Ciro Immobile (68' Bobby Adekanye), Jony. Coach: Simone Inzaghi.
Goals: 31', 87' Joris Gnagnon 1-0, 2-0.
Referee: Srdjan Jovanovic (SRB)   Attendance: 25,082.

12.12.19 Stadionul Dr. Constantin Radulescu, Cluj-Napoca:
CFR Cluj – Celtic FC 2-0 (0-0)
CFR Cluj: Giedrius Arlauskis, Mateo Susic, Camora, Mike Cestor, Andrei Burca, Emmanuel Culio, Ciprian Deac (85' Ovidiu Hoban), Damjan Djokovic (83' Luís Aurélio), Mihai Bordeianu, Lacina Traoré, Billel Omrani (74' Catalin Golofca). Coach: Dan Petrescu.
Celtic FC: Craig Gordon, Christopher Jullien (46' Kristoffer Ajer), Moritz Bauer, Boli Bolingoli Mbombo, Scott Sinclair, Nir Bitton, Olivier Ntcham, Lewis Morgan (67' Vakoun Bayo), Scott Robertson, Leigh Griffiths, Mikey Johnston (72' Karamoko Dembélé). Coach: Neil Lennon.
Goals: 49' Andrei Burca 1-0, 70' Damjan Djokovic 2-0.
Referee: Halis Özkahya (TUR)   Attendance: 12,890.

GROUP F

19.09.19 Commerzbank-Arena, Frankfurt am Main:
Eintracht Frankfurt – Arsenal FC 0-3 (0-1)
Eintracht Frankfurt: Kevin Trapp, Makoto Hasebe, David Abraham, Martin Hinteregger, Danny da Costa (74' Timothy Chandler), Filip Kostic, Dominik Kohr, Djibril Sow, Daichi Kamada, Bas Dost (66' Gonçalo Paciência), André Silva. Coach: Adi Hütter.
Arsenal FC: Emiliano Martínez, David Luiz, Shkodran Mustafi, Sead Kolasinac (80' Ainsley Maitland-Niles), Calum Chambers, Granit Xhaka, Lucas Torreira, Joseph Willock (72' Dani Ceballos), Emile Smith-Rowe (60' Nicolas Pépé), Bukayo Saka, Pierre-Emerick Aubameyang. Coach: Unai Emery.
Goals: 38' Joseph Willock 0-1, 85' Bukayo Saka 0-2, 88' Pierre-Emerick Aubameyang 0-3.
Referee: Davide Massa (ITA)   Attendance: 47,000.
Sent off: 79' Dominik Kohr.

19.09.19 Stade Maurice Dufrasne, Liège: Standard Liège – Vitória de Guimarães 2-0 (0-0)
Standard Liège: Vanja Milinkovic-Savic, Kostas Laifis, Nicolas Gavory, Mergim Vojvoda, Mehdi Carcela-González (85' Aleksandar Boljevic), Gojko Cimirot, Anthony Limbombe (81' Zinho Vanheusden), Paul M'Poku, Merveille Bopé Bokadi, Samuel Bastien, Renaud Emond (68' Felipe Avenatti). Coach: Michel Preud'homme.
Vitória de Guimarães: João Miguel Silva, Florent Hanin, Valeriy Bondarenko, Falaye Sacko, Edmond Tapsoba, Mikel Agu (70' Pêpê Rodrigues), Lucas Evangelista (77' André Pereira), Rochinha, Denis Poha, Léo Bonatini (57' Bruno Duarte), Davidson. Coach: Ivo Vieira.
Goals: 66' Florent Hanin 1-0 (og), 90+1' Paul M'Poku 2-0.
Referee: Sergey Ivanov (RUS)   Attendance: 13,477.

03.10.19 Estádio Dom Afonso Henriques, Guimarães:
Vitória de Guimarães – Eintracht Frankfurt 0-1 (0-1)
Vitória de Guimarães: João Miguel Silva, Florent Hanin, "Pedrão" Pedro Henrique, Falaye Sacko (65' Rochinha), Edmond Tapsoba, Mikel Agu, Lucas Evangelista, Denis Poha, Marcus Edwards, Léo Bonatini (65' Bruno Duarte), Davidson (78' André Pereira). Coach: Ivo Vieira.
Eintracht Frankfurt: Frederik Rønnow, Martin Hinteregger, Erik Durm (78' Danny da Costa), Almamy Touré, Evan Obite N'Dicka, Gelson Fernandes, Sebastian Rode (60' Daichi Kamada), Filip Kostic, Djibril Sow, Gonçalo Paciência (68' Bas Dost), André Silva. Coach: Adi Hütter.
Goal: 36' Evan Obite N'Dicka 0-1.
Referee: Radu Petrescu (ROM)   Attendance: 15,187.

03.10.19 Emirates Stadium, London: Arsenal FC – Standard Liège 4-0 (3-0)
Arsenal FC: Emiliano Martínez, Shkodran Mustafi, Héctor Bellerín, Kieran Tierney, Rob Holding, Ainsley Maitland-Niles (66' Nicolas Pépé), Dani Ceballos, Lucas Torreira, Joseph Willock (74' Mattéo Guendouzi), Reiss Nelson (79' Pierre-Emerick Aubameyang), Gabriel Martinelli. Coach: Unai Emery.
Standard Liège: Vanja Milinkovic-Savic, Kostas Laifis, Nicolas Gavory, Mergim Vojvoda, Zinho Vanheusden, Maxime Lestienne (80' Selim Amallah), Gojko Cimirot, Paul M'Poku, Aleksandar Boljevic (58' Mehdi Carcela-González), Samuel Bastien, Renaud Emond (73' Felipe Avenatti). Coach: Michel Preud'homme.
Goals: 13', 16' Gabriel Martinelli 1-0, 2-0, 22' Joseph Willock 3-0, 57' Dani Ceballos 4-0.
Referee: Sandro Schärer (SUI)   Attendance: 58,725.

24.10.19 Emirates Stadium, London: Arsenal FC – Vitória de Guimarães 3-2 (1-2)
Arsenal FC: Emiliano Martínez, Shkodran Mustafi, Héctor Bellerín, Kieran Tierney, Rob Holding, Ainsley Maitland-Niles (46' Mattéo Guendouzi), Lucas Torreira, Joseph Willock (46' Dani Ceballos), Emile Smith-Rowe, Alexandre Lacazette (75' Nicolas Pépé), Gabriel Martinelli. Coach: Unai Emery.
Vitória de Guimarães: João Miguel Silva, Florent Hanin, Victor García, Frederico Venâncio, Edmond Tapsoba, Mikel Agu, Denis Poha, Marcus Edwards (71' André Pereira), André Almeida (64' Pêpê Rodrigues), Davidson (87' Rochinha), Bruno Duarte. Coach: Ivo Vieira.
Goals: 9' Marcus Edwards 0-1, 32' Gabriel Martinelli 1-1, 37' Bruno Duarte 1-2, 80', 90+3' Nicolas Pépé 2-2, 3-2.
Referee: Serdar Gözübüyük (HOL)   Attendance: 60,195.

24.10.19 Commerzbank-Arena, Frankfurt am Main:
            Eintracht Frankfurt – Standard Liège 2-1 (1-0)
Eintracht Frankfurt: Frederik Rønnow, Makoto Hasebe, David Abraham, Martin Hinteregger, Danny da Costa, Sebastian Rode, Filip Kostic (83' Timothy Chandler), Mijat Gacinovic (75' Dominik Kohr), Djibril Sow, Daichi Kamada (88' Gelson Fernandes), Gonçalo Paciência. Coach: Adi Hütter.
Standard Liège: Vanja Milinkovic-Savic, Kostas Laifis, Nicolas Gavory, Collins Fai (85' Paul M'Poku), Dimitri Lavalée, Mehdi Carcela-González (75' Obbi Oularé), Gojko Cimirot, Aleksandar Boljevic, Samuel Bastien, Selim Amallah, Duje Cop (72' Maxime Lestienne). Coach: Michel Preud'homme.
Goals: 28' David Abraham 1-0, 73' Martin Hinteregger 2-0, 82' Selim Amallah 2-1.
Referee: Daniel Stefanski (POL)   Attendance: 47,000.

06.11.19 Estádio Dom Afonso Henriques, Guimarães:
            Vitória de Guimarães – Arsenal FC 1-1 (0-0)
Vitória de Guimarães: Douglas Jesus, Victor García, Rafa Soares, Frederico Venâncio, Edmond Tapsoba, Mikel Agu, Lucas Evangelista (82' Léo Bonatini), Pêpê Rodrigues (61' Denis Poha), Marcus Edwards, Davidson (68' Rochinha), Bruno Duarte. Coach: Ivo Vieira.
Arsenal FC: Emiliano Martínez, Sokratis Papastathopoulos, Shkodran Mustafi, Kieran Tierney, Rob Holding, Ainsley Maitland-Niles, Dani Ceballos (54' Mattéo Guendouzi), Joseph Willock (78' Lucas Torreira), Bukayo Saka (65' Alexandre Lacazette), Nicolas Pépé, Gabriel Martinelli. Coach: Unai Emery.
Goals: 81' Shkodran Mustafi 0-1, 90+1' Bruno Duarte 1-1.
Referee: Halis Özkahya (TUR)   Attendance: 17,822.

07.11.19   Stade Maurice Dufrasne, Liège: Standard Liège – Eintracht Frankfurt 2-1 (0-0)
Standard Liège: Arnaud Bodart, Kostas Laifis, Nicolas Gavory, Collins Fai, Zinho Vanheusden, Mehdi Carcela-González (81' Maxime Lestienne), Gojko Cimirot, Samuel Bastien, Selim Amallah (73' Paul M'Poku), Duje Cop (81' Obbi Oularé), Renaud Emond.
Coach: Michel Preud'homme.
Eintracht Frankfurt: Frederik Rønnow, Makoto Hasebe, David Abraham, Martin Hinteregger, Danny da Costa (89' Timothy Chandler), Gelson Fernandes, Sebastian Rode, Filip Kostic, Djibril Sow, Gonçalo Paciência (73' Bas Dost), André Silva (62' Daichi Kamada).
Coach: Adi Hütter.
Goals: 56' Zinho Vanheusden 1-0, 65' Filip Kostic 1-1, 90+4' Maxime Lestienne 2-1.
Referee: Matej Jug (SVN)   Attendance: 15,952.

28.11.19   Estádio Dom Afonso Henriques, Guimarães:
Vitória de Guimarães – Standard Liège 1-1 (1-1)
Vitória de Guimarães: Douglas Jesus, Florent Hanin, "Pedrão" Pedro Henrique, Falaye Sacko, Edmond Tapsoba, Mikel Agu, Lucas Evangelista, Denis Poha, Marcus Edwards (76' Rochinha), André Pereira (86' Léo Bonatini), Bruno Duarte (45' Davidson). Coach: Ivo Vieira.
Standard Liège: Arnaud Bodart, Kostas Laifis, Nicolas Gavory, Mergim Vojvoda, Zinho Vanheusden, Mehdi Carcela-González, Maxime Lestienne (71' Selim Amallah), Gojko Cimirot, Paul M'Poku (82' Duje Cop), Samuel Bastien, Renaud Emond (69' Obbi Oularé).
Coach: Michel Preud'homme.
Goals: 40' Maxime Lestienne 0-1 (p), 45+2' André Pereira 1-1.
Referee: Serhiy Boyko (UKR)   Attendance: 11,221.

28.11.19   Emirates Stadium, London: Arsenal FC – Eintracht Frankfurt 1-2 (1-0)
Arsenal FC: Emiliano Martínez, David Luiz (31' Mattéo Guendouzi), Sokratis Papastathopoulos, Shkodran Mustafi (76' Lucas Torreira), Calum Chambers, Kieran Tierney, Granit Xhaka, Joseph Willock, Bukayo Saka, Pierre-Emerick Aubameyang, Gabriel Martinelli (60' Mesut Özil). Coach: Unai Emery.
Eintracht Frankfurt: Frederik Rønnow, Makoto Hasebe, David Abraham, Martin Hinteregger, Danny da Costa, Gelson Fernandes (46' Dominik Kohr), Filip Kostic, Djibril Sow, Daichi Kamada, Gonçalo Paciência, André Silva (46' Mijat Gacinovic). Coach: Adi Hütter.
Goals: 45+1' Pierre-Emerick Aubameyang 1-0, 55', 64' Daichi Kamada 1-1, 1-2.
Referee: Ruddy Buquet (FRA)   Attendance: 49,419.

12.12.19   Commerzbank-Arena, Frankfurt am Main:
Eintracht Frankfurt – Vitória de Guimarães 2-3 (2-1)
Eintracht Frankfurt: Frederik Rønnow, Makoto Hasebe, David Abraham, Martin Hinteregger, Danny da Costa, Sebastian Rode (78' Gelson Fernandes), Filip Kostic, Djibril Sow, Daichi Kamada, Gonçalo Paciência, André Silva (73' Mijat Gacinovic). Coach: Adi Hütter.
Vitória de Guimarães: João Miguel Silva, Florent Hanin, Victor García, "Pedrão" Pedro Henrique, Frederico Venâncio, Rochinha (70' Marcus Edwards), Pêpê Rodrigues, Denis Poha (82' Bruno Duarte), Almoatasembellah Ali Mohamed Elmusrati, Davidson, André Pereira (66' Léo Bonatini). Coach: Ivo Vieira.
Goals: 8' Rochinha 0-1, 31' Danny da Costa 1-1, 38' Daichi Kamada 2-1, 85' Almoatasembellah Ali Mohamed Elmusrati 2-2, 87' Marcus Edwards 2-3.
Referee: Gediminas Mazeika (LTU)   Attendance: 47,000.

12.12.19 Stade Maurice Dufrasne, Liège: Standard Liège – Arsenal FC 2-2 (0-0)
Standard Liège: Arnaud Bodart, Kostas Laifis, Nicolas Gavory, Collins Fai, Zinho Vanheusden, Mehdi Carcela-González, Gojko Cimirot, Paul M'Poku, Samuel Bastien, Selim Amallah (85' Maxime Lestienne), Renaud Emond (46' Felipe Avenatti).
Coach: Michel Preud'homme.
Arsenal FC: Emiliano Martínez, David Luiz, Sokratis Papastathopoulos (69' Gabriel Martinelli), Konstantinos Mavropanos, Ainsley Maitland-Niles (78' Calum Chambers), Joseph Willock, Mattéo Guendouzi, Emile Smith-Rowe (85' Pierre-Emerick Aubameyang), Bukayo Saka, Alexandre Lacazette, Reiss Nelson. Coach: Freddie Ljungberg.
Goals: 47' Samuel Bastien 1-0, 69' Selim Amallah 2-0, 78' Alexandre Lacazette 2-1, 81' Bukayo Saka 2-2.
Referee: Andreas Ekberg (SWE)   Attendance: 21,797.

GROUP G

19.09.19 Estádio Do Dragão, Porto: FC Porto – BSC Young Boys 2-1 (2-1)
FC Porto: Agustín Marchesín, Pepe, Ivan Marcano, Alex Telles, Danilo Pereira, Mateus Uribe, Otavinho, Luis Díaz (66' Romário Baró), Tiquinho Soares (81' Fábio Silva), Jesús Corona, Moussa Marega (70' Wilson Manafá). Coach: Sérgio Conceição.
BSC Young Boys: David von Ballmoos, Fabian Lustenberger, Frederik Sørensen, Saidy Janko, Ulisses Garcia, Nicolas Bürgy, Cédric Zesiger, Christian Fassnacht (73' Gianluca Gaudino), Vincent Sierro (69' Michel Aebischer), Jean-Pierre Nsamé (61' Guillaume Hoarau), Roger Assalé. Coach: Gerardo Seoane.
Goals: 8' Tiquinho Soares 1-0, 15' Jean-Pierre Nsamé 1-1 (p), 29' Tiquinho Soares 2-1.
Referee: Andris Treimanis (LAT)   Attendance: 32,929.

19.09.19 Ibrox Stadium, Glasgow: Glasgow Rangers FC – Feyenoord Rotterdam 1-0 (1-0)
Glasgow Rangers FC: Allan McGregor, James Tavernier, Connor Goldson, Filip Helander, Borna Barisic, Steven Davis, Scott Arfield (90' Andy King), Ryan Jack, Glen Kamara (82' Joe Aribo), Sheyi Ojo (74' Brandon Barker), Alfredo Morelos. Coach: Steven Gerrard.
Feyenoord Rotterdam: Kenneth Vermeer, Eric Botteghin, Edgar Ié, Ridgeciano Haps, Rick Karsdorp, Leroy Fer, Renato Tapia, Orkun Kökçü (65' Luciano Narsingh), Steven Berghuis, Sam Larsson (78' Nicolai Jørgensen), Luis Sinisterra (86' Jens Toornstra). Coach: Jaap Stam.
Goal: 24' Sheyi Ojo 1-0.
Referee: Antonio Mateu Lahoz (ESP)   Attendance: 46,858.

James Tavernier missed a penalty kick (10').

03.10.19 De Kuip, Rotterdam: Feyenoord Rotterdam – FC Porto 2-0 (0-0)
Feyenoord Rotterdam: Kenneth Vermeer, Eric Botteghin, Edgar Ié, Ridgeciano Haps, Rick Karsdorp (85' Lutsharel Geertruida), Leroy Fer, Jens Toornstra, Renato Tapia, Steven Berghuis, Sam Larsson (83' Marcos Senesi), Luis Sinisterra (83' Luciano Narsingh). Coach: Jaap Stam.
FC Porto: Agustín Marchesín, Pepe, Ivan Marcano, Alex Telles, Wilson Manafá, Danilo Pereira (81' Fábio Silva), Shoya Nakajima (53' Luis Díaz), Mateus Uribe, Otavinho, Zé Luís (62' Tiquinho Soares), Moussa Marega. Coach: Sérgio Conceição.
Goals: 49' Jens Toornstra 1-0, 80' Rick Karsdorp 2-0.
Referee: Sergei Karasev (RUS)   Attendance: 41,000.

03.10.19   Stade de Suisse, Bern: BSC Young Boys – Glasgow Rangers FC 2-1 (0-1)
BSC Young Boys: David von Ballmoos, Fabian Lustenberger, Frederik Sørensen, Saidy Janko, Ulisses Garcia, Cédric Zesiger, Gianluca Gaudino (73' Nicolas Moumi Ngamaleu), Christian Fassnacht, Michel Aebischer, Jean-Pierre Nsamé, Roger Assalé (67' Jordan Lotomba).
Coach: Gerardo Seoane.
Glasgow Rangers FC: Allan McGregor, James Tavernier, Connor Goldson, Filip Helander, Borna Barisic, Steven Davis, Scott Arfield, Ryan Jack (65' Greg Stewart), Glen Kamara, Sheyi Ojo, Alfredo Morelos. Coach: Steven Gerrard.
Goals: 44' Alfredo Morelos 0-1, 50' Roger Assalé 1-1, 90+3' Christian Fassnacht 2-1.
Referee: Manuel Schüttengruber (AUT)   Attendance: 26,348.

24.10.19   Stade de Suisse, Bern: BSC Young Boys – Feyenoord Rotterdam 2-0 (2-0)
BSC Young Boys: David von Ballmoos, Fabian Lustenberger (42' Gianluca Gaudino), Frederik Sørensen, Saidy Janko, Jordan Lotomba, Cédric Zesiger, Nicolas Moumi Ngamaleu, Christian Fassnacht (86' Ulisses Garcia), Michel Aebischer, Jean-Pierre Nsamé, Roger Assalé (66' Nicolas Bürgy). Coach: Gerardo Seoane.
Feyenoord Rotterdam: Kenneth Vermeer, Edgar Ié (37' Eric Botteghin), Tyrell Malacia (82' Ridgeciano Haps), Marcos Senesi, Lutsharel Geertruida, Leroy Fer, Jens Toornstra, Orkun Kökçü (74' Luciano Narsingh), Steven Berghuis, Sam Larsson, Luis Sinisterra.
Coach: Jaap Stam.
Goals: 14' Roger Assalé 1-0 (p), 28' Jean-Pierre Nsamé 2-0 (p).
Referee: Jakob Kehlet (DEN)   Attendance: 27,641.

24.10.19   Estádio Do Dragão, Porto: FC Porto – Glasgow Rangers FC 1-1 (1-1)
FC Porto: Agustín Marchesín, Pepe, Ivan Marcano, Alex Telles, Danilo Pereira, Mateus Uribe, Otavinho (60' Bruno Costa), Luis Díaz (63' Shoya Nakajima), Zé Luís (76' Tiquinho Soares), Jesús Corona, Moussa Marega. Coach: Sérgio Conceição.
Glasgow Rangers FC: Allan McGregor, James Tavernier, Connor Goldson, Filip Helander, Borna Barisic, Steven Davis, Ryan Jack (83' Scott Arfield), Glen Kamara, Alfredo Morelos, Brandon Barker (84' Sheyi Ojo), Ryan Kent (76' Joe Aribo). Coach: Steven Gerrard.
Goals: 36' Luis Díaz 1-0, 44' Alfredo Morelos 1-1.
Referee: Nikola Dabanovic (MNE)   Attendance: 31,307.

07.11.19   De Kuip, Rotterdam: Feyenoord Rotterdam – BSC Young Boys 1-1 (1-0)
Feyenoord Rotterdam: Kenneth Vermeer, Jan-Arie van der Heijden, Edgar Ié (73' Marcos Senesi), Ridgeciano Haps, Rick Karsdorp, Jens Toornstra, Renato Tapia, Orkun Kökçü, Nicolai Jørgensen, Steven Berghuis, Luis Sinisterra (73' Sam Larsson). Coach: Dick Advocaat.
BSC Young Boys: David von Ballmoos, Fabian Lustenberger, Frederik Sørensen, Ulisses Garcia, Jordan Lotomba (68' Saidy Janko), Cédric Zesiger, Nicolas Moumi Ngamaleu (68' Marvin Spielmann), Christian Fassnacht, Michel Aebischer, Jean-Pierre Nsamé, Roger Assalé (87' Felix Mambimbi). Coach: Gerardo Seoane.
Goals: 18' Steven Berghuis 1-0 (p), 71' Marvin Spielmann 1-1.
Referee: Pawel Gil (POL)   Attendance: 45,022.

07.11.19 Ibrox Stadium, Glasgow: Glasgow Rangers FC – FC Porto 2-0 (0-0)
Glasgow Rangers FC: Allan McGregor, James Tavernier, Connor Goldson, Filip Helander, Borna Barisic, Steven Davis, Ryan Jack, Glen Kamara, Alfredo Morelos (85' Jermain Defoe), Brandon Barker (65' Scott Arfield), Ryan Kent (83' Joe Aribo). Coach: Steven Gerrard.
FC Porto: Agustín Marchesín, Pepe (49' Luis Díaz), Ivan Marcano, Alex Telles, Chancel Mbemba, Wilson Manafá, Danilo Pereira, Mateus Uribe, Otavinho (74' Fábio Silva), Tiquinho Soares (64' Zé Luís), Jesús Corona. Coach: Sérgio Conceição.
Goals: 69' Alfredo Morelos 1-0, 73' Steven Davis 2-0.
Referee: Davide Massa (ITA)   Attendance: 49,645.

28.11.19 Stade de Suisse, Bern: BSC Young Boys – FC Porto 1-2 (1-0)
BSC Young Boys: David von Ballmoos, Fabian Lustenberger (70' Jordan Lotomba), Frederik Sørensen, Saidy Janko (81' Guillaume Hoarau), Ulisses Garcia, Cédric Zesiger, Nicolas Moumi Ngamaleu, Christian Fassnacht, Michel Aebischer, Jean-Pierre Nsamé, Roger Assalé (57' Christopher Martins Pereira). Coach: Gerardo Seoane.
FC Porto: Agustín Marchesín, Pepe, Ivan Marcano, Alex Telles, Chancel Mbemba (46' Wilson Manafá), Danilo Pereira, Otavinho, Mamadou Loum N'Diaye (74' Luis Díaz), Vincent Aboubakar, Jesús Corona (84' Diogo Leite), Moussa Marega. Coach: Sérgio Conceição.
Goals: 6' Christian Fassnacht 1-0, 76', 79' Vincent Aboubakar 1-1, 1-2.
Referee: Tamás Bognár (HUN)   Attendance: 31,120.

28.11.19 De Kuip, Rotterdam: Feyenoord Rotterdam – Glasgow Rangers FC 2-2 (1-0)
Feyenoord Rotterdam: Nick Marsman, Eric Botteghin, Tyrell Malacia, Marcos Senesi, Lutsharel Geertruida, Leroy Fer, Jens Toornstra (85' Yassin Ayoub), Orkun Kökçü, Steven Berghuis, Sam Larsson (69' Luciano Narsingh), Luis Sinisterra. Coach: Dick Advocaat.
Glasgow Rangers FC: Allan McGregor, James Tavernier, Connor Goldson, Filip Helander, Borna Barisic, Steven Davis, Ryan Jack, Glen Kamara, Sheyi Ojo (77' Scott Arfield), Alfredo Morelos, Ryan Kent. Coach: Steven Gerrard.
Goals: 33' Jens Toornstra 1-0, 53', 65' Alfredo Morelos 1-1, 1-2, 68' Luis Sinisterra 2-2.
Referee: Damir Skomina (SVN)   Attendance: 47,500.

12.12.19 Estádio Do Dragão, Porto: FC Porto – Feyenoord Rotterdam 3-2 (3-2)
FC Porto: Agustín Marchesín, Pepe, Ivan Marcano, Alex Telles, Danilo Pereira, Mateus Uribe, Otavinho, Luis Díaz (74' Sérgio Oliveira), Tiquinho Soares (75' Zé Luís), Jesús Corona, Moussa Marega (84' Chancel Mbemba). Coach: Sérgio Conceição.
Feyenoord Rotterdam: Nick Marsman, Eric Botteghin, Tyrell Malacia, Marcos Senesi, Lutsharel Geertruida, Leroy Fer, Jens Toornstra (72' Yassin Ayoub), Orkun Kökçü (75' Renato Tapia), Steven Berghuis, Sam Larsson, Luis Sinisterra (72' Luciano Narsingh). Coach: Dick Advocaat.
Goals: 14' Luis Díaz 1-0, 16' Tyrell Malacia 2-0 (og), 19' Eric Botteghin 2-1, 22' Sam Larsson 2-2, 34' Tiquinho Soares 3-2.
Referee: Deniz Aytekin (GER)   Attendance: 28,507.

12.12.19   Ibrox Stadium, Glasgow: Glasgow Rangers FC – BSC Young Boys 1-1 (1-0)
Glasgow Rangers FC: Allan McGregor, James Tavernier, Connor Goldson, Borna Barisic, Nikola Katic, Scott Arfield, Ryan Jack, Glen Kamara, Joe Aribo, Alfredo Morelos, Ryan Kent (78' Sheyi Ojo). Coach: Steven Gerrard.
BSC Young Boys: David von Ballmoos, Frederik Sørensen, Saidy Janko, Ulisses Garcia, Nicolas Bürgy, Christopher Martins Pereira (73' Felix Mambimbi), Nicolas Moumi Ngamaleu (61' Marvin Spielmann), Christian Fassnacht, Michel Aebischer, Jean-Pierre Nsamé (61' Guillaume Hoarau), Roger Assalé. Coach: Gerardo Seoane.
Goals: 30' Alfredo Morelos 1-0, 89' Borna Barisic 1-1 (og).
Referee: Felix Brych (GER)   Attendance: 49,015.
Sent off: 90+3' Ryan Jack.

GROUP H

19.09.19   Ludogorets Arena, Razgrad: PFC Ludogorets Razgrad – CSKA Moscow 5-1 (0-1)
PFC Ludogorets Razgrad: Renan, Dragos Grigore, Cicinho, Rafael Forster, Anton Nedyalkov, Anicet Andrianantenaina, Wanderson, Stéphane Badji, Claudiu Keserü (86' Dan Biton), Marcelinho (74' Jacek Góralski), Jody Lukoki (84' Jorginho). Coach: Stanislav Genchev.
CSKA Moscow: Igor Akinfeev, Mário Fernandes, Hördur Magnússon, Igor Diveev, Vadim Karpov, Nikola Vlasic, Kristijan Bistrovic, Konstantin Kuchaev (71' Lucas Santos), Ivan Oblyakov, Jaka Bijol (53' Fedor Chalov), Takuma Nishimura (54' Ilzat Akhmetov). Coach: Victor Goncharenko.
Goals: 11' Igor Diveev 0-1, 48' Wanderson 1-1, 5-0' Jody Lukoki 2-1, 52', 68', 73' Claudiu Keserü 3-1, 4-1, 5-1 (p).
Referee: Irfan Peljto (BIH)   Attendance: 8,423.

19.09.19   RCDE Stadium, Cornellà de Llobregat: RCD Espanyol – Ferencvárosi TC 1-1 (0-1)
RCD Espanyol: Diego López, Bernardo Espinosa, Dídac Vilà (67' Adrià Pedrosa), Javi López, Naldo, Granero, Marc Roca, Matías Vargas (74' Víctor Campuzano), Pol Lozano, Melendo (56' Jonathan Calleri), Lei Wu. Coach: David Gallego.
Ferencvárosi TC: Dénes Dibusz, Marcel Heister, Endre Botka (66' Gergö Lovrencsics), Miha Blazic, Lasha Dvali, Dávid Sigér, Igor Kharatin, Oleksandr Zubkov, Danylo Ignatenko (85' Abraham Frimpong), Isael (65' Nikolay Signevich), Tokmac Nguen. Coach: Serhiy Rebrov.
Goals: 10' Javi López 0-1 (og), 60' Matías Vargas 1-1.
Referee: Nikola Dabanovic (MNE)   Attendance: 18,125.

03.10.19   Groupama Aréna, Budapest: Ferencvárosi TC – PFC Ludogorets Razgrad 0-3 (0-2)
Ferencvárosi TC: Dénes Dibusz, Marcel Heister, Miha Blazic, Abraham Frimpong, Gergö Lovrencsics, Dávid Sigér (73' Nikolay Signevich), Igor Kharatin, Oleksandr Zubkov (80' Roland Varga), Isael, Tokmac Nguen, Franck Boli (73' Michal Skvarka).
Coach: Serhiy Rebrov.
PFC Ludogorets Razgrad: Plamen Iliev, Dragos Grigore, Cicinho (69' Jordan Ikoko), Rafael Forster, Anton Nedyalkov, Anicet Andrianantenaina, Wanderson, Stéphane Badji, Claudiu Keserü, Marcelinho (46' Cosmin Moti), Jody Lukoki (57' Jacek Góralski).
Coach: Stanislav Genchev.
Goals: 1' Jody Lukoki 0-1, 40', 64' Rafael Forster 0-2, 0-3.
Goals: Bartosz Frankowski (POL)   Attendance: 16,163.
Sent off: 43' Dragos Grigore.

03.10.19   VEB Arena, Moscow: CSKA Moscow – RCD Espanyol 0-2 (0-0)
CSKA Moscow: Igor Akinfeev, Mário Fernandes, Hördur Magnússon, Zvonimir Sarlija, Igor Diveev (46' Cédric Gogoua), Nikola Vlasic, Ilzat Akhmetov (76' Jaka Bijol), Kristijan Bistrovic, Arnór Sigurdsson, Konstantin Kuchaev (67' Ivan Oblyakov), Fedor Chalov.
Coach: Victor Goncharenko.
RCD Espanyol: Diego López, Sébastien Corchia, David López, Adrià Pedrosa, Fernando Calero, Granero (90' Pol Lozano), Víctor Sánchez, Marc Roca, Matías Vargas, Lei Wu (76' Pablo Piatti), Jonathan Calleri (22' Víctor Campuzano). Coach: David Gallego.
Goals: 64' Lei Wu 0-1, 90+5' Víctor Campuzano 0-2.
Referee: Ali Palabiyik (TUR)   Attendance: 22,288.

24.10.19   VEB Arena, Moscow: CSKA Moscow – Ferencvárosi TC 0-1 (0-0)
CSKA Moscow: Igor Akinfeev, Mário Fernandes, Hördur Magnússon, Igor Diveev, Vadim Karpov, Nikola Vlasic, Ilzat Akhmetov (75' Lucas Santos), Arnór Sigurdsson (80' Jaka Bijol), Konstantin Kuchaev (61' Kristijan Bistrovic), Ivan Oblyakov, Fedor Chalov.
Coach: Victor Goncharenko.
Ferencvárosi TC: Dénes Dibusz, Endre Botka, Miha Blazic, Eldar Civic, Gergö Lovrencsics, Dávid Sigér, Igor Kharatin, Oleksandr Zubkov (89' Lasha Dvali), Danylo Ignatenko, Tokmac Nguen (84' Roland Varga), Franck Boli (72' Isael). Coach: Serhiy Rebrov.
Goal: 86' Roland Varga 0-1.
Referee: Pavel Orel (CZE)   Attendance: 18,518.

24.10.19   Ludogorets Arena, Razgrad: PFC Ludogorets Razgrad – RCD Espanyol 0-1 (0-1)
PFC Ludogorets Razgrad: Plamen Iliev, Cosmin Moti, Cicinho, Rafael Forster, Anton Nedyalkov, Anicet Andrianantenaina (67' Dan Biton), Wanderson, Stéphane Badji, Marcelinho, Jody Lukoki (59' Jakub Swierczok), Mavis Tchibota. Coach: Stanislav Genchev.
RCD Espanyol: Diego López, Bernardo Espinosa, Dídac Vilá, Sébastien Corchia, Javi López, Lluís López, Granero, Iturraspe, Melendo (69' Marc Roca), Lei Wu (61' Matías Vargas), Víctor Campuzano (78' Facundo Ferreyra). Coach: Pablo Machín.
Goal: 13' Víctor Campuzano 0-1.
Referee: Aliyar Agayev (AZE)   Attendance: 10,334.
Sent off: 88' Javi López.

07.11.19   Groupama Aréna, Budapest: Ferencvárosi TC – CSKA Moscow 0-0
Ferencvárosi TC: Dénes Dibusz, Endre Botka, Miha Blazic, Eldar Civic, Michal Skvarka (84' Roland Varga), Gergö Lovrencsics, Igor Kharatin, Oleksandr Zubkov, Danylo Ignatenko, Tokmac Nguen (90' Abraham Frimpong), Franck Boli (82' Isael). Coach: Serhiy Rebrov.
CSKA Moscow: Igor Akinfeev, Mário Fernandes, Hördur Magnússon (81' Kirill Nababkin), Igor Diveev, Vadim Karpov, Nikola Vlasic, Ilzat Akhmetov (59' Kristijan Bistrovic), Arnór Sigurdsson, Ivan Oblyakov, Jaka Bijol (63' Konstantin Kuchaev), Fedor Chalov.
Coach: Victor Goncharenko.
Referee: Aleksandar Stavrev (MCD)   Attendance: 18,153.
Sent off: 90+1' Kirill Nababkin.

07.11.19 RCDE Stadium, Cornellà de Llobregat:
RCD Espanyol – PFC Ludogorets Razgrad 6-0 (3-0)
RCD Espanyol: Diego López, Bernardo Espinosa (46' Adrià Pedrosa), Dídac Vilá, Sébastien Corchia, Lluís López, Fernando Calero, Granero, Matías Vargas, Pol Lozano, Melendo (72' Lei Wu), Víctor Campuzano (65' Facundo Ferreyra). Coach: Pablo Machín.
PFC Ludogorets Razgrad: Plamen Iliev, Cicinho, Georgi Terziev, Rafael Forster, Anton Nedyalkov, Wanderson (77' Svetoslav Dyakov), Jacek Góralski, Stéphane Badji, Claudiu Keserü (39' Anicet Andrianantenaina), Marcelinho (21' Jordan Ikoko), Jody Lukoki. Coach: Aleksi Zhelyazkov.
Goals: 4' Melendo 1-0 19' Lluís López 2-0, 36' Matías Vargas 3-0 (p), 52' Víctor Campuzano 4-0, 73' Adrià Pedrosa 5-0, 76' Facundo Ferreyra 6-0.
Referee: François Letexier (FRA) Attendance: 13,963.
Sent off: 12' Rafael Forster, 34' Jacek Góralski.

28.11.19 VEB Arena, Moscow: CSKA Moscow – PFC Ludogorets Razgrad 1-1 (0-0)
CSKA Moscow: Igor Akinfeev, Mário Fernandes, Hördur Magnússon, Igor Diveev, Vadim Karpov (76' Jaka Bijol), Nikola Vlasic, Kristijan Bistrovic, Arnór Sigurdsson (64' Ilzat Akhmetov), Konstantin Kuchaev (54' Alan Dzagoev), Ivan Oblyakov, Fedor Chalov. Coach: Victor Goncharenko.
PFC Ludogorets Razgrad: Plamen Iliev, Dragos Grigore, Cicinho, Georgi Terziev, Anton Nedyalkov, Anicet Andrianantenaina, Wanderson (81' Mavis Tchibota), Stéphane Badji, Claudiu Keserü (87' Jakub Swierczok), Marcelinho (76' Svetoslav Dyakov), Jody Lukoki. Coach: Aleksi Zhelyazkov.
Goals: 66' Claudiu Keserü 0-1, 76' Fedor Chalov 1-1.
Referee: Jakob Kehlet (DEN) Attendance: 12,948.

28.11.19 Groupama Aréna, Budapest: Ferencvárosi TC – RCD Espanyol 2-2 (1-1)
Ferencvárosi TC: Dénes Dibusz, Miha Blazic, Abraham Frimpong, Eldar Civic, Gergö Lovrencsics, Dávid Sigér (86' Michal Skvarka), Igor Kharatin, Isael, Roland Varga (61' Oleksandr Zubkov), Tokmac Nguen, Franck Boli (83' Nikolay Signevich). Coach: Serhiy Rebrov.
RCD Espanyol: Diego López, Dídac Vilá, Sébastien Corchia, Lluís López, Pipa Ávila, Fernando Calero, Granero (69' Mohamed Ezzarfani), Iturraspe, Pol Lozano, Melendo (81' Jonathan Calleri), Víctor Campuzano (88' Sergi Darder). Coach: Pablo Machín.
Goals: 23' Dávid Sigér 1-0, 31' Melendo 1-1, 90+1' Michal Skvarka 2-1 (p), 90+6' Sergi Darder 2-2.
Referee: Tiago Martins (POR) Attendance: 19,111.
Sent off: 90+4' Eldar Civic.

Isael missed a penalty kick (77').

12.12.19   Ludogorets Arena, Razgrad: PFC Ludogorets Razgrad – Ferencvárosi TC 1-1 (1-0)
PFC Ludogorets Razgrad: Plamen Iliev, Dragos Grigore, Cicinho, Georgi Terziev, Anton Nedyalkov, Anicet Andrianantenaina, Wanderson (85' Svetoslav Dyakov), Stéphane Badji, Claudiu Keserü (90+1' Jordan Ikoko), Marcelinho, Jody Lukoki (77' Mavis Tchibota).
Coach: Aleksi Zhelyazkov.
Ferencvárosi TC: Dénes Dibusz, Marcel Heister, Endre Botka, Miha Blazic, Abraham Frimpong, Dávid Sigér (79' Michal Skvarka), Igor Kharatin (84' Danylo Ignatenko), Oleksandr Zubkov, Isael, Tokmac Nguen, Franck Boli (84' Nikolay Signevich).
Coach: Serhiy Rebrov.
Goals: 24' Jody Lukoki 1-0, 90+5' Nikolay Signevich 1-1.
Referee: Matej Jug (SVN)   Attendance: 5,528.

12.12.19   RCDE Stadium, Cornellà de Llobregat: RCD Espanyol – CSKA Moscow 0-1 (0-0)
RCD Espanyol: Andrés Prieto, Javi López, Naldo (86' Jonathan Calleri), Lluís López, Pipa Ávila, Adrià Pedrosa, Pablo Piatti (72' Granero), Iturraspe, Pol Lozano, Facundo Ferreyra, Víctor Campuzano (46' Lei Wu). Coach: Pablo Machín.
CSKA Moscow: Ilya Pomazun, Mário Fernandes, Hördur Magnússon, Igor Diveev, Vadim Karpov, Nikola Vlasic (86' Jaka Bijol), Ilzat Akhmetov (81' Georgiy Shchennikov), Kristijan Bistrovic, Konstantin Kuchaev (78' Arnór Sigurdsson), Ivan Oblyakov, Fedor Chalov.
Coach: Victor Goncharenko.
Goal: 84' Nikola Vlasic 0-1.
Referee: Kevin Blom (HOL)   Attendance: 10,615.

GROUP I

19.09.19   GHELAMCO-arena, Gent: KAA Gent – AS Saint-Étienne 3-2 (2-1)
KAA Gent: Thomas Kaminski, Nana Asare, Mikael Lustig, Igor Plastun, Michael Ngadeu-Ngadjui, Vadis Odjidja-Ofoe, Sven Kums (90+3' Brecht Dejaegere), Elisha Owusu, Laurent Depoitre, Roman Yaremchuk (81' Dylan Bronn), Jonathan David (90+4' Giorgi Kvilitaia).
Coach: Jess Thorup.
AS Saint-Étienne: Stéphane Ruffier, Loïc Perrin, Mathieu Debuchy, Timothée Kolodziejczak, Miguel Trauco, Harold Moukoudi (72' Robert Beric), Yohan Cabaye (65' Denis Bouanga), Yann M'Vila, Romain Hamouma (72' Arnaud Nordin), Zaydou Youssouf, Wahbi Khazri.
Coach: Ghislain Printant.
Goals: 2' Jonathan David 1-0, 38' Wahbi Khazri 1-1, 43' Jonathan David 2-1, 64' Loïc Perrin 3-1 (og), 75' Thomas Kaminski 3-2 (og).
Referee: Roi Reinshreiber (ISR)   Attendance: 14,928.

19.09.19   Volkswagen Arena, Wolfsburg: VfL Wolfsburg – FC Oleksandriya 3-1 (2-0)
VfL Wolfsburg: Pavao Pervan, Robin Knoche, Jérôme Roussillon, Marcel Tisserand (70' Jeffrey Bruma), Kevin Mbabu, Yannick Gerhardt, Admir Mehmedi (86' Renato Steffen), Josuha Guillavogui, Maximilian Arnold, Josip Brekalo (76' Lukas Nmecha), Wout Weghorst.
Coach: Oliver Glasner.
FC Oleksandriya: Yuri Pankiv, Kaspars Dubra, Pavlo Pashayev, Valeri Luchkevych (81' Yevhen Protasov), Denis Miroshnichenko, Glib Bukhal, Oleksiy Dovgiy (46' Kirilo Kovalets), Dmytro Grechyshkin, Eugene Banada, Maksym Tretyakov (65' Dmytro Shastal), Artem Sitalo.
Coach: Volodymyr Sharan.
Goals: 20' Maximilian Arnold 1-0. 24' Admir Mehmedi 2-0, 66' Eugene Banada 2-1, 67' Josip Brekalo 3-1.
Referee: Halis Özkahya (TUR)   Attendance: 10,112.

03.10.19 Arena Lviv, Lviv: FC Oleksandriya – KAA Gent 1-1 (0-1)
FC Oleksandriya: Yuri Pankiv, Kaspars Dubra, Pavlo Pashayev, Valeri Luchkevych (86'
Denys Bezborodko), Denis Miroshnichenko, Glib Bukhal, Dmytro Grechyshkin, Kirilo
Kovalets (75' Oleksiy Dovgiy), Eugene Banada, Maksym Tretyakov, Artem Sitalo (80'
Dmytro Shastal). Coach: Volodymyr Sharan.
KAA Gent: Thomas Kaminski, Nana Asare, Mikael Lustig, Igor Plastun, Michael Ngadeu-
Ngadjui, Vadis Odjidja-Ofoe, Sven Kums, Elisha Owusu, Laurent Depoitre (85' Giorgi
Kvilitaia), Roman Yaremchuk (89' Yūya Kubo), Jonathan David. Coach: Jess Thorup.
Goals: 6' Laurent Depoitre 0-1, 60' Artem Sitalo 1-1.
Referee: Jens Maae (DEN) Attendance: 7,588.

FC Oleksandriya played their home matches at Arena Lviv, Lviv, instead of their regular home stadium CSC Nika Stadium Oleksandriya, as it did not meet UEFA requirements.

03.10.19 Stade Geoffroy-Guichard, Saint-Étienne:
AS Saint-Étienne – VfL Wolfsburg 1-1 (1-1)
AS Saint-Étienne: Jessy Moulin, Loïc Perrin, Mathieu Debuchy (60' Harold Moukoudi),
Timothée Kolodziejczak, William Saliba, Yann M'Vila, Romain Hamouma, Arnaud Nordin,
Zaydou Youssouf, Wahbi Khazri (86' Charles Abi), Robert Beric (65' Denis Bouanga).
Coach: Ghislain Printant.
VfL Wolfsburg: Pavao Pervan, Jeffrey Bruma, Robin Knoche, Jérôme Roussillon (83' Renato
Steffen), Marcel Tisserand, William, Josuha Guillavogui, Felix Klaus, Maximilian Arnold,
Josip Brekalo (72' João Victor), Wout Weghorst (60' Lukas Nmecha). Coach: Oliver Glasner.
Goals: 13' Timothée Kolodziejczak 1-0, 15' William 1-1.
Referee: Craig Pawson (ENG) Attendance: 24,815.

24.10.19 Stade Geoffroy-Guichard, Saint-Étienne:
AS Saint-Étienne – FC Oleksandriya 1-1 (1-1)
AS Saint-Étienne: Stéphane Ruffier, Mathieu Debuchy, Timothée Kolodziejczak, Gabriel
Silva, William Saliba, Yann M'Vila, Romain Hamouma, Jean-Eudes Aholou (46' Ryad
Boudebouz), Arnaud Nordin (63' Charles Abi), Zaydou Youssouf, Robert Beric (74' Denis
Bouanga). Coach: Claude Puel.
FC Oleksandriya: Yuri Pankiv, Kaspars Dubra, Pavlo Pashayev, Valeri Luchkevych (80'
Dmytro Shastal), Denis Miroshnichenko, Glib Bukhal, Dmytro Grechyshkin, Kirilo Kovalets
(83' Oleksiy Dovgiy), Eugene Banada, Maksym Tretyakov (90+3' Vladislav Baboglo), Artem
Sitalo. Coach: Volodymyr Sharan.
Goals: 8' Gabriel Silva 1-0, 14' Gabriel Silva 1-1 (og).
Referee: Espen Eskås (NOR) Attendance: 28,573.

24.10.19 GHELAMCO-arena, Gent: KAA Gent – VfL Wolfsburg 2-2 (1-2)
KAA Gent: Thomas Kaminski, Nana Asare, Mikael Lustig, Igor Plastun, Michael Ngadeu-
Ngadjui, Vadis Odjidja-Ofoe, Sven Kums (87' Jean-Luc Dompé), Elisha Owusu (60' Roman
Bezus), Laurent Depoitre (73' Giorgi Kvilitaia), Roman Yaremchuk, Jonathan David.
Coach: Jess Thorup.
VfL Wolfsburg: Pavao Pervan, Jeffrey Bruma, Robin Knoche, Marcel Tisserand, William (46'
Kevin Mbabu), Josuha Guillavogui, Maximilian Arnold, Renato Steffen (79' Jérôme
Roussillon), Josip Brekalo (66' Lukas Nmecha), Wout Weghorst, João Victor.
Coach: Oliver Glasner.
Goals: 3' Wout Weghorst 0-1, 24' João Victor 0-2, 41', 90+4' Roman Yaremchuk 1-2, 2-2.
Referee: Sergey Ivanov (RUS) Attendance: 15,437.

07.11.19 Arena Lviv, Lviv: FC Oleksandriya – AS Saint-Étienne 2-2 (0-1)
FC Oleksandriya: Yuri Pankiv, Kaspars Dubra, Pavlo Pashayev, Valeri Luchkevych (78' Maksym Zaderaka), Denis Miroshnichenko, Glib Bukhal, Dmytro Grechyshkin, Kirilo Kovalets, Eugene Banada, Maksym Tretyakov (84' Timur Stetskov), Dmytro Shastal (46' Denys Bezborodko). Coach: Volodymyr Sharan.
AS Saint-Étienne: Stéphane Ruffier, Loïc Perrin, Mathieu Debuchy, Timothée Kolodziejczak, Wesley Fofana, Jean-Eudes Aholou, Denis Bouanga, Arnaud Nordin (87' Ryad Boudebouz), Zaydou Youssouf, Wahbi Khazri (72' Gabriel Silva), Robert Beric (55' Mahdi Camara). Coach: Claude Puel.
Goals: 24' Wahbi Khazri 0-1 (p), 72' Mahdi Camara 0-2, 84' Denys Bezborodko 1-2, 90+1' Maksym Zaderaka 2-2.
Referee: João Pedro Pinheiro (POR)   Attendance: 6,361.

07.11.19 Volkswagen Arena, Wolfsburg: VfL Wolfsburg – KAA Gent 1-3 (1-0)
VfL Wolfsburg: Pavao Pervan, Jeffrey Bruma, Robin Knoche (82' Felix Klaus), Marcel Tisserand, William, Josuha Guillavogui, Maximilian Arnold (70' Lukas Nmecha), Renato Steffen, Josip Brekalo (66' Yunus Malli), Wout Weghorst, João Victor. Coach: Oliver Glasner.
KAA Gent: Thomas Kaminski, Nana Asare, Mikael Lustig, Igor Plastun, Michael Ngadeu-Ngadjui, Vadis Odjidja-Ofoe, Sven Kums, Elisha Owusu, Laurent Depoitre (90+1' Giorgi Kvilitaia), Roman Yaremchuk (81' Alessio Castro-Montes), Jonathan David. Coach: Jess Thorup.
Goals: 20' João Victor 1-0, 50' Roman Yaremchuk 1-1, 65' Laurent Depoitre 1-2, 76' Michael Ngadeu-Ngadjui 1-3.
Referee: Massimiliano Irrati (ITA)   Attendance: 11,620.

28.11.19 Stade Geoffroy-Guichard, Saint-Étienne: AS Saint-Étienne – KAA Gent 0-0
AS Saint-Étienne: Stéphane Ruffier, Loïc Perrin, Timothée Kolodziejczak, Wesley Fofana, Yann M'Vila (80' Robert Beric), Ryad Boudebouz, Jean-Eudes Aholou (64' Arnaud Nordin), Denis Bouanga, Mahdi Camara, Loïs Diony (73' Zaydou Youssouf), Franck Honorat. Coach: Claude Puel.
KAA Gent: Thomas Kaminski, Mikael Lustig, Igor Plastun, Michael Ngadeu-Ngadjui, Milad Mohammadi, Vadis Odjidja-Ofoe, Sven Kums, Elisha Owusu, Laurent Depoitre (78' Alessio Castro-Montes), Roman Yaremchuk (71' Giorgi Kvilitaia), Jonathan David (80' Brecht Dejaegere). Coach: Jess Thorup.
Referee: Irfan Peljto (BIH)   Attendance: 25,315.
Sent off: 76' Michael Ngadeu-Ngadjui.

28.11.19 Arena Lviv, Lviv: FC Oleksandriya – VfL Wolfsburg 0-1 (0-1)
FC Oleksandriya: Yuri Pankiv, Kaspars Dubra, Pavlo Pashayev, Valeri Luchkevych (86' Maksym Zaderaka), Denis Miroshnichenko, Vladislav Baboglo, Andriy Zaporozhan, Dmytro Grechyshkin, Kirilo Kovalets (39' Denys Bezborodko), Eugene Banada, Dmytro Shastal (55' Maksym Tretyakov). Coach: Volodymyr Sharan.
VfL Wolfsburg: Koen Casteels, Jeffrey Bruma, Jérôme Roussillon, Marcel Tisserand, John Anthony Brooks, William (90+1' Kevin Mbabu), Admir Mehmedi (80' Felix Klaus), Josuha Guillavogui, Maximilian Arnold, Wout Weghorst, João Victor (61' Renato Steffen). Coach: Oliver Glasner.
Goal: 45+1' Wout Weghorst 0-1 (p).
Referee: Manuel Schüttengruber (AUT)   Attendance: 7,118.

12.12.19 GHELAMCO-arena, Gent: KAA Gent – FC Oleksandriya 2-1 (2-0)
KAA Gent: Thomas Kaminski, Nana Asare, Mikael Lustig, Igor Plastun, Alessio Castro-Montes, Vadis Odjidja-Ofoe, Sven Kums, Roman Bezus (80' Jean-Luc Dompé), Elisha Owusu, Laurent Depoitre (90+3' Giorgi Kvilitaia), Roman Yaremchuk (73' Giorgi Chakvetadze). Coach: Jess Thorup.
FC Oleksandriya: Yuri Pankiv, Kaspars Dubra, Pavlo Pashayev, Valeri Luchkevych, Denis Miroshnichenko, Vladislav Baboglo, Andriy Zaporozhan (46' Oleksiy Dovgiy), Dmytro Grechyshkin, Kirilo Kovalets, Maksym Tretyakov (79' Maksym Zaderaka), Denys Bezborodko (86' João Teixeira). Coach: Volodymyr Sharan.
Goals: 7', 16' Laurent Depoitre 1-0, 2-0, 54' Denis Miroshnichenko 2-1.
Referee: Radu Petrescu (ROM)   Attendance: 13,156.

12.12.19 Volkswagen Arena, Wolfsburg: VfL Wolfsburg – AS Saint-Étienne 1-0 (0-0)
VfL Wolfsburg: Pavao Pervan, Robin Knoche, Marcel Tisserand, Paulo Otávio (79' Jérôme Roussillon), Kevin Mbabu, Yannick Gerhardt, Renato Steffen, Xaver Schlager (64' Yunus Malli), Josip Brekalo, Elvis Rexhbeçaj, Daniel Ginczek (64' Lukas Nmecha).
Coach: Oliver Glasner.
AS Saint-Étienne: Jessy Moulin, Timothée Kolodziejczak, Sergi Palencia, Harold Moukoudi, Yann M'Vila, Romain Hamouma (55' Bilal Benkhedim), Jean-Eudes Aholou (46' Franck Honorat), Assane Dioussé (77' Gabriel Silva), Arnaud Nordin, Zaydou Youssouf, Robert Beric. Coach: Claude Puel.
Goal: 52' Paulo Otávio 1-0.
Referee: Paul Tierney (ENG)   Attendance: 10,802.

GROUP J

19.09.19 Stadio Olimpico, Roma: AS Roma – Istanbul Basaksehir FK 4-0 (1-0)
AS Roma: Pau López, Aleksandar Kolarov, Federico Fazio, Juan Jesus, Leonardo Spinazzola, Javier Pastore (64' Lorenzo Pellegrini), Bryan Cristante (72' Jordan Veretout), Amadou Diawara, Nicolò Zaniolo, Edin Dzeko (74' Nikola Kalinic), Justin Kluivert.
Coach: Paulo Fonseca.
Istanbul Basaksehir FK: Mert Günok, Gaël Clichy, Júnior Caiçara, Ponck, Arda Turan (64' Enzo Crivelli), Mehmet Topal, Mahmut Tekdemir, Danijel Aleksic (69' Azubuike Okechukwu), Edin Visca, Irfan Kahveci, Fredrik Gulbrandsen (77' Demba Ba).
Coach: Okan Buruk.
Goals: 42' Júnior Caiçara 1-0 (og), 58' Edin Dzeko 2-0, 71' Nicolò Zaniolo 3-0, 90+3' Justin Kluivert 4-0.
Referee: Xavier Estrada Fernández (ESP)   Attendance: 21,348.

19.09.19   Stadion im Borussia-Park, Mönchengladbach:
Borussia Mönchengladbach – Wolfsberger AC 0-4 (0-3)
Borussia Mönchengladbach: Yann Sommer, Stefan Lainer, Matthias Ginter, Nico Elvedi, Ramy Bensebaini, Christoph Kramer, László Bénes, Florian Neuhaus (46' Breel Embolo), Denis Zakaria, Alassane Pléa (72' Patrick Herrmann), Marcus Thuram (71' Raffael).
Coach: Marco Rose.
Wolfsberger AC: Alexander Kofler, Nemanja Rnic, Lukas Schmitz, Michael Sollbauer, Michael Novak, Michael Liendl, Mario Leitgeb, Marcel Ritzmaier (86' Christopher Wernitznig), Anderson Niangbo (90+1' Marc Andre Schmerböck), Romano Schmid, Shon Weissman (84' Alexander Schmidt). Coach: Gerhard Struber.
Goals: 13' Shon Weissman 0-1, 31' Mario Leitgeb 0-2, 41' Marcel Ritzmaier 0-3, 68' Mario Leitgeb 0-4.
Referee: Tamás Bornár (HUN)   Attendance: 34,846.

03.10.19   Merkur Arena, Graz: Wolfsberger AC – AS Roma 1-1 (0-1)
Wolfsberger AC: Alexander Kofler, Nemanja Rnic, Lukas Schmitz, Michael Sollbauer, Michael Novak, Michael Liendl (88' Marc Andre Schmerböck), Mario Leitgeb, Marcel Ritzmaier (90+2' Christopher Wernitznig), Anderson Niangbo, Romano Schmid, Shon Weissman (81' Alexander Schmidt). Coach: Gerhard Struber.
AS Roma: Antonio Miranta, Federico Fazio, Davide Santon, Leonardo Spinazzola (80' Aleksandar Kolarov), Gianluca Mancini, Javier Pastore (77' Mirko Antonucci), Bryan Cristante (82' Jordan Veretout), Amadou Diawara, Nicolò Zaniolo, Nikola Kalinic, Justin Kluivert. Coach: Paulo Fonseca.
Goals: 27' Leonardo Spinazzola 0-1, 51' Michael Liendl 1-1.
Referee: Tiago Martins (POR)   Attendance: 11,169.

Wolfsberger AC played their home matches at Merkur Arena, Graz, instead of their regular home stadium Lavanttal-Arena, Wolfsberg.

03.10.19   Basaksehir Fatih Terim Stadyumu, Istanbul:
Istanbul Basaksehir FK – Borussia Mönchengladbach 1-1 (0-0)
Istanbul Basaksehir FK: Mert Günok, Gaël Clichy, Martin Skrtel, Júnior Caiçara, Ponck, Mahmut Tekdemir, Danijel Aleksic (46' Azubuike Okechukwu), Edin Visca, Irfan Kahveci (89' Mehmet Topal), Fredrik Gulbrandsen, Enzo Crivelli (78' Eljero Elia).
Coach: Okan Buruk.
Borussia Mönchengladbach: Yann Sommer, Oscar Wendt (76' Ramy Bensebaini), Stefan Lainer, Matthias Ginter, Nico Elvedi, Christoph Kramer (64' Patrick Herrmann), Florian Neuhaus, Denis Zakaria, Alassane Pléa (46' Raffael), Breel Embolo, Marcus Thuram.
Coach: Marco Rose.
Goals: 55' Edin Visca 1-0, 90+1' Patrick Herrmann 1-1.
Referee: Stuart Attwell (ENG)   Attendance: 5,646.

24.10.19   Basaksehir Fatih Terim Stadyumu, Istanbul:
           Istanbul Basaksehir FK – Wolfsberger AC 1-0 (0-0)
Istanbul Basaksehir FK: Mert Günok, Gaël Clichy, Martin Skrtel, Júnior Caiçara, Ponck, Mehmet Topal, Mahmut Tekdemir (46' Azubuike Okechukwu), Edin Visca (90' Ugur Uçar), Irfan Kahveci, Fredrik Gulbrandsen (64' Robinho), Enzo Crivelli. Coach: Okan Buruk.
Wolfsberger AC: Alexander Kofler, Nemanja Rnic, Lukas Schmitz (90+1' Marc Andre Schmerböck), Michael Sollbauer, Michael Novak, Michael Liendl, Mario Leitgeb, Marcel Ritzmaier, Anderson Niangbo (76' Alexander Schmidt), Romano Schmid, Shon Weissman. Coach: Gerhard Struber.
Goal: 78' Irfan Kahveci 1-0.
Referee: Irfan Peljto (BIH)   Attendance: 4,101.

24.10.19   Stadio Olimpico, Roma: AS Roma – Borussia Mönchengladbach 1-1 (1-0)
AS Roma: Pau López, Aleksandar Kolarov, Federico Fazio, Chris Smalling, Leonardo Spinazzola, Gianluca Mancini, Javier Pastore (62' Diego Perotti), Jordan Veretout, Nicolò Zaniolo (77' Mirko Antonucci), Edin Dzeko, Justin Kluivert (84' Alessandro Florenzi). Coach: Paulo Fonseca.
Borussia Mönchengladbach: Yann Sommer, Tony Jantschke, Stefan Lainer, Nico Elvedi, Ramy Bensebaini, Christoph Kramer (76' László Bénes), Florian Neuhaus, Denis Zakaria, Patrick Herrmann (62' Jonas Hofmann), Breel Embolo (76' Lars Stindl), Marcus Thuram. Coach: Marco Rose.
Goals: 32' Nicolò Zaniolo 1-0, 90+5' Lars Stindl 1-1 (p).
Referee: William Collum (SCO)   Attendance: 29,037.

07.11.19   Merkur Arena, Graz: Wolfsberger AC – Istanbul Basaksehir FK 0-3 (0-0)
Wolfsberger AC: Alexander Kofler, Nemanja Rnic, Lukas Schmitz, Michael Sollbauer, Michael Novak, Michael Liendl, Mario Leitgeb (87' Manfred Gollner), Marcel Ritzmaier, Anderson Niangbo (81' Alexander Schmidt), Romano Schmid, Shon Weissman. Coach: Gerhard Struber.
Istanbul Basaksehir FK: Mert Günok, Gaël Clichy, Martin Skrtel, Júnior Caiçara, Ponck, Mehmet Topal, Edin Visca, Berkay Özcan (80' Arda Turan), Azubuike Okechukwu (89' Eljero Elia), Fredrik Gulbrandsen (88' Aziz Behich), Enzo Crivelli. Coach: Okan Buruk.
Goals: 73' Edin Visca 0-1 (p), 84', 87' Enzo Crivelli 0-2, 0-3.
Referee: Sandro Schärer (SUI)   Attendance: 5,286.
Sent off: 72' Nemanja Rnic.

07.11.19   Stadion im Borussia-Park, Mönchengladbach:
           Borussia Mönchengladbach – AS Roma 2-1 (1-0)
Borussia Mönchengladbach: Yann Sommer, Oscar Wendt (85' Ramy Bensebaini), Tony Jantschke (28' Jonas Hofmann), Stefan Lainer, Matthias Ginter, Nico Elvedi, Lars Stindl, László Bénes, Florian Neuhaus (73' Alassane Pléa), Denis Zakaria, Marcus Thuram. Coach: Marco Rose.
AS Roma: Pau López, Aleksandar Kolarov, Federico Fazio, Davide Santon, Chris Smalling, Gianluca Mancini (59' Amadou Diawara), Javier Pastore (80' Diego Perotti), Jordan Veretout, Nicolò Zaniolo (76' Cengiz Ünder), Edin Dzeko, Justin Kluivert. Coach: Paulo Fonseca.
Goals: 35' Federico Fazio 1-0 (og), 64' Federico Fazio 1-1, 90+5' Marcus Thuram 2-1.
Referee: Jesús Gil Manzano (ESP)   Attendance: 44,570.

28.11.19 Basaksehir Fatih Terim Stadyumu, Istanbul:
Istanbul Basaksehir FK – AS Roma 0-3 (0-3)
Istanbul Basaksehir FK: Mert Günok, Gaël Clichy, Martin Skrtel (52' Berkay Özcan), Alexandru Epureanu (46' Robinho), Ponck, Mehmet Topal, Edin Visca, Irfan Kahveci, Azubuike Okechukwu, Fredrik Gulbrandsen (16' Aziz Behich), Enzo Crivelli.
Coach: Okan Buruk.
AS Roma: Pau López, Aleksandar Kolarov (53' Leonardo Spinazzola), Davide Santon, Chris Smalling, Gianluca Mancini, Jordan Veretout, Lorenzo Pellegrini (71' Cengiz Ünder), Amadou Diawara, Nicolò Zaniolo, Edin Dzeko (72' Henrikh Mkhitaryan), Justin Kluivert.
Coach: Paulo Fonseca.
Goals: 30' Jordan Veretout 0-1 (p), 41' Justin Kluivert 0-2, 45+1' Edin Dzeko 0-3.
Referee: Ovidiu Hategan (ROM)   Attendance: 12,879.

28.11.19 Merkur Arena, Graz: Wolfsberger AC – Borussia Mönchengladbach 0-1 (0-0)
Wolfsberger AC: Alexander Kofler, Lukas Schmitz, Michael Sollbauer, Manfred Gollner, Michael Novak, Michael Liendl, Mario Leitgeb, Marcel Ritzmaier, Anderson Niangbo (85' Marc Andre Schmerböck), Romano Schmid (75' Christopher Wernitznig), Shon Weissman. Coach: Mohamed Sahli.
Borussia Mönchengladbach: Yann Sommer, Oscar Wendt, Stefan Lainer, Ramy Bensebaini, Lars Stindl (74' Breel Embolo), Tobias Strobl, Jonas Hofmann, László Bénes, Denis Zakaria, Alassane Pléa (77' Patrick Herrmann), Marcus Thuram (89' Raffael). Coach: Marco Rose.
Goal: 60' Lars Stindl 0-1.
Referee: Serdar Gözübüyük (HOL)   Attendance: 12,073.

12.12.19 Stadio Olimpico, Roma: AS Roma – Wolfsberger AC 2-2 (2-1)
AS Roma: Antonio Mirante (62' Pau López), Federico Fazio, Leonardo Spinazzola, Alessandro Florenzi, Gianluca Mancini, Henrikh Mkhitaryan, Jordan Veretout, Cengiz Ünder (66' Lorenzo Pellegrini), Amadou Diawara, Edin Dzeko, Diego Perotti (67' Nicolò Zaniolo). Coach: Paulo Fonseca.
Wolfsberger AC: Alexander Kofler, Nemanja Rnic, Lukas Schmitz, Michael Sollbauer, Michael Novak, Michael Liendl, Christopher Wernitznig (76' Lukas Schöfl), Sven Sprangler, Anderson Niangbo (90+4' Joshua Steiger), Romano Schmid, Shon Weissman (90+2' Amar Hodzic). Coach: Mohamed Sahli.
Goals: 7' Diego Perotti 1-0 (p), 10' Alessandro Florenzi 1-1 (og), 19' Edin Dzeko 2-1, 64' Shon Weissman 2-2.
Referee: Craig Pawson (ENG)   Attendance: 21,672.

12.12.19 Stadion im Borussia-Park, Mönchengladbach:
Borussia Mönchengladbach – Istanbul Basaksehir FK 1-2 (1-1)
Borussia Mönchengladbach: Yann Sommer, Oscar Wendt, Stefan Lainer, Matthias Ginter, Nico Elvedi, Christoph Kramer (90+2' Ramy Bensebaini), Florian Neuhaus (78' Lars Stindl), Denis Zakaria, Patrick Herrmann, Breel Embolo (78' Alassane Pléa), Marcus Thuram.
Coach: Marco Rose.
Istanbul Basaksehir FK: Mert Günok, Gaël Clichy, Alexandru Epureanu, Júnior Caiçara, Ponck, Eljero Elia, Mehmet Topal (88' Berkay Özcan), Danijel Aleksic (67' Demba Ba), Edin Visca, Irfan Kahveci (90+3' Azubuike Okechukwu), Enzo Crivelli. Coach: Okan Buruk.
Goals: 33' Marcus Thuram 1-0, 44' Irfan Kahveci 1-1, 90+1' Enzo Crivelli 1-2.
Referee: José María Sánchez Martínez (ESP)   Attendance: 40,046.

GROUP K

19.09.19 Národný Futbalový Stadión, Bratislava: Slovan Bratislava – Besiktas JK 4-2 (1-2)
Slovan Bratislava: Dominik Greif, Vasil Bozhikov, Vernon, Jurij Medvedev, Myenty Abena, Ibrahim Rabiu (89' Kenan Bajric), Dávid Holman, Joeri de Kamps (82' Marin Ljubicic), "Moha" Mohammed Rharsalla, Andraz Sporar, Dejan Drazic (76' Erik Daniel).
Coach: Ján Kozák.
Besiktas JK: Loris Karius, Domagoj Vida, Douglas Pereira, Víctor Ruíz (74' Atiba Hutchinson), Pedro Rebocho, Adem Ljajic, Mohamed Elneny, Georges-Kévin N'Koudou (82' Güven Yalçin), Dorukhan Toköz, Abdoulay Diaby (79' Jeremain Lens), Mehmet Umut Nayir.
Coach: Abdullah Avci.
Goals: 14' Andraz Sporar 1-0, 29' Adem Ljajic 1-1 (p), 45+1' Vasil Bozhikov 1-2 (og), 58' Andraz Sporar 2-2, 90+3' Marin Ljubicic 3-2, 90+4' "Moha" Mohammed Rharsalla 4-2.
Referee: Kristo Tohver (EST)   Attendance: 5,273.

Officially, the match was played behind closed doors due to punishment by UEFA, but Slovan Bratislava used the UEFA regulation, which allows such matches to be visited by children under 14 years to allow a crowd to attend.

19.09.19   Molineux Stadium, Wolverhampton:
            Wolverhampton Wanderers – Sporting Braga 0-1 (0-0)
Wolverhampton Wanderers: Rui Patrício, Ryan Bennett, Willy Boly, Matt Doherty (80' Adama Traoré), Conor Coady, Jonny Castro, Leander Dendoncker (76' Diogo Jota), Rúben Neves, Morgan Gibbs-White (67' João Moutinho), Raúl Jiménez, Patrick Cutrone.
Coach: Nuno Espírito Santo.
Sporting Braga: Matheus Magalhães, Ricardo Esgaio, Nuno Sequeira, Pablo Santos, Bruno Viana, Fransérgio, João Palhinha, André Horta (88' Murilo), Paulinho, Ricardo Horta (86' João Novais), Galeno (84' Francisco Trincão). Coach: Sá Pinto.
Goal: 71' Ricardo Horta 0-1.
Referee: Jakob Kehlet (DEN)   Attendance: 28,314.

03.10.19   Estádio Municipal de Braga, Braga: Sporting Braga – Slovan Bratislava 2-2 (1-1)
Sporting Braga: Eduardo, Ricardo Esgaio, Nuno Sequeira, Pablo Santos, Bruno Viana, Fransérgio (88' Rui Fonte), João Palhinha, André Horta (70' João Novais), Paulinho, Ricardo Horta (71' Francisco Trincão), Galeno. Coach: Sá Pinto.
Slovan Bratislava: Dominik Greif, Artem Sukhotskiy (80' Erik Daniel), Vernon, Jurij Medvedev, Myenty Abena, Ibrahim Rabiu, Dávid Holman (68' Dejan Drazic), Joeri de Kamps (68' Marin Ljubicic), Kenan Bajric, "Moha" Mohammed Rharsalla, Andraz Sporar.
Coach: Ján Kozák.
Goals: 31' Bruno Viana 1-0, 45+4' Andraz Sporar 1-1, 63' Galeno 2-1, 87' Bruno Viana 2-2 (og).
Referee: Adrien Jaccottet (SUI)   Attendance: 9,077.

Andraz Sporar missed a penalty kick (45+4').

03.10.19   Vodafone Park, Istanbul: Besiktas JK – Wolverhampton Wanderers 0-1 (0-0)
Besiktas JK: Loris Karius, Caner Erkin, Domagoj Vida, Douglas Pereira, Pedro Rebocho, Jeremain Lens (84' Gökhan Gönül), Adem Ljajic, Necip Uysal, Mohamed Elneny, Dorukhan Toköz (79' Oguzhan Özyakup), Güven Yalçin (27' Mehmet Umut Nayir).
Coach: Abdullah Avci.
Wolverhampton Wanderers: Rui Patrício, Willy Boly, Matt Doherty, Conor Coady, Jonny Castro, João Moutinho, Romain Saïss, Rúben Neves, Morgan Gibbs-White (62' Leander Dendoncker), Raúl Jiménez (79' Patrick Cutrone), Pedro Neto (46' Adama Traoré).
Coach: Nuno Espírito Santo.
Goal: 90+3' Willy Boly 0-1.
Referee: Harald Lechner (AUT)   Attendance: 22,670.

24.10.19   Vodafone Park, Istanbul: Besiktas JK – Sporting Braga 1-2 (0-1)
Besiktas JK: Loris Karius, Caner Erkin, Domagoj Vida, Enzo Roco, Pedro Rebocho, Adem Ljajic, Necip Uysal (67' Mehmet Umut Nayir), Oguzhan Özyakup (61' Kartal Yilmaz), Mohamed Elneny, Tyler Boyd (84' Erdem Seçgin), Güven Yalçin. Coach: Abdullah Avci.
Sporting Braga: Matheus Magalhães, Ricardo Esgaio, Nuno Sequeira, Pablo Santos, Bruno Viana, João Novais (75' Uche Agbo), João Palhinha, André Horta (75' Wilson Eduardo), Paulinho (83' Rui Fonte), Ricardo Horta, Galeno. Coach: Sá Pinto.
Goals: 38' Ricardo Horta 0-1, 71' Mehmet Umut Nayir 1-1, 80' Wilson Eduardo 1-2.
Referee: Alejandro Hernández Hernández (ESP)   Attendance: 20,956.

Adem Ljajic missed a penalty kick (74').

24.10.19   Národny Futbalovy Stadión, Bratislava:
           Slovan Bratislava – Wolverhampton Wanderers 1-2 (1-0)
Slovan Bratislava: Dominik Greif, Vasil Bozhikov, Vernon, Jurij Medvedev, Myenty Abena, Ibrahim Rabiu (81' Aleksandar Cavric), Dávid Holman (57' Marin Ljubicic), Joeri de Kamps, Erik Daniel (66' Rafael Ratão), "Moha" Mohammed Rharsalla, Andraz Sporar.
Coach: Ján Kozák.
Wolverhampton Wanderers: Rui Patrício, Willy Boly, Matt Doherty, Conor Coady, Rúben Vinagre, Max Kilman, João Moutinho, Romain Saïss (76' Leander Dendoncker), Morgan Gibbs-White (59' Diogo Jota), Raúl Jiménez, Patrick Cutrone (46' Adama Traoré). Coach: Nuno Espírito Santo.
Goals: 11' Andraz Sporar 1-0, 58' Romain Saïss 1-1, 64' Raúl Jiménez 1-2 (p).
Referee: Yevhen Aranovskyi (UKR)   Attendance: 20,333.
Sent off: 87' Diogo Jota.

07.11.19   Estádio Municipal de Braga, Braga: Sporting Braga – Besiktas JK 3-1 (2-1)
Sporting Braga: Eduardo, Ricardo Esgaio, Nuno Sequeira, Wallace, Bruno Viana, Fransérgio, João Palhinha, André Horta (77' Francisco Trincão), Paulinho (67' Rui Fonte), Ricardo Horta (60' Wilson Eduardo), Galeno. Coach: Sá Pinto.
Besiktas JK: Loris Karius, Caner Erkin (63' Pedro Rebocho), Domagoj Vida, Enzo Roco, Jeremain Lens, Necip Uysal, Oguzhan Özyakup, Kartal Yilmaz (72' Mohamed Elneny), Tyler Boyd, Mehmet Umut Nayir, Güven Yalçin (88' Erdem Seçgin). Coach: Abdullah Avci.
Goals: 14' Paulinho 1-0, 29' Tyler Boyd 1-1, 37' Paulinho 2-1, 81' Wilson Eduardo 3-1.
Referee: Gediminas Mazeika (LTU)   Attendance: 8,833.
Sent off: 44' Jeremain Lens.

07.11.19 Molineux Stadium, Wolverhampton:
Wolverhampton Wanderers – Slovan Bratislava 1-0 (0-0)
Wolverhampton Wanderers: Rui Patrício, Matt Doherty, Conor Coady, Rúben Vinagre (90+7' Jonny Castro), Max Kilman, João Moutinho, Leander Dendoncker, Rúben Neves, Raúl Jiménez, Adama Traoré (90+10' Ryan Bennett), Pedro Neto (69' Patrick Cutrone).
Coach: Nuno Espírito Santo.
Slovan Bratislava: Dominik Greif, Vasil Bozhikov, Vernon, Jurij Medvedev, Myenty Abena, Ibrahim Rabiu (90+7' Erik Daniel), Joeri de Kamps, Kenan Bajric (89' Marin Ljubicic), Andraz Sporar, Rafael Ratão (70' Artem Sukhotskiy), Dejan Drazic. Coach: Ján Kozák.
Goal: 90+2' Raúl Jiménez 1-0.
Referee: Bas Nijhuis (HOL)   Attendance: 29,789.

Rúben Neves missed a penalty kick (51').

28.11.19 Vodafone Park, Istanbul: Besiktas JK – Slovan Bratislava 2-1 (0-1)
Besiktas JK: Loris Karius, Caner Erkin, Domagoj Vida, Enzo Roco, Pedro Rebocho (46' Adem Ljajic), Necip Uysal, Oguzhan Özyakup (76' Güven Yalçin), Mohamed Elneny, Abdoulay Diaby, Tyler Boyd (46' Georges-Kévin N'Koudou), Mehmet Umut Nayir.
Coach: Abdullah Avci.
Slovan Bratislava: Dominik Greif, Vasil Bozhikov, Vernon, Myenty Abena, Ibrahim Rabiu, Dávid Holman (83' Marin Ljubicic), Joeri de Kamps, Erik Daniel (86' Rafael Ratão), Kenan Bajric, "Moha" Mohammed Rharsalla (76' Dejan Drazic), Andraz Sporar. Coach: Ján Kozák.
Goals: 35' Erik Daniel 0-1, 75' Enzo Roco 1-1, 90+2' Adem Ljajic 2-1 (p).
Referee: Enea Jorgji (ALB)   Attendance: 11,526.

28.11.19 Estádio Municipal de Braga, Braga:
Sporting Braga – Wolverhampton Wanderers 3-3 (1-3)
Sporting Braga: Eduardo, Ricardo Esgaio, Nuno Sequeira, Wallace (58' Wilson Eduardo), Bruno Viana, Fransérgio, João Palhinha, André Horta, Paulinho (87' Pablo Santos), Ricardo Horta (73' Rui Fonte), Galeno. Coach: Sá Pinto.
Wolverhampton Wanderers: Rui Patrício, Matt Doherty, Conor Coady, Jonny Castro, João Moutinho, Romain Saïss, Leander Dendoncker, Rúben Neves, Raúl Jiménez (70' Pedro Neto), Adama Traoré (75' Rúben Vinagre), Diogo Jota (80' Patrick Cutrone).
Coach: Nuno Espírito Santo.
Goals: 6' André Horta 1-0, 14' Raúl Jiménez 1-1, 34' Matt Doherty 1-2, 35' Adama Traoré 1-3, 65' Paulinho 2-3, 79' Fransérgio 3-3.
Referee: Aleksei Kulbakov (BLS)   Attendance: 12,058.

12.12.19 Národný Futbalový Štadión, Bratislava:
Slovan Bratislava – Sporting Braga 2-4 (1-1)
Slovan Bratislava: Dominik Greif, Vasil Bozhikov, Vernon, Jurij Medvedev, Myenty Abena, Marin Ljubicic, Nono Delgado (76' Kenan Bajric), Erik Daniel, "Moha" Mohammed Rharsalla, Andraz Sporar, Dejan Drazic (78' Rafael Ratão). Coach: Ján Kozák.
Sporting Braga: Tiago Sá, Ricardo Esgaio, Pablo Santos, Caju (59' Diogo Viana), Bruno Viana, Fransérgio, João Novais, Uche Agbo, Rui Fonte (82' Paulinho), Ricardo Horta, Francisco Trincão (83' Galeno). Coach: Sá Pinto.
Goals: 42' Andraz Sporar 1-0, 44' Rui Fonte 1-1, 70' "Moha" Mohammed Rharsalla 2-1, 72' Francisco Trincão 2-2, 75' Vasil Bozhikov 2-3 (og), 90+3' Paulinho 2-4.
Referee: Pawel Gil (POL)   Attendance: 10,856.

12.12.19   Molineux Stadium, Wolverhampton:
Wolverhampton Wanderers – Besiktas JK 4-0 (0-0)
Wolverhampton Wanderers: John Ruddy, Ryan Bennett, Conor Coady, Oskar Buur, Rúben Vinagre, Max Kilman, João Moutinho (70' Taylor Perry), Leander Dendoncker (73' Owen Otasowie), Rúben Neves (56' Diogo Jota), Patrick Cutrone, Pedro Neto.
Coach: Nuno Espírito Santo.
Besiktas JK: Utku Yuvakuran, Pedro Rebocho, Kerem Kalafat (76' Enzo Roco), Erdogan Kaya, Jeremain Lens (81' Abdoulay Diaby), Necip Uysal, Oguzhan Özyakup, Erdem Seçgin, Tyler Boyd, Mehmet Umut Nayir, Güven Yalçin (64' Mohamed Elneny).
Coach: Abdullah Avci.
Goals: 58', 63' Diogo Jota 1-0, 2-0, 67' Leander Dendoncker 3-0, 69' Diogo Jota 4-0.
Referee: Andris Treimanis (LAT)   Attendance: 27,866.

GROUP L

19.09.19   Stadion Partizana, Beograd: Partizan Beograd – AZ Alkmaar 2-2 (1-1)
Partizan Beograd: Vladimir Stojkovic, Bojan Ostojic, Nemanja Miletic (I), Slobodan Urosevic, Strahinja Pavlovic, Bibras Natcho, Zoran Tosic (63' Lazar Markovic), Aleksandar Scekic (80' Seydouba Soumah), Sasa Zdjelar, Takuma Asano, Umar Sadiq (88' Petar Gigic).
Coach: Savo Milosevic.
AZ Alkmaar: Marco Bizot, Ron Vlaar, Stijn Wuytens (54' Pantelis Hatzidiakos), Jonas Svensson, Owen Wijndal, Fredrik Midtsjø, Dani de Wit, Teun Koopmeiners, Oussama Idrissi (31' Yukinari Sugawara), Myron Boadu, Calvin Stengs (84' Jordy Clasie). Coach: Arne Slot.
Goals: 13' Calvin Stengs 0-1, 42', 61' Bibras Natcho 1-1 (p), 2-1, 67' Myron Boadu 2-2.
Referee: Marco Guida (ITA)   Attendance: 22,564.
Sent off: 27' Jonas Svensson.

Partizan Beograd were supposed to play two matches behind closed doors following racist behaviour of supporters against Turkish club Yeni Malatyaspor at the third qualifying round. However, Partizan used a UEFA regulation allowing matches to be visited by children under 14 years to allow a crowd to attend, for their Europa League matches against AZ Alkmaar and Manchester United.

19.09.19   Old Trafford, Manchester: Manchester United – FK Astana 1-0 (0-0)
Manchester United: Sergio Romero, Marcos Rojo (78' Ashley Young), Phil Jones, Diogo Dalot, Axel Tuanzebe, Nemanja Matic, Fred, Angel Gomes (68' Mata), Marcus Rashford, Tahith Chong (68' Jesse Lingard), Mason Greenwood. Coach: Ole Gunnar Solskjær.
FK Astana: Nenad Eric, Antonio Rukavina, Dmitriy Shomko, Zarko Tomasevic, Evgeny Postnikov, Luka Simunovic (46' Yuriy Logvinenko), Rúnar Sigurjónsson, Marin Tomasov, Ivan Maevski, Roman Murtazaev (46' Rangelo Janga), Dorin Rotariu (82' Ndombe Mubele).
Coach: Roman Grygorchuk.
Goal: 73' Mason Greenwood 1-0.
Referee: François Letexier (FRA)   Attendance: 50,783.

03.10.19 Astana Arena, Nur-Sultan: FK Astana – Partizan Beograd 1-2 (0-1)
FK Astana: Nenad Eric, Antonio Rukavina, Dmitriy Shomko, Zarko Tomasevic (15' Evgeny Postnikov), Abzal Beysebekov (79' Rangelo Janga), Luka Simunovic, Rúnar Sigurjónsson, Ivan Maevski, Yuri Pertsukh, Sergey Khizhnichenko (46' Roman Murtazaev), Dorin Rotariu.
Coach: Roman Grygorchuk.
Partizan Beograd: Vladimir Stojkovic, Bojan Ostojic, Nemanja Miletic (I), Slobodan Urosevic, Strahinja Pavlovic, Bibras Natcho, Zoran Tosic (77' Lazar Markovic), Seydouba Soumah (66' Aleksandar Scekic), Sasa Zdjelar, Takuma Asano (79' Rajko Brezancic), Umar Sadiq.
Coach: Savo Milosevic.
Goals: 29', 73' Umar Sadiq 0-1, 0-2, 85' Rúnar Sigurjónsson 1-2.
Referee: Mohammed Al-Hakim (SWE)   Attendance: 20,137.

03.10.19   Cars Jeans Stadion, The Hague: AZ Alkmaar – Manchester United 0-0
AZ Alkmaar: Marco Bizot, Ron Vlaar, Stijn Wuytens, Owen Wijndal, Yukinari Sugawara, Fredrik Midtsjø, Dani de Wit (87' Pantelis Hatziidiakos), Teun Koopmeiners, Oussama Idrissi, Myron Boadu, Calvin Stengs. Coach: Arne Slot.
Manchester United: David de Gea, Marcos Rojo, Victor Lindelöf, Diogo Dalot, Brandon Williams, Mata (83' Scott McTominay), Nemanja Matic, Fred, Daniel James (63' Marcus Rashford), Angel Gomes, Mason Greenwood (77' Jesse Lingard).
Coach: Ole Gunnar Solskjær.
Referee: Gediminas Mazeika (LTU)   Attendance: 13,863.

AZ Alkmaar played their home matches at Cars Jeans Stadion, The Hague, instead of their regular home stadium AFAS Stadion, Alkmaar due to the latter's roof collapse.

24.10.19   Cars Jeans Stadion, The Hague: AZ Alkmaar – FK Astana 6-0 (2-0)
AZ Alkmaar: Marco Bizot, Ron Vlaar (69' Pantelis Hatziidiakos), Stijn Wuytens (80' Jordy Clasie), Jonas Svensson, Owen Wijndal, Fredrik Midtsjø, Dani de Wit (71' Yukinari Sugawara), Teun Koopmeiners, Oussama Idrissi, Myron Boadu, Calvin Stengs.
Coach: Arne Slot.
FK Astana: Nenad Eric (26' Aleksandr Mokin), Yuriy Logvinenko (69' Evgeny Postnikov), Dmitriy Shomko, Abzal Beysebekov (43' Antonio Rukavina), Luka Simunovic, Ivan Maevski, Serikzhan Muzhikov, Didar Zhalmukan, Yuri Pertsukh, Rangelo Janga, Dorin Rotariu.
Coach: Roman Grygorchuk.
Goals: 39' Teun Koopmeiners 1-0 (p), 43' Myron Boadu 2-0, 77' Calvin Stengs 3-0, 83' Teun Koopmeiners 4-0 (p), 85' Yukinari Sugawara 5-0, 90+2' Oussama Idrissi 6-0.
Referee: Enea Jorgji (ALB)   Attendance: 8,123.

24.10.19   Stadion Partizana, Beograd: Partizan Beograd – Manchester United 0-1 (0-1)
Partizan Beograd: Vladimir Stojkovic, Bojan Ostojic, Nemanja Miletic (I), Slobodan Urosevic, Strahinja Pavlovic, Bibras Natcho, Zoran Tosic (75' Filip Stevanovic), Seydouba Soumah (83' Lazar Pavlovic), Sasa Zdjelar, Takuma Asano (90+3' Djordje Ivanovic), Umar Sadiq.
Coach: Savo Milosevic.
Manchester United: Sergio Romero, Marcos Rojo, Phil Jones, Harry Maguire, Aaron Wan-Bissaka (60' Daniel James), Brandon Williams, Mata, Jesse Lingard, Scott McTominay, James Garner (82' Andreas Pereira), Anthony Martial (60' Marcus Rashford).
Coach: Ole Gunnar Solskjær.
Goal: 43' Anthony Martial 0-1 (p).
Referee: Xavier Estrada Fernández (ESP)   Attendance: 25,627.

07.11.19 Astana Arena, Nur-Sultan: FK Astana – AZ Alkmaar 0-5 (0-1)
FK Astana: Nenad Eric, Antonio Rukavina, Yuriy Logvinenko, Dmitriy Shomko, Abzal Beysebekov (74' Serikzhan Muzhikov), Evgeny Postnikov, Marin Tomasov, Ivan Maevski, Yuri Pertsukh, Sergey Khizhnichenko, Dorin Rotariu (71' Roman Murtazaev).
Coach: Roman Grygorchuk.
AZ Alkmaar: Marco Bizot, Stijn Wuytens, Jonas Svensson (61' Yukinari Sugawara), Pantelis Hatzidiakos, Owen Wijndal, Fredrik Midtsjø (67' Jordy Clasie), Dani de Wit, Teun Koopmeiners, Oussama Idrissi, Myron Boadu, Calvin Stengs (77' Zakaria Aboukhlal).
Coach: Arne Slot.
Goals: 29' Myron Boadu 0-1, 52' Fredrik Midtsjø 0-2, 57' Oussama Idrissi 0-3, 76' Pantelis Hatzidiakos 0-4, 77' Myron Boadu 0-5.
Referee: Mads-Kristoffer Kristoffersen (DEN)   Attendance: 11,584.

07.11.19 Old Trafford, Manchester: Manchester United – Partizan Beograd 3-0 (2-0)
Manchester United: Sergio Romero, Ashley Young, Marcos Rojo, Harry Maguire, Aaron Wan-Bissaka, Mata, Fred (63' James Garner), Scott McTominay (75' Jesse Lingard), Anthony Martial, Marcus Rashford (67' Andreas Pereira), Mason Greenwood.
Coach: Ole Gunnar Solskjær.
Partizan Beograd: Vladimir Stojkovic, Bojan Ostojic, Nemanja Miletic (I), Slobodan Urosevic, Strahinja Pavlovic, Bibras Natcho (60' Zoran Tosic), Aleksandar Scekic, Seydouba Soumah, Sasa Zdjelar, Takuma Asano (70' Filip Stevanovic), Umar Sadiq (86' Djordje Ivanovic).
Coach: Savo Milosevic.
Goals: 22' Mason Greenwood 1-0, 33' Anthony Martial 2-0, 49' Marcus Rashford 3-0.
Referee: Mattias Gestranius (FIN)   Attendance: 62,955.

28.11.19 Astana Arena, Nur-Sultan: FK Astana – Manchester United 2-1 (0-1)
FK Astana: Nenad Eric, Antonio Rukavina, Yuriy Logvinenko, Dmitriy Shomko, Abzal Beysebekov, Evgeny Postnikov, Rúnar Sigurjónsson, Ivan Maevski, Sergey Khizhnichenko (85' Yuri Pertsukh), Roman Murtazaev (90+1' Rangelo Janga), Dorin Rotariu.
Coach: Roman Grygorchuk.
Manchester United: Lee Grant, Luke Shaw, Axel Tuanzebe, Di'Shon Bernard, Ethan Laird, Jesse Lingard, Angel Gomes (89' Ethan Galbraith), Dylan Levitt, James Garner (84' Largie Ramazani), Tahith Chong (65' D'Mani Bughail-Mellor), Mason Greenwood.
Coach: Ole Gunnar Solskjær.
Goals: 10' Jesse Lingard 0-1, 55' Dmitriy Shomko 1-1, 62' Di'Shon Bernard 2-1 (og).
Referee: Donatas Rumsas (LTU)   Attendance: 28,949.

28.11.19 Cars Jeans Stadion, The Hague: AZ Alkmaar – Partizan Beograd 2-2 (0-2)
AZ Alkmaar: Marco Bizot, Stijn Wuytens (60' Yukinari Sugawara), Jonas Svensson, Pantelis Hatzidiakos (54' Ferdy Druijf), Owen Wijndal, Fredrik Midtsjø, Dani de Wit (71' Jordy Clasie), Teun Koopmeiners, Oussama Idrissi, Myron Boadu, Calvin Stengs. Coach: Arne Slot.
Partizan Beograd: Vladimir Stojkovic, Bojan Ostojic, Nemanja Miletic (I), Slobodan Urosevic, Strahinja Pavlovic, Bibras Natcho (90+2' Igor Vujacic), Zoran Tosic (69' Rajko Brezancic), Seydouba Soumah (75' Aleksandar Scekic), Sasa Zdjelar, Takuma Asano, Umar Sadiq.
Coach: Savo Milosevic.
Goals: 16' Takuma Asano 0-1, 27' Seydouba Soumah 0-2, 88' 90+2' Ferdy Druijf 1-2, 2-2.
Referee: Daniel Stefanski (POL)   Attendance: 9,092.
Sent off: 83' Myron Boadu.

12.12.19 Stadion Partizana, Beograd: Partizan Beograd – FK Astana 4-1 (3-0)
Partizan Beograd: Vladimir Stojkovic (70' Filip Kljajic), Bojan Ostojic, Slobodan Urosevic, Strahinja Pavlovic, Zoran Tosic, Aleksandar Scekic, Seydouba Soumah (64' Lazar Pavlovic), Sasa Zdjelar, Takuma Asano, Aleksandar Lutovac, Umar Sadiq (83' Filip Stevanovic).
Coach: Savo Milosevic.
FK Astana: Nenad Eric, Antonio Rukavina, Yuriy Logvinenko, Dmitriy Shomko, Abzal Beysebekov, Evgeny Postnikov, Rúnar Sigurjónsson (85' Rangelo Janga), Ivan Maevski, Sergey Khizhnichenko, Roman Murtazaev (47' Yuri Pertsukh), Dorin Rotariu.
Coach: Roman Grygorchuk.
Goals: 4' Seydouba Soumah 1-0, 22' Umar Sadiq 2-0, 26' Takuma Asano 3-0, 76' Umar Sadiq 4-0, 79' Dorin Rotariu 4-1.
Referee: Filip Glova (SVK)   Attendance: 8,075.

12.12.19   Old Trafford, Manchester: Manchester United – AZ Alkmaar 4-0 (0-0)
Manchester United: Sergio Romero, Ashley Young (68' Ethan Laird), Harry Maguire (68' Phil Jones), Axel Tuanzebe, Brandon Williams, Mata, Nemanja Matic, Andreas Pereira, James Garner, Anthony Martial (59' Tahith Chong), Mason Greenwood.
Coach: Ole Gunnar Solskjær.
AZ Alkmaar: Marco Bizot, Stijn Wuytens, Jonas Svensson, Owen Wijndal, Yukinari Sugawara (68' Ron Vlaar), Jordy Clasie, Fredrik Midtsjø, Dani de Wit (63' Ferdy Druijf), Teun Koopmeiners, Oussama Idrissi (77' Thomas Ouwejan), Calvin Stengs. Coach: Arne Slot.
Goals: 53' Ashley Young 1-0, 58' Mason Greenwood 2-0, 62' Mata 3-0 (p), 64' Mason Greenwood 4-0.
Referee: Sandro Schärer (SUI)   Attendance: 65,773.

KNOCKOUT PHASE
ROUND OF 32

AFC Ajax, Red Bull Salzburg, Internazionale, SL Benfica, Bayer Leverkusen, Shakhtar Donetsk, Olympiacos Piraeus, Club Brugge KV entered the UEFA Europa League as the group stage third-placed teams eliminated from the UEFA Champions League.

20.02.20   Estádio José Alvalade, Lisboa: Sporting CP – Istanbul Basaksehir FK 3-1 (2-0)
Sporting CP: Luís Maximiano, Neto, Sebastián Coates, Stefan Ristovski, Rodrigo Battaglia, Wendel, Yannick Bolasie (89' Gonzalo Plata), Marcos Acuña, Andraz Sporar (71' Pedro Mendes), Luciano Vietto, Jovane Cabral (81' Idrissa Doumbia). Coach: Silas.
Istanbul Basaksehir FK: Mert Günok, Gaël Clichy, Martin Skrtel (70' Eljero Elia), Júnior Caiçara, Carlos Ponck, Mahmut Tekdemir, Edin Visca, Irfan Kahveci (81' Danijel Aleksic), Demba Ba, Fredrik Gulbrandsen (46' Berkay Özcan), Enzo Crivelli. Coach: Okan Buruk.
Goals: 3' Sebastián Coates 1-0, 44' Andraz Sporar 2-0, 51' Luciano Vietto 3-0, 77' Edin Visca 3-1 (p).
Referee: Anthony Taylor (ENG)   Attendance: 27,392.

20.02.20   Coliseum Alfonso Pérez, Getafe: Getafe CF – AFC Ajax 2-0 (1-0)
Getafe CF: David Soria, Allan Nyom, Damián Suárez, Etxeita, Djené Dakonam Ortega, Cururella (88' Kenedy), Mathías Olivera, Nemanja Maksimovic, Mauro Arambarri, Mata (72' Jorge Molina), Deyverson (57' Ángel). Coach: José Bordalás.
AFC Ajax: Bruno Varela, Daley Blind, Nicolás Tagliafico, Edson Álvarez (67' Perr Schuurs), Lisandro Martínez, Sergiño Dest, Hakim Ziyech, Donny van de Beek, Ryan Babel, Dusan Tadic, Lassina Traoré (67' Klaas Jan Huntelaar). Coach: Erik ten Hag.
Goals: 38' Deyverson 1-0, 90+3' Kenedy 2-0.
Referee: Ruddy Buquet (FRA)   Attendance 14,039

20.02.20   Telia Parken, København: FC København – Celtic FC 1-1 (0-1)
FC København: Kalle Johnsson, Ragnar Sigurdsson (86' Sotirios Papagiannopoulos), Bryan Oviedo (73' Pierre Bengtsson), Guillermo Varela, Victor Nelsson, Rasmus Falk, Zeca, Pep Biel Mas, Jens Stage, Dame N'Doye, Michael Santos (73' Mikkel Kaufmann).
Coach: Ståle Solbakken.
Celtic FC: Fraser Forster, Christopher Jullien, Kristoffer Ajer, Jeremie Frimpong (84' Jozo Simunovic), Scott Brown (73' Nir Bitton), Jonny Hayes, James Forrest, Callum McGregor, Jules Olivier Ntcham (60' Mohamed Elyounoussi), Ryan Christie, Odsonne Édouard.
Coach: Neil Lennon.
Goals: 14' Odsonne Édouard 0-1, 52' Dame N'Doye 1-1.
Referee: Sergei Karasev (RUS)   Attendance: 34,346.

(Jens Stage missed a penalty kick 79').

20.02.20   Stadionul Dr. Constantin Radulescu, Cluj-Napoca: CFR Cluj – Sevilla FC 1-1 (0-0)
CFR Cluj: Giedrius Arlauskis, Paulo Vinícius, Camora, Andrei Burca, Cristian Manea, Ciprian Deac, Damjan Djokovic, Mihai Bordeianu, Adrian Paun (74' Ovidiu Hoban), Lacina Traoré (83' Mário Rondón), Billel Omrani (86' Catalin Golofca). Coach: Dan Petrescu.
Sevilla FC: Tomás Vaclík, Jesús Navas (73' Youssef En-Nesyri), Escudero, Diego Carlos, Jules Koundé, Fernando, Nemanja Gudelj, Lucas Ocampos (78' Rony Lopes), Suso (90+1' Franco Vázquez), Joan Jordán, Luuk de Jong. Coach: Lopetegui.
Goals: 59' Ciprian Deac 1-0 (p), 82' Youssef En-Nesyri (82').
Referee: Deniz Aytekin (GER)   Attendance: 14,820.

20.02.20   Jan Breydelstadion, Brugge: Club Brugge KV – Manchester United 1-1 (1-1)
Club Brugge KV: Simon Mignolet, Clinton Mata, Éder Álvarez Balanta (47' Ruud Vormer), Simon Deli, Brandon Mechele, Maxim De Cuyper (73' Siebe Schrijvers), Odilon Kossounou, Mats Rits, Hans Vanaken, Percy Tau (62' Charles De Ketelaere), Emmanuel Dennis Bonaventure. Coach: Philippe Clement.
Manchester United: Sergio Romero, Victor Lindelöf, Harry Maguire, Luke Shaw, Diogo Dalot (81' Bruno Fernandes), Brandon Williams, Mata, Nemanja Matic, Jesse Lingard, Andreas Pereira (71' Fred), Anthony Martial (67' Odion Ighalo). Coach: Ole Gunnar Solskjær.
Goals: 15' Emmanuel Dennis Bonaventure 1-0, 36' Anthony Martial 1-1.
Referee: Aleksei Kulbakov (BLS)   Attendance: 27,006.

20.02.20   Ludogorets Arena, Razgrad: PFC Ludogorets Razgrad – Internazionale 0-2 (0-0)
PFC Ludogorets Razgrad: Plamen Iliev, Dragos Grigore, Cicinho, Georgi Terziev, Anton Nedyalkov, Svetoslav Dyakov (67' Stéphane Badji), Anicet Andrianantenaina, Wanderson, Cauly (90' Dan Biton), Marcelinho, Jakub Swierczok (76' Mavis Tchibota).
Coach: Pavel Vrba.
Internazionale: Daniele Padelli, Diego Godín, Andrea Ranocchia, Danilo D'Ambrosio, Cristiano Biraghi (81' Ashley Young), Borja Valero, Victor Moses (72' Nicolò Barella), Christian Eriksen, Matías Vecino, Alexis Sánchez, Lautaro Martínez (64' Romelu Lukaku).
Coach: Antonio Conte.
Goals: 71' Christian Eriksen 0-1, 90+5' Romelu Lukaku 0-2 (p).
Referee: Carlos del Cerro Grande (ESP)   Attendance: 10,024.

20.02.20   Commerzbank-Arena, Frankfurt am Main:
            Eintracht Frankfurt – Red Bull Salzburg 4-1 (2-0)
Eintracht Frankfurt: Kevin Trapp, Makoto Hasebe, David Abraham, Almamy Touré, Evan Obite N'Dicka, Stefan Ilsanker (86' Erik Durm), Sebastian Rode, Filip Kostic, Djibril Sow, Daichi Kamada (81' Danny da Costa), André Silva (75' Gonçalo Paciência).
Coach: Adi Hütter.
Red Bull Salzburg: Cican Stankovic, Andreas Ulmer, Patrick Farkas, Jérôme Onguéné, Max Wöber, Zlatko Junuzovic, Masaya Okugawa (46' Karim Adeyemi), Dominik Szoboszlai (71' Mohamed Camara), Enock Mwepu, Hwang Hee-Chan, Patson Daka (46' Sékou Koïta).
Coach: Jesse Marsch.
Goals: 12' Daichi Kamada 1-0, 43' Daichi Kamada 2-0, 53' Daichi Kamada 3-0, 56' Filip Kostic 4-0, 85' Hwang Hee-Chan 4-1 (p).
Referee: Ali Palabiyik (TUR)   Attendance: 47,000.

20.02.20   Metalist Stadium, Kharkiv: Shakhtar Donetsk – SL Benfica 2-1 (0-0)
Shakhtar Donetsk: Andriy Pyatov, Sergiy Kryvtsov, Ismaily, Mykola Matviyenko, Marlos (83' Yevhen Konoplyanka), Taras Stepanenko, Taison (90+4' Tetê), Alan Patrick (80' Marcos Antônio), Sergiy Bolbat, Viktor Kovalenko, Júnior Moraes. Coach: Luís Castro.
SL Benfica: Odisseas Vlachodimos, Álex Grimaldo, Rúben Dias, Francisco Reis Ferreira, Tomás Tavares, Adel Taarabt, Pizzi (90+2' Andreas Samaris), Franco Cervi, Chiquinho (79' Rafa Silva), Florentino Luís, Haris Seferovic (69' Carlos Vinícius). Coach: Bruno Lage.
Goals: 56' Alan Patrick 1-0, 67' Pizzi 1-1 (p), 72' Viktor Kovalenko 2-1.
Referee: Bobby Madden (SCO)   Attendance: 24,429.

Shakhtar Donetsk played their home match at Metalist Stadium, Kharkiv, instead of their regular home stadium Donbass Arena, Donetsk, due to the war conditions in Eastern Ukriane.

20.02.20   Molineux Stadium, Wolverhampton:
            Wolverhampton Wanderers – RCD Espanyol 4-0 (1-0)
Wolverhampton Wanderers: Rui Patricio, Willy Boly, Matt Doherty, Conor Coady, Jonny Castro, João Moutinho, Romain Saïss, Rúben Neves, Raúl Jiménez (75' Pedro Neto), Adama Traoré (61' Leander Dendoncker), Diogo Jota (83' Daniel Podence).
Coach: Nuno Espírito Santo.
RCD Espanyol: Andrés Prieto, Dídac Vilà, Naldo, Fernando Calero, Víctor Gómez Perea (75' Sergi Darder), Víctor Sánchez, Iturraspe (61' David López), Matías Vargas, Melendo (62' Jonathan Calleri), Facundo Ferreyra, Lei Wu. Coach: Abelardo.
Goals: 15' Diogo Jota 1-0, 52' Rúben Neves 2-0, 67', 81' Diogo Jota 3-0, 4-0.
Referee: Tobias Stieler (GER)   Attendance: 30,435.

20.02.20 BayArena, Leverkusen: Bayer Leverkusen – Porto 2-1 (1-0)
Bayer Leverkusen: Lukás Hrádecky, Sven Bender, Daley Sinkgraven, Edmond Tapsoba, Lars Bender, Charles Aránguiz (72' Julian Baumgartlinger), Kerem Demirbay, Nadiem Amiri, Kai Havertz, Kevin Volland (90+4' Paulinho), Lucas Alario (80' Leon Bailey). Coach: Peter Bosz.
FC Porto: Agustín Marchesín, Ivan Marcano, Alex Telles, Chancel Mbemba, Wilson Manafá (61' Shoya Nakajima), Sérgio Oliveira, Mateus Uribe, Luis Díaz (77' Danilo Pereira), Tiquinho Soares (63' Zé Luís), Jesús Corona, Moussa Marega. Coach: Sérgio Conceição.
Goals: 29' Lucas Alario 1-0, 57' Kai Havertz 2-0 (p), 73' Luis Díaz 2-1.
Referee: Slavko Vincic (SVN)   Attendance: 26,839.

20.02.20 Neo GSP Stadium, Nicosia: APOEL Nicosia – FC Basel 0-3 (0-1)
APOEL Nicosia: Vid Belec, Giorgios Merkis, Praxitelis Vouros, Nicholas Ioannou (80' Christos Wheeler), Mike Jensen, Dragan Mihajlovic, Uros Matic, Tomás De Vincenti (71' Antonio Jakolis), Alef, Moussa Al Tamari, Andrija Pavlovic (56' Linus Hallenius). Coach: Marinos Ouzounidis.
FC Basel: Jonas Omlin, Silvan Widmer, Omar Alderete, Raoul Petretta (80' Afimico Pululu), Eray Cömart, Blas Riveros, Valentin Stocker, Fabian Frei (85' Orges Bunjaku), Taulant Xhaka, Samuele Campo, Arthur Cabral (74' Kemal Ademi). Coach: Marcel Koller.
Goals: 16' Raoul Petretta 0-1, 53' Valentin Stocker 0-2, 66' Arthur Cabral 0-3.
Referee: Orel Grinfeld (ISR)   Attendance: 8,191.

20.02.20 Stadio Georgios Karaiskáki, Piraeus: Olympiacos Piraeus – Arsenal FC 0-1 (0-0)
Olympiacos Piraeus: José Sá, Omar Elabdellaoui, Rúben Semedo, Kostas Tsimikas, Ousseynou Ba, Mathieu Valbuena, Guilherme, Andreas Bouchalakis (65' Kostas Fortounis), Georgios Masouras (75' Maximiliano Lovera), Mady Camara, Youssef El-Arabi. Coach: Pedro Martins.
Arsenal FC: Bernd Leno, David Luiz, Sokratis Papastathopoulos (90+2' Ainsley Maitland-Niles), Shkodran Mustafi, Granit Xhaka, Joseph Willock (75' Nicolas Pépé), Mattéo Guendouzi, Bukayo Saka, Pierre-Emerick Aubameyang, Alexandre Lacazette, Gabriel Martinelli (58' Dani Ceballos). Coach: Mikel Arteta.
Goal: 81' Alexandre Lacazette 0-1.
Referee: Felix Zwayer (GER)   Attendance: 31,456.

20.02.20 AFAS Stadion, Alkmaar: AZ Alkmaar – LASK Linz 1-1 (0-1)
AZ Alkmaar: Marco Bizot, Ramon Leeuwin, Jonas Svensson, Owen Wijndal, Jordy Clasie, Dani de Wit, Teun Koopmeiners, Håkon Evjen (73' Yukinari Sugawara), Oussama Idrissi (81' Ferdy Druijf), Myron Boadu, Calvin Stengs. Coach: Arne Slot.
LASK Linz: Alexander Schlager, Petar Filipovic, Gernot Trauner, Reinhold Ranftl, Philipp Wiesinger, James Holland, Thomas Goiginger, Peter Michorl, René Renner (56' Marvin Potzmann), Dominik Frieser (76' Husein Balic), Marko Raguz (56' Klauss). Coach: Valérien Ismaël.
Goals: 26' Marko Raguz 0-1, 86' Teun Koopmeiners 1-1 (p).
Referee: Mattias Gestranius (FIN)   Attendance: 12,526.

20.02.20   Volkswagen Arena, Wolfsburg: VfL Wolfsburg – Malmö FF 2-1 (0-0)
VfL Wolfsburg: Koen Casteels, Robin Knoche, Jérôme Roussillon (46' Paulo Otávio), John Anthony Brooks, Kevin Mbabu, Yannick Gerhardt, Admir Mehmedi, Maximilian Arnold, Xaver Schlager (71' Renato Steffen), Josip Brekalo (90+3' Daniel Ginczek), Wout Weghorst. Coach: Oliver Glasner.
Malmö FF: Johan Dahlin, Behrang Safari, Rasmus Bengtsson, Eric Larsson, Anel Ahmedhodzic, Anders Christiansen, Fouad Bachirou, Arnór Ingvi Traustason (22' Søren Rieks, 58' Jo Inge Berget), Adi Nalic, Marcus Antonsson, Isaac Kiese Thelin. Coach: Jon Dahl Tomasson.
Goals: 47' Isaac Kiese Thelin 0-1 (p), 49' Josip Brekalo 1-1, 62' Isaac Kiese Thelin 2-1 (og).
Referee: Gediminas Mazeika (LTU)   Attendance: 13,801.

20.02.20   Stadio Olimpico, Roma: AS Roma – KAA Gent 1-0 (1-0)
AS Roma: Pau López, Aleksandar Kolarov, Federico Fazio, Chris Smalling, Leonardo Spinazzola (69' Davide Santon), Jordan Veretout, Bryan Cristante, Lorenzo Pellegrini (79' Henrikh Mkhitaryan), Edin Dzeko, Diego Perotti (82' Justin Kluivert), Carles Pérez. Coach: Paulo Fonseca.
KAA Gent: Thomas Kaminski, Mikael Lustig, Igor Plastun, Michael Ngadeu-Ngadjui, Milad Mohammadi, Vadis Odjidja-Ofoe, Sven Kums (90+1' Sulayman Marreh), Roman Bezus (74' Giorgi Chakvetadze), Elisha Owusu, Laurent Depoitre, Jonathan David. Coach: Jess Thorup.
Goal: 13' Carles Pérez 1-0).
Referee: Georgi Kabakov (BUL)   Attendance: 28,248.

20.02.20   Ibrox Stadium, Glasgow: Glasgow Rangers FC – Sporting Braga 3-2 (0-1)
Glasgow Rangers FC: Allan McGregor, James Tavernier, Connor Goldson, Borna Barisic (73' Greg Stewart), Nikola Katic, Steven Davis, Scott Arfield, Glen Kamara (54' Joe Aribo), Ianis Hagi, Alfredo Morelos, Ryan Kent (68' Florian Kamberi). Coach: Steven Gerrard.
Sporting Braga: Matheus Magalhães, Raúl Silva, Ricardo Esgaio, Nuno Sequeira, Wallace (12' Galeno), Bruno Viana, Fransérgio, João Palhinha (83' João Novais), Paulinho, Abel Ruiz (70' Ricardo Horta), Francisco Trincão. Coach: Micael Sequeira.
Goals: 11' Fransérgio 0-1, 59' Abel Ruiz 0-2, 67' Ianis Hagi 1-2, 75' Joe Aribo 2-2, 82' Ianis Hagi 3-2.
Referee: Xavier Estrada Fernández (ESP)   Attendance: 49,378.

26.02.20   Estádio Municipal de Braga, Braga:
           Sporting Braga – Glasgow Rangers FC 0-1 (0-0)
Sporting Braga: Matheus Magalhães, Raúl Silva (52' Galeno), Ricardo Esgaio, Nuno Sequeira, Bruno Viana, David Carmo (64' Abel Ruiz), Fransérgio, João Palhinha (46' João Novais), Paulinho, Ricardo Horta, Francisco Trincão. Coach: Micael Sequeira.
Glasgow Rangers FC: Allan McGregor, James Tavernier, Connor Goldson, Borna Barisic, Samuel George Edmundson, Steven Davis, Scott Arfield, Ryan Jack, Ianis Hagi (72' Joe Aribo), Ryan Kent, Florian Kamberi (78' Sheyi Ojo). Coach: Steven Gerrard.
Goal: 61' Ryan Kent 0-1.
Referee: Andreas Ekberg (SWE)   Attendance: 18,113.

(Ianis Hagi missed a penalty kick 45+1').

27.02.20   RCDE Stadium, Cornellà de Llobregat:
           RCD Espanyol – Wolverhampton Wanderers 3-2 (1-1)
RCD Espanyol: Andrés Prieto, Naldo, David López, Adrià Pedrosa, Fernando Calero, Víctor Gómez Perea, Víctor Sánchez (61' Pol Lozano), Sergi Darder (67' Lei Wu), Matías Vargas, Melendo (75' Pipa Ávila), Jonathan Calleri. Coach: Abelardo.
Wolverhampton Wanderers: Rui Patricio, Willy Boly, Matt Doherty, Conor Coady, Rúben Vinagre (58' Romain Saïss), Max Kilman, João Moutinho, Leander Dendoncker, Daniel Podence, Morgan Gibbs-White (64' Pedro Neto), Adama Traoré (78' Bruno Jordåo). Coach: Nuno Espírito Santo.
Goals: 16' Jonathan Calleri 1-0, 22' Adama Traoré 1-1, 57' Jonathan Calleri 2-1 (p), 79' Matt Doherty 2-2, 90+1' Jonathan Calleri 3-2.
Referee: Marco Guida (ITA)   Attendance: 14,525.

27.02.20   Basaksehir Fatih Terim Stadyumu, Istanbul:
           Istanbul Basaksehir – Sporting CP 4-1 (2-0, 3-1) (a.e.t.)
Istanbul Basaksehir FK: Mert Günok, Gaël Clichy, Martin Skrtel, Alexandru Epureanu, Júnior Caiçara, Eljero Elia (85' Fredrik Gulbrandsen), Danijel Aleksic, Edin Visca (120' Carlos Ponck), Irfan Kahveci (89' Robinho), Azubuike Okechukwu (77' Berkay Özcan), Demba Ba. Coach: Okan Buruk
Sporting CP: Luís Maximiano, Sebastián Coates, Stefan Ristovski, Tiago Ilori, Rodrigo Battaglia, Wendel (90+1' Eduardo Henrique), Yannick Bolasie (60' Gonzalo Plata), Marcos Acuña, Andraz Sporar (108' Pedro Mendes), Luciano Vietto, Jovane Cabral (73' Idrissa Doumbia). Coach: Emanuel Ferro.
Goals: 31' Martin Skrtel 1-0, 45' Danijel Aleksic 2-0, 68' Luciano Vietto 2-1, 90+2', 119' Edin Visca 3-1, 4-1 (p).
Referee: Antonio Mateu Lahoz (ESP)   Attendance: 5,892.

Istanbul Basaksehir won after extra time.

27.02.20   Estádio Do Dragão, Porto: FC Porto – Bayer Leverkusen 1-3 (0-1)
FC Porto: Agustín Marchesín, Ivan Marcano, Alex Telles, Chancel Mbemba, Sérgio Oliveira, Mateus Uribe (46' Pepe), Otavinho, Luis Díaz (29' Shoya Nakajima), Zé Luís (64' Tiquinho Soares), Jesús Corona, Moussa Marega. Coach: Sérgio Conceição.
Bayer Leverkusen: Lukás Hrádecky, Sven Bender (67' Aleksandar Dragovic), Jonathan Tah, Daley Sinkgraven, Edmond Tapsoba, Lars Bender (46' Mitchell Weiser), Kerem Demirbay, Nadiem Amiri, Kai Havertz, Lucas Alario, Moussa Diaby (83' Leon Bailey).
Coach: Peter Bosz.
Goals: 10' Lucas Alario 0-1, 50' Kerem Demirbay 0-2, 58' Kai Havertz 0-3, 65' Moussa Marega 1-3.
Referee: István Kovács (ROM)   Attendance: 30,292.
Sent off: 85' Tiquinho Soares.

27.02.20   St. Jakob-Park, Basel: FC Basel – APOEL Nicosia 1-0 (1-0)
FC Basel: Djordje Nikolic, Emil Bergström, Raoul Petretta (46' Edon Zhegrova), Eray Cömart, Blas Riveros, Elis Isufi, Valentin Stocker, Fabian Frei (70' Ramires), Taulant Xhaka, Samuele Campo, Kemal Ademi (32' Arthur Cabral). Coach: Marcel Koller.
APOEL Nicosia: Boy Waterman, Vujadin Savic, Giorgios Merkis, Praxitelis Vouros, Nicholas Ioannou, Mike Jensen, Stathis Aloneftis (62' Giorgos Efrem), Dragan Mihajlovic, Antonio Jakolis (46' Tomás De Vincenti), Uros Matic, Moussa Al Tamari (70' Andrija Pavlovic). Coach: Marinos Ouzounidis.
Goal: 38' Fabian Frei 1-0 (p).
Referee: Pavel Královec (CZE)   Attendance: 14,428.

(Tomás De Vincenti missed a penalty kick 74').

27.02.20   Linzer Stadion, Linz: LASK Linz – AZ Alkmaar 2-0 (1-0)
LASK Linz: Alexander Schlager, Petar Filipovic, Gernot Trauner, Reinhold Ranftl, Philipp Wiesinger, James Holland, Thomas Goiginger (89' Christian Ramsebner), Peter Michorl, René Renner, Dominik Frieser (61' Husein Balic), Marko Raguz (69' Klauss).
Coach: Valérien Ismaël.
AZ Alkmaar: Marco Bizot, Ramon Leeuwin (63' Ferdy Druijf), Jonas Svensson (76' Håkon Evjen), Owen Wijndal, Jordy Clasie, Fredrik Midtsjø, Dani de Wit, Teun Koopmeiners, Oussama Idrissi, Myron Boadu, Calvin Stengs. Coach: Arne Slot.
Goals: 44', 50' Marko Raguz 1-0 (p), 2-0.
Referee: Srdjan Jovanovic (SRB)   Attendance: 12,855.
Sent off: 88' Philipp Wiesinger.

27.02.20   Swedbank Stadion Malmö: Malmö FF – VfL Wolfsburg 0-3 (0-1)
Malmö FF: Johan Dahlin, Behrang Safari, Rasmus Bengtsson (76' Lasse Nielsen), Anel Ahmedhodzic, Søren Rieks, Anders Christiansen, Fouad Bachirou, Oscar Lewicki, Adi Nalic (56' Jo Inge Berget), Marcus Antonsson, Isaac Kiese Thelin. Coach: Jon Dahl Tomasson.
VfL Wolfsburg: Koen Casteels, Robin Knoche, John Anthony Brooks, Paulo Otávio, Yannick Gerhardt, Admir Mehmedi, Maximilian Arnold, Renato Steffen, Xaver Schlager (59' João Victor), Josip Brekalo (79' Felix Klaus), Wout Weghorst (70' Daniel Ginczek).
Coach: Oliver Glasner.
Goals: 42' Josip Brekalo 0-1, 65' Yannick Gerhardt 0-2, 69' João Victor 0-3.
Referee: William Collum (SCO)   Attendance: 20,500.

27.02.20   GHELAMCO-arena, Gent: Gent – AS Roma 1-1 (1-1)
KAA Gent: Thomas Kaminski, Igor Plastun (80' Anderson Niangbo), Michael Ngadeu-Ngadjui, Milad Mohammadi, Alessio Castro-Montes, Vadis Odjidja-Ofoe, Sven Kums, Roman Bezus (66' Giorgi Chakvetadze), Elisha Owusu, Laurent Depoitre (66' Giorgi Kvilitaia), Jonathan David. Coach: Jess Thorup.
AS Roma: Pau López, Aleksandar Kolarov, Chris Smalling, Leonardo Spinazzola (67' Davide Santon), Gianluca Mancini, Henrikh Mkhitaryan, Jordan Veretout (78' Federico Fazio), Bryan Cristante, Edin Dzeko, Carles Pérez (83' Gonzalo Villar), Justin Kluivert.
Coach: Paulo Fonseca.
Goals: 25' Jonathan David 1-0, 29' Justin Kluivert 1-1.
Referee: José María Sánchez Martínez (ESP)   Attendance: 17,557.

27.02.20   Johan Cruijff ArenA, Amsterdam: AFC Ajax – Getafe CF 2-1 (1-1)
AFC Ajax: André Onana, Daley Blind, Perr Schuurs, Lisandro Martínez, Sergiño Dest, Donny van de Beek, Carel Eiting, Ryan Gravenberch (75' Klaas Jan Huntelaar), Ryan Babel, Dusan Tadic, Danilo (46' Quincy Promes). Coach: Erik ten Hag.
Getafe CF: David Soria, Allan Nyom, Damián Suárez, Etxeita, Djené Dakonam Ortega, Cururella (90+4' Kenedy), Mathías Olivera, Nemanja Maksimovic, Mauro Arambarri, Mata (90+1' David Timor), Deyverson (70' Jorge Molina). Coach: José Bordalás.
Goals: 5' Mata 0-1, 10' Danilo 1-1, 63' Mathías Olivera 2-1 (og).
Referee: Anastasios Sidropoulos (GRE)   Attendance: 51,487.

27.02.20   Celtic Park, Glasgow: Celtic FC – FC København 1-3 (0-0)
Celtic FC: Fraser Forster, Jozo Simunovic, Christopher Jullien, Kristoffer Ajer, Greg Taylor, Scott Brown, James Forrest, Callum McGregor, Mohamed Elyounoussi (70' Leigh Griffiths), Tom Rogic, Odsonne Édouard. Coach: Neil Lennon.
FC København: Kalle Johnsson, Pierre Bengtsson, Ragnar Sigurdsson, Guillermo Varela, Victor Nelsson, Rasmus Falk, Zeca, Pep Biel Mas (86' Andreas Bjelland), Jens Stage, Dame N'Doye, Mikkel Kaufmann (45' Michael Santos, 88' Mohammed Daramy).
Coach: Ståle Solbakken.
Goals: 51' Michael Santos 0-1, 83' Odsonne Édouard 1-1 (p), 85' Pep Biel Mas 1-2, 88' Dame N'Doye 1-3.
Referee: Artur Soares Dias (POR)   Attendance: 56,172.

27.02.20   Estadio Ramón Sánchez Pizjuán, Sevilla: Sevilla FC – CFR Cluj 0-0
Sevilla FC: Yassine Bounou, Jesús Navas (76' Youssef En-Nesyri), Diego Carlos, Reguilón, Jules Koundé, Fernando, Nemanja Gudelj, Lucas Ocampos, Suso (67' Nolito), Joan Jordán (57' Éver Banega), Luuk de Jong. Coach: Lopetegui.
CFR Cluj: Giedrius Arlauskis, Paulo Vinícius, Camora, Andrei Burca (27' Kévin Boli), Cristian Manea, Ciprian Deac, Damjan Djokovic (78' Mário Rondón), Mihai Bordeianu, Adrian Paun, Lacina Traoré, Billel Omrani (84' Catalin Golofca). Coach: Dan Petrescu.
Referee: Andris Treimanis (LAT)   Attendance: 31,338.
Sent off: 90+1' Mihai Bordeianu.

Sevilla FC won on away goals.

27.02.20   Emirates Stadium, London: Arsenal – Olympiacos 1-2 (0-0, 0-1) (a.e.t.)
Arsenal FC: Bernd Leno, David Luiz, Shkodran Mustafi (103' Sokratis Papastathopoulos), Héctor Bellerín (84' Joseph Willock), Mesut Özil, Granit Xhaka, Dani Ceballos (72' Lucas Torreira), Bukayo Saka, Pierre-Emerick Aubameyang, Alexandre Lacazette (105' Gabriel Martinelli), Nicolas Pépé. Coach: Mikel Arteta.
Olympiacos Piraeus: José Sá, Omar Elabdellaoui, Kostas Tsimikas (114' Maximiliano Lovera), Pape Cissé, Ousseynou Ba, Mathieu Valbuena (86' Bruno Gaspar), Guilherme (117' Avraam Papadopoulos), Andreas Bouchalakis, Lazar Randjelovic (77' Georgios Masouras), Mady Camara, Youssef El-Arabi. Coach: Pedro Martins.
Goals: 53' Pape Cissé 0-1, 113' Pierre-Emerick Aubameyang 1-1, 119' Youssef El-Arabi 1-2.
Referee: Davide Massa (ITA)   Attendance: 60,242.

Olympiacos Piraeus won after extra time.

27.02.20 Old Trafford, Manchester: Manchester United – Club Brugge KV 5-0 (3-0)
Manchester United: Sergio Romero, Harry Maguire, Luke Shaw, Eric Bailly, Aaron Wan-Bissaka, Mata, Fred, Bruno Fernandes (65' Jesse Lingard), Daniel James (46' Tahith Chong), Scott McTominay (72' Mason Greenwood), Odion Ighalo. Coach: Ole Gunnar Solskjær.
Club Brugge KV: Simon Mignolet, Clinton Mata (62' Matej Mitrovic), Simon Deli, Brandon Mechele, Federico Ricca, Maxim De Cuyper, Odilon Kossounou, Mats Rits (79' Charles De Ketelaere), Hans Vanaken, Percy Tau (61' Krépin Diatta), David Okereke.
Coach: Philippe Clement.
Goals: 27' Bruno Fernandes 1-0 (p), 34' Odion Ighalo 2-0, 41' Scott McTominay 3-0, 82', 90+3' Fred 4-0, 5-0.
Referee: Serdar Gözübüyük (HOL)   Attendance: 70,397.
Sent off: 22' Simon Deli.

27.02.20 Stadio Giuseppe Meazza, Milan:
           Internazionale – PFC Ludogorets Razgrad 2-1 (2-1)
Internazionale: Daniele Padelli, Diego Godín, Andrea Ranocchia, Danilo D'Ambrosio (76' Alessandro Bastoni), Cristiano Biraghi, Borja Valero, Victor Moses, Christian Eriksen, Nicolò Barella (46' Marcelo Brozovic), Alexis Sánchez, Romelu Lukaku (62' Sebastiano Esposito).
Coach: Antonio Conte.
PFC Ludogorets Razgrad: Plamen Iliev, Dragos Grigore, Cicinho, Georgi Terziev, Anton Nedyalkov, Svetoslav Dyakov, Wanderson (70' Mavis Tchibota), Stéphane Badji, Cauly, Claudiu Keserü (64' Jakub Swierczok), Marcelinho (83' Dan Biton). Coach: Pavel Vrba.
Goals: 26' Cauly 0-1, 32' Cristiano Biraghi 1-1, 45+4' Romelu Lukaku 2-1.
Referee: Daniel Siebert (GER)

The match was played behind closed doors due to the outbreak of COVID-19 in Italy.

27.02.20 Estádio do Sport Lisboa e Benfica, Lisboa:
           SL Benfica – Shakhtar Donetsk 3-3 (2-1)
SL Benfica: Odisseas Vlachodimos, Álex Grimaldo, Rúben Dias, Francisco Reis Ferreira "Ferro", Tomás Tavares, Adel Taarabt, Pizzi (79' João Filipe "Jota"), Rafa Silva, Julian Weigl, Chiquinho (67' Haris Seferovic), Dyego Sousa (79' Carlos Vinícius). Coach: Bruno Lage.
Shakhtar Donetsk: Andriy Pyatov, Sergiy Kryvtsov, Ismaily, Mykola Matviyenko, Dodô, Marlos (62' Tetê), Taras Stepanenko, Taison (86' Yevhen Konoplyanka), Alan Patrick (90+2' Davit Khocholava), Marcos Antônio, Júnior Moraes. Coach: Luís Castro.
Goals: 9' Pizzi 1-0, 12', 36' Rúben Dias 1-1 (og), 2-1, 47' Rafa Silva 3-1, 49' Taras Stepanenko 3-2, 71' Alan Patrick 3-3.
Referee: Björn Kuipers (HOL)   Attendance: 48,302.

28.02.20   Red Bull Arena, Wals-Siezenheim:
　　　　　　Red Bull Salzburg – Eintracht Frankfurt 2-2 (1-1)
Red Bull Salzburg: Cican Stankovic, Andreas Ulmer, André Ramalho, Albert Vallci, Jérôme Onguéné, Dominik Szoboszlai (86' Antoine Bernède), Enock Mwepu (76' Mërgim Berisha), Mohamed Camara, Hwang Hee-Chan, Patson Daka, Sékou Koïta (66' Noah Okafor).
Coach: Jesse Marsch.
Eintracht Frankfurt: Kevin Trapp, David Abraham, Martin Hinteregger, Almamy Touré, Evan Obite N'Dicka, Stefan Ilsanker, Sebastian Rode, Filip Kostic (88' Timothy Chandler), Djibril Sow, Daichi Kamada (73' Danny da Costa), André Silva (88' Gonçalo Paciência).
Coach: Adi Hütter.
Goals: 10' Andreas Ulmer 1-0, 30' André Silva 1-1, 72' Jérôme Onguéné 2-1, 83' André Silva 2-2.
Referee: Benoît Bastien (FRA)　　Attendance: 29,000.

This match was originally scheduled to be played on 27th February 2020 in Wals-Siezenheim, but was postponed to 28th February 2020, due to a storm warning.

ROUND OF 16

12.03.20   Basaksehir Fatih Terim Stadyumu, Istanbul:
　　　　　　Istanbul Basaksehir – FC København 1-0 (0-0)
Istanbul Basaksehir FK: Mert Günok, Gaël Clichy, Martin Skrtel, Alexandru Epureanu, Júnior Caiçara, Mahmut Tekdemir (85' Fredrik Gulbrandsen), Danijel Aleksic, Edin Visca (90+1' Azubuike Okechukwu), Irfan Kahveci, Demba Ba, Enzo Crivelli (74' Robinho).
Coach: Okan Buruk.
FC København: Kalle Johnsson, Pierre Bengtsson, Andreas Bjelland, Guillermo Varela, Victor Nelsson, Rasmus Falk, Zeca, Pep Biel Mas (89' Karlo Bartolec), Jens Stage, Michael Santos (82' Viktor Fischer), Mohammed Daramy (62' Mikkel Kaufmann). Coach: Ståle Solbakken.
Goal: 88' Edin Visca 1-0 (p).
Referee: William Collum (SCO)　　Attendance: 12,205.

12.03.20   Commerzbank-Arena, Frankfurt am Main: Eintracht Frankfurt – FC Basel 0-3 (0-1)
Eintracht Frankfurt: Kevin Trapp, Makoto Hasebe (74' Stefan Ilsanker), David Abraham, Martin Hinteregger, Almamy Touré, Evan Obite N'Dicka, Sebastian Rode, Filip Kostic, Djibril Sow (46' Gonçalo Paciência), Daichi Kamada (78' Mijat Gacinovic), André Silva.
Coach: Adi Hütter.
FC Basel: Jonas Omlin, Silvan Widmer, Omar Alderete, Raoul Petretta (68' Kevin Bua), Eray Cömart, Blas Riveros, Valentin Stocker (90+2' Edon Zhegrova), Fabian Frei, Taulant Xhaka, Samuele Campo (78' Jasper van der Werff), Arthur Cabral. Coach: Marcel Koller.
Goals: 27' Samuele Campo 0-1, 73' Kevin Bua 0-2, 85' Fabian Frei 0-3.
Referee: Andreas Ekberg (SWE)

This match was played behind closed doors due to the effects of the COVID-19 pandemic.

12.03.20   Linzer Stadion, Linz: LASK Linz – Manchester United 0-5 (0-1)
LASK Linz: Alexander Schlager, Christian Ramsebner, Gernot Trauner, Reinhold Ranftl, James Holland (76' Stefan Haudum), Peter Michorl, René Renner, Dominik Frieser (71' Husein Balic), Dominik Reiter, Samuel Tetteh (61' Marko Raguz), Klauss.
Coach: Valérien Ismaël.
Manchester United: Sergio Romero, Harry Maguire, Luke Shaw, Eric Bailly, Brandon Williams, Mata, Fred, Bruno Fernandes (78' Andreas Pereira), Daniel James (71' Tahith Chong), Scott McTominay, Odion Ighalo (85' Mason Greenwood).
Coach: Ole Gunnar Solskjær.
Goals: 28' Odion Ighalo 0-1, 58' Daniel James 0-2, 82' Mata 0-3, 90+2' Mason Greenwood 0-4, 90+3' Andreas Pereira 0-5.
Referee: Artur Soares Dias (POR)

LASK Linz played their home match at Linzer Stadion, Linz, instead of their regular home stadium Waldstadion, Pasching.

This match was played behind closed doors due to the effects of the COVID-19 pandemic.

12.03.20   Stadio Georgios Karaiskáki, Piraeus:
           Olympiacos Piraeus – Wolverhampton Wanderers 1-1 (0-0)
Olympiacos Piraeus: José Sá, Omar Elabdellaoui, Rúben Semedo, Kostas Tsimikas, Ousseynou Ba, Mathieu Valbuena (84' Bruno Gaspar), Guilherme, Andreas Bouchalakis, Georgios Masouras (34' Pape Cissé), Mady Camara, Youssef El-Arabi (74' Kostas Fortounis).
Coach: Pedro Martins.
Wolverhampton Wanderers: Rui Patricio, Willy Boly, Matt Doherty (46' Pedro Neto), Conor Coady, Rúben Vinagre (79' Daniel Podence), João Moutinho (85' Leander Dendoncker), Romain Saïss, Rúben Neves, Raúl Jiménez, Adama Traoré, Diogo Jota.
Coach: Nuno Espírito Santo.
Goals: 54' Youssef El-Arabi 1-0, 67' Pedro Neto 1-1.
Referee: Clément Turpin (FRA)
Sent off: 28' Rúben Semedo.

This match was played behind closed doors due to the effects of the COVID-19 pandemic.

12.03.20   Ibrox Stadium, Glasgow: Glasgow Rangers FC – Bayer Leverkusen 1-3 (0-1)
Glasgow Rangers FC: Allan McGregor, James Tavernier (85' Matt Polster), Connor Goldson, Borna Barisic, Samuel George Edmundson, Steven Davis, Scott Arfield, Glen Kamara (68' Ianis Hagi), Joe Aribo (53' Florian Kamberi), Alfredo Morelos, Ryan Kent.
Coach: Steven Gerrard.
Bayer Leverkusen: Lukás Hrádecky, Aleksandar Dragovic, Mitchell Weiser, Wendell, Jonathan Tah, Edmond Tapsoba (68' Paulinho), Charles Aránguiz, Karim Bellarabi (62' Leon Bailey), Kerem Demirbay (81' Julian Baumgartlinger), Kai Havertz, Moussa Diaby.
Coach: Peter Bosz.
Goals: 37' Kai Havertz 0-1 (p), 67' Charles Aránguiz 0-2, 75' Samuel George Edmundson 1-2, 88' Leon Bailey 1-3.
Referee: Szymon Marciniak (POL)   Attendance: 47,494.

12.03.20   Volkswagen Arena, Wolfsburg: VfL Wolfsburg – Shakhtar Donetsk 1-2 (0-1)
VfL Wolfsburg: Koen Casteels, Robin Knoche, John Anthony Brooks, Paulo Otávio, Yannick Gerhardt, Admir Mehmedi (80' Daniel Ginczek), Maximilian Arnold, Renato Steffen, Xaver Schlager (73' João Victor), Josip Brekalo, Wout Weghorst. Coach: Oliver Glasner.
Shakhtar Donetsk: Andriy Pyatov, Sergiy Kryvtsov, Ismaily (68' Davit Khocholava), Mykola Matviyenko, Dodô, Taison (88' Yevhen Konoplyanka), Alan Patrick, Viktor Kovalenko (66' Maycon), Marcos Antônio, Tetê, Júnior Moraes. Coach: Luís Castro.
Goals: 17' Júnior Moraes 0-1, 48' John Anthony Brooks 1-1, 73' Marcos Antônio 1-2.
Referee: Damir Skomina (SVN)

Viktor Kovalenko missed a penalty kick (22').
Wout Weghorst missed a penalty kick (45+2').

This match was played behind closed doors due to the effects of the COVID-19 pandemic.

Due to the effects of the COVID-19 pandemic, the competition was postponed and play did note resume until August 2020. All remaining matches were played behind closed doors.

For the two ties that had not played their first legs, the matches were instead played in a single-leg format, at neutral venues in Germany.

05.08.20   Telia Parken, København: FC København – Istanbul Basaksehir FK 3-0 (1-0)
FC København: Kalle Johnsson, Andreas Bjelland, Nicolai Boilesen (69' Pierre Bengtsson), Guillermo Varela, Victor Nelsson, Rasmus Falk (84' Karlo Bartolec), Zeca, Pep Biel Mas (84' Bryan Oviedo), Robert Mudrazija (53' Jens Stage), Jonas Wind, Mikkel Kaufmann (53' Mohammed Daramy). Coach: Ståle Solbakken.
Istanbul Basaksehir FK: Mert Günok, Gaël Clichy, Martin Skrtel, Alexandru Epureanu, Júnior Caiçara, Mehmet Topal (54' Danijel Aleksic), Mahmut Tekdemir (54' Eljero Elia), Edin Visca, Irfan Kahveci (71' Berkay Özcan), Demba Ba, Enzo Crivelli (79' Fredrik Gulbrandsen). Coach: Okan Buruk.
Goals: 4', 53' Jonas Wind 1-0, 2-0 (p), 62' Rasmus Falk 3-0.
Referee: Daniele Orsato (ITA)

05.08.20   NSK Olimpijs'kyj, Kiev: Shakhtar Donetsk – VfL Wolfsburg 3-0 (0-0)
Shakhtar Donetsk: Andriy Pyatov, Sergiy Kryvtsov, Davit Khocholava, Mykola Matviyenko, Dodô, Marlos (77' Manor Solomon), Taras Stepanenko, Taison (86' Yevhen Konoplyanka), Alan Patrick, Marcos Antônio (74' Viktor Kovalenko), Júnior Moraes. Coach: Luís Castro.
VfL Wolfsburg: Koen Casteels, Jérôme Roussillon (83' Felix Klaus), Marcel Tisserand, John Anthony Brooks, Marin Pongracic, Maximilian Arnold, Xaver Schlager, Josip Brekalo (75' Josuha Guilavogui), Daniel Ginczek (62' Omar Marmoush), Wout Weghorst, João Victor. Coach: Oliver Glasner.
Goals: 89' Júnior Moraes 1-0, 90+1' Manor Solomon 2-0, 90+3' Júnior Moraes 3-0.
Referee: Ivan Kruzliak (SVK)
Sent off: 67' Davit Khocholava, 70' John Anthony Brooks.

05.08.20   Veltins-Arena, Gelsenkirchen (GER): Internazionale – Getafe CF 2-0 (1-0)
Internazionale: Samir Handanovic, Diego Godín, Stefan de Vrij, Alessandro Bastoni, Nicolò Barella, Roberto Gagliardini, Danilo D'Ambrosio (84' Cristiano Biraghi), Marcelo Brozovic (82' Christian Eriksen), Ashley Young, Romelu Lukaku, Lautaro Martínez (70' Alexis Sánchez). Coach: Antonio Conte.
Getafe CF: David Soria, Damián Suárez, Djené Dakonam Ortega, Etxeita, Mathías Olivera (88' Portillo), Nemanja Maksimovic (56' Ángel), David Timor, Allan Nyom (69' Jason), Mauro Arambarri (89' Hugo Duro), Cururella, Mata (69' Jorge Molina). Coach: José Bordalás.
Goals: 33' Romelu Lukaku 1-0, 83' Christian Eriksen 2-0.
Referee: Anthony Taylor (ENG)

Jorge Molina missed a penalty kick (76').

The result of this tie was decided in a single match played at a neutral venue in Germany.

05.08.20   Old Trafford, Manchester: Manchester United – LASK Linz 2-1 (0-0)
Manchester United: Sergio Romero, Harry Maguire, Eric Bailly, Timothy Fosu-Mensah (84' Teden Mengi), Brandon Williams (72' Tahith Chong), Mata, Fred (64' Andreas Pereira), Jesse Lingard (63' Paul Pogba), Daniel James (84' Anthony Martial), Scott McTominay, Odion Ighalo. Coach: Ole Gunnar Solskjær.
LASK Linz: Alexander Schlager, Gernot Trauner, Reinhold Ranftl, Philipp Wiesinger (73' Thomas Sabitzer), Andrés Andrade (80' Petar Filipovic), James Holland, Peter Michorl, René Renner, Dominik Frieser, Husein Balic (66' Dominik Reiter), Marko Raguz.
Coach: Dominik Thalhammer
Goals: 55' Philipp Wiesinger 0-1, 57' Jesse Lingard 1-1, 88' Anthony Martial 2-1.
Referee: Anasthasios Sidiropoulos (GRE)

06.08.20   BayArena, Leverkusen: Bayer Leverkusen – Glasgow Rangers 1-0 (0-0)
Bayer Leverkusen: Lukás Hrádecký, Sven Bender (77' Jonathan Tah), Daley Sinkgraven, Edmond Tapsoba, Lars Bender (68' Aleksandar Dragovic), Charles Aránguiz, Exequiel Palacios (87' Adrian Stanilewicz), Kai Havertz, Florian Wirtz (68' Julian Baumgartlinger), Kevin Volland, Moussa Diaby (68' Leon Bailey). Coach: Peter Bosz.
Glasgow Rangers FC: Allan McGregor, James Tavernier (77' Nathan Patterson), Connor Goldson, Filip Helander, Borna Barisic, Steven Davis (66' Scott Arfield), Ryan Jack, Joe Aribo, Alfredo Morelos (77' Greg Stewart), Brandon Barker (60' Ianis Hagi), Ryan Kent (66' Jordan Jones). Coach: Steven Gerrard.
Goal: 51' Moussa Diaby 1-0.
Referee: Danny Makkelie (HOL)

06.08.20   Schauinsland-Reisen-Arena, Duisburg (GER): Sevilla FC – AS Roma 2-0 (2-0)
Sevilla FC: Yassine Bounou, Jesús Navas, Jules Koundé, Diego Carlos, Sergio Reguilón, Fernando, Éver Banega, Joan Jordán, Lucas Ocampos (90+6' Franco Vázquez), Youssef En-Nesyri (90+3' Luuk de Jong), Suso (67' Munir). Coach: Lopetegui.
AS Roma: Pau López, Gianluca Mancini, Ibañez, Aleksandar Kolarov (78' Gonzalo Villar), Bruno Peres, Amadou Diawara (57' Carles Pérez), Bryan Cristante, Leonardo Spinazzola, Nicolò Zaniolo (57' Lorenzo Pellegrini), Henrikh Mkhitaryan, Edin Dzeko.
Coach: Paulo Fonseca.
Goals: 22' Sergio Reguilón 1-0, 44' Youssef En-Nesyri 2-0.
Referee: Björn Kuipers (HOL)
Sent off: 90+10' Gianluca Mancini.

The result of this tie was decided in a single match played at a neutral venue in Germany.

06.08.20 Molineux Stadium, Wolverhampton:
Wolverhampton Wanderers – Olympiacos Piraeus 1-0 (1-0)
Wolverhampton Wanderers: Rui Patrício, Willy Boly, Matt Doherty, Conor Coady, Jonny Castro (17' Rúben Vinagre), João Moutinho, Romain Saïss, Rúben Neves, Daniel Podence (71' Leander Dendoncker), Raúl Jiménez, Adama Traoré (57' Diogo Jota). Coach: Nuno Espírito Santo.
Olympiacos Piraeus: Bobby Allain, Omar Elabdellaoui, Kostas Tsimikas, Pape Cissé, Ousseynou Ba, Mathieu Valbuena, Guilherme (82' Café), Andreas Bouchalakis (46' Kostas Fortounis), Georgios Masouras (46' Lazar Randjelovic), Mady Camara (65' Kouka), Youssef El-Arabi. Coach: Pedro Martins.
Goal: 8' Raúl Jiménez 1-0 (p).
Referee: Szymon Marciniak (POL)

06.08.20 St. Jakob-Park, Basel: FC Basel – Eintracht Frankfurt 1-0 (0-0)
FC Basel: Djordje Nikolic, Silvan Widmer, Omar Alderete, Raoul Petretta, Eray Cömart, Valentin Stocker (66' Ricky van Wolfswinkel), Fabian Frei, Taulant Xhaka (87' Yannick Marchand), Samuele Campo, Arthur Cabral (80' Kemal Ademi), Afimico Pululu (67' Jasper van der Werff). Coach: Marcel Koller.
Eintracht Frankfurt: Kevin Trapp, David Abraham, Martin Hinteregger, Danny da Costa (67' Timothy Chandler), Evan Obite N'Dicka (46' Makoto Hasebe), Sebastian Rode (67' Stefan Ilsanker), Filip Kostic, Dominik Kohr, Daichi Kamada, Bas Dost, André Silva (46' Gonçalo Paciência). Coach: Adi Hütter.
Goal: 88' Fabian Frei 1-0.
Referee: Antonio Mateu Lahoz (ESP)

QUARTER-FINALS

Due to the effects of the COVID-19 pandemic, all ties from the quarter-final stage onwards were played as a single match at a neutral venue in Germany with no specators allowed.

10.08.20 RheinEnergieStadion, Köln:
Manchester United – FC København 1-0 (0-0, 0-0) (a.e.t)
Manchester United: Sergio Romero, Harry Maguire, Eric Bailly (71' Victor Lindelöf), Aaron Wan-Bissaka, Brandon Williams, Paul Pogba, Fred (70' Nemanja Matic), Bruno Fernandes, Anthony Martial (120+1' Scott McTominay), Marcus Rashford (113' Jesse Lingard), Mason Greenwood (90' Mata). Coach: Ole Gunnar Solskjær.
FC København: Kalle Johnsson, Andreas Bjelland, Nicolai Boilesen (15' Pierre Bengtsson), Guillermo Varela (105' Karlo Bartolec), Victor Nelsson, Rasmus Falk (111' William Bøving Vick), Zeca, Pep Biel Mas (57' Bryan Oviedo), Jens Stage (105' Robert Mudrazija), Mohammed Daramy (57' Mikkel Kaufmann), Jonas Wind. Coach: Ståle Solbakken.
Goal: 95' Bruno Fernandes 1-0 (p).
Referee: Clément Turpin (FRA)

Manchester United won after extra-time.

10.08.20   Merkur Spiel-Arena, Düsseldorf: Internazionale – Bayer Leverkusen 2-1 (2-1)
Internazionale: Samir Handanovic, Ashley Young, Diego Godín, Stefan de Vrij, Danilo D'Ambrosio (59' Victor Moses), Alessandro Bastoni (84' Milan Skriniar), Marcelo Brozovic, Roberto Gagliardini (59' Christian Eriksen), Nicolò Barella, Romelu Lukaku, Lautaro Martínez (64' Alexis Sánchez). Coach: Antonio Conte.
Bayer Leverkusen: Lukás Hrádecký, Jonathan Tah, Daley Sinkgraven (68' Wendell), Edmond Tapsoba, Lars Bender (85' Karim Bellarabi), Julian Baumgartlinger (68' Nadiem Amiri), Kerem Demirbay, Exequiel Palacios (59' Leon Bailey), Kai Havertz, Kevin Volland (85' Lucas Alario), Moussa Diaby. Coach: Peter Bosz.
Goals: 15' Nicolò Barella 1-0, 21' Romelu Lukaku 2-0, 24' Kai Havertz 2-1.
Referee: Carlos del Cerro Grande (ESP)

11.08.20   Veltins-Arena, Gelsenkirchen: Shakhtar Donetsk – FC Basel 4-1 (2-0)
Shakhtar Donetsk: Andriy Pyatov, Sergiy Kryvtsov, Mykola Matviyenko, Valeriy Bondar, Dodô, Marlos (72' Manor Solomon), Taras Stepanenko, Taison (85' Tetê), Alan Patrick (78' Viktor Kovalenko), Marcos Antônio (85' Maycon), Júnior Moraes (85' Fernando). Coach: Luís Castro.
FC Basel: Djordje Nikolic, Silvan Widmer, Omar Alderete, Raoul Petretta, Jasper van der Werff (73' Ramires), Valentin Stocker (73' Ricky van Wolfswinkel), Fabian Frei, Taulant Xhaka (60' Yannick Marchand), Samuele Campo, Arthur Cabral (73' Kemal Ademi), Afimico Pululu. Coach: Marcel Koller.
Goals: 2' Júnior Moraes 1-0, 22' Taison 2-0, 75' Alan Patrick 3-0 (p), 88' Dodô 4-0, 90+2' Ricky van Wolfswinkel 4-1.
Referee: Michael Oliver (ENG)

11.08.20   Schauinsland-Reisen-Arena, Duisburg:
              Wolverhampton Wanderers – Sevilla FC 0-1 (0-0)
Wolverhampton Wanderers: Rui Patrício, Willy Boly, Matt Doherty, Conor Coady, Rúben Vinagre, João Moutinho (71' Pedro Neto), Romain Saïss, Leander Dendoncker, Rúben Neves, Raúl Jiménez, Adama Traoré (79' Diogo Jota). Coach: Nuno Espírito Santo.
Sevilla FC: Yassine Bounou, Jesús Navas, Diego Carlos, Sergio Reguilón, Jules Koundé, Éver Banega, Fernando, Lucas Ocampos, Suso (89' Munir), Joan Jordán (85' Franco Vázquez), Youssef En-Nesyri (85' Luuk de Jong). Coach: Lopetegui.
Goal: 88' Lucas Ocampos 0-1.
Referee: Daniele Orsato (ITA)

Raúl Jiménez missed a penalty kick (13').

SEMI-FINALS

16.08.20 RheinEnergieStadion, Köln: Sevilla FC – Manchester United 2-1 (1-1)
Sevilla FC: Yassine Bounou, Jesús Navas, Diego Carlos, Sergio Reguilón, Jules Koundé, Éver Banega, Fernando, Lucas Ocampos (56' Munir), Suso (75' Franco Vázquez), Joan Jordán (87' Nemanja Gudelj), Youssef En-Nesyri (56' Luuk de Jong). Coach: Lopetegui.
Manchester United: David de Gea, Victor Lindelöf, Harry Maguire, Aaron Wan-Bissaka (87' Daniel James), Brandon Williams (87' Timothy Fosu-Mensah), Paul Pogba, Fred, Bruno Fernandes, Anthony Martial, Marcus Rashford (87' Mata), Mason Greenwood (90+3' Odion Ighalo). Coach: Ole Gunnar Solskjær.
Goals: 9' Bruno Fernandes 0-1 (pen), 26' Suso 1-1, 78' Luuk de Jong 2-1.
Referee: Dr. Felix Brych (Germany)

17.08.20 Merkur Spiel-Arena, Düsseldorf: Internazionale – Shakhtar Donetsk 5-0 (1-0)
Internazionale: Samir Handanovic, Ashley Young (66' Cristiano Biraghi), Diego Godín, Stefan de Vrij, Danilo D'Ambrosio (81' Victor Moses), Alessandro Bastoni, Marcelo Brozovic (85' Stefano Sensi), Roberto Gagliardini, Nicolò Barella, Romelu Lukaku (85' Sebastiano Esposito), Lautaro Martínez (81' Christian Eriksen). Coach: Antonio Conte.
Shakhtar Donetsk: Andriy Pyatov, Sergiy Kryvtsov, Davit Khocholava, Mykola Matviyenko, Dodô, Marlos (75' Yevhen Konopyanka), Taras Stepanenko, Taison, Alan Patrick (59' Manor Solomon), Marcos Antônio, Júnior Moraes. Coach: Luís Castro.
Goals: 19' Lautaro Martínez 1-0, 64' Danilo D'Ambrosio 2-0, 74' Lautaro Martínez 3-0, 78', 84' Romelu Lukaku 4-0, 5-0.
Referee: Szymon Marciniak (POL)

FINAL

21.08.20 RheinEnergieStadion, Köln: Sevilla FC – Internazionale 3-2 (2-2)
Sevilla FC: Yassine Bounou, Jesús Navas, Diego Carlos (86' Nemanja Gudelj), Sergio Reguilón, Jules Koundé, Éver Banega, Fernando, Lucas Ocampos (71' Munir), Suso (78' Franco Vázquez), Joan Jordán, Luuk de Jong (85' Youssef En-Nesyri). Coach: Lopetegui.
Internazionale: Samir Handanovic, Ashley Young, Diego Godín (90' Antonio Candreva), Stefan de Vrij, Danilo D'Ambrosio (78' Victor Moses), Alessandro Bastoni, Marcelo Brozovic, Roberto Gagliardini (78' Christian Eriksen), Nicolò Barella, Romelu Lukaku, Lautaro Martínez (78' Alexis Sánchez). Coach: Antonio Conte.
Goals: 5' Romelu Lukaku 0-1 (pen), 12', 33' Luuk de Jong 1-1, 2-1, 36' Diego Godín 2-2, 74' Romelu Lukaku 3-2 (og).
Referee: Danny Makkelie (HOL)

UEFA EUROPA LEAGUE
2020-2021

PRELIMINARY ROUND

18.08.20   Estadi Comunal, Andorra la Vella: UE Engordany – FK Zeta Golubovci 1-3 (0-1)
UE Engordany: Coca, Lucas Sousa, Pedro Muñoz, Matías Rudler, Edson (75' Guillaume Lopez), Mario Spano, Kyllan Ramé (87' João Teixeira), Sébastien Aguéro, Luigi San Nicolas (67' Morgan Lafont), Aaron Sánchez, Sebastián Gómez. Coach: José Prades.
FK Zeta Golubovci: Zoran Akovic, Aleksandar Milic, Ognjen Djinovic, Zvonko Ceklic, Goran Milojko, Srdjan Krstovic, Lazar Lambulic (89' Ilija Tripunovic), Amel Tuzovic, Mijat Lambulic (81' Matija Lambulic), Vasko Kalezic, Ivan Vuksevic (89' Nemanja Djurovic). Coach: Dejan Ragonovic.
Goals: 45+1' Ivan Vukcevic 0-1, 54' Mijat Lambulic 0-2, 63' Lazar Lambulic 0-3, 90+4' Sebastián Gómez 1-3 (p).
Referee: Juxhin Xhaja (ALB)

20.08.20   Victoria Stadium, Gibraltar: St Joseph's FC – B36 Tórshavn 1-2 (1-2)
St Joseph's FC: Mateo, Pecci, Federico Villar, Ezequiel, Carlos Carrasco (77' Ángel Guirado), Nano, Alain Pons (87' Aymen Mouelhi), Juanma González, Domingo Ferrer (61' Pedro Fernández), Boro, Juanfri. Coach: Raúl Procopio.
B36 Tórshavn: Rói Hentze, Andrias Eriksen, Bjarni Petersen (61' Benjamin Heinesen), Sonni Nattestad, Alex Mellemgaard (79' Erling Jacobsen), Magnus Holm Jacobsen (86' Stefan Radosavljevic), Eli Nielsen, Árni Frederiksberg, Meinhard Olsen, Sebastian Pingel, Michal Przybylski. Coach: Jákup á Borg.
Goals: 28' Michal Przybylski 0-1, 30' Boro 1-1, 43' Alex Mellemgaard 1-2 (p).
Referee: Jasmin Sabotic (LUX)

20.08.20   Svangaskard, Toftir: NSÍ Runavík – Barry Town United 5-1 (0-0)
NSÍ Runavík: Tórdur Thomsen, Oddur Højgaard, Jóhan Davidsen, Rógvi Nielsen, Jesper Christjansen (82' Aron Knudsen), Petur Knudsen, Jann Benjaminsen, Mórits Heini Mortensen, Bárdur Jógvansson-Hansen (60' Pætur Skipanes), Salmundur Bech, Klæmint Olsen (79' Steffan Abrahamsson Løkin. Coach: Glenn Leif Ståhl.
Barry Town United: Mike Lewis, Chris Hugh, Luke Cooper, Luke Cummings, Robbie Patten (70' Michael George), David Cotterill (70' Jordan Cotterill), Theo Wharton, Clayton Green, Evan Press, Kayne McLaggon, Nathaniel Jarvis (82' Keyon Reffell). Coach: Gavin Chesterfield.
Goals: 52', 63' Klæmint Olsen 1-0, 2-0, 67' Petur Kundsen 3-0, 74' Klæmint Olsen 4-0, 83' Steffan Abrahamsson Løkin 5-0, 88' Kayne McLaggon 5-1.
Referee: Pavel Rejzek (CZE)

NSÍ Runavík played their home match at Svangaskard, Toftir, instead of their regular stadium Vid Løkin, Runavík, which did not meet UEFA requirements.

20.08.20 Estadi Comunal, Andorra la Vella:
FC Santa Coloma – Iskra Danilovgrad 0-0 (a.e.t.)
FC Santa Coloma: Casals, Moisés San Nicolas, Juanma Miranda, Álex Sánchez, Aleix Cistero, Txus Rubio, Marc Rebés (116' Javi Camochu), Enric Pi (46' Diego Nájero), Jordi Aláez, Luis Blanco (81' Pedro Santos), Alexandre Martínez (90' Hamza Bouharma). Coach: Jorquera.
Iskra Danilovgrad: Srdjan Blazic, Nikola Kumburovic, Luka Malesevic, Milos Drincic, Irfan Sahman, Balsa Boricic, Vladislav Rogosic (89' Bogdan Milic), Miroje Jovanovic (113' Ognjen Obradovic), Aldin Adzovic (68' Milan Djurisic), Sho Yamamoto (81' Bogdan Mandic), Ivan Vukovic. Coach: Aleksandar Nedovic.
Referee: Keith Kennedy (NIR)
Sent off: 40' Jordi Aláez.

Iskra Danilovgrad won on penalties after extra-time (4-3).
Penalties: Djurisic 1-0, Cisteró 1-1, Obradovic 2-1, Miranda 2-2, Vukovic 3-2,
Bouharma missed, Boricic missed, Camochu 3-3, Drincic 4-3, Santos missed.

20.08.20 The Oval, Belfast: Glentoran Belfast – HB Tórshavn 1-0 (1-0)
Glentoran Belfast: Dayle Coleing, Patrick McClean, Caolan Marron, Keith Cowan, Marcus Kane, Gaël Bigirimana, Chris Gallagher, Seanan Clucas (68' Luke McCullough), Rory Donnelly (83' Cameron Stewart), Robbie McDaid, Paul O'Neill (72' Jamie McDonagh). Coach: Mick McDermott.
HB Tórshavn: Teitur Gestsson, Jógvan Davidsen (62' René Joensen), Delphin Tshiembe, Daniel Johansen, Bartal Wardum, Hedin Hansen, Dan í Soylu (75' Mads Mikkelsen), Pætur Petersen (46' Adrian Justinussen), Mathias Nygaard, Hilmar Leon Jakobsen, Mikkel Dahl. Coach: Jens Berthel Askou.
Goal: 42' Robbie McDaid 1-0.
Referee: Lukas Fähndrich (SUI)

20.08.20 The Showgrounds, Coleraine: Coleraine FC – SP La Fiorita 1-0 (0-0)
Coleraine FC: Gareth Deane, Lyndon Kane, Aaron Canning, Ben Doherty, Stephen O'Donnell, Aaron Jarvis, Stephen Lowry, Josh Carson (46' Stewart Nixon), Aaron Traynor, James McLaughlin, Curtis Allen (62' Eoin Bradley). Coach: Oran Kearney.
SP La Fiorita: Gianluca Vivan, Andrea Brighi, Roberto Di Maio, Andrea Grandoni, Marco Gasperoni, Simone Errico (65' Tommaso Guidi), Simone Loiodice, Armando Amati, Christian Damiano (74' Michele Pieri), Danilo Rinaldi, Lucio Peluso (79' Marcello Mularoni). Coach: Nicola Berardi.
Goal: 89' James McLaughlin 1-0.
Referee: Christian-Petru Ciochirca (AUT)

21.08.20 San Marino Stadium, Serravalle: SP Tre Penne – KF Gjilani 1-3 (1-1)
SP Tre Penne: Mattia Migani, Christofer Genestreti, Nicolas Lombardi, Riccardo Mezzadri, Luca Patregnani, Alex Gasperoni (68' Davide Cesarini), Nicola Gai, Michael Battistini, Luca Sorrentino, Luca Ceccaroli (50' Enrico Cibelli), Alessandro Chiurato (74' Riccardo Pieri). Coach: Stefano Ceci.
KF Gjilani: Enea Koliçi, Oltion Rapa, Armend Halili (83' Ylber Kastrati), Erlis Frashëri, Franc Veliu, Ardit Hila, Muhamed Useini, Fiton Hajdari (79' Muhamed Dubova), Fjoart Jonuzi (50' Edvin Kuc), Darko Nikac, Gerhard Progni. Coach: Gentian Mezani.
Goals: 16' Nicola Gai 1-0, 24' Darko Nikac 1-1, 64' Fiton Hajdari 1-2, 68' Ardir Hila 1-3.
Referee: Alex Troleis (FRO)
Sent off: 43' Luca Sorrentino.

The match was originally scheduled to be played on 20th August 2020, but was postponed until 21st August 2020, after a player from KF Gjilani tested positive for SARS-2 coronavirus.

22.08.20 Victoria Stadium, Gibraltar: Lincoln Red Imps – Prishtina KF 3-0
Referee: David Munro (SCO)

The match was originally scheduled to be played on 18th August 2020, but was postponed until 22nd August 2020, after several members from Prishtina's delegation tested positive for the SARS-2 coronavirus and the whole team was put into quarantine by the Gibraltarian authorities. On 22nd August 2020 it was clear that the match could not be played due to eight players from Prishtina KF testing positive for SARS-2 coronavirus and the whole second team being put into quarantine by the Gibraltarian authorities. Lincoln Red Imps were subsequently awarded a technical 3-0 victory by UEFA according to the regulations related to COVID-19.

FIRST QUALIFYING ROUND

25.08.20 LFF stadionas, Vilnius: FK Riteriai – Derry City 3-2 (1-1, 2-2) (a.e.t.)
FK Riteriai: Tadas Simaitis, Akseli Kalermo, Ricardas Sveikauskas, Dominykas Barauskas, Ángel Lezama, Deividas Malzinskas, Mindaugas Grigaravicius (116' Bright Godwin), Tomas Dombrauskis (88' Matas Ramanauskas, Lajo Traore (77' Dominyk Kodz), Donatas Kazlauskas, Gytis Paulauskas (101' Rokas Filipavicius). Coach: Tommi Petteri Pikkarainen.
Derry City: Peter Cherrie, Ciarán Coll, Darren Cole, Colm Horgan, Eoin Toal, Adam Hammill, Conor McCormack, Joe Thomson (73' Connor Clifford, 112' Gerardo Bruna), Jake Dunwoody (56' Stephen Mallon), James Akintunde, Ibrahim Meité (85' Ciaron Harkin).
Coach: Declan Devine.
Goals: 18' Joe Thomson 0-1, 39', 49' Gytis Paulauskas 1-1, 2-1 , 63' Eoin Toal 2-2, 91' Donatas Kazlauskas 3-2.
Referee: Ville Nevalainen (FIN)

FK Riteriai won after extra time.

26.08.20   Stade Municipal de Differdange, Differdange:
            Progrès Niederkorn – FK Zeta Golubovci 3-0 (1-0)
Progrès Niederkorn: Sebastian Flauss, Tom Laterza, Adrien Ferino, Metin Karayer, Aldin Skenderovic, Sébastien Thill, Kevin Holtz (67' Belmin Muratovic), Christian Silaj, Ryad Habbas (78' Antonio Luisi), Kempes Tekiela, Irvin Latic (86' Florik Shala).
Coach: Roland Vrabec.
FK Zeta Golubovci: Zoran Akovic, Aleksandar Milic, Zvonko Ceklic (67' Nemanja Djurovic), Ognjen Djinovic, Alphonse Soppo, Goran Milojko, Vasko Kalezic (62' Elom Nya-Vedji), Amel Tuzovic, Srdjan Krstovic, Ivan Vukcevic, Mijat Lambulic (55' Lazar Lambulic).
Coach: Dejan Roganovic.
Goals: 11', 55' Kempes Tekiela 1-0, 2-0 (p), 90+3' Sébastien Thill 3-0.
Referee: Rahim Hasanov (AZE)

Progrès Niederkorn played their home match at Stade Municipal de Differdange, Differdange, instead of their regular stadium Stade Jos Haupert, Niederkorn, which did not meet UEFA requirements.

27.08.20   Olimpiska centra Ventspils Stadiona, Ventspils:
            FK Ventspils – Dinamo-Auto 2-1 (1-1)
FK Ventspils: Dele Alampasu, Giorgi Rekhviashvili, Andriy Sakhnevich, Giorgi Mchedlishvili, Dmitrijs Litvinskis, Guga Palavandishvili, Giorgi Eristavi, Lucas Villela, Abdulla Genaev (70' Daniils Ulimbasevs), Kaspars Svārups (80' Chris Ondong Mba), Evgeny Kozlov. Coach: Viorel Frunza.
Dinamo-Auto: Victor Straistari, Radu Rogac, Oleksandr Masalov, Dmitri Nagiyev (78' Octavian Bulat), Vadim Dijinari, Maxim Mihaliov, Vadim Paireli, Alexandr Belousov, Artiom Bilinschii, Yehor Kondratyuk, Dumitru Rogac. Coach: Igor Dobrovolskiy.
Goals: 15' Dumitru Rogac 0-1, 22' Lucas Villela 1-1, 75' Evgeny Kozlov 2-1 (p).
Referee: Eldorjan Hamiti (ALB)
Sent off: 90+4' Guga Palavandishvili.

27.08.20   Stadion Qajimuqan Munaytpasov, Shymkent: FK Ordabasy – FC Botosani 1-2 (1-2)
FK Ordabasy: Bekkhan Shayzada, Viktor Dmitrenko (84' Mirzad Mehanovic), Pablo Fontanello, Damir Dautov, João Paulo (76' Toktar Zhangylyshbay), Abdoulaye Diakhaté, May Mahlangu, Ziguy Badibanga, Rúben Brígido, Timur Dosmagambetov, Sergey Khizhnichenko (46' Aleksandar Simcevic). Coach: Kakhaber Tskhadadze.
FC Botosani: Eduard Pap, Marcel Holzmann, Stefan Ashkovski (89' Alexandru Tiganasu), Alin Seroni, Denis Harut, Andrei Chindris, Bryan Mendoza, Eduard Florescu, Jonathan Rodriguez, Reagy Ofosu (74' Hamidou Keyta), Marko Dugandzic (90+2' Mihai Roman).
Coach: Marius Croitoru.
Goals: 25' Marcel Holzmann 0-1, 31' May Mahlangu 1-1, 33' Marko Dugandzic 1-2.
Referee: Rauf Jabbarov (AZE)

27.08.20 Ortaliq Stadion, Almaty: KF Kairat – FC Noah 4-1 (2-1)
KF Kairat: Stas Pokatilov, Dino Mikanovic, Rade Dugalic, Nuraly Alip, Kamo Hovhannisyan, Nebojsa Kosovic, Jacek Góralski, Konrad Wrzesinski (59' Aybol Abiken), Gulzhygit Alykulov (74' Daniyar Uzenov), Vágner Love, Abat Aymbetov (79' Aderinsola Eseola).
Coach: Aleksey Shpilevskiy.
FC Noah: Valerio Vimercati, Vladislav Kryuchkov, Mikhail Kovalenko (71' Saná Gomes), Soslan Kagermazov, Denis Dedechko, Pavel Deobald (46' Artem Simonyan), Vladimir Azarov (72' Benik Hovhannisyan), Eduards Emsis, Dmitri Lavrishchev, Kirill Bor, Danu Spataru.
Coach: Vladimir Japalau.
Goals: 8' Kirill Bor 0-1, 12' Gulzhygit Alykulov 1-1, 35', 70' Vágner Love 2-1, 3-1, 90+4' Aderinsola Eseola 4-1.
Referee: Kristoffer Karlsson (SWE)

27.08.20 Stadiumi Niko Dovana, Durrës: KF Teuta Durrës – Beitar Jerusalem 2-0 (1-0)
KF Teuta Durrës: Stivi Frashëri, Renato Arapi, Blagoja Todorovski, Rustem Hoxha, Alexandros Kouros, Fabjan Beqja (63' Ildi Gruda), Emiljano Vila, Albano Aleksi, Florent Avdyli (90+2' Ledjo Beqja), Blerim Krasniqi (65' Rubin Hebaj), Lorenco Vila.
Coach: Edi Martini.
Beitar Jerusalem: Itamar Nitzan, Orel Dgani, Diogo Verdasca, Oren Biton (76' Uri Magbo), Shay Konstantini, Ofir Kriaf, Ali Mohamed Muhammad, Liran Rotman (46' Gleofilo Hasselbaink Vlijter), Idan Vered, Eliran Atar (70' Shalom Edri), Shlomi Azulay.
Coach: Roni Levy.
Goals: 6' Blerim Krasniqi 1-0, 87' Rubin Hebaj 2-0.
Referee: Nikolas Neokleous (CYP)

27.08.20 Gradski Stadion, Banja Luka: Borac Banja Luka – FK Sutjeska Niksic 1-0 (1-0)
Borac Banja Luka: Bojan Pavlovic, Nemanja Janicic, Marko Jovanovic, Djordje Cosic, Stojan Vranjes, Goran Zakaric, Sinisa Dujakovic (79' Sasa Kajkut), Marko Brtan (63' Aleksandar Vojinovic), Almedin Dino Ziljkic, Vladan Danilovic, Jovo Lukic (72' Aleksandar Radulovic).
Coach: Vlado Jagodic.
FK Sutjeska Niksic: Vladan Giljen, Darko Bulatovic, Nikola Stijepovic, Filip Mitrovic, Dragan Grivic, Marko Cetkovic, Damir Kojasevic (10' Milivoje Raicevic), Branislav Jankovic (74' Bozo Markovic), Milutin Osmajic, Balsa Dubljevic (67' Aleksa Marusic), Admir Adrovic.
Coach: Dragan Radojicic.
Goal: 35' Stojan Vranjes 1-0.
Referee: Morten Krogh (DEN)

27.08.20 Stadyen Dynamo, Minsk: Dinamo Minsk – Piast Gliwice 0-2 (0-1)
Dinamo Minsk: Evgeniy Pomazan, Sergey Matveychik, Igor Shitov, Artem Sukhotskyi, Miha Goropevsek, Dominik Dinga, Edgar Olekhnovich (73' Kirill Vergeychik), Vladislav Klimovich, Ivan Bakhar, Silas (59' Mikhail Kozlov), Yevgeniy Shikavka (79' Vladimir Khvashchinskiy). Coach: Leonid Kuchuk.
Piast Gliwice: Frantisek Plach, Mikkel Kirkeskov, Jakub Czerwinski, Tomás Huk, Martin Konczkowski, Gerard Badía (72' Dominik Steczyk), Patryk Lipski, Patryk Sokolowski, Jakub Swierczok, Krisztófer Vida (82' Sebastian Milewski), Piotr Parzyszek (55' Michal Zyro).
Coach: Waldemar Fornalik.
Goals: 10' Patryk Lipski 0-1, 56' Jakub Swierczok 0-2.
Referee: Lazar Lukic (SRB)

27.08.20 Victoria Stadium, Gilbraltar: Lincoln Red Imps – Union Titus Pétange 2-0 (1-0)
Lincoln Red Imps: Lolo Soler, Scott Wiseman, Bernardo Lopes, Roy Chipolina, Ethan Britto, Mustapha Yahaya, Jack Sergeant, Graeme Torilla, Anthony Hernandez (73' Kyle Casciaro), Lee Casciaro (78' James Coombes), Kike Gómez (85' Eric Same). Coach: William.
Union Titur Pétange: Tom Ottele, Alexandre Laurienté, Mike Schneider (75' Joel Rodrigues da Cruz), Mounir Hamzaoui, Allan Hauguel, Yannick Kakoko, Boyou Kodjia, Bilel El Hamzaoui, Abdoul Kabore, Robert Maah (63' Jonathan Nanizayamo), Luca Duriatti (55' Eliot Gashi). Coach: Ismaël Bouzid.
Goals: 36' Lee Casciaro 1-0, 90+5' Mustapha Yahaya 2-0.
Referee: Helgi Mikael Jónasson (ISL)

27.08.20 Bakcell Arena, Baku: Neftçi PFK – KF Shkupi 2-1 (0-0)
Neftçi PFK: Aqil Mammadov, Thallyson (90+2' Vojislav Stankovic), Mamadou Mbodj, Anton Krivotsyuk, Dzhabir Amirli, Steeven Joseph-Monrose (90' Mirabdulla Abbasov), Emin Makhmudov, Namiq Alasgarov, Sabir Bougrine, Mamadou Kane, Yusuf Lawal. Coach: Fuzuli Mammadov.
KF Shkupi: Kristijan Naumovski, Darko Glisic, Filip Gligorov, Besart Krivanjeva, Bianor, Sabit Bilalli, Besar Iseni (65' Freddy Álvarez), Lamine Diack, Dembo Darboe, Ilirid Ademi (73' Fatjon Jusufi), Oumar Goudiaby. Coaches: Muharem Bajrami & Vladimir Kolev.
Goals: 66' Sabir Bougrine 1-0, 88' Anton Krivotsyuk 2-0, 90+3' Dembo Darboe 2-1.
Referee: Aleksandrs Golubevs (LAT)
Sent off: 70' Oumar Goudiaby.

27.08.20 Aspmyra Stadion, Bodø: FK Bodø/Glimt – Kauno Zalgiris 6-1 (2-0)
FK Bodø/Glimt: Nikita Haikin, Marius Høibråten, Marius Lode (59' Ole Amund Sveen), Alfons Sampsted, Fredrik Bjørkan (62' Aleksander Foosnæs), Ulrik Saltnes, Patrick Berg, Jens Hauge, Philip Zinckernagel (77' Sebastian Tounekti), Sondre Fet, Victor Boniface.
Coach: Kjetil Knutsen.
Kauno Zalgiris: Deividas Mikelionis, Steven Trichot, Egidijus Vaitkunas, Martynas Dapkus, Rudinilson Silva, Karolis Silkaitis, Linas Pilibaitis (73' Deividas Sesplaukis), Yuriy Bushman, Simonas Urbys (82' Benas Anisas), Gratas Sirgedas, Emmanuel David (61' Philip Otele).
Coach: Rokas Garastas.
Goals: 27', 36' Philip Zinckernagel 1-0, 2-0, 52', 59' Jens Hauge 3-0, 4-0 (p), 78' Philip Otele 4-1, 79' Victor Boniface 5-1, 81' Sebastian Tounekti 6-1.
Referee: Kaarlo Oskari Hämäläinen (FIN)

27.08.20 Neo GSP Stadium, Nicosia: Apollon Limassol – FC Saburtalo Tbilisi 5-1 (2-0)
Apollon Limassol: Joël Mall, Valentin Roberge, Attila Szalai, Ioannis Pittas, Nicolas Diguiny (64' Sasa Markovic), Héctor Yuste, Florentin Matei (75' Petros Psychas), Esteban Sachetti, Djordje Denic (64' Diego Aguirre), Bagaliy Dabo, Giannis Gianniotas.
Coach: Sofronis Avgousti.
FC Saburtalo Tbilisi: Lazare Kupatadze, Levan Kakubava, Tedore Grigalashvili, Gagi Margvelashvili, Nikoloz Mali, Olivier Boumal (78' Giorgi Gocholeishvili), Jeroen Lumu (63' Giorgi Guliashvili), Sandro Altunashvili, Alwyn Tera (66' Anri Chichinadze), Iuri Tabatadze, Beka Kavtaradze. Coach: Teimuraz Shalamberidze.
Goals: 3', 32' Bagaliy Dabo 1-0, 2-0, 59' Nicolas Diguiny 3-0, 69' Giorgi Guliashvili 3-1, 76' Bagaliy Dabo 4-1, 86' Giannis Gianniotas 5-1.
Referee: Adrien Jaccottet (SUI)
Sent off: 81' Anri Chichinadze.

Apollon Limassol played their home match at Neo GSP Stadium, Nicosia, instead of their regular stadium Tsirio Stadium, Limassol, which did not meet UEFA requirements.

27.08.20 Vazgen Sargsyan anvan Hanrapetakan Marzadasht, Yerevan:
  FC Alashkert – FK Renova 0-1 (0-0)
FC Alashkert: Ognjen Cancarevic, Risto Mitrevski, Taron Voskanyan, Igor Gonchar, Bryan Garcia, Tiago Cametá (67' Aghvan Papikyan), Artak Grigoryan (80' Nikita Tankov), Thiago Galvão, Wangu Gome, Perdigão (61' Pape Camara), Aleksandar Glisic.
Coach: Eghishe Melikyan.
FK Renova: Hadis Velii, Nenad Miskovski, Xhelil Abdulla, Bashkim Velija, Argjent Gafuri (86' Artan Veliu), Saimir Fetai, Burim Sadiki, Emran Ramadani (71' Alen Jasaroski), Alush Gavazaj, Remzi Selmani (63' Filip Stojchevski), Shefit Shefiti. Coach: Bujar Islami.
Goal: 58' Nenad Miskovski 0-1.
Referee: Nick Walsh (SCO)

FC Alashkert played their home match at Vazgen Sargsyan anvan Hanrapetakan Marzadasht, Yerevan, instead of their regular stadium Alashkert Stadium Yerevan, which did not meet UEFA requirements.

27.08.20 Kapital Bank Arena, Sumgayit: Sumgayit FK – KF Shkëndija 79 0-2 (0-0)
Sumgayit FK: Mekhti Dzhenetov, Vurgun Hüseynov, Elvin Badalov, Dzhamaldin Khodzhaniyazov, Tellur Mütallimov, Elvin Mammadov (73' Rüfat Abdullazade), Vüqar Mustafayev, Rahim Sadikhov, Khayal Najafov (63' Sabuhi Abdullazade), Süleyman Ahmadov (62' Adam Hemati), Ali Ghorbani. Coach: Aykhan Abbasov.
KF Shkëndija 79: Kostadin Zahov, Mevlan Murati (90+5' Medzit Neziri), Antonio Pavic, Egzon Bejtulai, Ján Krivák, Bruno Dita, Valon Ahmedi, Ennur Totre, Omar Imeri (77' Arbin Zejnullai), Besart Ibraimi, Ljupco Doriev (90+3' Abou Baker Es Sahhal).
Coach: Ernest Gjoka.
Goals: 56' Besart Ibraimi 0-1 (p), 89' Ljupco Doriev 0-2 (p).
Referee: Arman Ismuratov (KAZ)
Sent off: 89' Tellur Mütallimov.

27.08.20 Stadion Stozice, Ljubljana:
  Olimpija Ljubljana – Víkingur Reykjavík 2-1 (0-1, 1-1) (a.e.t.)
Olimpija Ljubljana: Ziga Frelih, Uros Korun, Miral Samardzic, Jan Andrejasic (46' Matic Fink), Enrik Ostrc, Timi Elsnik, Angel Lyaskov (91' Michael Pavlovic), Mihail Caimacov, Ante Vukusic (71' Jucie Lupeta), Drazen Bagaric (58' Jakov Blagaic), Radivoj Bosic.
Coach: Dino Skender.
Víkingur Reykjavík: Ingvar Jónsson, Sölvi Ottesen, Kári Árnason, Halldór Sigurdsson, Atli Barkarson, David Atlason (96' Dofri Snorrason), Július Magnússon (60' Viktor Örlygur Andrason), Erlingur Agnarsson, Nikolaj Hansen (60' Halldór Thórdarson, 110' Helgi Gudjónsson), Óttar Karlsson, Ágúst Edvald Hlynsson. Coach: Arnar Gunnlaugsson.
Goals: 27' Óttar Karlsson 0-1, 88' Matic Fink 1-1, 106' Radivoj Bosic 2-1.
Referee: Walter Altmann (AUT)
Sent off: 5' Sölvi Ottesen.

Olimpija Ljubljana won after extra time.

27.08.20   MOL Aréna Sóstó, Székesfehérvár:
Fehérvar FC – Bohemians FC 1-1 (1-1, 1-1) (a.e.t.)
Fehérvár FC: Ádam Kovácsik, Attila Fiola, Loïc Négo, Stopira, Adrián Rus, Ivan Petryak (109' Krisztián Géresi), Lyes Houri, Alef (75' Máté Pátkai), Nemanja Nikolic (74' Armin Hodzic), Evandro (101' Boban Nikolov), Funsho Bamgboye. Coach: Gábor Márton.
Bohemians FC: Stephen McGuinness, Robert Cornwall (71' James Finnerty), Anto Breslin, Dan Casey, Andy Lyons, Keith Ward (83' Dawson Devoy), Keith Buckley (109' Daniel Mandroiu), Kris Twardek, Jonathan Lunney (79' Conor Levingston), Andre Wright, Daniel Grant. Coach: Keith Long.
Goals: 22' Keith Ward 0-1, 37' Nemanja Nikolic 1-1 (p).
Referee: Timotheos Christofi (CYP)

Fehérvár FC won on penalties after extra time (4-2).
Penalties: Hodzic missed, Mandroiu 0-1, Nikolov 1-1, Levingston 1-2, Géresi 2-2, Casey missed, Stopira 3-2, Twardek missed, Houri 4-2.

27.08.20   Vilniaus LFF stadionas, Vilnius: FK Zalgiris – Paide Linnameeskond 2-0 (2-0)
FK Zalgiris: Martin Berkovec, Donovan Slijngard, Ivan Tatomirovic, Nemanja Ljubisavljevic, Saulius Mikoliūnas, Hugo Vidémont (90+1' Francis Kyeremeh), Domantas Simkus, Modestas Vorobjovas, Karlo Kamenar (68' Mantas Kuklys), Andrija Kaludjerovic, Liviu Antal (81' Richie Ennin). Coach: Aleksei Baga.
Paide Linnameeskond: Mait Toom, Karl Mööl, Martin Kase, Kristjan Pelt, Sander Sinilaid (46' Bruno Caprioli), Sergei Mosnikov, Andre Frolov (76' Deabeas Owusu-Sekyere), Siim Luts (63' Edrisa Lubega), Joseph Saliste, Henri Anier, Edgar Tur. Coach: Vjatseslav Zahovaiko.
Goals: 9' Andrija Kaludjerovic 1-0, 32' Liviu Antal 2-0.
Referee: Petri Viljanen (FIN)

27.08.20   Lerkendal Stadion, Trondheim: Rosenborg BK – Breidablik 4-2 (4-0)
Rosenborg BK: Julian Lund, Tore Reginiussen, Even Hovland, Vegar Hedenstad (80' Waren Kamanzi), Erlend Reitan, Gjermund Åsen, Kristoffer Zachariassen, Edvard Tagseth (61' Filip Brattbakk), Torgeir Børven, Dino Islamovic, Carl Holse. Coach: Trond Henriksen.
Breidablik: Anton Ari Einarsson, Damir Muminovic, Elfar Helgason, Andri Yeoman (39' Oliver Sigurjónsson), Höskuldur Gunnlaugsson, Gísli Eyjólfsson, Viktor Einarsson, Brynjólfur Willumsson, Róbert Thorkelsson (78' Viktor Örn Margeirsson), Thomas Mikkelsen, Alexander Sigurdarson (70' Kristinn Steindórsson). Coach: Óskar Hrafn Thorvaldsson.
Goals: 3' Torgeir Børven 1-0, 17' Tore Reginiussen 2-0, 24' Even Hovland 3-0, 29' Torgeir Børven 4-0, 60' Viktor Einarsson 4-1, 90+1' Thomas Mikkelsen 4-2 (p).
Referee: Matthew De Gabriele (MLT)

27.08.20   Tele2 Arena, Stockholm: Hammarby IF – Puskás Akadémia FC 3-0 (2-0)
Hammarby IF: David Ousted, David Fällman, Mads Fenger, Mohanad Jeahze (80' Vladimir Rodic), Imad Khalili, Abdul Khalili (77' Alexander Kacaniklic), Darijan Bojanic, Jeppe Andersen, Tim Söderström, Paulinho, Muamer Tankovic (55' Aron Jóhannsson).
Coach: Stefan Billborn.
Puskás Akadémia FC: Martin Auerbach, Kamen Hadzhiev, Roland Szolnoki, Csaba Spandler, Zsolt Nagy, László Deutsch, Jakub Plsek, Liridon Latifi (61' György Komáromi), Tamás Kiss (81' Benedek Kalmár), Márton Radics, Weslen Júnior (69' Marius Corbu).
Coach: Zsolt Hornyák.
Goals: 14' Abdul Khalili 1-0, 32' Darijan Bojanic 2-0, 84' Paulinho 3-0.
Referee: Mario Zebec (CRO)

27.08.20   Eleda Stadion, Malmö: Malmö FF – KS Cracovia Kraków 2-0 (2-0)
Malmö FF: Marko Johansson, Eric Larsson, Jonas Knudsen, Franz Brorsson, Anel Ahmedhodzic, Søren Rieks, Anders Christiansen, Oscar Lewicki, Erdal Rakip (75' Arnór Traustason), Jo Inge Berget (67' Amin Sarr), Isaac Kiese Thelin. Coach: Jon Dahl Tomasson.
KS Cracovia Kraków: Lukás Hrosso, Cornel Rapa, David Jablonský, Michal Helik, Michal Siplak (58' Diego Ferraresso), Sergiu Hanca, Pelle van Amersfoort, Mateusz Wdowiak, Florian Loshaj, Marcos Álvarez (79' Tomás Vestenický), Rivaldinho (46' Milan Dimun). Coach: Michal Probierz.
Goals: 1' Jo Inge Berget 1-0, 44' Søren Rieks 2-0.
Referee: Urs Schnyder (SUI)

27.08.20   Ceres Park & Arena, Aarhus: Aarhus GF – FC Honka 5-2 (3-1)
Aarhus GF: William Eskelinen, Casper Højer Nielsen, Alexander Munksgaard, Frederik Tingager, Sebastian Hausner, Nikolai Poulsen, Patrick Olsen, Bror Blume (86' Benjamin Hvidt), Jón Dagur Thorsteinsson (70' Søren Tengstedt), Gift Links (78' Milan Jevtovic), Patrick Mortensen. Coach: David Nielsen.
FC Honka: Tim Murray, Henri Aalto (69' Macoumba Kandji), Dani Hatakka, Jonas Levänen, Robert Ivanov, Konsta Rasimus, Javi Hervás, Jerry Voutilainen, Lucas Kaufmann, Jean Dongou, Borjas Martín (79' Arlind Sejdiu). Coach: Vesa Vasara.
Goals: 21' Frederik Tingager 1-0, 29' Patrick Mortensen 2-0, 35' Borjas Martín 2-1, 45+2' Patrick Mortensen 3-1 (p), 64' Lucas Kaufmann 3-2, 90+1' Patrick Olsen 4-2, 90+2' Søren Tengstedt 5-2.
Referee: Ioannis Papadopoulos (GRE)

27.08.20   Rheinpark Stadion, Vaduz: FC Vaduz – Hibernians FC 0-2 (0-1)
FC Vaduz: Benjamin Büchel, Denis Simani, Pius Dorn (75' Matteo Di Giusto), Yannick Schmid, Cédric Gasser, Sandro Wieser, Gabriel Lüchinger (67' Nicolae Milinceanu), Sebastian Santin (67' Nico Hug), Mohamed Coulibaly, Manuel Sutter, Tunahan Çiçek. Coach: Mario Frick.
Hibernians FC: Matthew Calleja Cremona, Leandro Almeida, Andrei Agius, Zachary Grech, Gabriel Izquier, Bjorn Kristensen, Jake Grech, Wilkson (63' Rundell Winchester), Shola Shodiya (75' Timothy Tabone Desira), Jurgen Degabriele, Ayrton Attard (70' Edafe Uzeh). Coach: Stefano Sanderra.
Goals: 34', 57' Jurgen Degabriele 0-1, 0-2.
Referee: Luís Teixeira (POR)
Sent off: 64' Bjorn Kristensen.

27.08.20   ASK Arena, Baku: Kesla FK – KF Laçi 0-0 (a.e.t.)
Kesla FK: Stanislav Namasco, Mijusko Bojovic, Ilkin Qirtimov, Azer Salahli, Shahriyar Aliyev, Artur (81' Dzhavid Imamverdiyev), Rahman Hadzhiyev, John Kamara, Dmytro Klyots, Vüsal Isgendarli (119' Tural Akhundov), Alexander Cristovão (64' Silvio). Coach: Yunis Hüseynov.
KF Laçi: Alen Sherri, Aleksandar Ignjatovic, Rudolf Turkaj, Adolf Selmani, Ardit Deliu (99' Donald Rapo), Regi Lushkja, Lucas Ramos, Albion Marku, Teco (120' Mentor Mazrekaj), Kyrian Nwabueze, Redon Xhixha (105' Klejdi Rapo). Coach: Armando Cungu.
Referee: Georgi Kikacheishvili (GEO)
Sent off: 72' Lucas Ramos, 112' Shahriyar Aliyev.

KF Laçi won on penalties after extra time (5-4)
Penalties: Nwabueze 1-0, Klyots 1-1, Lushkja 2-1, Silvio 2-2, D.Rapo 3-2, Akhundov 3-3, Mazrekaj 4-3, Hajyev 4-4, Ignjatovic 5-4, Qirtimov missed.

27.08.20   Stadion Balgarska Armija, Sofia: CSKA Sofia – Sirens FC 2-1 (0-0)
CSKA Sofia: Busatto, Jurgen Mattheij, Plamen Galabov, Bradley Mazikou, Valentin Antov, Graham Carey (57' Georgi Yomov), Tiago Rodrigues, Amos Youga (71' Ahmed Ahmedov), Stefano Beltrame (65' Younousse Sankharé), Ali Sowe, Henrique. Coach: Stamen Belchev.
Sirens FC: David Cassar, Adrian Borg, Ryan Scicluna, Sergio Raphael, Thiaguinho, Manuel Bustos, Romeu (30' Jacob Walker), Terence Agius (82' Ryan Grech), Wilfried Domoraud, Maxuell Samurai, Wellington Petinha (79' Michael Mifsud). Coach: Stephen D'Aamto.
Goals: 69' Maxuell Samurai 0-1, 75' Ahmed Ahmedov 1-1, 90+1' Ali Sowe 2-1.
Referee: Krzysztof Jakubik (POL)

Maxuell Samurai missed a penalty kick (48').

27.08.20   Mikheil Meskhis Sakhelobis Stadionis Satadarigo Moedani, Tbilisi:
             Lokomotivi Tbilisi – CS Universitatea Craiova 2-1 (0-0)
Lokomotivi Tbilisi: Giorgi Mamardashvili, Nika Sandokhadze (77' Aleksandre Andronikashvili), Giorgi Gabadze, Aleksandre Gureshidze, Daviti Ubilava, Temur Shonia, Davit Samurkasovi (80' Nika Tchanturia), Tornike Kirkitadze, Beka Dartsmelia, Imran Oulad Omar (69' Tornike Dzebniauri), Irakli Sikharulidze. Coach: Giorgi Chiabrishvili.
CS Universitatea Craiova: Mirko Pigliacelli, Marius Constantin, Bogdan Vatajelu, Nicusor Bancu, Stephane Acka, Alexandru Mateiu (67' Vladimir Screciu), Dan Nistor (77' Stefan Baiaram), Cristian Barbut (61' Valentin Mihaila), Alexandru Cicâldau, Elvir Koljic, Andrei Ivan. Coach: Cristiano Bergodi.
Goals: 57' Irakli Sikharulidze 1-0, 61' Imran Oulad Omar 2-0, 90+4' Stefan Baiaram 2-1.
Referee: Milos Djordjic (SRB)

27.08.20   Stadiumi Fadil Vokrri, Pristina: KF Gjilani – APOEL Nicosia 0-2 (0-0, 0-0) (a.e.t.)
KF Gjilani: Enea Koliçi, Franc Veliu, Jackson (105' Arbër Prekazi), Oltion Rapa (72' Erlis Frashëri), Ylber Kastrati, Muhamed Useini (77' Edvin Kuc), Ardit Hila (96' Fjoart Jonuzi), Keita Lanzeni Aziz, Gerhard Progni, Darko Nikac, Fiton Hajdari. Coach: Gentian Mezani.
APOEL Nicosia: Miguel Silva, Giorgios Merkis, Nicholas Ioannou, Rafael Santos, Mike Jensen (117' Christos Shelis), Dragan Mihajlovic, Tomás De Vincenti, Marius Lundemo, Ghayas Zahid (67' Ben Sahar), Moussa Al Taamari (90' Giorgos Efrem), Viktor Klonaridis (79' Dieumerci Ndongala). Coach: Marinos Ouzounidis.
Goals: 102' Giorgos Efrem 0-1, 116' Dieumerci Ndongala 0-1.
Referee: Yigal Frid (ISR)

Musa Al Taamari missed a penalty kick (78').

APOEL Nicosia won after extra time.

KF Gjilani played their home match at Stadiumi Fadil Vokrri, Pristina, instead of their regular stadium Gjilan City Stadium, Gjilan, which was under reconstruction.

27.08.20   Stadion Kaplakrikavöllur, Hafnarfjördur:
  FH Hafnarfjördur – DAC Dunajská Streda 0-2 (0-1)
FH Hafnarfjördur: Gunnar Nielsen, Pétur Vidarsson, Gudmann Thórisson, Hördur Ingi Gunnarsson, Daníel Hafsteinsson (71' Atli Gudnason), Thórir Jóhann Helgason, Gudmundur Kristjánsson, Eggert Jónsson, Björn Sverrisson (82' Baldur Sigurdsson), Olafur Finsen (58' Jónathan Jónsson), Steven Lennon. Coaches: Eidur Gudjohnsen & Logi Ólafsson.
DAC Dunajská Streda: Martin Jedlicka, Éric Davis, Jannik Müller, Dominik Kruzliak, César Blackman, Zsolt Kalmár, Andrija Balic, Sidney Friede, András Schäfer, Eric Ramírez, Marko Divkovic (71' Andrej Fábry). Coach: Bernd Storck.
Goals: 23' Andrija Balic 0-1, 76' Eric Ramírez 0-2.
Referee: Jason Lee Barcelo (GIB)

27.08.20   Stadyen Budaunik (Stroitel), Soligorsk:
  Shakhter Soligorsk – FC Sfintul Gheorghe 0-0 (a.e.t.)
Shakhter Soligorsk: Alyaksandr Gutor, Aleksandr Sachivko, Igor Burko, Roman Begunov (105' Viktor Sotnikov), Ruslan Khadarkevich, Yuri Kendysh (68' Július Szöke), Aleksandr Selyava, Igor Ivanovic (46' Sergey Balanovich), Dmitri Podstrelov, Darko Bodul, Artem Arkhipov (46' Jasurbek Yakhshiboev). Coach: Yuriy Vernydub.
FC Sfintul Gheorghe: Nicolae Cebotari, Andrey Novicov, Maxim Focsa, Serghei Svinarenco, Eugeniu Slivca, Petru Ojog, Sidy Sagna (84' Vitalie Plamadeala), Yevhen Smirnov, Dimitrii Mandrîcenco (90+1' Alexandru Suvorov), Rienat Mochulyak (79' Maxim Iurcu), Roman Volkov. Coach: Sergiu Cebotari.
Referee: Dragan Petrovic (BIH)
Sent off: 28' Darko Bodul, 121' Maxim Railean *(not used sub)*.

FC Sfintul Gheorghe won on penalties after extra time (4-1).
Penalties: Suvorov 1-0, Sachivko 1-1, Volkov 2-1, Sotnikov missed, Iurcu 3-1,
  Yakhshiboev missed, Slivca 4-1

27.08.20   Park Hall Stadium, Oswestry: The New Saints – MSK Zilina 3-1 (0-0, 1-1) (a.e.t.)
The New Saints: Paul Harrison, Simon Spender (48' Ryan Harrington), Chris Marriott, Blaine Hudson, Ryan Astles, Daniel Redmond (104' Jon Routledge), Ryan Brobbel (81' Leo Smith), Tom Holland, Jamie Mullan, Dean Ebbe, Louis Robles (87' Adrian Cieslewicz).
Coach: Scott Ruscoe.
MSK Zilina: Samuel Petrás, Jan Minárik, Kristián Vallo, Branislav Sluka, Adam Kopas, Jakub Paur (85' Dawid Kurminowski), Ján Bernát (90+3' Vahan Bichakhchyan), Patrik Myslovic, Miroslav Gono, Dávid Duris (118' Adrián Kaprálik), Patrik Ilko (101' Matús Rusnák).
Coach: Pavol Stano.
Goals: 56' Louis Robles 1-0, 77' Patrik Myslovic 1-1 (p), 100' Leo Smith 2-1, 108' Adrian Cieslewicz 3-1 (p).
Referee: Manfredas Lukjancukas (LIT)
Sent off: 108' Branislav Sluka.

The New Saints won after extra time.

27.08.20   HaMoshava Stadium, Petak Tikva: Hapoel Be'er Sheva – Dinamo Batumi 3-0 (2-0)
Hapoel Be'er Sheva: Ohad Levita, Miguel Vítor (79' Loai Taha), Shir Tzedek, Sean Goldberg, Elton Acolatse, Or Dadya, Sintayehu Sallalich, Josué, Marwan Kabha (62' Tomer Yosefi), David Keltjens, Itamar Shviro (75' Gaëtan Varenne). Coach: Yossi Abukasis.
Dinamo Batumi: Mikheil Alavidze, Giorgi Navalovski (45' Lasha Chaladze), Mamuka Kobakhidze, Godfrey Oboabona, Jambuli Jighauri, Benjamin Teidi, Vladimer Mamuchashvili, Giuly Mandzgaladze (79' Tornike Gaprindashvili), Giorgi Nikabadze (64' Reynaldo), Vagner Gonçalves, Flamarion. Coach: George Geguchadze.
Goals: 9' Josué 1-0, 21' Mamuka Kobakhidze 2-0 (og), 61' Josué 3-0.
Referee: Aleksandrs Anufrijevs (LAT)

Hapoel Be'er Sheva played their home match at HaMoshava Stadium, Petak Tikva, instead of their regular stadium Turner Stadium, Beersheba, which was temporarily closed for structural problems fixing on its roof.

27.08.20   Tórsvøllur, Tórshavn: B36 Tórshavn – FCI Levadia Tallinn 4-3 (0-0, 2-2) (a.e.t.)
B36 Tórshavn: Rói Hentze, Alex Mellemgaard, Sonni Nattestad, Eli Nielsen (69' Andrass Johansen, 115' Bjarni Petersen), Árni Frederiksberg, Benjamin Heinesen, Andrias Eriksen, Michal Przybylski, Magnus Holm Jacobsen (90+1' Ragnar Samuelsen), Stefan Radosavljevic (60' Hannes Agnarsson), Sebastian Pingel. Coach: Jákup á Borg.
FCI Levadia Tallinn: Artur Kotenko, Markus Jürgenson, Dmitri Kruglov, Maksim Podholjuzin, Trevor Elhi, Zurab Ochihava, Brent Lepistu, Mark Roosnupp (115' Rasmus Peetson), Elysee Kouadio, Karl Õigus, Artjom Komlov (105' Marko Lipp).
Coach: Vladimir Vassiljev.
Goals: 52' Karl Õigus 0-1, 72', 76' Sebastian Pingel 1-1, 2-1, 80' Trevor Elhi 2-2, 101' Elysee Kouadio 2-3, 107' Ragnar Samuelsen 3-3, 113' Hannes Agnarsson 4-3.
Referee: Donald Robertson (SCO)

B36 Tórshavn won after extra time.

B36 Tórshavn played their home match at Tórsvøllur, Tórshavn, instead of their regular stadium Gundadalur, Tórshavn, which did not meet UEFA requirements.

27.08.20   Stadion pod Bijelim Brijegom, Mostar:
           Zrinjski Mostar – FC Differdange 03 3-0 (2-0)
Zrinjski Mostar: Ivan Brkic, Mario Ticinovic, Tomislav Barbaric, Pero Stojkic, Slobodan Jakovljevic, Ognjen Todorovic (82' Miljan Govedarica), Dinko Trebotic, Milos Filipovic (74' Ivan Basic), Ivan Enin, Nemanja Bilbija, Anes Masic (64' Josip Ivancic).
Coach: Mladen Zizovic.
FC Differdange 03: Kevin Strauss, Geoffrey Franzoni, Maxime De Taddeo, Dylan Lempereur, Théo Brusco, Gonçalo Almeida (84' Shean Garlito y Romo), Quentin Leite Pereira (80' Fadel Gobitaka), Mamadou Sanoussy Baldé (46' Hugo Komano), Kilian Gulluni, Aurélien Joachim, Andreas Buch. Coach: Paolo Amodio.
Goals: 37' Nemanja Bilbija 1-0, 40' Milos Filipovic 2-0, 79' Josip Ivancic 3-0.
Referee: Aristotelis Diamantopoulos (GRE)

27.08.20 MFA Centenary Stadium, Ta'Qali: Valletta FC – Bala Town FC 0-1 (0-1)
Valletta FC: Henry Bonello, Jonathan Caruana, Mihailo Jovanovic, Jean Borg, Rowen Muscat, Enmy Peña, Shaun Dimech (68' Taisei Marukawa), Santiago Malano, Miguel Alba (46' Kyrian Nwoko), Matteo Piciollo (60' Taylon), Mario Fontanella. Coach: Jesmond Zerafa.
Bala Town FC: Alex Ramsay, Anthony Stephens, Sean Smith, Jonathan Spittle, Antony Kay, Steven Leslie (69' Kieran Smith), Chris Venables, Will Evans, Oliver Shannon, Lassana Mendes, Raul Correia (79' Henry Jones). Coach: Colin Caton.
Goal: 38' Chris Venables 0-1.
Referee: Luca Barbeno (SMR)

Mario Fontanella missed a penalty kick (62').

27.08.20 Air Albania Stadium, Tirana: FK Kukësi – Slavia Sofia 2-1 (0-0)
FK Kukësi: Dashamir Xhika, Kenan Horic, Edis Malikji, Erhun Obanor, Bruno Telushi, Emiljano Musta, Eduart Rroca, Besar Musolli, Enis Gavazaj (46' Albin Gashi), Vesel Limaj (65' Zenel Gavazaj), Patrick Eze (66' Godberg Cooper). Coach: Skënder Gega.
Slavia Sofia: Antonis Stergiakis, Hristo Popadiyn, Petar Patev, Andrea Hristov, Georgi Valchev (73' Ventsislav Bengyuzov), Milen Gamakov, Emil Stoev (87' Dimitar Stoyanov), Yanis Karabelyov, Filip Krastev, Dimitar Rangelov (62' Ivailo Dimitrov), Kaloyan Krastev. Coach: Zlatomir Zagorcic.
Goals: 56' Patrick Eze 1-0 (p), 81' Kaloyan Krastev 1-1, 85' Godberg Cooper 2-1.
Referee: Arda Kardesler (TUR)

FK Kukësi played their home match at Air Albania Stadium, Tirana, instead of their regular stadium Zeqir Ymeri Stadium, Kukës, which was under reconstruction.

27.08.20 Stadionul Zimbru, Chisina: CS Petrocub Hîncesti – TSC Backa Topola 0-2 (0-1)
CS Petrocub Hîncesti: Cristian Avram, Petru Racu, Ion Jardan, Iaser Turcan (68' Victor Bogaciuc), Andrei Cojocari, Artiom Rozgoniuc, Dan Taras (53' Alexandru Bejan), Vladimir Ambros (68' Ilie Damascan), Jacques Onana Ndzomo, Donalio Melachio Douanla, Sergiu Platica. Coach: Lilian Popescu.
TSC Backa Topola: Nenad Filipovic, Goran Antonic, Dajan Ponjevic, Filip Babic, Nenad Lukic, Sasa Tomanovic, Boris Varga, Djuro Zec (90+1' Vasilije Djuric), Vladimir Siladji (44' Nemanja Petrovic), Dejan Milicevic, Borko Duronjic (74' Mihajlo Banjac).
Coach: Zoltán Szabó.
Goals: 17' Sasa Tomanovic 0-1, 55' Nenad Lukic 0-2 (p).
Referee: Sebastian Coltescu (ROM)
Sent off: 31' Boris Varga, 54' Artiom Rozgoniuc.

CS Petrocub Hîncesti played their home match at Stadionul Zimbru, Chisinau, instead of their regular stadium Stadionul Municipal, Hîncesti, which did not meet UEFA requirements.

27.08.20   Stadion Pod Goricom, Podgorica: Iskra Danilovgrad – Lokomotiv Plovdiv 0-1 (0-0)
Iskra Danilovgrad: Marko Kordic, Luka Malesevic, Nikola Kumburovic, Milos Drincic, Miroje Jovanovic, Kōhei Katō, Irfan Sahman, Balsa Boricic (82' Milan Djuricic), Ivan Vukovic, Aldin Adzovic (78' Bogdan Milic), Zoran Petrovic (73' Vladislav Rogosic).
Coach: Aleksandar Nedovic.
Lokomotiv Plovdiv: Martin Lukov, Milos Petrovic, Dinis Almeida, Lucas Masoero, Momchil Tsvetanov, Parvizchon Umarbaev (90' Nikolay Nikolaev), Petar Vitanov, Lucas Salinas (65' Christian Ilic), Dimitar Iliev, Birsent Karagaren, Ante Aralica (73' Georgi Minchev).
Coach: Bruno Akrapovic.
Goal: 75' Dimitar Iliev 0-1 (p).
Referee: Gergö Bogár (HUN)

Iskra Danilovgrad played their home match at Stadion Pod Goricom, Podgorica, instead of their regular stadium Braca Velasevic Stadium, Danilovgrad, which did not meet UEFA requirements.

27.08.20   Stade de Genève, Geneva: Servette Genève – MFK Ruzomberok 3-0 (0-0)
Servette Genève: Jérémy Frick, Anthony Sauthier, Vincent Sasso, Steve Rouiller, Arial Mendy, Miroslav Stevanovic, Gaël Ondoua, Timothé Cognat (87' Andrea Maccoppi), Varol Tasar (69' Alexis Antunes), Kastriot Imeri (76' Boris Cespedes), Grejohn Kyei.
Coach: Alain Geiger.
MFK Ruzomberok: Matús Macík, Ján Maslo, Matej Curma, Matej Madlenák, Alexander Mojzis, Matej Kochan, Dalibor Takác (60' Peter Dungel), Marek Zsigmund, Timotej Múdry (65' Adam Brenkus), Stefan Gerec, Ladislav Almási (70' Tomás Bobcek). Coach: Ján Haspra.
Goals: 54' Miroslav Stevanovic 1-0, 77' Arial Mendy 2-0, 86' Alexis Antunes 3-0.
Referee: Viktor Kopiievskyi (UKR)

27.08.20   Arena Nationala, Bucharest: FCSB – Shirak FC 3-0 (1-0)
FCSB: Andrei Vlad, Valentin Cretu, Iulian Cristea, George Andrei Miron, Ionut Pantîru, Ovidiu Popescu, Darius Olaru, Sergiu Bus (46' Alexandru Buziuc), Florin Tanase (86' Ionut Vina), Florinel Coman, Dennis Man (78' Olimpiu Morutan). Coach: Anton Petrea.
Shirak FC: Vsevolod Ermakov, Hrayr Mkoyan, Aghvan Davoyan, Marko Prijevic, Zhirayr Margaryan, Edgar Malakyan, Davit Manoyan (69' Solomon Udo), Karen Muradyan, Arman Aslanyan (74' Junior Avo Leibe), Urus Nenadovic (74' Artem Gevorkyan), Mory Kone.
Coach: Tigran Davtyan.
Goals: 34' Darius Olaru 1-0, 65' Florin Tanase 2-0 (p), 83' Alexandru Buziuc 3-0.
Referee: Admir Sehovic (BIH)

27.08.20 Ljudski vrt, Maribor: NK Maribor – Coleraine FC 1-1 (0-0, 1-1) (a.e.t.)
NK Maribor: Azbe Jug, Mitja Viler, Martin Milec, Nemanja Mitrovic, Spiro Pericic, Rok Kronaveter (84' Jan Mlakar), Alexandru Cretu, Aleks Pihler (102' Amir Dervisevic), Martin Kramaric (61' Marcos Tavares), Jasmin Mesanovic, Aljosa Matko (61' Rudi Vancas Pozeg).
Coach: Sergej Jakirovic.
Coleraine FC: Gareth Deane, Aaron Canning, Aaron Traynor (105' Gareth McConaghie), Stephen O'Donnell, Lyndon Kane, Stephen Lowry, Josh Carson, Ben Doherty, Aaron Jarvis (72' Ronan Wilson), James McLaughlin (95' Ian Parkhill), Stewart Nixon (85' Eoin Bradley).
Coach: Oran Kearney.
Goals: 62' James McLaughlin 0-1, 65' Rudi Vancas Pozeg 1-1.
Referee: Kai Erik Steen (NOR)

Amir Dervesevic missed a penalty kick (105').

Coleraine FC won on penalties after extra time (5-4).
Penalties: Dervesevic 1-0, Parkhill 1-1, Mlakar 2-1, Kane 2-2, Marcos Tavares 3-2, McConaghie 3-3, Mesanovic 4-3, Bradley 4-4, Vancas Pozeg missed, Doherty 4-5.

27.08.20 Pittodrie Stadium, Aberdeen: Aberdeen FC – NSÍ Runavík 6-0 (2-0)
Aberdeen FC: Joe Lewis, Andrew Considine, Scott McKenna, Jonny Hayes, Marley Watkins (73' Bruce Anderson), Matthew Kennedy, Dylan McGeouch, Ross McCrorie, Lewis Ferguson, Curtis Main (46' Ryan Hedges), Scott Wright (82' Niall McGinn). Coach: Derek McInnes.
NSÍ Runavík: Tórdur Thomsen, Oddur Højgaard, Jóhan Davidsen, Bárdur Jógvansson-Hansen (59' Jákup Jakobsen), Rógvi Nielsen, Jesper Christjansen, Salmundur Bech (88' Aron Knudsen), Petur Knudsen, Mórits Heini Mortensen (70' Steffan Abrahamsson Løken), Jann Benjaminsen, Klæmint Olsen. Coach: Glenn Leif Ståhl.
Goals: 37' Lewis Ferguson 1-0, 43' Curtis Main 2-0, 50', 59' Ryan Hedges 3-0, 4-0, 60' Jonny Hayes 5-0, 87' Ryan Hedges 6-0 (p).
Referee: Ívar Orri Kristjánsson (ISL)

27.08.20 Fir Park, Motherwell: Motherwell FC – Glentoran Belfast 5-1 (0-0)
Motherwell FC: Trevor Carson, Declan Gallagher, Stephen O'Donnell (82' Harry Robinson), Ricki Lamie, Liam Grimshaw (60' Sherwin Seedorf), Bevis Mugabi, Liam Polworth, Mark O'Hara, Allan Campbell, Chris Long, Callum Lang (70' Tony Watt).
Coach: Stephen Robinson.
Glentoran Belfast: Dayle Coleing, Keith Cowan, Patrick McClean, Caolan Marron, Marcus Kane, Gaël Bigirimana, Seanan Clucas, Chris Gallagher (78' Ciarán O'Connor), Rory Donnelly (73' Cameron Stewart), Robbie McDaid, Paul O'Neill (62' Jamie McDonagh).
Coach: Mick McDermott.
Goals: 58' Callum Lang 1-0, 72' Stephen O'Donnell 2-0, 75' Liam Polworth 3-0, 78' Tony Watt 4-0, 87' Chris Long 5-0, 90' Robbie McDaid 5-1 (p).
Referee: Bram Van Driessche (BEL)
Sent off: 52' Seanan Clucas.

27.08.20   Hidegkuti Nándor Stadion, Budapest:
Budapest Honvéd – FC Inter Turku 2-1 (0-0, 1-1) (a.e.t.)
Budapest Honvéd: Tomás Tujvel, Eke Uzoma, Ivan Lovric, Botond Baráth (46' Mohamed Mezghrani), Bence Batík, Patrik Hidi (107' Djordje Kamber), Barna Kesztyüs, Donát Zsótér, Dániel Gazdag, Roland Ugrai (120' Naser Aliji), Kristóf Tóth-Gábor (72' Boubacar Traoré).
Coach: Tamás Bódog.
FC Inter Turku: Henrik Moisander, Jesper Engström (106' Kevin Kouassivi-Benissan), Juuso Hämäläinen, Rick Ketting, Arttu Hoskonen, Anthony Annan, Álvaro Muñiz (106' Taiki Kagayama), Aleksi Paananen (65' Matias Ojala), Connor Ruane, Timo Furuholm, Benjamin Källman (89' Liliu). Coach: Jose Riveiro.
Goals: 90' Boubacar Traoré 1-0, 90+1' Liliu 1-1, 105' Juuso Hämäläinen 2-1 (og).
Referee: Gal Leibovitz (ISR)

Budapest Honvéd won after extra time.

Budapest Honvéd played their home match at Hidegkuti Nándor Stadion, Budapest, instead of their regular stadium Bozsik József Stadion (1913), Budapest, as it was demolished to be replaced by their new stadium Bozsik József Aréna, Budapest.

27.08.20   Tallaght Stadium, Dublin: Shamrock Rovers – Ilves Tampere 2-2 (1-1, 2-2) (a.e.t.)
Shamrock Rovers: Alan Mannus, Joey O'Brien, Roberto Lopes, Liam Scales, Ronan Finn, Aaron McEneff, Jack Byrne, Gary O'Neill, Neil Farrugia (78' Dean Williams), Aaron Greene (105+2' Danny Lafferty), Graham Burke (64' Dylan Watts). Coach: Stephen Bradley.
Ilves Tampere: Mika Hilander, Felipe Aspegren (111' Doni Arifi), Tatu Miettunen, Diogo Tomas, Mikael Almen, Joona Veteli (83' Tuure Siira), Lauri Ala-Myllymäki, Jair, Naatan Skyttä, Eero Tamminen (102' Eetu Mömmö), Ilari Mettälä (79' Eemeli Raittinen).
Coach: Jarkko Wiss.
Goals: 10' Lauri Ala-Myllymäki 0-1 (p), 14' Graham Burke 1-1, 62' Joona Veteli 1-2, 78' Roberto Lopes 2-2.
Referee: Michal Ocenás (SVK)
Sent off: 88' Liam Scales.

Shamrock Rovers won on penalties after extra time (12-11).
Penalties: Ala-Myllymäki 1-0, Byrne missed, Jair missed, O'Brien 1-1, Raittinen 2-1, Watts 2-2, Siira 3-2, O'Neill 3-3, Skyttä 4-3, McEneff 4-4, Mömmö 5-4, Williams 5-5, Tomas 6-5, Roberto Lopes 6-6, Almén 7-6, Lafferty 7-7, Miettunen 8-7, Finn 8-8, Hilander 9-8, Mannus 9-9, Ala-Myllymäki 10-9, Watts 10-10, Jair 11-10, McEneff 11-11, Raittinen missed, O'Brien 11-12.

27.08.20   Stadion Partizana, Beograd: Partizan Beograd – FK Rīgas Futbola skola 1-0 (0-0)
Partizan Beograd: Vladimir Stojkovic, Uros Vitas, Nemanja Miletic, Macky Frank Bagnack, Slobodan Urosevic, Bibras Natcho (90+2' Milan Smiljanic), Aleksandar Scekic, Sasa Zdjelar, Takuma Asano (90+5' Dennis Stojkovic), Umar Sadiq, Filip Stevanovic (72' Seydouba Soumah). Coach: Savo Milosevic.
FK Rīgas Futbola skola: Danylo Kucher, Aleksandrs Solovjovs, Vitālijs Jagodinskis, Ziga Lipuscek, Tomás Simkovic (71' Chinonso Nnamdi), Tomislav Saric, Roberts Savalnieks, Jānis Ikaunieks, Leonel Strumia, Darko Lemajic, Alain Cedric Kouadio (70' Baiano).
Coach: Viktors Morozs.
Goal: 52' Bibras Natcho 1-0 (p).
Referee: Zaven Hovhannisyan (ARM)

27.08.20   INEA stadion, Poznan: KKS Lech Poznan – Valmiera FC 3-0 (0-0)
KKS Lech Poznan: Filip Bednarek, Lubomir Satka, Djordje Crnomarkovic, Robert Gumny, Tymoteusz Puchacz, Pedro Tiba (80' Filip Marchwinski), Dani Ramírez, Kamil Józwiak, Jakub Moder, Jacub Kaminski (63' Alan Czerwinski), Mikael Ishak (88' Filip Szymczak).
Coach: Dariusz Zuraw.
Valmiera FC: Rūdolfs Soloha, Julien Celestine, Olaide Badmus, Pape Yaré Fall, Kriss Kārkliņs, Mykola Musolitin, Luka Silagadze (46' Mootez Zaddem), Alvis Jaunzems (83' Daniils Skopenko), Mohamed Victor Diagne, Jorge Teixeira (76' Djibril Gueyé), Toluwalase Arokodare. Coach: Tamaz Pertia.
Goals: 59', 78' Mikael Ishak 1-0, 2-0, 88' Filip Szymczak 3-0.
Referee: Ondrej Pechanec (CZE)

09.09.20   Sammy Ofer Stadium, Haifa: Maccabi Haifa – Zeljeznicar Sarajevo 3-1 (1-1)
Maccabi Haifa: Josh Cohen, Ernest Mabouka, Sun Menachem, Ayed Habashi, Ofri Arad, Tjaronn Chery, Yuval Ashkenazi, Neta Lavi, Mohammad Abu Fani (54' Dolev Haziza), Nikita Rukavytsya (76' Stav Nachmani), Yanic Wildschut (69' Yarden Shua). Coach: Barak Bakhar.
Zeljeznicar Sarajevo: Irfan Fejzic, Sinisa Stevanovic, Aleksandar Kosoric, Luka Miletic, Mehmed Alispahic (75' Damir Sadikovic), Semir Stilic, Mladen Veselinovic (63' Mustafa Mujezinovic), Haris Hajdarevic, Eldar Sehic (75' Luka Juricic), Ivan Lendric, Ante Blazevic. Coach: Amar Osim.
Goals: 34' Ivan Lendric 0-1, 38' Tjaronn Chery 1-1, 59' Nikita Rukavytsya 2-1, 66' Yuval Ashkenazi 3-1.
Referee: Jørgen Burchardt (DEN)

The match, originally scheduled to be played on 27th August 2020, at Sammy Ofer Stadium, Haifa, was postponed to 9th September 2020, after five members from Zeljeznicar's delegation tested positive for SARS-2 coronavirus, the whole team being put into quarantine by the Israeli authorities.

10.09.20   Szusza Ferenc Stadion, Budapest (HUN): JK Nõmme Kalju – NS Mura 0-4 (0-4)
JK Nõmme Kalju: Marko Meerits, Kirill Aleksandr Antonov (89' Frank Kenneth Liblikmann), Sander Puri, Andreas Raudsepp, Kaspar Paur, Marcus Suurväli, Kaarel Usta, Arthur Jersov (46' Kirill Sustov), Jevgeni Demidov, Alex Matthias Tamm, Kristjan Rattasepp.
Coach: Marko Kristal.
NS Mura: Matko Obradovic, Ziga Kous, Klemen Sturm, Jan Gorenc, Zan Kamiczik, Matic Marusko (46' Kai Cipot), Nino Kouter (78' Amadej Marosa), Alen Kozar (66' Marko Brkic), Tomi Horvat, Kevin Zizek, Andrija Filipovic. Coach: Ante Simundza.
Goals: 17', 27' Kevin Zizek 0-1, 0-2, 32' Ziga Kous 0-3, 36' Alen Kozar 0-4.
Referee: Robert Hennessy (IRL)

Nino Kouter missed a penalty kick (27').

The match, originally scheduled to be played on 27th August 2020, at Kadriorg Stadium, Tallinn, was postponed to 10th September 2020, and moved to Szusza Ferenc Stadium, Budapest (Hungary), after one player from JK Nõmme Kalju and one player from NS Mura testing positive for SARS-2 coronavirus following Meistriliiga and Slovenian PrvaLiga matches on 22nd August 2020. Both teams were put into quarantine by the Estonian authorities.

SECOND QUALIFYING ROUND

16.09.20 Stade Parc des Sports, Differdange: Progrès Niederkorn – Willem II 0-5 (0-3)
Progrès Niederkorn: Sebastian Flauss, Mathias Jänisch (64' Metin Karayer), Adrien Ferino, Aldin Skenderovic, Yannis Dublin, Yannick Bastos, Kevin Holtz (64' Florik Shala), Christian Silaj, Ryad Habbas (46' Antonio Luisi), Kempes Tekiela, Irvin Latic. Coach: Roland Vrabec.
Willem II: Robbin Ruiter, Jordens Peters, Miquel Nelom (62' Derrick Köhn), Freek Heerkens (41' Victor van den Bogert), Sebastian Holmén, Pol Llonch (62' Driess Saddiki), Görkem Saglam, Mike Trésor, Vangelis Pavlidis, Mats Köhlert, Ché Nunnely. Coach: Adrie Koster.
Goals: 20' Vangelis Pavlidis 0-1, 28' Görkem Saglam 0-2, 34' Vangelis Pavlidis 0-3, 46' Ché Nunnely 0-4, 65' Mike Trésor 0-5.
Referee: Mykola Balakin (UKR)

Progrès Niederkorn played their home match at Stade Parc des Sports, Differdange, instead of their regular stadium Stade Jos Haupert, Niederkorn, which did not meet UEFA requirements.

16.09.20 Tele2 Arena, Stockholm: Hammarby IF – KKS Lech Poznan 0-3 (0-0)
Hammarby IF: David Ousted, David Fällman (46' Richárd Magyar), Mads Fenger, Mohanad Jeahze, Kalle Björklund, Serge-Junior Martinsson-Ngouali, Abdul Khalili, Jeppe Andersen, Paulinho (77' Alexander Kacaniklic), Aron Jóhannsson, Gustav Ludwigson.
Coach: Stefan Billborn.
KKS Lech Poznan: Filip Bednarek, Lubomir Satka, Alan Czerwinski, Djordje Crnomarkovic, Tymoteusz Puchacz, Jan Sýkora (73' Michal Skóras), Pedro Tiba (84' Filip Marchwinski), Dani Ramírez, Jakub Moder, Jacub Kaminski, Mikael Ishak (90+1' Mohamad Awaed).
Coach: Dariusz Zuraw.
Goals: 56' Pedro Tiba 0-1, 89' Jakub Kaminski 0-2, 90+3' Filip Marchwinski 0-3.
Referee: Sascha Stegemann (GER)
Sent off: 63' Jeppe Andersen.

16.09.20 Tórsvøllur, Tórshavn: B36 Tórshavn – The New Saints 2-2 (0-0, 1-1) (a.e.t.)
B36 Tórshavn: Rói Hentze, Alex Mellemgaard, Sonni Nattestad, Eli Nielsen, Árni Frederiksberg (68' Hannes Agnarsson), Benjamin Heinesen, Andrias Eriksen (111' Erling Jacobsen), Michal Przybylski, Magnus Holm Jacobsen (113' Andrass Johansen), Ragnar Samuelsen (86' Stefan Radosavljevic), Sebastian Pingel. Coach: Jákup á Borg.
The New Saints: Paul Harrison, Keston Davies (30' Ben Clark), Ryan Harrington, Jon Routledge (71' Leo Smith), Daniel Redmond, Ryan Brobbel (77' Adrian Cieslewicz), Ryan Astles, Tom Holland, Jamie Mullan, Dean Ebbe, Louis Robles (116' Greg Draper).
Coach: Scott Ruscoe.
Goals: 47' Michal Przybylski 1-0, 80' Leo Smith 1-1, 112' Dean Ebbe 1-2, 120+2' Stefan Radosavljevic 2-2.
Referee: Ian McNabb (NIR)

B36 Tórshavn won on penalties after extra time (5-4).
Penalties: Nattestad 1-0, Harrison 1-1, Mellemgaard 2-1, Cieslewicz 2-2, Heinesen 3-2, Draper 3-3, Przybylski missed, Smith 3-4, Radosavljevic 4-4, Ebbe missed, Pingel 5-4, Redmond missed.

B36 Tórshavn played their home match at Tórsvøllur, Tórshavn, instead of their regular stadium Gundadalur, Tórshavn, which did not meet UEFA requirements.

17.09.20   Stadion Qajimuqan Muñaytpasov, Shymkent:
Kaysar Kyzylorda – APOEL Nicosia 1-4 (1-2)
Kaysar Kyzylorda: Aleksandr Zarutskiy, Ilyas Amirseitov (89' Dinmukhamed Kashken), Ivan Graf, Aleksandr Marochkin, Bagdat Kairov, Clarence Bitang, Ashkat Tagybergen (85' Mark Gurman), Duman Narzildaev (58' Aleksandar Stanisavljevic), Aleksandar Kolev, Elguja Lobjanidze, Maksim Fedin. Coach: Stoicho Mladenov.
APOEL Nicosia: Miguel Silva, Emilio N'Sue, Christos Wheeler, Christos Shelis, Rafael Santos, Tomás De Vincenti, Ghayas Zahid, Anuar Tuhami, Ben Sahar (58' Moussa Al Taamari), Viktor Klonaridis (46' Omer Atzili), Dieumerci Ndongala (85' Atdhe Nuhiu). Coach: Marinos Ouzounidis.
Goals: 6' Elguja Lobjanidze 1-0, 15' Tomás De Vincenti 1-1, 25' Anuar Tuhami 1-2, 48' Omer Atzili 1-3, 90+4' Tomás De Vincenti 1-4.
Referee: Jens Maae (DEN)

Kaysar Kyzylorda played their home match at Stadion Qajimuqan Muñaytpasov, Shymkent, instead of their regular stadium Gani Murathbayev Stadium, Kyzylorda.

17.09.20   Olimpiskā centra Ventspils Stadionā, Ventspils:
FK Ventspils – Rosenborg BK 1-5 (1-3)
FK Ventspils: Dele Alampasu, Abdoul Mamah, Giorgi Rekhviashvili, Andriy Sakhnevich, Giorgi Mchedlishvili, Dmitrijs Litvinskis, Giorgi Eristavi (53' Dumte Pyagbara), Daniils Ulimbasevs, Lucas Villela, Kaspars Svārups (75' Kazeem Ojo Aderounmu), Evgeny Kozlov (81' Kaspars Kokins). Coach: Viorel Frunza.
Rosenborg BK: André Hansen, Even Hovland, Vegar Hedenstad, Gustav Valsvik, Erlend Reitan, Per Skjelbred, Anders Konradsen (71' Gjermund Åsen), Kristoffer Zachariassen, Dino Islamovic (90' Torgeir Børven), Samuel Adegbenro (58' Emil Ceïde), Carl Holse. Coach: Åge Hareide.
Goals: 5' Evgeny Kozlov 1-0, 14' Dino Islamovic 1-1 (p), 37' Anders Konradsen 1-2, 45+2' Dino Islamovic 1-3, 64' Carl Holse 1-4, 71' Kristoffer Zachariassen 1-5.
Referee: Paul McLaughlin (IRL)
Sent off: 63' Dmitrijs Litvinskis.

17.09.20   Trening centar Petar Milosevski, Skopje: FK Renova – Hajduk Split 0-1 (0-1)
FK Renova: Hadis Velii, Nenad Miskovski, Xhelil Abdulla, Bashkim Velija, Arbër Shala, Argjent Gafuri, Saimir Fetai (46' Suhejlj Muharem), Burim Sadiki (72' Artan Veliu), Emran Ramadani (77' Alen Jasaroski), Alush Gavazaj, Shefit Shefiti. Coach: Bujar Islami.
Hajduk Split: Josip Posavec, Darko Todorovic, David Colina, Nihad Mujakic, Mario Vuskovic, Ádám Gyurcsó (65' Ivan Dolcek), Mijo Caktas, Stanko Juric, Darko Nejasmic (77' Jani Atanasov), Jairo (82' Marin Jakolis), Dimitrios Diamantakos. Coach: Hari Vukas.
Goal: 4' Mijo Caktas 0-1.
Referee: João Pedro Pinheiro (POR)

FK Renova played their home match at Trening centar Petar Milosevski, Skopje, instead of their regular stadium Ecolog Arena, Tetovo.

17.09.20   Stadiumi Niko Dovana, Durrës: KF Teuta Durrës – Granada CF 0-4 (0-3)
KF Teuta Durrës: Stivi Frashëri, Renato Arapi, Rustem Hoxha, Alexandros Kouros, Fabjan Beqja, Emiljano Vila, Asion Daja (46' Ildi Gruda), Albano Aleksi, Florent Avdyli (56' Rubin Hebaj), Blerim Krasniqi (68' Ledjo Beqja), Lorenco Vila. Coach: Edi Martini.
Granada CF: Rui Silva, Víctor Díaz, Germán Sánchez, Domingos Duarte (46' Jesús Vallejo), Carlos Neva, Montoro (58' Fede Vico), Maxime Gonalons, Antonio Puertas, Kenedy, Yangel Herrera, Soldado (46' Jorge Molina). Coach: Diego Martínez.
Goals: 5' Soldado 0-1, 10' Kenedy 0-2, 31', 46' Yangel Herrera 0-3, 0-4.
Referee: Willy Delajod (FRA)
Sent off: 80' Fabjan Beqja.

17.09.20   Ortaliq Stadion, Almaty: FK Astana – FK Buducnost Podgorica 0-1 (0-1)
FK Astana: Nenad Eric, Evgeny Postnikov, Uros Radakovic, Luka Simunovic, Rúnar Sigurjónsson, Dmitriy Shomko (50' Abzal Beysebekov), Ivan Maevski, Maks Ebong (86' Aleksey Shchetkin), Tigran Barseghyan, Pieros Sotiriou, Dorin Rotariu (57' Marin Tomasov). Coach: Paul Ashworth.
FK Buducnost Podgorica: Milos Dragojevic, Vladan Adzic, Luka Mirkovic, Igor Cukovic, Nemanja Sekulic, Petar Grbic, Milos Raickovic, Vasilije Terzic (89' Aleksandar Vujacic), Petar Vuksevic (9' Bogdan Milic), Igor Ivanovic, Panagiotis Moraitis (90+5' Miomir Djurickovic). Coach: Mladen Milinkovic.
Goal: 25' Vasilije Terzic 0-1.
Referee: Dumitri Muntean (MOL)

FK Astana played their home match at Ortaqil Stadion, Almaty, instead of their regular stadium Astana Arena, Nur-Sultan.

17.09.20   Yazgen Sargsyan Republican Stadium, Yerevan:
            FC Ararat-Armenia – CS Fola Esch 4-3 (1-1, 3-3) (a.e.t.)
FC Ararat-Armenia: Stefan Cupic, Alemão, Sergiy Vakulenko, Ângelo Meneses, Alex Christian Júnior, Yoan Gouffran (84' Louis Ogana), Kódjo Alphonse (70' Sargis Shahinyan), Furdjel Narsingh, Yusuf Otubanjo (60' Mailson), Zakaria Sanogo, Jeisson Martínez (96' Armen Ambartsumyan). Coach: David Campaña.
CS Fola Esch: Thomas Hym, Julien Klein, Jean Sylvio Ouassiero, Cédric Sacras, Rodrigues Dikaba, Bruno Freire (84' Tiago Semedo Monteiro), Diogo Pimentel, Stefano Bensi (87' Billy Bernard), Gilson Delgado, Jules Diallo (70' Achraf Drif), Zachary Hadji (117' Guillaume Mura). Coach: Sébastian Grandjean.
Goals: 16' Jeisson Martínez 1-0, 19' Diogo Pimentel 1-1, 56' Stefano Bensi 1-2 (p), 81' Zachary Hadji 1-3, 90+1', 90+4' Mailson 2-3 (p), 3-3 (p), 113' Sergiy Vakulenko 4-3.
Referee: Enea Jorgji (ALB)
Sent off: 43' Alex Christian Júnior, 90' Diogo Pimentel.

FC Ararat-Armenia played their home match at Vazgen Sargsyan Republican Stadium, Yerevan, instead of their regular stadium Yerevan Football Academy Stadium, Yerevan.

17.09.20 Victoria Stadium, Gibraltar: Lincoln Red Imps – Glasgow Rangers FC 0-5 (0-2)
Lincoln Red Imps: Kyle Goldwin, Scott Wiseman (56' Diego Gámez), Bernardo Lopes, Roy Chipolina, Ethan Britto, Mustapha Yahaya, Jack Sergeant (68' Jesús Toscano), Graeme Torilla, Anthony Hernandez (52' Tjay De Barr), Lee Casciaro, Kike Gómez. Coach: William.
Glasgow Rangers FC: Allan McGregor, James Tavernier (46' Alfredo Morelos), Connor Goldson, Borna Barisic, George Edmundson, Scott Arfield, Glen Kamara, Ianis Hagi, Greg Stewart, Kemar Roofe (42' Nathan Patterson), Cedric Itten (66'Jermain Defoe).
Coach: Steven Gerrard.
Goals: 21' James Tavernier 0-1, 45+4' Connor Goldson 0-2, 67' Alfredo Morelos 0-3, 84' Jermain Defoe 0-4, 88' Alfredo Morelos 0-5.
Referee: Iwan Arwel Griffith (WAL)

17.09.20 Savon Sanomat Areena, Kuopio:
Kuopion PS – Slovan Bratislava 1-1 (0-0, 0-0) (a.e.t.)
Kuopion PS: Otso Virtanen, Artur Pikk, Juho Pirttijoki (88' Luc Tabi Manga), Nuno Tomás, Petteri Pennanen, Ville Saxman (115' Igors Tarasovs), Bismark Adjei-Boateng, Ilmari Niskanen, Urho Nissilä, Saku Savolainen (115' Usman Sale), Rangel (87' Aniekpeno Udoh).
Coach: Arne Erlandsen.
Slovan Bratislava: Dominik Greif, Lukás Pauschek, Kenan Bajric, Vernon De Marco, Myenty Abena, Ibrahim Rabiu (69' Nono Delgado), Dávid Holman (103' Dejan Drazic), Joeri de Kamps, Erik Daniel (69' Aleksandar Cavric), Rafael Ratão, Zan Medved (114' Alen Ozbolt).
Coach: Darko Milanic.
Goals: 111' Zan Medved 0-2, 120' Aniekpeno Udoh 1-1.
Referee: Volen Chinkov (BUL)

Kuopion PS won on penalties after extra time (4-3).
Penalties: Pennanen 1-0, Vernon De Marco 1-1, Udoh 2-1, Ozbolt 2-2, Niskanen missed, de Kamps 2-3, Nuno Tomás 3-3, Rafael Ratão missed, Adjei-Boateng 4-3, Nono missed

17.09.20 Stadionul Municipal, Botosani: FC Botosani – KF Shkëndija 79 0-1 (0-1)
FC Botosani: Eduard Pap, Alexandru Tiganasu, Alin Seroni, Denis Harut, Andrei Chindris, David Babunski (79' Mihai Roman), Eduard Florescu (71' Andrei Patache), Jonathan Rodriguez, Reagy Ofosu, Stefan Ashkovski (46') Hamidou Keyta, Marko Dugandzic.
Coach: Marius Croitoru.
KF Shkëndija 79: Kostadin Zahov, Mevlan Murati, Antonio Pavic, Egzon Bejtulai, Ján Krivák, Armend Alimi, Bruno Dita, Valon Ahmedi, Ennur Totre (75' Arbin Zejnullai), Besart Ibraimi (88' Zija Merdzhani), Ljupco Doriev (70' Valmir Nafiu). Coach: Ernest Gjoka.
Goal: 2' Besart Ibraimi 0-1.
Referee: Mohammed Al-Hakim (SWE)
Sent off: 67' Armend Alimi.

17.09.20   Stadion Lokomotiv, Plovdiv: Lokomotiv Plovdiv – Tottenham Hotspur 1-2 (0-0)
Lokomotiv Plovdiv: Martin Lukov, Milos Petrovic, Dinis Almeida, Lucas Masoero, Momchil Tsvetanov, Parvizchon Umarbaev (68' Georgi Minchev), Petar Vitanov (81' Filip Mihaljevic), Lucas Salinas, Dimitar Iliev, Birsent Karagaren, Ante Aralica (68' Christian Ilic).
Coach: Bruno Akrapovic.
Tottenham Hotspur: Hugo Lloris, Matt Doherty, Ben Davies, Davinson Sánchez (72' Lucas Moura), Moussa Sissoko (61' Tanguy NDombèlé), Pierre-Emile Højbjerg, Eric Dier, Giovani Lo Celso, Son Heung-Min, Harry Kane, Steven Bergwijn (70' Érik Lamela).
Coach: José Mourinho.
Goals: 71' Georgi Minchev 1-0, 80' Harry Kane 1-1 (p), 84' Tanguy NDombèlé 1-2.
Referee: Harm Osmers (GER)
Sent off: 78' Dinis Almeida, 79' Birsent Karagaren.

17.09.20   Baki Olimpiya Stadionu, Baku: Neftçi PFK – Galatasaray 1-3 (0-1)
Neftçi PFK: Aqil Mammadov, Vojislav Stankovic, Mamadou Mbodj, Anton Krivotsyuk, Omar Buludov, Emin Makhmudov, Namiq Alasgarov (65' Thallyson), Saman Nariman Jahan (70' Sabir Bougrine), Mamadou Kane, Yusuf Lawal, Prince Ibara (76' Mirabdulla Abbasov).
Coach: Fuzuli Mammadov.
Galatasaray: Fatih Öztürk, Ömer Bayram, Martin Linnes, Marcão Teixeira, Marcelo Saracchi, Christian Luyindama Nekadio, Younès Belhanda (46' Sofiane Féghouli), Taylan Antalyali, Emre Kilinç (68' Arda Turan), Ryan Babel (83' Jimmy Durmaz), Mbaye Diagne.
Coach: Fatih Terim.
Goals: 19' Mbaye Diagne 0-1, 46' Mamadou Mbodj 1-1,
48' Christian Luyindama Nekadio 1-2, 63' Mbaye Diagne 1-3.
Referee: Kevin Clancy (SCO)

17.09.20   Gamla Ullivi, Göteborg: IFK Göteborg – FC København 1-2 (0-0)
IFK Göteborg: Giannis Anestis, Mattias Bjärsmyr, André Calisir, Alexander Jallow (87' Hosam Aiesh), Yahya Kalley (69' Emil Holm), Jakob Johansson, Pontus Wernbloom, Tobias Sana, Alexander Farnerud (65' Sargon Abraham), August Erlingmark, Alhassan Yusuf.
Coach: Roland Nilsson.
FC København: Kalle Johnsson, Pierre Bengtsson, Andreas Bjelland (78' Robert Mudrazija), Guillermo Varela, Victor Nelsson, Rasmus Falk, Zeca, Viktor Fischer (78' Mikkel Kaufmann), Jens Stage (78' Pep Biel Mas), Kamil Wilczek, Jonas Wind. Coach: Ståle Solbakken.
Goals: 73' Tobias Sana 1-0, 82' Robert Mudrazija 1-1, 85' Jonas Wind 1-2.
Referee: Guillermo Cuadra (ESP)

17.09.20   Vilniaus LFF stadionas, Vilnius: FK Riteriai – Slovan Liberec 1-5 (0-2)
FK Riteriai: Tadas Simaitis, Valdemars Borovskis (83' Dovydas Virksas), Ricardas Sveikauskas, Dominykas Barauskas, Ángel Lezama, Deividas Malzinskas, Mindaugas Grigaravicius, Tomas Dombrauskis (62' Rokas Filipavicius), Lajo Traore (40' Matas Ramanauskas), Donatas Kazlauskas, Gytis Paulauskas. Coach: Tommi Petteri Pikkarainen.
Slovan Liberec: Filip Nguyen, Taras Kacharaba, Jan Mikula, Martin Koscelník, Mohamed Tijani, Jhon Mosquera, Jakub Hromada (80' Matej Chalus), Jakub Pesek (88' Jan Matousek), Kamso Mara, Michal Beran (63' Michael Rabusic), Abdulla Yusuf Helal.
Coach: Pavel Hoftych.
Goals: 12' Kamso Mara 0-1 (p), 20' Jakub Hromada 0-2, 61' Ángel Lezama 1-2,
84' Michael Rabusci 1-3, 89' Abdulla Yusuf Helal 1-4 (p), 90+3' Jan Matousek 1-5.
Referee: Espen Eskås (NOR)

17.09.20 Aspmyra Stadion, Bodø: FK Bodø/Glimt – FK Zalgiris 3-1 (2-1)
FK Bodø/Glimt: Nikita Haikin, Marius Høibråten, Marius Lode, Fredrik Bjørkan, Ulrk Saltnes, Morten Konradsen (72' Alfons Sampsted), Patrick Berg, Jens Hauge, Philip Zinckernagel, Sondre Fet (78' Ola Solbakken), Victor Boniface (89' Ole Amund Sveen).
Coach: Kjetil Knutsen.
FK Zalgiris: Martin Berkovec, Saulius Mikoliūnas, Donovan Slijngard, Ivan Tatomirovic, Nemanja Ljubisavljevic, Hugo Vidémont, Domantas Simkus (84' Mantas Kuklys), Modestas Vorobjovas, Andrija Kaludjerovic, Liviu Antal, Francis Kyeremeh (68' Marko Karamarko).
Coach: Aleksei Baga.
Goals: 20' Philip Zinckernagel 1-0, 26' Liviu Antal 1-1, 32' Victor Boniface 2-1, 81' Fredrik Bjørkan 3-1.
Referee: Peter Královic (SVK)

17.09.20 Stadion Stozice, Ljubljana:
Olimpija Ljubljana – Zrinjski Mostar 2-3 (1-0, 2-2) (a.e.t.)
Olimpija Ljubljana: Ziga Frelih, Uros Korun, Miral Samardzic, Matic Fink, Enrik Ostrc (56' Michael Pavlovic), Nik Kapun (105' Gal Kurez), Timi Elsnik, Angel Lyaskov (90' Drazen Bagaric), Mihail Caimacov, Andrés Vombergar (85' Ante Vukusic), Djordje Ivanovic.
Coach: Dino Skender.
Zrinjski Mostar: Ivan Brkic, Mario Ticinovic (78' Josip Corluka), Tomislav Barbaric, Pero Stojkic (73' Luis Ibáñez), Slobodan Jakovljevic, Ognjen Todorovic, Dinko Trebotic (66' Damir Zlomislic), Milos Filipovic, Ivan Enin, Nemanja Bilbija, Josip Ivancic (96' Anes Masic). Coach: Mladen Zizovic.
Goals: 19' Djordje Ivanovic 1-0, 51' Nemanja Bilbija 1-1, 81' Andrés Vombergar 2-1, 84' Nemanja Bilbija 2-2, 92' Josip Ivancic 2-3.
Referee: Ricardo De Burgos Bengoetxea (ESP)

Zrinjski Mostar won after extra time.

17.09.20 A. Le Coq Arena, Tallinn: FC Flora Tallinn – KR Reykjavík 2-1 (2-0)
FC Flora Tallinn: Matvei Igonen, Märten Kuusk, Henrik Pürg, Marco Lukka, Michael Lilander, Konstantin Vassiljev, Martin Miller (46' Markus Soomets), Vladislavs Kreida, Rauno Alliku (74' Frank Liivak), Rauno Sappinen (81' Mark Lepik), Vlasiy Sinyavskiy.
Coach: Jürgen Henn.
KR Reykjavík: Beitir Ólafsson, Arnór Adalsteinsson, Kristinn Jónsson, Finnur Tómas Pálmason (66' Óskar Hauksson), Pálmi Pálmason, Finnur Margeirsson (6' Pablo Punyed), Atli Sigurjónsson, Stefán Árni Geirsson, Kennie Chopart, Kristján Finnbogason, Ægir Jónasson.
Coach: Rúnar Kristinsson.
Goals: 7' Rauno Sappinen 1-0, 37' Michael Lilander 2-0, 74' Kristján Finnbogason 2-1.
Referee: Sigurd Smehus Kringstad (NOR)
Sent off: 58' Ægir Jónasson.

17.09.20 Stadionul Zimbru, Chisinau:
FC Sfântul Gheorghe – Partizan Beograd 0-1 (0-0, 0-0) (a.e.t.)
FC Sfântul Gheorghe: Nicolae Calancea, Andrey Novicov (90' Valerii Stepanenko), Serghei Svinarenko, Eugeniu Slivca, Vitalie Plamadeala, Petru Ojog, Sidy Sagna, Yevhen Smirnov, Dimitrii Mandrîcenco, Rienat Mochulyak (86' Mihail Ghecev), Roman Volkov (57' Sergiu Istrati). Coach: Sergiu Cebotari.
Partizan Beograd: Vladimir Stojkovic, Aleksandar Miljkovic, Uros Vitas, Bojan Ostojic, Slobodan Urosevic, Bibras Natcho, Seydouba Soumah (110' Aleksandar Scekic), Sasa Zdjelar, Takuma Asano (90' Aleksandar Lutovac), Umar Sadiq (78' Bojan Matic), Filip Stevanovic (63' Lazar Markovic). Coach: Aleksandar Stanojevic.
Goal: 104' Bibras Natcho 0-1 (p).
Referee: Juri Frischer (EST)

FC Sfântul Gheorghe played their home match at Stadionul Zimbru, Chisinau, instead of their regular stadium Suruceni Stadium, Suruceni.

17.09.20 Mikheil Meskhis Sakhelobis Stadionis Satadarigo Moedani, Tbilisi:
Lokomotivi Tbilisi – Dinamo Moskva 2-1 (0-0)
Lokomotivi Tbilisi: Giorgi Mamardashvili, Nika Sandokhadze, Giorgi Gabadze, Aleksandre Gureshidze, Daviti Ubilava, Temur Shonia, Davit Samurkasovi (62' Tornike Dzebniauri), Tornike Kirkitadze (83' Aleksandr Kobakhidze), Beka Dartsmelia, Imran Oulad Omar (65' Mamia Gavashelushvili), Irakli Sikharulidze. Coach: Giorgi Chiabrishvili.
Dinamo Moskva: Anton Shunin, Sergey Parshivlyuk, Ivan Ordets, Dmitriy Skopintsev (46' Grigori Morozov), Roman Evgenjev, Charles Kaboré, Maximilian Philipp (69' Sylvester Igboun), Daniil Fomin, Sebastian Szymanski, Clinton N'Jie (61' Daniil Lesovoy), Nikolay Komlichenko. Coach: Kirill Novikov.
Goals: 54' Irakli Sikharulidze 1-0, 76' Mamia Gavashelishvili 2-0, 90' Nikolay Komlichenko 2-1 (p).
Referee: Karim Abed (FRA)

17.09.20 Stadion Bâlgarska Armija, Sofia: CSKA Sofia – BATE Borisov 2-0 (1-0)
CSKA Sofia: Busatto, Jurgen Mattheij, Plamen Galabov, Geferson, Bradley Mazikou, Valentin Antov, Younousse Sankharé (68' Tiago Rodrigues), Amos Youga, Georgi Yomov (73' Jules Keita), Ali Sowe, Henrique (79' Graham Carey). Coach: Stamen Belchev.
BATE Borisov: Denis Shcherbitskiy, Egor Filipenko, Bojan Nastic, Aleksander Filipovic, Jakov Filipovic, Pavel Nekhaychik, Dmitriy Baga (77' Hervaine Moukam), Evgeni Yablonski (69' Aleksandr Volodko), Willum Thór Willumsson, Nemanja Milic (80' Bojan Dubajic), Maksim Skavysh. Coach: Kirill Alshevskiy.
Goals: 44' Ali Sowe 1-0, 90+5' Graham Carey 2-0.
Referee: Horatiu Fesnic (ROM)

17.09.20   Elbasan Arena, Elbasan: KF Laçi – Hapoel Be'er Sheva 1-2 (0-0)
KF Laçi: Alen Sherri, Aleksandar Ignjatovic, Rudolf Turkaj, Adolf Selmani, Ardit Deliu, Regi Lushkja, Juljan Shehu (46' Endrit Marku), Albion Marku (46' Donald Rapo), Teco, Kyrian Nwabueze (89' Renato Malota), Redon Xhixha. Coach: Armando Cungu.
Hapoel Be'er Sheva: Ohad Levita, Miguel Vítor, Loai Taha, Sean Goldberg, Elton Acolatse, Or Dadya, Sintayehu Sallalich (74' Rotem Hatuel), Josué, Marwan Kabha, Tomer Yosefi (61' Jhonatan Agudelo), Itamar Shviro (61' Gaëtan Varenne). Coach: Yossi Abukasis.
Goals: 59' Kyrian Nwabueze 1-0, 90' Jhonatan Agudelo 1-1, 90+3' Gaëtan Varenne 1-2.
Referee: Jochem Kamphuis (HOL)
Sent off: 86' Ardit Deliu.

KF Laçi played their home match at Elbasan Arena, Elbasan, instead of their regular stadium Laçi Stadium, Laçi.

17.09.20   MFA Centenary Stadium, Ta'Qali: Hibernians FC – Fehérvár FC 0-1 (0-0)
Hibernians FC: Matthew Calleja Cremona, Leandro Almeida, Andrei Agius, Ferdinando Apap, Zachary Grech (64' Rundell Winchester), Gabriel Izquier, Jake Grech, Wilkson (74' Edafe Uzeh), Shola Shodiya, Jurgen Degabriele, Ayrton Attard (83' Dustan Vella). Coach: Stefano Sanderra.
Fehérvár FC: Ádam Kovácsik, Attila Fiola, Loïc Négo, Stopira, Visar Musliu, Bendegúz Bolla, Ivan Petryak (83' Evandro), Boban Nikolov, Lyes Houri, Alef (51' Máté Pátkai), Budu Zivzivadze (88' Nemanja Nikolic). Coach: Gábor Márton.
Goals: 61' Boban Nikolov 0-1.
Referee: Ivaylo Stoyanov (BUL)
Sent off: 90+3' Shola Shodiya.

17.09.20   Stadio Thódoros Vardinoyánnis, Heraklion:
             OFI Crete – Apollon Limassol 0-1 (0-0)
OFI Crete: Boy Waterman, Konstantinos Giannoulis (80' Nikos Korovesis), Nikolaos Marinakis (68' Adil Nabi), Praxitelis Vouros, Vahid Selimovic, Abul Rahman Oues, Miguel Mellado, Paschalis Staikos (68' Nazareno Solis), Juan Neira, Adrián Sardinero, João Figueiredo. Coach: Georgios Simos.
Apollon Limassol: Demetris Demetriou, Valentin Roberge, Attila Szalai, Nicolas Diguiny, Héctor Yuste, Florentin Matei (46' Charlison Benschop), Diego Aguirre, Esteban Sachetti, Djordje Denic, João Pedro (46' Ioannis Pittas), Bagaliy Dabo (79' Giannis Gianniotas). Coach: Sofronis Avgousti.
Goal: 50' Attila Szalai 0-1.
Referee: Fabio Maresca (ITA)

17.09.20   Tele2 Arena, Stockholm: Djurgårdens IF – Europa FC 2-1 (1-0)
Djurgårdens IF: Per Bråtveit, Elliot Käck, Jacob Une-Larsson, Aslak Witry, Haris Radetinac (84' Jonathan Ring), Magnus Eriksson, Fredrik Ulvestad, Jesper Karlström, Curtis Edwards (64' Jonathan Augustinsson), Karl Holmberg, Edward Chilufya (72' Emir Kujovic). Coach: Kim Bergstrand.
Europa FC: Javi Muñoz, Olmo González, Ethan Jolley, Jayce Olivero, Álex Quillo, Polaco (85' Mitchell Gibson), Juampe Rico (79' Michael Yome), Liam Walker, Marco Rosa (36' Kwadwo Poku), Ale Carrascal, Adrián Gallardo. Coach: Rafael Escobar.
Goals: 42' Curtis Edwards 1-0, 57' Adrián Gallardo 1-1, 69' Fredrik Ulvestad 2-1 (p).
Referee: Stéphanie Frappart (FRA)
Sent off: 62' Álex Quillo.

17.09.20   Racecourse Ground, Wrexham:
Connah's Quay Nomads FC – Dinamo Tbilisi 0-1 (0-0)
Connah's Quay Nomads FC: Lewis Brass, John Disney, Daniel Davies, Kris Owens, Callum Roberts, Priestley Farquharson, Aeron Edwards, Jay Owen, Declan Poole, Sameron Dool, Jamie Insall (87' Aron Williams). Coach: Andy Morrison.
Dinamo Tbilisi: Roin Kvaskhvadze, Giorgi Kimadze, Nodar Iashvili, Davit Kobouri, Simon Ghegnon, Giorgi Papava, Nodar Kavtaradze (90+5' Rodney Klooster), Bakar Kardava, Giorgi Zaria (80' Tornike Kapanadze), Giorgi Gabedava, Filip Orsula (59' José Vitor Pernambuco). Coach: Xisco Muñoz.
Goal: 90+7' Giorgi Gabedava 0-1 (p).
Referee: Alain Durieux (LUX)

17.09.20   Sammy Ofer Stadium, Haifa: Maccabi Haifa – KF Kairat 2-1 (1-1)
Maccabi Haifa: Josh Cohen, Ernest Mabouka, Sun Menachem, Ayed Habashi, Ofri Arad, Tjaronn Chery, Yuval Ashkenazi (55' Dolev Haziza), Neta Lavi, Mohammad Abu Fani, Nikita Rukavytsya (84' José Rodríguez), Yanic Wildschut (74' Bogdan Planic). Coach: Barak Bakhar.
KF Kairat: Stas Pokatilov, Gafurzhan Suyumbayev, Dino Mikanovic, Rade Dugalic, Nuraly Alip, Nebojsa Kosovic, Jacek Góralski, Aybol Abiken (87' Yerkebulan Tungyshbayev), Gulzhygit Alykulov (81' Konrad Wrzesinski), Vágner Love, Abat Aymbetov (64' Aderinsola Eseola). Coach: Aleksey Shpilevskiy.
Goals: 31' Yuval Ashkenazi 1-0, 45+1' Vágner Love 1-1, 72' Nikita Rukavytsya 2-1.
Referee: Mads-Kristoffer Kristoffersen (DEN)

17.09.20   Estadi Comunal d'Andorra la Vella, Andorra la Vella:
Inter Club d'Escaldes – Dundalk FC 0-1 (0-1)
Inter Club d'Escaldes: Josep Gómes, Ildefons Lima, Federico Bessone, Jordi Rubio (86' Óscar Reyes), Emili García, Raul Feher, Marc Pujol, Albert Reyes, Sergi Moreno (82' Jordi Roca), Genis Soldevila, Jordi Betriu (78' Bruninho). Coach: Adolfo Baines.
Dundalk FC: Gary Rogers, Brian Gartland, Andrew Boyle, Sean Hoare, Darragh Leahy, Chris Shields, Sean Murray (70' John Mountney), Gregory Sloggett, Stefan Colovic (60' Sean Gannon), David McMillan (71' Patrick Hoban), Michael Duffy. Coach: Shane Keegan.
Goal: 14' David McMillan 0-1.
Referee: Viktor Shimusik (BLS)
Sent off: 58' Andrew Boyle.

17.09.20   Tallaght Stadium, Dublin: Shamrock Rovers – AC Milan 0-2 (0-1)
Shamrock Rovers: Alan Mannus, Joey O'Brien, Roberto Lopes, Lee Grace, Ronan Finn, Aaron McEneff, Jack Byrne, Gary O'Neill (70' Dylan Watts), Neil Farrugia (83' Sean Kavanagh), Aaron Greene (88' Dean Williams), Graham Burke. Coach: Stephen Bradley.
AC Milan: Gianluigi Donnarumma, Simon Kjær, Davide Calabria, Theo Hernández, Matteo Gabbia, Hakan Çalhanoglu (84' Brahim Díaz), Samu Castillejo, Franck Kessié, Ismaël Bennacar (84' Sandro Tonali), Alexis Saelemaekers (74' Rade Krunic), Zlatan Ibrahimovic. Coach: Stefano Pioli.
Goals: 23' Zlatan Ibrahimovic 0-1, 67' Hakan Çalhanoglu 0-2.
Referee: Ádám Farkas (HUN)

17.09.20   Stadion Miejski, Gliwice: Piast Gliwice – TSV Hartberg 3-2 (1-1)
Piast Gliwice: Frantisek Plach, Piotr Malarczyk (89' Bartosz Rymaniak), Mikkel Kirkeskov, Jakub Czerwinski, Tomás Huk, Martin Konczkowski, Tomasz Jodlowiec, Krisztófer Vida (78' Dominik Steczyk), Patryk Lipski, Patryk Sokolowski, Piotr Parzyszek (55' Michal Zyro). Coach: Waldemar Fornalik.
TSV Hartberg: Rene Swete, Andreas Lienhart (73' Stefan Gölles), Christian Klem, Manfred Gollner (67' Julius Ertlthaler), Thomas Rotter, Tobias Kainz, Felix Luckeneder, Lukas Ried, Samson Tijani (89' Michael Huber), Dario Tadic, Rajko Rep. Coach: Markus Schopp.
Goals: 10' Martin Konczkowski 1-0, 33' Tobias Kainz 1-1, 62' Patryk Sokolowski 2-1, 75' Lukas Ried 2-2, 84' Michal Zyro 3-2.
Referee: Erik Lambrechts (BEL)

17.09.20   Stade Maurice Dufrasne, Liège: Standard Liège – Bala Town FC 2-0 (2-0)
Standard Liège: Arnaud Bodart, Kostas Laifis, Nicolas Gavory, Collins Fai, Zinho Vanheusden, Mehdi Carcela-González, Gojko Cimirot (72' Merveille Bopé Bokadi), Eden Shamir, Selim Amallah (67' Jackson Muleka), Felipe Avenatti (84' Obbi Oularé), Michel Balikwisha. Coach: Philippe Montanier.
Bala Town FC: Alex Ramsay, Antony Kay (81' Anthony Stephens), Nathan Peate, Sean Smith, Jonathan Spittle, Steven Leslie (81' Henry Jones), Chris Venables, Will Evans, Oliver Shannon, Lassana Mendes, Raul Correia (57' Kieran Smith). Coach: Colin Caton.
Goals: 19' Felipe Avenatti 1-0 (p), 34' Selim Amallah 2-0.
Referee: Trustin Farrugia Cann (MLT)

17.09.20   Stadio Harilaou Klénthis Vikelídis, Saloniki:
              Aris Saloniki – Kolos Kovalivka 1-2 (0-0)
Aris Saloniki: Julián Cuesta, Lindsay Rose, Toni Datkovic, Cristian Ganea (69' Dimitrios Manos), Bruno Gama, Javier Matilla, Facundo Bertoglio, Ioannis Fetfatzidis, Lucas Sasha (78' Daniel Mancini), James Jeggo, Cristian López. Coach: Michael Oenning.
Kolos Kovalivka: Evgen Volynets, Vitaly Gavrish, Evgen Novak, Kyrylo Petrov, Oleksy Zozulya (51' Yevgeniy Morozko), Vladislav Emets, Evgeniy Zadoya, Andriy Bogdanov, Yevgeniy Smyrnyi (88' Denys Kostyshyn), Vladimir Lisenko (64' Yevhen Seleznyov), Denys Antyukh. Coach: Ruslan Kostyshyn.
Goals: 47' Evgen Novak 0-1, 55' Bruno Gama 1-1, 62' Denys Antyukh 1-2.
Referee: Lionel Tschudi (SUI)

17.09.20   Gradski Stadion, Banja Luka: Borac Banja Luka – Rio Ave FC 0-2 (-0)
Borac Banja Luka: Bojan Pavlovic, Marko Jovanovic, Djordje Cosic, Djordje Milojevic, Stojan Vranjes, Goran Zakaric, Sinisa Dujakovic (90+5' Boban Georgiev), Marko Brtan (90+1' Aleksandar Vojinovic), Almedin Dino Ziljkic, Vladan Danilovic, Jovo Lukic (87' Sasa Kajkut). Coach: Vlado Jagodic.
Rio Ave FC: Pawel Kieszek, Ivo Pinto, Aderllan Santos, Matheus Reis, Toni Borevkovic, Tarantini, Filipe Augusto, Francisco "Chico" Geraldes (75' Gelson Dala), Bruno Moreira (90+3' Nikola Jambor), Carlos Mané, Lucas Piazón (90+5' Gabrielzinho). Coach: Mário Silva.
Goals: 90' Tarantini 0-1, 90+6' Nikola Jambor 0-2.
Referee: Peter Kjærsgaard-Andersen (DEN)

17.09.20   Air Albania Stadium, Tirana: FK Kukësi – VfL Wolfsburg 0-4 (0-2)
FK Kukësi: Entonjo Elezaj, Kenan Horic, Edis Malikji, Erhun Obanor, Besir Demiri, Bruno Telushi, Emiljano Musta (46' Albin Gashi), Eduart Rroca (70' Godberg Cooper), Besar Musolli (60' Zenel Gavazaj), Vesel Limaj, Patrick Eze. Coach: Skënder Gega.
VfL Wolfsburg: Koen Casteels, Paulo Otávio, Maxence Lacroix, Admir Mehmedi, Josuha Guilavogui, Felix Klaus (68' Jérôme Roussillon), Maximilian Arnold (36' Yannick Gerhardt), Renato Steffen, Xaver Schlager, Josip Brekalo (74' João Victor), Wout Weghorst.
Coach: Oliver Glasner.
Goals: 21' Wout Weghorst 0-1, 33' Maxence Lacroix 0-2, 74' Wout Weghorst 0-3, 89' Admir Mehmedi 0-4.
Referee: Duje Strukan (CRO)

Eduart Rroca missed a penalty kick (35').

FK Kukësi played their home match at Air Albania Stadium, Tirana, instead of their regular stadium Zeqir Ymeri Stadium, Kukës, which was under reconstruction.

17.09.20   Tose Proeski Arena, Skopje: Sileks Kratova – Drita Gjilan 0-2 (0-0)
Sileks Kratova: Daniel Bozhinovski, Srdjan Draskovic, Hristijan Grozdanoski, Denis Ristov (81' Bojan Spirkoski), Angelce Timovski, Burhan Mustafov, Dejan Tanturovski, Viktor Serafimovski, Daniel Karcheski, Pepi Gorgiev (55' Stefan Djuric), Ivan Ivanovski (46' Kristijan Kostovski). Coach: Goran Simov.
Drita Gjilan: Faton Maloku, Ardijan Cuculi, Fidan Gërbeshi, Ardian Limani, Ilir Blakçori, Erjon Vucaj (76' Bujar Shabani), Xhevdet Shabani (67' Vladica Brdarovski), Hamdi Namani, Almir Ajzeraj, Astrit Fazliu (88' Ergyn Ahmeti), Betim Haxhimusa. Coach: Ardijan Nuhiji.
Goals: 48' Fidan Gërbeshi 0-1 (p), 81' Ardian Limani 0-2.
Referee: Andy Madley (ENG)
Sent off: 78' Hristijan Grozdanoski.

Sileks Kratova played their home match at Tose Proeski Arena, Skopje, instead of their regular stadium Gradski stadion Kratova, Kratova.

17.09.20   Mestni Stadion Fazanerija, Murska Soboto: NS Mura – Aarhus GF 3-0 (1-0)
NS Mura: Matko Obradovic, Ziga Kous, Klemen Sturm, Jan Gorenc, Zan Karniczik, Nino Kouter (90+2' Amadej Marosa), Alen Kozar, Luka Bobicanec (82' Dragan Lovric), Kevin Zizek, Andrija Filipovic (69' Tomi Horvat), Kai Cipot. Coach: Ante Simundza.
Aarhus GF: William Eskelinen, Niklas Backman, Casper Højer Nielsen, Alexander Munksgaard, Frederik Tingager, Nikolai Poulsen, Patrick Olsen, Bror Blume (73' Nicklas Helenius), Jón Dagur Thorsteinsson (76' Albert Erlykke), Gift Links (30' Søren Tengstedt), Patrick Mortensen. Coach: David Nielsen.
Goals: 37' Jan Gorenc 1-0, 72' Kevin Zizek 2-0, 90+5' Amadej Marosa 3-0.
Referee: Giorgi Kruashvili (GEO)

17.09.20　The Snowgrounds, Coleraine: Coleraine FC – Motherwell FC 2-2 (0-2, 2-2) (a.e.t.)
Coleraine FC: Gareth Deane, Aaron Traynor (74' Ian Parkhill), Gareth McConaghie, Stephen O'Donnell, Lyndon Kane, Stephen Lowry, Josh Carson, Ben Doherty, Aaron Jarvis (8' Jamie Glackin), James McLaughlin (117' Curtis Allen), Stewart Nixon (52' Eoin Bradley).
Coach: Oran Kearney.
Motherwell FC: Trevor Carson, Declan Gallagher, Stephen O'Donnell, Ricki Lamie, Nathan McGinley (65' Sherwin Seedorf), Bevis Mugabi, Liam Polworth (87' Barry Maguire), Mark O'Hara, Allan Campbell (91' Chris Long), Tony Watt, Callum Lang (87' Jake Hastie).
Coach: Stephen Robinson.
Goals: 16' Callum Lang 0-1, 37' Tony Watt 0-2, 49', 90' Ben Doherty 1-2 (p), 2-2 (p).
Referee: Antti Mumukka (FIN)
Sent off: 89' Bevis Mugabi.

Motherwell FC won on penalties after extra time (3-0).
Penalties: O'Hara 1-0, Parkhill missed, Watt 2-0, Kane missed, O'Donnell 3-0, McConaghie missed.

17.09.20　SR-Bank Arena, Stavanger: Viking FK – Aberdeen FC 0-2 (0-1)
Viking FK: Iven Austbø, Rolf Vikstøl, Viljar Vevatne (76' Sondre Bjørshol), Alex Andrésson (76' Tommy Høiland), Henrik Heggheim, Fredrik Torsteinbø, Zymer Bytyqi, Joe Bell, Veton Berisha, Yann-Erik de Lanlay (85' Even Østensen), Yildren Ibrahimaj.
Coach: Bjarne Berntsen.
Aberdeen FC: Joe Lewis, Andrew Considine, Tommie Hoban, Scott McKenna, Jonny Hayes, Marley Watkins (90+1' Curtis Main), Dylan McGeouch (73' Shay Logan), Ryan Hedges, Ross McCrorie, Lewis Ferguson, Scott Wright (72' Funso Ojo). Coach: Derek McInnes.
Goals: 44' Ross McCrorie 0-1, 78' Ryan Hedges 0-2.
Referee: Filip Glova (SVK)

17.09.20　MOL Aréna, Dunajská Streda:
　　　　　DAC Dunajská Streda – FK Jablonec 5-3 (1-1, 3-3) (a.e.t.)
DAC Dunajská Streda: Martin Jedlicka, Éric Davis, Jannik Müller, Dominik Kruzliak, César Blackman, Zsolt Kalmár (120+2' Sainey Njie), Andrija Balic (105' Martin Bednár), Andrej Fábry (78' Ion Nilolaescu), András, Schäfer, Eric Ramírez, Marko Divkovic (113' Danilo Beskorovayniy). Coach: Bernd Storck.
FK Jablonec: Jan Hanus, Jakub Prodaný, Jaroslav Zelený (110' Dominik Plestil), Vojtech Kubista, Libor Holík, Jakub Martinec, Tomáš Hübschman, Jakub Povazanez (98' Václav Pilar), Tomáš Ladra (86' Vladimir Jovovic), Ivan Schranz, Tomáš Cvancara (79' Martin Dolezal). Coach: Petr Rada.
Goals: 6' Marko Divkovic 1-0, 25' Jaroslav Zelený 1-1, 57' Ivan Schranz 1-2, 65' Marko Divkovic 2-2, 71' Ivan Schranz 2-3 (p), 85', 96' Ion Nicolaescu 3-3, 4-3, 114' Éric Davis 5-3.
Referee: Marco Di Bello (ITA)

DAC Dunajská Streda won after extra time.

17.09.20   Stade de Genève, Carouge: Servette Genève – Stade de Reims 0-1 (0-1)
Servette Genève: Jérémy Frick, Anthony Sauthier, Vincent Sasso, Steve Rouiller, Arial Mendy (85' Moussa Diallo), Miroslav Stevanovic, Gaël Ondoua, Timothé Cognat, Varol Tasar (46' Koro Koné), Kastriot Imeri (74' Alex Schalk), Grejohn Kyei. Coach: Alain Geiger.
Stade de Reims: Predrag Rajkovic, Thomas Foket, Wout Faes, Ghislain Konan, Valon Berisha, Xavier Chavalerin, Dereck Kutesa (65' Kaj Sierhuis), Moreto Cassamá (81' Mathieu Cafaro), Marshall Munetsi, Boulaye Dia (90+2' Arber Zeneli), El Bilal Touré. Coach: David Guion.
Goal: 4' Valon Berisha 0-1.
Referee: Stuart Steven Attwell (ENG)

17.09.20   Stadion Gradski vrt, Osijek: NK Osijek – FC Basel 1-2 (0-2)
NK Osijek: Ivica Ivusic, Mile Skoric, Ante Majstorovic, Igor Carioca, Talys Oliveira, Vedran Jugovic, László Kleinheisler (76' Marin Pilj), Petar Bockaj (81' Alen Grgic), Mihael Zaper, Ante Erceg, Eros Grezda (64' Ramón Miérez). Coach: Nenad Bjelica.
FC Basel: Djordje Nikolic, Silvan Widmer, Omar Alderete, Eray Cömert, Andrea Padula, Valentin Stocker, Fabian Frei, Samuele Campo (85' Jasper van der Werff), Ricky van Wolfswinkel, Arthur Cabral (63' Kemal Ademi), Afimico Pululu (70' Julian von Moos). Coach: Ciriaco Sforza.
Goals: 18' Arthur Cabral 0-1, 44' Valentin Stocker 0-2, 84' Ante Majstorovic 1-2.
Referee: José Luis Munuera Montero (ESP)

17.09.20   Windsor Park, Belfast: Linfield FC – Floriana FC 0-1 (0-1)
Linfield FC: Christopher Johns, Matthew Clarke (62' Andrew Waterworth), Niall Quinn, Ethan Boyle, Jamie Mulgrew, Jimmy Callacher, Bastien Héry (78' Daniel Kearns), Stephen Fallon, Navid Nasseri (61' Christy Manzinga), Shayne Lavery, Ross Larkin.
Coach: David Healy.
Floriana FC: Ini Akpan, Enzo Ruiz, Jurgen Pisani, Ryan Camenzuli, Diego Venancio Silva, Nicola Leone, Brandon Paiber (61' Ulises Arias, 86' Moustapha Beye), Matías García, Kristian Keqi (83' Flávio Carioca), Tiago Adan, Marcelo Dias. Coach: Vincenzo Potenza.
Goal: 10' Matías Dias 0-1.
Referee: David Munro (SCO)
Sent off: 74' Ross Larkin.

17.09.20   Gradski Stadion, Senta: TSC Backa Topola – FCSB 6-6 (2-1, 4-4) (a.e.t.)
TSC Backa Topola: Nenad Filipovic, Goran Antonic, Dajan Ponjevic, Filip Babic (64' Mihajlo Banjac), Bojan Balaz, Janko Tumbasevic, Nenad Lukic (75' Vladimir Siladji), Sasa Tomanovic, Djuro Zec, Dejan Milicevic (115' Vasilije Djuric), Borko Duronjic (45+1' Nemanja Petrovic). Coach: Zoltán Szabó.
FCSB: Razvan Ducan, Valentin Cretu, Marius Briceag, Ionut Pantîru, Grigoras Pantea (21' Adrian Petre), Olimpiu Morutan, Gabriel Simion, Ovidiu Perianu, Alexandru Buziuc (46' Robert Ion), Florinel Coman (73' Ovidiu Horsia), Dennis Man. Coach: Anton Petrea.
Goals: 11' Dejan Milicevic 1-0, 14' Borko Duronjic 2-0, 25' Florinel Coman 2-1, 50' Dennis Man 2-2, 51' Goran Antonic 3-2, 63' Dennis Man 3-3 (p), 90+2' Bojan Balaz 3-4 (og), 90+4' Sasa Tomanovic 4-4, 1-5' Dennis Man 4-5, 105+1' Janko Tumbasevic 5-5, 108' Adrian Petre 5-6, 117' Sasa Tomanovic 6-6.
Referee: Dennis Higler (HOL)
Sent off: 44' Dajan Ponjevic, 103' Vladimir Siladji.

FCSB won on penalties after extra time (5-4).
Penalties: Tomanovic 1-0, Morutan 1-1, Zec 2-1, Perianu 2-2, Banjac missed, Pantîru 2-3, Antonic 3-3, Petre 3-4, Djuric 4-4, Man 4-5.

TSC Backa Topola played their home match at Gradski Stadion, Senta, instead of their regular stadium City Stadium in Backa Topola.

17.09.20   Hidegkuti Nándor Stadion, Budapest: Budapest Honvéd – Malmö FF 0-2 (0-1)
Budapest Honvéd: Tomás Tujvel, Botond Baráth, Bence Batik, Naser Aliji, Mohamed Mezghrani, Patrik Hidi, Donát Zsótér (46' Norbert Szendrei), Dániel Gazdag, Bertalan Bocskay (84' Barna Kesztyüs), Roland Ugrai, Norbert Balogh (69' Boubacar Traoré). Coach: Tamás Bódog.
Malmö FF: Marko Johansson, Eric Larsson, Lasse Nielsen, Jonas Knudsen, Anel Ahmedhodzic, Søren Rieks (79' Arnór Traustason), Oscar Lewicki (90+3' Samuel Adrian), Erdal Rakip, Ola Toivonen, Jo Inge Berget, Amin Sarr (67' Adi Nalic). Coach: Jon Dahl Tomasson.
Goals: 42' Ola Toivonen 0-1, 86' Arnór Traustason 0-2.
Referee: Anastasios Papapetrou (GRE)

Budapest Honvéd played their home match at Hidegkuti Nándor Stadion, Budapest, instead of their regular stadium Bozsik József Stadion (1913), Budapest, as it was demolished to be replaced by their new stadium Bozsik József Aréna, Budapest.

18.09.20   Stadions Skonto, Riga: Riga FC – SP Tre Fiori 1-0 (0-0)
Riga FC: Roberts Ozols, Elvis Stuglis, Herdi Prenga, Vladimirs Kamess, Ritvars Rugins, Felipe Brisola, Pedrinho (85' Vyacheslav Sharpar), Stefan Panic, Jordan N'Kololo, Vladislavs Fjororovs, Stefan Milosevic (78' Kule Mbombo). Coach: Oleg Kononov.
SP Tre Fiori: Aldo Simoncini, Davide Simoncini, Giovanni Bonini, Angelo Gregorio, Luca Angelini (83' Pablo Martini), Paolo Vandi (90+1' Lorenzo Perotto), Pier Figone, Lounseny Kalissa, Nicholas Santoni (79' Durell Bilendo Duma), Joel Apezteguía Hijuelos, Bojan Gjurchinoski. Coach: Matteo Cecchetti.
Goal: 57' Pedrinho 1-0.
Referee: Kári Jóannesarson á Høvdanum (FRO)

THIRD QUALIFYING ROUND

Byes: KF Tirana, PFC Ludogorets Razgrad.

23.09.20   Neo GSP Stadium, Nicosia: Apollon Limassol – KKS Lech Poznan 0-5 (0-1)
Apollon Limassol: Demetris Demetriou, Valentin Roberge, Attila Szalai, Ioannis Pittas (46' Daniel Larsson), Nicolas Diguiny, Diego Aguirre, Esteban Sachetti (66' Sasa Markovic), Djordje Denic, Fanos Katelaris, Charlison Benschop, Bagaliy Dabo (14' Giannis Gianniotas).
Coach: Sofronis Avgousti.
KKS Lech Poznan: Filip Bednarek, Lubomir Satka, Alan Czerwinski, Djordje Crnomarkovic, Tymoteusz Puchacz, Jan Sýkora, Pedro Tiba, Dani Ramírez, Jakub Moder (73' Karlo Muhar), Jakub Kaminski (76' Michal Skóras), Mikael Ishak (67' Nika Kacharava).
Coach: Dariusz Zuraw.
Goals: 42' Pedro Tiba 0-1, 47' Mikael Ishak 0-2, 58' Jakub Kaminski 0-3, 81' Jan Sýkora 0-4, 90+1' Pedro Tiba 0-5.
Referee: Mattias Gestranius (FIN)

Apollon Limassol played their home match at Neo GSP Stadium, Nicosia, instead of their regular stadium Tsirio Stadium, Limassol.

24.09.20   FFA Academy Stadium, Yerevan:
            FC Ararat-Armenia – NK Celje 1-0 (0-0, 0-0) (a.e.t.)
FC Ararat-Armenia: Stefan Cupic, Alemão, Sergiy Vakulenko, Ângelo Meneses, David Humanes (83' Yusuf Otubanjo), Yoan Gouffran (105' Armen Ambartsumyan), Sargis Shahinyan, Furdjel Narsingh, Zakaria Sanogo, Mailson, Jeisson Martínez (120+1' Louis Ogana). Coach: David Campaña.
NK Celje: Matjaz Rozman, Denis Marandici, Amadej Brecl, Zan Zaletel, Dusan Stojinovic, Matic Vrbanec (91' Nino Pungarsek), Lan Stravs (99' Zan Benedicic), Mitja Lotric, Filip Dangubic, Ivan Bozic (112' Mico Kuzmanovic), Luka Kerin (86' Jakob Novak).
Coach: Dusan Kosic.
Goal: 111' Sergiy Vakalenko 1-0.
Referee: John Beaton (SCO)

FC Ararat-Armenia won after extra time.

24.09.20   Savon Sanomat Areena, Kuopio: Kuopion PS – FK Sūdova Marijampolé 2-0 (1-0)
Kuopion PS: Otso Virtanen, Igors Tarasovs, Artur Pikk, Nuno Tomás, Petteri Pennanen, Bismark Adjei-Boateng, Urho Nissilä, Ats Purje, Saku Savolainen, Rangel (86' Aniekpeno Udoh), Usman Sale. Coach: Arne Erlandsen.
FK Sūdova Marijampolé: Ivan Kardum, Vaidas Slavickas, Thomas Salamon, Andro Svrljuga, Aleksandar Zivanovic, Semir Kerla, Ivan Haldík, Nicolás Gorobsov (66' Domagoj Pusic), Giedrius Matulevicius (76' Eligijus Jankauskas), Josip Tadic, Valērijs Sabala (59' Mihret Topcagic). Coach: Saulius Sirmelis.
Goals: 31' Rangel 1-0, 72' Igors Tarasovs 2-0.
Referee: Manuel Schüttengruber (AUT)

24.09.20   MOL Aréna Sóstó, Székesfehérvár: Fehérvár FC – Stade de Reims 0-0 (a.e.t.)
Fehérvár FC: Ádam Kovácsik, Attila Fiola, Loïc Négo, Stopira, Visar Musliu, Szilveszter Hangya, Bendegúz Bolla, Ivan Petryak (76' Armin Hodzic), Boban Nikolov, Lyes Houri, Budu Zivzivadze (68' Evandro). Coach: Gábor Márton.
Stade de Reims: Predrag Rajkovic, Yunis Abdelhamid, Thomas Foket, Wout Faes, Ghislain Konan, Valon Berisha (80' El Bilal Touré), Xavier Chavalerin, Dereck Kutesa (69' Anastasios Donis), Marshall Munetsi, Arber Zeneli (63' Kaj Sierhuis), Boulaye Dia. Coach: David Guion.
Referee: Matej Jug (SVN)
Sent off: 115' Thomas Foket.

Fehérvár FC won on penalties after extra time (4-1).
Penalties: Evandro 1-0, Dia missed, Stopira 2-0, Abdelhamid missed, Hodzic 3-0, Konan 3-1, Négo 4-1.

24.09.20   Doosan Aréna, Plzen: FC Viktoria Plzen – SønderjyskE 3-0 (2-0)
FC Viktoria Plzen: Ales Hruska, David Limberský, Jakub Brabec, Lukás Hejda, Milan Havel, Jan Kopic, Ales Cermák (90' Pavel Bucha), Miroslav Kácer, Lukás Kalvach, Adriel D'Avila Ba Loua (71' Joel Kayamba), Zdenek Ondrásek (79' Jean-David Beauguel).
Coach: Adrián Gula.
SønderjyskE: Lawrence Thomas, Pierre Kanstrup, Marc Hende, Patrick Banggaard, Stefan Gartenmann, Mads Albæk (72' Emil Frederiksen), Alexander Bah, Victor Ekani, Johan Absalonsen (74' Haji Wright), Anders Jacobsen, Rilwan Hassan (31' Julius Eskesen).
Coach: Glen Riddersholm.
Goals: 35' Zdenek Ondrásek 1-0 (p), 41' Adriel D'Avila Ba Loua 2-0, 51' Miroslav Kácer 3-0.
Referee: Donatas Rumsas (LTU)

24.09.20   Rostov Arena, Rostov-na-Donu: FK Rostov – Maccabi Haifa 1-2 (1-1)
FK Rostov: Sergei Pesyakov, Aleksey Kozlov, Evgeniy Chernov, Maksim Osipenko, Roman Eremenko (64' Kento Hashimoto), Aleksey Ionov, Khoren Bayramyan (64' Dmitriy Poloz), Mathias Normann, Dennis Hadzikadunic, Danil Glevoc, Eldor Shomurodov (82' David Tosevski). Coach: Valeriy Karpin.
Maccabi Haifa: Josh Cohen, Ernest Mabouka, Bogdan Planic, Sun Menachem, Ayed Habashi, Ofri Arad, Tjaronn Chery, Neta Lavi, Mohammad Abu Fani (83' José Rodríguez), Nikita Rukavytsya (89' Stav Nachmani), Dolev Haziza (84' Yuval Ashkenazi). Coach: Barak Bakhar.
Goals: 9' Eldor Shomurodov 1-0, 20' Nikita Rukavytsya 1-1, 60' Mohammad Abu Fani 1-2.
Referee: Petr Ardeleánu (CZE)
Sent off: 68' Danil Glebov.

24.09.20   Mestni Stadion Fazanerija, Murska Sobota: NS Mura – PSV Eindhoven 1-5 (1-2)
NS Mura: Matko Obradovic, Ziga Kous, Klemen Sturm, Jan Gorenc, Zan Karniczik, Nino Kouter, Alen Kozar, Luka Bobicanec, Tomi Horvat (76' Marko Brkic), Kevin Zizek (81' Amadej Marosa), Andrija Filipovic (76' Luka Maric). Coach: Ante Simundza.
PSV Eindhoven: Yvon Mvogo, Philipp Max, Olivier Boscagli, Denzel Dumfries, Jordan Teze, Ryan Thomas (76' Michal Sadílek), Mauro Júnior, Pablo Rosario, Bruma, Maximiliano Romero (11' Cody Gakpo), Donyell Malen (86' Noni Madueke). Coach: Roger Schmidt.
Goals: 17' Donyell Malen 0-1, 21' Nino Kouter 1-1, 28' Mauro Júnior 1-2, 54' Cody Gakpo 1-3, 65' Donyell Malen 14, 90' Cody Gakpo 1-5.
Referee: Sandro Schärer (SUI)

24.09.20   Stade du Pays de Charleroi, Charleroi:
Sporting Charleroi – Partizan Beograd 2-1 (1-0, 1-1) (a.e.t.)
Sporting Charleroi: Nicolas Penneteau, Dorian Dessoleil, Steeven Willems, Maxime Busi, Ryota Morioka, Marco Ilaimaharitra, Joris Kayembe (114' Ivan Goranov), Mamadou Fall (109' Ken Nkuba), Ali Gholizadeh (112' Lucas Ribeiro Costa), Kaveh Rezaei (118' Guillaume Gillet), Shamar Nicholson. Coach: Karim Belhocine.
Partizan Beograd: Vladimir Stojkovic, Aleksandar Miljkovic, Uros Vitas (91' Bojan Ostojic), Macky Bagnack, Slobodan Urosevic, Bibras Natcho (98' Aleksandar Scekic), Lazar Markovic, Sasa Zdjelar, Takuma Asano (111' Dennis Stojkovic), Umar Sadiq, Filip Stevanovic (46' Seydouba Soumah). Coach: Aleksandar Stanojevic.
Goals: 10' Dorian Dessoleil 1-0, 53' Seydouba Soumah 1-1, 108' Kaveh Rezaei 2-1.
Referee: Robert Madden (SCO)

Sporting Charleroi won after extra time.

24.09.20   Eleda Stadion, Malmö: Malmö FF – Lokomotiva Zagreb 5-0 (3-0)
Malmö FF: Marko Johansson, Eric Larsson, Lasse Nielsen, Jonas Knudsen (46' Behrang Safari), Anel Ahmedhodzic, Søren Rieks (76' Amin Sarr), Oscar Lewicki, Erdal Rakip (63' Bonke Innocent), Adi Nalic, Jo Inge Berget, Isaac Kiese Thelin. Coach: Jon Dahl Tomasson.
Lokomotiva Zagreb: Krunoslav Hendija, Denis Kolinger, Stipo Markovic, Dominik Kovacic, Marko Djira (75' Ivan Celikovic), Fran Karacic, Jon Mersinaj, Jorge Sammir (69' Indrit Tuci), Oliver Petrak, Sherif Kallaku (84' Reuben Acquah), Enis Çokaj. Coach; Goran Tomic.
Goals: 5', 17' Isaac Kiese Thelin 1-0, 2-0, 31' Adi Nalic 3-0, 52' Eric Larsson 4-0, 72' Søren Rieks 5-0.
Referee: François Letexier (FRA)

24.09.20   Lerkendal Stadion, Trondheim: Rosenborg BK – Alanyaspor 1-0 (0-0)
Rosenborg BK: André Hansen, Tore Reginiussen, Hólmar Eyjólfsson, Vegar Hedenstad, Pa Konate, Per Skjelbred, Anders Konradsen, Kristoffer Zachariassen, Dino Islamovic, Samuel Adegbenro (71' Edvard Tagseth), Carl Holse (81' Erlend Reitan). Coach: Åge Hareide.
Alanyaspor: Marafona, Giorgos Tzavellas, Steven Caulker, François Moubandje, Juanfran (85' Onur Bulut), Fatih Aksoy (90+3' Khouma Babacar), Efecan Karaca (81' Mustafa Pektemek), Salih Uçan, Anastasios Bakasetas, Davidson, Adam Bareiro. Coach: Semih Tokatli.
Goal: 59' Anders Konradsen 1-0.
Referee: Kristo Tohver (EST)
Sent off: 66' Anders Konradsen, 90+3' Khouma Babacar.

24.09.20   Vodafone Park, Istanbul: Besiktas JK – Rio Ave FC 1-1 (1-0, 1-1) (a.e.t.)
Besiktas JK: Utku Yuvakuran, Welinton Souza, Javi Montero, Ridvan Yilmaz, Jeremain Lens (101' Ajdin Hasic), Adem Ljalic (72' Bernard Mensah), Necip Uysal, Oguzhan Özyakup, Dorukhan Toköz, Tyler Boyd (84' Gökhan Töre), Güven Yalçin (64' Cyle Larin).
Coach: Sergen Yalçin.
Rio Ave FC: Pawel Kieszek, Ivo Pinto (79' Nikola Jambor), Aderllan Santos, Matheus Reis, Toni Borevkovic, Tarantini (79' Ryotaro Meshino), Filipe Augusto, Francisco "Chico" Geraldes (97' Gabrielzinho), Bruno Moreira, Carlos Mané, Lucas Piazón (69' Diego Lopes).
Coach: Mário Silva.
Goals: 15' Güven Yalçin 1-0, 85' Bruno Moreira 1-1.
Referee: Daniel Siebert (GER)

Rio Ave FC won on penalties after extra time (4-2).
Penalties: Mensah 1-0, Bruno Moreira 1-1, Töre 2-1, Aderllan Santos 2-2, Welinton Souza missed, Jambor 2-3, Larin missed, Matheus Reis 2-4.

24.09.20   Stadion Bâlgarska Armija, Sofia: CSKA Sofia – B36 Tórshavn 3-1 (2-0)
CSKA Sofia: Busatto, Jurgen Mattheij, Plamen Galabov, Geferson (61' Tiago Rodrigues), Bradley Mazikou, Valentin Antov, Younousse Sankharé, Graham Carey (84' Henrique), Amos Youga, Georgi Yomov (69' Jules Keita), Ali Sowe. Coach: Stamen Belchev.
B36 Tórshavn: Símun Rógvi Hansen, Erling Jacobsen, Alex Mellemgaard, Eli Nielsen (59' Stefan Radosavljevic), Árni Frederiksberg, Benjamin Heinesen, Andrias Eriksen, Michal Przybylski, Magnus Holm Jacobsen (68' Andrass Johansen), Ragnar Samuelsen (59' Hannes Agnarsson), Sebastian Pingel. Coach: Jákup á Borg.
Goals: 27' Ali Sowe 1-0, 38' Georgi Yomov 2-0, 61' Sebastian Pingel 2-1, 83' Jules Keita 3-1.
Referee: Tamás Bognár (HUN)

24.09.20   Stadions Skonto, Riga: Riga FC – Celtic FC 0-1 (0-0)
Riga FC: Roberts Ozols, Armands Pētersons, Elvis Stuglis, Herdi Prenga, Vladimirs Kamess, Ritvars Rugins, Stefan Panic, Marko Djurisic, Roger, Roman Debelko (67' Stefan Milosevic, 90+1' Jordan N'Kololo), Wesley Natã (71' Felipe Brisola). Coach: Oleg Kononov.
Celtic FC: Vassilis Barkas, Shane Duffy, Kristoffer Ajer, Greg Taylor, Scott Brown, Nir Bitton, James Forrest (34' Jeremie Frimpong), Callum McGregor, Olivier Ntcham (72' Albian Ajeti), Ryan Christie, Odsonne Édouard (82' Mohamed Elyounoussi). Coach: Neil Lennon.
Goal: 90' Mohamed Elyounoussi 0-1.
Referee: Fábio Veríssimo (POR)

24.09.20   Tele2 Arena, Stockholm: Djurgårdens IF – CFR Cluj 0-1 (0-0)
Djurgårdens IF: Per Bråtveit, Elliot Käck, Jacob Une-Larsson, Aslak Witry, Jonathan Augustinsson, Haris Radetinac, Magnus Eriksson, Fredrik Ulvestad, Jesper Karlström, Curtis Edwards (78' Emir Kujovic), Edward Chilufya (72' Jonathan Ring). Coach: Kim Bergstrand.
CFR Cluj: Cristian Balgradean, Paulo Vinícius, Mateo Susic, Camora, Andrei Burca, Ciprian Deac, Damjan Djokovic, Mihai Bordeianu, Adrian Paun (89' Michaël Pereira), Mário Rondón (90+3' Ovidiu Hoban), Billel Omrani (86' Gabriel Debeljuh). Coach: Dan Petrescu.
Goal: 56' Paulo Vinícius 0-1.
Referee: Bartosz Frankowski (POL)

24.09.20 Ta'Qali National Stadium, Ta'Qali: Floriana FC – FC Flora Tallinn 0-0 (a.e.t.)
Floriana FC: Ini Akpan, Enzo Ruiz, Jurgen Pisani, Ryan Camenzuli, Diego Venancio Silva, Nicola Leone (118' Jan Busuttil), Brandon Paiber (81' Flávio Carioca), Matías García, Kristian Keqi, Tiago Adan, Marcelo Dias. Coach: Vincenzo Potenza.
FC Flora Tallinn: Matvei Igonen, Märten Kuusk, Henrik Pürg, Marco Lukka, Michael Lilander, Konstantin Vassiljev (90' Markus Poom), Markus Soomets, Vladislavs Kreida, Rauno Alliku (69' Martin Miller), Rauno Sappinen (81' Mark Lepik), Vlasiy Sinyavskiy (106' Frank Liivak). Coach: Jürgen Henn.
Referee: Irfan Peljto (BIH)
Sent off: 130' Rauno Sappinen.

FC Flora Tallinn won after extra time on penalties (4:2).
Penalties: Lilander 1-0, Keqi missed, Kreida 2-0, Diego Venancio Silva missed, Poom missed, Tiago Adan 2-1, Kuusk 3-1, Busuttil 3-2, Liivak 4-2.

24.09.20 Stadionul Marin Anastasovici, Giurgiu: FCSB – Slovan Liberec 0-2 (0-0)
FCSB: Catalin Straton, Aristides Soiledis, Ionut Pantîru, Gabriel Enache, David Caiado, Adrian Sut, Gabriel Simion, Stefan Cana, Ovidiu Perianu, Goran Karanovic (10' Octavian Popescu), Adrian Petre (68' Robert Ion). Coach: Anton Petrea.
Slovan Liberec: Filip Nguyen, Taras Kacharaba, Jan Mikula, Martin Koscelník, Mohamed Tijani, Jhon Mosquera, Jakub Hromada (88' Matej Chalus), Jakub Pesek (84' Jan Matousek), Kamso Mara, Michal Beran (51' Michael Rabusic), Abdulla Yusuf Helal.
Coach: Pavel Hoftych.
Goals: 64' Abdulla Yusuf Helal 0-1, 82' Michael Rabusic 0-2.
Referee: Äliyar Agayev (AZE)
Sent off: 20' Stefan Cana.

FCSB played their home match at Stadionul Marin Anastasovic, Giurgiu, instead of their regular stadium Arena Nationala, Bucharest.

24.09.20 HaMoshava Stadium, Petach-Tikva: Hapoel Be'er Sheva – Motherwell FC 3-0 (1-0)
Hapoel Be'er Sheva: Ohad Levita, Miguel Vítor, Loai Taha, Sean Goldberg, Elton Acolatse (86' Tomer Yosefi), Lucas Bareiro, Or Dadya, Sintayehu Sallalich (86' Marcelo Meli), Josué, Marwan Kabha, Jhonatan Agudelo (59' Gaëtan Varenne). Coach: Yossi Abukasis.
Motherwell FC: Trevor Carson, Declan Gallagher, Stephen O'Donnell, Ricki Lamie, Liam Grimshaw, Nathan McGinley, Liam Polworth (86' Barry Maguire), Mark O'Hara, Allan Campbell, Tony Watt (75' Jordan White), Chris Long (72' Callum Lang).
Coach: Stephen Robinson.
Goals: 43' Miguel Vítor 1-0, 71' Josué 2-0 (p), 82' Elton Acolatse 3-0.
Referee: Sergey Boyko (UKR)
Sent off: 70' Declan Gallagher.

Hapoel Be'er Sheva played their home match at HaMoshava Stadium, Petach Tikva, instead of their regular stadium Turner Stadium, Beersheba, which was temporarily closed for structural problems with the roof.

24.09.20 Tose Proeski Arena, Skopje: KF Shkëndija 79 – Tottenham Hotspur 1-2 (0-1)
KF Shkëndija 79: Kostadin Zahov, Mevlan Murati, Antonio Pavic, Egzon Bejtulai, Ján Krivák, Bruno Dita (77' Arbin Zejnullai), Valon Ahmedi, Ennur Totre, Besart Ibraimi, Valmir Nafiu (85' Florent Ramadani), Ljupco Doriev (85' Zija Merdzhani). Coach: Ernest Gjoka.
Tottenham Hotspur: Joe Hart, Toby Alderweireld, Serge Aurier, Ben Davies, Davinson Sánchez, Érik Lamela, Dele Alli (60' Harry Kane), Harry Winks (59' Giovani Lo Celso), Tanguy NDombèlé, Son Heung-Min, Steven Bergwijn (65' Lucas Moura).
Coach: José Mourinho.
Goals: 5' Érik Lamela 0-1, 55' Valmir Nafiu 1-1, 70' Son Heung-Min 1-2, 79' Harry Kane 1-3.
Referee: Ali Palabiyik (TUR)

KF Shkëndija 79 played their home match at Tose Proeski Arena, Skopje, instead of their regular stadium Ecolog Arena, Tetovo.

24.09.20 Estadio Nuevo Los Cármenes, Granada: Granada CF – Lokomotivi Tbilisi 2-0 (0-0)
Granada CF: Rui Silva, Víctor Díaz, Germán Sánchez, Jesús Vallejo, Carlos Neva, Montoro, Maxime Gonalons, Luis Milla, Kenedy (62' Alberto Soro), Soldado (67' Jorge Molina), Darwin Machís (80' Antonio Puertas). Coach: Diego Martínez.
Lokomotivi Tbilisi: Giorgi Mamardashvili, Nika Sandokhadze, Giorgi Gabadze, Aleksandre Gureshidze, Daviti Ubilava, Temur Shonia, Davit Samurkasovi (60' Rati Mtchedlishvili), Tornike Kirkitadze (75' Mamia Gavashelushvili), Beka Dartsmelia, Imran Oulad Omar (71' Aleksandr Kobakhidze), Irakli Sikharulidze. Coach: Giorgi Chiabrishvili.
Goals: 48' Darwin Machís 1-0, 90+1' Jorge Molina 2-0.
Referee: Serdar Gözübüyük (HOL)
Sent off: 59' Giorgi Gabadze.

24.09.20 Stade Maurice Dufrasne, Liège:
Standard Liège – Vojvodina Novi Sad 2-1 (0-0, 1-1) (a.e.t.)
Standard Liège: Arnaud Bodart, Kostas Laifis, Nicolas Gavory, Collins Fai, Zinho Vanheusden, Mehdi Carcela-González (98' Duje Cop), Gojko Cimirot (92' Eden Shamir), Merveille Bopé Bokadi, Selim Amallah, Nicolas Raskin (107' Noë Dussenne), Felipe Avenatti (72' Jackson Muleka). Coach: Philippe Montanier.
Vojvodina Novi Sad: Goran Vuklis, Stefan Djordjevic, Slavko Bralic, Nikola Andric, Sinisa Sanicanin (105' Novica Maksimovic), Arandel Stojkovic (105' Dejan Zukic), Nikola Drincic, Petar Bojic, Miljan Vukadinovic (86' Miodrag Gemovic), Nemanja Covic, Momcilo Mrkaic (59' Ognjen Djuricin). Coach: Nenad Lalatovic.
Goals: 47' Felipe Avenatti 1-0 (p), 75' Petar Bojic 1-1, 91' Selim Amallah 2-1.
Referee: Harald Lechner (AUT)

Standard Liège won after extra time.

24.09.20 Türk Telekom Stadyumu, Istanbul: Galatasaray – Hajduk Split 2-0 (0-0)
Galatasaray: Fatih Öztürk, Ömer Bayram (71' Younès Belhanda), Martin Linnes, Emre Tasdemir (80' Omar Elabdellaoui), Marcão Teixeira, Ryan Donk, Sofiane Féghouli (89' Emre Kilinç), Taylan Antalyali, Oghenekaro Etebo, Ryan Babel, Mbaye Diagne. Coach: Fatih Terim.
Hajduk Split: Josip Posavec, David Colina, Nihad Mujakic, Mario Vuskovic, Ádám Gyurcsó (84' Leon Krekovic), Mijo Caktas, Bassel Jradi (84' Jani Atanasov), Stanko Juric (74' Darko Nejasmic), Jairo, Dimitrios Diamantakos, Marin Jakolis. Coach: Hari Vukas.
Goals: 77' Younès Belhanda 1-0, 86' Ryan Babel 2-0.
Referee: Craig Pawson (ENG)

24.09.20   Telia Parken, Copenhagen: FC København – Piast Gliwice 3-0 (1-0)
FC København: Kalle Johnsson, Pierre Bengtsson, Ragnar Sigurdsson (68' Marios Oikonomou), Guillermo Varela, Victor Nelsson, Rasmus Falk (53' Robert Mudrazija), Zeca, Viktor Fischer (75' Jens Stage), Pep Biel Mas, Kamil Wilczek, Jonas Wind.
Coach: Ståle Solbakken.
Piast Gliwice: Frantisek Plach, Mikkel Kirkeskov, Jakub Czerwinski, Tomás Huk, Jakub Holúbek, Martin Konczkowski, Tomasz Jodlowiec, Krisztófer Vida, Patryk Lipski (82' Sebastian Milewski), Patryk Sokolowski (62' Michal Zyro), Piotr Parzyszek (89' Dominik Steczyk). Coach: Waldemar Fornalik.
Goals: 14' Kamil Wilczek 1-0, 58' Jonas Wind 2-0, 90+5' Pep Biel Mas 3-0.
Referee: Roi Reinshreiber (ISR)

24.09.20   Neo GSP Stadium, Nicosia: APOEL Nicosia – Zrinjski Mostar 2-2 (2-1, 2-2) (a.e.t.)
APOEL Nicosia: Miguel Silva, Emilio N'Sue, Geraldes, Artur Jorge, Rafael Santos, Tomás De Vincenti, Ghayas Zahid (64' Mike Jensen), Anuar Tuhami (86' Marius Lundemo), Atdhe Nuhiu (98' Ben Sahar), Dieumerci Ndongala (73' Moussa Al Taamari), Omer Atzili.
Coach: Marinos Ouzounidis.
Zrinjski Mostar: Ivan Brkic, Luis Ibáñez, Tomislav Barbaric (57' Almir Bekic), Slobodan Jakovljevic, Ognjen Todorovic, Dinko Trebotic (66' Damir Zlomislic), Milos Filipovic, Josip Corluka (105' Rijad Sadiku), Ivan Enin, Nemanja Bilbija, Josip Ivancic (76' Miljan Govedarica). Coach: Mladen Zizovic.
Goals: 11' Josip Ivancic 0-1, 14' Omer Atzili 1-1, 26' Atdhe Nuhiu 2-1,
69' Nemanja Bilbija 2-2.
Referee: Daniel Stefanski (POL)

APOEL won on penalties after extra time (4-2).
Pelanties: Jensen1-0, Filipovic 1-1, Atzili missed, Ibáñez missed, Sahar 2-1, Bilbija missed,
Moussa Al Tamari 3-1, Govedarica 3-2, De Vincenti 4-2.

24.09.20   Bolshaya Sportivnaya Arena, Tiraspol:
FC Sheriff Tiraspol – Dundalk FC 1-1 (1-1, 1-1) (a.e.t.)
FC Sheriff Tiraspol: Zvonimir Mikulic, Veaceslav Posmac, Andrei Peteleu (64' Charles Petro), Ousmane N'Diaye, Faith Obilor, William Parra, Cristiano, Dimitrios Kolovos (88' Dabney dos Santos), Andriy Bliznichenko (46' Rifet Kapic), Benedik Mioc (99' Max Veloso), Frank Castañeda. Coach: Zoran Zekic.
Dundalk FC: Gary Rogers, Brian Gartland, Sean Gannon (13' John Mountney, 88' Daniel Kelly), Sean Hoare, Daniel Cleary, Darragh Leahy, Chris Shields, Sean Murray (72' Patrick McEleney), Gregory Sloggett, Patrick Hoban, Michael Duffy (102' Stefan Colovic).
Coach: Shane Keegan.
Goals: 8' Veaceslav Posmac 1-0, 45+1' Sean Murray 1-1.
Referee: Aleksandar Stavrev (MKD)

Dundalk FC won on penalties after extra time (5-3).
Penalties: Colovic 1-0, Kapic 1-1, Hoban 2-1, Obilor missed, Hoare 3-1, Veloso 3-2,
McEleney 4-2, Parra 4-3, Shields 5-3.

24.09.20 Stadion Bilino Polje, Zenica: FK Sarajevo – FK Buducnost Podgorica 2-1 (1-1)
FK Sarajevo: Vladan Kovacevic, Amer Dupovac, Besim Serbecic, Selmir Pidro, Mirko Oremus, Aleksandr Pejovic, Tino-Sven Suric (58' Andrej Djokanovic), Amar Rahmanovic, Mersudin Ahmetovic (81' Haris Handzic), Matthias Fanimo (90+1' Krste Velkoski), Benjamin Tatar. Coach: Vinko Marinovic.
FK Buducnost Podgorica: Milos Dragojevic, Vladan Adzic, Luka Mirkovic, Igor Cukovic, Nemanja Sekulic, Bogdan Milic, Petar Grbic, Milos Raickovic, Vasilije Terzic (85' Aleksandar Vujacic), Igor Ivanovic, Panagiotis Moraitis. Coach: Mladen Milinkovic.
Goals: 4' Benjamin Tatar 1-0, 44' Panagiotis Moraitis 1-1, 67' Matthias Fanimo 2-1.
Referee: José Sánchez Martínez (ESP)
Sent off: 75' Amar Rahmanovic.

FK Sarajevo played their home match at Stadion Bilino Polje, Zenica, instead of their regular stadium Kosevo City Stadium, Sarajevo.

24.09.20 Tórsvøllur, Tórshavn: KÍ Klaksvík – Dinamo Tbilisi 6-1 (1-0)
KÍ Klaksvík: Kristian Joensen, Odmar Færø, Heini Vatnsdal, Jesper Brinck, Deni Pavlovic (75' David Skrbec), Jákup Andreasen, Jóannes Bjartalid, Jóannes Danielsen, Páll Klettskard (82' Jonn Johannesen), Patrik Johannesen (89' Boris Dosljak), Ole Erik Midtskogen. Coach: Mikkjal Thomassen.
Dinamo Tbilisi: Roin Kvaskhvadze, Giorgi Kimadze, Nodar Iashvili, Davit Kobouri (74' Giorgi Kukhianidze), Simon Ghegnon, Giorgi Papava, Nodar Kavtaradze, Bakar Kardava, Giorgi Zaria (61' Giorgi Kutsia), Giorgi Gabedava, Filip Orsula (52' José Vitor Pernambuco). Coach: Xisco Muñoz.
Goals: 22' Deni Pavlovic 1-0, 58' Patrik Johannesen 2-0, 60', 69' Páll Klettskard 3-0, 4-0, 71' José Vitor Pernambuco 4-1, 73' Páll Klettskard 5-1, 85' Jonn Johannesen 6-1.
Referee: Thorvaldur Árnason (ISL)

KÍ Klaksvík played their home match at Tórsvøllur, Tórshavn, instead of their regular stadium Vid Djúpumyrar, Klaksvík, which did not meet UEFA requirements.

24.09.20 AOK Stadion, Wolfsburg: VfL Wolfsburg – Desna Chernigov 2-0 (1-0)
VfL Wolfsburg: Koen Casteels, Jérôme Roussillon, Maxence Lacroix (62' John Anthony Brooks), Admir Mehmedi, Josuha Guilavogui, Maximilian Arnold, Renato Steffen, Xaver Schlager, João Victor, Wout Weghorst (78' Daniel Ginczek), Omar Marmoush (59' Paulo Otávio). Coach: Oliver Glasner.
Desna Chernigov: Evgen Past, Joonas Tamm, Andriy Gitchenko, Andriy Mostovyi, Yukhym Konoplya, Vladislav Ogirya, Vladislav Kalitvintsev, Egor Kartushov (46' Oleksiy Gutsulyak), Andriy Totovytskyi, Andriy Dombrovskyi (65' Vitaliy Ermakov), Pylyp Budkivskyi (84' Ilya Shevtsov). Coach: Oleksandr Ryabokon.
Goals: 16' Josuha Guilavogui 1-0, 90+2' Daniel Ginczek 2-0.
Referee: Lawrence Visser (BEL)
Sent off: 60' Joonas Tamm.

VfL Wolfsburg played their home match at AOK Stadion, Wolfsburg, instead of their regular stadium Volfkswagen Arena, Wolfsburg, as a cost-saving measure.

24.09.20 Stadion Kybunpark, St. Gallen: FC St. Gallen – AEK Athens 0-1 (0-0)
FC St. Gallen: Lawrence Ati-Zigi, Miro Muheim, Leonidas Stergiou, Jordi Quintillà, Basil Stillhart (74' André Ribeiro), Kwadwo Duah (62' Florian Kamberi), Alessandro Kräuchi, Betim Fazliji, Lukas Görtler, Victor Ruiz (74' Élie Youan), Jérémy Guillemenot.
Coach: Peter Zeidler.
AEK Athens: Panagiotis Tsintotas, Dmytro Chygrynskiy, Emanuel Insúa, Stavros Vasilantonopoulos, Efstratios Svarnas, Nenad Krsticic, Petros Mandalos, André Simões, Karim Ansarifard (68' Levi García), Nélson Oliveira, Marko Livaja (90' Yevhen Shakhov).
Coach: Massimo Carrera.
Goal: 72' Nélson Oliveira 0-1.
Referee: Alejandro Hernández Hernández (ESP)
Sent off: 90+5' Lukas Görtler.

Nélson Oliveira missed a penalty kick (71').

24.09.20 Linzer Stadion, Linz: LASK Linz – DAC Dunajská Streda 7-0 (2-0)
LASK Linz: Alexander Schlager, Petar Filipovic (58' Christian Ramsebner), Gernot Trauner, Reinhold Ranftl, Philipp Wiesinger, James Holland, Peter Michorl, René Renner, Husein Balic (72' Thomas Sabitzer), Andreas Gruber (58' Dominik Reiter), Marko Raguz.
Coach: Dominik Thalhammer.
DAC Dunajská Streda: Martin Jedlicka, Éric Davis, Jannik Müller, Dominik Kruzliak, César Blackman, Zsolt Kalmár, Andrija Balic, Andrej Fábry (36' Danilo Beskorovayniy), András Schäfer, Eric Ramírez (60' Ion Nilolaescu), Marko Divkovic (60' Martin Bednár).
Coach: Bernd Storck.
Goals: 6', 16' Marko Raguz 1-0, 2-0, 46' Petar Filipovic 3-0, 51' Peter Michori 4-0, 53' Andreas Gruber 5-0, 55' Husein Balic 6-0, 77' Thomas Sabitzer 7-0.
Referee: Jérôme Brisard (FRA)
Sent off: 48' César Blackman.

24.09.20 Stadio Giuseppe Meazza, Milano: AC Milan – FK Bodø/Glimt 3-2 (2-1)
AC Milan: Gianluigi Donnarumma, Simon Kjær, Davide Calabria, Theo Hernández, Matteo Gabbia, Hakan Çalhanoglu, Samu Castillejo (66' Rade Krunic), Franck Kessié, Ismaël Bennacar (80' Sandro Tonali), Alexis Saelemaekers, Lorenzo Colombo (57' Daniel Maldini).
Coach: Stefano Pioli.
FK Bodø/Glimt: Nikita Haikin, Brede Moe, Marius Lode, Alfons Sampsted (83' Ola Solbakken), Fredrik Bjørkan, Ulrik Saltnes, Patrick Berg, Jens Hauge, Kasper Junker (90' Victor Boniface), Philip Zinckernagel, Sondre Fet (65' Morten Konradsen).
Coach: Kjetil Knutsen.
Goals: 15' Kasper Junker 0-1, 16' Hakan Çalhanoglu 1-1, 32' Lorenzo Colombo 2-1, 50' Hakan Çalhanoglu 3-1, 55' Jens Hauge 3-2.
Referee: Fran Jovic (CRO)

24.09.20   St. Jakob-Park, Basel: FC Basel – Anorthosis Famagusta FC 3-2 (3-1)
FC Basel: Djordje Nikolic, Silvan Widmer, Omar Alderete, Eray Cömert, Andrea Padula, Valentin Stocker (76' Dimitri Oberlin), Fabian Frei, Samuele Campo (85' Jasper van der Werff), Ricky van Wolfswinkel, Arthur Cabral, Afimico Pululu (60' Julian von Moos).
Coach: Ciriaco Sforza.
Anorthosis Famagusta FC: Giorgi Loria, Gordon Schildenfeld, Evgen Selin (78' Georgios Galitsios), Branko Vrgoc, Hovhannes Hambardzumyan, Anderson Correia (46' Dimitris Christofi), Murtaz Daushvili, Renato Margaça (61' Dor Micha), Tornike Okriashvili, Kanagiotis Artymatas, Giorgi Kvilitaia. Coach: Temur Ketsbaia.
Goals: 3' Silvan Widmer 1-0, 12' Samuele Campo 2-0, 21' Hovhannes Hambardzumyan 3-0 (og), 45' Branko Vrgoc 3-1, 67' Giorgi Kvilitaia 3-2 (p).
Referee: Radu Marían Petrescu (ROM)
Sent off: 50' Tornike Okriashvili, 88' Julian von Moos.

24.09.20   Stadion Miejski Legii Warszawa im. Marszalka Józefa Pilsudskiego, Warszawa:
Legia Warszawa – Drita Gjilan 2-0 (2-0)
Legia Warszawa: Artur Boruc, Artur Jedrzejczyk, Filip Mladenovic, Mateusz Wieteska, Josip Juranovic, Michal Karbownik, Pawel Wszolek, Bartosz Slisz, Luquinhas (67' Bartosz Kapustka), Tomás Pekhart (72' José Kanté), Joel Valencia (63' Valeriane Gvilia).
Coach: Czeslaw Michniewicz.
Drita Gjilan: Faton Maloku, Ardijan Cuculi, Vladica Brdarovski (66' Erjon Vucaj), Fidan Gërbeshi, Ilir Blakçori, Bujar Shabani, Xhevdet Shabani, Hamdi Namani, Almir Ajzeraj (74' Festim Alidema), Kastriot Rexha (56' Betim Haxhimusa), Astrit Fazliu. Coach: Ardijan Nuhiji.
Goals: 24' Pawel Wszolek 1-0, 43' Tomás Pekhart 2-0.
Referee: Halis Özkahya (TUR)

24.09.20   Stadion HNK Rijeka, Rijeka: HNK Rijeka – Kolos Kovalivka 2-0 (0-0, 0-0) (a.e.t.)
HNK Rijeka: Ivan Nevistic, Ivan Tomecak (90+1' Momcilo Raspopovic), Darko Velkovski (91' João Escoval), Daniel Stefulj, Hrvoje Smolcic, Franko Andrijasevic, Domagoj Pavicic (71' Sandro Kulenovic), Luka Capan, Robert Muric, Stjepan Loncar, Adam Gnezda Cerin (99' Ivan Lepinjica). Coach: Simon Rozman.
Kolos Kovalivka: Evgen Volynets, Vitaly Gavrish, Evgen Novak, Kyrylo Petrov (109' Pavel Orikhovskyi), Vladislav Emets, Evgeniy Zadoya, Andriy Bogdanov, Mykyta Kravchenko, Yevgeniy Smyrnyi (84' Denys Kostyshyn), Vladimir Lisenko (71' Yevhen Seleznyov), Denys Antyukh (90+4' Yevgeniy Morozko). Coach: Ruslan Kostyshyn.
Goals: 1-2' João Escoval 1-0, 115' Franko Andrijasevic 2-0.
Referee: Tiago Martins (POR)

HNK Rijeka won after extra time.

24.09.20   Koning Willem II Stadion, Tilburg: Willem II – Glasgow Rangers FC 0-4 (0-2)
Willem II: Robbin Ruiter, Jordens Peters (73' Victor van den Bogert), Miquel Nelom, Sebastian Holmén, Derrick Köhn, Pol Llonch, Görkem Saglam, Driess Saddiki (59' John Yeboah), Mike Trésor, Vangelis Pavlidis, Ché Nunnely (60' Mats Köhlert).
Coach: Adrie Koster.
Glasgow Rangers FC: Allan McGregor, James Tavernier, Connor Goldson, Filip Helander, Borna Barisic (74' Calvin Bassey), Steven Davis, Scott Arfield, Glen Kamara, Ianis Hagi, Alfredo Morelos (79' Cedric Itten), Ryan Kent (72' Jordan Jones). Coach: Steven Gerrard.
Goals: 22' James Tavernier 0-1 (p), 25' Ryan Kent 0-2, 55' Filip Helander 0-3, 71' Connor Goldson 0-4.
Referee: Maurizio Mariani (ITA)

24.09.20   Estádio José Alvalade, Lisboa: Sporting CP – Aberdeen FC 1-0 (1-0)
Sporting CP: Antonio Adán, Luis Carlos Neto, Sebastián Coates, Zouhair Feddal, Pedro Porro (88' Gonzalo Plata), Nuno Mendes, Wendel (86' Daniel Bragança), Matheus Nunes, Luciano Vietto, Jovane Cabral, Tiago Tomás (77' Andraz Sporar). Coach: Emanuel Ferro.
Aberdeen FC: Joe Lewis, Andrew Considine, Shay Logan (83' Connor McLennan), Ash Taylor, Tommie Hoban, Jonny Hayes, Marley Watkins (81' Ryan Edmondson), Dylan McGeouch (69' Scott Wright), Ryan Hedges, Ross McCrorie, Lewis Ferguson.
Coach: Derek McInnes.
Goal: 7' Tiago Tomás 1-0.
Referee: Nikola Dabanovic (MNE)

PLAY-OFF ROUND

01.10.20   Stadionul Dr. Constantin Radulescu, Cluj-Napoca:
           CFR Cluj – Kuopion PS 3-1 (2-0)
CFR Cluj: Cristian Balgradean, Paulo Vinícius, Mateo Susic, Camora, Andrei Burca, Ciprian Deac (78' Michaël Pereira), Damjan Djokovic, Mihai Bordeianu, Adrian Paun (86' Ovidiu Hoban), Mário Rondón, Gabriel Debeljuh (83' Billel Omrani). Coach: Dan Petrescu.
Kuopion PS: Otso Virtanen, Igors Tarasovs, Artur Pikk, Nuno Tomás, Petteri Pennanen, Ville Saxman (76' Arttu Heinonen), Bismark Adjei-Boateng, Urho Nissilä (77' Ats Purje), Saku Savolainen, Rangel (82' Aniekpeno Udoh), Usman Sale. Coach: Arne Erlandsen.
Goals: 5' Mário Rondón 1-0, 42' Gabriel Debeljuh 2-0, 56' Mário Rondón 3-0, 90+1' Aniekpeno Udoh 3-1.
Referee: Ivan Bebek (CRO)

01.10.20   Stadion Maksimir, Zagreb: Dinamo Zagreb – FC Flora Tallinn 3-1 (2-0)
Dinamo Zagreb: Dominik Livakovic, Marin Leovac, Kévin Théophile-Catherine, Petar Stojanovic, Josko Gvardiol, Arijan Ademi, Kristijan Jakic, Lovro Majer (84' Lirim Kastrati), Mario Gavranovic (65' Luka Ivanusec), Mislav Orsic (68' Amer Gojak), Bruno Petkovic.
Coach: Zoran Mamic.
FC Flora Tallinn: Matvei Igonen, Märten Kuusk, Henrik Pürg, Marco Lukka, Michael Lilander, Konstantin Vassiljev, Markus Soomets (81' Martin Miller), Vladislavs Kreida (88' Markus Poom), Rauno Alliku, Frank Liivak (76' Mark Lepik), Vlasiy Sinyavskiy.
Coach: Jürgen Henn.
Goals: 11' Mario Gavranovic 1-0, 26' Arijan Ademi 2-0, 65' Vlasiy Sinyavskiy 2-1, 87' Arijan Ademi 3-1.
Referee: Ali Palabiyik (TUR)

01.10.20   Neo GSP Stadium, Nicosia (CYP):
FC Ararat-Armenia – Crvena Zvezda Beograd 1-2 (0-1)
FC Ararat-Armenia: Stefan Cupic, Alemão (65' Yusuf Otubanjo), Sergiy Vakulenko, Ângelo Meneses, David Humanes, Yoan Gouffran, Sargis Shahinyan (70' Armen Ambartsumyan), Furdjel Narsingh, Zakaria Sanogo, Mailson, Jeisson Martínez. Coach: David Campaña.
Crvena Zvezda Beograd: Milan Borjan, Milan Rodic, Milos Degenek, Milan Gajic, Radovan Pankov, Aleksandar Katai (77' Zeljko Gavric), Guélor Kanga (65' Njegos Petrovic), Mirko Ivanic, Veljko Nikolic, Diego Falcinelli, El Fardou Ben Nabouhane (81' Marko Gobeljic). Coach: Dejan Stankovic.
Goals: 45' Aleksandar Katai 0-1, 60' Diego Falcinelli 0-2, 71' Mailson 1-2.
Referee: Anasthasios Sidiropoulos (GRE)

Match originally to be played at Vazgen Sargsyan Republican Stadium, Yerevan, was moved to Neo GSP Stadium, Nicosia (Cyprus), due to the 2020 Nagorno-Karabakh conflict.

01.10.20   Lerkendal Stadion, Trondheim: Rosenborg BK – PSV Eindhoven 0-2 (0-1)
Rosenborg BK: André Hansen, Tore Reginiussen, Hólmar Eyjólfsson, Vegar Hedenstad (77' Erlend Reitan), Pa Konate, Per Skjelbred, Markus Henriksen, Kristoffer Zachariassen, Dino Islamovic, Samuel Adegbenro (65' Pál André Helland), Carl Holse. Coach: Åge Hareide.
PSV Eindhoven: Yvon Mvogo, Philipp Max (60' Nick Viergever), Olivier Boscagli, Denzel Dumfries, Jordan Teze, Ryan Thomas (21' Jorrit Hendrix), Mauro Júnior, Pablo Rosario, Eran Zahavi (90+3' Noni Madueke), Donyell Malen, Cody Gakpo. Coach: Roger Schmidt.
Goals: 22' Eran Zahavi 0-1, 61' Cody Gakpo 0-2.
Referee: Davide Massa (ITA)

01.10.20   Stade du Pays de Charleroi: Sporting Charleroi – KKS Lech Poznan 1-2 (0-2)
Sporting Charleroi: Nicolas Penneteau, Dorian Dessoleil, Steeven Willems (83' David Henen), Maxime Busi (57' Modou Diagne), Ryota Morioka, Marco Ilaimaharitra (89' Lucas Ribeiro Costa), Joris Kayembe, Mamadou Fall, Ali Gholizadeh, Kaveh Rezaei, Shamar Nicholson. Coach: Karim Belhocine.
KKS Lech Poznan: Filip Bednarek, Lubomir Satka, Alan Czerwinski, Vasyl Kravets (71' Michal Skóras), Djordje Crnomarkovic, Tymoteusz Puchacz, Pedro Tiba, Dani Ramírez (79' Thomas Rogne), Jakub Moder, Jakub Kaminski, Mikael Ishak (87' Filip Marchwinski). Coach: Dariusz Zuraw.
Goals: 33' Dani Ramírez 0-1, 42' Tymoteusz Puchacz 0-2, 56' Mamadou Fall 1-2.
Referee: Felix Zwayer (GER)
Sent off: 77' Lubomír Satka.

Kaveh Rezaei missed a penalty kick (51').

01.10.20   Eleda Stadion, Malmö: Malmö FF – Granada CF 1-3 (1-1)
Malmö FF: Marko Johansson, Eric Larsson, Jonas Knudsen, Franz Brorsson, Anel Ahmedhodzic, Søren Rieks (71' Arnór Traustason), Oscar Lewicki, Erdal Rakip (71' Anders Christiansen), Ola Toivonen, Jo Inge Berget, Isaac Kiese Thelin (77' Adi Nalic). Coach: Jon Dahl Tomasson.
Granada CF: Rui Silva, Víctor Díaz, Germán Sánchez, Domingos Duarte, Carlos Neva, Montoro, Maxime Gonalons, Antonio Puertas (74' Kenedy), Yangel Herrera, Soldado (81' Jorge Molina), Darwin Machís (89' Dimitri Foulquier). Coach: Diego Martínez.
Goals: 30' Darwin Machís 0-1, 45' Jo Inge Berget 1-1, 58' Antonio Puertas 1-2, 85' Yangel Herrera 1-3.
Referee: Danny Makkelie (HOL)

01.10.20   Stadion u Nisy, Liberec: Slovan Liberec – APOEL Nicosia 1-0 (0-0)
Slovan Liberec: Filip Nguyen, Taras Kacharaba, Jan Mikula, Martin Koscelník, Mohamed Tijani, Jhon Mosquera, Jakub Hromada, Jakub Pesek (80' Jan Matousek), Kamso Mara, Michal Beran (55' Michael Rabusic), Abdulla Yusuf Helal. Coach: Pavel Hoftych.
APOEL Nicosia: Miguel Silva, Emilio N'Sue, Geraldes, Artur Jorge, Christos Shelis, Tomás De Vincenti, Ghayas Zahid, Anuar Tuhami (90+4' Giorgios Merkis), Atdhe Nuhiu, Dieumerci Ndongala (68' Omer Atzili), Moussa Al Taamari (82' Viktor Klonaridis).
Coach: Marinos Ouzounidis.
Goal: 90+5' Kamso Mara 1-0 (p).
Referee: Andreas Ekberg (SWE)

01.10.20   HaMoshava Stadium, Petach-Tikva:
Hapoel Be'er Sheva – FC Viktoria Plzen 1-0 (1-0)
Hapoel Be'er Sheva: Ohad Levita, Miguel Vítor, Loai Taha, Sean Goldberg, Elton Acolatse (81' Tomer Yosefi), Lucas Bareiro, Or Dadya, Sintayehu Sallalich (90+1' David Keltjens), Josué, Marwan Kabha, Jhonatan Agudelo (75' Gaëtan Varenne). Coach: Yossi Abukasis.
FC Viktoria Plzen: Ales Hruska, David Limberský, Jakub Brabec, Lukás Hejda, Milan Havel, Jan Kopic, Ales Cermák, Lukás Kalvach, Adriel D'Avila Ba Loua (62' Joel Kayamba), Pavel Bucha (89' Ludek Pernica), Zdenek Ondrásek (80' Jean-David Beauguel).
Coach: Adrián Gula.
Goal: 4' Josué 1-0 (p).
Referee: Srdjan Jovanovic (SRB)

Hapoel Be'er Sheva played their home match at HaMoshava Stadium, Petach Tikva, instead of their regular stadium Turner Stadium, Beersheba, which was temporarily closed for structural problems with the roof.

01.10.20   Stadyen Dynamo, Minsk: FK Dynamo Brest – PFC Ludogorets Razgrad 0-2 (0-0)
FK Dynamo Brest: Sergey Ignatovich, Maksim Vitus, Yevhen Khacheridi, Gaby Kiki, Sergey Kislyak, Pavel Savitskiy, Artem Bykov (80' Sergey Krivets), Roman Yuzepchuk (88' Kirill Pechenin), Pavel Sedko, David Tweh, Abdoulaye Diallo (46' Mikhail Gordeychuk).
Coach: Sergey Kovalchuk.
PFC Ludogorets Razgrad: Plamen Iliev, Cosmin Moti, Cicinho, Anton Nedyalkov, Olivier Verdon, Stéphane Badji, Cauly (88' Jordan Ikoko), Alex Santana, Dominik Yankov, Claudiu Keserü (77' Higinio Marín), Bernard Tekpetey (66' Elvis Manu). Coach: Pavel Vrba.
Goals: 73' Elvis Manu 0-1, 79' Higinio Marín 0-2.
Referee: Slavko Vincic (SVN)

01.10.20   Stadion Bilino Polje, Zenica: FK Sarajevo – Celtic FC 0-1 (0-0)
FK Sarajevo: Vladan Kovacevic, Amer Dupovac, Selmir Pidro, Andrej Djokanovic (86' Ivan Jukic), Mirko Oremus, Aleksandr Pejovic, Hrvoje Milicevic, Tino-Sven Suric, Mersudin Ahmetovic (68' Haris Handzic), Matthias Fanimo (86' Krste Velkoski), Benjamin Tatar.
Coach: Vinko Marinovic.
Celtic FC: Vassilis Barkas, Shane Duffy, Kristoffer Ajer, Greg Taylor, Jeremie Frimpong, Scott Brown, Nir Bitton (11' Hatem Abd Elhamed), Callum McGregor, Mohamed Elyounoussi, Ryan Christie (86' Olivier Ntcham), Odsonne Édouard (78' Patryk Klimala).
Coach: Neil Lennon.
Goal: 70' Odsonne Édouard 0-1.
Referee: Benoît Bastien (FRA)

FK Sarajevo played their home match at Stadion Bilino Polje, Zenica, instead of their regular stadium Kosevo City Stadium, Sarajevo.

01.10.20   Stadion Miejski Legii Warszawa im. Marszalka Józefa Pilsudskiego, Warszawa:
Legia Warszawa – Qarabag FK 0-3 (0-0)
Legia Warszawa: Artur Boruc, Artur Jedrzejczyk, Igor Lewczuk, Filip Mladenovic, Josip Juranovic, Domagoj Antolic (63' Luquinhas), Bartosz Kapustka (66' Michal Karbownik), Bartosz Slisz, Tomás Pekhart, Rafael Lopes (56' Pawel Wszolek), Joel Valencia.
Coach: Czeslaw Michniewicz.
Qarabag FK: Sahrudin Mahammadaliyev, Maksim Medvedev, Qara Qarayev, Badavi Hüseynov, Abbas Hüseynov, Kevin Medina, Uros Matic, Filip Ozobic (75' Jaime Romero), Abdellah Zoubir (63' Mahir Emreli), Patrick Andrade, Owusu Kwabena (84' Elvin Dzhafarquliyev). Coach: Gurban Gurbanov.
Goals: 50' Patrick Andrade 0-1, 62' Abdellah Zoubir 0-2, 70' Filip Ozobic 0-3.
Referee: Tobias Stieler (GER)

01.10.20   Telia Parken, Copenhagen: FC København – HNK Rijeka 0-1 (0-1)
FC København: Kalle Johnsson, Pierre Bengtsson, Ragnar Sigurdsson, Peter Andersen (67' Karlo Bartolec), Victor Nelsson, Zeca, Viktor Fischer (46' Mikkel Kaufmann), Pep Biel Mas, Jens Stage (56' Robert Mudrazija), Kamil Wilczek, Jonas Wind. Coach: Ståle Solbakken.
HNK Rijeka: Ivan Nevistic, Ivan Tomecak (90+1' Momcilo Raspopovic), Darko Velkovski, Daniel Stefulj, Hrvoje Smolcic, Franko Andrijasevic, Domagoj Pavicic (76' Ivan Lepinjica), Luka Capan, Stjepan Loncar, Adam Gnezda Cerin, Sandro Kulenovic (83' João Escoval).
Coach: Simon Rozman.
Goal: 20' Peter Ankersen 0-1 (og).
Referee: Chris Kavanagh (ENG)

01.10.20   Stade Maurice Dufrasne, Liège: Standard Liège – Fehérvár FC 3-1 (0-1)
Standard Liège: Arnaud Bodart, Kostas Laifis (59' Noë Dussenne), Nicolas Gavory, Collins Fai, Zinho Vanheusden, Mehdi Carcela-González (82' Eden Shamir), Gojko Cimirot, Merveille Bopé Bokadi (46' Michel Balikwisha), Selim Amallah, Nicolas Raskin, Jackson Muleka. Coach: Philippe Montanier.
Fehérvár FC: Ádám Kovácsik, Attila Fiola, Loïc Négo, Stopira, Visar Musliu, Szilveszter Hangya, Bendegúz Bolla, Ivan Petryak (63' Funsho Bamgboye), Boban Nikolov, Lyes Houri (89' Armin Hodzic), Nemanja Nikolic (65' Budu Zivzivadze). Coach: Gábor Márton.
Goals: 10' Nemanja Nikolic 0-1, 50' Nicolas Gavory 1-1, 77', 85' Selim Amallah 2-1 (p), 3-1 (p).
Referee: William Collum (SCO)

01.10.20   Stadion Wankdorf, Bern: BSC Young Boys – KF Tirana 3-0 (1-0)
BSC Young Boys: David von Ballmoos, Fabian Lustenberger, Jordan Lefort, Ulisses Garcia, Silvan Hefti, Mohamed Camara, Nicolas Moumi Ngamaleu (66' Gianluca Gaudino), Christian Fassnacht (72' Felix Mambimbi), Vincent Sierro, Jean-Pierre Nsamé (73' Theoson Siebatcheu), Meschack Elia. Coach: Gerardo Seoane.
KF Tirana: Visar Bekaj, Kristi Vangjeli, Kristijan Tosevski, Marsel Ismajlgeci, Filip Najdovski, Idriz Batha, Jurgen Çelhaka, Agustin Torassa, Elton Calé (89' Grent Halili), Winful Cobbinah (71' Derrick Sasraku), Ernest Muçi (85' Erion Hoxhallari). Coach: Ndubuisi Egbo.
Goals: 42' Christian Fassnacht 1-0, 52', 64' Jean-Pierre Nsamé 2-0, 3-0.
Referee: Sergei Karasev (RUS)
Sent off: 67' Agustin Torassa.

01.10.20   St. Jakob-Park, Basel: FC Basel – CSKA Sofia 1-3 (0-0)
FC Basel: Djordje Nikolic, Silvan Widmer, Omar Alderete, Eray Cömert, Andrea Padula, Valentin Stocker (90+1' Aldo Kalulu), Fabian Frei, Orges Bunjaku (90+1' Samuele Campo), Ricky van Wolfswinkel, Arthur Cabral (77' Edon Zhegrova), Afimico Pululu.
Coach: Ciriaco Sforza.
CSKA Sofia: Busatto, Jurgen Mattheij, Plamen Galabov, Geferson (59' Tiago Rodrigues), Bradley Mazikou, Valentin Antov, Younousse Sankharé (90+1' Ahmed Ahmedov), Amos Youga, Georgi Yomov, Ali Sowe, Jules Keita (60' Henrique). Coach: Stamen Belchev.
Goals: 54' Arthur Cabral 1-0 (p), 72', 88' Tiago Rodrigues 1-1, 1-2,
90+6' Ahmed Ahmedov 1-3.
Referee: Ivan Kruzliak (SVK)

01.10.20   Aviva Stadium, Dublin: Dundalk FC – KÍ Klaksvík 3-1 (1-0)
Dundalk FC: Gary Rogers, Brian Gartland, Sean Hoare, Daniel Cleary, Darragh Leahy, Patrick McEleney (81' John Mountney), Sean Murray, Gregory Sloggett, Stefan Colovic (71' Daniel Kelly), Patrick Hoban (71' David McMillan), Michael Duffy. Coach: Shane Keegan.
KÍ Klaksvík: Kristian Joensen, Odmar Færø, Heini Vatnsdal, Jesper Brinck, Deni Pavlovic (86' Jonn Johannesen), Jákup Andreasen, Jóannes Bjartalid, Jóannes Danielsen, Páll Klettskard (55' Boris Dosljak), Patrik Johannesen, Ole Erik Midtskogen. Coach: Mikkjal Thomassen.
Goals: 33' Sean Murray 1-0, 48' Daniel Cleary 2-0, 66' Ole Erik Midtskogen 2-1, 79' Daniel Kelly 3-1.
Referee: Maurizio Mariana (ITA)

Dundalk FC played their home match at Aviva Stadium, Dublin, instead of their regular stadium Oriel Park, Dundalk.

01.10.20   Olympiako Stadio Spyros Louis, Athens: AEK Athens – VfL Wolfsburg 2-1 (0-1)
AEK Athens: Panagiotis Tsintotas, Dmytro Chygrynskiy, Emanuel Insúa, Stavros Vasilantonopoulos, Efstratios Svarnas, Nenad Krsticic, Yevhen Shakhov, Petros Mandalos (63' Marko Livaja), André Simões, Nélson Oliveira (87' Karim Ansarifard), Levi García (81' Theodosis Macheras). Coach: Massimo Carrera.
VfL Wolfsburg: Pavao Pervan, Jérôme Roussillon, Paulo Otávio, Maxence Lacroix, Admir Mehmedi, Josuha Guilavogui, Maximilian Arnold, Renato Steffen, Xaver Schlager (61' Yannick Gerhardt), Josip Brekalo (79' Bartosz Bialek), Wout Weghorst.
Coach: Oliver Glasner.
Goals: 45+1' Admir Mehmedi 0-1, 64' André Simões 1-1, 90+4' Karim Ansarifard 2-1.
Referee: Artur Soares Dias (POR)

Petros Mandalos missed a penalty kick (20')

01.10.20   Ibrox Stadium, Glasgow: Glasgow Rangers FC – Galatasaray 2-1 (0-0)
Glasgow Rangers FC: Allan McGregor, James Tavernier, Connor Goldson, Filip Helander, Borna Barisic, Steven Davis, Scott Arfield, Glen Kamara, Ianis Hagi (78' Ryan Jack), Alfredo Morelos (87' Cedric Itten), Ryan Kent. Coach: Steven Gerrard.
Galatasaray: Fatih Öztürk, Martin Linnes, Omar Elabdellaoui, Marcão Teixeira, Christian Luyindama, Sofiane Féghouli (73' Mbaye Diagne), Younès Belhanda (66' Oghenekaro Etebo), Taylan Antalyali, Emre Kilinç, Ryan Babel (65' Ömer Bayram), Radamel Falcao.
Coach: Fatih Terim.
Goals: 52' Scott Arfield 1-0, 59' James Tavernier 2-0, 87' Marcão Teixeira 2-1.
Referee: Andris Treimanis (LAT)

01.10.20   Estádio José Alvalade, Lisboa: Sporting CP – LASK Linz 1-4 (1-1)
Sporting CP: Antonio Adán, Luis Carlos Neto, Sebastián Coates, Zouhair Feddal, Pedro Porro, Nuno Mendes, Wendel, Matheus Nunes (71' Andraz Sporar), Luciano Vietto (67' Pedro Gonçalves), Nuno Santos (78' Antunes), Tiago Tomás. Coach: Emanuel Ferro.
LASK Linz: Alexander Schlager, Petar Filipovic (78' Andrés Andrade), Gernot Trauner, Reinhold Ranftl, Philipp Wiesinger, James Holland, Peter Michorl (87' Lukas Grgic), René Renner, Husein Balic, Andreas Gruber (74' Patrick Plojer), Marko Raguz.
Coach: Dominik Thalhammer.
Goals: 14' Gernot Trauner 0-1, 42' Tiago Tomás 1-1, 58' Marko Raguz 1-2, 65' Peter Michorl 1-3, 68' Andreas Gruber 1-4.
Referee: Aleksei Kulbakov (BLS)
Sent off: 63' Sebastián Coates.

01.10.20   Estádio do Rio Ave Futebol Clube, Vila do Conde:
Rio Ave FC – AC Milan 2-2 (0-0, 1-1) (a.e.t.)
Rio Ave FC: Pawel Kieszek, Ivo Pinto, Aderllan Santos, Nélson Monte, Toni Borevkovic, Tarantini (75' Nikola Jambor), Filipe Augusto, Diego Lopes (66' Francisco "Chico" Geraldes), Bruno Moreira (86' Gelson Dala), Carlos Mané (109' Gabrielzinho), Lucas Piazón.
Coach: Mário Silva.
AC Milan: Gianluigi Donnarumma, Simon Kjær, Davide Calabria, Theo Hernández, Matteo Gabbia, Hakan Çalhanoglu, Samu Castillejo (46' Brahim Díaz), Franck Kessié (105' Sandro Tonali), Ismaël Bennacar, Alexis Saelemaekers (95' Lorenzo Colombo), Daniel Maldini (67' Rafael Leão). Coach: Stefano Pioli.
Goals: 51' Alexis Saelemaekers 0-1, 72' Francisco "Chico" Geraldes 1-1, 91' Gelson Dala 2-1, 120+2' Hakan Çalhanoglu 2-2.
Referee: Jesús Gil Manzano (ESP)
Sent off: 120' Toni Borevkovic.

AC Milan won on penalties after extra time (9-8).
Penalties: Bennacer 1-0, Francisco "Chico" Geraldes 1-1, Kjær 2-1, Aderllan Santos 2-2,
   Hernández 3-2, Jambor 3-3, Brahim Díaz 4-3, Lucas Piazón 4-4, Çalhanoglu 5-4,
   Filipe Augusto 5-5, Calabria 6-5, Gelson Dala 6-6, Tonali 7-6, Gabrielzinho 7-7,
   Colombo missed, Nélson Monte missed, Rafael Leão 8-7, Ivo Pinto 8-8,
   Donnarumma missed, Kieszak missed, Bennacer missed,
   Francisco "Chico" Geraldes missed, Kjær 9-8, Aderllan Santos missed.

01.10.20 Tottenham Hotspur Stadium, London:
Tottenham Hotspur – Maccabi Haifa 7-2 (4-1)
Tottenham Hotspur: Joe Hart, Toby Alderweireld, Matt Doherty, Ben Davies, Davinson Sánchez, Lucas Moura, Pierre-Emile Højbjerg (63' Moussa Sissoko), Harry Winks, Giovani Lo Celso (46' Dele Alli), Harry Kane (75' Reguilón), Steven Bergwijn. Coach: José Mourinho.
Maccabi Haifa: Josh Cohen, Ernest Mabouka, Bogdan Planic, Sun Menachem, Ayed Habashi, Ofri Arad (71' Godsway Donyoh), Tjaronn Chery, Neta Lavi, Mohammad Abu Fani (87' Yuval Ashkenazi), Nikita Rukavytsya, Dolev Haziza (84' José Rodríguez).
Coach: Barak Bakhar.
Goals: 2' Harry Kane 1-0, 17' Tjaronn Chery 1-1, 20' Lucas Moura 2-1, 36', 39' Giovanni Lo Celso 3-1, 4-1, 52' Nikita Rukavytsya 4-2 (p), 56', 74' Harry Kane 5-2 (p), 6-2, 90+1' Dele Alli 7-2 (p).
Referee: Ruddy Buquet (FRA)

GROUP STAGE

GROUP A

AS Roma	6	4	1	1	13	-	5	13
BSC Young Boys	6	3	1	2	9	-	7	10
CFR Cluj	6	1	2	3	4	-	10	5
CSKA Sofia	6	1	2	3	3	-	7	5

GROUP B

Arsenal FC	6	6	0	0	20	-	5	18
Molde FK	6	3	1	2	9	-	11	10
SK Rapid Wien	6	2	1	3	11	-	13	7
Dundalk FC	6	0	0	6	8	-	19	0

GROUP C

Bayer Leverkusen	6	5	0	1	21	-	8	15
Slavia Praha	6	4	0	2	11	-	10	12
Hapoel Be'er Sheva	6	2	0	4	7	-	13	6
OGC Nice	6	1	0	5	8	-	16	3

GROUP D

Glasgow Rangers FC	6	4	2	0	13	-	7	14
SL Benfica	6	3	3	0	18	-	9	12
Standard Liège	6	1	1	4	7	-	14	4
KKS Lech Poznan	6	1	0	5	6	-	14	3

GROUP E

PSV Eindhoven	6	4	0	2	12	-	9	12
Granada CF	6	3	2	1	6	-	3	11
PAOK Saloniki	6	1	3	2	8	-	7	6
Omonia Nicosia	6	1	1	4	5	-	12	4

GROUP F

SSC Napoli	6	3	2	1	7	-	4	11
Real Sociedad	6	2	3	1	5	-	4	9
AZ Almaar	6	2	2	2	7	-	5	8
HNK Rijeka	6	1	1	4	6	-	12	4

GROUP G

Leicester City	6	4	1	1	14 -	5	13
Sporting Braga	6	4	1	1	14 -	10	13
Zorya Luhansk	6	2	0	4	6 -	11	6
AEK Athens	6	1	0	5	7 -	15	3

GROUP H

AC Milan	6	4	1	1	12 -	7	13
Lille Olympique	6	3	2	1	14 -	8	11
AC Sparta Praha	6	2	0	4	10 -	12	6
Celtic FC	6	1	1	4	10 -	19	4

GROUP I

Villarreal CF	6	5	1	0	17 -	5	16
Maccabi Tel Aviv	6	3	2	1	6 -	7	11
Sivasspor	6	2	0	4	9 -	11	6
Qarabag FK	6	0	1	5	4 -	13	1

GROUP J

Tottenham Hotspur	6	4	1	1	15 -	5	13
Royal Antwerp FC	6	4	0	2	8 -	5	12
LASK Linz	6	3	1	2	11 -	12	10
PFC Ludogorets Razgrad	6	0	0	6	7 -	19	0

GROUP K

Dinamo Zagreb	6	4	2	0	9 -	1	14
Wolfsberger AC	6	3	1	2	7 -	6	10
Feyenoord Rotterdam	6	1	2	3	4 -	8	5
CSKA Moscow	6	0	3	3	3 -	8	3

GROUP L

1899 Hoffenheim	6	5	1	0	17 -	2	16
Crvena Zvezda Beograd	6	3	2	1	9 -	4	11
Slovan Liberec	6	2	1	3	4 -	13	7
KAA Gent	6	0	0	6	4 -	15	0

The top 2 teams in each group advanced to the knockout phase.

GROUP STAGE
GROUP A

22.10.20 Stadion Wankdorf, Bern: BSC Young Boys – AS Roma 1-2 (1-0)
BSC Young Boys: David von Ballmoos, Fabian Lustenberger, Nicolas Bürgy, Cédric Zesiger, Silvan Hefti, Quentin Maceiras, Nicolas Moumi Ngamaleu (65' Felix Mambimbi), Christian Fassnacht (65' Meschack Elia), Vincent Sierro (79' Gianluca Gaudino), Fabian Rieder (70' Michel Aebischer), Jean-Pierre Nsamé (79' Theoson Siebatcheu). Coach: Gerardo Seoane.
AS Roma: Pau López, Federico Fazio, Bruno Peres, Juan Jesus (69' Lorenzo Pellegrini), Rick Karsdorp (46' Leonardo Spinazzola), Marash Kumbulla, Bryan Cristante, Gonzalo Villar (59' Jordan Veretout), Pedro (59' Henrikh Mkhitaryan), Borja Mayoral (59' Edin Dzeko), Carles Pérez. Coach: Paulo Fonseca.
Goals: 14' Jean-Pierre Nsamé 1-0 (p), 69' Bruno Peres 1-1, 73' Marash Kumbulla 1-2.
Referee: Carlos del Cerro Grande (ESP)   Attendance: 600.

22.10.20 Vasil Levski National Stadium, Sofia: CSKA Sofia – CFR Cluj 0-2 (0-0)
CSKA Sofia: Busatto, Jurgen Mattheij, Thibaut Vion, Bradley Mazikou, Valentin Antov, Younousse Sankharé (71' Ahmed Ahmedov), Tiago Rodrigues (81' Stefano Beltrame), Amos Youga, Georgi Yomov (80' Henrique), Ali Sowe, Jerome Sinclair (63' Jules Keita). Coach: Stamen Belchev.
CFR Cluj: Cristian Balgradean, Paulo Vinícius, Mateo Susic, Camora, Andrei Burca, Ciprian Deac (78' Alexandru Chipciu), Ovidiu Hoban, Damjan Djokovic, Adrian Paun (83' Michaël Pereira), Mário Rondón (87' Nicolae Cârnat), Gabriel Debeljuh (87' Jakub Vojtus). Coach: Dan Petrescu.
Goals: 53' Mário Rondón 0-1, 74' Ciprian Deac 0-2 (p).
Referee: Halil Umut Meler (TUR)   Attendance: 11,958.

CSKA Sofia played the home matches at Vasil Levski National Stadium, Sofia, instead of their regular stadium Stadion Balgarska Armia, Sofia.

29.10.20 Stadio Olimpico, Roma: AS Roma – CSKA Sofia 0-0
AS Roma: Pau López, Federico Fazio, Chris Smalling (56' Juan Jesus), Bruno Peres, Leonardo Spinazzola (46' Rick Karsdorp), Marash Kumbulla, Henrikh Mkhitaryan (46' Pedro), Bryan Cristante, Gonzalo Villar, Borja Mayoral (71' Edin Dzeko), Carles Pérez (75' Lorenzo Pellegrini). Coach: Paulo Fonseca.
CSKA Sofia: Busatto, Petar Zanev, Thibaut Vion (89' Ivan Turitsov), Geferson (80' Tiago Rodrigues), Bradley Mazikou, Valentin Antov, Younousse Sankharé (89' Ahmed Ahmedov), Amos Youga (82' Stefano Beltrame), Georgi Yomov, Ali Sowe, Jerome Sinclair (64' Henrique). Coach: Daniel Morales.
Referee: Aleksei Kulbakov (BLS)

29.10.20 Stadionul Dr. Constantin Radulescu, Cluj-Napoca:
CFR Cluj – BSC Young Boys 1-1 (0-0)
CFR Cluj: Cristian Balgradean, Paulo Vinícius (14' Cristian Manea), Mateo Susic, Camora, Andrei Burca, Ciprian Deac (63' Alexandru Chipciu), Ovidiu Hoban (79' Catalin Itu), Damjan Djokovic, Adrian Paun (79' Michaël Pereira), Mário Rondón, Gabriel Debeljuh (46' Billel Omrani). Coach: Dan Petrescu.
BSC Young Boys: David von Ballmoos, Fabian Lustenberger, Cédric Zesiger, Silvan Hefti (63' Ulisses Garcia), Mohamed Camara (74' Miralem Sulejmani), Quentin Maceiras, Nicolas Moumi Ngamaleu (74' Theoson Siebatcheu), Christian Fassnacht, Michel Aebischer (75' Vincent Sierro), Jean-Pierre Nsamé, Meschack Elia (63' Gianluca Gaudino).
Coach: Gerardo Seoane.
Goals: 62' Mário Rondón 1-0, 69' Christian Fassnacht 1-1.
Referee: Glenn Nyberg (SWE)

05.11.20 Stadio Olimpico, Roma: AS Roma – CFR Cluj 5-0 (3-0)
AS Roma: Pau López, Federico Fazio, Bruno Peres, Leonardo Spinazzola (46' Juan Jesus), Marash Kumbulla, Ibañez (61' Chris Smalling), Henrikh Mkhitaryan (46' Lorenzo Pellegrini), Jordan Veretout (46' Pedro), Bryan Cristante (74' Tommaso Milanese), Gonzalo Villar, Borja Mayoral. Coach: Paulo Fonseca.
CFR Cluj: Cristian Balgradean, Mateo Susic (78' Iasmin Latovlevici), Camora, Cristian Manea, Denis Ciobotariu, Ciprian Deac (46' Michaël Pereira), Ovidiu Hoban, Damjan Djokovic, Catalin Itu (46' Adrian Paun), Mário Rondón (90' Andrei Joca), Gabriel Debeljuh (67' Nicolae Cârnat). Coach: Dan Petrescu.
Goals: 1' Henrikh Mkhitaryan 1-0, 24' Ibañez 2-0, 34', 84' Borja Mayoral 3-0, 4-0, 89' Pedro 5-0.
Referee: Matej Jug (SVN)

05.11.20 Stadion Wankdorf, Bern: BSC Young Boys – CSKA Sofia 3-0 (3-0)
BSC Young Boys: David von Ballmoos, Fabian Lustenberger, Jordan Lefort, Silvan Hefti, Mohamed Camara (63' Ulisses Garcia), Miralem Sulejmani (70' Gianluca Gaudino), Christian Fassnacht, Vincent Sierro (62' Michel Aebischer), Fabian Rieder, Jean-Pierre Nsamé (69' Theoson Siebatcheu), Felix Mambimbi (70' Meschack Elia). Coach: Gerardo Seoane.
CSKA Sofia: Busatto, Jurgen Mattheij, Thibaut Vion (87' Ivan Turitsov), Bradley Mazikou, Valentin Antov, Younousse Sankharé (87' Ahmed Ahmedov), Amos Youga, Georgi Yomov (79' Jules Keita), Ali Sowe, Jerome Sinclair (69' Graham Carey), Adalberto Peñaranda (68' Tiago Rodrigues). Coach: Daniel Morales.
Goals: 2' Felix Mambimbi 1-0, 18' Miralem Sulejmani 2-0, 32' Felix Mambimbi 3-0.
Referee: Lawrence Visser (BEL)

26.11.20 Vasil Levski National Stadium, Sofia: CSKA Sofia – BSC Young Boys 0-1 (0-1)
CSKA Sofia: Busatto, Petar Zanev, Jurgen Mattheij, Valentin Antov, Ivan Turitsov (59' Jerome Sinclair), Younousse Sankharé (75' Amos Youga), Graham Carey, Tiago Rodrigues (75' Ahmed Ahmedov), Stefano Beltrame (90' Jules Keita), Georgi Yomov (75' Adalberto Peñaranda), Ali Sowe. Coach: Bruno Akrapovic.
BSC Young Boys: David von Ballmoos, Fabian Lustenberger (74' Jordan Lefort), Ulisses Garcia, Silvan Hefti, Mohamed Camara, Nicolas Moumi Ngamaleu (87' Nicolas Bürgy), Christian Fassnacht (74' Felix Mambimbi), Vincent Sierro, Fabian Rieder (74' Gianluca Gaudino), Jean-Pierre Nsamé, Meschack Elia (60' Michel Aebischer). Coach: Gerardo Seoane.
Goal: 34' Jean-Pierre Nsamé 0-1.
Referee: Fábio Veríssimo (POR)

26.11.20   Stadionul Dr. Constantin Radulescu, Cluj-Napoca: CFR Cluj – AS Roma 0-2 (0-0)
CFR Cluj: Cristian Balgradean, Mateo Susic, Camora, Andrei Burca, Cristian Manea, Damjan Djokovic, Michaël Pereira, Adrian Paun (71' Nicolae Cârnat), Catalin Itu (51' Alexandru Chipciu), Mário Rondón, Gabriel Debeljuh (70' Jakub Vojtus). Coach: Dan Petrescu.
AS Roma: Pau López, Bruno Peres, Juan Jesus, Leonardo Spinazzola (64' Henrikh Mkhitaryan), Riccardo Calafiori, Bryan Cristante, Lorenzo Pellegrini (46' Jordan Veretout), Gonzalo Villar, Amadou Diawara (77' Tommaso Milanese), Borja Mayoral (63' Edin Dzeko), Carles Pérez (84' Filippo Tripi). Coach: Paulo Fonseca.
Goals: 49' Gabriel Debeljuh 0-1 (og), 67' Jordan Veretout 0-2 (p).
Referee: Harald Lechner (AUT)

03.12.20   Stadio Olimpico, Roma: AS Roma – BSC Young Boys 3-1 (1-1)
AS Roma: Pau López, Bruno Peres, Juan Jesus, Ibañez (46' Leonardo Spinazzola), Riccardo Calafiori, Bryan Cristante (65' Federico Fazio), Gonzalo Villar (60' Lorenzo Pellegrini), Amadou Diawara, Pedro (46' Henrikh Mkhitaryan), Borja Mayoral (60' Edin Dzeko), Carles Pérez. Coach: Paulo Fonseca.
BSC Young Boys: David von Ballmoos, Jordan Lefort, Ulisses Garcia (68' Meschack Elia), Cédric Zesiger, Silvan Hefti, Mohamed Camara, Nicolas Moumi Ngamaleu (76' Felix Mambimbi), Christian Fassnacht, Michel Aebischer (67' Gianluca Gaudino), Fabian Rieder (58' Vincent Sierro), Jean-Pierre Nsamé (76' Theoson Siebatcheu). Coach: Gerardo Seoane.
Goals: 34' Jean-Pierre Nsamé 0-1, 44' Borja Mayoral 1-1, 59' Riccardo Calafiori 2-1, 81' Edin Dzeko 3-1.
Referee: Fran Jovic (CRO)
Sent off: 82' Mohamed Camara.

03.12.20   Stadionul Dr. Constantin Radulescu, Cluj-Napoca: CFR Cluj – CSKA Sofia 0-0
CFR Cluj: Cristian Balgradean, Mateo Susic, Camora, Andrei Burca, Cristian Manea, Alexandru Chipciu, Damjan Djokovic, Michaël Pereira (61' Ciprian Deac), Adrian Paun (75' Nicolae Cârnat), Mário Rondón, Gabriel Debeljuh (86' Jakub Vojtus). Coach: Dan Petrescu.
CSKA Sofia: Busatto, Petar Zanev, Jurgen Mattheij, Thibaut Vion, Geferson, Valentin Antov, Younousse Sankharé (78' Tiago Rodrigues), Graham Carey, Amos Youga, Georgi Yomov (77' Henrique), Ali Sowe. Coach: Bruno Akrapovic.
Referee: Amaury Delerue (FRA)
Sent off: 85' Alexandru Chipciu.

10.12.20   Stadion Wankdorf, Bern: BSC Young Boys – CFR Cluj 2-1 (0-0)
BSC Young Boys: David von Ballmoos, Jordan Lefort, Ulisses Garcia, Nicolas Bürgy (86' Theoson Siebatcheu), Silvan Hefti, Miralem Sulejmani (58' Gianluca Gaudino), Nicolas Moumi Ngamaleu (82' Cédric Zesiger), Michel Aebischer, Fabian Rieder (58' Christopher Martins Pereira), Jean-Pierre Nsamé, Felix Mambimbi (58' Meschack Elia).
Coach: Gerardo Seoane.
CFR Cluj: Cristian Balgradean, Paulo Vinícius, Camora, Andrei Burca, Cristian Manea, Ciprian Deac (90+2' Grzegorz Sandomierski *goalkeeper*), Ovidiu Hoban, Damjan Djokovic, Michaël Pereira (88' Mateo Susic), Adrian Paun (74' Gabriel Debeljuh), Mário Rondón.
Coach: Edward Iordanescu.
Goals: 84' Gabriel Debeljuh 0-1, 90+3' Jean-Pierre Nsamé 1-1 (p), 90+6' Gianluca Gaudino 2-1.
Referee: Benoît Bastien (FRA)
Sent off: 90' Cristian Balgradean, 90+5' Jean-Pierre Nsamé, 90+7' Damjan Djokovic.

10.12.20   Vasil Levski National Stadium, Sofia: CSKA Sofia – AS Roma 3-1 (2-1)
CSKA Sofia: Busatto, Petar Zanev, Jurgen Mattheij, Geferson, Bradley Mazikou, Valentin Antov, Younousse Sankharé (63' Stefano Beltrame), Tiago Rodrigues (81' Henrique), Amos Youga (74' Plamen Galabov), Georgi Yomov (63' Thibaut Vion), Ali Sowe (74' Ahmed Ahmedov). Coach: Bruno Akrapovic.
AS Roma: Pietro Boer, Federico Fazio, Bruno Peres (81' Filippo Tripi), Juan Jesus, Marash Kumbulla (46' Chris Smalling), Amadou Diawara, Tommaso Milanese (62' Gonzalo Villar), Pedro, Borja Mayoral, Carles Pérez, Mory Bamba (62' Rick Karsdorp). Coach: Paulo Fonseca.
Goals: 5' Tiago Rodrigues 1-0, 22' Tommaso Milanese 1-1, 34', 55' Ali Sowe 2-1, 3-1.
Referee: Irfan Peljto (BIH)

GROUP B

22.10.20   Tallaght Stadium, Dublin: Dundalk FC – Molde FK 1-2 (1-0)
Dundalk FC: Gary Rogers, Brian Gartland, Sean Gannon (77' David McMillan), Daniel Cleary, Darragh Leahy (77' Cameron Dummigan), Chris Shields, Sean Murray (77' Andy Boyle), John Mountney, Gregory Sloggett (64' Patrick McEleney), Patrick Hoban, Michael Duffy (80' Stefan Colovic). Coach: Shane Keegan.
Molde FK: Andreas Linde, Kristoffer Haugen, Martin Bjørnbak, Stian Gregersen, Marcus Pedersen, Magnus Wolff Eikrem (82' Martin Ellingsén), Etzaz Hussain, Eirik Hestad, Fredrik Aursnes, Mathis Bolly (69' Erling Knudtzon), Ohi Omoijuanfo (90+4' Ola Brynhildsen). Coach: Erling Moe.
Goals: 35' Sean Murray 1-0, 62' Etzaz Hussain 1-1, 72' Ohi Omoijuanfo 1-2 (p).
Referee: Petri Viljanen (FIN)

Dundalk FC played their home match at Tallaght Stadium, Dublin, instead of their regular stadium Oriel Park, Dundalk.

22.10.20   Allianz Stadion, Vienna: SK Rapid Wien – Arsenal FC 1-2 (0-0)
SK Rapid Wien: Richard Strebinger, Filip Stojkovic, Maximilian Hofmann, Maximilian Ullmann, Mateo Barac, Marcel Ritzmaier (88' Christoph Knasmüllner), Srdjan Grahovac, Dejan Ljubicic, Taxiarchis Fountas, Ercan Kara (76' Koya Kitagawa), Kelvin Arase (79' Thorsten Schick). Coach: Dietmar Kühbauer.
Arsenal FC: Bernd Leno, David Luiz, Cédric Soares (61' Héctor Bellerín), Sead Kolasinac, Gabriel Magalhães, Bukayo Saka (84' Kieran Tierney), Mohamed Elneny, Thomas Partey, Alexandre Lacazette (84' Joseph Willock), Nicolas Pépé (90+4' Reiss Nelson), Eddie Nketiah (61' Pierre-Emerick Aubameyang). Coach: Mikel Arteta.
Goals: 51' Taxiarchis Fountas 1-0, 70' David Luiz 1-1, 74' Pierre-Emerick Aubameyang 1-2.
Referee: Pavel Krátovec (CZE)   Attendance: 3,000.

29.10.20 Emirates Stadium, London: Arsenal FC – Dundalk FC 3-0 (2-0)
Arsenal FC: Rúnar Alex Rúnarsson, Shkodran Mustafi (61' Dani Ceballos), Cédric Soares, Sead Kolasinac, Granit Xhaka (74' Kieran Tierney), Mohamed Elneny, Ainsley Maitland-Niles, Joseph Willock, Nicolas Pépé (62' Willian), Eddie Nketiah (74' Folarin Balogun), Reiss Nelson. Coach: Mikel Arteta.
Dundalk FC: Gary Rogers, Brian Gartland, Andy Boyle, Daniel Cleary (53' Sean Hoare), Cameron Dummigan, Chris Shields (62' Sean Gannon), Patrick McEleney (53' Jordan Flores), Sean Murray (46' Gregory Sloggett), John Mountney, Patrick Hoban, Michael Duffy (70' Stefan Colovic). Coach: Shane Keegan.
Goals: 42' Eddie Nketiah 1-0, 44' Joseph Willock 2-0, 46' Nicolas Pépé 3-0.
Referee: Filip Glova (SVK)

29.10.20 Åker Stadion, Molde: Molde FK – SK Rapid Wien 1-0 (0-0)
Molde FK: Andreas Linde, Kristoffer Haugen, Martin Bjørnbak, Stian Gregersen, Magnus Wolff Eikrem (83' Leke James), Eirik Hestad (68' Mathis Bolly), Fredrik Aursnes, Martin Ellingsen, Henry Wingo, Ola Brynhildsen (77' Etzaz Hussain), Ohi Omoijuanfo. Coach: Erling Moe.
SK Rapid Wien: Paul Gartler, Filip Stojkovic, Maximilian Ullmann, Mateo Barac, Leo Greiml, Thorsten Schick (46' Kelvin Arase), Marcel Ritzmaier, Srdjan Grahovac (77' Melih Ibrahimoglu), Dejan Ljubicic, Koya Kitagawa (59' Christoph Knasmüllner), Ercan Kara. Coach: Dietmar Kühbauer.
Goal: 65' Ohi Omoijuanfo 1-0.
Referee: Petr Ardeleánu (CZE)   Attendance: 600.

05.11.20 Allianz Stadion, Vienna: SK Rapid Wien – Dundalk FC 4-3 (1-1)
SK Rapid Wien: Paul Gartler, Filip Stojkovic, Maximilian Hofmann, Maximilian Ullmann, Mateo Barac (54' Mario Sonnleitner), Christoph Knasmüllner (72' Yusuf Demir), Thorsten Schick, Dejan Petrovic (72' Srdjan Grahovac), Dejan Ljubicic, Ercan Kara, Kelvin Arase. Coach: Dietmar Kühbauer.
Dundalk FC: Aaron McCarey, Andy Boyle, Sean Gannon (65' John Mountney), Sean Hoare, Daniel Cleary, Darragh Leahy (65' Cameron Dummigan), Chris Shields, Gregory Sloggett, Jordan Flores (76' Sean Murray), Patrick Hoban (76' David McMillan), Michael Duffy (72' Nathan Oduwa). Coach: Shane Keegan.
Goals: 7' Patrick Hoban 0-1, 22' Dejan Ljubicic 1-1, 79' Kelvin Arase 2-1,
82' David McMillan 2-2 (p), 87' Maximilian Hofmann 3-2, 90' Yusuf Demir 4-2,
90+6' David McMillan 4-3 (p).
Referee: Trustin Farrugia Cann (MLT)

05.11.20 Emirates Stadium, London: Arsenal FC – Molde FK 4-1 (1-1)
Arsenal FC: Bernd Leno, David Luiz, Shkodran Mustafi, Sead Kolasinac, Granit Xhaka (80' Kieran Tierney), Ainsley Maitland-Niles (63' Cédric Soares), Dani Ceballos (80' Mohamed Elneny), Joseph Willock, Willian (63' Bukayo Saka), Nicolas Pépé, Eddie Nketiah.
Coach: Mikel Arteta.
Molde FK: Andreas Linde, Kristoffer Haugen, Martin Bjørnbak, Stian Gregersen (46' Sheriff Sinyan), Magnus Wolff Eikrem (74' Ola Brynhildsen), Etzaz Hussain, Fredrik Aursnes, Martin Ellingsen (86' Mattias Moström), Henry Wingo, Mathis Bolly (63' Erling Knudtzon), Ohi Omoijuanfo (74' Leke James). Coach: Erling Moe.
Goals: 22' Martin Ellingsen 0-1, 45+1' Kristoffer Haugen 1-1 (og),
62' Sheriff Sinyan 2-1 (og), 69' Nicolas Pépé 3-1, 88' Joseph Willock 4-1.
Referee: Halil Umut Meler (TUR)

26.11.20   Åker Stadion, Molde: Molde FK – Arsenal FC 0-3 (0-0)
Molde FK: Andreas Linde, Stian Gregersen (85' Erling Knudtzon), Birk Risa (82' Marcus Pedersen), Sheriff Sinyan, Magnus Wolff Eikrem (81' Ola Brynhildsen), Etzaz Hussain (61' Mathis Bolly), Eirik Hestad, Fredrik Aursnes, Martin Ellingsen, Henry Wingo, Leke James (61' Ohi Omoijuanfo). Coach: Erling Moe.
Arsenal FC: Rúnar Alex Rúnarsson, David Luiz (46' Rob Holding), Shkodran Mustafi, Cédric Soares, Granit Xhaka (62' Dani Ceballos), Ainsley Maitland-Niles, Joseph Willock (75' Kieran Tierney), Alexandre Lacazette (75' Emile Smith-Rowe), Nicolas Pépé, Eddie Nketiah (82' Folarin Balogun), Reiss Nelson. Coach: Mikel Arteta.
Goals: 50' Nicolas Pépé 0-1, 55' Reiss Nelson 0-2, 83' Folarin Balogun 0-3.
Referee: Irfan Peljto (BIH)   Attendance: 600.

26.11.20   Aviva Stadium, Dublin: Dundalk FC – SK Rapid Wien 1-3 (0-2)
Dundalk FC: Gary Rogers, Andy Boyle, Sean Gannon, Sean Hoare (46' Daniel Kelly), Daniel Cleary, Cameron Dummigan (81' Darragh Leahy), Chris Shields, Gregory Sloggett (72' Sean Murray), Stefan Colovic (46' Patrick McEleney), David McMillan (46' Nathan Oduwa), Michael Duffy. Coach: Shane Keegan.
SK Rapid Wien: Paul Gartler, Filip Stojkovic, Maximilian Hofmann, Maximilian Ullmann, Mateo Barac, Christoph Knasmüllner (81' Yusuf Demir), Thorsten Schick, Srdjan Grahovac, Melih Ibrahimoglu (55' Kelvin Arase), Taxiarchis Fountas (66' Lion Schuster), Ercan Kara (66' Koya Kitagawa). Coach: Dietmar Kühbauer.
Goals: 11' Christoph Knasmüllner 0-1, 37', 58' Ercan Kara 0-2, 0-3, 63' Chris Shields 1-3 (p).
Referee: Tamás Bognár (HUN)

Nathan Oduwa missed a penalty kick (49').

Dundalk FC played their home match at Aviva Stadium, Dublin, instead of their regular stadium Oriel Park, Dundalk.

03.12.20   Emirates Stadium, London: Arsenal FC – SK Rapid Wien 4-1 (3-0)
Arsenal FC: Rúnar Alex Rúnarsson, Shkodran Mustafi (70' Calum Chambers), Cédric Soares, Pablo Marí, Sead Kolasinac, Mohamed Elneny (63' Dani Ceballos), Ainsley Maitland-Niles, Alexandre Lacazette (63' Emile Smith-Rowe), Nicolas Pépé, Eddie Nketiah (81' Folarin Balogun), Reiss Nelson (63' Willian). Coach: Mikel Arteta.
SK Rapid Wien: Richard Strebinger, Mario Sonnleitner, Maximilian Hofmann (46' Mateo Barac), Maximilian Ullmann (46' Thorsten Schick), Leo Greiml, Marcel Ritzmaier (65' Christoph Knasmüllner), Lion Schuster, Deni Alar (77' Lukas Sulzbacher), Koya Kitagawa (65' Ercan Kara), Kelvin Arase, Yusuf Demir. Coach: Dietmar Kühbauer.
Goals: 10' Alexandre Lacazette 1-0, 17' Pablo Marí 2-0, 44' Eddie Nketiah 3-0, 47' Koya Kitagawa 3-1, 66' Emile Smith-Rowe 4-1.
Referee: Radu Marian Petrescu (ROM)   Attendance: 2,000.

03.12.20 Åker Stadion, Molde: Molde FK – Dundalk FC 3-1 (2-0)
Molde FK: Andreas Linde, Stian Gregersen (68' Etzaz Hussain), Birk Risa, Sheriff Sinyan, Magnus Wolff Eikrem (78' Leke James), Eirik Hestad (79' Mattias Moström), Fredrik Aursnes (78' Tobias Christensen), Martin Ellingsen, Henry Wingo, Erling Knudtzon, Ohi Omoijuanfo (86' Mathis Bolly). Coach: Erling Moe.
Dundalk FC: Gary Rogers, Brian Gartland, Andy Boyle (61' Daniel Cleary), Sean Gannon, Sean Hoare, Cameron Dummigan, Chris Shields (68' John Mountney), Gregory Sloggett (61' Patrick McEleney), Jordan Flores, Daniel Kelly (73' David McMillan), Nathan Oduwa (61' Michael Duffy). Coach: Shane Keegan.
Goals: 30' Magnus Wolff Eikrem 1-0, 41' Ohi Omoijuanfo 2-0, 67' Martin Ellingsen 3-0, 90+4' Jordan Flores 3-1.
Referee: Daniel Siebert (GER)   Attendance: 600.

10.12.20 Aviva Stadium, Dublin: Dundalk FC – Arsenal FC 2-4 (1-2)
Dundalk FC: Gary Rogers, Andy Boyle (46' Brian Gartland), Sean Gannon (54' John Mountney), Sean Hoare, Daniel Cleary, Darragh Leahy, Chris Shields, Patrick McEleney (78' Stefan Colovic), Jordan Flores, David McMillan (53' Daniel Kelly), Michael Duffy (77' Jamie Wynne). Coach: Shane Keegan.
Arsenal FC: Rúnar Alex Rúnarsson, Shkodran Mustafi, Cédric Soares, Pablo Marí, Calum Chambers, Mohamed Elneny (62' Dani Ceballos), Ainsley Maitland-Niles, Joseph Willock (83' Miguel Azeez), Emile Smith-Rowe (77' Ben Cottrell), Nicolas Pépé, Eddie Nketiah (62' Folarin Balogun). Coach: Mikel Arteta.
Goals: 12' Eddie Nketiah 0-1, 18' Mohamed Elneny 0-2, 22' Jordan Flores 1-2, 67' Joseph Willock 1-3, 80' Folarin Balogun 1-4, 85' Sean Hoare 2-4.
Referee: Ivan Bebek (CRO)

Dundalk FC played their home match at Aviva Stadium, Dublin, instead of their regular stadium Oriel Park, Dundalk.

10.12.20 Allianz Stadion, Vienna: SK Rapid Wien – Molde FK 2-2 (1-1)
SK Rapid Wien: Paul Gartler, Filip Stojkovic, Maximilian Hofmann, Maximilian Ullmann, Mateo Barac, Christoph Knasmüllner (46' Taxiarchis Fountas), Thorsten Schick, Marcel Ritzmaier (61' Melih Ibrahimoglu), Srdjan Grahovac, Ercan Kara (75' Koya Kitagawa), Kelvin Arase (46' Yusuf Demir). Coach: Dietmar Kühbauer.
Molde FK: Andreas Linde, Stian Gregersen, Birk Risa, Sheriff Sinyan, Marcus Pedersen, Magnus Wolff Eikrem (57' Etzaz Hussain), Eirik Hestad (45' Erling Knudtzon), Fredrik Aursnes, Martin Ellingsen, Ola Brynhildsen (56' Ohi Omoijuanfo), Leke James (85' Henry Wingo). Coach: Erling Moe.
Goals: 12' Magnus Wolff Eikrem 0-1, 43' Marcel Ritzmaier 1-1, 46' Magnus Wolff Eikrem 1-2, 90' Melih Ibrahimoglu 2-2.
Referee: Marco Guida (ITA)

GROUP C

22.10.20 BayArena, Leverkusen: Bayer Leverkusen – OGC Nice 6-2 (2-1)
Bayer Leverkusen: Lukás Hrádecký, Sven Bender (81' Jonathan Tah), Lars Bender (82' Aleksandar Dragovic), Wendell, Edmond Tapsoba, Julian Baumgartlinger, Nadiem Amiri, Exequiel Palacios (74' Florian Wirtz), Lucas Alario (74' Karim Bellarabi), Leon Bailey, Moussa Diaby. Coach: Peter Bosz.
OGC Nice: Walter Benítez, Dante, Jordan Lotomba (79' Youcef Atal), Stanley N'Soki (63' Rony Lopes), Robson Bambu, Morgan Schneiderlin, Hassane Kamara, Pierre Lees-Melou (79' Dan N'Doye), Hichem Boudaoui (63' Alexis Claude-Maurice), Kasper Dolberg (71' Myziane Maolida), Amine Gouiri. Coach: Patrick Vieira.
Goals: 11' Nadiem Amiri 1-0, 16' Lucas Alario 2-0, 31' Amine Gouiri 2-1, 61' Moussa Diaby 3-1, 79, 83' Karim Bellarabi 4-1, 5-1, 87' Florian Wirtz 6-1, 90' Alexis Claude-Maurice 6-2.
Referee: Fran Jovic (CRO)

22.10.20 HaMoshava Stadium, Petach-Tikva: Hapoel Be'er Sheva – Slavia Praha 3-1 (1-0)
Hapoel Be'er Sheva: Ohad Levita, Miguel Vítor, Loai Taha (46' Shir Tzedek), Sean Goldberg, Elton Acolatse (89' Gaëtan Varenne), Lucas Bareiro, Or Dadya, Sintayehu Sallalich (79' Tomer Yosefi), Josué (90' David Keltjens), Marwan Kabha, Jhonatan Agudelo (70' César Marcelo Meli). Coach: Yossi Abukasis.
Slavia Praha: Ondrej Kolár, Ondrej Kúdela, Jan Boril, David Hovorka, Tomás Malinský (58' Lukás Masopust), Petr Sevcík (75' Ondrej Lingr), Lukás Provod, Ibrahim Traoré (46' Nicolae Stanciu), Oscar Dorley (89' Abdallah Sima), Stanislav Tecl (57' Jan Kuchta), Petar Musa. Coach: Jindrich Trpisovský.
Goals: 45' Jhonatan Agudelo 1-0, 75' Lukás Provod 1-1, 86', 88' Elton Acolatse 2-1, 3-1.
Referee: Lawrence Visser (BEL)   Attendance: 40.

Hapoel Be'er Sheva played their home match at HaMoshava Stadium, Petach Tikva, instead of their regular stadium Turner Stadium, Beersheba, which was temporarily closed for structural problems with the roof.

29.10.20 Sinobo Stadium, Prague: Slavia Praha – Bayer Leverkusen 1-0 (0-0)
Slavia Praha: Ondrej Kolár, Ondrej Kúdela, Jan Boril, Tomás Holes (61' Nicolae Stanciu), David Zima, Tomás Malinský (71' Abdallah Sima), Lukás Masopust, Petr Sevcík, Lukás Provod (76' Ibrahim Traoré), Ondrej Lingr (46' Petar Musa), Oscar Dorley (61' Peter Olayinka). Coach: Jindrich Trpisovský.
Bayer Leverkusen: Lukás Hrádecký, Aleksandar Dragovic, Wendell, Tin Jedvaj, Jonathan Tah, Julian Baumgartlinger, Kerem Demirbay, Florian Wirtz (67' Nadiem Amiri), Karim Bellarabi, Lucas Alario (46' Leon Bailey), Moussa Diaby. Coach: Peter Bosz.
Goal: 80' Peter Olayinka 1-0.
Referee: William Collum (SCO)
Sent off: 22' Karim Bellarabi.

Nicolae Stanciu missed a penalty kick (65').

29.10.20   Allianz Riviera, Nice: OGC Nice – Hapoel Be'er Sheva 1-0 (1-0)
OGC Nice: Walter Benítez, Dante, Stanley N'Soki (46' Andy Pelmard), Youcef Atal (68' Jordan Lotomba), Robson Bambu, Morgan Schneiderlin, Hassane Kamara, Alexis Claude-Maurice (58' Jeff Reine-Adélaïde), Khéphren Thuram-Ulien, Kasper Dolberg (85' Hichem Boudaoui), Amine Gouiri (69' Myziane Maolida). Coach: Patrick Vieira.
Hapoel Be'er Sheva: Ohad Levita, Miguel Vítor, Loai Taha, Sean Goldberg (76' Gaëtan Varenne), Elton Acolatse (88' Dudu Twito), Lucas Bareiro (81' Ramzi Safouri), Or Dadya, Sintayehu Sallalich (76' César Marcelo Meli), Josué, Marwan Kabha, Tomer Yosefi (46' Jhonatan Agudelo). Coach: Yossi Abukasis.
Goal: 23' Amine Gouiri 1-0.
Referee: Chris Kavanagh (ENG)

05.11.20   Sinobo Stadium, Prague: Slavia Praha – OGC Nice 3-2 (2-1)
Slavia Praha: Ondrej Kolár, Tomás Holes, David Hovorka (86' Jakub Kristan), David Zima, Lukás Masopust, Petr Sevcík, Peter Olayinka, Ondrej Lingr (70' Ibrahim Traoré), Oscar Dorley, Jan Kuchta (77' Stanislav Tecl), Abdallah Sima. Coach: Jindrich Trpisovský.
OGC Nice: Walter Benítez, Jordan Lotomba, Robson Bambu, Andy Pelmard, Flavius Daniliuc, Morgan Schneiderlin, Hassane Kamara (88' Dan N'Doye), Pierre Lees-Melou (65' Alexis Claude-Maurice), Rony Lopes (65' Jeff Reine-Adélaïde), Kasper Dolberg (81' Youcef Atal), Amine Gouiri. Coach: Patrick Vieira.
Goals: 16' Jan Kuchta 1-0, 33' Amine Gouiri 1-1, 43' Abdallah Sima 2-1, 71' Jan Kuchta 3-1, 90+3' Dan N'Doye 3-2.
Referee: Jakob Kehlet (DEN)

05.11.20   HaMoshava Stadium, Petach-Tikva:
            Hapoel Be'er Sheva – Bayer Leverkusen 2-4 (2-2)
Hapoel Be'er Sheva: Ohad Levita, Miguel Vítor, Loai Taha, Sean Goldberg (84' Ramzi Safouri), Elton Acolatse (89' César Marcelo Meli), Lucas Bareiro, Or Dadya, Sintayehu Sallalich (64' Itamar Shviro), Josué, Marwan Kabha (84' Gaëtan Varenne), Jhonatan Agudelo (64' Tomer Yosefi). Coach: Yossi Abukasis.
Bayer Leverkusen: Lukás Hrádecký, Aleksandar Dragovic, Wendell, Tin Jedvaj (62' Lars Bender), Jonathan Tah, Kerem Demirbay, Nadiem Amiri, Exequiel Palacios, Florian Wirtz, Lucas Alario (46' Moussa Diaby), Leon Bailey. Coach: Peter Bosz.
Goals: 5' Leon Bailey 0-1, 11', 25' Elton Acolatse 1-1, 2-1, 39' Or Dadya 2-2 (og), 75' Leon Bailey 2-3, 88' Florian Wirtz 2-4.
Referee: Radu Marian Petrescu (ROM)

26.11.20   Bay Arena, Leverkusen: Bayer Leverkusen – Hapoel Be'er Sheva 4-1 (1-0)
Bayer Leverkusen: Lukás Hrádecký, Aleksandar Dragovic, Wendell, Tin Jedvaj, Jonathan Tah, Kerem Demirbay, Nadiem Amiri (90+1' Julian Baumgartlinger), Florian Wirtz (80' Daley Sinkgraven), Karim Bellarabi (80' Emrehan Gedikli), Patrik Schick (68' Lucas Alario), Leon Bailey (68' Moussa Diaby). Coach: Peter Bosz.
Hapoel Be'er Sheva: Ohad Levita, Loai Taha, Sean Goldberg (70' Dudu Twito), Lucas Bareiro, Or Dadya, Sintayehu Sallalich (70' Jhonatan Agudelo, 85' Gaëtan Varenne), Marwan Kabha, César Marcelo Meli (81' Ilay Madmon), David Keltjens, Tomer Yosefi, Itamar Shviro (80' Rotem Hatuel). Coach: Yossi Abukasis.
Goals: 29' Patrik Schick 1-0, 48' Leon Bailey 2-0, 58' Itamar Shviro 2-1, 76' Kerem Demirbay 3-1, 80' Lucas Alario 4-1.
Referee: Pawel Gil (POL)

26.11.20   Allianz Riviera, Nice: OGC Nice – Slavia Praha 1-3 (0-1)
OGC Nice: Walter Benítez, Jordan Lotomba, Stanley N'Soki, Youcef Atal (66' Dan N'Doye), Robson Bambu, Morgan Schneiderlin, Jeff Reine-Adélaïde, Alexis Claude-Maurice (72' Hichem Boudaoui), Rony Lopes, Myziane Maolida, Amine Gouiri (78' Andy Pelmard).
Coach: Patrick Vieira.
Slavia Praha: Ondrej Kolár, Ondrej Kúdela, Jan Boril, Tomás Holes (87' Ondrej Karafiát), David Zima, Lukás Masopust, Petr Sevcík, Peter Olayinka (88' Tomás Malínský), Ondrej Lingr (63' Ibrahim Traoré), Jan Kuchta (82' Lukás Provod), Abdallah Sima (87' Stanislav Tecl). Coach: Jindrich Trpisovský.
Goals: 14' Ondrej Lingr 0-1, 61' Amine Gouiri 1-1, 64' Peter Olayinka 1-2, 75' Abdallah Sima 1-3.
Referee: Glenn Nyberg (SWE)
Sent off: 90+1' Hichem Boudaoui.

03.12.20   Sinobo Stadium, Prague: Slavia Praha – Hapoel Be'er Sheva 3-0 (2-0)
Slavia Praha: Ondrej Kolár, Ondrej Kúdela, Tomás Holes, David Zima, Nicolae Stanciu (64' Ondrej Lingr), Lukás Masopust (81' Lukás Provod), Petr Sevcík (80' Ibrahim Traoré), Peter Olayinka, Oscar Dorley (61' Jan Boril), Jan Kuchta (81' Petar Musa), Abdallah Sima.
Coach: Jindrich Trpisovský.
Hapoel Be'er Sheva: Ohad Levita, Loai Taha (81' Noam Gamon), Shir Tzedek, Lucas Bareiro (46' Ilay Madmon), Dudu Twito, Or Dadya, Sintayehu Sallalich (62' Tomer Yosefi), Josué (76' Rotem Hatuel), Marwan Kabha, David Keltjens, Gaëtan Varenne (61' Itamar Shviro).
Coach: Yossi Abukasis.
Goals: 31' Abdallah Sima 1-0, 36' Nicolae Stanciu 2-0, 85' Dudu Twito 3-0 (og).
Referee: Tamás Bognár (HUN)   Attendance: 600.

03.12.20   Allianz Riviera, Nice: OGC Nice – Bayer Leverkusen 2-3 (1-2)
OGC Nice: Walter Benítez, Jordan Lotomba, Stanley N'Soki, Robson Bambu, Flavius Daniliuc, Hassane Kamara (72' Racing Coly), Danilo Barbosa (67' Khéphren Thuram-Ulien), Jeff Reine-Adélaïde, Alexis Claude-Maurice, Myziane Maolida (29' Dan N'Doye), Amine Gouiri (72' Alexis Trouillet). Coach: Patrick Vieira.
Bayer Leverkusen: Lukás Hrádecký, Lars Bender (46' Edmond Tapsoba), Aleksandar Dragovic, Wendell, Jonathan Tah, Julian Baumgartlinger, Kerem Demirbay (86' Florian Wirtz), Nadiem Amiri (68' Cem Türkmen), Karim Bellarabi, Patrik Schick (46' Leon Bailey), Moussa Diaby (68' Emrehan Gedikli). Coach: Peter Bosz.
Goals: 22' Moussa Diaby 0-1, 26' Hassane Kamara 1-1, 32' Aleksandar Dragovic 1-2, 47' Dan N'Doye 2-2, 51' Julian Baumgartlinger 2-3.
Referee: Maurizio Mariani (ITA)

10.12.20   Bay Arena, Leverkusen: Bayer Leverkusen – Slavia Praha 4-0 (2-0)
Bayer Leverkusen: Niklas Lomb, Aleksandar Dragovic, Wendell, Tin Jedvaj, Daley Sinkgraven (62' Samed Onur), Edmond Tapsoba, Julian Baumgartlinger (62' Lars Bender), Nadiem Amiri (74' Cem Türkmen), Karim Bellarabi, Patrik Schick (46' Emrehan Gedikli), Leon Bailey (46' Moussa Diaby). Coach: Peter Bosz.
Slavia Praha: Ondrej Kolár, Jan Boril, David Zima, Lukás Masopust, Petr Sevcík (19' Nicolae Stanciu), Peter Olayinka, Ibrahim Traoré (82' Ondrej Karafiát), Ondrej Lingr (82' Tomás Rigo), Oscar Dorley, Petar Musa (53' Stanislav Tecl), Abdallah Sima (82' Matej Jarásek).
Coach: Jindrich Trpisovský.
Goals: 8', 32' Leon Bailey 1-0, 2-0, 59' Moussa Diaby 3-0, 90+1' Karim Bellarabi 4-0.
Referee: Anastasios Sidiropoulos (GRE)

10.12.20   HaMoshava Stadium, Petach-Tikva: Hapoel Be'er Sheva – OGC Nice 1-0 (0-0)
Hapoel Be'er Sheva: Raz Rahamim, Loai Taha, Shir Tzedek, Noam Gamon, Dudu Twito, Marwan Kabha, David Keltjens, Tomer Yosefi (66' Josué), Ilay Madmon, Gaëtan Varenne (65' Itamar Shviro, 76' Ramzi Safouri), Rotem Hatuel (84' Sintayehu Sallalich).
Coach: Yossi Abukasis.
OGC Nice: Yoan Cardinale, Racine Coly (28' Hicham Mahou), Robson Bambu, Andy Pelmard, Théo Pionnier-Bertrand (82' Noah Crétier), Morgan Schneiderlin (46' Hichem Boudaoui), Alexis Claude-Maurice, Alexis Trouillet, Khéphren Thuram-Ulien, Rony Lopes (46' Selim Ben Seghir), Dan N'Doye. Coach: Adrian Ursea.
Goal: 71' Rotem Hatuel 1-0.
Referee: Kristo Tohver (EST)

GROUP D

22.10.20   Stade Maurice Dufrasne, Liège: Standard Liège – Glasgow Rangers FC 0-2 (0-1)
Standard Liège: Arnaud Bodart, Noë Dussenne (78' Laurent Jans), Nicolas Gavory, Collins Fai (63' Mehdi Carcela-González), Zinho Vanheusden, Maxime Lestienne (72' Felipe Avenatti), Gojko Cimirot, Merveille Bopé Bokadi, Samuel Bastien, Selim Amallah (72' Duje Cop), Jackson Muleka (46' Obbi Oularé). Coach: Philippe Montanier.
Glasgow Rangers FC: Allan McGregor, Leon Balogun, James Tavernier, Connor Goldson, Borna Barisic (43' Calvin Bassey Ughelumba), Scott Arfield, Ryan Jack, Glen Kamara, Ianis Hagi (67' Joe Ayodele-Aribo), Alfredo Morelos (74' Kemar Roofe), Ryan Kent.
Coach: Steven Gerrard.
Goals: 19' James Tavernier 0-1 (p), 90+3' Kemar Roofe 0-2.
Referee: Jakob Kehlet (DEN)   Attendance: 3,139.

22.10.20   INEA stadion, Poznan: KKS Lech Poznan – SL Benfica 2-4 (1-2)
KKS Lech Poznan: Filip Bednarek, Alan Czerwinski, Tomasz Dejewski, Djordje Crnomarkovic, Tymoteusz Puchacz (74' Vasyl Kravets), Pedro Tiba, Dani Ramírez (67' Karlo Muhar), Jakub Moder, Michal Skóras (90+1' Mohamed Awaed), Jakub Kaminski (67' Filip Marchwinski), Mikael Ishak (74' Nika Kacharava). Coach: Dariusz Zuraw.
SL Benfica: Odisseas Vlachodimos, Jan Vertonghen, Nicolás Otamendi, Gabriel, Álex Grinaldo (67' Nuno Tavares), Adel Taarabt (62' Julian Weigl), Pizzi (46' Rafa Silva), Gabriel, Éverton (87' Jardel), Luca Waldschmidt (62' Pedrinho), Darwin Núñez. Coach: Jorge Jesus.
Goals: 9' Pizzi 0-1 (p), 15' Mikael Ishak 1-1, 42' Darwin Núñez 1-2, 48' Mikael Ishak 2-2, 60', 90+3' Darwin Núñez 2-3, 2-4.
Referee: Nikola Dabanovic (MNE)

29.10.20   Estádio do Sport Lisboa e Benfica, Lisboa: SL Benfica – Standard Liège 3-0 (0-0)
SL Benfica: Odisseas Vlachodimos, Jan Vertonghen, Nicolás Otamendi, Nuno Tavares, Pizzi (79' Gonçalo Ramos), Gabriel (72' Julian Weigl), Diogo Gonçalves, Éverton, Pedrinho (46' Rafa Silva), Luca Waldschmidt (68' Adel Taarabt), Darwin Núñez (72' Haris Seferovic).
Coach: Jorge Jesus.
Standard Liège: Arnaud Bodart, Noë Dussenne, Nicolas Gavory, Collins Fai, Zinho Vanheusden (76' Kostas Laifis), Mehdi Carcela-González, Gojko Cimirot (75' Joachim Carcela-González), Merveille Bopé Bokadi, Samuel Bastien, Selim Amallah (80' Felipe Avenatti), Obbi Oularé (70' Aleksandar Boljevic). Coach: Philippe Montanier.
Goals: 49' Pizzi 1-0 (p), 66' Luca Waldschmidt 2-0 (p), 76' Pizzi 3-0.
Referee: François Letexier (FRA)   Attendance: 4,750

29.10.20 Ibrox Stadium, Glasgow: Glasgow Rangers FC – KKS Lech Poznan 1-0 (0-0)
Glasgow Rangers FC: Allan McGregor, Leon Balogun, James Tavernier, Connor Goldson, Borna Barisic, Steven Davis, Scott Arfield (80' Ryan Jack), Glen Kamara, Ianis Hagi (69' Joe Ayodele-Aribo), Kemar Roofe (63' Alfredo Morelos), Ryan Kent (81' Brandon Barker).
Coach: Steven Gerrard.
KKS Lech Poznan: Filip Bednarek, Thomas Rogne, Lubomír Satka, Alan Czerwinski, Vasyl Kravets, Tymoteusz Puchacz, Dani Ramírez (87' Nika Kacharava), Jakub Moder, Michal Skóras (74' Jan Sýkora), Filip Marchwinski (82' Mohamed Awaed), Mikael Ishak.
Coach: Dariusz Zuraw.
Goal: 68' Alfredo Morelos 1-0.
Referee: Kristo Tohver (EST)   Attendance: 11.

05.11.20 Estádio do Sport Lisboa e Benfica, Lisboa:
SL Benfica – Glasgow Rangers FC 3-3 (1-2)
SL Benfica: Odisseas Vlachodimos, Jan Vertonghen, Nicolás Otamendi, Nuno Tavares (46' Álex Grimaldo), Adel Taarabt, Pizzi (21' Jardel), Rafa Silva, Julian Weigl, Diogo Gonçalves (46' Gilberto), Éverton (67' Luca Waldschmidt), Haris Seferovic (60' Darwin Núñez).
Coach: Jorge Jesus.
Glasgow Rangers FC: Allan McGregor, James Tavernier, Connor Goldson, Filip Helander, Borna Barisic, Steven Davis, Ryan Jack, Glen Kamara, Joe Ayodele-Aribo (69' Scott Arfield), Alfredo Morelos, Ryan Kent. Coach: Steven Gerrard.
Goals: 2' Connor Goldson 1-0 (og), 24' Diogo Gonçalves 1-1 (og), 25' Glen Kamara 1-2, 51' Alfredo Morelos 1-3, 77' Rafa Silva 2-3, 90+1' Darwin Núñez 3-3.
Referee: Jesús Gil Manzano (ESP)
Sent off: 19' Nicolás Otamendi.

05.11.20 INEA stadion, Poznan: KKS Lech Poznan – Standard Liège 3-1 (2-1)
KKS Lech Poznan: Filip Bednarek, Thomas Rogne, Lubomír Satka, Alan Czerwinski, Tymoteusz Puchacz, Pedro Tiba (81' Karlo Muhar), Dani Ramírez (81' Mohamed Awaed), Jakub Moder, Michal Skóras (62' Jan Sýkora), Filip Marchwinski (62' Jakub Kaminski), Mikael Ishak (85' Nika Kacharava). Coach: Dariusz Zuraw.
Standard Liège: Arnaud Bodart, Noë Dussenne, Laurent Jans, Nicolas Gavory (46' Hugo Siquet), Maxime Lestienne (73' Obbi Oularé), Gojko Cimirot (88' Joachim Carcela-González), Merveille Bopé Bokadi, Samuel Bastien, Selim Amallah (60' Aleksandar Boljevic), Nicolas Raskin (73' Mehdi Carcela-González), Michel Balikwisha. Coach: Philippe Montanier.
Goals: 14' Michal Skóras 1-0, 22' Mikael Ishak 2-0, 29' Maxime Lestienne 2-1, 48' Mikael Ishak 3-1.
Referee: Manuel Schüttengruber (AUT)

26.11.20 Stade Maurice Dufrasne, Liège: Standard Liège – KKS Lech Poznan 2-1 (0-0)
Standard Liège: Arnaud Bodart, Noë Dussenne, Kostas Laifis, Nicolas Gavory (76' Laurent Jans), Collins Fai, Maxime Lestienne (46' Aleksandar Boljevic), Gojko Cimirot, Merveille Bopé Bokadi (46' Abdoul Tapsoba), Nicolas Raskin (76' Samuel Bastien), Obbi Oularé, Michel Balikwisha (76' Felipe Avenatti). Coach: Philippe Montanier.
KKS Lech Poznan: Filip Bednarek, Thomas Rogne, Bogdan Butko, Djordje Crnomarkovic, Tymoteusz Puchacz, Jan Sýkora (64' Vasyl Kravets), Pedro Tiba (78' Filip Marchwinski), Dani Ramírez, Jakub Moder (78' Lubomír Satka), Michal Skóras (64' Alan Czerwinski), Mikael Ishak (83' Nika Kacharava). Coach: Dariusz Zuraw.
Goals: 61' Mikael Ishak 0-1, 63' Abdoul Tapsoba 1-1, 90+4' Kostas Laifis 2-1.
Referee: Petr Ardeleánu (CZE)
Sent off: 45+2' Obbi Oularé, 74' Djordje Crnomarkovic.

26.11.20 Ibrox Stadium, Glasgow: Glasgow Rangers FC – SL Benfica 2-2 (1-0)
Glasgow Rangers FC: Allan McGregor, Leon Balogun, James Tavernier, Connor Goldson, Borna Barisic, Steven Davis, Scott Arfield, Glen Kamara, Kemar Roofe, Alfredo Morelos, Ryan Kent. Coach: Steven Gerrard.
SL Benfica: Helton Leite, Jan Vertonghen, Jardel, Gilberto (70' Gonçalo Ramos), Álex Grimaldo, Gabriel, Rafa Silva, Éverton, Chiquinho (56' Pizzi), Haris Seferovic (90+3' Ferro), Luca Waldschmidt (56' Diogo Gonçalves). Coach: Jorge Jesus.
Goals: 7' Scott Arfield 1-0, 69' Kemar Roofe 2-0, 78' James Tavernier 2-1 (og), 81' Pizzi 2-2.
Referee: Radu Marian Petrescu (ROM)

03.12.20 Estádio do Sport Lisboa e Benfica, Lisboa:
SL Benfica – KKS Lech Poznan 4-0 (1-0)
SL Benfica: Odisseas Vlachodimos, Jan Vertonghen, Nicolás Otamendi, Gilberto, Álex Grimaldo, Pizzi (59' Luca Waldschmidt), Gabriel, Rafa Silva (77' Franco Cervi), Éverton (70' Pedrinho), Chiquinho (60' Julian Weigl), Darwin Núñez (60' Haris Seferovic).
Coach: Jorge Jesus.
KKS Lech Poznan: Filip Bednarek, Bogdan Butko, Lubomír Satka, Tomasz Dejewski, Tymoteusz Puchacz, Jan Sýkora (63' Vasyl Kravets), Karlo Muhar, Michal Skóras (63' Alan Czerwinski), Filip Marchwinski (82' Jakub Moder), Nika Kacharava (42' Mikael Ishak), Mohamad Awaed (63' Dani Ramírez). Coach: Dariusz Zuraw.
Goals: 36' Jan Vertonghen 1-0, 57' Darwin Núñez 2-0, 58' Pizzi 3-0, 89' Julian Weigl 4-0.
Referee: Srdjan Jovanovic (SRB)

03.12.20 Ibrox Stadium, Glasgow: Glasgow Rangers FC – Standard Liège 3-2 (2-2)
Glasgow Rangers FC: Allan McGregor, Leon Balogun, James Tavernier, Connor Goldson, Borna Barisic (89' Calvin Bassey Ughelumba), Steven Davis, Scott Arfield (86' Bongani Zungu), Glen Kamara, Kemar Roofe (89' Cedric Itten), Alfredo Morelos (79' Joe Ayodele-Aribo), Ryan Kent. Coach: Steven Gerrard.
Standard Liège: Arnaud Bodart, Noë Dussenne, Laurent Jans (86' Nicolas Gavory), Kostas Laifis, Collins Fai, Maxime Lestienne (71' Felipe Avenatti), Eden Shamir (71' Nicolas Raskin), Merveille Bopé Bokadi, Samuel Bastien, Duje Cop (46' Michel Balikwisha), Abdoul Tapsoba. Coach: Philippe Montanier.
Goals: 6' Maxime Lestienne 0-1, 39' Connor Goldson 1-1, 41' Duje Cop 1-2, 45+1' James Tavernier 2-2 (p), 63' Scott Arfield 3-2.
Referee: Bojan Pandzic (SWE)

10.12.20 Stade Maurice Dufrasne, Liège: Standard Liège – SL Benfica 2-2 (1-1)
Standard Liège: Arnaud Bodart, Laurent Jans, Kostas Laifis, Nicolas Gavory, Gojko Cimirot, Eden Shamir (59' Collins Fai), Merveille Bopé Bokadi, Samuel Bastien, Nicolas Raskin (80' Joachim Carcela-González), Abdoul Tapsoba (72' Obbi Oularé), Michel Balikwisha (59' Jackson Muleka). Coach: Philippe Montanier.
SL Benfica: Helton Leite, Jan Vertonghen, Jardel, Nuno Tavares (80' Franco Cervi), João Ferreira, Adel Taarabt (83' Haris Seferovic), Julian Weigl (80' Gabriel), Éverton, Pedrinho (64' Rafa Silva), Luca Waldschmidt (64' Pizzi), Darwin Núñez. Coach: Jorge Jesus.
Goals: 12' Nicolas Raskin 1-0, 16' Éverton 1-1, 60' Abdoul Tapsoba 2-1, 67' Pizzi 2-2 (p).
Referee: Aleksei Kulbakov (BLS)

10.12.20   INEA stadion, Poznan: KKS Lech Poznan – Glasgow Rangers FC 0-2 (0-1)
KKS Lech Poznan: Filip Bednarek, Bogdan Butko, Lubomír Satka, Djordje Crnomarkovic, Tymoteusz Puchacz, Petro Tiba (46' Jakub Moder), Karlo Muhar, Michal Skóras (12' Jan Sýkora, 64' Dani Ramírez), Filip Marchwinski, Jakub Kaminski (46' Vasyl Kravets), Mikael Ishak (64' Mohamad Awaed). Coach: Dariusz Zuraw.
Glasgow Rangers FC: Jon McLaughlin, Leon Balogun (80' Calvin Bassey Ughelumba), Connor Goldson, Borna Barisic, Nathan Patterson (66' James Tavernier), Scott Arfield, Bongani Zungu (76' Brandon Barker), Glen Kamara, Joe Ayodele-Aribo, Ianis Hagi (77' Ryan Kent), Cedric Itten (80' Alfredo Morelos). Coach: Steven Gerrard.
Goals: 31' Cedric Itten 0-1, 72' Ianis Hagi 0-2.
Referee: José María Sánchez Martínez (ESP)

GROUP E

22.10.20   Philips Stadion, Eindhoven: PSV Eindhoven – Granada CF 1-2 (1-0)
PSV Eindhoven: Yvon Mvogo, Philipp Max, Timo Baumgartl, Olivier Boscagli, Denzel Dumfries, Mario Götze (46' Nick Viergever), Jorrit Hendrix, Mauro Júnior (73' Noni Madueke), Ibrahim Sangaré, Mohamed Ihattaren, Donyell Malen. Coach: Roger Schmidt.
Granada CF: Rui Silva, Germán Sánchez, Dimitri Foulquier, Jesús Vallejo, Carlos Neva, Maxime Gonalons (35' Montero), Antonio Puertas, Luis Milla (81' Yan Eteki), Yangel Herrera, Jorge Molina (69' Luis Suárez), Darwin Machís (81' Alberto Soro). Coach: Diego Martínez.
Goals: 45+1' Mario Götze 1-0, 57' Jorge Molina 1-1, 66' Darwin Machís 1-2.
Referee: Felix Zwayer (GER)

22.10.20   Stadio Toumbas, Thessaloniki: PAOK Saloniki – Omonia Nicosia 1-1 (0-1)
PAOK Saloniki: Zivko Zivkovic, Léo Matos (61' Rodrigo Alves), Fernando Varela, Sverrir Ingason, Dimitris Giannoulis, Giannis Michailidis, Stefan Schwab, Thomas Murg (73' Diego Biseswar), Andrija Zivkovic (73' Christos Tzolis), Anderson Esiti (46' Douglas Augusto), Antonio Colak (61' Karol Swiderski). Coach: Abel Ferreira.
Omonia Nicosia: Fabiano, Jan Lecjaks, Tomás Hubocan, Michael Lüftner, Ádám Lang, Jordi Gómez (74' Ioannis Kousoulos), Éric Bauthéac (90+2' Loizos Loizou), Vítor Gomes, Marinos Tzionis, Michal Duris (76' Andronikos Kakoullis), Fotis Papoulis (75' Ernest Asante). Coach: Henning Berg.
Goals: 16' Éric Bauthéac 0-1, 56' Thomas Murg 1-1.
Referee: Robert Madden (SCO)

29.10.20   Neo GSP Stadium, Nicosia: Omonia Nicosia – PSV Eindhoven 1-2 (1-1)
Omonia Nicosia: Fabiano, Jan Lecjaks, Tomás Hubocan, Michael Lüftner, Ádám Lang, Jordi Gómez, Éric Bauthéac (90+3' Ioannis Kousoulos), Vítor Gomes, Marinos Tzionis, Michal Duris (81' Andronikos Kakoullis), Fotis Papoulis (81' Ernest Asante). Coach: Henning Berg.
PSV Eindhoven: Yvon Mvogo, Philipp Max, Olivier Boscagli, Jordan Teze, Mario Götze, Ryan Thomas, Jorrit Hendrix, Ibrahim Sangaré, Mohamed Ihattaren, Donyell Malen, Noni Madueke (83' Adrian Fein). Coach: Roger Schmidt.
Goals: 29' Jordi Gómez 1-0, 40', 90+3' Donyell Malen 1-1, 1-2.
Referee: Donatas Rumsas (LTU)

29.10.20 Estadio Nuevo Los Cármenes, Granada: Granada CF – PAOK Saloniki 0-0
Granada CF: Rui Silva, Germán Sánchez, Jesús Vallejo, Carlos Neva, Maxime Gonalons (90' Yan Eteki), Antonio Puertas, Luis Milla, Kenedy (73' Montoro), Yangel Herrera (59' Jorge Molina), Darwin Machís (90' Domingos Duarte), Luis Suárez (73' Alberto Soro).
Coach: Diego Martínez.
PAOK Saloniki: Zivko Zivkovic, José Ángel Crespo, Fernando Varela, Sverrir Ingason, Rodrigo Alves (74' Moussa Wagué), Dimitris Giannoulis, Stefan Schwab, Thomas Murg (70' Omar El Kaddouri), Andrija Zivkovic, Douglas Augusto, Antonio Colak (69' Karol Swiderski). Coach: Abel Ferreira.
Referee: Tiago Martins (POR)

05.11.20 Stadio Toumbas, Thessaloniki: PAOK Saloniki – PSV Eindhoven 4-1 (0-1)
PAOK Saloniki: Zivko Zivkovic, José Ángel Crespo, Fernando Varela, Rodrigo Alves, Dimitris Giannoulis (71' Lefteris Lyratzis), Diego Biseswar (46' Christos Tzolis), Omar El Kaddouri (81' Theocharis Tsiggaras), Stefan Schwab, Andrija Zivkovic (84' Thomas Murg), Douglas Augusto, Antonio Colak (46' Karol Swiderski). Coach: Pablo García.
PSV Eindhoven: Yvon Mvogo, Philipp Max, Olivier Boscagli, Jordan Teze, Mario Götze (83' Ismael Saibari), Ryan Thomas (58' Noni Madueke), Ibrahim Sangaré (83' Richie Ledezma), Pablo Rosario (46' Adrian Fein), Mohamed Ihattaren (58' Mauro Júnior), Eran Zahavi, Donyell Malen. Coach: Roger Schmidt.
Goals: 20' Eran Zahavi 0-1 (p), 47' Stefan Schwab 1-1, 56' Andrija Zivkovic 2-1, 58' Christos Tzolis 3-1, 66' Andrija Zivkovic 4-1.
Referee: Daniel Stefanski (POL)

05.11.20 Neo GSP Stadium, Nicosia: Omonia Nicosia – Granada CF 0-2 (0-1)
Omonia Nicosia: Fabiano, Jan Lecjaks, Tomás Hubocan, Michael Lüftner, Ádám Lang, Jordi Gómez (46' Abdullahi Shehu), Éric Bauthéac (46' Ernest Asante), Vítor Gomes, Marinos Tzionis (72' Thiago Santos), Michal Duris, Fotis Papoulis (46' Ioannis Kousoulos).
Coach: Henning Berg.
Granada CF: Rui Silva, Germán Sánchez, Domingos Duarte, Carlos Neva, Pepe Sánchez (89' Nehuén Pérez), Montoro (46' Luis Milla), Maxime Gonalons, Kenedy (76' Alberto Soro), Yangel Herrera (90' Yan Eteki), Darwin Machís, Luis Suárez (75' Jorge Molina).
Coach: Diego Martínez.
Goals: 4' Yangel Herrera 0-1, 63' Luis Suárez 0-2.
Referee: Ivan Bebek (CRO)
Sent off: 41' Michal Duris.

26.11.20 Philips Stadion, Eindhoven: PSV Eindhoven – PAOK Saloniki 3-2 (1-2)
PSV Eindhoven: Yvon Mvogo, Philipp Max, Olivier Boscagli, Denzel Dumfries, Jordan Teze, Ibrahim Sangaré, Pablo Rosario, Eran Zahavi (71' Jorrit Hendrix), Donyell Malen (90+2' Richie Ledezma), Cody Gakpo, Noni Madueke (78' Mauro Júnior). Coach: Roger Schmidt.
PAOK Saloniki: Zivko Zivkovic, José Ángel Crespo (86' Moussa Wagué), Fernando Varela, Sverrir Ingason, Rodrigo Alves, Omar El Kaddouri (85' Diego Biseswar), Stefan Schwab, Andrija Zivkovic, Theocharis Tsiggaras (69' Douglas Augusto), Antonio Colak (69' Karol Swiderski), Christos Tzolis (58' Thomas Murg). Coach: Pablo García.
Goals: 4' Fernando Varela 0-1, 13' Christos Tzolis 0-2, 20' Cody Gakpo 1-2, 51' Noni Madueke 2-2, 53' Donyell Malen 3-2.
Referee: Andris Treimanis (LAT)

26.11.20 Estadio Nuevo Los Cármenes, Granada: Granada CF – Omonia Nicosia 2-1 (1-0)
Granada CF: Rui Silva, Jesús Vallejo, Domingos Duarte, Carlos Neva, Nehuén Pérez (66' Dimitri Foulquier), Maxime Gonalons (66' Darwin Machís), Luis Milla, Yangel Herrera, Alberto Soro (79' Antonio Puertas), Soldado (79' Jorge Molina), Luis Suárez (79' Yan Eteki). Coach: Diego Martínez.
Omonia Nicosia: Fabiano, Tomás Hubocan, Michael Lüftner, Ádám Lang, Kiko (59' Jan Lecjaks), Ioannis Kousoulos, Éric Bauthéac (36' Ernest Asante), Charis Mavrias, Abdullahi Shehu (58' Jordi Gómez), Marinos Tzionis (59' Thiago Santos), Andronikos Kakoullis (74' Mamadou Kaly Sene). Coach: Henning Berg.
Goals: 8' Luis Suárez 1-0, 60' Ernest Asante 1-1, 73' Alberto Soro 2-1.
Referee: Stéphanie Frappart (FRA)

03.12.20 Estadio Nuevo Los Cármenes, Granada: Granada CF – PSV Eindhoven 0-1 (0-1)
Granada CF: Rui Silva, Germán Sánchez (56' Dimitri Foulquier), Jesús Vallejo, Domingos Duarte, Carlos Neva, Maxime Gonalons, Luis Milla (76' Jorge Molina), Yangel Herrera, Alberto Soro (56' Luis Suárez), Soldado (83' Antonio Puertas), Darwin Machís. Coach: Diego Martínez.
PSV Eindhoven: Yvon Mvogo, Philipp Max, Olivier Boscagli, Denzel Dumfries (71' Timo Baumgartl), Jordan Teze, Mario Götze, Ibrahim Sangaré, Pablo Rosario, Donyell Malen, Cody Gakpo, Noni Madueke (38' Eran Zahavi, 88' Jorrit Hendrix). Coach: Roger Schmidt.
Goal: 38' Donyell Malen 0-1.
Referee: Roi Reinshreiber (ISR)

03.12.20 Neo GSP Stadium, Nicosia: Omonia Nicosia – PAOK Saloniki 2-1 (1-1)
Omonia Nicosia: Fabiano, Tomás Hubocan, Michael Lüftner, Ádám Lang, Kiko (59' Jan Lecjaks), Ioannis Kousoulos (60' Jordi Gómez), Vítor Gomes, Marinos Tzionis, Andronikos Kakoullis (21' Abdullahi Shehu), Mamadou Kaly Sene (59' Michal Duris), Loizos Loizou (85' Ernest Asante). Coach: Henning Berg.
PAOK Saloniki: Zivko Zivkovic, José Ángel Crespo, Fernando Varela, Rodrigo Alves, Moussa Wagué (46' Dimitris Giannoulis), Omar El Kaddouri, Stefan Schwab (46' Thomas Murg), Andrija Zivkovic, Theocharis Tsiggaras (79' Diego Biseswar), Karol Swiderski, Christos Tzolis. Coach: Pablo García.
Goals: 9' Andronikos Kakoullis 1-0, 39' Christos Tzolis 1-1, 84' Jordi Gómez 2-1 (p).
Referee: Craig Pawson (ENG)

10.12.20 Philips Stadion, Eindhoven: PSV Eindhoven – Omonia Nicosia 4-0 (1-0)
PSV Eindhoven: Yvon Mvogo, Nick Viergever, Philipp Max (46' Olivier Boscagli), Timo Baumgartl, Denzel Dumfries (81' Jordan Teze), Jorrit Hendrix, Pablo Rosario (46' Ibrahim Sangaré), Richie Ledezma (17' Adrian Fein), Mohamed Ihattaren, Donyell Malen (46' Cody Gakpo), Joël Piroe. Coach: Roger Schmidt.
Omonia Nicosia: Fabiano, Michael Lüftner, Ádám Lang, Kiko (60' Jan Lecjaks), Ioannis Kousoulos (60' Jordi Gómez), Vítor Gomes, Abdullahi Shehu, Marinos Tzionis, Thiago Santos, Mamadou Kaly Sene (61' Michal Duris), Loizos Loizou. Coach: Henning Berg.
Goals: 35' Donyell Malen 1-0, 63' Denzel Dumfries 2-0 (p), 90+1', 90+3' Joël Piroe 3-0, 4-0.
Referee: Kevin Clancy (SCO)

Jordi Gómez missed a penalty kick (70').

10.12.20   Stadio Toumbas, Thessaloniki: PAOK Saloniki – Granada CF 0-0
PAOK Saloniki: Alexandros Paschalakis, José Ángel Crespo, Fernando Varela, Sverrir Ingason, Lefteris Lyratzis (63' Moussa Wagué), Omar El Kaddouri, Thomas Murg, Anderson Esiti (63' Douglas Augusto), Antonio Colak (81' Karol Swiderski), Christos Tzolis (46' Andrija Zivkovic), Giorgios Koutsias (46' Theocharis Tsiggaras). Coach: Pablo García.
Granada CF: Aarón Escandell, Germán Sánchez, Dimitri Foulquier, Nehuén Pérez, Pepe Sánchez (66' Carlos Neva), Antonio Puertas, Luis Milla (75' Maxime Gonalons), Kenedy (67' Luis Suárez), Yan Eteki (85' Soldado), Alberto Soro (75' Darwin Machís), Jorge Molina. Coach: Diego Martínez.
Referee: John Beaton (SCO)

GROUP F

22.10.20   Stadio San Paolo, Napoli: SSC Napoli – AZ Alkmaar 0-1 (0-0)
SSC Napoli: Alex Meret, Nikola Maksimovic, Kalidou Koulibaly, Elseid Hysaj (59' Mário Rui), Giovanni Di Lorenzo, Stanislav Lobotka (66' Diego Demme), Fabián Ruiz, Dries Mertens, Matteo Politano (83' Tiemoué Bakayoko), Hirving Lozano (59' Lorenzo Insigne), Victor Osimhen (66' Andrea Petagna). Coach: Gennaro Gattuso.
AZ Alkmaar: Marco Bizot, Bruno Martins Indi, Jonas Svensson, Pantelis Hatzidiakos, Owen Wijndal, Yukinari Sugawara, Fredrik Midtsjø (88' Ramon Leeuwin), Dani de Wit, Teun Koopmeiners, Jesper Karlsson (88' Albert Gudmundsson), Calvin Tengs. Coach: Arne Slot.
Goal: 57' Dani de Wit 0-1.
Referee: Daniel Stefanski (POL)   Attendance: 494.

22.10.20   Stadion Rujevica, Rijeka: HNK Rijeka – Real Sociedad 0-1 (0-0)
HNK Rijeka: Ivan Nevistic, Ivan Tomecak, Darko Velkovski, João Escoval, Daniel Stefulj, Hrvoje Smolcic, Franko Andrijasevic (63' Sterling Yatéké), Domagoj Pavicic, Stjepan Loncar (87' Luka Capan), Adam Gnezda Cerin, Sandro Kulenovic (77' Ivan Lepinjica). Coach: Simon Rozman.
Real Sociedad: Álex Remiro, Nacho Monreal, Aritz Elustondo, Andoni Gorosabel, Robin Le Normand, David Silva, Mikel Merino, Martín Zubimendi, Portu (89' Adnan Januzaj), Mikel Oyarzabal (85' Jon Bautista), Alexander Isak (72' Willian José). Coach: Imanol Alguacil.
Goal: 90+3' Jon Bautista 0-1.
Referee: Bartosz Frankowski (POL)   Attendance: 2,089.

29.10.20   Reale Arena, San Sebastián: Real Sociedad – SSC Napoli 0-1 (0-0)
Real Sociedad: Álex Remiro, Nacho Monreal, Andoni Gorosabel (79' Ander Barrenetxea), Robin Le Normand, Modibo Sagnan, David Silva, Mikel Merino (79' Martín Zubimendi), Guevara, Portu (67' Jon Bautista), Mikel Oyarzabal (86' Jon Guridi), Alexander Isak (67' Willian José). Coach: Imanol Alguacil.
SSC Napoli: David Ospina, Nikola Maksimovic, Mário Rui, Kalidou Koulibaly, Elseid Hysaj, Diego Demme (89' Fabián Ruiz), Tiemoué Bakayoko, Stanislav Lobotka (61' Dries Mertens), Lorenzo Insigne (22' Hirving Lozano), Matteo Politano (61' Giovanni Di Lorenzo), Andrea Petagna (61' Victor Osimhen). Coach: Gennaro Gattuso.
Goal: 56' Matteo Politano 0-1.
Referee: Craig Pawson (ENG)
Sent off: 90+2' Victor Osimhen.

29.10.20 AFAS Stadion, Alkmaar: AZ Alkmaar – HNK Rijeka 4-1 (2-0)
AZ Alkmaar: Marco Bizot, Bruno Martins Indi (90' Maxim Gullit), Jonas Svensson, Pantelis Hatzidiakos (60' Ramon Leeuwin), Owen Wijndal, Fredrik Midtsjø, Dani de Wit, Teun Koopmeiners, Albert Gudmundsson (90' Yusuf Barasi), Jesper Karlsson (67' Håkon Evjen), Calvin Tengs (66' Zakaria Aboukhlal). Coach: Arne Slot.
HNK Rijeka: Ivan Nevistic, Ivan Tomecak (80' Momcilo Raspopovic), Darko Velkovski (65' Ivan Lepinjica), João Escoval, Daniel Stefulj (80' Armando Anastasio), Hrvoje Smolcic, Franko Andrijasevic (64' Tibor Halilovic), Domagoj Pavicic, Stjepan Loncar, Luka Menalo (64' Sterling Yatéké), Sandro Kulenovic. Coach: Simon Rozman.
Goals: 6' Teun Koopmeiners 1-0 (p), 20' Albert Gudmundsson 2-0, 51' Jesper Karlsson 3-0, 60' Albert Gudmundsson 4-0, 72' Sandro Kulenovic 4-1.
Referee: Sergey Ivanov (RUS)

05.11.20 Reale Arena, San Sebastián: Real Sociedad – AZ Alkmaar 1-0 (0-0)
Real Sociedad: Moyà, Nacho Monreal, Aritz Elustondo, Robin Le Normand, Modibo Sagnan, David Silva, Mikel Merino (76' Martín Zubimendi), Guevara, Portu (76' Adnan Januzaj), Mikel Oyarzabal (89' Ander Barrenetxea), Alexander Isak (62' Willian José).
Coach: Imanol Alguacil.
AZ Alkmaar: Marco Bizot, Jonas Svensson, Pantelis Hatzidiakos (70' Timo Letschert), Owen Wijndal, Fredrik Midtsjø, Dani de Wit, Teun Koopmeiners, Albert Gudmundsson (63' Zakaria Aboukhlal), Jesper Karlsson (63' Ferdy Druijf), Myron Boadu (62' Håkon Evjen), Calvin Tengs (70' Tijs Velthuis). Coach: Arne Slot.
Goal: 58' Portu 1-0.
Referee: John Beaton (SCO)

05.11.20 Stadion Rujevica, Rijeka: HNK Rijeka – SSC Napoli 1-2 (1-1)
HNK Rijeka: Ivan Nevistic, Ivan Tomecak, Darko Velkovski, João Escoval, Filip Braut (64' Daniel Stefulj), Hrvoje Smolcic, Robert Muric (24' Sterling Yatéké, 64' Momcilo Raspopovic), Stjepan Loncar, Adam Gnezda Cerin, Luka Menalo, Sandro Kulenovic.
Coach: Simon Rozman.
SSC Napoli: Alex Meret, Nikola Maksimovic, Mário Rui (80' Piotr Zielinski), Kalidou Koulibaly, Giovanni Di Lorenzo, Diego Demme, Stanislav Lobotka (59' Lorenzo Insigne), Eljif Elmas (59' Fabián Ruiz), Dries Mertens, Matteo Politano (69' Hirving Lozano), Andrea Petagna (80' Faouzi Ghoulam). Coach: Gennaro Gattuso.
Goals: 13' Robert Muric 1-0, 43' Diego Demme 1-1, 62' Filip Braut 1-2 (og).
Referee: Mattias Gestranius (FIN)

26.11.20 Stadio San Paolo, Napoli: SSC Napoli – HNK Rijeka 2-0 (1-0)
SSC Napoli: Alex Meret, Nikola Maksimovic, Kalidou Koulibaly, Faouzi Ghoulam, Giovanni Di Lorenzo, Diego Demme (69' Stanislav Lobotka), Piotr Zielinski (64' Lorenzo Insigne), Tiemoué Bakayoko, Eljif Elmas (69' Dries Mertens), Matteo Politano (64' Hirving Lozano), Andrea Petagna (81' Fabián Ruiz). Coach: Gennaro Gattuso.
HNK Rijeka: Ivan Nevistic, Ivan Tomecak, Darko Velkovski, Nino Galovic, Armando Anastasio (80' Filip Braut), Daniel Stefulj, Hrvoje Smolcic, Franko Andrijasevic (87' Matija Grigan), Robert Muric (78' Sterling Yatéké), Stjepan Loncar, Adam Gnezda Cerin (87' Veldin Hodza). Coach: Simon Rozman.
Goals: 41' Matteo Politano 1-0, 75' Hiring Lozano 2-0.
Referee: Halis Özkahya (TUR)

26.11.20   AFAS Stadion, Alkmaar: AZ Alkmaar – Real Sociedad 0-0
AZ Alkmaar: Marco Bizot, Bruno Martins Indi, Jonas Svensson, Pantelis Hatzidiakos, Owen Wijndal, Fredrik Midtsjø, Dani de Wit, Teun Koopmeiners, Albert Gudmundsson (71' Myron Boadu), Jesper Karlsson (71' Zakaria Aboukhlal), Calvin Tengs. Coach: Arne Slot.
Real Sociedad: Álex Remiro, Nacho Monreal, Joseba Zaldúa, Aritz Elustondo, Robin Le Normand, Adnan Januzaj (73' Roberto López), Mikel Merino, Martín Zubimendi, Portu (82' Ander Barrenetxea), Mikel Oyarzabal (86' Martín Merquelanz), Alexander Isak (73' Willian José). Coach: Imanol Alguacil.
Referee: Aleksandar Stavrev (MKD)

03.12.20   AFAS Stadion, Alkmaar: AZ Alkmaar – SSC Napoli 1-1 (0-1)
AZ Alkmaar: Marco Bizot, Bruno Martins Indi, Pantelis Hatzidiakos, Owen Wijndal, Yukinari Sugawara, Fredrik Midtsjø, Dani de Wit, Teun Koopmeiners, Albert Gudmundsson (70' Myron Boadu), Calvin Tengs, Zakaria Aboukhlal (82' Jesper Karlsson). Coach: Arne Slot.
SSC Napoli: David Ospina, Nikola Maksimovic, Kalidou Koulibaly, Faouzi Ghoulam (66' Mário Rui), Giovanni Di Lorenzo, Piotr Zielinski (61' Andrea Petagna), Tiemoué Bakayoko, Fabián Ruiz (57' Eljif Elmas), Dries Mertens (66' Diego Demme), Lorenzo Insigne, Matteo Politano (61' Hirving Lozano). Coach: Gennaro Gattuso.
Goals: 6' Dries Mertens 0-1, 54' Bruno Martins Indi 1-1.
Referee: Ruddy Buquet (FRA)

Teun Koopmeiners missed a penalty kick (60').

03.12.20   Reale Arena, San Sebastián: Real Sociedad – HNK Rijeka 2-2 (0-1)
Real Sociedad: Álex Remiro, Nacho Monreal, Joseba Zaldúa (67' Andoni Gorosabel), Robin Le Normand, David Silva (68' Willian José), Adnan Januzaj (80' Portu), Mikel Merino, Zubeldía, Martín Zubimendi, Mikel Oyarzabal (80' Roberto López), Alexander Isak (58' Jon Bautista). Coach: Imanol Alguacil.
HNK Rijeka: Ivan Nevistic, Ivan Tomecak, Darko Velkovski (86' João Escoval), Nino Galovic, Daniel Stefulj, Franko Andrijasevic (86' Sterling Yatéké), Luka Capan, Robert Muric (75' Domagoj Pavicic), Tibor Halilovic, Stjepan Loncar, Luka Menalo (80' Armando Anastasio). Coach: Simon Rozman.
Goals: 38' Darko Velkovski 0-1, 69' Jon Bautista 1-1, 73' Stjepan Loncar 1-2, 79' Nacho Monreal 2-2.
Referee: João Pinheiro (POR)

10.12.20   Stadio Diego Armando Maradona, Napoli: SSC Napoli – Real Sociedad 1-1 (1-0)
SSC Napoli: David Ospina, Nikola Maksimovic, Mário Rui (82' Faouzi Ghoulam), Kalidou Koulibaly, Giovanni Di Lorenzo, Piotr Zielinski (74' Eljif Elmas), Tiemoué Bakayoko (70' Diego Demme), Fabián Ruiz, Dries Mertens (70' Andrea Petagna), Lorenzo Insigne, Hirving Lozano (70' Matteo Politano). Coach: Gennaro Gattuso.
Real Sociedad: Álex Remiro, Nacho Monreal (78' Aihen Muñoz), Joseba Zaldúa (46' Andoni Gorosabel), Robin Le Normand (78' Alexander Isak), Adnan Januzaj, Mikel Merino, Zubeldía, Guevara (78' Modibo Sagnan), Martín Zubimendi, Willian José, Portu (56' Ander Barrenetxea). Coach: Imanol Alguacil.
Goals: 35' Piotr Zielinski 1-0, 90+2' Willian José 1-1.
Referee: Orel Grinfeld (ISR)

10.12.20   Stadion Rujevica, Rijeka: HNK Rijeka – AZ Alkmaar 2-1 (0-0)
HNK Rijeka: Ivan Nevistic, Ivan Tomecak, Nino Galovic, Daniel Stefulj, Hrvoje Smolcic, Franko Andrijasevic, Luka Capan, Robert Muric (71' Sandro Kulenovic), Tibor Halilovic, Stjepan Loncar, Luka Menalo (71' Domagoj Pavicic). Coach: Simon Rozman.
AZ Alkmaar: Marco Bizot, Bruno Martins Indi (18' Timo Letschert), Pantelis Hatzidiakos, Owen Wijndal, Yukinari Sugawara, Fredrik Midtsjø, Teun Koopmeiners, Albert Gudmundsson (71' Zakaria Aboukhlal), Jesper Karlsson, Myron Boadu (89' Ferdy Druijf), Calvin Tengs. Coach: Pascal Jansen.
Goals: 52' Luka Menalo 1-0, 57' Owen Wijndal 1-1, 90+3' Ivan Tomecak 2-1.
Referee: Sergei Karasev (RUS)
Sent off: 80' Jesper Karlsson.

GROUP G

22.10.20   Estádio Municipal de Braga, Braga: Sporting Braga – AEK Athens 3-0 (1-0)
Sporting Braga: Matheus Magalhães, Ricardo Esgaio, Nuno Sequeira, Bruno Viana, David Carmo, Andre Castro (90+2' Guilherme Schettine), Fransérgio (84' Francisco Moura), Iuri Medeiros (59' André Horta), Paulinho, Ricardo Horta (90+2' João Novais), Galeno (84' Almoatasembellah Ali Al Musrati). Coach: Carlos Carvalhal.
AEK Athens: Panagiotis Tsintotas, Dmytro Chygrynskiy (61' Marko Livaja, 89' Theodosis Macheras), Hélder Lopes, Stavros Vasilantonopoulos, Ionut Nedelcearu, Efstratios Svarnas, Nenad Krsticic, Yevhen Shakhov, Petros Mandalos, Karim Ansarifard (62' Muamer Tankovic), Nélson Oliveira. Coach: Massimo Carrera.
Goals: 44' Galeno 1-0, 78' Paulinho 2-0, 88' Ricardo Horta 3-0.
Referee: Ruddy Buquet (FRA)   Attendance: 2,196.

22.10.20   King Power Stadium, Leicester: Leicester City – Zorya Luhansk 3-0 (2-0)
Leicester City: Kasper Schmeichel, Christian Fuchs, Jonny Evans (82' Wes Morgan), Timothy Castagne (82' James Justin), Wesley Fofana, Nampalys Mendy, Dennis Praet, Youri Tielemans (71' Hamza Choudhury), James Maddison (65' Cengiz Ünder), Harvey Barnes, Kelechi Iheanacho (72' Ayoze Pérez). Coach: Brendan Rodgers.
Zorya Luhansk: Mykyta Shevchenko, Vitaliy Vernydub, Dmitriy Ivanisenya, Denis Favorov (76' Agron Rufati), Dmytro Khomchenovsky (76' Andrejs Ciganiks), Vladlen Yurchenko, Lovro Cvek, Vladyslav Kochergin (85' Sergiy Gryn), Egor Nazaryna, Vladyslav Kabayev (64' Mihailo Perovic), Maksym Lunev (65' Oleksandr Gladkyi). Coach: Viktor Skripnik.
Goals: 29' James Maddison 1-0, 45' Harvey Barnes 2-0, 67' Kelechi Iheanacho 3-0.
Referee: Stéphanie Frappart (FRA)

29.10.20   Olympiako Stadio Spyros Louis, Athens: AEK Athens – Leicester City 1-2 (0-2)
AEK Athens: Panagiotis Tsintotas, Michalis Bakakis (86' Stavros Vasilantonopoulos), Hélder Lopes, Emanuel Insúa (87' Theodosis Macheras), Ionut Nedelcearu, Efstratios Svarnas, Nenad Krsticic, Yevhen Shakhov (86' Anel Sabanadzovic), Petros Mandalos, Karim Ansarifard (46' Nélson Oliveira), Marko Livaja (46' Muamer Tankovic). Coach: Massimo Carrera.
Leicester City: Kasper Schmeichel, Christian Fuchs (46' Luke Thomas), Wes Morgan, James Justin, Wesley Fofana, Marc Albrighton, Youri Tielemans, James Maddison (74' Harvey Barnes), Cengiz Ünder (66' Dennis Praet), Hamza Choudhury (66' Nampalys Mendy), Jamie Vardy (71' Kelechi Iheanacho). Coach: Brendan Rodgers.
Goals: 18' Jamie Vardy 0-1 (p), 39' Hamza Choudhury 0-2, 49' Muamer Tankovic 1-2.
Referee: Harald Lechner (AUT)

29.10.20   Slavutych-Arena, Zaporizhia: Zorya Luhansk – Sporting Braga 1-2 (0-2)
Zorya Luhansk: Nikola Vasilj, Vitaliy Vernydub, Dmitriy Ivanisenya, Denis Favorov (87' Joel Abu Hanna), Dmytro Khomchenovsky, Vladlen Yurchenko (87' Mihailo Perovic), Lovro Cvek, Vladyslav Kochergin, Egor Nazaryna, Vladyslav Kabayev (81' Allahyar Sayyadmanesh), Maksym Lunev (62' Oleksandr Gladkyi). Coach: Viktor Skripnik.
Sporting Braga: Matheus Magalhães, Raúl Silva, Ricardo Esgaio (90+1' Vítor Tormena), Bruno Viana, Francisco Moura, David Carmo, Andre Castro (79' Almoatasembellah Ali Al Musrati), Nicolás Gaitán (66' Iuri Medeiros), Fransérgio, Paulinho (79' Guilherme Schettine), Ricardo Horta (66' André Horta). Coach: Carlos Carvalhal.
Goals: 4' Paulinho 0-1, 11' Nicolás Gaitán 0-2, 90+6' Dmitriy Ivanisenya 1-2.
Referee: Giorgi Kruashvili (GEO)   Attendance: 853.

Zorya Luhansk played their home matches at Slavutych-Arena, Zaporizhia, instead of their regular stadium Avanhard Stadium, Luhansk, due to the war conditions in Eastern Ukraine.

05.11.20   King Power Stadium, Leicester: Leicester City – Sporting Braga 4-0 (1-0)
Leicester City: Kasper Schmeichel, Christian Fuchs, James Justin, Luke Thomas, Wesley Fofana, Marc Albrighton (62' Wes Morgan), Youri Tielemans (72' Harvey Barnes), James Maddison, Cengiz Ünder (62' Dennis Praet), Hamza Choudhury, Kelechi Iheanacho (72' Ayoze Pérez). Coach: Brendan Rodgers.
Sporting Braga: Matheus Magalhães, Raúl Silva, Ricardo Esgaio, Bruno Viana, David Carmo, João Novais, Almoatasembellah Ali Al Musrati (71' Andre Castro), André Horta (62' Iuri Medeiros), Paulinho (72' Nicolás Gaitán), Galeno (71' Francisco Moura), Abel Ruiz (62' Guilherme Schettine). Coach: Carlos Carvalhal.
Goals: 21', 48' Kelechi Iheanacho 1-0, 2-0, 67' Dennis Praet 3-0, 78' James Maddison 4-0.
Referee: Bas Nijhuis (HOL)

05.11.20   Slavutych-Arena, Zaporizhia: Zorya Luhansk – AEK Athens 1-4 (0-2)
Zorya Luhansk: Mykyta Shevchenko, Vitaliy Vernydub, Dmitriy Ivanisenya, Joel Abu Hanna, Artem Gromov (46' Allahyar Sayyadmanesh), Dmytro Khomchenovsky (59' Denis Favorov), Vladlen Yurchenko, Andrejs Ciganiks, Vladyslav Kochergin, Vladyslav Kabayev (59' Oleksandr Gladkyi), Maksym Lunev (46' Egor Nazaryna). Coach: Viktor Skripnik.
AEK Athens: Panagiotis Tsintotas, Dmitro Chygrynskiy, Emanuel Insúa, Stavros Vasilantonopoulos, Ionut Nedelcearu, Efstratios Svarnas, Nenad Krsticic (85' Konstantinos Galanopoulos), Yevhen Shakhov (70' Anel Sabanadzovic), Petros Mandalos (85' Giannis-Fivos Botos), Marko Livaja, Muamer Tankovic (75' Karim Ansarifard).
Coach: Massimo Carrera.
Goals: 7' Muamer Tankovic 0-1, 34' Petros Mandalos 0-2, 54' Marko Livaja 0-3, 81' Vladyslav Kochergin 1-3, 81' Marko Livaja 1-4.
Referee: William Collum (SCO)

26.11.20   Estádio Municipal de Braga, Braga: Sporting Braga – Leicester City 3-3 (2-1)
Sporting Braga: Matheus Magalhães, Ricardo Esgaio, Nuno Sequeira, Bruno Viana, Vítor Tormena, Andre Castro (87' André Horta), Almoatasembellah Ali Al Musrati, Iuri Medeiros (77' Fransérgio), Paulinho (87' Guilherme Schettine), Ricardo Horta (69' Raúl Silva), Galeno. Coach: Carlos Carvalhal.
Leicester City: Kasper Schmeichel, Christian Fuchs (46' Wesley Fofana), Jonny Evans, James Justin, Luke Thomas, Marc Albrighton, Dennis Praet (46' Youri Tielemans), Cengiz Ünder (62' Jamie Vardy), Hamza Choudhury, Harvey Barnes (62' James Maddison), Kelechi Iheanacho (68' Ayoze Pérez). Coach: Brendan Rodgers.
Goals: 4' Almoatasembellah Ali Al Musrati 1-0, 9' Harvey Barnes 1-1, 24' Paulinho 2-1, 79' Luke Thomas 2-2, 90+1' Fransérgio 3-2, 90+5' Jamie Vardy 3-3.
Referee: Daniele Orsato (ITA)

26.11.20   Olympiako Stadio Spyros Louis, Athens: AEK Athens – Zorya Luhansk 0-3 (0-0)
AEK Athens: Georgios Athanasiadis, Dmitro Chygrynskiy, Michalis Bakakis (65' Konstantinos Galanopoulos), Emanuel Insúa, Ionut Nedelcearu, Efstratios Svarnas (82' Stavros Vasilantonopoulos), Nenad Krsticic, Yevhen Shakhov, André Simões (87' Theodoros Macheras), Marko Livaja, Muamer Tankovic (75' Karim Ansarifard). Coach: Massimo Carrera.
Zorya Luhansk: Mykyta Shevchenko, Vitaliy Vernydub, Dmitriy Ivanisenya, Denis Favorov, Joel Abu Hanna, Artem Gromov (87' Sergiy Gryn), Vladlen Yurchenko (87' Mihailo Perovic), Andrejs Ciganiks, Vladyslav Kochergin (82' Maksym Lunev), Oleksandr Gladkyi (63' Egor Nazaryna), Vladyslav Kabayev (87' Allahyar Sayyadmanesh). Coach: Viktor Skripnik.
Goals: 61' Artem Gromov 0-1, 76' Vladyslav Kabayev 0-2, 86' Vladlen Yurchenko 0-3 (p).
Referee: Äliyar Aghayev (AZE)
Sent off: 48' Yevhen Shakhov.

03.12.20   Olympiako Stadio Spyros Louis, Athens: AEK Athens – Sporting Braga 2-4 (1-3)
AEK Athens: Panagiotis Tsintotas, Michalis Bakakis (46' Stavros Vasilantonopoulos), Emanuel Insúa, Ionut Nedelcearu, Nassim Hnid, Petros Mandalos (74' Levi García), André Simões, Konstantinos Galanopoulos, Nélson Oliveira (60' Karim Ansarifard), Marko Livaja, Christos Albanis (60' Muamer Tankovic). Coach: Massimo Carrera.
Sporting Braga: Matheus Magalhães, Ricardo Esgaio, Nuno Sequeira, Bruno Viana (46' David Carmo), Vítor Tormena, Andre Castro (78' João Novais), Almoatasembellah Ali Al Musrati (57' Fransérgio), Iuri Medeiros (57' André Horta), Paulinho (71' Guilherme Schettine), Ricardo Horta, Galeno. Coach: Carlos Carvalhal.
Goals: 8' Vítor Tormena 0-1, 10' Ricardo Esgaio 0-2, 31' Nélson Oliveira 1-2, 45' Ricardo Horta 1-3, 83' Galeno 1-4, 89' Stavros Vasilantonopoulos 2-4.
Referee: Georgi Kabakov (BUL)

03.12.20   Slavutych-Arena, Zaporizhia: Zorya Luhansk – Leicester City 1-0 (0-0)
Zorya Luhansk: Nikola Vasilj, Dmitriy Ivanisenya, Denis Favorov, Joel Abu Hanna, Artem Gromov (90+3' Mihailo Perovic), Vladlen Yurchenko, Andrejs Ciganiks, Vladyslav Kochergin, Egor Nazaryna, Oleksandr Gladkyi (81' Allahyar Sayyadmanesh), Vladyslav Kabayev. Coach: Viktor Skripnik.
Leicester City: Danny Ward, Wes Morgan (56' Christian Fuchs), Ricardo Pereira (46' Luke Thomas), Çaglar Söyüncü (17' Wesley Fofana), James Justin, Dennis Praet (77' James Maddison), Wilfred Ndidi (56' Nampalys Mendy), Cengiz Ünder, Hamza Choudhury, Harvey Barnes, Kelechi Iheanacho. Coach: Brendan Rodgers.
Goal: 84' Allahyar Sayyadmanesh 1-0.
Referee: Espen Eskås (NOR)

10.12.20   Estádio Municipal de Braga, Braga: Sporting Braga – Zorya Luhansk 2-0 (0-0)
Sporting Braga: Tiago Sá, Raúl Silva, Vítor Tormena, Zé Carlos (73' Bruno Viana), David Carmo, Fransérgio, João Novais (77' Almoatasembellah Ali Al Musrati), André Horta (67' Iuri Medeiros), Guilherme Schettine (68' Paulinho), Galeno, Abel Ruiz (68' Ricardo Horta).
Coach: Carlos Carvalhal.
Zorya Luhansk: Mykyta Shevchenko, Dmitriy Ivanisenya, Denis Favorov (87' Dmytro Khomchenovsky), Joel Abu Hanna, Artem Gromov (77' Sergiy Gryn), Vladlen Yurchenko, Andrejs Ciganiks, Vladyslav Kochergin (87' Dmytro Piddubnyi), Egor Nazaryna, Oleksandr Gladkyi (77' Mihailo Perovic), Vladyslav Kabayev (77' Maksym Lunev).
Coach: Viktor Skripnik.
Goals: 61' Joel Abu Hanna 1-0 (og), 68' Ricardo Horta 2-0.
Referee: Daniel Stefanski (POL)

10.12.20   King Power Stadium, Leicester: Leicester City – AEK Athens 2-0 (2-0)
Leicester City: Danny Ward, Jonny Evans, James Justin, Luke Thomas, Wesley Fofana (81' Wes Morgan), Dennis Praet, Youri Tielemans (82' Hamza Choudhury), Wilfred Ndidi (63' Nampalys Mendy), Cengiz Ünder, Harvey Barnes, Kelechi Iheanacho (67' Ayoze Pérez).
Coach: Brendan Rodgers.
AEK Athens: Panagiotis Tsintotas, Stavros Vasilantonopoulos, Ionut Nedelcearu, Efstratios Svarnas (56' Yevhen Shakhov), Nassim Hnid, Nenad Krsticic, Petros Mandalos (66' Christos Albanis), André Simões (81' Konstantinos Galanopoulos), Mario Mitaj, Karim Ansarifard (66' Nélson Oliveira), Levi García (55' Theodosis Macheras). Coach: Massimo Carrera.
Goals: 12' Cengiz Ünder 1-0, 14' Harvey Barnes 2-0.
Referee: Lawrence Visser (BEL)

GROUP H

22.10.20   Celtic Park, Glasgow: Celtic FC – AC Milan 1-3 (0-2)
Celtic FC: Vassilis Barkas, Shane Duffy, Diego Laxalt (77' Greg Taylor), Kristoffer Ajer, Stephen Welsh (46' Mohamed Elyounoussi), Jeremie Frimpong, Scott Brown (64' Tom Rogic), Callum McGregor, Olivier Ntcham, Leigh Griffiths (46' Ryan Christie), Albian Ajeti (77' Patryk Klimala). Coach: Neil Lennon.
AC Milan: Gianluigi Donnarumma, Simon Kjær, Alessio Romagnoli, Theo Hernández, Diogo Dalot, Samu Castillejo (79' Alexis Saelemaekers), Rade Krunic, Franck Kessié (66' Ismaël Bennacar), Sandro Tonali, Zlatan Ibrahimovic (66' Rafael Leão), Brahim Díaz (79' Jens Hauge). Coach: Stefano Pioli.
Goals: 14' Rade Krunic 0-1, 42' Brahim Díaz 0-2, 76' Mohamed Elyounoussi 1-2, 90+2' Jens Hauge 1-3.
Referee: Matej Jug (SVN)   Attendance: 316.

22.10.20   Generali Arena, Prague: AC Sparta Praha – Lille Olympique 1-4 (0-1)
AC Sparta Praha: Milan Heca, Andreas Vindheim, Matej Hanousek (90+1' Martin Minchev), David Lischka, Borek Dockal, David Pavelka, Michal Trávník (78' Adam Karabec), David Moberg-Karlsson (74' Matej Polidar), Michal Sácek (90+1' Martin Vitík), Ladislav Krejci (II), Lukás Julis (46' Adam Hlozek). Coach: Václav Kotal.
Lille Olympique: Mike Maignan, José Fonte, Jérémy Pied, Sven Botman (78' Adama Soumaoro), Domagoj Bradaric (63' Reinildo), Xeka, Jonathan Ikoné, Boubakary Soumaré, Yusuf Yazici (80' Timothy Weah), Jonathan Bamba (78' Luiz Araujo), Jonathan David (63' Burak Yilmaz). Coach: Christophe Galtier.
Goals: 45+1' Yusuf Yazici 0-1, 47' Borek Dockal 1-1, 60' Yusuf Yazici 1-2, 66' Jonathan Ikoné 1-3, 75' Yusuf Yazici 1-4.
Referee: Duje Strukan (CRO)
Sent off: 23' Ladislav Krejci (II).

29.10.20   Stadio Giuseppe Meazza, Milano: AC Milan – AC Sparta Praha 3-0 (1-0)
AC Milan: Ciprian Tatarusanu, Simon Kjær, Alessio Romagnoli (80' Léo Duarte), Davide Calabria (68' Andrea Conti), Diogo Dalot, Samu Castillejo, Rade Krunic (88' Daniel Maldini), Ismaël Bennacar (81' Franck Kessié), Sandro Tonali, Zlatan Ibrahimovic (46' Rafael Leão), Brahim Díaz. Coach: Stefano Pioli.
AC Sparta Praha: Milan Heca, Ondrej Celustka, Andreas Vindheim, Matej Hanousek, David Lischka (80' Dominik Plechatý), Borek Dockal (90' Vojtech Patrák), David Pavelka, Ladislav Krejci (I) (63' David Moberg-Karlsson), Michal Trávník (80' Adam Karabec), Michal Sácek, Lukás Julis (63' Libor Kozák). Coach: Václav Kotal.
Goals: 24' Brahim Díaz 1-0, 57' Rafael Leão 2-0, 67' Diogo Dalot 3-0.
Referee: Halis Özkahya (TUR)

Zlatan Ibrahimovic missed a penalty kick (36').

29.10.20   Stade Pierre-Mauroy, Villeneuve-d'Ascq: Lille Olympique – Celtic FC 2-2 (0-2)
Lille Olympique: Mike Maignan, Adama Soumaoro, Mehmet Zeki Çelik, Sven Botman, Domagoj Bradaric, Benjamin André (63' Renato Sanches), Jonathan Ikoné, Boubakary Soumaré, Yusuf Yazici (82' Timothy Weah), Jonathan Bamba (63' Luiz Araujo), Jonathan David (64' Burak Yilmaz). Coach: Christophe Galtier.
Celtic FC: Scott Bain, Shane Duffy, Diego Laxalt, Kristoffer Ajer (53' Nir Bitton), Jeremie Frimpong, Scott Brown (81' Ismaila Soro), Callum McGregor, Mohamed Elyounoussi, Olivier Ntcham (82' Stephen Welsh), Ryan Christie (81' Tom Rogic), Albian Ajeti (64' Odsonne Édouard). Coach: Neil Lennon.
Goals: 28', 33' Mohamed Elyounoussi 0-1, 0-2, 67' Mehmet Zeki Çelik 1-2, 75' Jonathan Ikoné 2-2.
Referee: Aleksandar Stavrev (MKD)

Jonathan David missed a penalty kick (40').

05.11.20 Celtic Park, Glasgow: Celtic FC – AC Sparta Praha 1-4 (0-2)
Celtic FC: Scott Bain, Shane Duffy, Diego Laxalt (80' Olivier Ntcham), Jeremie Frimpong, Scott Brown (60' Hatem Abd Elhamed), Nir Bitton, Callum McGregor, Mohamed Elyounoussi (59' Leigh Griffiths), Tom Rogic, Ryan Christie, Odsonne Édouard (80' Albian Ajeti). Coach: Neil Lennon.
AC Sparta Praha: Florin Nita, Andreas Vindheim, Dávid Hancko (73' David Lischka), Dominik Plechatý, David Pavelka, David Moberg-Karlsson (88' Srdjan Plavsic), Matej Polidar (79' Ladislav Krejci (I)), Michal Sácek (88' Borek Dockal), Ladislav Krejci (II), Adam Karabec (74' Michal Trávník), Lukás Julis. Coach: Václav Kotal.
Goals: 26', 45' Lukás Julis 0-1, 0-2, 65' Leigh Griffiths 1-2, 77' Lukás Julis 1-3, 90' Ladislav Krejci (I) 1-4.
Referee: István Kovács (ROM)   Attendance: 397.

05.11.20 Stadio Giuseppe Meazza, Milano: AC Milan – Lille Olympique 0-3 (0-1)
AC Milan: Gianluigi Donnarumma, Simon Kjær, Alessio Romagnoli, Theo Hernández, Diogo Dalot, Samu Castillejo (46' Rafael Leão), Rade Krunic (46' Hakan Çalhanoglu), Franck Kessié, Sandro Tonali (61' Ismaël Bennacar), Zlatan Ibrahimovic (61' Ante Rebic), Brahim Díaz (78' Jens Hauge). Coach: Stefano Pioli.
Lille Olympique: Mike Maignan, José Fonte, Mehmet Zeki Çelik, Sven Botman, Domagoj Bradaric, Renato Sanches (80' Boubakary Soumaré), Xeka (65' Benjamin André), Jonathan Ikoné (65' Isaac Lihadji), Yusuf Yazici (80' Burak Yilmaz), Jonathan Bamba (84' Reinildo), Jonathan David. Coach: Christophe Galtier.
Goals: 22', 55', 58' Yusuf Yazici 0-1 (p), 0-2, 0-3.
Referee: Bartosz Frankowski (POL)

26.11.20 Generali Arena, Prague: AC Sparta Praha – Celtic FC 4-1 (2-1)
AC Sparta Praha: Florin Nita, Andreas Vindheim, Matej Hanousek, Dávid Hancko (67' Filip Soucek), Dominik Plechatý, Borek Dockal, David Pavelka, Michal Trávník (76' Ladislav Krejci (I)), David Moberg-Karlsson (86' Srdjan Plavsic), Ladislav Krejci (II), Lukás Julis (86' Martin Minchev). Coach: Václav Kotal.
Celtic FC: Scott Bain, Hatem Abd Elhamed, Christopher Jullien, Diego Laxalt, Kristoffer Ajer, Scott Brown (66' Tom Rogic), Callum McGregor, Mohamed Elyounoussi, Olivier Ntcham, Ryan Christie, Odsonne Édouard (82' Patryk Klimala). Coach: Neil Lennon.
Goals: 15' Odsonne Édouard 0-1, 26' Dávid Hancko 1-1, 38', 80' Lukás Julis 2-1, 3-1, 90+4' Srdjan Plavsic 4-1.
Referee: Tobias Stieler (GER)

26.11.20 Stade Pierre-Mauroy, Villeneuve-d'Ascq: Lille Olympique – AC Milan 1-1 (0-0)
Lille Olympique: Mike Maignan, José Fonte, Jérémy Pied (79' Tiago Djaló), Reinildo, Sven Botman, Benjamin André, Xeka (63' Boubakary Soumaré), Yusuf Yazici (63' Jonathan Ikoné), Luiz Araujo (75' Isaac Lihadji), Jonathan Bamba, Jonathan David. Coach: Christophe Galtier.
AC Milan: Gianluigi Donnarumma, Simon Kjær, Theo Hernández, Diogo Dalot, Matteo Gabbia, Hakan Çalhanoglu (61' Brahim Díaz), Samu Castillejo, Ismaël Bennacar, Jens Hauge (77' Rade Krunic), Sandro Tonali, Ante Rebic (61' Lorenzo Colombo). Coach: Stefano Pioli.
Goals: 46' Samu Castillejo 0-1, 65' Jonathan Bamba 1-1.
Referee: Craig Pawson (ENG)

03.12.20   Stadio Giuseppe Meazza, Milano: AC Milan – Celtic FC 4-2 (2-2)
AC Milan: Gianluigi Donnarumma, Simon Kjær (11' Alessio Romagnoli), Theo Hernández, Diogo Dalot, Matteo Gabbia, Hakan Çalhanoglu (61' Brahim Díaz), Samu Castillejo, Rade Krunic (46' Sandro Tonali), Franck Kessié (62' Ismaël Bennacar), Jens Hauge, Ante Rebic (83' Lorenzo Colombo). Coach: Stefano Pioli.
Celtic FC: Vassilis Barkas, Hatem Abd Elhamed, Diego Laxalt, Kristoffer Ajer, Jeremie Frimpong, Scott Brown (78' Ismaila Soro), Nir Bitton, Callum McGregor, Tom Rogic (67' Olivier Ntcham), Ryan Christie (86' Patryk Klimala), Odsonne Édouard. Coach: Neil Lennon.
Goals: 7' Tom Rogic 0-1, 14' Odsonne Édouard 0-2, 24' Hakan Çalhanoglu 1-2, 26' Samu Castillejo 2-2, 50' Jens Hauge 3-2, 82' Brahim Díaz 4-2.
Referee: Ricardo de Burgos Bengoetxea (ESP)

03.12.20   Stade Pierre-Mauroy, Villeneuve-d'Ascq:
           Lille Olympique – AC Sparta Praha 2-1 (0-0)
Lille Olympique: Mike Maignan, José Fonte, Tiago Djaló (77' Timothy Weah), Sven Botman, Domagoj Bradaric (85' Reinildo), Benjamin André (85' Boubakary Soumaré), Xeka, Yusuf Yazici (77' Burak Yilmaz), Luiz Araujo (68' Jonathan Ikoné), Jonathan Bamba, Jonathan David. Coach: Christophe Galtier.
AC Sparta Praha: Florin Nita, Ondrej Celustka, Andreas Vindheim, Dominik Plechatý, Borek Dockal (89' Adam Karabec), David Pavelka, Ladislav Krejci (I) (89' Martin Minchev), David Moberg-Karlsson (46' Srdjan Plavsic), Ladislav Krejci (II), Filip Soucek (81' Michal Trávník), Lukás Julis (81' Matej Hanousek). Coach: Václav Kotal.
Goals: 71' Ladislav Krejci (II) 0-1, 80', 84' Burak Yilmaz 1-1, 2-1.
Referee: Xavier Estrada Fernández (ESP)
Sent off: 64' Ondrej Celustka.

10.12.20   Celtic Park, Glasgow: Celtic FC – Lille Olympique 3-2 (2-1)
Celtic FC: Conor Hazard, Shane Duffy, Christopher Jullien, Diego Laxalt, Kristoffer Ajer (87' Stephen Welsh), Jeremie Frimpong (30' Ewan Henderson), Callum McGregor, Mohamed Elyounoussi, David Turnbull (87' Tom Rogic), Ismaila Soro, Patryk Klimala (78' Albian Ajeti). Coach: Neil Lennon.
Lille Olympique: Mike Maignan, José Fonte (46' Sven Botman), Tiago Djaló, Domagoj Bradaric, Xeka, Jonathan Ikoné (66' Isaac Lihadji), Boubakary Soumaré (66' Benjamin André), Yusuf Yazici, Cheikh Niasse (71' Jonathan Bamba), Timothy Weah (78' Reinildo), Jonathan David. Coach: Christophe Galtier.
Goals: 21' Christopher Jullien 1-0, 24' Jonathan Ikoné 1-1, 28' Callum McGregor 2-1 (p), 71' Timothy Weah 2-2, 75' David Turnbull 3-2.
Referee: Fábio Veríssimo (POR)   Attendance: 300.

10.12.20   Generali Arena, Prague: AC Sparta Praha – AC Milan 0-1 (0-1)
AC Sparta Praha: Milan Heca, David Lischka, Tomás Wiesner, Dominik Plechatý, Martin Vitík, Srdjan Plavsic (65' David Moberg-Karlsson), Matej Polidar, Michal Sácek (82' Ladislav Krejci (I)), Martin Minchev (65' Lukás Julis), Filip Soucek, Adam Karabec (45' Ladislav Krejci (II)). Coach: Václav Kotal.
AC Milan: Ciprian Tatarusanu, Andrea Conti, Diogo Dalot, Léo Duarte, Pierre Kalulu, Samu Castillejo, Rade Krunic, Jens Hauge (90' Brahim Díaz), Sandro Tonali, Lorenzo Colombo (67' Rafael Leão), Daniel Maldini (78' Franck Kessié). Coach: Stefano Pioli.
Goal: 23' Jens Hauge 0-1.
Referee: Daniel Siebert (GER)
Sent off: 77' Dominik Plechatý.

GROUP I

22.10.20   Estadio de la Cerámica, Villarreal: Villarreal CF – Sivasspor 5-3 (2-2)
Villarreal CF: Gerónimo Rulli, Raúl Albiol, Jaume Costa (70' Alfonso Pedraza), Juan Foyth, Francis Coquelin (79' Yeremi Pino), Manu Trigueros (58' Moi Gómez), Rubén Peña, Samuel Chukwueze, Takefusa Kubo, Álex Baena (46' Iborra), Carlos Bacca (70' Paco Alcácer).
Coach: Unai Emery.
Sivasspor: Mamadou Samassa, Caner Osmanpasa, Ugur Çiftçi, Samba Camara (79' Claudemir), Hakan Arslan, Fayçal Fajr, Isaac Cofie, Robin Yalçin, Mustapha Yatabaré, Max Gradel (82' Yasin Öztekin), Olarenwaju Kayode (82' Arouna Koné). Coach: Riza Çalimbary.
Goals: 12' Takefusa Kubo 1-0, 20' Carlos Bacca 2-0, 33' Olarenwaju Kayode 2-1, 43' Mustapha Yatabaré 2-2, 57' Juan Foyth 3-2, 64' Max Gradel 3-3, 74', 78' Paco Alcácer 4-3, 5-3.
Referee: Pawel Raczkowski (POL)

Carlos Bacca missed a penalty kick (37').

22.10.20   Bloomfield Stadium, Tel Aviv: Maccabi Tel Aviv – Qarabag FK 1-0 (1-0)
Maccabi Tel Aviv: Daniel Tenenbaum, Sheran Yeini, Eitan Tibi, Ofir Davidzada (46' Ben Bitton), Saborit (84' Luis Hernández), Maor Kandil, Eyal Golasa (78' Tal Ben Haim), Dor Peretz, Dan Glazer, Itay Shechter (46' Eduardo Guerrero), Yonatan Cohen (69' Avi Rikan). Coach: Georgios Donis.
Qarabag FK: Sahrudin Mahammadaliyev, Maksim Medvedev, Qara Qarayev (81' Ismayil Ibrahimli), Abbas Hüseynov, Kevin Medina, Jaime Romero (86' Musa Qurbanly), Uros Matic (60' Owusu Kwabena), Filip Ozobic (80' Elvin Dzhafarquliyev), Wilde-Donald Guerrier, Abdellah Zoubir (86' Tural Bayramov), Patrick Andrade. Coach: Gurban Gurbanov.
Goal: 10' Yonatan Cohen 1-0.
Referee: John Beaton (SCO)

29.10.20   Basaksehir Fatih Terim Stadyumu, Istanbul (TUR):
            Qarabag FK – Villarreal CF 1-3 (0-0)
Qarabag FK: Sahrudin Mahammadaliyev, Qara Qarayev, Abbas Hüseynov, Kevin Medina, Rahil Mammadov, Jaime Romero (61' Uros Matic), Filip Ozobic (61' Mahir Emreli), Wilde-Donald Guerrier, Abdellah Zoubir (82' Elvin Dzhafarquliyev), Patrick Andrade (90+2' Ismayil Ibrahimli), Owusu Kwabena (90+2' Tural Bayramov). Coach: Gurban Gurbanov.
Villarreal CF: Gerónimo Rulli, Jaume Costa (74' Moi Gómez), Pau Torres, Juan Foyth (90+2' Ramiro Funes Mori), Iborra, Manu Trigueros, Rubén Peña, Alfonso Pedraza, Samuel Chukwueze (86' Álex Baena), Takefusa Kubo (74' Paco Alcácer), Carlos Bacca (74' Yeremi Pino). Coach: Unai Emery.
Goals: 78' Owusu Kwabena 1-0, 80' Yeremi Pino 1-1, 84', 90+6' Paco Alcácer 1-2, 1-3 (p).
Referee: Pavel Orel (CZE)

Qarabag FK played their home matches at the neutral venue Basaksehir Fatih Terim Stadyumu, Istanbul (Turkey), instead of their regular home stadium Tofiq Bahramov adina Respublika stadionu, Baku, as UEFA announced on 20 October 2020 to temporarily suspend all UEFA matches taking place in Armenia and Azerbaijan until further notice due to the 2020 Nagorno-Karabakh conflict.

29.10.20   Yeni Sivas 4 Eylül Stadyumu, Sivas: Sivasspor – Maccabi Tel Aviv 1-2 (0-0)
Sivasspor: Mamadou Samassa, Caner Osmanpasa, Ugur Çiftçi, Samba Camara, Claudemir (81'
Arouna Koné), Hakan Arslan, Fayçal Fajr, Robin Yalçin, Mustapha Yatabaré, Max Gradel (78'
Casimir Ninga), Olarenwaju Kayode (75' Isaac Cofie). Coach: Riza Çalimbary.
Maccabi Tel Aviv: Daniel Tenenbaum, Sheran Yeini, Eitan Tibi, Ofir Davidzada, Luis
Hernández, Maor Kandil (65' Eyal Golasa), Avi Rikan (88' Eden Karzev), Dor Peretz (90+1'
Saborit), Dan Glazer, Dan Biton (88' Yonatan Cohen), Itay Shechter (65' Aleksandar Pesic).
Coach: Georgios Donis.
Goals: 55' Olarenwaju Kayode 1-0, 69' Dan Biton 1-1 (p), 74' Dor Petetz 1-2.
Referee: Irfan Peljto (BIH)   Attendance: 348.
Sent off: 67' Samba Camara.

05.11.20   Yeni Sivas 4 Eylül Stadyumu, Sivas: Sivasspor – Qarabag FK 2-0 (1-0)
Sivasspor: Mamadou Samassa, Caner Osmanpasa, Ugur Çiftçi, Marcelo Goiano, Claudemir
(90+1' Isaac Cofie), Hakan Arslan, Fayçal Fajr, Robin Yalçin, Erdogan Yesilyurt (59' Max
Gradel), Mustapha Yatabaré (59' Olarenwaju Kayode), Casimir Ninga (67' Yasin Öztekin).
Coach: Riza Çalimbary.
Qarabag FK: Sahrudin Mahammadaliyev, Maksim Medvedev (85' Rahil Mammadov), Qara
Qarayev, Badavi Hüseynov (61' Abbas Hüseynov), Kevin Medina, Uros Matic (84' Ismayil
Ibrahimli), Filip Ozobic (62' Jaime Romero), Wilde-Donald Guerrier, Abdellah Zoubir, Patrick
Andrade (46' Mahir Emreli), Owusu Kwabena. Coach: Gurban Gurbanov.
Goals: 11' Caner Osmanpasa 1-0, 88' Olarenwaju Kayode 2-0.
Referee: Sandro Schärer (SUI)   Attendance: 296.

05.11.20   Estadio de la Cerámica, Villarreal: Villarreal CF – Maccabi Tel Aviv 4-0 (1-0)
Villarreal CF: Gerónimo Rulli, Raúl Albiol, Jaume Costa (65' Moi Gómez), Ramiro Funes
Mori, Iborra (59' Manu Trigueros), Dani Parejo (59' Pervis Estupiñán), Rubén Peña, Takefusa
Kubo, Álex Baena (74' Gerard Moreno), Yeremi Pino, Carlos Bacca (74' Fer Niño).
Coach: Unai Emery.
Maccabi Tel Aviv: Daniel Tenenbaum, Eitan Tibi, Ben Biton, Luis Hernández, Saborit, Tal
Ben Haim (61' Dan Biton), Dan Glazer (68' Dor Peretz), Matan Baltaxa, Eden Karzev (61'
Eyal Golasa), Nick Blackman (51' Aleksandar Pesic), Yonatan Cohen (68' Itay Shechter).
Coach: Georgios Donis.
Goals: 4', 52' Carlos Bacca 1-0, 2-0, 71' Álex Baena 3-0, 81' Fer Niño 4-0.
Referee: Nikola Dabanovic (MNE)

26.11.20   Bloomfield Stadium, Tel Aviv: Maccabi Tel Aviv – Villarreal CF 1-1 (0-1)
Maccabi Tel Aviv: Daniel Tenenbaum, Eitan Tibi, Luis Hernández, Saborit, Maor Kandil, Eyal
Golasa (90+2' Ofir Davidzada), Dor Peretz, Dan Glazer (54' Nick Blackman), Dan Biton (85'
Sheran Yeini), Aleksandar Pesic (85' Avi Rikan), Yonatan Cohen (90+2' Eden Karzev).
Coach: Georgios Donis.
Villarreal CF: Gerónimo Rulli, Ramiro Funes Mori, Juan Foyth, Francis Coquelin, Manu
Trigueros (63' Yeremi Pino), Rubén Peña, Alfonso Pedraza, Samuel Chukwueze (63' Dani
Parejo), Takefusa Kubo (63' Gerard Moreno), Álex Baena (75' Iborra), Carlos Bacca (63' Fer
Niño). Coach: Unai Emery.
Goals: 44' Álex Baena 0-1, 47' Aleksandar Pesic 1-1.
Referee: Tiago Martins (POR)
Sent off: 89' Saborit.

26.11.20   Basaksehir Fatih Terim Stadyumu, Istanbul (TUR):
Qarabag FK – Sivasspor 2-3 (1-1)
Qarabag FK: Sahrudin Mahammadaliyev, Qara Qarayev, Kevin Medina, Uros Matic, Wilde-Donald Guerrier, Abdellah Zoubir, Ismayil Ibrahimli, Tural Bayramov (66' Jaime Romero), Elvin Dzhafarquliyev, Mahir Emreli, Owusu Kwabena. Coach: Gurban Gurbanov.
Sivasspor: Mamadou Samassa, Caner Osmanpasa, Ugur Çiftçi, Marcelo Goiano, Aaron Appindangoyé, Claudemir, Yasin Öztekin (90+3' Samba Camara), Robin Yalçin (20' Isaac Cofie), Arouna Koné, Max Gradel, Casimir Ninga (57' Olarenwaju Kayode).
Coach: Riza Çalimbary.
Goals: 8' Abdellah Zoubir 1-0, 40' Arouna Koné 1-1 (p), 51' Uros Matic 2-1, 58' Olarenwaju Kayode 2-2, 79' Arouna Koné 2-3.
Referee: Jakob Kehlet (DEN)

03.12.20   Basaksehir Fatih Terim Stadyumu, Istanbul (TUR):
Qarabag FK – Maccabi Tel Aviv 1-1 (1-1)
Qarabag FK: Sahrudin Mahammadaliyev, Qara Qarayev, Kevin Medina, Jaime Romero (72' Tural Bayramov), Uros Matic, Filip Ozobic (83' Rahil Mammadov), Wilde-Donald Guerrier, Abdellah Zoubir, Ismayil Ibrahimli, Elvin Dzhafarquliyev, Owusu Kwabena.
Coach: Gurban Gurbanov.
Maccabi Tel Aviv: Daniel Tenenbaum, Sheran Yeini, Eitan Tibi, Ofir Davidzada, Luis Hernández, Maor Kandil (69' Dan Glazer), Eyal Golasa (83' Itay Shechter), Dor Peretz (83' Tal Ben Haim), Dan Biton, Nick Blackman (65' Eduardo Guerrero), Yonatan Cohen.
Coach: Georgios Donis.
Goals: 22' Yonatan Cohen 0-1 (p), 37' Jaime Romero 1-1.
Referee: Robert Hennessy (IRL)

03.12.20   Yeni Sivas 4 Eylül Stadyumu, Sivas: Sivasspor – Villarreal CF 0-1 (0-0)
Sivasspor: Mamadou Samassa, Caner Osmanpasa, Ziya Erdal, Samba Camara, Aaron Appindangoyé, Yasin Öztekin, Fayçal Fajr, Isaac Cofie (82' Claudemir), Robin Yalçin (77' Arouna Koné), Mustapha Yatabaré (80' Casimir Ninga), Max Gradel. Coach: Riza Çalimbary.
Villarreal CF: Gerónimo Rulli, Jaume Costa (77' Pervis Estupiñán), Ramiro Funes Mori, Juan Foyth, Iborra, Francis Coquelin (68' Manu Trigueros), Rubén Peña, Samuel Chukwueze (76' Gerard Moreno), Takefusa Kubo (58' Yeremi Pino), Álex Baena (68' Dani Parejo), Fer Niño.
Coach: Unai Emery.
Goal: 75' Samuel Chukwueze 0-1.
Referee: Duje Strukan (CRO)

10.12.20   *Estadio de la Cerámica, Villarreal: Villarreal CF – Qarabag FK 3-0 **(awarded)***
Referee: *Mykola Balakin (UKR)*

Match was cancelled and awarded as a 3-0 win to Villarreal CF after several players of the Qarabag FK squad tested positive for the SARS-CoV-2 coronavirus.

10.12.20 Bloomfield Stadium, Tel Aviv: Maccabi Tel Aviv – Sivasspor 1-0 (0-0)
Maccabi Tel Aviv: Daniel Tenenbaum, Eitan Tibi, Luis Hernández, Saborit (85' Sheran Yeini), Maor Kandil, Eyal Golasa (74' Tal Ben Haim), Dor Peretz, Dan Glazer, Dan Biton (63' Ofir Davidzada), Aleksandar Pesic (85' Nick Blackman), Yonatan Cohen (74' Avi Rikan).
Coach: Georgios Donis.
Sivasspor: Mamadou Samassa, Caner Osmanpasa, Samba Camara, Aaron Appindangoyé, Claudemir (63' Arouna Koné), Hakan Arslan, Fayçal Fajr, Robin Yalçin, Mustapha Yatabaré, Max Gradel, Olarenwaju Kayode. Coach: Riza Çalimbary.
Goal: 66' Saborit 1-0.
Referee: Andris Treimanis (LAT)

GROUP J

22.10.20 Tottenham Hotspur Stadium, London: Tottenham Hotspur – LASK Linz 3-0 (2-0)
Tottenham Hotspur: Joe Hart, Matt Doherty, Ben Davies, Davinson Sánchez, Reguilón, Érik Lamela (62' Dele Alli), Lucas Moura (78' Giovani Lo Celso), Pierre-Emile Højbjerg (62' Moussa Sissoko), Harry Winks, Gareth Bale (62' Son Heung-Min), Carlos Vinícius (86' Jack Clarke). Coach: José Mourinho.
LASK Linz: Alexander Schlager, Gernot Trauner, Reinhold Ranftl, Philipp Wiesinger, James Holland (5' Lukas Grgic), Peter Michorl, René Renner (39' Petar Filipovic), Husein Balic (78' Thomas Goiginger), Andrés Andrade (46' Marvin Potzmann), Andreas Gruber (46' Johannes Eggestein), Marko Raguz. Coach: Dominik Thalhammer.
Goals: 18' Lucas Moura 1-0, 27' Andrés Andrade 2-0 (og), 84' Son Heung-Min 3-0.
Referee: Mohammed Al-Hakim (SWE)

22.10.20 Huvepharma Arena, Razgrad:
PFC Ludogorest Razgrad – Royal Antwerp FC 1-2 (0-0)
PFC Ludogorets Razgrad: Plamen Iliev, Cicinho, Georgi Terziev, Anton Nedyalkov, Olivier Verdon, Stéphane Badji (83' Anicet Andrianantenaina), Cauly (78' Claudiu Keserü), Alex Santana, Dominik Yankov (77' Bernard Tekpetey), Kiril Despodov (45+1' Elvis Manu), Higinio Marín. Coach: Pavel Vrba.
Royal Antwerp FC: Jean Butez, Ritchie De Laet, Simen Juklerød, Dylan Batubinsika, Jérémy Gelin, Faris Haroun, Lior Refaelov (72' Buta), Cristián Benavente (59' Nana Ampomah), Pieter Gerkens, Koji Miyoshi, Martin Hongla Yma (80' Birger Verstraete). Coach: Ivan Leko.
Goals: 46' Higinio Marín 1-0, 63' Pieter Gerkens 1-1, 70' Lior Refaelov 1-2.
Referee: Roi Reinshreiber (ISR)   Attendance: 2,321.

29.11.20 Linzer Stadion, Linz: LASK Linz – PFC Ludogorets Razgrad 4-3 (3-1)
LASK Linz: Alexander Schlager, Petar Filipovic, Gernot Trauner, Reinhold Ranftl, Philipp Wiesinger, Peter Michorl, Lukas Grgic, Husein Balic (63' Johannes Eggestein), Andrés Andrade, Andreas Gruber (63' Thomas Goiginger), Marko Raguz.
Coach: Dominik Thalhammer.
PFC Ludogorets Razgrad: Plamen Iliev, Cosmin Moti, Cicinho, Anton Nedyalkov, Olivier Verdon, Anicet Andrianantenaina, Stéphane Badji (53' Cauly), Alex Santana, Dominik Yankov (80' Mavis Tchibota), Elvis Manu, Bernard Tekpetey (88' Jordan Ikoko).
Coach: Stanislav Genchev.
Goals: 2' Husein Balic 1-0, 11' Andreas Gruber 2-0, 15' Elvis Manu 2-1, 35' Marko Raguz 3-1, 56' Olivier Verdon 4-1 (og), 67', 73' Elvis Manu 4-2, 4-3 (p).
Referee: Xavier Estrada Fernández (ESP)   Attendance: 1,487.
Sent off: 73' Lukas Grgic.

LASK Linz played their home matches at Linzer Stadion, Linz, instead of their regular home stadium Waldstation, Pasching.

29.10.20 Bosuilstadion, Antwerp: Royal Antwerp FC – Tottenham Hotspur 1-0 (1-0)
Royal Antwerp FC: Jean Butez, Ritchie De Laet, Simen Juklerød, Jérémy Gelin, Abdoulaye Seck, Faris Haroun, Lior Refaelov (88' Cristián Benavente), Pieter Gerkens, Koji Miyoshi (58' Buta), Martin Hongla Yma (70' Birger Verstraete), Dieumerci Mbokani. Coach: Ivan Leko.
Tottenham Hotspur: Hugo Lloris, Serge Aurier, Ben Davies, Davinson Sánchez, Reguilón, Dele Alli (46' Érik Lamela), Harry Winks, Giovani Lo Celso (46' Pierre-Emile Højbjerg), Gareth Bale (58' Harry Kane), Steven Bergwijn (46' Lucas Moura), Carlos Vinícius (46' Son Heung-Min). Coach: José Mourinho.
Goal: 29' Lior Refaelov 1-0.
Referee: Maurizio Mariana (ITA)

05.11.20 Huvepharma Arena, Razgrad:
PFC Ludogorets Razgrad – Tottenham Hotspur 1-3 (0-2)
PFC Ludogorets Razgrad: Plamen Iliev, Georgi Terziev, Jordan Ikoko, Anton Nedyalkov, Olivier Verdon, Anicet Andrianantenaina (59' Alex Santana), Stéphane Badji (90+2' Ivan Yordanov), Cauly, Dominik Yankov (80' Mavis Tchibota), Claudiu Keserü (59' Dimitar Mitkov), Elvis Manu (46' Bernard Tekpetey). Coach: Stanislav Genchev.
Tottenham Hotspur: Joe Hart, Toby Alderweireld, Matt Doherty, Ben Davies, Moussa Sissoko (46' Pierre-Emile Højbjerg), Lucas Moura (61' Son Heung-Min), Eric Dier, Harry Winks, Giovani Lo Celso (72' Tanguy NDombélé), Gareth Bale (65' Steven Bergwijn), Harry Kane (46' Carlos Vinícius). Coach: José Mourinho.
Goals: 13' Harry Kane 0-1, 32' Lucas Moura 0-2, 50' Claudiu Keserü 1-2, 62' Giovani Lo Celso 1-3.
Referee: Fran Jovic (CRO)

05.11.20 Bosuilstadion, Antwerp: Royal Antwerp FC – LASK Linz 0-1 (0-0)
Royal Antwerp FC: Jean Butez, Ritchie De Laet, Simen Juklerød (75' Cristián Benavente), Abdoulaye Seck, Faris Haroun (87' Frank Boya), Lior Refaelov (87' Jordan Lukaku), Pieter Gerkens, Birger Verstraete (64' Nana Ampomah), Koji Miyoshi (64' Buta), Martin Hongla Yma, Dieumerci Mbokani. Coach: Ivan Leko.
LASK Linz: Alexander Schlager, Petar Filipovic, Gernot Trauner, Reinhold Ranftl, Philipp Wiesinger, James Holland, Peter Michorl, René Renner, Husein Balic, Andreas Gruber (66' Thomas Goiginger), Marko Raguz (40' Johannes Eggestein). Coach: Dominik Thalhammer.
Goal: 54' Johannes Eggestein 0-1.
Referee: Yevhen Aranovskiy (UKR)
Sent off: 68' James Holland.

26.11.20 Linzer Stadion, Linz: LASK Linz – Royal Antwerp FC 0-2 (0-0)
LASK Linz: Alexander Schlager, Petar Filipovic (73' Marvin Potzmann), Gernot Trauner, Reinhold Ranftl, Philipp Wiesinger, Peter Michorl, René Renner, Husein Balic, Mads Madsen (53' Andrés Andrade), Andreas Gruber (60' Thomas Goiginger), Johannes Eggestein. Coach: Dominik Thalhammer.
Royal Antwerp FC: Jean Butez, Ritchie De Laet, Simen Juklerød (81' Buta), Dylan Batubinsika, Abdoulaye Seck, Faris Haroun, Lior Refaelov (88' Manuel Benson), Cristián Benavente (67' Nana Ampomah), Pieter Gerkens, Koji Miyoshi (81' Jordan Lukaku), Martin Hongla Yma. Coach: Ivan Leko.
Goals: 52' Lior Refaelov 0-1, 83' Pieter Gerkens 0-2.
Referee: Donatas Rumsas (LTU)
Sent off: 50' Gernot Trauner.

26.11.20 Tottenham Hotspur Stadium, London:
Tottenham Hotspur – PFC Ludogorets Razgrad 4-0 (2-0)
Tottenham Hotspur: Joe Hart (82' Alfie Whiteman), Matt Doherty, Ben Davies, Davinson Sánchez, Japhet Tanganga, Lucas Moura (82' Dane Scarlett), Dele Alli (82' Harvey White), Harry Winks, Tanguy NDombélé (61' Pierre-Emile Højbjerg), Gareth Bale (68' Jack Clarke), Carlos Vinícius. Coach: José Mourinho.
PFC Ludogorets Razgrad: Plamen Iliev, Cosmin Moti, Dragos Grigore, Jordan Ikoko, Anton Nedyalkov, Olivier Verdon, Anicet Andrianantenaina (68' Cauly), Stéphane Badji (89' Ivan Yordanov), Dominik Yankov (90' Dimitar Mitkov), Claudiu Keserü (68' Mavis Tchibota), Kiril Despodov (64' Bernard Tekpetey). Coach: Stanislav Genchev.
Goals: 16', 34' Carlos Vinícius 1-0, 2-0, 63' Harry Winks 3-0, 73' Lucas Moura 4-0.
Referee: Giorgi Kruashvili (GEO)

03.12.20 Linzer Stadion, Linz: LASK Linz – Tottenham Hotspur 3-3 (1-1)
LASK Linz: Alexander Schlager, Reinhold Ranftl, Philipp Wiesinger, James Holland, Peter Michorl, René Renner, Andrés Andrade, Mads Madsen, Thomas Goiginger (69' Mamoudou Karamoko), Andreas Gruber (69' Dominik Reiter), Johannes Eggestein.
Coach: Dominik Thalhammer.
Tottenham Hotspur: Joe Hart, Matt Doherty, Ben Davies, Davinson Sánchez, Japhet Tanganga, Lucas Moura (65' Moussa Sissoko), Pierre-Emile Højbjerg, Tanguy NDombélé (65' Steven Bergwijn), Giovani Lo Celso (71' Eric Dier), Gareth Bale (82' Serge Aurier), Son Heung-Min (82' Dele Alli). Coach: José Mourinho.
Goals: 42' Peter Michorl 1-0, 45+2' Gareth Bale 1-1 (p), 56' Son Heung-Min 1-2, 84' Johannes Eggestein 2-2, 87' Dele Alli 2-3 (p), 90+3' Mamoudou Karamoko 3-3.
Referee: Pawel Raczkowski (POL)

03.12.20 Bosuilstadion, Antwerp: Royal Antwerp FC – PFC Ludogorets Razgrad 3-1 (1-0)
Royal Antwerp FC: Jean Butez, Ritchie De Laet, Simen Juklerød (64' Manuel Benson), Jérémy Gelin, Abdoulaye Seck, Faris Haroun, Lior Refaelov (77' Buta), Cristián Benavente (64' Nana Ampomah), Pieter Gerkens (84' Dieumerci Mbokani), Koji Miyoshi, Martin Hongla Yma (77' Frank Boya). Coach: Ivan Leko.
PFC Ludogorets Razgrad: Vladislav Stoyanov, Dragos Grigore, Jordan Ikoko (44' Georgi Terziev), Anton Nedyalkov, Olivier Verdon, Anicet Andrianantenaina, Mavis Tchibota (67' Bernard Tekpetey), Stéphane Badji (83' Alex Santana), Cauly, Claudiu Keserü (67' Elvis Manu), Kiril Despodov (83' Dimitar Mitkov). Coach: Stanislav Genchev.
Goals: 19' Martin Hongla Yma 1-0, 53' Kiril Despodov 1-1, 72' Ritchie De Laet 2-1, 87' Manuel Benson 3-1.
Referee: Pavel Orel (CZE)
Sent off: 90' Dragos Grigore.

10.12.20 Tottenham Hotspur Stadium, London:
Tottenham Hotspur – Royal Antwerp 2-0 (0-0)
Tottenham Hotspur: Joe Hart, Matt Doherty, Ben Davies, Davinson Sánchez, Reguilón (47' Steven Bergwijn), Japhet Tanganga, Lucas Moura (68' Moussa Sissoko), Harry Winks (59' Tanguy NDombélé), Giovani Lo Celso, Gareth Bale (58' Son Heung-Min), Carlos Vinícius (59' Harry Kane). Coach: José Mourinho.
Royal Antwerp FC: Alireza Beiranvand, Jordan Lukaku (61' Simen Juklerød), Dylan Batubinsika, Buta, Jérémy Gelin, Abdoulaye Seck (72' Birger Verstraete), Faris Haroun, Lior Refaelov (46' Nana Ampomah), Cristián Benavente, Martin Hongla Yma (61' Frank Boya), Manuel Benson (72' Koji Miyoshi). Coach: Ivan Leko.
Goals: 57' Carlos Vinícius 1-0, 71' Giovani Lo Celso 2-0.
Referee: Jesús Gil Manzano (ESP) Attendance: 2,000.

10.12.20 Huvepharma Arena, Razgrad: PFC Ludogorets Razgrad – LASK Linz 1-3 (0-0)
PFC Ludogorets Razgrad: Plamen Iliev, Cicinho, Josué Sá, Jordan Ikoko (70' Georgi Terziev), Olivier Verdon, Mavis Tchibota (46' Elvis Manu), Stéphane Badji (77' Anicet Andrianantenaina), Cauly (77' Dominik Yankov), Alex Santana, Claudiu Keserü (77' Bernard Tekpetey), Kiril Despodov. Coach: Stanislav Genchev.
LASK Linz: Alexander Schlager, Reinhold Ranftl (74' Marvin Potzmann), Philipp Wiesinger (86' Christian Ramsebner), Yevgen Cheberko, James Holland, René Renner, Andrés Andrade, Dominik Reiter (63' Andreas Gruber), Mads Madsen, Thomas Goiginger (62' Husein Balic), Johannes Eggestein (73' Patrick Plojer). Coach: Dominik Thalhammer.
Goals: 46' Elvis Manu 1-0, 56' Philipp Wiesinger 1-1, 61' René Renner 1-2 (p), 67' Mads Madsen 1-3.
Referee: Vitali Meshkov (RUS)
Sent off: 61' Alex Santana.

Thomas Golginger missed a penalty kick (45').

GROUP K

22.10.20   Stadion Maksimir, Zagreb: Dinamo Zagreb – Feyenoord Rotterdam 0-0
Dinamo Zagreb: Dominik Livakovic, Kévin Théophile-Catherine, Petar Stojanovic, Rasmus Lauritsen, Josko Gvardiol, Arijan Ademi, Kristijan Jakic (71' Bartol Franjic), Lovro Majer, Mario Gavranovic (54' Bruno Petkovic), Mislav Orsic, Lirim Kastrati (I) (54' Luka Ivanusec). Coach: Zoran Mamic.
Feyenoord Rotterdam: Justin Bijlow, Uros Spajic, Ridgeciano Haps, Bart Nieuwkoop, Marcos Senesi, Jens Toornstra, João Carlos Teixeira, Mark Diemers (81' Nicolai Jørgensen), Orkun Kökçü (74' Eric Botteghin), Bryan Linssen, Steven Berghuis. Coach: Dick Advocaat.
Referee: Mattias Gestranius (FIN)   Attendance: 1,271.
Sent off: 73' Marcos Senesi.

Steven Berghuis missed a penalty kick (8').

22.10.20   Wörthersee Stadion, Klagenfurt am Wörthersee:
Wolfsberger AC – CSKA Moscow 1-1 (1-1)
Wolfsberger AC: Alexander Kofler, Michael Novak, Jonathan Scherzer (84' Mario Pavelic), Dominik Baumgartner, Luka Lochoshvili, Michael Liendl, Mario Leitgeb, Christopher Wernitznig (73' Eliel Peretz), Matthäus Taferner, Cheikhou Dieng (78' Marc Andre Schmerböck), Dejan Joveljic. Coach: Ferdinand Feldhofer.
CSKA Moscow: Igor Akinfeev, Viktor Vasin (46' Alan Dzagoev), Hördur Magnússon, Igor Diveev, Nikola Vlasic (86' Kristijan Bistrovic), Baktiyor Zaynutdinov, Konstantin Kuchaev (76' Ilzat Akhmetov), Ivan Oblyakov, Nayair Tiknizyan (46' Chidera Ejuke), Konstantin Maradishvili, Adolfo Gaich (61' Fedor Chalov). Coach: Victor Goncharenko.
Goals: 5' Adolfo Gaich 0-1, 42' Michael Liendl 1-1 (p).
Referee: Sascha Stegemann (GER)   Attendance: 3,000.

Wolfsberger AC played their home matches at Wörthersee Stadion, Klagenfurt am Wörthersee, instead of their regular home stadium Lavanttal-Arena, Wolfsberg.

29.10.20   VEB Arena, Moscow: CSKA Moscow – Dinamo Zagreb 0-0
CSKA Moscow: Igor Akinfeev, Mário Fernandes (84' Kristijan Bistrovic), Hördur Magnússon, Igor Diveev, Nikola Vlasic, Baktiyor Zaynutdinov, Konstantin Kuchaev (81' Ilzat Akhmetov), Ivan Oblyakov (80' Alan Dzagoev), Konstantin Maradishvili, Fedor Chalov (74' Adolfo Gaich), Chidera Ejuke (75' Arnór Sigurdsson). Coach: Victor Goncharenko.
Dinamo Zagreb: Dominik Livakovic, Petar Stojanovic, Dino Peric (81' Lirim Kastrati (I)), Rasmus Lauritsen, Josko Gvardiol, Arijan Ademi, Luka Ivanusec (66' Kristijan Jakic), Lovro Majer, Bartol Franjic, Mislav Orsic (90+3' Sadegh Moharrami), Bruno Petkovic (65' Mario Gavranovic). Coach: Zoran Mamic.
Referee: Radu Marian Petrescu (ROM)   Attendance: 6,411.

29.10.20   De Kuip, Rotterdam: Feyenoord Rotterdam – Wolfsberger AC 1-4 (0-2)
Feyenoord Rotterdam: Justin Bijlow, Eric Botteghin, Uros Spajic, Ridgeciano Haps, Bart Nieuwkoop (46' Luciano Narsingh), Lutsharel Geertruida, Jens Toornstra, Mark Diemers, Orkun Kökçü, Bryan Linssen (76' Naoufal Bannis), Steven Berghuis. Coach: Dick Advocaat.
Wolfsberger AC: Alexander Kofler, Michael Novak, Jonathan Scherzer, Dominik Baumgartner, Luka Lochoshvili, Michael Liendl, Mario Leitgeb, Christopher Wernitznig (82' Eliel Peretz), Matthäus Taferner (60' Kai Stratznig), Cheikhou Dieng (82' Dario Vizinger), Dejan Joveljic (67' Nemanja Rnic). Coach: Ferdinand Feldhofer.
Goals: 4', 13' Michael Liendl 0-1 (p), 0-2 (p), 53' Steven Berghuis 1-2, 60' Michael Liendl 1-3, 66' Dejan Joveljic 1-4 (p).
Referee: Srdjan Jovanovic (SRB)

05.11.20   Stadion Maksimir, Zagreb: Dinamo Zagreb – Wolfsberger AC 1-0 (0-0)
Dinamo Zagreb: Danijel Zagorac, Dino Peric (15' Marin Leovac), Sadegh Moharrami (74' Iyayi Atiemwen), Rasmus Lauritsen, Josko Gvardiol, Arijan Ademi, Kristijan Jakic (46' Lirim Kastrati (I)), Lovro Majer, Bartol Franjic, Mario Gavranovic (90+2' Robbie Burton), Mislav Orsic. Coach: Zoran Mamic.
Wolfsberger AC: Alexander Kofler, Michael Novak, Mario Pavelic (81' Amar Hodzic), Dominik Baumgartner, Luka Lochoshvili, Christopher Wernitznig, Eliel Peretz (80' Marc Andre Schmerböck), Matthäus Taferner, Kai Stratznig, Cheikhou Dieng (54' Dario Vizinger), Dejan Joveljic (46' Stefan Peric). Coach: Ferdinand Feldhofer.
Goal: 76' Iyayi Atiemwen 1-0.
Referee: Jérôme Brisard (FRA)
Sent off: 45' Matthäus Taferner.

05.11.20   De Kuip, Rotterdam: Feyenoord Rotterdam – CSKA Moscow 3-1 (0-0)
Feyenoord Rotterdam: Justin Bijlow, Uros Spajic, Ridgeciano Haps, Tyrell Malacia, Marcos Senesi, Lutsharel Geertruida, Jens Toornstra, Mark Diemers, Orkun Kökçü (76' João Carlos Teixeira), Bryan Linssen, Steven Berghuis. Coach: Dick Advocaat.
CSKA Moscow: Igor Akinfeev, Mário Fernandes (31' Alan Dzagoev), Hördur Magnússon (77' Viktor Vasin), Igor Diveev, Nikola Vlasic, Baktiyor Zaynutdinov, Arnór Sigurdsson, Konstantin Kuchaev (68' Fedor Chalov), Ivan Oblyakov (77' Kristijan Bistrovic), Konstantin Maradishvili, Chidera Ejuke (76' Nayair Tiknizyan). Coach: Victor Goncharenko.
Goals: 63' Ridgeciano Haps 1-0, 71' Orkun Kökçü 2-0, 72' Lutsharel Geertruida 3-0, 79' Marcos Senesi 3-1 (og).
Referee: Roi Reinshreiber (ISR)

26.11.20   VEB Arena, Moscow: CSKA Moscow – Feyenoord Rotterdam 0-0
CSKA Moscow: Igor Akinfeev, Georgiy Shchennikov (64' Ilzat Akhmetov), Hördur Magnússon, Igor Diveev, Nikola Vlasic, Baktiyor Zaynutdinov, Arnór Sigurdsson (63' Ilya Shkurin), Ivan Oblyakov (71' Kristijan Bistrovic), Konstantin Maradishvili, Fedor Chalov (80' Nayair Tiknizyan), Chidera Ejuke (81' Adolfo Gaich). Coach: Victor Goncharenko.
Feyenoord Rotterdam: Nick Marsman, Uros Spajic, Bart Nieuwkoop, Marcos Senesi, Lutsharel Geertruida, Jens Toornstra (71' Jordy Wehrmann), Mark Diemers, Orkun Kökçü, Bryan Linssen, Nicolai Jørgensen, Steven Berghuis (82' Eric Botteghin). Coach: Dick Advocaat.
Referee: Kristo Tohver (EST)   Attendance: 5,407.
Sent off: 48' Nicolai Jørgensen.

26.11.20 Wörthersee Stadion, Klagenfurt am Wörthersee:
Wolfsberger AC – Dinamo Zagreb 0-3 (0-0)
Wolfsberger AC: Manuel Kuttin, Michael Novak, Jonathan Scherzer (82' Guram Giorbelidze), Dominik Baumgartner (46' Nemanja Rnic), Luka Lochoshvili, Michael Liendl, Mario Leitgeb, Christopher Wernitznig (66' Dejan Joveljic), Eliel Peretz, Kai Stratznig (72' Sven Sprangler), Dario Vizinger (82' Marc Andre Schmerböck). Coach: Ferdinand Feldhofer.
Dinamo Zagreb: Dominik Livakovic, Kévin Théophile-Catherine, Sadegh Moharrami, Rasmus Lauritsen, Josko Gvardiol, Arijan Ademi (90+2' Robbie Burton), Kristijan Jakic (83' Marko Tolic), Lovro Majer (74' Bartol Franjic), Mislav Orsic (74' Luka Ivanusec), Bruno Petkovic, Lirim Kastrati (I). Coach: Zoran Mamic.
Goals: 60' Lovro Majer 0-1, 75' Bruno Petkovic 0-2, 90+1' Luka Ivanusec 0-3.
Referee: Serhiy Boyko (UKR)

03.12.20 VEB Arena, Moscow: CSKA Moscow – Wolfsberger AC 0-1 (0-1)
CSKA Moscow: Igor Akinfeev, Georgiy Shchennikov (63' Nayair Tiknizyan), Hördur Magnússon, Igor Diveev, Nikola Vlasic, Ilzat Akhmetov (64' Kristijan Bistrovic), Baktiyor Zaynutdinov, Konstantin Kuchaev (46' Chidera Ejuke), Ivan Oblyakov (76' Arnór Sigurdsson), Konstantin Maradishvili, Fedor Chalov (46' Adolfo Gaich).
Coach: Victor Goncharenko.
Wolfsberger AC: Alexander Kofler, Michael Novak, Jonathan Scherzer, Dominik Baumgartner, Luka Lochoshvili, Michael Liendl (81' Christopher Wernitznig), Mario Leitgeb, Sven Sprangler (82' Nemanja Rnic), Eliel Peretz, Matthäus Taferner (61' Kai Stratznig), Dario Vizinger (70' Dejan Joveljic). Coach: Ferdinand Feldhofer.
Goal: 22' Dario Vizinger 0-1.
Referee: Nikola Dabanovic (MNE)   Attendance: 4,321.

03.12.20 De Kuip, Rotterdam: Feyenoord Rotterdam – Dinamo Zagreb 0-2 (0-1)
Feyenoord Rotterdam: Nick Marsman, Uros Spajic (46' Eric Botteghin), Tyrell Malacia, Marcos Senesi, Lutsharel Geertruida, Jens Toornstra, Mark Diemers (69' João Carlos Teixeira), Orkun Kökçü, Bryan Linssen (36' Naoufal Bannis), Luciano Narsingh, Steven Berghuis. Coach: Dick Advocaat.
Dinamo Zagreb: Dominik Livakovic, Kévin Théophile-Catherine, Sadegh Moharrami, Rasmus Lauritsen, Josko Gvardiol, Arijan Ademi, Kristijan Jakic, Luka Ivanusec (72' Mislav Orsic), Lovro Majer (65' Bartol Franjic), Bruno Petkovic (88' Marko Tolic), Lirim Kastrati (I) (88' Dino Peric). Coach: Zoran Mamic.
Goals: 45+5' Bruno Petkovic 0-1 (p), 53' Lovro Majer 0-2.
Referee: Chris Kavanagh (ENG)

10.12.20 Stadion Maksimir, Zagreb: Dinamo Zagreb – CSKA Moscow 3-1 (2-0)
Dinamo Zagreb: Dominik Livakovic, Martin Leovac (20' Dino Peric), Kévin Théophile-Catherine, Sadegh Moharrami, Josko Gvardiol, Arijan Ademi (35' Bartol Franjic), Kristijan Jakic, Lovro Majer (78' Marko Tolic), Mario Gavranovic (78' Iyayi Atiemwen), Mislav Orsic (78' Mario Cuze), Lirim Kastrati (I). Coach: Zoran Mamic.
CSKA Moscow: Igor Akinfeev, Viktor Vasin, Georgiy Shchennikov (71' Adolfo Gaich), Igor Diveev (78' Vadim Karpov), Ilzat Akhmetov (63' Nayair Tiknizyan), Baktiyor Zaynutdinov, Kristijan Bistrovic, Arnór Sigurdsson, Ivan Oblyakov, Konstantin Maradishvili, Ilya Shkurin (63' Fedor Chalov). Coach: Victor Goncharenko.
Goals: 28' Josko Gvardiol 1-0, 41' Mislav Orsic 2-0, 75' Lirim Kastrati (I) 3-0, 76' Kristijan Bistrovic 3-1.
Referee: Tiago Martins (POR)

10.12.20   Wörthersee Stadion, Klagenfurt am Wörthersee:
Wolfsberger AC – Feyenoord Rotterdam 1-0 (1-0)
Wolfsberger AC: Alexander Kofler, Michael Novak, Jonathan Scherzer, Dominik Baumgartner, Luka Lochoshvili, Michael Liendl, Mario Leitgeb, Sven Sprangler, Matthäus Taferner (68' Nemanja Rnic), Dario Vizinger (83' Kai Stratznig), Dejan Joveljic (56' Eliel Peretz). Coach: Ferdinand Feldhofer.
Feyenoord Rotterdam: Nick Marsman, Uros Spajic (72' João Carlos Teixeira), Tyrell Malacia (79' Naoufal Bannis), Marcos Senesi, Lutsharel Geertruida, Jens Toornstra, Mark Diemers, Orkun Kökçü, Bryan Linssen (72' Luis Sinisterra), Nicolai Jørgensen, Steven Berghuis.
Coach: Dick Advocaat
Goal: 31' Dejan Joveljic 1-0.
Referee: Pawel Raczkowski (POL)

GROUP L

22.10.20   PreZero Arena, Sinsheim: 1899 Hoffenheim – Crvena Zvezda Beograd 2-0 (0-0)
1899 Hoffenheim: Oliver Baumann, Kevin Vogt, Kevin Akpoguma, Stefan Posch, Sebastian Rudy, Florian Grillitsch (46' Diadié Samassékou), Mijat Gacinovic (46' Dennis Geiger), Christoph Baumgartner (78' Ihlas Bebou), Ryan Sessegnon (90' Robert Skov), Ishak Belfodil (78' Jacob Bruun Larsen), Munas Dabour. Coach: Sebastian Hoeneß.
Crvena Zvezda Beograd: Milan Borjan, Nemanja Milunovic, Milan Rodic, Milos Degenek, Milan Gajic (85' Veljko Simic), Strahinja Erakovic, Aleksandar Katai (75' Aleksa Vukanovic), Srdjan Spiridonovic (76' El Fardou Ben Nabouhane), Sékou Sanogo (76' Njegos Petrovic), Veljko Nikolic, Diego Falcinelli (85' Milan Pavkov). Coach: Dejan Stankovic.
Goals: 64' Christoph Baumgartner 1-0, 90+3' Munas Dabour 2-0.
Referee: Alejandro José Hernández Hernández (ESP)

Coach Dejan Stankovic was sent to the stands (65').

22.10.20   Stadion u Nisy, Liberec: Slovan Liberec – KAA Gent 1-0 (1-0)
Slovan Liberec: Filip Nguyen, Jakub Jugas, Jan Mikula, Martin Koscelník, Mohamed Tijani, Jhon Mosquera, Jakub Hromada (79' Matej Chalus), Jakub Pesek (68' Jan Matousek), Kamso Mara, Michal Beran (57' Michal Sadílek), Abdulla Yusuf Helal (58' Michael Rabusic).
Coach: Pavel Hoftych.
KAA Gent: Davy Roef, Jordan Botaka (77' Anderson Niangbo), Michael Ngadeu-Ngadjui, Núrio Fortuna (87' Igor Plastun), Andreas Hanche-Olsen, Alessio Castro-Montes, Sven Kums, Sulayman Marreh, Roman Yaremchuk, Tim Kleindienst (76' Laurent Depoitre), Osman Bukari. Coach: Wim De Decker.
Goal: 29' Abdulla Yusuf Helal 1-0.
Referee: Manuel Schüttengruber (AUT)

29.10.20   GHELAMCO-arena, Gent: KAA Gent – 1899 Hoffenheim 1-4 (0-1)
KAA Gent: Davy Roef, Michael Ngadeu-Ngadjui, Núrio Fortuna, Andreas Hanche-Olsen, Milad Mohammadi, Alessio Castro-Montes (77' Sulayman Marreh), Sven Kums (69' Tim Kleindienst), Roman Bezus (56' Vadis Odjidja-Ofoe), Niklas Dorsch (77' Jordan Botaka), Roman Yaremchuk (69' Anderson Niangbo), Osman Bukari. Coach: Wim De Decker.
1899 Hoffenheim: Oliver Baumann, Kevin Vogt, Kevin Akpoguma, Stefan Posch (82' Munas Dabour), Sebastian Rudy (67' Mijat Gacinovic), Florian Grillitsch (77' Christoph Baumgartner), Diadié Samassekou, Ryan Sessegnon, Ishak Belfodil (77' Klauss), Ihlas Bebou (67' Sargis Adamyan), Robert Skov. Coach: Sebastian Hoeneß.
Goals: 35' Ishak Belfodil 0-1 (p), 52' Florian Grillitsch 0-2, 73' Mijat Gacinovic 0-3, 90+3' Tim Kleindienst 1-3, 90+4' Munas Dabour 1-4.
Referee: Sandro Schärer (SUI)

Roman Yaremchuk missed a penalty kick (14').

29.10.20   Stadion Rajko Mitic, Beograd: Crvena Zvezda Beograd – Slovan Liberec 5-1 (2-1)
Crvena Zvezda Beograd: Milan Borjan, Nemanja Milunovic, Milan Rodic (75' Marko Gobeljic), Milos Degenek, Milan Gajic, Aleksandar Katai (88' Aleksa Vukanovic), Sékou Sanogo, Mirko Ivanic (83' Zeljko Gavric), Veljko Nikolic, Diego Falcinelli (88' Radovan Pankov), El Fardou Ben Nabouhane (83' Njegos Petrovic). Coach: Dejan Stankovic.
Slovan Liberec: Filip Nguyen, Jan Mikula, Martin Koscelník, Matej Chalus, Mohamed Tijani, Jhon Mosquera (90' Michal Fukala), Jakub Hromada (86' Jan Sulc), Michal Sadílek, Jan Matousek (75' Michal Beran), Kamso Mara (90+1' Jakub Barac), Abdulla Yusuf Helal (75' Michael Rabusic). Coach: Pavel Hoftych.
Goals: 7', 22' El Fardou Ben Nabouhane 1-0, 2-0, 41' Jan Matousek 2-1, 50' Milan Gajic 3-1, 67' Aleksandar Katai 4-1, 69' Diego Falcinelli 5-1.
Referee: Fábio Veríssimo (POR)

05.11.20   Stadion Rajko Mitic, Beograd: Crvena Zvezda Beograd – KAA Gent 2-1 (1-1)
Crvena Zvezda Beograd: Milan Borjan, Nemanja Milunovic, Milos Degenek, Marko Gobeljic, Milan Gajic, Aleksandar Katai (90+1' Veljko Nikolic), Sékou Sanogo, Guélor Kanga (83' Radovan Pankov), Mirko Ivanic (64' Njegos Petrovic), Diego Falcinelli, El Fardou Ben Nabouhane (90+1' Srdjan Spiridonovic). Coach: Dejan Stankovic.
KAA Gent: Colin Coosemans, Jordan Botaka (63' Anderson Niangbo), Andreas Hanche-Olsen, Milad Mohammadi, Alessio Castro-Montes, Vadis Odjidja-Ofoe (80' Tim Kleindienst), Sulayman Marreh, Niklas Dorsch, Elisha Owusu (75' Sven Kums), Roman Yaremchuk, Osman Bukari. Coach: Wim De Decker.
Goals: 12' Guélor Kanga 1-0, 31' Vadis Odjidja-Ofoe 1-1, 59' Aleksandar Katai 2-1.
Referee: Michael Fabbri (ITA)

05.11.20   PreZero Arena, Sinsheim: 1899 Hoffenheim – Slovan Liberec 5-0 (2-0)
1899 Hoffenheim: Oliver Baumann, Kevin Vogt (46' Florian Grillitsch), Kevin Akpoguma (60' Håvard Nordtveit), Melayro Bogarde, Sebastian Rudy (46' Diadié Samassekou), Mijat Gacinovic, Christoph Baumgartner (73' Ishak Belfodil), Munas Dabour (61' Sargis Adamyan), Ihlas Bebou, Robert Skov, Klauss. Coach: Sebastian Hoeneß.
Slovan Liberec: Lukás Hasalík, Taras Kacharaba, Jan Mikula, Martin Koscelník, Daniel Kosek (90+1' Matyás Kazda), Marios Pourzitidis, David Cancola (90+1' Miroslav Dvorák), Jakub Hromada (77' Kristian Michal), Ales Nesický (90+1' Radim Cernický), Kamso Mara, Imad Rondic (67' Lukás Csáno). Coach: Pavel Hoftych.
Goals: 22', 29' Munas Dabour 1-0, 2-0, 59' Florian Grillitsch 3-0, 71', 76' Sargis Adamyan 4-0, 5-0.
Referee: Sergei Karasev (RUS)

26.11.20   GHELAMCO-arena, Gent: KAA Gent – Crvena Zvezda Beograd 0-2 (0-1)
KAA Gent: Sinan Bolat, Jordan Botaka (46' Alessio Castro-Montes), Michael Ngadeu-Ngadjui, Núrio Fortuna, Andreas Hanche-Olsen, Milad Mohammadi, Sven Kums (84' Wouter George), Roman Bezus, Niklas Dorsch, Elisha Owusu (58' Vadis Odjidja-Ofoe), Osman Bukari (66' Anderson Niangbo). Coach: Wim De Decker.
Crvena Zvezda Beograd: Milan Borjan, Nemanja Milunovic, Milos Degenek, Milan Gajic, Radovan Pankov, Mirko Ivanic, Njegos Petrovic (72' Strahinja Erakovic), Veljko Nikolic, Diego Falcinelli (87' Richmond Boakye), El Fardou Ben Nabouhane (72' Srdjan Spiridonovic), Aleksa Vukanovic (87' Andrija Radulovic). Coach: Dejan Stankovic.
Goals: 1' Njegos Petrovic 0-1, 58' Nemanja Milunovic 0-1.
Referee: Filip Glova (SVK)

26.11.20   Stadion u Nisy, Liberec: Slovan Liberec – 1899 Hoffenheim 0-2 (0-0)
Slovan Liberec: Filip Nguyen, Jakub Jugas, Taras Kacharaba, Jan Mikula, Martin Koscelník, Matej Chalus (83' Imad Rondic), Jhon Mosquera, Jakub Pesek (83' Jan Matousek), Michal Sadílek, Kamso Mara (89' Michal Beran), Abdulla Yusuf Helal (70' Michael Rabusic). Coach: Pavel Hoftych.
1899 Hoffenheim: Oliver Baumann, Håvard Nordtveit, Kasim Adams Nuhu, Melayro Bogarde, Sebastian Rudy (61' Ihlas Bebou), Florian Grillitsch (78' Diadié Samassekou), Mijat Gacinovic, Christoph Baumgartner (78' Dennis Geiger), Ryan Sessegnon (46' Robert Skov), Klauss, Maximilian Beier (60' Andrej Kramaric). Coach: Sebastian Hoeneß.
Goals: 77' Christoph Baumgartner 0-1, 89' Andrej Kramaric 0-2 (p).
Referee: Jérôme Brisard (FRA)

03.12.20   GHELAMCO-arena, Gent: KAA Gent – Slovan Liberec 1-2 (0-1)
KAA Gent: Sinan Bolat, Dino Arslanagic, Núrio Fortuna, Andreas Hanche-Olsen, Milad Mohammadi, Alessio Castro-Montes (56' Tim Kleindienst), Sven Kums, Niklas Dorsch, Elisha Owusu (62' Roman Bezus), Roman Yaremchuk, Osman Bukari. Coach: Wim De Decker.
Slovan Liberec: Filip Nguyen, Jakub Jugas, Taras Kacharaba, Jan Mikula, Martin Koscelník, Jhon Mosquera, Jakub Pesek (75' Jan Matousek), Michal Sadílek, Kamso Mara, Michal Beran (68' Jakub Hromada), Abdulla Yusuf Helal (70' Michael Rabusic). Coach: Pavel Hoftych.
Goals: 32' Kamso Mara 0-1, 55' Taras Kacharaba 0-2, 59' Roman Yaremchuk 1-2.
Referee: Kateryna Monzul (UKR)

03.12.20   Stadion Rajko Mitic, Beograd: Crvena Zvezda Beograd – 1899 Hoffenheim 0-0
Crvena Zvezda Beograd: Milan Borjan, Nemanja Milunovic, Milos Degenek, Milan Gajic, Radovan Pankov, Srdjan Spiridonovic (46' Aleksa Vukanovic), Sékou Sanogo, Guélor Kanga (81' Veljko Nikolic), Njegos Petrovic, Diego Falcinelli (89' Richmond Boakye), El Fardou Ben Nabouhane (81' Strahinja Erakovic). Coach: Dejan Stankovic.
1899 Hoffenheim: Oliver Baumann, Håvard Nordtveit, Kevin Vogt, Melayro Bogarde, Sebastian Rudy (72' Kasim Adams Nuhu), Mijat Gacinovic (72' Christoph Baumgartner), Dennis Geiger (58' Florian Grillitsch), Marco John, Munas Dabour (46' Andrej Kramaric), Robert Skov (89' Ryan Sessegnon), Klauss. Coach: Sebastian Hoeneß.
Referee: Robert Madden (SCO)

10.12.20 PreZero Arena, Sinsheim: 1899 Hoffenheim – KAA Gent 4-1 (2-0)
1899 Hoffenheim: Philipp Pentke, Kevin Akpoguma, Stefan Posch (46' Håvard Nordtveit), Kasim Adams Nuhu, Mijat Gacinovic, Dennis Geiger (75' Alfons Amade), Marco John, Munas Dabour, Robert Skov (61' Ishak Belfodil), Klauss (62' Andrej Kramaric), Maximilian Beier (75' Christoph Baumgartner). Coach: Sebastian Hoeneß.
KAA Gent: Dany Roef, Igor Plastun, Dino Arslanagic, Michel Ngadeu-Ngadjui, Milad Mohammadi (46' Núrio Fortuna), Alessio Castro-Montes (76' Jordan Botaka), Roman Bezus, Niklas Dorsch (56' Sven Kums), Elisha Owusu (56' Vadis Odjidja-Ofoe), Tim Kleindienst, Osman Bukari (56' Roman Yaremchuk). Coach: Hein Vanhaezebrouck.
Goals: 21' Maximilian Beier 1-0, 26' Robert Skov 2-0, 49' Maximilian Beier 3-0, 64' Andrej Kramaric 4-0, 81' Núrio Fortuna 4-1.
Referee: Anastasios Papapetrou (GRE)

10.12.20 Stadion u Nisy, Liberec: Slovan Liberec – Crvena Zvezda Beograd 0-0
Slovan Liberec: Milan Knobloch, Jakub Jugas, Taras Kacharaba, Jan Mikula, Martin Koscelník, Jhon Mosquera (89' Michal Fukala), Jakub Pesek (68' Jan Matousek), Michal Sadílek, Kamso Mara, Michal Beran (68' Jakub Hromada), Abdulla Yusuf Helal (75' Michael Rabusic). Coach: Pavel Hoftych.
Crvena Zvezda Beograd: Milan Borjan, Nemanja Milunovic, Milan Rodic (71' Marko Gobeljic), Milos Degenek (80' Radovan Pankov), Milan Gajic, Sékou Sanogo, Guélor Kanga (53' Veljko Nikolic), Mirko Ivanic (71' Richmond Boakye), Njegos Petrovic, Diego Falcinelli, El Fardou Ben Nabouhane (81' Strahinja Erakovic). Coach: Dejan Stankovic.
Referee: Mattias Gestranius (FIN)

KNOCKOUT PHASE

ROUND OF 32

Manchester United, Club Brugge KV, Shakhtar Donetsk, AFC Ajax, FK Krasnodar, Red Bull Salzburg, Dynamo Kyiv and Olympiakos Piraeus entered the UEFA Europa League as the group stage third-placed teams of the UEFA Champions League.

18.02.21 NSK Olimpijs'kyj Stadium, Kyiv: Dynamo Kyiv – Club Brugge KV 1-1 (0-0)
Dynamo Kyiv: Georgiy Bushchan, Tomasz Kedziora (81' Oleksandr Karavayev), Denys Popov, Vitali Mykolenko, Illia Zabarnyi, Sergiy Sydorchuk, Vitaliy Buyalskyi, Carlos de Pena (72' Gerson Rodrigues), Viktor Tsygankov, Mykola Shaparenko (73' Volodymyr Shepelyev), Artem Besedin (81' Vladyslav Supryaga). Coach: Mircea Lucescu.
Club Brugge KV: Simon Mignolet, Clinton Mata, Brandon Mechele, Federico Ricca, Odilon Kossounou, Ruud Vormer, Nabil Dirar (70' Ignace Van Der Brempt), Éder Balanta, Charles De Ketelaere, Bas Dost (90+2' Maxim De Cuyper), David Okereke (69' Youssouph Badji). Coach: Philippe Clement.
Goals: 62' Vitaliy Buyalskyi 1-0, 67' Brandon Mechele 1-1.
Referee: Mattias Gestranius (FIN)   Attendance: 3,284.

18.02.21   Puskás Aréna, Budapest (HUN): Wolfsberger AC – Tottenham Hotspur 1-4 (0-3)
Wolfsberger AC: Alexander Kofler, Michael Novak (81' Mario Pavelic), Jonathan Scherzer, Dominik Baumgartner, Luka Lochoshvili, Michael Liendl, Christopher Wernitznig, Sven Sprangler (65' Guram Giorbelidze), Matthäus Taferner (46' Gustav Henriksson), Dario Vizinger (46' Kai Stratznig), Dejan Joveljic (65' Cheikhou Dieng).
Coach: Ferdinand Feldhofer.
Tottenham Hotspur: Hugo Lloris, Toby Alderweireld, Matt Doherty, Ben Davies, Moussa Sissoko (78' Pierre-Emile Højbjerg), Lucas Moura (64' Steven Bergwijn), Dele Alli (78' Tanguy NDombèlé), Eric Dier, Harry Winks, Gareth Bale (64' Érik Lamela), Son Heung-Min (46' Carlos Vinícius). Coach: José Mourinho.
Goals: 13' Son Heung-Min 0-1, 28' Gareth Bale 0-2, 34' Lucas Moura 0-3, 55' Michael Liendl 1-3 (p), 88' Calos Vinícius 1-4.
Referee: Ali Palabiyik (TUR)

The match, originally to be played at Wörthersee Stadion, Klagenfurt am Wörthersee, instead of the Wolfsberger AC regular stadium Lavanttal-Arena, Wolfsberg, was moved to Puskás Aréna, Budapest (Hungary) due to travel restrictions related to the COVID-19 pandemic.

18.02.21   Allianz Stadium, Torino (ITA): Real Sociedad – Manchester United 0-4 (0-1)
Real Sociedad: Álex Remiro, Nacho Monreal, Joseba Zaldúa (73' Andoni Gorosabel), Robin Le Normand, David Silva, Illarramendi (73' Guevara), Adnan Januzaj (79' Portu), Mikel Merino, Zubeldía, Mikel Oyarzabal (86' Jon Bautista), Alexander Isak (80' Ander Barrenetxea). Coach: Imanol Alguacil.
Manchester United: Dean Henderson, Alex Telles, Harry Maguire, Eric Bailly, Aaron Wan-Bissaka, Fred, Bruno Fernandes (83' Mata), Daniel James, Scott McTominay (60' Nemanja Matic), Marcus Rashford (68' Anthony Martial), Mason Greenwood (83' Amad Diallo).
Coach: Ole Gunnar Solskjær.
Goals: 27', 57' Bruno Fernandes 0-1, 0-2, 64' Marcus Rashford 0-3, 90' Daniel James 0-4.
Referee: Sandro Schärer (SUI)

The match, originally to be played at Anoeta Stadium, San Sebastián, was moved to Allianz Stadium, Torino (Italy), due to travel restrictions related to the COVID-19 pandemic.

18.02.21   Stadion Rajko Mitic, Beograd: Crvena Zvezda Beograd – AC Milan 2-2 (0-1)
Crvena Zvezda Beograd: Milan Borjan, Nemanja Milunovic, Milan Rodic, Milos Degenek, Marko Gobeljic (74' Milan Gajic), Radovan Pankov, Guélor Kanga, Mirko Ivanic (80' Axel Bakayoko), Njegos Petrovic (81' Sékou Sanogo), Diego Falcinelli (80' Milan Pavkov), Fardou Ben Nabouhane (62' Filippo Falco). Coach: Dejan Stankovic.
AC Milan: Gianluigi Donnarumma, Alessio Romagnoli, Fikayo Tomori, Theo Hernández (78' Diogo Dalot), Pierre Kalulu, Soualiho Meïté, Samu Castillejo, Rade Krunic, Ismaël Bennacer (39' Sandro Tonali), Mario Mandzukic (82' Hakan Çalhanoglu), Ante Rebic (46' Rafael Leão). Coach: Stefano Pioli.
Goals: 42' Radovan Pankov 0-1 (og), 52' Guélor Kanga 1-1 (p), 61' Theo Hernández 1-2 (p), 90+3' Milan Pavkov 2-2.
Referee: Anastasios Sidiropoulos (GRE)
Sent off: 77' Milan Rodic.

18.02.21   Sinobo Stadium, Prague: Slavia Praha – Leicester City 0-0
Slavia Praha: Ondrej Kolár, Ondrej Kúdela, Jan Boril, Tomás Holes (30' Jakub Hromada), Alexander Bah, David Zima, Nicolae Stanciu (73' Ibrahim Traoré), Lukás Provod (90+1' Ondrej Lingr), Peter Olayinka, Jan Kuchta (73' Lukás Masopust), Abdallah Sima.
Coach: Jindrich Trpisovský.
Leicester City: Kasper Schmeichel, Jonny Evans, Daniel Amartey, Çaglar Söyüncü, Luke Thomas, Marc Albrighton (64' Cengiz Ünder), Youri Tielemans, Wilfred Ndidi, James Maddison (76' Hamza Choudhury), Harvey Barnes, Jamie Vardy (64' Kelechi Iheanacho).
Coach: Brendan Rodgers.
Referee: Marco Guida (ITA)   Attendance: 600.

18.02.21   Estádio Municipal de Braga, Braga: Sporting Braga – AS Roma 0-2 (0-1)
Sporting Braga: Matheus Magalhães, Raúl Silva, Ricardo Esgaio, Nuno Sequeira, Vítor Tormena, Nicolás Gaitán (57' Zé Carlos), Fransérgio (69' André Horta), Ali Al Musrati, Andraz Sporar (62' Abel Ruiz), Ricardo Horta (62' Lucas Piazón), Galeno (70' Cristian Borja).
Coach: Carlos Carvalhal.
AS Roma: Pau López, Leonardo Spinazzola, Rick Karsdorp, Gianluca Mancini, Ibañez (53' Gonzalo Villar), Henrikh Mkhitaryan, Jordan Veretout, Bryan Cristante (7' Bruno Peres), Amadou Diawara, Edin Dzeko (70' Borja Mayoral), Pedro (71' Stephan El Shaarawy).
Coach: Paulo Fonseca.
Goals: 5' Edin Dzeko 0-1, 86' Borja Mayoral 0-2.
Referee: István Kovács (ROM)
Sent off: 54' Ricardo Esgaio.

18.02.21   Stadion FK Krasnodar, Krasnodar: FK Krasnodar – Dinamo Zagreb 2-3 (1-1)
FK Krasnodar: Evgeniy Gorodov, Igor Smolnikov, Aleksandr Martynovich, Evgeniy Chernov (80' Aleksey Ionov), Rémy Cabella, Victor Claesson, Tonny Vilhena, Kristoffer Olsson (62' Yuri Gazinskiy), Kaio Pantaleão, Marcus Berg, Magomed Suleymanov (46' Wanderson).
Coach: Murad Musaev.
Dinamo Zagreb: Dominik Livakovic, Kévin Théophile-Catherine, Stefan Ristovski, Rasmus Lauritsen, Josko Gvardiol, Arijan Ademi, Kristijan Jakic, Luka Ivanusec (78' Bartol Franjic), Lovro Majer (64' Iyayi Atiemwen), Mislav Orsic (90+4' Josip Misic), Bruno Petkovic.
Coach: Zoran Mamic.
Goals: 15' Bruno Petkovic 0-1, 28' Marcus Berg 1-1, 54' Bruno Petkovic 1-2, 69' Victor Claesson 2-2, 75' Iyayi Atiemwen 1-2.
Referee: Bartosz Frankowski (POL)   Attendance: 9,897.

18.02.21   Stadion Wankdorf, Bern: BSC Young Boys – Bayer Leverkusen 4-3 (3-0)
BSC Young Boys: David von Ballmoos, Fabian Lustenberger, Jordan Lefort (74' Miralem Sulejmani), Cédric Zesiger, Silvan Hefti, Nicolas Moumi Ngamaleu (58' Ulisses Garcia), Christian Fassnacht (80' Gianluca Gaudino), Sandro Lauper (81' Fabian Rieder), Michel Aebischer, Theoson Siebatcheu, Meschack Elia (74' Felix Mambimbi).
Coach: Gerardo Seoane.
Bayer Leverkusen: Niklas Lomb, Aleksandar Dragovic, Jonathan Tah, Daley Sinkgraven, Jeremie Frimpong, Kerem Demirbay, Nadiem Amiri (46' Edmond Tapsoba), Demarai Gray, Florian Wirtz, Patrik Schick, Leon Bailey (65' Moussa Diaby). Coach: Peter Bosz.
Goals: 3' Christian Fassnacht 1-0, 19' Theoson Siebatcheu 2-0, 44' Meschack Elia 3-0, 49', 52' Patrik Schick 3-1, 3-2, 68' Moussa Diaby 3-3, 89' Theoson Siebatcheu 4-3.
Referee: Antonio Mateu Lahoz (ESP)

18.02.21   Stadio Georgios Karaiskáki, Piraeus:
Olympiakos Piraeus – PSV Eindhoven 4-2 (3-2)
Olympiakos Piraeus: José Sá, Sokratis Papastathopoulos, Kenny Lala (80' Athanasios Androutsos), Oleg Reabciuk, Ousseynou Ba, Mathieu Valbuena (68' Georgios Masouras), Yann M'Vila (80' Marios Vrousai), Andreas Bouchalakis, Mohamed Camara, Youssef El-Arabi (75' Kostas Fortounis), Bruma (80' Koka). Coach: Pedro Martins.
PSV Eindhoven: Yvon Mvogo, Philipp Max, Olivier Boscagli (38' Timo Baumgartl), Denzel Dumfries, Jordan Teze, Mario Götze (70' Mauro Júnior), Ryan Thomas (85' Marco van Ginkel), Ibrahim Sangaré (71' Yorbe Vertessen), Pablo Rosario, Eran Zahavi (85' Érick Gutiérrez), Donyell Malen. Coach: Roger Schmidt.
Goals: 9' Andreas Bouchalakis 1-0, 14' Eran Zahavi 1-1, 37' Yann M'Vila 2-1, 39' Eran Zahavi 2-2, 45+2' Youssef El-Arabi 3-2, 83' Georgios Masouras 4-2.
Referee: Andreas Ekberg (SWE)

18.02.21   Stadio Olimpico, Roma (ITA): SL Benfica – Arsenal FC 1-1 (0-0)
SL Benfica: Helton Leite, Jan Vertonghen, Nicolás Otamendi, Álex Grimaldo, Lucas Veríssimo (85' Chiquinho), Adel Taarabt (77' Gabriel), Pizzi (64' Éverton), Julian Weigl, Diogo Gonçalves, Luca Waldschmidt (46' Rafa Silva), Darwin Núñez (64' Haris Seferovic). Coach: Jorge Jesus.
Arsenal FC: Bernd Leno, David Luiz, Cédric Soares (64' Kieran Tierney), Héctor Bellerín, Gabriel Magalhães, Granit Xhaka, Martin Ødegaard (90' Willian), Dani Ceballos (90' Mohamed Elneny), Emile Smith-Rowe (77' Gabriel Martinelli), Bukayo Saka, Pierre-Emerick Aubameyang (77' Nicolas Pépé). Coach: Mikel Arteta.
Goals: 55' Pizzi 1-0 (p), 57' Bukayo Saka 1-1.
Referee: Cüneyt Çakir (TUR)

The match, originally to be played at Estádio da Luz, Lisboa, was moved to Stadio Olimpico, Roma (Italy), due to travel restrictions related to the COVID-19 pandemic.

18.02.21   Bosuilstadion, Antwerp: Royal Antwerp FC – Glasgow Rangers FC 3-4 (2-1)
Royal Antwerp FC: Alireza Beiranvand (77' Ortwin De Wolf), Ritchie De Laet, Maxime Le Marchand, Jordan Lukaku, Buta, Abdoulaye Seck, Lior Refaelov (90+2' Nana Ampomah), Pieter Gerkens (90+2' Koji Miyoshi), Frank Boya (69' Birger Verstraete), Martin Hongla Yma (90+1' Jérémy Gelin), Felipe Avenatti. Coach: Frank Vercauteren.
Glasgow Rangers FC: Allan McGregor, James Tavernier (24' Leon Balogun), Connor Goldson, Filip Helander, Borna Barisic, Steven Davis, Scott Arfield (74' Ryan Jack), Glen Kamara (74' Ianis Hagi), Joe Ayodele-Aribo, Kemar Roofe (45+5' Ryan Kent), Alfredo Morelos. Coach: Steven Gerrard.
Goals: 39' Joe Ayodele-Aribo 0-1, 45' Felipe Avenatti 1-1, 45+8' Lior Refaelov 2-1 (p), 59' Borna Barisic 2-2 (p), 67' Martin Hongla Yma 3-2, 83' Ryan Kent 3-3, 90' Borna Barisic 3-4 (p).
Referee: Georgi Kabakov (BUL)
Sent off: 88' Abdoulaye Seck.

18.02.21   Red Bull Arena, Wals-Siezenheim: Red Bull Salzburg – Villarreal CF 0-2 (0-1)
Red Bull Salzburg: Cican Stankovic, Andreas Ulmer, Albert Vallçi, Rasmus Kristensen, Oumar Solet, Zlatko Junuzovic (74' Antoine Bernède), Enock Mwepu, Brenden Aaronson (61' Karim Adeyemi), Luka Sucic (61' Noah Okafor), Mërgim Berisha, Patson Daka.
Coach: Jesse Marsch.
Villarreal CF: Gerónimo Rulli, Raúl Albiol, Pervis Estupiñán, Pau Torres, Étienne Capoue (74' Jaume Costa), Dani Parejo, Moi Gómez (60' Pedraza), Manu Trigueros, Rubén Peña (46' Juan Foyth), Paco Alcácer (60' Fer Niño), Gerard Moreno (83' Yeremi Pino). Coach: Unai Emery.
Goals: 41' Paco Alcácer 0-1, 71' Fer Niño 0-2.
Referee: Andris Treimanis (LAT)

Paco Alcácer missed a penalty kick (29').

18.02.21   Estadio de la Cerámica, Villarreal (ESP): Molde FK – 1899 Hoffenheim 3-3 (1-3)
Molde FK: Andreas Linde, Kristoffer Haugen, Martin Bjørnbak, Stian Gregersen, Marcus Pedersen, Magnus Wolff Eikrem, Eirik Andersen (86' Tobias Christensen), Fredrik Aursnes, Martin Ellingsen, Björn Sigurdarson (64' David Fofana), Mathis Bolly (64' Erling Knudtzon).
Coach: Erling Moe.
1899 Hoffenheim: Oliver Baumann, Kevin Vogt, Kasim Adams Nuhu (83' Melayro Bogarde), Chris Richards, Sebastian Rudy, Mijat Gacinovic (26' Pavel Kaderábek), Diadié Samassékou (62' Florian Grillitsch), Christoph Baumgartner, Marco John, Munas Dabour (83' Georginio Rutter), Ihlas Bebou (62' Sargis Adamyan). Coach: Sebastian Hoeneß.
Goals: 8', 28' Munas Dabour 0-1, 0-2, 41' Martin Ellingsen 1-2, 45+3' Christoph Baumgartner 1-3, 70' Eirik Andersen 2-3, 74' David Fofana 3-3.
Referee: Stéphanie Frappart (FRA)

Munas Dabour missed a penalty kick (63').

The match, originally to be played at Åker Stadion, Molde, was moved to Estadio de la Cerámica, Villarreal (Spain), due to Norwegian quarantine restrictions in place because of the COVID-19 pandemic.

18.02.21   Estadio Nuevo Los Cármenes, Granada: Granada CF – SSC Napoli 2-0 (2-0)
Granada CF: Rui Silva, Dimitri Foulquier, Jesús Vallejo (23' Germán Sánchez), Domingos Duarte, Carlos Neva (78' Víctor Díaz), Montoro, Maxime Gonalons (78' Yan Eteki), Kenedy (70' Alberto Soro), Yangel Herrera, Jorge Molina, Darwin Machís (70' Antonio Puertas).
Coach: Diego Martínez.
SSC Napoli: Alex Meret, Nikola Maksimovic, Mário Rui, Giovanni Di Lorenzo, Amir Rrahmani, Stanislav Lobotka (64' Tiemoué Bakayoko), Fabián Ruiz, Eljif Elmas, Lorenzo Insigne, Matteo Politano (46' Piotr Zielinski), Victor Osimhen. Coach: Gennaro Gattuso.
Goals: 19' Yangel Herrera 1-0, 21' Kenedy 2-0.
Referee: Sergei Karasev (RUS)

18.02.21   Bloomfield Stadium, Tel Aviv: Maccabi Tel Aviv – Shakhtar Donetsk 0-2 (0-1)
Maccabi Tel Aviv: Daniel Tenenbaum, Eitan Tibi, Luis Hernández, Saborit, Geraldes, Avi Rikan (63' Eyal Golasa), Dor Peretz, Dan Glazer, Dan Biton (46' Matan Hozez), Tal Ben Haim (63' Nick Blackman), Aleksandar Pesic (84' Eduardo Guerrero).
Coach: Patrick van Leeuwen.
Shakhtar Donetsk: Anatolii Trubin, Sergiy Kryvtsov, Mykola Matvienko, Dodô, Vitão, Marlos (77' Maycon), Taras Stepanenko, Taison (77' Yevhen Konoplyanka), Alan Patrick (88' Marcos Antônio), Manor Solomon (73' Mateus Martins Tetê), Júnior Moraes (89' Fernando).
Coach: Luís Castro.
Goals: 31' Alan Patrick 0-1, 90+3' Mateus Martins Tetê 0-2.
Referee: François Letexier (FRA)

18.02.21   Stade Pierre-Mauroy, Villeneuve-d'Ascq: Lille Olympique – AFC Ajax 1-2 (0-0)
Lille Olympique: Mike Maignan, José Fonte, Reinildo (82' Domagoj Bradaric), Zeki Çelik, Sven Botman, Renato Sanches, Boubakary Soumaré, Yusuf Yazici (62' Luiz Araujo), Jonathan Bamba, Timothy Weah, Jonathan David (78' Jonathan Ikoné). Coach: Christophe Galtier.
AFC Ajax: Maarten Stekelenburg, Daley Blind, Nicolás Tagliafico, Edson Álvarez, Lisandro Martínez, Jurriën Timber, Devyne Rensch (82' Perr Schuurs), Davy Klaassen, Dusan Tadic, David Neres (74' Brian Brobbey), Antony (82' Oussama Idrissi). Coach: Erik ten Hag.
Goals: 72' Timothy Weah 1-0, 87' Dusan Tadic 1-1 (p), 89' Brian Brobbey 1-2.
Referee: Ivan Kruzliak (SVK)

24.02.21   Tottenham Hotspur Stadium, London:
             Tottenham Hotspur – Wolfsberger AC 4-0 (1-0)
Tottenham Hotspur: Joe Hart, Toby Alderweireld, Matt Doherty (74' Marcel Lavinier), Ben Davies, Moussa Sissoko (81' Nile John), Érik Lamela (68' Gareth Bale), Dele Alli (81' Dane Scarlett), Eric Dier, Harry Winks, Steven Bergwijn (69' Lucas Moura), Carlos Vinícius.
Coach: José Mourinho.
Wolfsberger AC: Manuel Kuttin, Michael Novak (46' Mario Pavelic), Jonathan Scherzer (65' Stefan Peric), Dominik Baumgartner (65' Guram Giorbelidze), Luka Lochoshvili, Gustav Henriksson, Michael Liendl, Christopher Wernitznig, Kai Stratznig (79' Nemanja Rnic), Cheikhou Dieng, Dario Vizinger (46' Dejan Joveljic). Coach: Ferdinand Feldhofer.
Goals: 11' Dele Alli 1-0, 50' Carlos Vinícius 2-0, 73' Gareth Bale 3-0, 83' Carlos Vinícius 4-0
Referee: Matej Jug (SVN)

25.02.21   Stadio Georgios Karaiskáki, Piraeus (GRE): Arsenal FC – SL Benfica 3-2 (1-1)
Arsenal FC: Bernd Leno, David Luiz, Héctor Bellerín (78' Alexandre Lacazette), Kieran Tierney, Gabriel Magalhães, Granit Xhaka, Martin Ødegaard (90' Mohamed Elneny), Dani Ceballos (63' Thomas Partey), Emile Smith-Rowe (63' Willian), Bukayo Saka (90' Calum Chambers), Pierre-Emerick Aubameyang. Coach: Mikel Arteta.
SL Benfica: Helton Leite, Jan Vertonghen, Nicolás Otamendi, Álex Grimaldo (85' Nuno Tavares), Lucas Veríssimo, Adel Taarabt (58' Gabriel), Pizzi (58' Éverton), Rafa Silva, Julian Weigl (90' Luca Waldschmidt), Diogo Gonçalves, Haris Seferovic (57' Darwin Núñez).
Coach: Jorge Jesus.
Goals: 21' Pierre-Emerick Aubameyang 1-0, 43' Diogo Gonçalves 1-1, 61' Rafa Silva 1-2, 67' Kieran Tierney 2-2, 87' Pierre-Emerick Aubameyang 3-2.
Referee: Björn Kuipers (HOL)

The match, originally to be played at Emirates Stadium, London, was moved to Stadio Georgios Karaiskáki, Piraeus (Greece), due to travel restrictions related to the COVID-19 pandemic.

25.02.21   Ibrox Stadium, Glasgow: Glasgow Rangers FC – Royal Antwerp FC 5-2 (1-1)
Glasgow Rangers FC: Allan McGregor, Leon Balogun (46' Nathan Patterson), Connor Goldson, Filip Helander, Borna Barisic, Steven Davis (82' Bongani Zungu), Glen Kamara, Joe Ayodele-Aribo, Ianis Hagi (71' Scott Arfield), Alfredo Morelos (85' Cedric Itten), Ryan Kent (82' Scott Wright). Coach: Steven Gerrard.
Royal Antwerp FC: Ortwin De Wolf, Ritchie De Laet, Maxime Le Marchand, Jordan Lukaku (75' Nana Ampomah), Buta, Jérémy Gelin (46' Frank Boya), Lior Refaelov, Pieter Gerkens (75' Felipe Avenatti), Birger Verstraete, Martin Hongla Yma (82' Koji Miyoshi), Didier Lamkel Zé. Coach: Frank Vercauteren.
Goals: 9' Alfredo Morelos 1-0, 32' Lior Refaelov 1-1, 46' Nathan Patterson 2-1, 55' Ryan Kent 3-1, 57' Didier Lamkel Zé 3-2, 79' Borna Barisic 4-2 (p), 90+2' Cedric Itten 5-2 (p).
Referee: Pawel Raczkowski (POL)

25.02.21   Estadio de la Cerámica, Villarreal: Villarreal CF – Red Bull Salzburg 2-1 (1-1)
Villarreal CF: Gerónimo Rulli, Raúl Albiol, Jaume Costa (82' Juan Foyth), Pervis Estupiñán, Pau Torres, Étienne Capoue, Dani Parejo (90' Álex Baena), Manu Trigueros, Pedraza (66' Moi Gómez), Paco Alcácer (66' Samuel Chukwueze), Gerard Moreno (90' Fer Niño). Coach: Unai Emery.
Red Bull Salzburg: Cican Stankovic, Andreas Ulmer, André Ramalho, Albert Vallçi (46' Max Wöber), Rasmus Kristensen (90+2' Oumar Solet), Zlatko Junuzovic, Antoine Bernède (60' Karim Adeyemi), Enock Mwepu, Brenden Aaronson (60' Luka Sucic), Mërgim Berisha, Patson Daka (90+2' Antonín Svoboda). Coach: Jesse Marsch.
Goals: 17' Mërgim Berisha 0-1, 40', 89' Gerard Moreno 1-1, 2-1 (p).
Referee: Felix Zwayer (GER)

25.02.21   PreZero Arena, Sinsheim: 1899 Hoffenheim – Molde FK 0-2 (0-1)
1899 Hoffenheim: Oliver Baumann, Kevin Vogt, Pavel Kaderábek (70' Sargis Adamyan), Chris Richards, Sebastian Rudy, Florian Grillitsch, Diadié Samassékou (83' Georginio Rutter), Christoph Baumgartner (56' Andrej Kramaric), Marco John (70' Ryan Sessegnon), Munas Dabour, Ihlas Bebou. Coach: Sebastian Hoeneß.
Molde FK: Andreas Linde, Kristoffer Haugen, Birk Risa, Sheriff Sinyan, Marcus Pedersen, Magnus Wolff Eikrem, Eirik Andersen, Fredrik Aursnes, Martin Ellingsen, Björn Sigurdarson (63' Mathis Bolly), Erling Knudtzon (79' Eirik Hestad). Coach: Erling Moe.
Goals: 19', 90+4' Eirik Andersen 0-1, 0-2.
Referee: Aleksey Kulbakov (BLS)

25.02.21   Stadio Diego Armando Maradona, Napoli: SSC Napoli – Granada CF 2-1 (1-1)
SSC Napoli: Alex Meret, Nikola Maksimovic (46' Faouzi Ghoulam), Kalidou Koulibaly, Giovanni Di Lorenzo, Amir Rrahmani, Piotr Zielinski, Tiemoué Bakayoko, Fabián Ruiz, Eljif Elmas (60' Dries Mertens), Lorenzo Insigne, Matteo Politano. Coach: Gennaro Gattuso.
Granada CF: Rui Silva, Germán Sánchez (56' Yangel Herrera), Dimitri Foulquier, Domingos Duarte, Carlos Neva (46' Nehuén Pérez), Montoro (83' Jesús Vallejo), Maxime Gonalons (45+2' Víctor Díaz), Antonio Puertas, Kenedy, Yan Eteki, Jorge Molina (84' Soldado). Coach: Diego Martínez.
Goals: 3' Piotr Zielinksi 1-0, 25' Montoro 1-1, 59' Fabián Ruiz 2-1.
Referee: Daniel Siebert (GER)

25.02.21   NSK Olimpijs'kyj Stadium, Kyiv: Shakhtar Donetsk – Maccabi Tel Aviv 1-0 (0-0)
Shakhtar Donetsk: Anatolii Trubin, Sergiy Kryvtsov, Mykola Matvienko, Dodô, Vitão (78' Viktor Kornienko), Marlos (46' Marcos Antônio), Taison (78' Yevhen Konoplyanka), Alan Patrick, Manor Solomon (46' Mateus Martins Tetê), Maycon, Júnior Moraes (78' Fernando). Coach: Luís Castro.
Maccabi Tel Aviv: Daniel Tenenbaum, Eitan Tibi, Luis Hernández, Saborit, Geraldes, Eyal Golasa (77' Avi Rikan), Dor Peretz, Dan Glazer, Tal Ben Haim (68' Eduardo Guerrero), Aleksandar Pesic (68' Nick Blackman), Matan Hozez (77' Dan Biton). Coach: Patrick van Leeuwen.
Goal: 67' Júnior Moraes 1-0 (p).
Referee: José María Sánchez Martínez (ESP)   Attendance: 10,217.

Shakhtar Donetsk played their home match at NSK Olimpijs'kyj Stadium, Kyiv, instead of their regular stadium Donbass Arena, Donetsk, due to the political disputes in Eastern Ukraine.

25.02.21   Johan Cruijff ArenA, Amsterdam: AFC Ajax – Lille Olympique 2-1 (1-0)
AFC Ajax: Maarten Stekelenburg, Daley Blind, Edson Álvarez, Lisandro Martínez, Jurriën Timber, Devyne Rensch, Davy Klaassen, Ryan Gravenberch (90' Mohammed Kudus), Dusan Tadic, David Neres (89' Oussama Idrissi), Antony (55' Brian Brobbey). Coach: Erik ten Hag.
Lille Olympique: Mike Maignan, Zeki Çelik (62' Jérémy Pied), Tiago Djaló, Sven Botman, Domagoj Bradaric, Renato Sanches, Xeka (70' Boubakary Soumaré), Jonathan Ikoné (62' Luiz Araujo), Yusuf Yazici, Jonathan Bamba (62' Jonathan David), Timothy Weah (78' Isaac Lihadji). Coach: Christophe Galtier.
Goals: 15' Davy Klaassen 1-0, 78' Yusuf Yazici 1-1 (p), 88' David Neres 2-1.
Referee: William Collum (SCO)

25.02.21   Jan Breydel Stadion, Brugge: Club Brugge KV – Dynamo Kyiv 0-1 (0-0)
Club Brugge KV: Simon Mignolet, Eduard Sobol (84' Maxim De Cuyper), Clinton Mata, Brandon Mechele, Federico Ricca, Odilon Kossounou, Ruud Vormer, Nabil Dirar (84' David Okereke), Éder Balanta, Thomas Van Den Keybus (46' Ignace Van Der Brempt), Bas Dost (58' Youssouph Badji). Coach: Philippe Clement.
Dynamo Kyiv: Georgiy Bushchan, Tomasz Kedziora (77' Oleksandr Karavayev), Vitali Mykolenko, Oleksandr Syrota, Illia Zabarnyi, Sergiy Sydorchuk, Vitaliy Buyalskyi (86' Oleksandr Andrievsky), Viktor Tsygankov, Volodymyr Shepelyev (58' Mykola Shaparenko), Gerson Rodrigues, Artem Besedin. Coach: Mircea Lucescu.
Goal: 83' Vitaliy Buyalskyi 0-1.
Referee: Srdjan Jovanovic (SRB)

25.02.21   Old Trafford, Manchester: Manchester United – Real Sociedad 0-0
Manchester United: Dean Henderson, Alex Telles, Victor Lindelöf, Eric Bailly, Aaron Wan-Bissaka (46' Brandon Williams), Nemanja Matic, Fred (46' Axel Tuanzebe), Bruno Fernandes (46' Marcus Rashford), Daniel James (59' Amad Diallo), Anthony Martial, Mason Greenwood (76' Shola Shoretire). Coach: Ole Gunnar Solskjær.
Real Sociedad: Álex Remiro, Andoni Gorosabel (46' Jon Bautista), Modibo Sagnan, Aihen Muñoz, Adnan Januzaj (66' Martín Merquelanz), Mikel Merino, Zubeldía, Guevara (72' Jon Guridi), Martín Zubimendi, Mikel Oyarzabal (46' Ander Barrenetxea), Alexander Isak (46' Portu). Coach: Imanol Alguacil.
Referee: Lawrence Visser (BEL)

Mikel Oyarzabal missed a penalty kick (13').

25.02.21   Stadio Giuseppe Meazza, Milano: AC Milan – Crvena Zvezda Beograd 1-1 (1-1)
AC Milan: Gianluigi Donnarumma, Alessio Romagnoli, Davide Calabria (66' Theo Hernández), Fikayo Tomori, Diogo Dalot, Hakan Çalhanoglu, Soualiho Meïté, Samu Castillejo (66' Alexis Saelemaekers), Rade Krunic (46' Ante Rebic), Franck Kessié, Rafael Leão (46' Zlatan Ibrahimovic). Coach: Stefano Pioli.
Crvena Zvezda Beograd: Milan Borjan, Milos Degenek, Marko Gobeljic, Milan Gajic, Radovan Pankov, Slavoljub Srnic (46' Njegos Petrovic), Sékou Sanogo, Guélor Kanga (69' Aleksandar Katai), Mirko Ivanic (84' Veljko Nikolic), Diego Falcinelli (72' Milan Pavkov), Fardou Ben Nabouhane (69' Filippo Falco). Coach: Dejan Stankovic.
Goals: 9' Franck Kessié 1-0 (p), 24' Fardou Ben Nabouhane 1-1.
Referee: Jesús Gil Manzano (ESP)
Sent off: 70' Marko Gobeljic.

AC Milan won on away goals.

25.02.21   King Power Stadium, Leicester: Leicester City – Slavia Praha 0-2 (0-0)
Leicester City: Kasper Schmeichel, Jonny Evans, Daniel Amartey (61' Ricardo Pereira), Çaglar Söyüncü, Luke Thomas, Marc Albrighton (61' Timothy Castagne), Youri Tielemans, Wilfred Ndidi, Cengiz Ünder (80' Sidnei Tavares), Hamza Choudhury (61' Harvey Barnes), Jamie Vardy. Coach: Brendan Rodgers.
Slavia Praha: Ondrej Kolár, Ondrej Kúdela, Jan Boril, Alexander Bah, David Zima, Nicolae Stanciu (69' Oscar Dorley), Lukás Provod, Jakub Hromada (75' Ondrej Lingr), Peter Olayinka, Jan Kuchta (84' Lukás Masopust), Abdallah Sima. Coach: Jindrich Trpisovský.
Goals: 49' Lukás Provod 0-1, 79' Abdallah Sima 0-2.
Referee: Serdar Gözübüyük (HOL)

25.02.21   Stadio Olimpico, Roma: AS Roma – Sporting Braga 3-1 (1-0)
AS Roma: Pau López, Bruno Peres, Rick Karsdorp, Gianluca Mancini, Jordan Veretout (59' Leonardo Spinazzola), Bryan Cristante, Gonzalo Villar (46' Lorenzo Pellegrini), Amadou Diawara, Edin Dzeko (67' Borja Mayoral), Pedro (77' Henrikh Mkhitaryan), Stephan El Shaarawy (59' Carles Pérez). Coach: Paulo Fonseca.
Sporting Braga: Tiago Sá, Rolando, Nuno Sequeira (70' Cristian Borja), Vítor Tormena, Zé Carlos, Nicolás Gaitán (60' Ricardo Horta), João Novais, André Horta, Lucas Piazón (60' Fransérgio), Andraz Sporar (60' Abel Ruiz), Galeno (77' Hernâni Infande Silva). Coach: Carlos Carvalhal.
Goals: 24' Edin Dzeko 1-0, 75' Carles Pérez 2-0, 88' Bryan Cristante 2-1 (og), 90+1' Borja Mayoral 3-1.
Referee: Andreas Ekberg (SWE)

Lorenzo Pellegrini missed a penalty kick (72').

25.02.21   Stadion Maksimir, Zagreb: Dinamo Zagreb – FK Krasnodar 1-0 (1-0)
Dinamo Zagreb: Dominik Livakovic, Kévin Théophile-Catherine, Stefan Ristovski, Rasmus Lauritsen, Josko Gvardiol, Arijan Ademi, Kristijan Jakic, Luka Ivanusec (83' Iyayi Atiemwen), Lovro Majer (69' Josip Misic), Mislav Orsic, Bruno Petkovic (87' Mario Gavranovic).
Coach: Zoran Mamic.
FK Krasnodar: Stanislav Agkatsev, Igor Smolnikov (70' Magomed Suleymanov), Aleksandr Martynovich, Evgeniy Chernov, Aleksey Ionov, Rémy Cabella, Yuri Gazinskiy (69' Ari), Victor Claesson, Tonny Vilhena (60' Kristoffer Olsson), Kaio Pantaleão, Wanderson.
Coach: Murad Musaev.
Goal: 31' Mislav Orsic 1-0.
Referee: Halil Umut Meler (TUR)

25.02.21   BayArena, Leverkusen: Bayer Leverkusen – BSC Young Boys 0-2 (0-0)
Bayer Leverkusen: Niklas Lomb, Aleksandar Dragovic (63' Demarai Gray), Jonathan Tah, Daley Sinkgraven, Jeremie Frimpong (78' Nadiem Amiri), Edmond Tapsoba, Charles Aránguiz, Florian Wirtz, Patrik Schick, Leon Bailey (63' Lucas Alario), Moussa Diaby.
Coach: Peter Bosz.
BSC Young Boys: David von Ballmoos, Fabian Lustenberger, Jordan Lefort, Cédric Zesiger, Silvan Hefti, Nicolas Moumi Ngamaleu (69' Fabian Rieder), Christian Fassnacht (87' Gianluca Gaudino), Sandro Lauper, Michel Aebischer (87' Vincent Sierro), Theoson Siebatcheu (78' Marvin Spielmann), Meschack Elia (78' Felix Mambimbi). Coach: Gerardo Seoane.
Goals: 48' Theoson Siebatcheu 0-1, 86' Christian Fassnacht 0-2.
Referee: Davide Massa (ITA)

25.02.21   Philips Stadion, Eindhoven: PSV Eindhoven – Olympiakos Piraeus 2-1 (2-0)
PSV Eindhoven: Yvon Mvogo, Nick Viergever, Philipp Max, Olivier Boscagli, Denzel Dumfries, Jordan Teze, Mario Götze (89' Yorbe Vertessen), Ryan Thomas (90' Mauro Júnior), Pablo Rosario, Eran Zahavi, Donyell Malen. Coach: Roger Schmidt.
Olympiakos Piraeus: José Sá, Kenny Lala (79' Athanasios Androutsos), Rúben Semedo, Oleg Reabciuk, Ousseynou Ba, Mathieu Valbuena (46' Georgios Masouras), Yann M'Vila, Andreas Bouchalakis (46' Kostas Fortounis), Mohamed Camara, Youssef El-Arabi (90' Sokratis Papastathopoulos), Bruma (79' Koka). Coach: Pedro Martins.
Goals: 23', 44' Eran Zahavi 1-0, 2-0, 88' Koka 2-1.
Referee: Clément Turpin (FRA)

ROUND OF 16

11.03.21   Johan Cruijff ArenA, Amsterdam: AFC Ajax – BSC Young Boys 3-0 (0-0)
AFC Ajax: Maarten Stekelenburg, Nicolás Tagliafico, Edson Álvarez, Lisandro Martínez, Jurriën Timber, Devyne Rensch (67' Perr Schuurs), Davy Klaassen, Ryan Gravenberch, Dusan Tadic, David Neres (83' Brian Brobbey), Antony (68' Oussama Idrissi). Coach: Erik ten Hag.
BSC Young Boys: Guillaume Faivre, Fabian Lustenberger, Jordan Lefort, Silvan Hefti, Mohamed Ali Camara (34' Cédric Zesiger), Miralem Sulejmani (46' Nicolas Moumi Ngamaleu), Christian Fassnacht (84' Theoson Siebatcheu), Sandro Lauper (71' Vincent Sierro), Michel Aebischer, Jean-Pierre Nsame, Meschack Elia (71' Felix Mambimbi).
Coach: Gerardo Seoane.
Goals: 62' Davy Klaassen 1-0, 82' Dusan Tadic 2-0, 90+2' Brian Brobbey 3-0.
Referee: Marco Guida (ITA)

11.03.21   NSK Olimpijs'kyj Stadium, Kyiv: Dynamo Kyiv – Villarreal CF 0-2 (0-1)
Dynamo Kyiv: Georgiy Bushchan, Tomasz Kedziora (84' Oleksandr Karavayev), Vitali Mykolenko, Oleksandr Syrota, Illia Zabarnyi, Sergiy Sydorchuk (68' Oleksandr Andrievsky), Vitaliy Buyalskyi, Viktor Tsygankov, Mykola Shaparenko (68' Volodymyr Shepelyev), Gerson Rodrigues, Artem Besedin. Coach: Mircea Lucescu.
Villarreal CF: Gerónimo Rulli, Raúl Albiol, Pau Torres (46' Ramiro Funes Mori), Juan Foyth, Étienne Capoue, Dani Parejo, Manu Trigueros (85' Moi Gómez), Pedraza, Samuel Chukwueze (84' Jaume Costa), Paco Alcácer (63' Carlos Bacca), Gerard Moreno (90' Álex Baena).
Coach: Unai Emery.
Goals: 30' Pau Torres 0-1, 52' Raúl Albiol 0-2.
Referee: Michael Oliver (ENG)   Attendance: 12,751.

11.03.21   Old Trafford, Manchester: Manchester United – AC Milan 1-1 (0-0)
Manchester United: Dean Henderson, Alex Telles, Harry Maguire, Eric Bailly, Aaron Wan-Bissaka (74' Brandon Williams), Nemanja Matic, Bruno Fernandes (74' Fred), Daniel James (74' Luke Shaw), Scott McTominay, Anthony Martial (46' Amad Diallo), Mason Greenwood. Coach: Ole Gunnar Solskjær.
AC Milan: Gianluigi Donnarumma, Simon Kjær, Davide Calabria (74' Pierre Kalulu), Fikayo Tomori, Diogo Dalot, Soualiho Meïté, Rade Krunic, Franck Kessié, Alexis Saelemaekers (69' Samu Castillejo), Rafael Leão, Brahim Díaz (69' Sandro Tonali). Coach: Stefano Pioli.
Goals: 50' Amad Diallo 1-0, 90+2' Simon Kjær 1-1.
Referee: Slavko Vincic (SVN)

11.03.21   Sinobo Stadium, Prague: Slavia Praha – Glasgow Rangers FC 1-1 (1-1)
Slavia Praha: Ondrej Kolár, Ondrej Kúdela, Jan Boril, Tomás Holes, Alexander Bah, David Zima, Nicolae Stanciu (76' Ondrej Lingr), Lukás Provod, Peter Olayinka (46' Lukás Masopust), Jan Kuchta (71' Oscar Dorley), Abdallah Sima. Coach: Jindrich Trpisovský.
Glasgow Rangers FC: Allan McGregor, Connor Goldson, Filip Helander, Borna Barisic, Nathan Patterson, Steven Davis, Glen Kamara (88' Bongani Zungu), Joe Ayodele-Aribo (81' Kemar Roofe), Ianis Hagi (63' Scott Arfield), Alfredo Morelos, Ryan Kent.
Coach: Steven Gerrard.
Goals: 7' Nicolae Stanciu 1-0, 36' Filip Helander 1-1.
Referee: Ovidiu Hategan (ROM)   Attendance: 300.

11.03.21   Stadio Olimpico, Roma: AS Roma – Shakhtar Donetsk 3-0 (1-0)
AS Roma: Pau López, Leonardo Spinazzola (78' Bruno Peres), Rick Karsdorp, Gianluca Mancini, Marash Kumbulla, Henrikh Mkhitaryan (35' Borja Mayoral), Bryan Cristante, Lorenzo Pellegrini (78' Carles Pérez), Gonzalo Villar, Amadou Diawara (79' Ibañez), Pedro (62' Stephan El Shaarawy). Coach: Paulo Fonseca.
Shakhtar Donetsk: Anatolii Trubin, Ismaily, Mykola Matvienko, Dodô, Vitão, Marlos (88' Marcos Antônio), Taison (79' Manor Solomon), Alan Patrick (79' Heorhii Sudakov), Maycon, Mateus Martins Tetê (87' Yevhen Konoplyanka), Júnior Moraes (76' Dentinho).
Coach: Luís Castro.
Goals: 23' Lorenzo Pellegrini 1-0, 73' Stephan El Shaarawy 2-0, 77' Gianluca Mancini 3-0.
Referee: Artur Soares Dias (POR)

11.03.21   Stadio Georgios Karaiskáki, Piraeus: Olympiakos Piraeus – Arsenal FC 1-3 (0-1)
Olympiakos Piraeus: José Sá, Sokratis Papastathopoulos, Kenny Lala, Oleg Reabciuk (46' José Holebas), Mathieu Valbuena (46' Kostas Fortounis), Yann M'Vila, Andreas Bouchalakis, Georgios Masouras (86' Athanasios Androutsos), Mohamed Camara, Youssef El-Arabi (77' Koka), Bruma (59' Lazar Randjelovic). Coach: Pedro Martins.
Arsenal FC: Bernd Leno, David Luiz, Héctor Bellerín, Kieran Tierney, Gabriel Magalhães, Granit Xhaka, Thomas Partey (55' Dani Ceballos), Martin Ødegaard (82' Emile Smith-Rowe), Bukayo Saka (82' Nicolas Pépé), Willian (82' Mohamed Elneny), Pierre-Emerick Aubameyang (88' Alexandre Lacazette). Coach: Mikel Arteta.
Goals: 34' Martin Ødegaard 0-1, 58' Youssef El-Arabi 1-1, 80' Gabriel Magalhães 1-2, 85' Mohamed Elneny 1-3.
Referee: Daniel Siebert (GER)

11.03.21 Tottenham Hotspur Stadium, London:
Tottenham Hotspur – Dinamo Zagreb 2-0 (1-0)
Tottenham Hotspur: Hugo Lloris, Serge Aurier, Ben Davies, Davinson Sánchez, Moussa Sissoko, Érik Lamela (64' Gareth Bale), Dele Alli (64' Steven Bergwijn), Eric Dier, Tanguy NDombèlé (72' Pierre-Emile Højbjerg), Son Heung-Min (64' Lucas Moura), Harry Kane (84' Carlos Vinícius). Coach: José Mourinho.
Dinamo Zagreb: Dominik Livakovic, Marin Leovac, Kévin Théophile-Catherine, Stefan Ristovski, Rasmus Lauritsen, Arijan Ademi (90' Bartol Franjic), Kristijan Jakic, Luka Ivanusec, Lovro Majer (64' Lirim Kastrati), Mislav Orsic (64' Iyayi Atiemwen), Bruno Petkovic (78' Mario Gavranovic). Coach: Zoran Mamic.
Goals: 25', 70' Harry Kane 1-0, 2-0.
Referee: Serder Gözübüyük (HOL)

11.03.21 Estadio Nuevo Los Cármenes, Granada: Granada CF – Molde FK 2-0 (1-0)
Granada CF: Rui Silva, Víctor Díaz, Dimitri Foulquier, Domingos Duarte, Nehuén Pérez, Maxime Gonalons, Antonio Puertas (90+1' Jesús Vallejo), Kenedy, Yan Eteki, Soldado (81' Ismael Ruiz), Jorge Molina. Coach: Diego Martínez.
Molde FK: Andreas Linde, Kristoffer Haugen, Stian Gregersen, Sheriff Sinyan, Marcus Pedersen, Magnus Wolff Eikrem, Eirik Andersen (86' Mathis Bolly), Eirik Hestad (65' Erling Knudtzon), Fredrik Aursnes, Martin Ellingsen, Björn Sigurdarson (73' David Fofana). Coach: Erling Moe.
Goals: 26' Jorge Molina 1-0, 76' Soldado 2-0.
Referee: Pawel Raczkowski (POL)
Sent off: 71' Martin Ellingsen.

18.03.21 NSK Olimpijs'kyj Stadium, Kyiv: Shakhtar Donetsk – AS Roma 1-2 (0-0)
Shakhtar Donetsk: Anatolii Trubin, Sergiy Kryvtsov, Mykola Matvienko, Dodô (82' Sergiy Bolbat), Vitão, Alan Patrick (60' Yevhen Konoplyanka), Manor Solomon (77' Heorhii Sudakov), Maycon, Marcos Antônio, Mateus Martins Tetê (60' Marlos), Júnior Moraes (76' Dentinho). Coach: Luís Castro.
AS Roma: Pau López, Leonardo Spinazzola (58' Riccardo Calafiori), Rick Karsdorp (58' Bruno Peres), Marash Kumbulla, Ibañez (46' Gianluca Mancini), Bryan Cristante, Gonzalo Villar, Amadou Diawara (59' Lorenzo Pellegrini), Pedro (75' Stephan El Shaarawy), Borja Mayoral, Carles Pérez. Coach: Paulo Fonseca.
Goals: 48' Borja Mayoral 0-1, 59' Júnior Moraes 1-1, 72' Borja Mayoral 1-2.
Referee: Antonio Mateu Lahoz (ESP)

Shakhtar Donetsk played their home match at NSK Olimpijs'kyj Stadium, Kyiv, instead of their regular stadium Donbass Arena, Donetsk, due to the war conditions in Eastern Ukraine.

18.03.21 Emirates Stadium, London: Arsenal FC – Olympiakos Pireus 0-1 (0-0)
Arsenal FC: Bernd Leno, David Luiz, Héctor Bellerín (82' Calum Chambers), Kieran Tierney, Gabriel Magalhães, Granit Xhaka, Mohamed Elneny (57' Thomas Partey), Dani Ceballos (57' Martin Ødegaard), Emile Smith-Rowe (81' Gabriel Martinelli), Pierre-Emerick Aubameyang, Nicolas Pépé. Coach: Mikel Arteta.
Olympiakos Piraeus: José Sá, José Holebas, Sokratis Papastathopoulos, Oleg Reabciuk (84' Kenny Lala), Ousseynou Ba, Yann M'Vila, Kostas Fortounis (84' Andreas Bouchalakis), Georgios Masouras (63' Bruma), Athanasios Androutsos (62' Lazar Randjelovic), Mohamed Camara, Youssef El-Arabi. Coach: Pedro Martins.
Goal: 51' Youssef El-Arabi 0-1.
Referee: Carlos del Cerro Grande (ESP)
Sent off: 83' Ousseynou Ba.

18.03.21 Stadion Maksimir, Zagreb:
Dinamo Zagreb – Tottenham Hotspur 3-0 (0-0, 2-0) (a.e.t.)
Dinamo Zagreb: Dominik Livakovic, Kévin Théophile-Catherine, Stefan Ristovski (90' Petar Stojanovic), Rasmus Lauritsen, Arijan Ademi (118' Dino Peric), Kristijan Jakic (75' Iyayi Atiemwen), Luka Ivanusec, Lovro Majer (81' Mario Gavranovic), Bartol Franjic (81' Marin Leovac), Mislav Orsic, Bruno Petkovic (90' Josip Misic). Coach: Damir Krznar.
Tottenham Hotspur: Hugo Lloris, Serge Aurier (108' Steven Bergwijn), Ben Davies (90' Reguilón), Davinson Sánchez, Moussa Sissoko, Érik Lamela (60' Gareth Bale), Lucas Moura (85' Carlos Vinícius), Dele Alli (68' Giovani Lo Celso), Eric Dier, Harry Winks (68' Tanguy NDombèlé), Harry Kane. Coach: José Mourinho.
Goals: 62,' 83', 106' Mislav Orsic 1-0, 2-0, 3-0.
Referee: Davide Massa (ITA)

Dinamo Zagreb won after extra time.

18.03.21 Puskás Aréna, Budapest (HUN): Molde FK – Granada CF 2-1 (1-0)
Molde FK: Andreas Linde, Martin Bjørnbak, Stian Gregersen (46' Sheriff Sinyan), Birk Risa (77' Kristoffer Haugen), Emil Breivik (82' Etzaz Hussain), Marcus Pedersen, Magnus Wolff Eikrem, Eirik Andersen (77' Erling Knudtzon), Eirik Hestad, Fredrik Aursnes, Björn Sigurdarson (63' David Fofana). Coach: Erling Moe.
Granada CF: Rui Silva, Víctor Díaz, Germán Sánchez, Jesús Vallejo (83' Nehuén Pérez), Domingos Duarte, Montoro (83' Darwin Machís), Maxime Gonalons (76' Yan Eteki), Antonio Puertas, Kenedy, Yangel Herrera, Jorge Molina (64' Soldado). Coach: Diego Martínez.
Goals: 29' Jesús Vallejo 1-0 (og), 72' Soldado 1-1, 90' Eirik Hestad 2-1 (p).
Referee: Srdjan Jovanovic (SRB)

The match, originally to be played at Åker Stadion, Molde, was moved to Puskás Aréna, Budapest (HUN), due to Norwegian quarantine restrictions related to COVID-19.

18.03.21 Stadion Wankdorf, Bern: BSC Young Boys – AFC Ajax 0-2 (0-1)
BSC Young Boys: Guillaume Faivre, Fabian Lustenberger, Jordan Lefort (46' Quentin Maceiras), Silvan Hefti, Mohamed Ali Camara (65' Fabian Rieder), Miralem Sulejmani (71' Marvin Spielmann), Christian Fassnacht (71' Gianluca Gaudino), Vincent Sierro, Sandro Lauper, Jean-Pierre Nsame, Meschack Elia (65' Felix Mambimbi). Coach: Gerardo Seoane.
AFC Ajax: Maarten Stekelenburg, Daley Blind (65' Mohammed Kudus), Nicolás Tagliafico (74' Sean Klaiber), Edson Álvarez, Lisandro Martínez, Devyne Rensch (80' Perr Schuurs), Davy Klaassen, Ryan Gravenberch, Dusan Tadic, David Neres (65' Oussama Idrissi), Antony (81' Brian Brobbey). Coach: Erik ten Hag.
Goals: 21' David Neres 0-1, 49' Dusan Tadic 0-2 (p).
Referee: Bobby Madden (SCO)

18.03.21 Estadio de la Cerámica, Villarreal: Villarreal CF – Dynamo Kyiv 2-0 (2-0)
Villarreal CF: Asenjo, Raúl Albiol, Ramiro Funes Mori, Juan Foyth (63' Mario Gaspar), Étienne Capoue, Dani Parejo, Manu Trigueros (79' Jaume Costa), Pedraza, Samuel Chukwueze (71' Álex Baena), Carlos Bacca (63' Yeremi Pino), Gerard Moreno (79' Dani Raba). Coach: Unai Emery.
Dynamo Kyiv: Georgiy Bushchan, Tomasz Kedziora, Vitali Mykolenko (83' Sidcley), Oleksandr Syrota (83' Denys Popov), Illia Zabarnyi, Sergiy Sydorchuk, Vitaliy Buyalskyi, Oleksandr Andrievsky (65' Volodymyr Shepelyev), Carlos de Pena, Viktor Tsygankov (46' Vladyslav Supryaha), Gerson Rodrigues (65' Bohdan Lednev). Coach: Mircea Lucescu.
Goals: 13', 36' Gerard Moreno 1-0, 2-0.
Referee: Andreas Ekberg (SWE)

18.03.21   Stadio Giuseppe Meazza, Milano: AC Milan – Manchester United 0-1 (0-0)
AC Milan: Gianluigi Donnarumma, Simon Kjær, Fikayo Tomori, Theo Hernández, Pierre Kalulu (65' Diogo Dalot), Hakan Çalhanoglu, Soualiho Meïté, Samu Castillejo (65' Zlatan Ibrahimovic), Rade Krunic (72' Brahim Díaz), Franck Kessié, Alexis Saelemaekers.
Coach: Stefano Pioli.
Manchester United: Dean Henderson, Victor Lindelöf, Harry Maguire, Luke Shaw, Aaron Wan-Bissaka, Fred, Bruno Fernandes, Daniel James, Scott McTominay, Marcus Rashford (46' Paul Pogba), Mason Greenwood. Coach: Ole Gunnar Solskjær.
Goal: 49' Paul Pogba 0-1.
Referee: Dr. Felix Brych (GER)

18.03.21   Ibrox Stadium, Glasgow: Glasgow Rangers FC – Slavia Praha 0-2 (0-1)
Glasgow Rangers FC: Allan McGregor, Leon Balogun, Connor Goldson, Borna Barisic, Nathan Patterson (78' Jack Simpson), Steven Davis (83' Cedric Itten), Scott Arfield (55' Kemar Roofe), Glen Kamara, Joe Ayodele-Aribo, Alfredo Morelos (83' Scott Wright), Ryan Kent (82' Bongani Zungu). Coach: Steven Gerrard.
Slavia Praha: Ondrej Kolár (65' Matyás Vágner), Ondrej Kúdela, Jan Boril, Simon Deli, Alexander Bah, Nicolae Stanciu (90' Ondrej Lingr), Lukás Provod, Jakub Hromada (58' Tomás Holes), Oscar Dorley (58' Jan Kuchta), Peter Olayinka (58' Lukás Masopust), Abdallah Sima. Coach: Jindrich Trpisovský.
Goals: 14' Peter Olayinka 0-1, 74' Nicolae Stanciu 0-2.
Referee: Orel Grinfeld (ISR)
Sent off: 61' Kemar Roofe, 73' Leon Balogun.

QUARTER-FINALS

08.04.21   Estadio Nuevo Los Cármenes, Granada: Granada CF – Manchester United 0-2 (0-1)
Granada CF: Rui Silva, Víctor Díaz, Jesús Vallejo, Domingos Duarte (54' Germán Sánchez), Carlos Neva (74' Dimitri Foulquier), Montoro, Maxime Gonalons (86' Yan Eteki), Antonio Puertas, Kenedy (75' Darwin Machís), Yangel Herrera, Soldado (87' Luis Suárez).
Coach: Diego Martínez.
Manchester United: David de Gea, Victor Lindelöf, Harry Maguire, Luke Shaw (46' Alex Telles), Aaron Wan-Bissaka, Paul Pogba (74' Nemanja Matic), Bruno Fernandes, Daniel James, Scott McTominay, Marcus Rashford (66' Edinson Cavani), Mason Greenwood (85' Donny van de Beek). Coach: Ole Gunnar Solskjær.
Goals: 31' Marcus Rashford 0-1, 90' Bruno Fernandes 0-2 (p).
Referee: Artur Soares Dias (POR)

08.04.21   Emirates Stadium, London: Arsenal FC – Slavia Praha 1-1 (0-0)
Arsenal FC: Bernd Leno, Cédric Soares, Héctor Bellerín, Rob Holding, Gabriel Magalhães, Granit Xhaka, Thomas Partey (78' Mohamed Elneny), Emile Smith-Rowe (88' Dani Ceballos), Bukayo Saka (78' Nicolas Pépé), Willian (73' Gabriel Martinelli), Alexandre Lacazette (78' Pierre-Emerick Aubameyang). Coach: Mikel Arteta.
Slavia Praha: Ondrej Kolár, Jan Boril, Tomás Holes, Alexander Bah, David Zima, Nicolae Stanciu (84' Lukás Masopust), Lukás Provod, Jakub Hromada (46' Petr Sevcík), Oscar Dorley (69' Ondrej Lingr), Peter Olayinka (85' Ibrahim Traoré), Abdallah Sima (69' Jan Kuchta).
Coach: Jindrich Trpisovský.
Goals: 86' Nicolas Pépé 1-0, 90+4' Tomás Holes 1-1.
Referee: Andreas Ekberg (SWE)

08.04.21   Johan Cruijff ArenA, Amsterdam: AFC Ajax – AS Roma 1-2 (1-0)
AFC Ajax: Kjell Scherpen, Nicolás Tagliafico, Edson Álvarez, Lisandro Martínez, Jurriën Timber, Devyne Rensch (78' Sean Klaiber), Davy Klaassen, Ryan Gravenberch, Dusan Tadic, David Neres (64' Brian Brobbey), Antony (88' Oussama Idrissi). Coach: Erik ten Hag.
AS Roma: Pau López, Bruno Peres, Leonardo Spinazzola (29' Riccardo Calafiori), Gianluca Mancini, Ibañez, Jordan Veretout (77' Gonzalo Villar), Bryan Cristante, Lorenzo Pellegrini, Amadou Diawara, Edin Dzeko (77' Borja Mayoral), Pedro (89' Carles Pérez).
Coach: Paulo Fonseca.
Goals: 39' Davy Klaassen 1-0, 57' Lorenzo Pellegrini 1-1, 87' Ibañez 1-2.
Referee: Sergey Karasev (RUS)

Dusan Tadic missed a penalty kick (53').

08.04.21   Stadion Maksimir, Zagreb: Dinamo Zagreb – Villarreal CF 0-1 (0-1)
Dinamo Zagreb: Dominik Livakovic, Kévin Théophile-Catherine, Stefan Ristovski, Rasmus Lauritsen, Josko Gvardiol (71' Marin Leovac), Arijan Ademi, Kristijan Jakic (61' Lirim Kastrati), Luka Ivanusec, Iyayi Atiemwen (61' Bruno Petkovic), Lovro Majer (82' Bartol Franjic), Mislav Orsic (82' Marko Tolic). Coach: Damir Krznar.
Villarreal CF: Gerónimo Rulli, Raúl Albiol, Pau Torres, Juan Foyth, Étienne Capoue, Dani Parejo, Manu Trigueros (86' Rubén Peña), Pedraza, Samuel Chukwueze (69' Moi Gómez), Carlos Bacca (46' Paco Alcácer), Gerard Moreno. Coach: Unai Emery.
Goal: 44' Gerard Moreno 0-1 (p).
Referee: Daniel Siebert (GER)

15.04.21   Old Trafford, Manchester: Manchester United – Granada CF 2-0 (1-0)
Manchester United: David de Gea, Alex Telles, Victor Lindelöf, Axel Tuanzebe, Aaron Wan-Bissaka (82' Brandon Williams), Nemanja Matic, Paul Pogba (46' Donny van de Beek), Fred, Bruno Fernandes (73' Mata), Edinson Cavani (60' Daniel James), Mason Greenwood (82' Amad Diallo). Coach: Ole Gunnar Solskjær.
Granada CF: Rui Silva, Germán Sánchez (82' Nehuén Pérez), Dimitri Foulquier, Jesús Vallejo, Carlos Neva (74' Víctor Díaz), Montoro, Maxime Gonalons (32' Jorge Molina), Kenedy (46' Antonio Puertas), Yangel Herrera, Soldado (46' Luis Suárez), Darwin Machís.
Coach: Diego Martínez.
Goals: 6' Edinson Cavani 1-0, 90' Jesús Vallejo 2-0 (og).
Referee: István Kovács (ROM)

15.04.21   Sinobo Stadium, Prague: Slavia Praha – Arsenal FC 0-4 (0-3)
Slavia Praha: Ondrej Kolár, Jan Boril (46' Oscar Dorley), Tomás Holes, Alexander Bah (46' Denis Visinský), David Zima, Nicolae Stanciu (46' Ondrej Lingr), Petr Sevcík, Lukás Provod, Jakub Hromada (46' Lukás Masopust), Peter Olayinka, Jan Kuchta (71' Stanislav Tecl).
Coach: Jindrich Trpisovský.
Arsenal FC: Bernd Leno, Pablo Marí, Calum Chambers, Rob Holding, Granit Xhaka, Thomas Partey (79' Cédric Soares), Dani Ceballos, Emile Smith-Rowe (67' Mohamed Elneny), Bukayo Saka (79' Gabriel Martinelli), Alexandre Lacazette (79' Eddie Nketiah), Nicolas Pépé (88' Folarin Balogun). Coach: Mikel Arteta.
Goals: 18' Nicolas Pépé 0-1, 21' Alexandre Lacazette 0-2 (p), 24' Bukayo Saka 0-3, 77' Alexandre Lacazette 0-4.
Referee: Cüneyt Çakir (TUR)   Attendance: 750.

15.04.21 Stadio Olimpico, Roma: AS Roma – AFC Ajax 1-1 (0-0)
AS Roma: Pau López, Rick Karsdorp, Gianluca Mancini, Ibañez, Riccardo Calafiori (81' Gonzalo Villar), Henrikh Mkhitaryan (87' Pedro), Jordan Veretout, Bryan Cristante, Lorenzo Pellegrini, Amadou Diawara, Edin Dzeko (80' Borja Mayoral). Coach: Paulo Fonseca.
AFC Ajax: Maarten Stekelenburg, Nicolás Tagliafico, Sean Klaiber (22' Perr Schuurs, 83' Oussama Idrissi), Edson Álvarez (69' Mohammed Kudus), Lisandro Martínez, Jurriën Timber, Davy Klaassen, Ryan Gravenberch, Dusan Tadic, David Neres (83' Lassina Traoré), Antony (46' Brian Brobbey). Coach: Erik ten Hag.
Goals: 49' Brain Brobbey 0-1, 72' Edin Dzeko 1-1.
Referee: Anthony Taylor (ENG)

15.04.21 Estadio de la Cerámica, Villarreal: Villarreal CF – Dinamo Zagreb 2-1 (2-0)
Villarreal CF: Gerónimo Rulli, Raúl Albiol, Pau Torres, Juan Foyth, Étienne Capoue, Dani Parejo (84' Francis Coquelin), Manu Trigueros (63' Moi Gómez), Pedraza (90' Alberto Moreno), Samuel Chukwueze (90' Rubén Peña), Paco Alcácer (90' Ález Baena), Gerard Moreno. Coach: Unai Emery.
Dinamo Zagreb: Dominik Livakovic, Kévin Théophile-Catherine (82' Dino Peric), Stefan Ristovski (62' Petar Stojanovic), Rasmus Lauritsen, Josko Gvardiol, Arijan Ademi (82' Josip Misic), Kristijan Jakic, Luka Ivanusec (76' Iyayi Atiemwen), Lovro Majer (62' Bartol Franjic), Mislav Orsic, Bruno Petkovic. Coach: Damir Krznar.
Goals: 36' Paco Alcácer 1-0, 43' Gerard Moreno 2-0, 74' Mislav Orsic 2-1.
Referee: Danny Makkelie (HOL)

SEMI-FINALS

29.04.21 Old Trafford, Manchester: Manchester United – AS Roma 6-2 (1-2)
Manchester United: David de Gea, Victor Lindelöf, Harry Maguire, Luke Shaw, Aaron Wan-Bissaka, Paul Pogba, Fred (83' Nemanja Matic), Bruno Fernandes (89' Mata), Scott McTominay, Edinson Cavani, Marcus Rashford (76' Mason Greenwood).
Coach: Ole Gunnar Solskjær.
AS Roma: Pau López (27' Antonio Mirante), Chris Smalling, Leonardo Spinazzola (37' Bruno Peres), Rick Karsdorp, Ibañez, Henrikh Mkhitaryan, Jordan Veretout (5' Gonzalo Villar), Bryan Cristante, Lorenzo Pellegrini, Amadou Diawara, Edin Dzeko. Coach: Paulo Fonseca.
Goals: 9' Bruno Fernandes 1-0, 15' Lorenzo Pellegrini 1-1 (p), 34' Edin Dzeko 1-2, 48', 64' Edinson Cavani 2-3, 3-2, 71' Bruno Fernandes 4-2 (p), 75' Paul Pogba 5-2, 86' Mason Greenwood 6-2.
Referee: Carlos del Cerro Grande (ESP)

29.04.21 Estadio de la Cerámica, Villarreal: Villarreal CF – Arsenal FC 2-1 (2-0)
Villarreal CF: Gerónimo Rulli, Raúl Albiol, Pau Torres, Juan Foyth (70' Mario Gaspar), Étienne Capoue, Dani Parejo, Manu Trigueros (80' Moi Gómez), Pedraza (81' Alberto Moreno), Samuel Chukwueze, Paco Alcácer (46' Francis Coquelin), Gerard Moreno.
Coach: Unai Emery.
Arsenal FC: Bernd Leno, Pablo Marí, Calum Chambers, Rob Holding, Granit Xhaka, Thomas Partey, Martin Ødegaard (63' Gabriel Martinelli), Dani Ceballos, Emile Smith-Rowe (90+5' Mohamed Elneny), Bukayo Saka (85' Pierre-Emerick Aubameyang), Nicolas Pépé (90+5' Willian). Coach: Mikel Arteta.
Goals: 5' Manu Trigueros 1-0, 29' Raúl Albiol 2-0, 73' Nicolas Pépé 2-1 (p).
Referee: Artur Soares Dias (POR)
Sent off: 57' Dani Ceballos, 80' Étienne Capoue.

06.05.21   Stadio Olimpico, Roma: AS Roma – Manchester United 3-2 (0-1)
AS Roma: Antonio Mirante, Chris Smalling (30' Ebrima Darboe), Bruno Peres (69' Davide Santon), Rick Karsdorp, Gianluca Mancini, Ibañez, Henrikh Mkhitaryan, Bryan Cristante, Lorenzo Pellegrini, Edin Dzeko (76' Borja Mayoral), Pedro (76' Nicola Zalewski).
Coach: Paulo Fonseca.
Manchester United: David de Gea, Harry Maguire, Luke Shaw (46' Alex Telles), Eric Bailly, Aaron Wan-Bissaka (46' Brandon Williams), Paul Pogba (64' Nemanja Matic), Fred, Bruno Fernandes (84' Mata), Donny van de Beek, Edinson Cavani (73' Marcus Rashford), Mason Greenwood. Coach: Ole Gunnar Solskjær.
Goals: 39' Edinson Cavani 0-1, 57' Edin Dzeko 1-1, 60' Bryan Cristante 2-1, 68' Edinson Cavani 2-2, 83' Alex Telles 3-2 (og).
Referee: Dr. Felix Brych (GER)

06.05.21   Emirates Stadium, London: Arsenal FC – Villarreal CF 0-0
Arsenal FC: Bernd Leno, Pablo Marí, Héctor Bellerín (90+1' Eddie Nketiah), Kieran Tierney (80' Willian), Rob Holding, Thomas Partey, Martin Ødegaard (66' Gabriel Martinelli), Emile Smith-Rowe, Bukayo Saka, Pierre-Emerick Aubameyang (79' Alexandre Lacazette), Nicolas Pépé. Coach: Mikel Arteta.
Villarreal CF: Gerónimo Rulli, Raúl Albiol, Mario Gaspar, Pau Torres, Dani Parejo, Francis Coquelin, Manu Trigueros, Pedraza (90+1' Alberto Moreno), Samuel Chukwueze (29' Yeremi Pino, 90+1' Moi Gómez), Paco Alcácer (72' Carlos Bacca), Gerard Moreno.
Coach: Unai Emery.
Referee: Slavko Vincic (SVN)

FINAL

26.05.21   Polsat Plus Arena Gdansk, Gdansk (POL):
   Villarreal CF – Manchester United 1-1 (1-0, 1-1) (a.e.t.)
Villarreal CF: Gerónimo Rulli, Raúl Albiol, Pau Torres, Juan Foyth (88' Mario Gaspar), Étienne Capoue (120+3' Dani Raba), Dani Parejo, Manu Trigueros (77' Moi Gómez), Pedraza (88' Alberto Moreno), Yeremi Pino (77' Paco Alcácer), Carlos Bacca (60' Francis Coquelin), Gerard Moreno. Coach: Unai Emery.
Manchester United: David de Gea, Victor Lindelöf, Luke Shaw, Eric Bailly (116' Axel Tuanzebe), Aaron Wan-Bissaka (120+3' Mata), Paul Pogba (115' Daniel James), Bruno Fernandes, Scott McTominay (120+3' Alex Telles), Edinson Cavani, Marcus Rashford, Mason Greenwood (100' Fred). Coach: Ole Gunnar Solskjær.
Goals: 29' Gerard Moreno 1-0, 55' Edinson Cavani 1-1.
Referee: Clément Turpin (FRA)   Attendance: 9,412.

Villarreal CF won on penalties after extra time (11-10).
Penalties: Gerard Moreno 1-0, Mata 1-1, Dani Raba 2-1, Alex Telles 2-2, Paco Alcácer 3-2,
   Bruno Fernandes 3-3, Alberto Moreno 4-3, Rashford 4-4, Dani Parejo 5-4,
   Cavani 5-5, Moi Gómez 6-5, Fred 6-6, Albiol 7-6, James 7-7, Coquelin 8-7,
   Shaw 8-8, Mario Gaspar 9-8, Tuanzebe 9-9, Pau Torres 10-9, Lindelöf 10-10,
   Rulli 11-10, De Gea missed.

FAIRS CUP / UEFA CUP / EUROPA LEAGUE WINNERS

Fairs Cup (1958-1971), UEFA-Cup (1972-2009), Europa League (2010-2021).

1958	FC Barcelona	Spain
1960	FC Barcelona	Spain
1961	AS Roma	Italy
1962	Valencia CF	Spain
1963	Valencia CF	Spain
1964	Real Zaragoza	Spain
1965	Ferencvárosi TC	Hungary
1966	FC Barcelona	Spain
1967	Dinamo Zagreb	Croatia
1968	Leeds United	England
1969	Newcastle United	England
1970	Arsenal FC	England
1971	Leeds United	England
1972	Tottenham Hotspur	England
1973	Liverpool FC	England
1974	Feyenoord	Netherlands
1975	Borussia Mönchengladbach	Germany
1976	Liverpool FC	England
1977	Juventus	Italy
1978	PSV	Netherlands
1979	Borussia Mönchengladbach	Germany
1980	Eintracht Frankfurt	Germany
1981	Ipswich Town	England
1982	IFK Göteborg	Sweden
1983	RSC Anderlecht	Belgium
1984	Tottenham Hotspur	England
1985	Real Madrid	Spain
1986	Real Madrid	Spain
1987	IFK Göteborg	Sweden
1988	Bayer Leverkusen	Germany
1989	SSC Napoli	Italy
1990	Juventus	Italy
1991	Internazionale	Italy
1992	AFC Ajax	Netherlands
1993	Juventus	Italy
1994	Internazionale	Italy
1995	Parma AC	Italy
1996	Bayern München	Germany
1997	FC Schalke 04	Germany
1998	Internazionale	Italy
1999	Parma AC	Italy
2000	Galatasaray	Turkey
2001	Liverpool FC	England
2002	Feyenoord	Netherlands
2003	FC Porto	Portugal
2004	Valencia CF	Spain
2005	CSKA Moskva	Russia

2006	Sevilla FC	Spain
2007	Sevilla FC	Spain
2008	Zenith St. Petersburg	Russia
2009	Shakhtar Donetsk	Ukraine
2010	Atlético Madrid	Spain
2011	FC Porto	Portugal
2012	Atlético Madrid	Spain
2013	Chelsea FC	England
2014	Sevilla FC	Spain
2015	Sevilla FC	Spain
2016	Sevilla FC	Spain
2017	Manchester United	England
2018	Atlético Madrid	Spain
2019	Chelsea FC	England
2020	Sevilla FC	Spain
2021	Villarreal CF	Spain

ALL-TIME WINNERS – COUNTRY

Spain	19
England	13
Italy	10
Germany	6
Netherlands	4
Sweden	2
Portugal	2
Russia	2
Hungary	1
Croatia	1
Belgium	1
Turkey	1
Ukraine	1

ALL-TIME WINNERS – CLUB

Sevilla FC	6
Atlético Madrid	3
FC Barcelona	3
Juventus	3
Internazionale	3
Liverpool FC	3
Valencia CF	3
Leeds United	2
Borussia Mönchengladbach	2
IFK Göteborg	2
Tottenham Hotspur	2
Real Madrid	2
Parma AC	2
Feyenoord	2
FC Porto	2
AS Roma	1
Real Zaragoza	1
Ferencvárosi TC	1
Dinamo Zagreb	1
Newcastle United	1
Arsenal FC	1
PSV	1
Eintracht Frankfurt	1
Ipswich Town	1
RSC Anderlecht	1
Bayer Leverkusen	1
SSC Napoli	1
AFC Ajax	1
Bayern München	1
FC Schalke 04	1
Galatasaray	1
CSKA Moskva	1
Zenith St. Petersburg	1
Shakhtar Donetsk	1
Chelsea FC	2
Manchester United	1
Villarreal CF	1